FA Mann

FA Mann

The Lawyer and His Legacy

Edited Collection by

JASON GRANT ALLEN
AND
GERHARD DANNEMANN

OXFORD
UNIVERSITY PRESS

OXFORD
UNIVERSITY PRESS

Great Clarendon Street, Oxford, OX2 6DP,
United Kingdom

Oxford University Press is a department of the University of Oxford.
It furthers the University's objective of excellence in research, scholarship,
and education by publishing worldwide. Oxford is a registered trade mark of
Oxford University Press in the UK and in certain other countries

First Edition published in 2024

Published in the United States of America by Oxford University Press
198 Madison Avenue, New York, NY 10016, United States of America

British Library Cataloguing in Publication Data

Data available

Library of Congress Control Number: 2023948479

ISBN 978–0–19–888145–2

DOI: 10.1093/oso/9780198881452.001.0001

Printed and bound by
CPI Group (UK) Ltd, Croydon, CR0 4YY

Acknowledgements

We owe so much gratitude to a large number of people and institutions. Anne Kriken Mann, widow of FA Mann's son David, donated some 9,000 items of correspondence and the associated copyright to the archive of Humboldt University, Berlin, and provided generous financial support for the digitalization and indexing of these documents. Jessica Thomas and Nicola Beauman, daughters of FA Mann, were most helpful in identifying and donating further documents, as was grandson Martin Thomas. Grandson Richard Thomas provided valuable assistance in getting the process started. Grandson William Lacey attended several project meetings and added valuable information. Herbert Smith Freehills allowed us to inspect many more boxes of correspondence and kindly donated more than 3,000 documents. Many of FA Mann's former colleagues at this firm were most helpful in this process, in particular Lord Collins (who also contributes to the present volume), Geoffrey Lewis (who also arranged for various interviews with friends and colleagues of FA Mann), and Sir Adam Johnson, then partner at HSF and now High Court judge. Professors Horst Eidenmüller, Reinhard Zimmermann, Wolfgang Ernst (another contributor to the present volume), and Christian Waldhoff all played important parts in ensuring that the documents would end up in the archives of Humboldt University. More detail on this can be found in the Introduction, Section III.B.

We are grateful to many other former colleagues and friends of FA Mann who accompanied the project by participating in our workshops and conferences, including Professors Jochen A Frowein, Christian Tomuschat, Campbell McLachlan, and Wolfgang Schön. Professor McLachlan's presentation, 'Foreign Relations Law Revisited', at the 44th FA Mann lecture in November 2022 would have made a very fitting contribution to the present volume but could not be included due to time constraints and will eventually be published separately. The same applies to Professor Schön and his conference paper, 'International Jurisdiction to Tax: The Legacy of F.A. Mann in International Tax Law'.

We also owe gratitude to our institutional partners who helped to arrange our project workshops. The first event, which took place 10–11 June 2021, was to be held at the Max Planck Institute for Legal History and Legal Theory at Frankfurt, but was moved online due to the Covid pandemic; Professor Stefan Vogenauer and Ulrike Radden made very helpful arrangements. The second workshop was held at the British Institute of International and Comparative Law in London on 19 November 2021. Our thanks go to Professors Spiros Maniatis and Eva Lein as well as Leigham Strachan. The final project conference took place at the Centre for

British Studies at Humboldt University, in Berlin, from 15–16 September 2022. To Catherine Smith, Dr Kalika Mehta, and our team of student assistants we owe our sincere thanks for ensuring that it all went so smoothly.

We must also thank the *Deutsche Forschungsgemeinschaft* and the *Alexander von Humboldt-Stiftung* for having generously supported our work. In the first stage, the *Deutsche Forschungsgemeinschaft* kindly provided a grant which allowed Professor Gerhard Dannemann to take a research leave during summer term 2017, and covered the salaries of Christoph König (another contributor to the present volume) and Franziska Stamm as student assistants. This allowed us collectively to read and take notes of the entire correspondence of FA Mann which is now held by the archives of Humboldt University.[1] Dr Jason Allen (as he then was) joined the project on an Alexander von Humboldt fellowship in 2017. The *Deutsche Forschungsgemeinschaft* then generously provided a grant which allowed Dr Allen to work for the project full time and as joint principal investigator with Professor Dannemann, Christoph König to join with a PhD project on an academic biography of FA Mann, and Ricarda Callies and Marco Mauer to provide valuable support as student assistants throughout. The *Deutsche Forschungsgemeinschaft* also kindly covered the costs for the project workshops and conferences as well as further research. Dr Kalika Mehta took over from Dr Allen as research project coordinator in September 2022. We owe her much gratitude for her invaluable work in chasing, coordinating, and editing the contributions to the present volume. At Oxford University Press, our thanks go to Rachel Mullaly and Lisa Butts for their patient support, Kiruthiga Kasthuriswamy and her team of copy editors for their painstaking work, and also to an anonymous reviewer who suggested the present (and much better) title for this present volume. Last but not least, we want to thank all our co-authors for their rich contributions which help us to understand FA Mann and his lasting legacy.

Berlin and Singapore
June 2023
The Editors

[1] See Gerhard Dannemann, Christoph König, and Franziska Stamm, 'The Correspondence of Frederick Alexander Mann (1907–1991)', first published by the British Institute of International and Comparative Law on the occasions of its 60th anniversary in 2018 <https://www.biicl.org/documents/2054_letters_of_fa_mann.pdf> accessed 9 June 2023.

Contents

PART III: 'THE TASK OF THE JURIST TO DEFINE': THE LEGAL ASPECTS OF MONEY

Table of Cases

UNITED KINGDOM

COURT OF JUSTICE OF THE EUROPEAN UNION (CJEU)

INTERNATIONAL COURT OF JUSTICE (ICJ)

PERMANENT COURT OF INTERNATIONAL JUSTICE (PCIJ)

AUSTRALIA

CANADA

FRANCE

GERMANY

NEW ZEALAND

SWITZERLAND

UNITED STATES

List of Abbreviations

BGB	*Bürgerliches Gesetzbuch*, German Civil Code
BIS	Bank for International Settlements
CBDC	Central Bank Digital Currency
CISG	1980 Vienna Convention on International Contracts for the Sale of Goods
CJEU	The Court of Justice of the European Union
ECB	European Central Bank
HGB	*Handelsgesetzbuch*, Commercial Code
IBA	International Bar Association
ILA	International Law Association
ICC	International Chamber of Commerce
ICJ	International Court of Justice
ICSID	1965 Washington Convention on the Settlement of Investment Disputes between States and Nationals of Other States
IMF	International Monetary Fund
KWI	Kaiser-Wilhelm Institute
MOCOMILA	Monetary Committee of the International Law Association
MPI	Max-Planck Institute
PCIJ	Permanent Court of International Justice
PECL	Principles of European Contract Law
UCC	Uniform Commercial Code
UNCITRAL	The United Nations Commission on International Trade Law
UNIDROIT	International Institute for the Unification of Private Law
UPICC	UNIDROIT Principles of International Commercial Contracts

Authors' Bios

Jason Grant Allen is Associate Professor of Law at Singapore Management University Yong Pung How School of Law and Director of the SMU Centre for AI & Data Governance. He was formerly a Senior Research Fellow at the Humboldt-Universität zu Berlin Centre for British Studies.

Will Bateman is Professor and Associate Dean (Research) at the Australian National University's School of Law. His research focuses on the law, constitutional practice, and economics of central banking, sovereign debt markets, and fiscal institutions.

María Emilia Buccella is a Programme Coordinator at the Cambridge Centre for Alternative Finance, Cambridge Judge Business School. She obtained her degree in Economics at the University of Buenos Aires. She is pursuing research on international capital flows, corporate indebtedness, and macroeconomic performance, with emphasis on developing countries.

Lord Collins of Mapesbury (Lawrence Collins) is an arbitrator at 24 Lincoln's Inn Fields. He is a former justice of the UK Supreme Court and a former partner of Herbert Smith Freehills.

Giuditta Cordero-Moss is a Professor at the Oslo University, where she teaches International Commercial Law, Private International Law, and Contract Law. A former corporate lawyer, she practices as an arbitrator in international disputes under the rules of numerous institutions, as well as in ad hoc arbitration.

Gerhard Dannemann is Professor of English Law, British Economy, and Politics at the Centre for British Studies, Humboldt-Universität zu Berlin and Visiting Research Fellow at the Institute of European and Comparative Law, University of Oxford.

Wolfgang Ernst is Regius Professor of Civil Law in the University of Oxford and Fellow of All Souls College. Among his numerous works, he has co-edited (with David Fox) *Money in the Western Legal Tradition* (Oxford University Press 2016).

David Fox holds the Chair of Common Law at the University of Edinburgh. His interests lie in the private law applied to money, treated from historical and comparative perspectives, and in the treatment of digital assets in property law.

Simon Gleeson is a former partner at Clifford Chance and specializes in banking and financial markets. His experience includes advising governments, regulators, and public bodies as well as banks, investment firms, fund managers, and other financial institutions and he is described by all the major legal directories as one of the world's leading experts in financial services and banking, capital markets, and derivatives.

Christian Hofmann is an Associate Professor at the National University of Singapore where he is also the Deputy Director of the Centre for Asian Legal Studies and the Head of Financial Regulation at the Centre for Banking & Finance Law.

Christoph König is doctoral candidate at Humboldt-Universität zu Berlin, a researcher at BSP Business and Law School Berlin in Germany and at Universität Innsbruck in Austria. He regularly lectures at the University of Erfurt and Freie Universität Berlin. His doctoral thesis is a biographical work on FA Mann.

Rosa María Lastra holds the Sir John Lubbock Chair in Banking Law and Chair of the Institute of Banking and Finance Law at the Centre for Commercial Law Studies, Queen Mary University of London. She studied at Valladolid University, Madrid University, London School of Economics and Political Science, and Harvard Law School (as a Fulbright Fellow).

Frank Mecklenburg is the Mark M and Lottie Salton Senior Historian at Leo Baeck Institute in New York City, a research library and archive that documents the history and culture of German-speaking Jews, primarily in the 19th and 20th centuries, but also including documents dating back to the Middle Ages. He publishes mainly in the field of social and emigration history.

Reut Yael Paz is an Israeli scholar specializing in international law, European law, international relations, and legal history. She is the Principal Investigator of 'Seeing Antisemitism Through Law: High Promises or Indeterminacies?' and the German Federal Ministry of Education and Research-funded project entitled 'Struggling for Justice – *Antisemitismus als justizielle Herausforderung*' at the Faculty of Law, Justus-Liebig University Giessen.

Joseph H Sommer was legal counsel at the Federal Reserve Bank of New York. He is an expert on payments systems law and has served on legislative drafting committees. Sommer joined the New York Fed. in September 1988 as a law clerk, and retired in 2019.

FA Mann, His Correspondence, and This Book

*Gerhard Dannemann and Jason Grant Allen**

I. Introduction

Francis Mann, as he became known to the Anglophone world, was a German born and educated lawyer. He fled racial persecution in 1933 and settled in London, where he became one of the great lawyers of his time, equally versed and experienced in legal practice and legal scholarship. His book *The Legal Aspect of Money*, first published in 1938, opened an entire area for legal scholarship. His numerous publications, in particular on public international law, conflict of laws, commercial law, procedural law, and arbitration, eclipse those of many full-time academic lawyers. As a solicitor and partner at the law firm Herbert Smith, he was instrumental in transforming a legal profession in England which traditionally had left litigation to barristers, with solicitors using their clerks as go-betweens. Now solicitors would become actively involved and thus become the experts in international litigation for which London solicitors have since become famed. Drawing on some

* Parts of this introduction, in particular the biographical notes and the description of the correspondence, have been revised and updated from Gerhard Dannemann, Christoph König, and Franziska Stamm, 'The Correspondence of Frederick Alexander Mann (1907–1991)', which was first published by the British Institute of International and Comparative Law on the occasion of its 60th anniversary in 2018, <https://www.biicl.org/documents/2054_letters_of_fa_mann.pdf> accessed 6 June 2023 (hereafter Dannemann, König, and Stamm).

Gerhard Dannemann and Jason Grant Allen, *FA Mann, His Correspondence, and This Book* In: *FA Mann*. Edited by: Jason Grant Allen and Gerhard Dannemann, Oxford University Press. © Gerhard Dannemann and Jason Grant Allen 2024.
DOI: 10.1093/oso/9780198881452.003.0001

12,500 letters of Mann's personal correspondence with judges, academics, and legal practitioners, this book explores how Mann's biography, his equal familiarity with German and English law, and with academia and legal practice, and his wide range of legal interests have contributed to his lasting influence on law and legal scholarship until today.

This introductory chapter provides some biographical information (Section I), explains the provenance and relevance of the correspondence on which this book draws (Section II), and presents a short overview of the three substantive parts of this volume (Sections III–V). Part I of the book deals with biographical aspects, Part II discusses Mann's influence on international law (public, private, commercial and arbitration), and contributions in Part III of the book focus on Mann's influence on monetary law.

II. Personal and Professional Life

> Of all my learned friends, Francis Mann is the most learned of all. Long ago, as a young man, he came from Germany. Since then he has become the head of an important firm of City solicitors: and at the same time the exponent in our literature of a wealth of legal knowledge.[1]

Mann's personal and professional life is well documented, inter alia in a memoir written by Geoffrey Lewis[2] and in Mann's autobiography.[3] Born as Friedrich August Alexander Mann on 11 August 1907, he grew up as the only child of Richard Mann, a practising lawyer with a family background in banking, and his wife Ida, née Oppenheim. The Manns were an assimilated Jewish family who were well respected in their provincial hometown of Frankenthal in Palatinate, Germany. Fritz Mann, as he was then commonly called, studied law in Munich, Geneva, and Berlin, where after graduation he would work as a so-called faculty assistant for the great comparative, commercial, and conflicts lawyer, Professor Martin Wolff, who also supervised his doctoral thesis on the formation of a stock corporation through contributions in kind.[4]

1 A (Lord) Denning, *The Due Process of the Law* (OUP 1980) 4.

2 Geoffrey Lewis, *F.A. Mann: A Memoir* (Hart Publishing 2013) (hereafter Lewis, *F.A. Mann*). Lewis was a younger colleague of Mann, a family friend, and executor of Mann's will. See also Lawrence Collins, 'F.A. Mann (1907–1991)' in Jack Beatson and Reinhard Zimmermann (eds), *Jurists Uprooted. German-speaking Émigré Lawyers in Twentieth-century Britain* (OUP 2004) 381–440 (hereafter Collins, 'F.A. Mann').

3 FA Mann, *Life and Cases. Manuscript of an Autobiography*, ed. by Wolfgang Ernst (V&R Unipress 2021) (hereafter Mann, *Life and Cases*).

4 FA Mann, *Die Sachgründung im Aktienrecht* (Bensheimer 1932). On Wolff, see Gerhard Dannemann, 'Martin Wolff (1872–1953)' in Jack Beatson and Reinhard Zimmermann (eds), *Jurists Uprooted. German-speaking Émigré Lawyers in Twentieth-century Britain* (OUP 2004).

Even before Hitler came to power in January 1933, Mann and Lore Ehrlich, a fellow (and historically only the second female) law faculty assistant at Berlin University,[5] had decided to leave Germany for a joint future. After both had completed their professional qualifications, they married on 12 October 1933 and left Germany on the same day.[6] They made London their new home, where Mann had professional contacts with the law firm Swann, Hardmann & Co., which took him on as an articled clerk.[7] Nevertheless, they had to rely on financial support from their families until 1935 when legal work, initially mostly for the German refugee community and as an expert witness and consultant on German law,[8] began to provide sufficient income.[9] Fritz and Lore Mann's son David was born in 1935 and their daughter Jessica in 1937. Fritz Mann enrolled for an LLM at the London School of Economics in 1935 with a view to an academic career, graduating in 1936.[10] Between 1936 and the end of 1937, he wrote *The Legal Aspect of Money*,[11] which was instantly accepted for publication (in 1938) by the Clarendon Press and also as a doctoral thesis by the London School of Economics.

At heart a legal academic, who under other circumstances would have pursued an academic career,[12] and in legal practice more inclined towards the bar, Mann decided in 1938 for financial reasons to become a solicitor, taking his final examinations in 1941. Being admitted to the roll would have required British citizenship, for which Fritz and Lore Mann had qualified and applied in 1938.[13] With the outbreak of the Second World War in 1939, however, both became enemy aliens. Mann was persuaded to anglicize his first name to 'Francis' (with Lore opposing 'Fred' or 'Frederick'). Their third child, Nicola, was born in 1944. In 1946, both parents were eventually naturalized, and Mann changed his first names by deed poll to 'Frederick Alexander'.[14]

[5] A Lösch, *Der nackte Geist. Die Juristische Fakultät der Berliner Universität im Umbruch von 1933* (Mohr Siebeck 1999) 85; M Röwekamp, *Juristinnen. Lexikon zu Leben und Werk* (Nomos 2005) 239–41. Her doctoral thesis was published as L Ehrlich, *Der Verrat von Betriebsgeheimnissen nach englischem und nordamerikanischen Recht* (W de Gruyter 1930).

[6] Lewis, *F.A. Mann* (n 2) 34.

[7] Mann, *Life and Cases* (n 3) 47.

[8] Collins, 'F.A. Mann' (n 2) 384.

[9] Lewis, *F.A. Mann* (n 2) 39–43.

[10] Mann, *Life and Cases* (n 3) 52f, where, however, Mann erroneously states that his daughter Jessica was born in September 1936, when it was actually 13 September 1937. <www.theguardian.com/books/2018/jul/23/jessica-mann-obituary> accessed 6 April 2023.

[11] Collins, 'F.A. Mann' (n 2) 398.

[12] Mann estate, FA Mann to S Duggan, 1 August 1933, NLMann_0970: 'I am a German lawyer of Jewish extraction. Owing to the recent evolution in Germany I have lost my position and all chances for my future career. [. . .] I had the intention and the possibility of becoming a professor, and I had already begun to write a book on the own stock of companies. Besides lecturing at a university I had intended to go to the bar, and probably I would have achieved both aims during the following winter. I am 26 years old.'

[13] Mann, *Life and Cases* (n 3) 54–57.

[14] ibid 38, 41, 46.

In 1946, the British Government called on Mann to become their delegate to the Inter-Allied Legal Committee of the Allied Control Council in Berlin.[15] This period from mid- until late 1946 is well documented in some 60 letters which Mann wrote to his wife, Lore.[16]

Mann declined a fellowship at University College, Oxford, in 1945 because he felt that the remuneration could not support a family of five. He then pinned great hopes on a professorship in international law at the University of London, for which he was shortlisted in 1949, but he was not selected and the post remained vacant until 1959. 'At the time I learned that it was felt difficult not to appoint me, that one did not, however, wish to appoint a lawyer of foreign origin and that therefore one preferred not to make any appointment at all', wrote Mann about his great disappointment.[17] However, the University of Bonn, where he taught regularly, made him an honorary professor in 1960, a position which he held until his death.[18] He was also awarded honorary doctorates by the universities of Kiel (1978), Zurich (1983), and Oxford (1989).[19] He was invited four times to give the prestigious lectures at the Hague Academy of International Law (in 1959, 1964, 1971, and 1984).[20] Amongst these, his 1964 and 1984 lectures on 'The Doctrine of Jurisdiction in International Law', which straddle public and private international law, stand out as lasting contributions to a still ongoing debate.[21]

Mann's academic credentials and his expertise in legal practice and legislation were recognized in his appointment to the Lord Chancellor's Private International Law Committee in 1952, which also included Professor Geoffrey Cheshire, Gerald Fitzmaurice (later Sir Gerald, judge at the International Court of Justice (ICJ)), the later Law Lords Geoffrey Cross and Richard Wilberforce, and the later Lord Justice John Megaw. Chapter 6 will deal with some aspects of Mann's work in this committee.[22] In 1952, Mann was also appointed Rapporteur of the Monetary Law Committee of the International Law Association, a position which he held until 1973.[23]

A tragic car accident which killed Douglas Philipps, partner in Mann's law firm, soon presented a silver lining. Herbert Smith, a large, well-reputed, and one of

[15] Lewis, *F.A. Mann* (n 2) 66.

[16] The earliest dated letter is from July, the latest from October 1946. FA Mann writes in his autobiography (Mann, *Life and Cases* (n 3) 68) that he flew to Berlin 'in about April 1946'. For Mann's time in Berlin in 1946, see also Dannemann, König, and Stamm (n *) 12–13.

[17] Mann, *Life and Cases* (n 3) 55.

[18] HH Jakobs (ed.), *Gedenkreden auf Frederick Alexander Mann, Brigitte Knobbe-Keuk, Werner Flume* (Bonn University Press 2011) 27 (hereafter Jakobs (ed.), *Gedenkreden*).

[19] Biography, Recueil des Cours 186 (1984) III, 15 (Kiel and Zürich). See Collins, 'F.A. Mann' (n 2) 386.

[20] Collins, 'F.A. Mann' (n 2) 385; for further details see (n 12).

[21] FA Mann, 'The Doctrine of Jurisdiction in International Law' (1963) 111 Recueil des Cours 1 (hereafter Mann, 'Jurisdiction in International Law'); FA Mann, 'The Doctrine of Jurisdiction in International Law Revisited After Twenty Years' (1984) 186 Recueil des Cours 9. See further Chapter 6.

[22] See further Dannemann, König, and Stamm (n *) 13–15.

[23] Biography, Recueil des Cours 186 (1984) III, 15.

the oldest law firms in London, offered to take him on as partner.[24] Mann agreed on the condition that Herbert Smith remove from their premises numerous glass cases which presented to their clients hunting and fishing trophies of the firm's founder.[25] This was symbolic of the change that Mann, together with fellow partner John Barker, would bring to this traditional law firm. At Herbert Smith, litigation had for a long time 'been looked upon as a sort of necessary evil',[26] mostly dealt with by articled clerks liaising with barristers.[27] By contrast, Mann became the prototype of a modern solicitor who designs procedural tactics jointly with a barrister. He was instrumental in building up the reputation of Herbert Smith as one of the world's leading law firms in litigation.[28] Mann could draw upon: his unique combination of experiences and skills in legal scholarship as well as private practice, with an enormous breadth of knowledge in business law, public international law, private international law, procedural law, arbitration, and comparative law; his fluency in English, German, and French (plus some familiarity with Italian);[29] and his excellent contacts in academia, legal practice, business, and politics in the UK, Germany, France, and Switzerland, together with his extensive private and institutional networks.[30] Lewis observed his extraordinary ability to transform a case with his methodological approach:[31] 'You had only to sketch the outline facts for him to seize on its essential features and imbue it with energy and infectious excitement.'[32] As Collins notes, Mann possessed considerable advocacy skills, which shone 'in those tribunals where he had the right of audience (especially in arbitrations such as the *Young Loan* case and in the International Court of Justice in the *Barcelona Tractions* case) [where] he was a very effective advocate in the English manner'.[33]

Collins has traced the deep influence which Mann has exerted on English and international case law.[34] Famous cases in which he appeared include *Barcelona Traction, Light and Power Company, Limited (Belgium v Spain)* (representing Belgium),[35] *Belgium and others v Federal Republic of Germany* (Young Loan case, representing Germany),[36] *BP Exploration Company (Libya) Ltd v Libya* (representing BP),[37] *JH Rayner (Mincing Lane) Ltd v Department of Trade and*

24 Tom Phillips, A History of Herbert Smith (Herbert Smith 2007) 107 (hereafter Phillips, *History of Herbert Smith*).
25 ibid 111.
26 Letter by partner Rex Hare (1949), as quoted in Phillips, *History of Herbert Smith* (n 24) 101.
27 Interview by the first author with Tom Phillips, 28 October 2014; Phillips, *History of Herbert Smith* (n 24) 101.
28 Phillips, *History of Herbert Smith* (n 24) 101, 123.
29 Mann estate, FA Mann to Andrea Giardina, 4 July 1983, NLMann_0282.
30 See the section on 'Institutional Networks' in Dannemann, König, and Stamm (n *).
31 Lewis, *F.A. Mann* (n 2) V.
32 ibid.
33 Collins, 'F.A. Mann' (n 2) 387.
34 ibid.
35 [1970] ICJ Reports 3.
36 [1980] 59 ILR 494; 19 ILM [1980] 1357.
37 (1979) 53 ILR 297.

Industry (International Tin Council case),[38] *Broome v Cassell & Co Ltd*,[39] *Carl Zeiss Stiftung v Rayner & Keeler Ltd*,[40] and *Buttes Gas and Oil v Hammer*.[41] Many developments in English case law can be linked to Mann, such as the abolition of the rule that an English court could not make an award in a foreign currency.[42] However, the 'most dramatic example of Mann's academic influence on the case law'[43] is the decision of the House of Lords in *Oppenheimer v Cattermole*, a tax case where the outcome appeared to hang on whether the revocation of German citizenship imposed in 1941 on all expatriate German citizen of Jewish descent was to be recognized by English courts.[44] The House of Lords had already completed deliberations and were set to allow the appeal when an article published by Mann changed their mind.[45] In this article, Mann pointed out that Art. 116 para (2) of the German Basic Law of 1949 had revoked the 1941 legislation and allowed expatriates to have their German citizenship reinstated, but also that Oppenheimer would have lost any German citizenship held in 1948 when accepting British citizenship. As Lord Cross explained in his opinion, the House of Lords reopened argument on the strength of Mann's article and remitted the case back to the Commissioners for the Special Purposes of the Income Tax Act for further findings.[46]

The many honours which were bestowed on Mann include Commander of the British Empire (1980), the German Grand Cross of the Order of Merit (1977), with Star (1982), being the first solicitor to be made Queen's Counsel, and Honorary Bencher of Gray's Inn.[47] He received a Festschrift in his honour on his 70th birthday.[48]

[38] [1990] 2 AC 418.

[39] [1972] AC 1027.

[40] [1967] 1 AC 853.

[41] [1982] AC 888. For a fuller description and analysis of cases in which Mann was involved, see Collins, 'F.A. Mann' (n 2) 387–436.

[42] *Miliangos v George Frank (Textiles) Ltd* [1976] AC 443, with references to FA Mann, *The Legal Aspect of Money* (3rd edn, OUP 1971).

[43] For a full account of this case, see Collins, 'F.A. Mann' (n 2) 430–36.

[44] *Oppenheimer v Cattermole (HM Inspector of Taxes)* [1976] AC 249. See also the contribution by Lawrence Collins to the present volume, Chapter 5.

[45] ibid 268 (Lord Cross); FA Mann, 'The Present Validity of Nazi Nationality Laws' (1973) 89 LQR 194.

[46] *Oppenheimer v Cattermole* (n 44); see also Collins, 'F.A. Mann' (n 2) 434.

[47] Lawrence Collins 'In Memoriam Dr. FA Mann, QC, CBE, FBA' (1992) BYBIL xvi, xxi.

[48] W Flume and others (eds), *Internationales Recht und Wirtschaftsordnung: Festschrift für F.A. Mann zum 70. Geburstag am 11. August 1977* (CH Beck 1977). On Mann's involvement with his own Festschrift, see Dannemann, König, and Stamm (n *) 17.

III. The Documents

A. The collection

The 12,500 or so documents which have come to light can help to understand the full impact that Mann had on the development of many aspects of the law. The majority, more than 9,000, were passed on after Mann's death in 1991 to his son David and then, after his death in 2012, to his widow, Anne Kriken Mann. When she was reading the manuscript of Lewis' memoir on a plane and placed this on the armrest during a pause, this caught the attention of the person in the adjacent seat, who happened to be Professor Horst Eidenmüller, then of Munich, now of Oxford University. In the ensuing conversation, Professor Eidenmüller advised her to contact Professor Reinhard Zimmermann, Director of the Max Planck Institute for Comparative and International Private Law in Hamburg. When learning about the Mann correspondence, Professor Zimmermann suggested that Professor Wolfgang Ernst, then of Zurich, now of Oxford University, should inspect the boxes at the Mann family home in Basel.[49] Professor Ernst advised that these documents were most certainly worth keeping and contacted inter alia Professor Gerhard Dannemann, who, together with the then Dean of the Law Faculty of Humboldt University, Professor Christian Waldhoff, had no trouble convincing the then Registrar of the Humboldt University Archive, Dr Winfried Schultze, that the University Archive should provide a permanent home for the correspondence of its famous alumnus. Anne Kriken Mann helped further with generous donations to have the correspondence catalogued and digitized.

Gerhard Dannemann suspected that numerous additional documents would be held in the archives of Herbert Smith Freehills. With the helpful assistance of Lord Collins, an additional seven boxes could eventually be traced, which Herbert Smith Freehills kindly allowed Gerhard Dannemann to inspect. With the further kind help of Adam Johnson, then partner of Herbert Smith Freehills and now a High Court Judge, and also of Geoffrey Lewis, more than 3,000 additional documents (those of interest which were not subject to client confidentiality) were identified and kindly donated by Herbert Smith Freehills to the Archives of Humboldt University.

Further valuable help was offered by Mann's daughters, Jessica Thomas and Nicola Beauman. Jessica Thomas provided copies of some 60 more letters to close friends and copies of the letters which Mann had written to his wife Lore from Berlin in 1946.[50] Further documents, including the originals of the 1946 letters, were later donated by the family through Mann's grandson Martin Thomas.

[49] AK Mann, Wolfgang Ernst (personal communications).

[50] Jessica Thomas, a well-known crime novelist and broadcaster who published as Jessica Mann, died on 10 July 2018. For an obituary, see <https://www.theguardian.com/books/2018/jul/23/jessica-mann-obituary> accessed 6 April 2023.

B. Correspondents

The vast majority of documents in the collection are correspondence—letters written by Mann (nearly always in carbon copy) or addressed to him. They show Mann at the hub of several networks. Many correspondents are legal scholars. UK academic correspondents include Ian Brownlie, PB Carter, Geoffrey Cheshire, Roy Goode, Rosalyn Higgins (later President of the ICJ), Robert Y Jennings (also later President of the ICJ), FH Lawson, Sir Otto Kahn-Freund (a very close friend), Sir Elihu Lauterpacht, Sir Hersch Lauterpacht, Kurt Lipstein, John Morris, Peter North, and many others.

The large group of German correspondents includes inter alios Ernst von Caemmerer, Claus-Wilhelm Canaris, Helmut Coing, Karl Doehring, Ulrich Drobnig, Werner Flume, Axel Flessner, Jochen A Frowein, Hugo J Hahn, Andreas Heldrich, Dieter Heinrich, Bernd von Hoffmann, Horst H Jakobs, Erik Jayme, Gerhard Kegel, Hein Kötz, Wolfram Müller-Freienfels, Peter Schlosser, and Christian Tomuschat.

Mann's extensive contacts in Swiss academia are represented by, among others, Max Gutzwiller, Anton Heini, Frédéric-Edouard Klein, Pierre Lalive, Alfred von Overbeck, and Frank Vischer.

French correspondents include Henri Batiffol, Paul Largarde, and Pierre Mayer. Other European academic correspondents are Ignaz Seidl-Hohenveldern (Austria) and François Rigaux (Belgium).

Mann exchanged letters with many US academic lawyers such as Edgar Bodenheimer, Martin Domke, E Allan Farnsworth, Philip C Jessup, Andreas F Lowenfeld, Kurt Nadelmann, Stefan Riesenfeld, Ernst Stiefel, and Arthur T van Mehren. Other well-known international correspondents include Antonio Boggiano (Argentina), James Crawford, and John Fleming (both Australia).

Mann also corresponded with some well-known academics who were not lawyers, including Sir (later Lord) Ralf Dahrendorf, Ernst Fraenkel, and Nobel laureate Friedrich Hayek ('an old friend and client').[51]

Mann had extensive written contact with senior judges—including 14 (some future) Law Lords, namely Ackner, Bingham, Collins, Cross, Denning, Diplock, Hoffmann, Keith, Mackay, Mustill, Roskill, Scarman, Sumption, and Wilberforce. Other senior judges amongst the Mann correspondents include Lord Justice Michael Kerr, Pierre Pescatore (ECJ), Sir Gerald Fitzmaurice (ICJ and ECtHR), Roger Errera (Conseiller d'État, France), William Gummow (later justice at the High Court of Australia), and, as mentioned above, the later ICJ presidents Rosalyn Higgins and Robert Y Jennings. Correspondents well-known in the banking world

[51] Mann, *Life and Cases* (n 3) 235.

include Hermann Josef Abs (a client) and Georges R Delaume, who also worked in arbitration.

From his correspondence with barristers, three stand out, namely Sir Elihu Lauterpacht (mentioned above in his other capacity as scholar), John Foster, and Mark Littman.

Mann exchanged letters with a number of Jewish émigrés. Next to above-named legal scholars, these include Lord Weidenfeld and the Tannhauser family (close family friends and well-known benefactors of the arts). Furthermore, there is a substantial amount of correspondence with Mann's doctoral students at the University of Bonn, most of whom went on to hold senior positions in business, government, academia, or private practice.[52]

While the earliest letter is from 1931,[53] and some other documents from the 1930s to the 1960s have survived, most of the correspondence dates between 1973 and Mann's death in September 1991. Other earlier correspondence includes the letters Mann sent to his wife Lore from Berlin in 1946. Numerically, top correspondents are Professor Hugo J Hahn (over 400 letters), Sir Elihu Lauterpacht (some 150), and Professor Ian Brownlie (some 100).

C. Other documents

Besides correspondence, the donation includes drafts of publications by Mann and a number of personal documents, as well as documents which Mann received as a member of the Lord Chancellor's Private International Law Committee (1952–1962, committee dissolved in 1964). These documents have been used for Chapter 6 of this book.[54]

IV. Part I: 'A German Lawyer of Jewish Extraction' in England: FA Mann's Legal Biography

Part I of this book deals with Mann's personal and professional biography, providing the background for an evaluation of his legacy in the various legal systems in which he worked.

Quite apart from any content of a personal nature, the archival material provides a view into Mann's personality in a number of ways. For example, it reveals Mann as a reliable correspondent who kept meticulous papers: Mann kept a carbon copy

[52] See Dannemann, König, and Stamm (n *) 17–18.

[53] Mann estate, Professor Geiler to R Mann, 7 September 1931, NLMann_0940 advising that his son should contact a certain publisher.

[54] See further Dannemann, König, and Stamm (n *) 13–15.

of each of his replies, and filed these together with those of his correspondent in thematically and alphabetically organized binders. It also provides an overview of his professional activities and impressive global network, both of which help us to understand the nature and calibre of the jurist.

Part I itself comprises four chapters. Chapter 1 by Jason Grant Allen opens the part with an exploration of some considerations that arise for a project on a German Jewish émigré. This chapter was conceived about halfway through the project, when it became clear that the experience of running the project at a German university—indeed, Mann's *alma mater*—was quite a different experience to running such a project at, say, a London university.

There are two aspects to this chapter. The first is a framing of what the 'Jewish dimension' of a person's biography might mean: what questions are open to being asked, and what conjectures may validly be engaged in where answers are not immediately clear, and what conclusions may legitimately be drawn. In the case of Mann, and indeed many of his contemporaries, the dominant cultural mode in the late 19th and early 20th centuries was one of deliberate assimilation to the majority German culture (and a recasting of 'Jewishness' in the mould of Christian religious affiliation that could be relegated to the private sphere). Of course, this assimilationist project ended tragically in Germany; rejection from the German body politic became a determining influence in Mann's personal and professional life, and that of his cohort. Rather than proffering any substantive arguments in this context, the chapter seeks to frame the issue for other chapters in this part.

The other aspect is the contemporary situation in German-speaking Europe today. The 'new' Germany is often characterized by its flagship project of building an *Erinnerungskultur*—a culture of remembrance—around the Holocaust and what the majority population did to its Jewish compatriots and the Jews of other European countries under the Third Reich. This volume is itself a brick in the edifice of that *Erinnerungskultur*. But there are debates about the project's soundness, and even sincerity, and for various reasons some uncomfortable questions are only able to be asked now as decades—and generations—have passed. Because our volume embraces (and purports to record) Mann's legacy, it is essential to consider the way that it interacts with that broader context.

Chapter 2 by Frank Mecklenburg provides some of the historical background to Mann's life and times, including a granular look at the history of the Jews of the Rheinland (and of Mann's birthplace Frankenthal in particular). Mann's biography can only be fully understood against the background of a brief but intense flourishing of German Jewish culture in what Mecklenburg calls the 'Golden Years' of emancipation in the late 19th and early 20th centuries. This helps us to understand both Mann as an individual and the cultural moment in which he lived. As the social world of the Golden Years is lost, and largely forgotten, this chapter helps to contextualize Mann's impressive contributions to legal practice and scholarship.

Chapter 3, by Christoph König, explores Mann's legal socialization and methodological approach as a lawyer and legal scholar, which reflects the traditions both of his native Germany and his adopted England. König argues that Mann's specific style of thinking and writing were a product of his transnational biography—a biography that not only crosses borders but transcends points of origin and terminus. Mann's various contributions to legal practice and legal scholarship therefore provide us with a context in which to consider the evolution of 'legal science' in both England and Germany today—in particular, in relation to the changing role of statutory text and judicial pronouncement.

Chapter 4 by Reut Yael Paz explores the influence of German and Jewish traditions of cosmopolitan thought on Mann's approach to the law of money in particular. Paz speculates that Mann's approach to money was (though not at first sight) consistent with this tradition and that his pre-occupation with money may have been driven (perhaps not consciously) by his desire to rehabilitate the problematical, and often associated, figures of 'money' and 'the Jew' through law.

V. Part II: 'A Wealth of Legal Knowledge': The International Lawyer

Part II portrays Mann as 'The International Lawyer' and traces his influence on the interplay between public international and domestic law, and between public international and private international law, and on international commercial practice and international arbitration. Part II will be complemented by two articles written by project contributors which for time constraints will be published separately, namely Campbell McLachlan's presentation on 'Foreign Relations Law Revisited' as the 44th FA Mann lecture in November 2022, and Wolfgang Schön's presentation at the final project conference on 'International Jurisdiction to Tax: The Legacy of FA Mann in International Tax Law'.

In Chapter 5, Lawrence Collins writes on 'The Influence of FA Mann on English Case Law: The Validity of Acts of State Contrary to Human Rights and International Law and the Enforcement of Foreign Public Law'. While Mann's considerable influence on the development of English Law is not limited to one or two areas, Collins focuses on one which was particularly close to Mann's heart, and also where his influence was most prominent. Over several decades, both in writing articles and in litigating cases before English courts, Mann became a relentless critic of a traditional notion that acts of foreign states were sacrosanct and were not to be called into question in domestic courts. The previously mentioned case of *Oppenheimer v Cattermole*, in which an article published by Mann made the House of Lords rethink their draft judgment, is one such example. Collins shows how Mann's influence extended well beyond his death in 1991, and how he continues to inform recent developments in English case law. A posthumous triumph occurred in 2002, when the House of Lords quoted Mann's writing extensively in support of their decision that foreign expropriations (in this case: of commercial Kuwaiti aircraft by Iraq after the 1990 invasion) need not be recognized if these contravened international law (*Kuwait Airways Corporation v Iraqi Airways Company and Others* [2002] UKHL 19). Collins also traces Mann's influence on a number of other decisions which did much to refine the position on whether foreign public law should be applied or enforced in domestic courts; again, Mann continues to be cited extensively and quoted in support, as recently as in a 2022 case, *Skatteforvaltningen v Solo Capital Partners LLP* [2022] EWCA Civ 234 (also known as the Danish Tax Recovery case).

Chapter 6, written by Gerhard Dannemann and entitled 'Jurisdiction and Private International Law: FA Mann's *Unvollendete*?', carries Mann's influence on jurisdiction and public international law into the area of private international law. Mann was highly critical of the frequent inability of public international lawyers and private international lawyers to even understand what the others were talking about, leading to grave and avoidable misunderstandings where those two areas meet. Mann used jurisdiction as the linchpin for public law influences on private international law in both his Hague Lectures on the subject. Chapter 6 shows that Mann had plans to develop this further into a general textbook on private international law, or at least a general theory of private international law. Drawing on a somewhat neglected speech given on the occasion of the 50th anniversary of his doctorate, as well as on his autobiography and his correspondence with scholars and legislators, Dannemann shows that the strong views which Mann held on expropriations, excessive civil jurisdiction, and so-called overriding mandatory provisions could be easily integrated into such a general theory. On the other hand, Mann might have struggled to reconcile a more comprehensive treatment of public–private international law interactions with his perspective as an English solicitor. Mann had strong aversions to most legal change, in particular against using legislation to remedy any deficiencies in the law which a clever solicitor could write around in a contract. The same is true for his aversion to international courts interpreting uniform international law.

In Chapter 7, Giuditta Cordero-Moss tackles a third and related issue on the borderline of public international law: 'Delocalization and Re-localization in Commercial Law and the Law of Arbitration: The Continued Relevance of FA Mann's Thought'. This relates to the division between public international law and the domestic law of states. Mann was a fierce proponent of a strict separation between those two, in line with the dualist notion generally followed by common law legal systems. As a private international lawyer, he also insisted that any application of a law other than the domestic law of the forum would necessarily occur by virtue of a private international law rule which invoked a foreign domestic law. There was no in-between, no transnational law, no *lex mercatoria*. International commercial contracts would thus necessarily be connected with one or more particular domestic laws. Moreover, all arbitration would also be bound to this model, by the simple fact that the proceedings would be held in a state which would regulate arbitration, and by the further fact that any award resulting from this arbitration would have to be enforced in the same or another state. Mann's views were opposed by a strong movement which sought to delocalize law in general and arbitration in particular, leaving arbiters seemingly beyond the reach of national legal systems. Arbiters may have enjoyed what they saw as greater legroom under a delocalized approach. Cordero-Moss traces a current small renaissance of the localization of arbitration law, with Mann's views regaining ground in current practice and discussion some 30 years after his death. She also explores a division within international commercial practice between delocalization-friendly drafters of international contracts and practitioners who litigate international contracts and who tend to follow the classical localized approach favoured by Mann.

VI. Part III: 'The Task of the Jurist to Define': The Legal Aspects of Money

Part III of the book contains a wealth of learning in monetary law presented by way of engagement with Mann's considerable imprint on that discipline. Some chapters engage with Mann's immediate intellectual influences and the economic and legal historical background against which Mann worked, while others bring Mann's work into the 21st century.

The Legal Aspect of Money was first published in 1938. Since the fifth edition (1992), published after Mann's death, the book has undergone three revisions under the editorship of Charles Proctor and continues to be a seminal text in the study of monetary law, covering areas such as the nature and concept of money (including the principle of nominalism and the role of state legal authority in the constitution of monetary phenomena) and the private law (including especially the private international law) of monetary obligations. As the global monetary system evolved over the decades from the gold standard to the Bretton Woods system, the text grew to cover the emerging international law of money (especially the law of exchange controls, the International Monetary Fund (IMF), and the role of central banks). As monetary theorists grapple with whatever has followed Bretton Woods, the 2020s presents a timely and important juncture at which to reflect on Mann's impressive contributions to the field.

Wolfgang Ernst opens in Chapter 8 with the work of Martin Wolff—Mann's doctoral supervisor and life-long friend—on the topic of monetary law.[55] This chapter

[55] See Chapter 3 in the current volume by Christoph König, 'Pragmatism Meets *Praxisorientierung*: FA Mann and a Transnational Biography in Law' and Chapter 6 by Gerhard Dannemann, 'Jurisdiction and Private International Law: FA Mann's *Unvollendete*?'

provides an original description of the two men's work in the field, a comparison of their similarities and differences, and some speculation about how the teacher and student may have influenced each other's thinking over the decades. One of the insights we gain from a comparison of Wolff's work on money with Mann's is that Mann appears to have accepted and implemented Georg Knapp's 'state theory' of money more enthusiastically than Wolff, and that Mann may have influenced Wolff's later views in this respect. Another is that Mann and Wolff parted ways on certain important questions, such as the extra-territorial application of statutory interferences with gold clauses.

David Fox's Chapter 9 contains a systematic exploration of the treatment of gold clauses in contracts—a topic that engaged about one-sixth of the page count of Mann's first edition of *The Legal Aspect of Money* (1938). This is unsurprising, as these clauses were one of the most troublesome issues in international contracting in the inter-war years. The litigation over gold clauses was, observes Fox, a sign that the old monetary order based on the international gold standard was breaking down, despite the efforts of national governments and central banks to shore it up. In Fox's analysis, the gold clause cases Mann dealt with in his treatise offer a view into the changing of the guard between the gold standard and Bretton Woods. Mann's presentation of the gold clause cases only makes sense if we understand the contemporary monetary world—in particular, why parties inserted gold clauses in their contracts and then litigated their disputes in the courts. Gold clause litigation was a sign that the pre-war monetary world of the international gold standard was breaking down. All countries were on their way to developing fiat money systems, but the assumption of gold value remained a feature of the monetary world. Where Mann examined these cases from the legal perspective, Fox provides an examination of their economic and geopolitical background as well. In his analysis, they illustrate the movement of capital along channels carved by larger forces of international power relations, as investors subscribed to bonds in the financial markets of Europe and America that provided capital not only for infrastructure projects but also for the wars and calamitous changes in international politics of the era.

Joe Sommer's Chapter 10 delves into Mann's use of Georg Knapp's 'state theory' of money. Sommer credits Mann with a 'conservative revolution' in monetary law: although flying under the Knappian banner, Mann's concept of money differs in important respects to Knapp's and is much more a *legal* than a *state* theory of money. Knapp served Mann well enough to do one key thing: to up-end gold and replace it with the sovereign power of the state. His theory was beautifully suited to an era of more instability, less naturalism, and more nationalism. But his revolution was conservative: where other critics of the gold standard preceding Mann had wanted to tear down the throne and embrace the 'societary' construction of money, Mann only wanted to dethrone gold. According to Sommer, the less conservative revolutionaries are winning today.

In Chapter 11, Will Bateman ties some of these themes together, exploring the constitutional dimensions of monetary law with particular attention to the gold standard and the Bretton Woods system. Mann defined the field of monetary law by stipulation as much as description. As Christoph König's Chapter 3 explains, this was not atypical of Mann's approach as a jurist. It allowed him to focus his attention and effort, and it perhaps helps to explain his efficacy and impact as a scholar and practitioner. However, the world does not always divide as neatly as the chapters of a well-formed treatise. Bateman argues that understanding the constitutional dynamics of money allows a richer appreciation of the interconnections of state and market institutions, enriching our understandings of law, economics, and politics.

At this point, it is interesting to note that so many of our authors have engaged with the gold standard and Bretton Woods. This is for an important reason. Just as Mann wrote his treatise at the changing of the guard between monetary orders, those working on monetary law today are considering the end of the Bretton Woods system, the system that has replaced it, and how that system is developing in new directions today. Monetary systems, however, inform legal doctrines and paradigms as well as being shaped by them. Although both the gold standard and the Bretton Woods system are things of the (increasingly distant) past, they both sometimes cast a long shadow. Looking at the changeover from gold standard money to the Bretton Woods system is instructive for those conceptualizing the legal nature of money post-Bretton Woods.

María Emilia Buccella, Rosa Lastra, and Jason Allen explore in Chapter 12 the impact of Mann's treatise in Spanish-speaking Latin America—a region which has, for reasons they elaborate, been an important region for the development of theory and practice in international monetary law. In particular, Latin America has provided an important context in which to consider the operation of the IMF Articles of Association—especially Article VIII(2)(b), which disallows exchange controls except within certain limits. Generally, English and American courts have taken a conservative approach to this Article, but that approach became difficult in the wake of the Latin American debt crisis of the 1980s. Understanding this crisis and its causes provides some economic historical parallels to the gold clause cases in Fox's chapter, as well as the background to a seminal translation project of Mann's major work in monetary law.

It also reveals something of Mann's character. Mann remained committed to a restrictive interpretation of Article VIII(2)(b) that gave it rather a rather limited scope of application, disagreeing with numerous others (including Sir Joseph Gold) on the correct interpretation of the provision.[56] In the preface to the fifth edition of *The Legal Aspect of Money*, Mann opined in characteristically forceful terms

[56] See Joseph Gold, 'Article VIII, Section 2 (b), of the Fund Agreement and the Unenforceability of Certain Exchange Contracts: A Note' (1955) 4 (2) Staff Papers-International Monetary Fund 330–38.

that the United Kingdom should remove Article VIII(2)(b) from its municipal law (while remaining a Member State of the IMF), as the provision 'ought to have no place in the law of a modern State intent upon upholding international commercial practice'.[57]

Simon Gleeson's Chapter 13 explores what Mann's theory might have to say about privately issued cryptocurrencies, by way of an excursus through exchange control legislation. Mann defined money as a chattel 'issued by the authority of law'.[58] However, as we have seen, in practice the situation is more complex: tokens other than chattels issued by entities other than states circulate as 'money', or in a manner problematically similar to 'money', that fall within the purview of 'monetary law'. The nominalistic principle is, at base, that an issuer of money has the prerogative to stipulate its value. The notion of a *lex monetae*—a rule-set proper to any given type of money—embraces nominalism but extends some way further, including as a matter of private and public international law. The precise extent has been hard-fought in various contexts, not least in the context of exchange control legislation (and the effectiveness of such legislation outside its state). In Gleeson's analysis, the impossibility of a private *lex monetae* for privately issued money tokens (such as cryptocurrencies) illustrates some of the limits of the concept itself. The *lex monetae* embraces public and private law doctrines, and is an uncertain concept; however, it is unquestionably a hybrid of private and public law doctrines. Thus, although a private creator of money tokens may be able to replicate some of the attributes of a *lex monetae* by contract, there is no *lex monetae* of purely private money tokens which have not been in some way adopted by the state.

Finally, Christian Hoffmann's Chapter 14 turns to central bank digital currency (CBDC), another contemporary development that provides an opportunity to reflect on Mann's monetary conception. Unlike privately issued cryptocurrencies, CBDCs are by definition issued by a central bank and are more easily accommodated within Mann's state theory based approach. However, they are also definitionally intangible and do not fit within Mann's conception of money as a chattel, i.e. a physical token. All things considered, Hofmann argues that CDBC nevertheless should be welcomed from a traditional 'Mannian' perspective as the next generation of state-issued money to counteract the dominance of privately issued commercial bank money.

Bibliography

Collins L, 'F.A. Mann (1907–1991)' in Jack Beatson and Reinhard Zimmermann (eds), *Jurists Uprooted. German-speaking Émigré Lawyers in Twentieth-century Britain* (OUP 2004)

[57] FA Mann, *The Legal Aspect of Money* (5th edn, OUP 1992).

[58] ibid 8. The reason for citing this edition is that much of Mann's material relating to exchange control has been removed from later editions as the discipline has fallen into practical desuetude.

Collins L, 'In Memoriam Dr. FA Mann, QC, CBE, FBA' (1992) 63(1) BYBIL xvi, xxi

Dannemann G, 'Martin Wolff (1872–1953)' in Jack Beatson and Reinhard Zimmermann (eds), *Jurists Uprooted. German-speaking Émigré Lawyers in Twentieth-century Britain* (OUP 2004)

Dannemann G, König C, and Stamm F, 'The Correspondence of Frederick Alexander Mann (1907–1991)' (2018) British Institute of International and Comparative Law at <https://www.biicl.org/documents/2054_letters_of_fa_mann.pdf> accessed 6 June 2023

Ehrlich L, *Der Verrat von Betriebsgeheimnissen nach englischem und nordamerikanischen Recht* (W de Gruyter 1930)

Flume W and others (eds), *Internationales Recht und Wirtschaftsordnung: Festschrift für F.A. Mann zum 70. Geburstag am 11. August 1977* (CH Beck 1977)

Gold J, 'Article VIII, Section 2 (b), of the Fund Agreement and the Unenforceability of Certain Exchange Contracts: A Note' (1955) 4(2) Staff Papers-International Monetary Fund 330

Jakobs HH (ed), *Gedenkreden auf Frederick Alexander Mann, Brigitte Knobbe-Keuk, Werner Flume* (Bonn University Press 2011)

Lewis G, *F.A. Mann: A Memoir* (Hart Publishing 2013)

Lösch A, *Der nackte Geist. Die Juristische Fakultät der Berliner Universität im Umbruch von 1933* (Mohr Siebeck 1999)

Mann FA, 'The Doctrine of Jurisdiction in International Law' (1963) 111 Recueil des Cours 1

Mann FA, 'The Present Validity of Nazi Nationality Laws' (1973) 89 LQR 194

Mann FA, *Die Sachgründung im Aktienrecht* (Bensheimer 1932)

Mann FA, *Life and Cases: Manuscript of an Autobiography* (Wolfgang Ernst ed, V&R Unipress 2021)

Mann FA, *The Legal Aspect of Money* (5th edn, OUP 1992)

Phillips T, *A History of Herbert Smith* (Herbert Smith 2007)

Röwekamp M, *Juristinnen. Lexikon zu Leben und Werk* (Nomos 2005)

PART I

'A GERMAN LAWYER OF JEWISH EXTRACTION' IN ENGLAND

FA Mann's Legal Biography

1

Ein Bericht aus einer Akademie

Writing About Germany's Lost Jewish Scholars, 80 Years On

Jason Grant Allen[*]

I. Introduction

This volume explores the life and work of FA Mann—a German-born and (mostly) German-educated jurist who spent the operative parts of his professional life in the United Kingdom. The project on which the volume is based set out to understand Mann's life as a lawyer and describe his legacy—in English law, and also in German, European, and international law.

As set out in the introduction, the project was catalysed by a bequest of documents to the Humboldt-Universität zu Berlin, where Mann read law and began his academic career.[1] This archive has formed the focal point of discussions by

[*] This chapter is dedicated to I.S., my former host mother, with the greatest thanks and affection. I am writing this chapter near turapina/Ben Lomond in north-eastern lutruwita/Tasmania. I acknowledge the traditional ownership of this area by letteremairenner people and the role of today's palawa people in our evolving society and relationship to the land.

[1] Then the Friedrich-Wilhelms-Universität.

Jason Grant Allen, Ein Bericht aus einer Akademie In: *FA Mann.* Edited by: Jason Grant Allen and Gerhard Dannemann, Oxford University Press. © Jason Grant Allen 2024. DOI: 10.1093/oso/9780198881452.003.0002

subject-matter experts within the various fields of Mann's activity. Together with a memoir by Geoffrey Lewis[2] and Mann's recently published autobiography (edited minimally by Wolfgang Ernst),[3] the archive provides a unique view into Mann's life and work, his social network, and German and English society in the 20th century.

This part explores Mann's personal and professional biography. Following this chapter, Frank Mecklenburg's chapter explores what it meant to be 'German *and* Jewish' in what he calls the 'Golden Years'. This provides some essential background, because Mann was in many ways a product of the peculiar history of Rhenish Jews and the cultural flourishing of Jews in German-speaking lands. Christoph König's chapter explores Mann's methodological and doctrinal orientation as a lawyer, framed by his educational background and his migration. Reut Yael Paz then explores what this background might have meant for Mann's scholarship—particularly for his seminal work on money. In the vein of earlier work on German-speaking Jewish international lawyers (including Mann's friend Sir Hersch Lauterpacht), Paz situates Mann within distinctly Jewish and German traditions of cosmopolitan thought.[4]

Though not the primary focus of our project, discussion of the 'Jewish dimension' of Mann's biography arose at various times and in various contexts. My conclusion is that until one has brought order to some sticky and convoluted questions, one cannot know how to write about the legacy of an individual like Mann today. My aims in this chapter are thus to (i) provide some clarity on what those questions are, and (ii) to provide a few answers by way of my own opinion. These may help to 'frame' the Jewish dimension of our collective effort to understand Mann 'the lawyer' and describe 'his legacy'.

Although I am not an expert in Jewish Studies, what it means to belong to a group, the confluence of biological and social factors, and the legal treatment of identity has fascinated me from the beginning of my academic career.[5] Written at the end of a longer stint as a researcher in the German academy, this chapter also draws on my own experience over multiple periods in Germany and Austria in the 2010s and 2020s as an Australian Jew born in the 1980s.[6]

[2] Geoffrey Lewis, *F.A. Mann: A Memoir* (Hart 2013).

[3] See FA Mann, *Life and Cases: Manuscript of an Autobiography* (Wolfgang Ernst ed., Bonn University Press 2022) (hereafter Mann, *Life and Cases*).

[4] See Reut Yael Paz, *A Gateway Between a Distant God and a Cruel World* (Brill 2013). See also Leora Bilsky and Annette Weinke, *Jewish-European Émigré Lawyers: Twentieth Century International Humanitarian Law as Idea and Profession* (Wallstein 2021).

[5] The first paper I ever published was on this topic, in the context of my own country's legacy of genocide: see JG Allen, 'Group Consent and the Nature of Group Belonging: Genomics, Race, and Indigenous Rights' (2010) 20(2) Journal of Law, Information and Science 28. This gives me the position of being vicariously associated with two genocides—the victim community of one, and the perpetrator community of another.

[6] One must generalize from personal anecdotes carefully; however, lived experience *is* the value of sojourning in another society. Tongue firmly in cheek, 'gonzo ethnography' (in which the observer is an active participant in observed events) might capture something about reaching considered hypotheses on this basis: see EMI Sefcovic, 'Toward a Conception of "Gonzo" Ethnography' (1995) 19(1) Journal of Communication Enquiry 20. The value is the process of reflective equilibrium between what one *reads* about the world and one what *experiences* the world to be.

For his own part, Mann described his family as 'non-practicing Jews' that nonetheless 'felt Jews by background, history and tradition, although our noses were straight and our cultural status was wholly and firmly German'.[7] This tied into his motivation to write an autobiography:

> I write [an autobiography], because I am persuaded that it is my duty to tell the story of a world that has disappeared, but should not be forgotten,—the story of a highly cultured German Jewish bourgeois milieu which perished in Auschwitz, though my nearest and dearest succeeded in escaping. The history of the rise and fall of that social class merits to be preserved, but stands in danger of falling into oblivion.[8]

These statements by Mann about himself raise more questions than they give answers. What does it mean to have a 'wholly and firmly German' 'cultural status'? What were the defining characteristics of this 'milieu'? Which of its characteristics were 'German' and which 'Jewish'? Before and during Mecklenburg's Golden Years, how did the German and Jewish bourgeois worlds intersect, and how were they (still) disconnected? Given the outsized contribution of 'highly educated, bourgeois' Jews to German culture, can we separate the two? If not, how do we avoid subsuming the 'Jewish' into the 'German' or vice versa? Elsewhere, Mecklenburg asks how 'German' this culture was. The answer must be informed by the fact that 'being German' is a much broader cultural phenomenon than the post-1871 territorial entity we now call Germany; crucially, '[t]here is no Germany without Jews, and in turn German is one of the most important Jewish languages'.[9] However, although the idea that Jewish culture was central to German-speaking European culture is now well-established, on a social level Jews are still definitely conceptualized as the quintessential 'Other'.[10]

Writing 80 years on, there are good reasons to avoid laying too much stress on the 'Jewishness' of an assimilated, secular German Jew like Mann. In the worst case, such an over-emphasis distorts our understanding of Mann as an individual, and writes his legacy within the same categories that defined German society under National Socialism. However, if we stress his 'Germanness' too

[7] Mann, *Life and Cases* (n 3) 49. See also Nicola Gluckmann, 'Past Imperfect, Future Tense: A Mother's Letter about Loss, Storytelling, and the Profound Ambivalence of the German-Jewish Legacy' in Gideon Reuveni and Diana Franklin (eds), *The Future of the German-Jewish Past* (Purdue University Press 2021) 53–54 (hereafter Reuveni and Franklin (eds), *German-Jewish Past*). This hints at the complexity of our subject matter: was Mann here adopting the prosaic racial stereotype of Jews? (The phenomenon of Jewish antisemitism towards poorer, more religious, and often less-educated Jews from Eastern Europe is well-documented). Or is this written an in ironic style?

[8] Mann, *Life and Cases* (n 3) 13.

[9] Frank Mecklenburg, 'Jewish and German: The Leo Baeck Institute Archives and Library' in Reuveni and Franklin (eds), *German-Jewish Past* (n 7) 224.

[10] Lisa Silverman, 'Rethinking Jews, Antisemitism and Jewish Difference in Post-War Germany' in Reuveni and Franklin (eds), *German-Jewish Past* (n 7) 136.

much, we effectively expunge his legacy of a defining element. Worse still: in so doing, we both lose the opportunity to explore the uniquely Jewish contribution to German life, and erase the Jewish dimension of German culture from the historical record forever—the precise trend Mann sought to counter with his own autobiography.

In short, we must be open to the notion that Mann contributed so much to German cultural life not only because he was prosaically 'more German than the Germans', but also, somehow, *because he was a Jew*. This is, in turn, an important contribution to the effort of maintaining an authentic 'culture of remembrance' [*Erinnerungskultur*] in German-speaking Europe today. In the maintenance of such a culture, it is sometimes most important what we say 'by the by'—that is, in projects *not* specifically dedicated to Jewish Studies. A project like this, which is focused on Mann as a lawyer and on his substantive impact on the law, thus provides a context in which we can and must explore the Jewish dimension of his life and legacy.

II. Stating the Obvious, and Answering a Question with a Question

The impacts of National Socialism on Mann's life are one of the more obvious elements of his biography. Although Mann claims never to have experienced antisemitism in his early life,[11] it was characteristic of the society into which he was born. Walther Rathenau, a rough contemporary of Mann's father, wrote in 1911:

> In the early years of every German Jew, there is a painful moment that can never be forgotten [in which] he becomes aware that he entered the world as a second-class citizen and that no amount of talent or merit would free him of that status.[12]

Nicola Gluckmann writes of her relative, Sir Otto Kahn-Freund, a contemporary of Mann's at the London School of Economics and a lifelong correspondent and friend:

> 'The single most important fact about my life is that I was born a Jew', wrote Otto in his unfinished personal memoir of 1979. Not 'am a Jew' but '*born* a Jew'. Despite

[11] See Mann, *Life and Cases* (n 3).

[12] Cited in Shulamit Volkov, 'Rewriting German History: Jewish Experience as a Corrective' (63rd Leo Baeck Memorial Lecture, 24 April 2022) <https://digipres.cjh.org/delivery/DeliveryManagerServlet?dps_pid=FL12607487> 14 accessed 5 June 2023 (hereafter Volkov, 'Rewriting German History'). Rathenau was assassinated in 1922 by right-wing militiamen while serving as Foreign Minister.

> his choice to live in a determinedly secular world, here by Otto's own admission was acknowledgment that his life was nevertheless defined by this one fact.[13]

Being born a Jew has, indeed, been a singular defining fact in many societies over many ages.[14] Jean Paul Sartre famously wrote that '[t]he one thing Jews can never choose is *not* to be a Jew'.[15] Lisa Silverman explains that one who does so merely becomes an 'inauthentic Jew': 'For Sartre, this category is a theoretical impossibility, as a Jew who attempts this denial of subjectivity merely reinforces the terms that created them in the first place.'[16] Being born a Jew is, it seems, an inescapable condition.[17]

Twentieth-century Germany was an extreme example, as even second-generation converts to Christianity were rooted out of the German body politic. Rathenau's moment must have come for Mann, too, possibly at some point in the 1920s as he entered adulthood, and certainly no later than the rise of the National Socialists to power in 1933. According to Sheer Ganor, 'National Socialism violently negated claims to German-Jewishness as a culture and identity: its claimants and bearers faced expulsion and dispersion, or worse, deportation and annihilation'.[18] No doubt, this would have caused complex psychological reactions including self-alienation as the two halves of Mann's professed culture delaminated—that is, as his fundamentally liminal cultural status was exposed.

On a superficial level, it is trite to say that Mann's life would have unfolded differently but for the fact that he was Jewish.[19] Probably, like the vast majority of Germans, 'Counterfactual Mann' would have remained in the country during its degradation

[13] Nicola Gluckmann, 'Past Imperfect, Future Tense: A Mother's Letter about Loss, Storytelling, and the Profound Ambivalence of the German-Jewish Legacy' in Reuveni and Franklin (eds), *German-Jewish Past* (n 7) 52.

[14] Shulamit Volkov prefaces her 2006 book with a 1832 quote from Ludwig Börne: 'It is like a miracle! I have experienced it a thousand times and it remains forever new to me. One blames me for being a Jew; the other forgives me for it; the third even praises me on this account; but they all think of it. As if they were caged in that magical Jewish circle, no one can get out.' Shulamit Volkov, *Germans, Jews, and Antisemites: Trials in Emancipation* (Cambridge University Press 2006).

[15] Jean Paul Sartre, *Anti-Semite and Jew: An Exploration of the Etiology of Hate* (George Becker tr., Schoken Books 1944) 69.

[16] Lisa Silverman, 'Rethinking Jews, Antisemitism and Jewish Difference in Postwar Germany' in Reuveni and Franklin (eds), *German-Jewish Past* (n 7) 140.

[17] See also Samuel Farber, 'Deutscher and the Jews: On the Non-Jewish Jew—An Analysis and Personal Reflection' in Jack Jacobs (ed), *Jews and Leftist Politics: Judaism, Israel, Anti-Semitism and Gender* (Cambridge University Press 2017) 331.

[18] Sheer Ganor, 'Generation in Flux: Diasporic Reflections on the Future of German-Jewishness' in Reuveni and Franklin (eds), *German-Jewish Past* (n 7) 14.

[19] What do we mean by 'Jew' and 'Jewish', and what is the right set of terms to use? 'Of Jewish extraction'? 'Born to Jewish parents'? See, in particular, Frank Mecklenburg's chapter in this volume on what it meant to be 'German *and* Jewish' in the decades between emancipation and the rise of National Socialism. The experience of German Jews is most obviously distinguishable from the experience of Jews in Eastern Europe. For a contemporary account, see for example Jakob Wassermann, *Mein Weg als Deutscher und Jude* (Suhrkamp Jüdischer Verlag 2005). Some prefer to speak of 'German-speaking Jews' or 'Jews from German-speaking lands' to avoid eliding the fundamental problematic of what it meant to be 'German *and* Jewish' in the relevant period.

under National Socialism. We would then be considering a very different biography—probably one of a Berlin law professor rather than a London solicitor. Assuming that Counterfactual Mann would have had 'our Mann's' politics and temperament, we would now discuss how he navigated a treacherous landscape in which academic standards and integrity were debased, and how he rebuilt his life through the post-war period.[20] Counterfactual Mann's work would almost certainly have remained more specific to German law; it is highly unlikely that he would have been a scholar of English law, and Mann attributed his own interest in international law to his experience of forced migration (and his friendship with Sir Hersch Lauterpacht).[21] His legacy would have been very different, too—perhaps, for example, a legacy of one dedicated to rebuilding academic standards in Germany following the war.[22]

The obvious point, then, is that Mann's life took a very different course in response to world-historical developments in his lifetime. But is this all there is to be said about the 'Jewish dimension' of his life? On a deeper level, for example, can we be sure that Counterfactual Mann would have had the same politics and temperament if he had been born into a non-Jewish family? How might his background have informed (or even defined) Mann's outlook on life and indeed the law? For many of us, this is an exciting and very worthwhile avenue of enquiry—even if it requires some speculation.

For some good reasons, however, there is a natural instinct to avoid the 'problem of identity'. I will explore what I see as the main reasons for this in the sections that follow. And yet, it was a point of discussion over the course of our project. My aim in this chapter is, therefore, to interrogate the context in which the question of Mann's identity arises for us today: in a scholarly project, with both biographical and substantive legal aims, at a German university in the third decade of the 21st century.

At the risk of being bromidic (or even gauche), the best answer to 'the Jewish Question' is often 'a Jewish question'. In response to the question: 'Is there a Jewish art?' Harold Rosenberg (writing in the 1970s) suggested that the 'Gentile answer' is a yes or no; the 'Jewish answer' is: 'What do you mean by Jewish art?'[23] Terry

[20] For example, see Carl Schmitt, 'Die deutsche Rechtswissenschaft im Kampf gegen den jüdischen Geist: Schlusswort auf der Tagung der Reichsgruppe Hochschullehrer des NSRB vom 3. Und 4. Oktober 1936' (1936) 41(2) Deutsche Juristenzeitung 1194.

[21] Apparently, Lauterpacht's LSE lectures introduced him to international law; staying with it was a reaction to emigration: 'I continued my studies in the fields in which I felt a foreign-born and originally foreign trained lawyer could make the most valuable contribution, namely private international law and, later, public international law as well as their interrelationship.' See Mann, *Life and Cases* (n 3) 55. I am grateful to Christoph König for his input on this point.

[22] Indeed, despite having a 'highly ambivalent' attitude towards Germany, Mann felt 'considerable responsibility towards Germany'—for educating German youth (and giving them the opportunity to meet a Jew), and 'rebuilding a sound intellectual standard' after the debasement of the university system. See Lawrence Collins, 'F.A. Mann (1907—1991)' in Jack Beatson and Reinhard Zimmermann (eds), *Jurists Uprooted* (OUP 2004) 440 (hereafter Beatson and Zimmermann (eds), *Jurists Uprooted*).

[23] Harold Rosenberg, 'Is There a Jewish Art?' in Harold Rosenberg, *Discovering the Present: Three Decades in Art, Culture, and Politics* (Chicago 1973) 223.

Cooney explains that the range of responses reflects the ongoing debate over the place of ethnicity in 20th-century American culture:

> [A]ny answer to his question presumes an outlook not just on the relation of ethnicity to art but on its importance for intellectual and social life in general. In no way was Rosenberg's 'Jewish answer' meant to evade the question ... he went on to assert at the end of his argument that 'the most serious theme in Jewish life is the problem of identity.' To answer the question with a question recognized that there were multiple responses to this 'problem' and directed particular attention toward the context within which any specific answer might be framed.[24]

Understanding any individual's life requires an understanding of their social, political, and legal context. This is perhaps particularly true of someone who identified as a Jew, or was identified by others as a Jew, in 20th-century Germany: German, Jewish, and German-Jewish identity is particularly complex. Further, the context in which *we* are asking the question is just as important to grapple with as Mann's historical context. The place of ethnicity, and the relation between Jewishness, ethnicity, and religion, is no easier in early 21st-century Europe than it was in 20th-century America.

A person's lived experience, including their subjective feelings of cultural belonging and self-identification, must be placed in their historical context. Mecklenburg's chapter provides the immediate context, with a focus on the economic life of Rhenish Jews and the punctuated liberalization of the professions in German-speaking lands. As Miriam Thulin explains, the broader picture of Jewish networks is framed by Jews' history (since antiquity) of mobility across territories and political boundaries, shared language and customs, and high literacy rates. But Jewish networks were also framed by social exclusion and prejudice against Jews by the majority population:

> [A]t least in Christian Europe from the mid-fifteenth century until the elimination of the European Jewry by National Socialism, communication in the Jewish diaspora was characterised by a constant 'dialectic of assimilation', by a genuinely dialectical process between acculturation and self-assertion, between isolation and openness (towards wider society) in the history of the Jews. This is connected not only with problems related to the material environment of the Jews and their surrounding cultures, questions of relational history, the transfer processes, and interpretation and translation phenomena. Rather, it also involves questions of laws and demands towards the Jews like occupational limitations and social

[24] Terry A Cooney, 'New York Intellectuals and the Question of Jewish Identity' (1991) 80(3) American Jewish History 344, 344.

> discrimination, as well as ambivalent, usually anti-Jewish and anti-Semitic, perceptions and attributions. These attributions, which very early regarded certain Jewish forms and structures of communication as threatening, surfaced in the 19th century especially as conspiracy theories, as a variety of critiques of capitalism or, often closely related to the latter, in the form of criticism of Jews for allegedly lacking a genuine Jewish country, state or land.[25]

All of these themes play out in Mann's biography. Real professional freedom, for example, was only realized in 1918 and ended tragically in the 1930s, as Mann reached professional maturity. Paz's chapter explores the association of Jews and capitalism, using this as an avenue to situate Mann within a distinctively German and Jewish cosmopolitan tradition. In the balance of this chapter, we will see themes including conspiracy (e.g. the myth of the '*Dolchstoss* agenda') and the 'dialectic of assimilation' recur, as well.

III. The Travails of German-Jewish Identity

Identity is always a highly personal, and therefore idiosyncratic, question. It is full of paradoxes and self-contradictions. It is a sensitive matter. This is particularly so in the case of Jewish identity. Although most religious identities are mutually exclusive, with 'ethno-religions' like Judaism there are additional layers above and below one's beliefs. I have many friends who proudly identify as 'Jewish atheists', some in the third generation![26] In my experience, however, 'non-Jewish Jews' cause non-Jewish Germans some confusion. From the 19th century, German Jews adopted a rhetorical position by which Jewishness was couched as a matter of religious affiliation. This was a response to antisemitism more than it was as an expression of the Jewish tradition. Today, many Germans adopt the same approach, perhaps for want of any better starting point. The notion of secular Jewish culture is somewhat awkward in this scheme. Historical 'non-Jewish Jews' that happened to be

[25] Mirjam Thulin, 'Jewish Networks' (*European History Online*, 3 December 2010) <http://ieg-ego.eu/en/threads/european-networks/jewish-networks> accessed 15 December 2022, citing Amos Funkenstein, 'The Dialectics of Assimilation' (1995) 1(2) Jewish Social Studies 1.

[26] This suggests there is a 'Jewish' way of being an atheist, and/or that there is something to being 'Jewish' beyond religious belief and practice. Many non-religious Jews, especially progressive ones, have been described (and may describe themselves) as 'non-Jewish Jews', i.e. people who are a-religious or even anti-religion in a distinctively 'Jewish' way. See Isaac Deutscher, *The Non-Jewish Jew and Other Essays* (Verso Books 2017). In my mother's native New York, being Jewish is at least as much a question of descent and culture as religious affiliation. A Catholic New Yorker once told me that 'everyone from New York is half Jewish'. If history had played out differently, could one have said something similar of Berlin or Vienna? See Gabe Friedman, 'What's a "Jew of no Religion"? 3 American Jews on their Non-Religious Identities' *Times of Israel* (7 June 2021) <https://www.timesofisrael.com/whats-a-jew-of-no-religion-3-american-jews-on-their-non-religious-identities/> accessed 26 April 2023; see also Peter Elias, *A Few from Afar: Jewish Lives in Tasmania from 1804* (Hobart Hebrew Congregation 2003).

German are, too often, macadamized back into the category of 'German' without differentiation.

German-Jewish émigrés and refugees (and their descendants) face a peculiarly tortuous set of identity questions.[27] This is for many reasons, but I shall pick three illustrative ones. First, German Jews' sense of Jewish identity is likely to be less informed by active religious observance and religious community participation. Second, German Jews are more likely to have been 'assimilated' than (for example) their Eastern European counterparts, which is to say that they are more likely to have made active attempts to identify with the mainstream of German culture. Finally, the violent rejection of their bid at belonging to the political and cultural body of the 'German people' has added layers of complexity.

Nicola Gluckmann's open 'letter' to her children gives a sense of the nuances, paradoxes, and, at times, self-contradictions of German-Jewish identity—both in her parents' generation (as Holocaust-era refugees from Berlin) and in her own.[28] Describing the deliberate dissociation of her mother with the Anglo-Jewish community of post-war Britain, Gluckmann explains that her mother would identify as 'Jewish not by religion but by "by *race*"'.[29] She responded to expulsion from the German body politic by doubling down on universalist values of international socialism. (This stands in contrast to Mann's generally conservative political outlook, but is perhaps not dissimilar to Mann's wife, Eleonore *née* Ehrlich, often referred to as Lore.) The failure of that post-war dream, however, and the resurgence of antisemitism in post-war Europe, 'perhaps best explains some of the legacy of family ambivalence and alienation that [the younger generation has] inherited'.[30]

It would not be appropriate for me to conjecture about Mann in the way Gluckmann does about her mother. However, there are some facts of which we can take notice. As any migrant—let alone refugee—knows, identities are informed by trauma and dislocation as much as by agency; this has been observed to lead to complex psychological outcomes.[31] In effect, the destruction of European Jewry layered on top of the self-alienation implicit in the process of assimilation itself.[32] In retrospect, the figure of the 20th-century German Jew is a dignified but

[27] The choice of these terms—émigré *versus* refugee—is interesting in a few senses. First, it could be used to put distance between those who had the foresight and the means to leave before they became 'refugees'. Secondly, it could be used to draw lines of connection between Jews who were literally forced to leave by violent displacement and those who chose to uproot themselves even in happier times. In the European context, of course, hindsight casts all Jewish migrants in a similar light.

[28] See Nicola Gluckmann, 'Past Imperfect, Future Tense: A Mother's Letter about Loss, Storytelling, and the Profound Ambivalence of the German-Jewish Legacy' in Reuveni and Franklin (eds), *German-Jewish Past* (n 7).

[29] ibid 53.

[30] ibid.

[31] See, for example, Wendy Pearlman, 'How Homeland Experiences Shape Refugee Belonging: Rethinking Exile, Home, and Integration in the Syrian Case' (2023) 57(1) International Migration Review 160.

[32] The 'self-hatred' of assimilated Jews is proverbial. See, for example: Ritchie Robertson, *The 'Jewish Question' in German Literature 1749–1939* (OUP 2001), particularly ch 4 'Assimilation' on the

ultimately tragic one: the society to which he felt a powerful belonging never quite reciprocated, and ultimately rejected him violently. As Gluckmann's letter makes poignantly clear, it would in fact be an error to take what this generation had to say about itself at face value.

IV. The Minefield (and Why We Must Enter It)

The overall thrust of this chapter is that it is worthwhile and legitimate to explore the 'Jewish dimension' when writing about Mann, the lawyer, and his legacy. However, there are reasons to avoid overemphasizing it. I wish to be equally candid about these reasons and will attempt to do them justice, even if I do not ultimately think they are convincing.

The first has been discussed already. Given Mann's own views about Jewishness, we must not present a distorted or imbalanced picture of the man. This would obviously be a poor outcome for a biographical volume. For example, we might give the impression that Mann was outspoken about his Jewish identity or that he was religiously observant, both of which would be inaccurate. Several project members report that they had been unaware that Mann was a Jew when they first encountered his work. Others, who knew Mann personally, recalled that he avoided making too much of the matter—and expressed antipathy towards those that did.[33] While this must be taken seriously, it rather informs how we should go about our task than negates it.

The second is more serious. It can be difficult to talk about the influence of Jewish background on a person's life and work without falling unwittingly on stereotypes and prejudices about Jews—or appearing to.[34] On the one hand, there is a risk is of reductivism and essentializing the Jewish experience as one of dislocation and

'unusual self-description "a Jewish German"' adopted by Friedrich Blach and Jeffrey C Alexander, *The Civil Sphere* (OUP 2006), particularly ch 18 'The Jewish Question: Anti-Semitism and the Failure of Assimilation'; Theodor Lessing, *Jewish Self-Hate* (PC Appelbaum tr., Berghahn Books 2021); Philip Roth, *Portnoy's Complaint* (Random House 1969); for a controversial revision, see Paul Reitter, *On the Origins of Jewish Self-Hatred* (Princeton University Press 2012).

33 According to an anecdote shared by Wolfgang Schön in one of our meetings, Mann criticized so-called '*Berufsjuden*' who made a 'profession' out of being a Jew in the post-war years. (One could also translate *Beruf* as 'vocation', however, in which case these individuals might appear in a more sympathetic light.) Either way, I think it would be a serious error to read too much into this. Alan Posener describes that 'for many returning Jewish émigrés [like his father], keeping a low profile and not asking too many questions was not only a matter of pride and pity but also made professional and private sense'. He continues that his father considered Heinz Galinksi, the leader of the *Zentralrat der Juden* who remained 'visibly and uncompromisingly Jewish', an embarrassment, 'the kind of 'pushy' Jew he never wanted to be or be associated with'. However, his father also recognized that his own attitude 'was in essence antisemitic'. Alan Posener, 'No More Mr. Nice Guy: Questioning the Ideal of Assimilation' in Gideon Reuveni and Diana Franklin (eds), *The Personal, the Historical, and the Making of German-Jewish Memory* (Purdue University Press 2021) 5–6.

34 Robert Howse, 'Review of Reut Yael Paz, A Gateway between a Distant God and a Cruel World: The Contribution of Jewish German-Speaking Scholars to International Law' (2015) 26 European Journal of International Law , 557–58.

forced emigration. Jewish experiences differ over time and geography and must be considered in their context. On the other hand, exile and guest status actually *is* a central element of the Jewish experience. All Jewish narratives are informed by traditions of exile: it is a major theme in the tradition's canonical texts, and almost every Jewish community has a localized history of expulsion, often violent, humiliating, and impoverishing.[35] Outside of the United States, most Jewish families in the world today have experienced this in living memory.[36] Conversely, most of us who identify as Jews have experienced the thrill of meeting someone 'exotic', yet discovering an intimate sphere of shared Jewish identity and experience.[37]

As Charles Kadushin observed a decade ago, the big picture of Jewish social networks has not been explored in a systematic, scholarly fashion as opposed to a conventional historical manner or anecdotally.[38] On an anecdotal level, many of Mann's friends and professional contacts in England were Jewish émigrés and refugees, including (for example) Sir Hersch Lauterpacht[39] and Sir Otto Kahn-Freund. A more systematic historical network analysis of the archives may, in the future, enrich our understanding of Mann's social world. Perhaps this volume might provoke further exploration of the Jewish dimension of Mann's network—potentially linking up with other archives in a more systematic manner.

The third reason relates to the task before us most directly, and will occupy the balance of this chapter. Reducing Mann to *only* the 'Jewish dimension' of his biography would perpetrate the very wrong committed against him by the National Socialists.[40] Christoph König discusses Mann's displeasure, for example, at reading an article in the *Frankfurter Allgemeine Zeitung* (FAZ) which contained a 'tasteless' reference to Mann's friend and mentor: 'That one calls Martin Wolff ... "a great Jewish legal scholar" is below the dignity of the [newspaper].'[41] Obviously, we do

[35] Psalm 137: 'By the rivers of Babylon we sat and wept when we remembered Zion.' Between memories of estrangement in Egypt and Babylon and the great Diaspora under the Romans, exile is a major theme in the Jewish tradition. Local expulsions have been a persistent theme, too, in European history, including in Germany. Expulsion from the British Isles and the Iberian Peninsula should be mentioned as well. There are virtually no Jewish communities without their own localized histories of exile.

[36] This is not just a phenomenon of modernity, either: see Simon Schama, *The Story of the Jews: Finding the Words (1000 BCE—1492 CE)* (The Bodley Head 2013) and *The Story of the Jews: Belonging (1492 CE—1900 CE)* (The Bodley Head 2017), which treat Jewish 'deep' history in a grand sweep.

[37] For example, while in Berlin I met some Kurdish Jews who had organized a cross-community event with the Yazidi community. The contexts that permit an Anglophone Westerner to feel legitimate community with someone from Kurdistan is rare.

[38] See Charles Kadushin, 'Social Networks and Jews' (2011) 31 Contemporary Jewry 55, 59, mentioning examples of Diaspora networks over the millennia and noting some exceptions to this observation.

[39] Lauterpacht's status as an 'émigré' or just a migrant is debated—see, for example, Martti Koskenniemi, 'Sir Hersch Lauterpacht' in Beatson and Zimmermann (eds), *Jurists Uprooted* (n 22) 607. For my own part, looking at the ethno-political situation in Lauterpacht's Galicia and what ultimately happened to Jews there, I would tend toward calling him an 'émigré'.

[40] See Reinhard Zimmermann, 'Was Heimat hieß, nun heißt es Hölle' in Beatson and Zimmermann (eds), *Jurists Uprooted* (n 22) ch 1.

[41] FA Mann to Friedrich Fromme (Mann estate, NLMann_0260, 20 September 1978): '*Das bedauerliche ist nur, dass der Artikel von Herrn F.W. voll von Unrichtigkeiten ist, Wesentliches weglässt und eine Reihe von groben Geschmacklosigkeiten enthält. Dass man Martin Wolff (mit dem Flume übrigens nicht das mindeste zu tun hatte) einen "großen jüdischen Rechtsgelehrten" nennt, ist der FAZ nicht würdig.*'

not want to write the same error large in such a book as this. However, that puts on the horns of a dilemma.

A. The Dilemma of Writing About German Jews

Why did Mann object to Martin Wolff being identified as a 'great Jewish legal scholar'? He *was* a great Jewish legal scholar! The wrong done to Mann and his generation was to label them as 'Jews'—and (therefore) as 'non-Germans'—in an environment where Jews were despised and a raft of wicked legal consequences followed. This kind of attitude has always been latent within German (and indeed broader European) culture, erupting from time to time. Yet, the fact that a person is a Jew is an interesting data point from our modern perspective as people who (presumably) do not see anything inherently negative about being Jewish. David Dyzenhaus, for example, observes that many of the great and good in 20th-century jurisprudence were Jews: HLA Hart, as well as his main counterpart, Hans Kelsen, his successor Ronald Dworkin, and others such as Joseph Raz and Lon Fuller. As Dyzenhaus writes in his review of Nicola Lacey's Hart biography:

> It might seem that I am harping too much on the theme of the legal philosopher as the Jewish outsider. [Chapter 1 of Lacey's book is entitled 'An Outsider on the Inside'.] But it is striking that three of the four philosophers of law mentioned so far [the fourth being Carl Schmitt], and whose contributions to our thinking about the nature of law are likely the highpoints of the last century, are Jewish. And that theme manifests itself directly in Hart in a tension that runs throughout his work.[42]

That tension relates to the normativity of law and its relationship to moral normativity, which also preoccupied émigrés such as Gustav Radbruch.[43] This is a much easier argument to run for the case of a legal philosopher like Hart than for a jurist like Mann, but it provides some of the context for Paz's investigation of Mann's preoccupation with money. There, too, we might notice that the 'monetary law triumvirate' of Martin Wolff, Mann, and Arthur Nussbaum were all Jews who worked in Berlin in the early 20th century. It is a phenomenon in search of an explanation.

It was rather the lack of immediate contextual significance in the FAZ article that was problematic. There is a deeper background to all this. While studying for my LLM in Augsburg in 2009, I chanced across the report of a conference of German

[42] David Dyzenhaus, 'Reviewed Work: A Life of HLA Hart: The Nightmare and the Noble Dream by Nicola Lacey' (2005) 55(4) Journal of Legal Education 606, 607.

[43] See John Bell, 'Wolfgang Friedmann (1907–1972) (with an excursus on Gustav Radbruch [1978–1949])' in Jack Beatson and Reinhard Zimmermann (eds), *Jurists Uprooted: German-Speaking Emigré Lawyers in Twentieth Century Britain* (OUP 2006).

law professors held in Berlin in 1936 published in the *Deutsche Juristenzeitung* on the 'struggle against the Jewish spirit in German legal science'.[44] In his closing remarks, Carl Schmitt summarized the outcome of the conference:

> The necessary task regarding the bibliography is very difficult; it is self-evidently necessary to determine, as accurately as possible, who is a Jew and who is not a Jew. Only on the basis of an accurate register can we continue work in the direction of library cataloguing ... All legal writings by Jewish authors belong ... without distinction to the library catalogue of the department 'Judaica' ... [O]nly when we solve the issue of the quotations, we will be able to remove the Jewish-infected literature, and attain, instead, German legal literature.[45]

This was part of a general effort to 'Aryanise' knowledge across the board—including, I would later discover, Nobel laureate Philipp Lenard's four volumes on 'German Physics'[46] in reaction to the perceived 'Jewish' quality of Albert Einstein's relativity theory. Against this background, the first thing we want to avoid is the contextually inappropriate, reductive branding of a person as 'a Jew'. This effort to identify Jews continues in our own century through different means such as the 'echo' or triple parentheses that arose in 2014 and came to prominence in 2016.[47]

For these reasons, there is a persistent and very understandable tendency towards opening a project such as this with a nominal recognition of the 'Jewish dimension' (for example: 'X was a German of Jewish extraction' or 'X was born to Jewish parents'), coupled with an intentional disengagement from the possible impacts of that dimension on their life and especially on their work. The emphasis is on integration and similarity rather than an exploration of the mysterious but powerful element that led a tiny minority—less than one per cent of the German population—to make an outsized contribution to its intellectual and cultural life, particularly in law.

44 This text is (still) largely unknown, both within and outside Germany: see Reinhard Mehring, 'Carl Schmitt und der Antisemitismus: Ein unbekannter Text' (*Forum Historiae Iuris*, 31 March 2006) <http://www.forhistiur.de/zitat/0603mehring2.htm> accessed 21 March 2023. The easiest way to find the text is on the Neo-Nazi website *Der Sturmer*, and the only existing translation of which I am aware is from Sunic Tomasovic, an Alt-Right thinker and disgraced University of California professor.

45 Carl Schmitt, 'Schlußwort des Reichsgruppenwalters Staatsrat Prof. Dr. Carl Schmitt' (1936) 41(20) Deutsche Juristenzeitung 1194, 1194–200. There is little secondary literature on this conference in English. In German, see Otmar Jung, 'Der literarische Judenstern: Die Indizierung der 'jüdischen' Rechtsliteratur im nationalsozialistisschen Deutschland' (2006) 54(1) Vierteljahreshefte für Zeitgeschichte 25; Christian Busse, '"Eine Maske ist gefallen": Die Berliner Tagung "Das Judentum und die Rechtswissenschaft" vom 3./4. Oktober 1936' (2000) 33(4) Nomos 580.

46 Philipp Lenard, *Deutsche Physik in 4 Bänden* (JF Lehmann 1936).

47 See Amanda Hess, 'The Alt-Right, the Message is in the Punctuation' *New York Times* (10 June 2016) <https://www.nytimes.com/2016/06/11/arts/for-the-alt-right-the-message-is-in-the-punctuation.html> accessed 4 June 2023. For example, my name would be rendered (((Jason Allen))) in a Twitter post to identify me as a Jew.

Candidly, we came quite close to adopting such an approach in this volume, too. Above all, we do not want to relegate 'FA Mann: The Lawyer and his Legacy' to the 'Judaica' section of the library! A chapter such as this credibly runs the risk of doing just that: this is a chapter about German-Jewish identity, not about (for example) the law of money or arbitration. Giving the first horn of our dilemma, a wide berth is particularly understandable for our non-Jewish German colleagues. But that puts us on the second, less obvious horn of the dilemma.

The reasons are complex. True, there are some darker patterns of 'Jewish difference' manifesting variously as antisemitism and philosemitism, which I will come to later. As Mecklenburg writes, even 80 years on, 'national identities are still standing in the way of a more common understanding of the many shared aspects of society, politics, and culture'.[48] But for the most part, what leads us to the second horn of the dilemma is very human and very understandable.

A personal anecdote perhaps best illustrates what I am talking about. The title of this chapter draws on the title of Franz Kafka's short story about a chimpanzee called Rotpeter—*Ein Bericht für eine Akademie*.[49] In this story, Rotpeter is captured by humans, trained in the ways of humankind, and eventually gains a degree of recognition. The story is structured as a letter to a learned society, in which Rotpeter tells his life. Although he has adopted the trappings of humanity with superlative skill, his home life is that of a chimpanzee. In passages that smack of self-loathing, for example, we learn that his wife remains simian in her habits.

I studied Kafka's classical works during my undergraduate studies in German Language and Literature. Immediately, the story jumped out at me as an allegory of Jewish assimilation, and I raised this point in class. Bizarrely, my Austrian lecturer—who had in fact published widely on animal allegories in literature and even on German-speaking Jewish authors—summarily foreclosed the discussion. To interpret this story as an allegory of Jewish assimilation would place it on a Procrustean bed; it was an exploration of the human condition writ large, nothing less.

Kafka's *oeuvre* makes only a single explicit reference to Jewishness. It seems not to be a major theme in understanding his work. But as Walter Sokel argues, the conclusion that Jewishness was not important to his writing 'would miss an essential dimension'.[50] Kafka in fact developed an intense interest in Judaism right at the time he began his mature work. Sokel argues that his personal journey, his family history, and the experience of Bohemian Jews more broadly informed the

[48] Frank Mecklenburg, '"Jewish and German": The Leo Baeck Institute Archives and Library' in Reuveni and Franklin (eds), *German-Jewish Past* (n 7) 222.

[49] Franz Kafka, 'Ein Bericht für eine Akademie' (1917) 2(8) Der Jude 559.

[50] Walter Sokel, 'Kafka as a Jew' (1999) 30(4) New Literary History 837 (hereafter Sokel, 'Kafka as a Jew'). For an extensive discussion, including of the 'three impossibilities' Kafka said faced Jews writing in German, see Galili Shahar, 'The Dialectics of Tradition: German-Jewish Studies and the Future' in Reuveni and Franklin (eds), *German-Jewish Past* (n 7) 89, 91–92.

'profound discrepancy between the appearance of solidity and a reality of alienation and vague but persistent menace' characteristic of his writing.[51] Kafka is best understood against the historical conditions of Jews in the Hapsburg lands during their rapid industrialization and social transformation, including Jewish emancipation following the Revolution of 1848.

Although a universalist interpretation of the *Bericht* is plausible, a 'Jewish assimilationist' interpretation is historically *more* plausible—and didactically important.[52] Indeed, Kafka's friend (and later literary executor) Max Brod presented the story in precisely these terms:

> Franz Kafka tells the story of an ape, who, captured by [the firm] Hagenbeck, becomes human through violence. And what a human! The worst, the dross of humanity reward him for his imitation efforts. *Is this not the most genius satire for assimilation that has ever been written?* One can read it in the latest issue of *Der Jude*. The assimilated [Jew] does not desire freedom or infinity, only an escape, a pitiful escape! It is grotesque and inspired in one breath. The involuntary freedom of God stands, menacingly, behind the animal-human comedy.[53]

In a tragic sense, to expunge the 'Jewish dimension' of Kafka analysis is to erase the existence of his whole world—starting with the fact that there was a German language literary magazine called *Der Jude* ('The Jew') in Prague! My lecturer was a lovely woman who showed sensibility for the human condition, in all its complexity, and instilled in me a love of German-language literature. I do not believe that she intended this outcome. But she somehow froze when it came to the interpretation of the *Bericht*. I doubt that she could truly have been committed to her view; that would be an ignorant position, and she was no ignoramus. Why, then, did she 'cancel' it in her classroom? She might have been uncomfortable by the animal allegory, assimilating Jews to chimpanzees. She might have been concerned that other students might not be able to discuss a Jewish assimilation allegory with sufficient nuance. As Yascha Mounk has observed, 'the simplest interaction

[51] Kafka's parents reflected 'the situation of the strenuously assimilating, but not yet fully assimilated, rising Jewish bourgeoisie' trying to advance economically socially in a society that was not ready to receive them as integrated equals. See Sokel, 'Kafka as a Jew' (n 50) 838.

[52] See the classic argument in WC Rubinstein, 'Franz Kafka's "A Report to an Academy"' (1954) 55 MLQ 359; see Jay Geller, *Bestarium Judaicum: Unnatural Histories of the Jews* (Fordham University Press 2018) ch 4 for an extensive discussion. See also Karlheinz Fingerhut, '"Manchmal nur, in dunkeln Zeiten": Heine, Kafka, Celan—Schreibweisen jüdischer Selbstreflexion' in JA Kruse (ed), *Heine-Jahrbuch 2002* (Springer 2002).

[53] Cited in Jürgen Born, *Franz Kafka: Kritik und Rezensionen zu seinem Lebzeiten 1912–1924* (Fischer Verlag 1979) 128. Translation my own, emphasis added. For a particularly ham-fisted treatment of the matter (in a didactically focused journal), see George Schulz-Behrend, 'Kafka's "Ein Bericht für eine Akademie": An Interpretation' (1963) 55(1) Monatshefte für Deutschen Unterricht, Deutsche Sprache und Literatur 1.

between Jew and Gentile [in Germany today can] degenerate into a politically correct comedy of errors'.[54]

Our position is subtly analogous if we underplay the 'Jewish dimension' of Mann's generation. The German-Jewish culture that thrived before the Holocaust is, sadly, gone. Jewish life in Germany will never be what it was, let alone what it could have been but for its destruction between 1933 and 1945. Given Europe's loss of Jews through murder and emigration, German-speaking culture will never be the same, either. This leads me to the key argument in this chapter: *The way we choose to talk and write about Jews like Mann determines whether and how their world is remembered—and, just as importantly, how the German-speaking world understands itself today.* Though the need for balance is paramount, if anything I think we should err on the side that seeks to remember, understand, and celebrate the uniqueness and fertility of German-Jewish life in the early 20th century.

To put it pointedly: if we label Mann now as a 'German' without differentiation—if we fail to acknowledge adequately that he was *also* a Jew—we expunge the historical record of the fact that there were Jews in Germany, or that they made a contribution to German legal scholarship and culture. Einstein called this a 'titillating application' of his relativity theory, with a fair twist of irony himself:[55]

> If my theory of relativity is proven successful, Germany will claim me as a German and France will declare me a citizen of the world. Should my theory prove untrue, France will say that I am a German, and Germany will declare that I am a Jew.[56]

Further, if we avoid investigating what the fact of his 'Jewishness' might *actually* have meant for Mann's work and his contribution to law, we are in a sense both staying trapped within the Nazi categories and completing their 'cleansing' of German legal science—paradoxically, even more so than were we to put their works in the 'Judaica' section. We are then also presenting a distorted view of German-speaking culture and German legal science, as well.

[54] Yascha Mounk, *Stranger in My Own Country: A Jewish Family in Modern Germany* (Macmillan 2014) 31.

[55] 'Today, I am called in Germany a "German scholar" and in England a "Swiss Jew"; if I ever come into the position of being presented as a *bete noire*, then I would be the opposite—in Germany, a "Swiss Jew" and for the English a "German scholar".' Albert Einstein, 'Was ist Relativitäts-Theorie?' (28 November 1919) in Albert Einstein, *Mein Weltbild* (Querido Verlag 1934) 220, <http://germanhistorydocs.ghi-dc.org/docpage.cfm?docpage_id=5438&language=german> accessed 4 June 2023. Translation my own.

[56] Address at the Sorbonne, Paris, possibly early December 1929, in *New York Times* (16 February 1930), cited in <https://www.oxfordreference.com/view/10.1093/acref/9780191826719.001.0001/q-oro-ed4-00003988> accessed 4 June 2023.

B. Mann's impression of denazification

A robust and healthy *Erinnerungskultur* is often treated as an accomplished fact in modern Germany. However, it is in fact radically incomplete and remains a work in progress. The roots of this incompleteness stretch back to the earliest days of German defeat and the reconstruction of modern Germany. In an effort such as the present, it is important to take stock of where we are in the scheme of things. Perhaps the best place to start is with Mann's experiences in Berlin immediately post-war. It is beyond the scope of this chapter to explore the complexities of post-war Germany in detail.[57] The short point is that, especially from the late 1940s, an enormous number of former active Nazis were granted amnesty and reintegrated into German society. It is generally thought that this policy achieved, through education and 'soul searching', a kind of social alchemy: Nazis in, good democratic Germans out.

Mann, however, was not impressed by the process of 'denazification' and made some observations that are salutary to consider today. For starters, he took a dismal view of his immediate superiors, the efficacy of the whole system, and the state of cooperation between the Allied powers. His letters from this period to Lore reveal some precious insights into the state of Berlin society at the time and what must have been a truly surreal experience for him, returning after less than a decade to a very different world. It is hard to know what to make of them; profound, and profoundly sad, observations are made about the physical state of Berlin—clearly, from the perspective of someone who identifies with the place and its people:

> I came into contact with German students and professors and this morning I even saw something of the terrible problems of the refugees from the East. There are 7½ million of these people and the misery of these people surpasses anything I have yet seen. We must continuously think of the misery the Germans have done to people in the East, Jews etc—in order not to be overwhelmed by sympathy. But two wrongs don't make one right.[58]

Many of the contents are troubling. An early missive reports:

> I then took the *Stadtbahn* to *Zoo* where I happened to run into Reuss—you may remember him as a *Fakultätsassistent*. We recognised each other. He: '*Wir kennen*

[57] See, in particular, Norbert Frei, *Adenauer's Germany and the Nazi Past* (Joel Golb tr., Columbia University Press 2003), an English translation of a 1996 German classic.

[58] My wife's grandmother, who fled East Prussia (Königsberg/Kaliningrad), was one of these 7.5 million—many Germans have a grandparent from that cohort. While she had been a child, and had fled to what became the German Democratic Republic, her sister left for Australia and came into contact with other European refugees—including Jews. She saw herself much less a victim of historical circumstances and could articulate a coherent sense of collective responsibility as a German (whose brothers had fought in the East) without personal moral failure.

> *uns doch.* ['We know each other!'] I: '*Wir haben uns einmal gekannt.* ['We knew each other once.'] We got talking and he asked about [you] and others and altogether emphasised his anti-Nazidom. But I have not forgotten his efforts in the [unknown organization] and have asked [Miss S] to search for and send me the references. When I have them I intend to pay him a visit at his office in *Kurfüstendamm* where he carries on a lucrative practice as *Rechtsanwalt & Notar.* He is a Nazi all right, and altogether it is *zum Kotzen* [lit. it makes we want to vomit].[59]

We read of a visit to Walter Schmidt and family in August 1946:

> They are nice people and almost the first who told me that the Nazis are alive and kicking and preparing their new *Dolchstoss* Agenda [i.e. the conspiracy that German Jews 'stabbed Germany in the back' in the First World War]. I never doubted it. They also said that anti-Semitism was still the same.
>
> I asked them how many people they know who wanted Germany to lose the war. Their answer was that the question could not arise. Anti-Nazis thought the war was lost from the beginning. I am not so certain; I think this feeling began only in 1941. It was quite an interesting evening, because I learned a lot about conditions here.[60]

Mann describes the Kohlrausches as a German family of the 'best bourgeois' type. Probably because Eduard Kohlrausch was Lore's doctoral supervisor, the letters contain several passages on this family and their predicament:

> They asked a lot about old friends, your mother, E and all your family and their attitude towards what happened to the Jews is the same as ours ... Of course we avoided the purely political topics,—their wounds are too open, though insofar as Nazidom is concerned there did not appear to be any difference of opinion. What I mean is their condemnation of Nazidom is loud and largely genuine, particularly insofar as Jews are concerned, where particularly Mrs K.'s attitude was unambiguous.[61]

However, the basic difference of perspective between Jewish and non-Jewish Germans appears:

[59] Letter from FA Mann to Lore Mann (Mann estate, RS1000_NLMann_0984, undated 1946). In her seminal work on the subject, Anna-Maria Lösch opines that Reuss reached an accommodation with the Nazis but was treated with suspicion due to his former involvement with the Social Democrat Party (SPD): see Anna-Maria von Lösch, *Der nackte Geist: Die juristische Fakultät der Berliner* (Mohr Seibeck 1999) 237, 350.

[60] Letter from FA Mann to Lore Mann (Mann estate, RS1000_NLMann_0984, undated 1946).

[61] ibid.

> But the hopelessness of their situation is overpowering and my feeling also is that they make a sharp distinction between Nazis and the German people (including the *Wehrmacht* [i.e. the ordinary German military]) which I cannot accept and which we did not discuss. They did say, however, that there were so very few Nazis! It is a wall of protection and justification which they build for themselves.[62]

It may be that Mann gave Kohlrausch somewhat of a free pass, perhaps as Kohlrausch had taken some early steps to curb antisemitic excesses while Dean of the Law Faculty in Berlin (including a letter to Adolf Hitler in 1933 protesting the excesses of National Socialist student groups against Jews and burning books).[63] However, Kohlrausch was not a straightforward character, and may not have been completely straight with Mann. The leading study by Holger Karitzky concludes that Kohlrausch's conduct through the years of the National Socialist regime were characterized by 'ambivalence, changeability, incoherence, and transformative capacity'.[64] Kohlrausch's career had already stretched over the German Empire, Weimar Republic, and National Socialist period; with the end of the latter, Kohlrausch set about continuing his career 'as uninterruptedly as he had in 1933':[65]

> He was considered—and considered himself—a renowned expert who would be needed by the Allies (including the Soviets) for criminal law reform, and to a significant degree pushed forward his views in relevant commissions. But when his (generally known and initially undisputed) membership in the Gürtner Criminal Law Commission became a subject of political evaluation (possibly due to the emerging Cold War), he was relieved of his duties; tirelessly striving for his rehabilitation, he died in early 1948.[66]

For criminal law professors, these years were a time of 'extreme uncertainty and high mobility under difficult conditions', as they were 'concerned about uncertain career prospects, handicapped by denazification proceedings, and limited by precarious institutional settings'.[67] Although they were certainly no worse off than the

[62] ibid.

[63] See <https://perspectives.ushmm.org/item/telegram-regarding-the-action-against-the-un-german-spirit> accessed 16 March 2023.

[64] Holger Karitzky, *Eduard Kohlrausch: Kriminalpolitik in vier Systemen—Eine strafrechtsgeschichtliche Biographie* (Berliner Juristische Universitätsschriften 2002) 70, cited in Thomas Vormbaum, 'Eduard Kohlrausch (1874–1948) Opportunismus oder Kontinuität?' in Stefan Grundmann and others (eds), *Festschrift 200 Jahre Juristische Fakultät der Humboldt-Universität zu Berlin: Geschichte, Gegenwart und Zukunft* (De Gruyter 2010) 525.

[65] ibid 526.

[66] ibid.

[67] Petra Gödecke, 'Criminal Law after National Socialism: The Renaissance of Natural Law and the Beginnings of Penal Reform in West Germany' in Richard F Wetzell (ed.), *Crime and Criminal Justice in Modern Germany* (Berghahn Books 2014) 280 <https://library.oapen.org/bitstream/handle/20.500.12657/29607/1000326.pdf;jsessionid=E94A163712F8684F02DBD300D1086CA1?sequence=1> accessed 5 June 2023.

rest of the population, their living and working conditions were perhaps subjectively experienced as particularly difficult by this highly privileged social group.[68]

Mann describes his contact with the Heidelberg law professor and later politician Eduard Wahl:

> He is in a poor state. He is reinstated as Professor in Heidelberg; although he was a party-member (involuntarily, so he says), he was denazified on account of his close connexion with the events of July 1944 [i.e. the plot by German military leaders to assassinate Hitler]. He lost his wife and now lives with his mother-in-law [...] who looks after his three little girls of 6, 4 and 2. The youngest seems to be in very poor condition because of undernourishment and I gave him a few things which almost made him cry, and me too. It is terribly hard.
>
> He is a real German, though, with that typical *Wehleidigkeit* [self-pity] and incapacity of seeing or believing in the suffering of others. He is violently anti-Russian and proud of the achievements of the Germans in many ways and I am certain he would gladly give a second Hitler another chance. But in spite of all this it would be nonsensical to call him a Nazi,—his brother, a lunatic, was involved in September 1941 and this, probably, opened his eyes. He always was and still is an odd fellow, but quite likeable, very intelligent and from my point of view interesting, because he told me many things ... I cannot help saying the utter hopelessness pervading this man made a great impression on me and, since I am weak, evoked my sympathy.[69]

Consistent with this attitude, in 1949 Wahl became a politician in Konrad Adenauer's government and was an active member of the so-called *Heidelberger Juristenkreis*, which lobbied for amnesty for Nazi war criminals in the first half of the 1950s under a policy of drawing a *Schlussstrich* ['closing line'] under the Nazi past.[70]

Perhaps the most moving recollection is about a family friend called Lydia. Unfortunately, I could not decipher much of the passage. The upshot is: 'I could write volumes about Lydia who is the only real anti-Nazi (as opposed to non-Nazi) I have met here.'[71] Lydia was apparently suspected of being a *Mischling* (a person of mixed Jewish and German descent), though it appears from context that she was not. Mann writes of her: 'She does not complain about anything, but managed quite well (on RM 200 a month) and is happy that the war is lost.'[72]

[68] ibid.

[69] Letter from FA Mann to Lore Mann (Mann estate, RS1000_NLMann_0984, undated 1946). I am unsure of the reference to September 1941, but suspect it is to events in Operation Barbarossa in the East. I am also unsure whether the brother was a 'lunatic' in the sense of being a Nazi or more literally.

[70] See further Philipp Glahé, 'The Heidelberg Circle of Jurists and Its Struggle against Allied Jurisdiction: Amnesty-Lobbyism and Impunity-Demands for National Socialist War Criminals (1949–1955)' (2019) 22(1) Journal of the History of International Law / Revue d'histoire du droit international 1.

[71] Letter from FA Mann to Lore Mann (Mann estate, RS1000_NLMann_0984, undated 1946).

[72] ibid.

This is a powerful litmus test and, perhaps (still) identifying as a German, Mann has mentioned it twice in the above passages: from the point of view of any given person, was Germany 'liberated' from a vile regime, or was it 'defeated'? Even today, among third-generation beneficiaries of democratic rule in Germany, this debate can escalate quickly. It seems to be emotionally challenging for a great number of Germans to identify with the Allies (*qua* 'liberators') against their own grandparents, despite the greater degree of ideological alignment with the former.[73]

The attitude in the decades immediately post-war was clear: Germany had been defeated. This was also the position taken by the Allies in 1945.[74] In the 1980s the official line changed when the Federal Republic of Germany's President Richard von Weizsäcker adopted a liberation narrative of the Allied victory.[75] From that point, it might seem that all 'good' Germans are 'Lydias' now. The truth of it is more subtle, however. Although it is more morally comfortable for democratically minded Germans to feel society of mind with the Allies than with National Socialist Germany, the liberation narrative interacts with German victimhood narratives in problematical ways, as it posits a gap between the populace (as 'victims') and their government that is pure fiction.[76]

Contemporary opinion polls suggest that something is going quite wrong. In 2020, a poll run by *Die Zeit* found that more than half of Germans believe that a 'few criminals' instigated the Second World War and perpetrated the Holocaust.[77] This is, of course, total nonsense, perhaps best illustrated in the recent demolition of the 'innocent *Wehrmacht* myth' (to which, we have seen, Kohlrausch already subscribed).[78] In Austria and the former East Germany, the story is more complex

[73] Anecdotally, I have been told, unsolicited, that the Second World War was 'all the Allies fault'—that 'we would have taken care of Hitler eventually'. In my experience, such conversations tend to crop up after a certain time, as a friendship evolves. Perhaps they are to test the waters; in most cases, the budding friendship has not survived this fundamental difference of perspective and opinion. In other cases, where both parties have been willing to invest the effort, a deeper friendship has blossomed which is based on honesty, empathy, and even solidarity.

[74] See, for example, US 740.00119 Control (Germany)/4–2645, *Directive to Commander in Chief of United States Forces of Occupation Regarding the Military Government of Germany*, <https://history.state.gov/historicaldocuments/frus1945v03/d351#:~:text=Germany%20will%20not%20be%20occupied,just%20but%20firm%20and%20aloof> accessed 5 June 2023.

[75] See 'Excerpts from Speech by German President' *New York Times* (9 May 1985) <https://www.nytimes.com/1985/05/09/world/excerpts-from-speech-by-german-president.html> accessed 5 June 2023.

[76] A very competent op-ed treatment of the problematic is found in James Angelos, 'Was Nazi Germany Defeated or Liberated? Germans Can't Decide' *New York Times* (8 May 2021) <https://www.nytimes.com/2021/05/08/opinion/germany-v-e-day-liberation-nazi-history.html> accessed 26 April 2023.

[77] See Christian Staas, 'Das Ende der Selbstgewissheit' (*Die Zeit*, 28 April 2020) <https://www.zeit.de/2020/19/erinnerungskultur-nationalsozialismus-aufarbeitung-deutschland-rechtsextremismus-umfrage/komplettansicht accessed 26 April 2023> accessed 5 June 2023.

[78] This is the myth that the 'ordinary' German soldiers were largely ignorant, and innocent, of the atrocities committed by the SS and their ilk. See, e.g., DA Harrisville, *The Virtuous Wehrmacht: Crafting the Myth of the German Solider on the Eastern Front, 1941–1944* (Cornell University Press 2021); Hannes Heer and others (eds), *The Discursive Construction of History: Remembering the Wehrmacht's War of Annihilation* (Palgrave-Macmillan 2008).

still: in the latter, the official line was that the German Democratic Republic was the heir to the anti-fascist resistance and that its citizens were 'the good Germans'.[79] In Austrian historiography, much has been made of the *Anschluss* [annexation] and the view that the Austrians were 'Hitler's first victims', cancelling out their active participation.[80] In recent decades, a kind of resentment has become increasingly evident in the former West, too.[81] Alan Posener points to the rhetoric of Pope Benedict XVI which casts the German people as an unwitting instrument of the Nazis rather than as a political community committed to its government's course of action. This in turn bolsters the view that 'enough is enough' and that 'too much self-examination and breast-beating somehow damages the German psyche, that it is time for a new self-confidence, that the nation needs to see the Nazi crimes in perspective'.[82]

Another founding myth of the *Bundesrepublik* is of the so-called 'rubble women' (*Trümmerfrauen*) who cleared the German cities of rubble to be used in reconstruction. In fact, this myth is not only inaccurate but positively misleading. As Leonie Treber has demonstrated, most of the work was in fact done by men and machines. Most of the work was done as a form of punishment for National Socialist criminals, although a few volunteers (who were paid with extra food rations) of both sexes were employed as well.[83] The campaign to present these women as heroes of the German post-war miracle had already begun in 1945 and 1946, while Mann was still in Berlin; however, those who did so were either being punished for their political activities or were doing so out of economic necessity (sometimes because their accounts had been frozen for their political involvement). This explains Mann's otherwise jarring comment in a letter to Lore from Berlin:

[79] See, e.g., Edgar Wolfrum, 'Geschichte der Erinnerungskultur in der DDR und BRD' (Bundeszentrale für politische Bildung, 26 August 2008) <https://www.bpb.de/themen/erinnerung/geschichte-und-erinnerung/39814/geschichte-der-erinnerungskultur-in-der-ddr-und-brd/#node-content-title-2> accessed 26 April 2023. Anecdotally, this attitude remains widespread—along with the non sequitur that 'because we were anti-fascist, we cannot be antisemites' even while espousing revisionist and otherwise dubious opinions. This is, in my view, part of what is enabling the rise of contemporary right-wing extremism in the former East.

[80] See Julia Hitz, 'Austria Faces Up to Nazi Past' (*Deutsche Welle*, 10 December 2021) <https://www.dw.com/en/austria-faces-up-to-nazi-past-in-auschwitz/a-59471005> accessed 26 April 2023. See also Klaus Hödl, 'Jewish Studies without the "Other"' in Reuveni and Franklin (eds), *The German-Jewish Past* (n 7) 122. The admission by Austrian political leaders that Austrians had, indeed, been actively involved in the Holocaust only occurred in the 1990s.

[81] See, e.g., Emily Schultheiss, 'Teaching the Holocaust in Germany as a Resurgent Far Right Questions It' (*The Atlantic*, 10 April 2019) <https://www.theatlantic.com/international/archive/2019/04/germany-far-right-holocaust-education-survivors/586357/> accessed 26 April 2023.

[82] Alan Posener, 'Don't let Auschwitz be Forgotten' *The Guardian* (27 January 2010) <https://www.theguardian.com/commentisfree/belief/2010/jan/26/auschwitz-jews-germany-islam?CMP=gu_com> accessed 26 April 2023.

[83] See Leonie Trebers, *Mythos Trümmerfrauen: Von der Trümmerbeseitigung in der Kriegs- und Nachkriegszeit und der Enstehung eines deutschen Erinnerungsortes* (Klartext Verlag 2015), also printed under the same title in shorter form by the Bundeszentrum für politische Bildung (Schriftenreihe 1655) <https://www.bpb.de/system/files/dokument_pdf/Textauszug_Mythos%20Tr%C3%BCmmerfrauen.pdf> accessed 5 June 2023.

> Incidentally, a sight typical of Berlin and most pleasant for my eyes is a horde of women clearing away *débris* in terrible heat,—these are functionaires of *NS Frauenschaft*. If only one could be certain that the right ones have [been] selected, that justice has been done. I know that denunciations are so numerous that there is no certainty on this point.[84]

This reminds us that we must be sensitive to the ambiguity of it all. Mann recounts his meeting with a family called the Plochmanns in 1946:

> They are very nice people, and Mrs P. has particularly impressed me. I am certain that without her the husband would have gone down the drain a long time ago; it is curious that everywhere women are so much stronger than men. They did not complain about the loss of most of their property as about food. They realise that this and many other consequences of the war must not only be borne, but are justifiable and even just. But, as I have said before, it is his position that causes the trouble. I know he did join the party and he says himself others may have had greater strength of character. But it meant so little. He was no Nazi, and although he would have been open to severe blame if he had joined at an earlier date and although he must even be punished for having joined in 1943 or so, I cannot help feeling that it is just silly to debar him from useful work more than a year after the end of the war.[85]

Any project on a society-wide scale lets some of the worst offenders go and sanctions those who really should be allowed to get on with their lives. The problem, Mann concluded, is that the mechanical test of 'member or non-member' was too superficial a methodology for rooting out the National Socialist element from German society:

> In the later years of the regime things were by far too complicated for such crude distinction. [T]hey were not all Nazis in the real sense of the word. But of course they were German nationalists, 'patriots', militarists, soldiers, and it is for this reason that Germany cannot be kept in bondage,—and the 'good Germans', as e.g. Plochmann, will agree. If you think of Kohlrausch you will see what I mean. It is an impossible problem, and the only solution is: control at the top, but let them live their lives. *Forget the past except insofar as the real criminals are concerned. These should be hanged. They still amount to many hundred thousand.* And in my view they include those who brought the regime into power, but not those who were or became *Mitläufer* [i.e. those complicit but not active]. There were too many of them, and this is the practical difficulty. The Lydias are rare. And the

[84] Letter from FA Mann to Lore Mann (Mann estate, RS1000_NLMann_0984, undated 1946).
[85] ibid.

tantalising trouble is that, as everybody will tell you, the real Nazis are to a large extent still in their positions. Which is an additional reason for depriving 'denazification' of all sense.[86]

Lest Mann be misunderstood, it bears repeating: in this passage, he both (i) calls for a widespread amnesty and (ii) calls for the execution, by hanging, of 'many hundred thousand' individuals. That never happened. The modern Germany we know is a product of letting those many hundred thousand criminals resume their lives, careers, and family roles.

C. Relevance to our understanding of 'FA Mann: The Lawyer and his Legacy'

This introduces the broader context to our project, which embraces not only 'the lawyer' but also his legacy. We are attempting here to understand Mann's individual biography, in which 'being Jewish' (whatever that means) was a major catalyst for disruptive change. Mann did not wear his Jewishness on his sleeve (and, because he was able to leave Germany in time, he was never forced to). Likewise, Mann was not a religiously observant Jew; observance of the rites and customs of Judaism seems not have to been very important in the way he lived his life.[87] In his letters to Lore from 1946 Berlin, I read some (for me highly relatable) gems such as: 'I do not know how I should behave on Yom Kippur: go to a Committee Meeting? (No!) Go to the office? (No) Fast? (?)".[88] Or: 'Tonight is Jewish New Year. I feel rather bad that I am in Berlin without going to a Synagogue.'[89]

But religiosity is not really the aspect of 'Jewishness' with which we are concerned here. We are looking for whatever it meant for Mann to be 'Jewish by background and tradition' that was consistent with his notion of having 'German cultural status'. In this, religion and participation in a religious community is only part of the picture.

[86] ibid. Emphasis mine.

[87] Gluckmann's observations on Kahn-Freund's statement (about being 'born a Jew') provide an apt point of comparison: 'Otto wasn't trying to deny that he was Jewish, but he did want to be sure that his Jewishness could not be coopted by a religious Jewish community with whom he didn't identify.' Nicola Gluckmann, 'Past Imperfect, Future Tense: A Mother's Letter about Loss, Storytelling, and the Profound Ambivalence of the German-Jewish Legacy' in Reuveni and Franklin (eds), *German-Jewish Past* (n 7) 52. Jewish rites featured to a limited extent in Mann's death and burial. His funeral instructions stipulated that 'There should be a Rabbi who will say Kaddisch,—the prayer which millions have said when they were killed where I ought to have been. If he insists, he may read in English a psalm,—but this is all.' Lord Lawrence Collins was asked by Mann's family to say *kaddish* at his funeral as apparently no Rabbi could be found willing to officiate in the minimalist way that Mann stipulated. FA Mann (Mann estate, NLMann_1002).

[88] Letter from FA Mann to Lore Mann (Mann estate, RS1000_NLMann_0984, undated 1946).

[89] ibid.

Plausibly, Mann's self-description was a response to the common assertion that Jews could not be 'truly' or 'wholly' German (or English, or French, etc.). Even amongst German liberals of the late 19th and early 20th centuries, the attitude was widespread that Jews would have to sacrifice their distinctive 'Jewishness'. To cite but one example of many, Theodor Mommsen in 1887 argued that the Jews must 'pay the price [of] entry into a great nation' by 'detach[ing] themselves, on their own part, of their uniqueness [and] breaking down completely the barriers between themselves and the rest of the German citizenry'.[90] This was a project to which many Jews of Mann's generation were heavily committed. It ended disastrously. As Shulamit Volkov observes, a century of German Enlightenment still has to be rewritten from a Jewish perspective.[91]

So: being Jewish meant exile for Mann, with a whole cascade of practical consequences such as the decision (or imperative) to practice as a London solicitor. But exile must have entailed a cascade of more personal consequences, too. No person who identified, or was identified by others, as Jewish could feel the same in 1945 as they did before 1933. Mann says little directly about this, but there are hints. For example, we read:

> Today it poured for hours. I saw a few 'clients' in the morning and at 5.30 I went to *Deutsches Theater* to see *Nathan der Weise*. The theatre is completely undamaged and as beautiful as ever. The acting was excellent with the exception of the sultan who was too bad for words. *The play is of course moving for us*, but as a play it is not really good and I find it rather hard going to take in this sort of dialogue. The theatre was sold out, but my uniform procured a good seat without difficulty. The audience clearly appreciated the play and there was a great deal of applause. What puzzled me was that when the Patriarch (who was first rate) said: *Der Jude wird verbannt* ['the Jew is banished'] a proportion of the audience which was not quite negligible laughed. I have no explanation. *I thought people were looking well. Many were nice and obviously cultured people.* They were not elegant, but adequately and partly well dressed. All of them looked clean, which I find difficult to understand, with my knowledge of heating facilities, German soap, etc.[92]

[90] Theodor Mommsen, 'Auch ein Wort über unser Judentum in Walter Boehlich (ed), *Der Berliner Antisemitismusstreit* (Frankfurt 1965) 227. The liberal Karl Rotteck went further in his speech to the parliament of Baden in 1833 that the requirement of state uniformity required no less than the end of Jewish history and the 'dismantling of their nation': Reinhard Rürup, 'The Torturous and Thorny Path to Equality. "Jew Laws" and Emancipatory Legislation in Germany from the late 18th Century' (1986) 31 Leo Baeck Institute Yearbook 24 (hereafter Rürup, 'The Torturous and Thorny Path to Equality'). Both are cited in Volkov, 'Rewriting German History' (n 12).

[91] See Volkov, 'Rewriting German History' (n 12); see also Rürup, 'The Torturous and Thorny Path to Equality' (n 60).

[92] Letter from FA Mann to Lore Mann (Mann estate, RS1000_NLMann_0984, undated 1946).

Nathan der Weise is a play by Gotthold Ephraim Lessing that communicates a plea for religious tolerance, which Mann evidently found laid it on a bit thick. It is of course moving 'for us'—I presume 'us Jews'.[93] He is baffled by the fact that an apparently bourgeois German audience—an audience that he might have felt were birds of his feather—responded with derision at a dramatic high point and 'moral moment' in the play. These others did not identify with the same 'us'. They were living in the rubble of 1946 Berlin. Very many of them would have been personally implicated (in one way or another) with the murder of European Jews. Some were probably wearing stolen clothing.[94] Though understated, this vignette speaks volumes.

Beyond the unfortunate consequences of persecution under National Socialism, and indeed beyond the negative factor of antisemitism generally, the fact of a person being born into a Jewish family in early 20th-century Germany could mean a lot of things to their work. On one view, it is possible to approach Mann with no knowledge of the fact that he was a Jew and miss nothing of importance in his work. On the other hand, Mecklenburg's chapter in this volume illustrates just how special the 'Golden Years' of German emancipated Jewry were. It is important to remember how brief these years were, too: the exclusion of Jews from the civil service and the professions (including law) in 1935 occurred, after all, pursuant to a statute calling for the 'restoration' of the public service.[95] The civil service had only really opened to Jews in 1918; entry into the professions had been a generation earlier, and Mann's experience of being a German-Jewish lawyer in the third generation was highly unusual.

Given the space to rise, Jews had acted like leaven in German society. We are products of our social *milieu*, and that is a product of various factors working over historical time. Though they made up less than one per cent of the German population, German Jews during these Golden Years came to occupy whole fractions of the legal profession and academy. This is a phenomenon that demands explanation—and that explanation must surely look for the 'Jewish' element to their success, whatever it was.

Zooming out from Mann as an individual, this volume is also to evaluate his legacy. In the first instance, this involves an assessment of Mann's impact on various legal systems' literature and practices. It also involves a broader appreciation of the fact that a young man from Germany, who crossed borders literal and

[93] Lessing apparently modelled Nathan on his friend, Moses Mendelssohn, and perhaps his own experience of being banished for his free expression.

[94] The goods of deported Jews were auctioned in every German city, town, and village, especially from 1941, and this has been well-documented. See, for example, Wolfgang Dreßen, *Betrifft: Aktion 3: Deutsche verwerten jüdische Nachbarn. Dokumente zur Arisierung* (Aufbau Verlag 1998). Auctions for household items such as crockery and clothing are documented to have brought the state over 300 million *Reichsmark*, and participation was truly widespread. See also the 2018 *Mitteldeutsche Rundfunk* documentary by Jan Lorenzen und Michael Schönherr, *Die Versteigerer – Profiteure des Holocaust.*

[95] The *Gesetz zur Wiederherstellung* [lit. re-establishment] *des Berufbeamtentums vom 7. April 1933.*

metaphorical, out of necessity as much as volition, had such an impact at all. In this, the 'Jewish dimension' looms even larger than in our consideration of Mann as an individual. The aim is to situate Mann alongside an important cohort who both shared an uncommon fate in Germany and made an uncommon contribution to their new homelands. As Matthias Greffrath noted in his 1978 edited collection *Zerstörung einer Zukunft* [lit. 'Destruction of a Future']:

> Some 3,000 professors left the German universities during fascism, the majority because they were Jews, leaving a deficit in intellectual and academic life that I think is felt to this day. The pro-fascists and collaborators that remained were none too eager to repatriate their exiled colleagues or indeed bring attention to the gap they left. It was rather the student movement of the 1960s that looked back to the 'lost intellectuals' of the Weimar period with anger and nostalgia, as they had been deprived of minds that would have had immense value for German intellectual and political life.[96]

Every time we write about Mann's generation, we lay another brick in the edifice of this history. How we lay each brick informs, tacitly, its historiography. The operative question is, again, not just Mann's identity (i.e., how Mann identified himself) but about *our identification of Mann*. In other words, the task before us invites (and requires) some conclusions about what it meant to have, or claim to have, a 'wholly and firmly German' 'cultural status'—which cannot have been, and indeed was not, unchanged by the events of 1933–1945. Our understanding of Mann's Jewish identity, therefore, is inextricably bound with our understanding of *German* identity and the way that Germans have negotiated their own identity politics in the wake of the Holocaust.[97] That is part of the story that must be told, up to the present, if we are to understand Mann's life and legacy.

Another thing to mention from this perspective is that Holocaust studies and the cultural dynamics between Jews and Germans is not the monopoly of German Jews any more than it is the monopoly of non-Jewish Germans. More than anything else, the Holocaust made it the legitimate concern of every Jew. Understanding the complexities of German-Jewish relations, therefore, is a topic of legitimate concern to us all—and it justifies some probing of non-Jewish Germans and also of German Jews like Mann. We cannot really examine an émigré like Mann without making it mean something beyond him *qua* individual. As Zipes observed some time ago:

[96] Matthias Grefrath, *Zerstörung einer Zukunft: Gespräche mit emigrierten Sozialwissenschaftlern* (Rohwolt Taschenbuch 1979). The excerpt here is cited in Jack Zipes, 'The Holocaust and the Vicissitudes of Jewish Identity' (1980) 20(2) New German Critique 155 (hereafter Zipes, 'The Holocaust and the Vicissitudes of Jewish Identity'), 167.

[97] On the importance of (non-Jewish) German identity to the historiography of the Holocaust—what we might call a kind of 'culture war' of its own—see A Dirk Moses, 'The Non-German German and the German German: Dilemmas of Identity after the Holocaust' (2007) 101 New German Critique 45 (hereafter Moses, 'Identity After the Holocaust').

> The vicissitudes of Jewish identity ... must be carefully qualified by the fact that [studies of the subject often] represent the experiences of middle-class Jewish intellectuals who have generally remained at a distance from the mainstream of organized Jewish life. There is something dangerous and grotesque about historical-biographical anthologies which single out 'special Jews' for treatment. There is a hint that the major crime of the Holocaust was that it deprived Germany of great Jewish intellectuals and scientists, as if the little Jewish tailor Hans Cohn was expendable, but the great minds like Einstein had to be saved—and were saved—at all costs. Such careful distinctions were not made by the Nazis, unless money and public pressure were used to bribe them to release prominent Jews. Otherwise, all Jews were equal under fascism, and their *common* suffering, beliefs, and fate are not revealed in these books. West German readers learn mainly about the vicissitudes of Jewish identity from a special point of view.[98]

Engaging with the context into which Mann's legacy extends—our contemporary social circumstances—is an implicit part of our task. At this point, we can observe that despite our best efforts to understand what it meant to be 'German *and* Jewish', a binary system of mutually exclusive 'German' and 'Jewish' categories tends to slip back into our thinking. Recall Einstein's relativity metaphor, cited earlier. The appropriateness of the metaphor is that certain features of reality depend on the observer, and change in virtue of being observed. If Jewish identity is relative to the perspective of the observer, we must ask ourselves what our own position is. What are we seeking to achieve in a project like this, at a German university 80 years on? We are not, and cannot be, purely 'descriptive' when speaking and writing about Jews, Germans, and the Holocaust. As I will explain in the next section, there is a kind of struggle for the heart and soul of German-speaking Europe on this exact question. We desperately need to find new ways of dealing with the past and integrating the concept of 'being Jewish' into German-speaking Europe's self-conception.

The tragedy of our failure would not just be one for Jews. Given the outsized contribution that Jews made to life and culture in Germany (and other German-speaking lands) over the centuries, we would lose something essential to understanding German culture as a whole. Modern Germany would not be what it is today without the positive contribution of Jews, or the negative consequences of their expulsion and destruction. Especially following the Holocaust, 'German German' identity can no more exist independently of its dialectic relationship with 'Jewish German' identity than the reverse.

98 Zipes, 'The Holocaust and the Vicissitudes of Jewish Identity' (n 66) 176.

V. The Contemporary Context

At this stage, it is necessary to delve into the contemporary context of our project. As Grefrath's quote, above, suggests, the interest in exploring German-Jewish émigrés in recent decades is partly a product of the nostalgia and good intentions of German scholars of the post-war generation—often those associated with the student movement of 1968, dubbed affectionately the *68er*. But despite these good intentions, we are still some way from the goal. Surprisingly, conditions within the Germany academy have only recently become amenable to having honest conversations about the matter.

The dominant narrative of post-war Germany revolves around a project of 'overcoming the past' [*Vergangenheitsbewältigung*], first and foremost through building an *Erinnerungskultur* around the Holocaust as an accomplished fact in German-speaking Europe. It is tempting to take this project as a successful *fait accompli*. As A Dirk Moses wrote in 2007, the proposition 'that the Federal Republic has adopted a healthy democratic culture around the memory of the Holocaust has almost become a platitude'.[99] In the Anglosphere (and among liberal Anglophone Jews), this fact tends to be accepted unreflectingly, and it has been lauded as an example of how to deal with some of our own dirty laundry.[100] This vision of 'Germanness' is represented in popular culture, too—for example, by the diverse group (including punks, Birkenstock-wearing muesli-eaters, and a Haredi Jew with *payot*) in the comedian Jan Böhmermann's 2016 satirical music video 'Be Deutsch!'.[101]

This is a comforting story. However, my experience of the *Vergangenheitsbewältigung* is not so straightforward. As Moses observes, the dominant narrative is 'explicitly Whiggish'.[102] Its success—and sincerity—is hotly debated in German-speaking Europe. The 2000s were rocked by scandalous revelations about the *éminences grises* of Germany society (and the academy), leading to a 'virulent identity crisis of the Germans'[103] which is both historically and conceptually bound up with the question of Jewish identity and identification. As Böhmermann's video makes clear, one's attitude towards diversity in Germany—and Jews in particular—is integral to what it means to 'be Deutsch' today. However, let us not forget that Böhmermann's song was composed in response to the rise of the New Right; the vision of Germanness it portrays is mythic. It is good public relations, but wholly unreflective of any stable notion of German identity I have encountered.

[99] Moses, 'Identity After the Holocaust' (n 67).

[100] See, for example, Susan Nieman, *Learning from the Germans: Race and the Memory of Evil* (Macmillan 2019).

[101] See ZDF, 'Be Deutsch!' (*Magazine Royale*, 2016) <https://www.youtube.com/watch?v=HMQkV5cTuoY> accessed 26 April 2023.

[102] Moses, 'Identity After the Holocaust' (n 67).

[103] Thomas Lindemann, 'Es kommt spat, aber zur rechten Zeit' (*Die Welt*, 8 May 2005), cited in Moses, 'Identity After the Holocaust' (n 67) 49.

The main (and most challenging) polemical thrust of this chapter is, then, that if we were to tell Mann's story *as if* the project of *Vergangenheitsbewältigung* had been unproblematically successful, we would do ourselves, our readers, and indeed Mann's legacy a disservice. Let us postulate (as neutrally as we can) that *Vergangenheitsbewältigung* is 'incomplete'. Paradoxically, far from being over, we may be among the very first to look this problem in the eye. Failing, therefore, to engage with the Jewish dimension of Mann's biography would be an abdication of our responsibility, in the present day, to situate his dislocation within its broader historical context in a way that is meaningful for the present and future generations.

VI. A Contested Work in Progress

Although it is uncomfortable to say it out loud, modern Germany is (still) a product of its past. The 'many hundred thousand' that Mann would have hanged came from all walks of life—including academics. For several decades, this was intentionally ignored—even as the official project of overcoming the past through building a culture of remembrance was launched. In a sense, perhaps the *Erinnerungskultur* was the *quid pro quo* for the desired *Schlussstrich*: stylized remembrance, focused on a 'few criminals' and divorced from the lived realities of the National Socialist era.

The best illustration of this is controversy that arose from the *Deutscher Historikertag*, the leading annual historical conference in Germany, held in Frankfurt in 1998. One of the panels dealt with the role of leading German historians in the Third Reich. The upshot was that the luminaries of the historical academy had been more deeply implicated in the regime than they had let on. They had been silent or even obscured their involvement. While this is unsurprising in itself, the extent of the problem, and its implications for the historiography of what had been written about the Third Reich up to the turn of the millennium, sent shockwaves throughout the German historical academy. In parallel developments, a seminal publication of 1997 by Saul Friedländer brought, to a unique extent, the Jewish perspective into the historical narrative for the first time.[104] As Volkov explains, even German historians concerned with antisemitism had excluded the Jewish ('victim') perspective from scholarly studies—on the grounds that it overshadowed academic rigour.[105]

[104] Saul Friedländer, *Nazi Germany and the Jews: The Years of Persecution, 1933–1939* (HarperCollins 1997); see also Saul Friedländer, *Nazi Germany and the Jews: The Years of Extermination, 1939–1945* (HarperCollins 2007).

[105] See Martin Broszat and Saul Friedländer, 'Um die Historisierung des Nationalsozialismus. Ein Briefwechsel' (1988) 36 Vierteljahresheft für Zeitgeschichte 339.

Why did this occur only in the late 1990s? The 'second generational' change played an important role, as Hannah Feesche writes.[106] In Germany, the teacher–student relationship is peculiarly characterized by dependency and patronage; this discouraged critical questioning.[107] By 1998, most of the offending historians were dead, such that reckonings could be made without the appearance of a personal denunciation. Reunification in 1990 had brought a new set of historical sources and points of comparison. As Max Planck said of the sciences, historiography also advances one funeral at a time.[108] According to Volkov, '[o]nly a younger generation of historians finally learned to listen to the Jewish voice and found it advantageous for their work'.[109] This generation in turn made genuine and extensive efforts to unravel the silence they confronted as teenagers, and deliver on the promise of a genuine culture of remembrance.

However, their efforts remain incomplete: as a mentor of mine once said, '*wir sind auf halber Strecke geblieben*'.[110] There are blind spots in the post-war generation's view of German-Jewish relations, too. In many respects, a second phase of work is just beginning now. This position frames our investigation of Mann, because it is this context in which we ourselves are writing.

A. Complicated, with Highs and Lows

Despite the official policy of shining light in dark corners [*Aufklärungspolitik*, where *Aufklärung* means 'clarification' and 'enlightenment'], a typical poll finds that almost half of young Germans report knowing little about the Holocaust; in Austria, 12 per cent of young people said they had never heard of the Holocaust and four out of 10 Austrian adults said that they knew 'just a little' about it.[111] Then German Foreign Minister Heiko Maas rightly declared this ignorance to be 'dangerous' in 2019.[112] It shows that the school-based approach to dealing with the past

[106] Hannah Feesche, 'Warum erst jetzt?' (Göttinger Institut für Demokratieforschung, 22 September 2014) <https://www.ifdem.de/beitraege/warum-erst-jetzt/> accessed 13 November 2023, translation my own.

[107] Of the Austrian universities, Klaus Hödl explains that a 'secluded intellectual atmosphere' prevails in which 'scholarly innovations occur not because of—but rather despite—given structures'. See Klaus Hödl, 'Jewish Studies without the "Other"' in Reuveni and Franklin (eds), *The German-Jewish Past* (n 7) 123. Hödl was describing an incident at the Karl-Franzens-Universität in Graz, where I spent an exchange summer in 2005.

[108] 'A new scientific truth does not triumph by convincing its opponents and making them see the light, but rather because its opponents eventually die, and a new generation grows up that is familiar with it.' Max Planck, *Scientific Autobiography and Other Papers* (Philosophical Library 195) 33, 97.

[109] Volkov, 'Rewriting German History' (n 12) 18.

[110] Literally, 'we got stuck halfway'.

[111] Richard Allen Greene, 'A Shadow Over Europe: Antisemitism in Europe' (*CNN*, 2018) <https://edition.cnn.com/interactive/2018/11/europe/antisemitism-poll-2018-intl/> accessed 26 April 2023 (hereafter Greene, 'A Shadow Over Europe').

[112] Heiko Maas, 'Das Unwissen der jungen Deutschen ist gefährlich' (*Die Welt*, 27 January 2019) <https://www.welt.de/debatte/kommentare/article187748332/Heiko-Maas-Das-Unwissen-der-jungen-Deutschen-ist-gefaehrlich.html> accessed 26 April 2023.

has not been effective. Recently, we have witnessed the rise of the New Right in Germany, as elsewhere, and a perceptible shift in the public debate about the past. This is typified by the rise of the populist party *Alternative für Deutschland* (AfD), whose Björn Höcke called for a '180 degree turn in the policy of remembrance' in a 2017 speech:

> We Germans, our people, are the only people in the whole world that has planted a memorial of shame in the heart of its capital city. And today we are not in the position to grieve our own victims [i.e. fallen *Wehrmacht* soldiers]. Instead of bringing the next generation in contact with the great philanthropists, the renowned, world-changing philosophers, the musicians, the genius explorers and inventors, of which we have so many … German history is made mean and ridiculous. And this stupid policy of overcoming the past [*Bewältigungspolitik*] lames us even more than in Franz Joseph Strauß's times. We need nothing short of a 180 degree turn in the policy of remembrance. It cannot, it must not, and it will not continue so. There is no moral duty of self-nullification.[113]

This attitude is not, however, new: the speech itself calls back to Strauß, a conservative politician from the south, who in 1969 called for an end to the 'eternal *Vergangenheitsbewältigung* as a societal task of perpetual atonement' and the 'cult of guilt'.[114] Posener describes Strauß's Germany, to which his father returned in the 1960s, as an uncomfortable place for Jews.[115] The difference is that we are unaccustomed to hearing such sentiments expressed in public discourse after a decade or two of thinking the job was done.

In view of these continuities, some modern scholars fundamentally doubt the sincerity of the post-war project. Samuel Salzborn, for example, calls it the country's 'biggest lie'.[116] According to Salzborn's analysis, invocations of the standard formulae are undermined by private denial, relativization, and counter-narratives of German victimhood that are grossly mis-calibrated. Over the decades, old structures of thinking about Jews have been remarkably persistent, and they are working their way further and further into the mainstream today.[117] Beyond the

[113] 'Die Höcke-Rede von Dresden in Wortlaut-Auszügen' <https://www.zeit.de/news/2017-01/18/parteien-die-hoecke-rede-von-dresden-in-wortlaut-auszuegen-18171207?utm_referrer=https%3A%2F%2Fwww.google.com%2F> accessed 5 June 2023.

[114] See Robert D Meyer, 'Der "Schlussstrich" hilft dem Ressentiment Die NS-Zeit als Vogelschiss der Geschichte zu betrachten, ist Beschlusslage der AfD' (*ND Aktuell*, 15 June 2018) <https://www.nd-aktuell.de/artikel/1091312.geschichtspolitik-der-afd-der-schlussstrich-hilft-dem-ressentiment.html> accessed 26 April 2023.

[115] Alan Posener, 'No More Mr Nice Guy: Questioning the Ideal of Assimilation' in Reuveni and Franklin (eds), *The German-Jewish Past* (n 7) 5.

[116] Samuel Salzborn, *Kollektive Unschuld: Die Abwehr der Shoah im deutschen Erinnern* (Hentrich und Hentrich Verlag Berlin 2020).

[117] See, e.g., Monika Schwarz-Friesel, Evyatar Friesel, and Jehuda Reinharz, *Aktueller Antisemitismus – ein Phänomen der Mitte* (De Gruyter 2010).

AfD, resurgence in antisemitic tropes in the context of the Covid-19 pandemic,[118] for example, again revealed that they are a fixture of German political culture.[119]

This manifests in what Salzborn calls '*Schuldabwehrantisemitismus*' [lit. 'guilt-avoidance antisemitism']. His argument is an exegesis on a familiar theme in Holocaust studies since Theodor Adorno's essay observing the role-reversal of victim and perpetrator.[120] The psychological response to guilt is guilt-avoidance [*Schuldabwehr*], and the best way to do this is to find reasons that justify the wrong done to the victim while laying emphasis on the perpetrator's own suffering. The desire to avoid guilt is particularly complex when it is a collective guilt for which one does not, and indeed should not, feel personal moral responsibility. The impulse to *Schuldabwehr* is, however, utterly corrosive of the very idea of an *Erinnerungskultur*. As Adorno wrote: 'the past is no longer safe from the present, which is again dedicated to forgetting in the act of remembering.'[121]

Younger Jewish voices include writers such as Max Czollek, who labels the *Erinnerungspolitik* a 'Theatre of Reconciliation'. According to Czollek, Germans carry out ritualized acts of remembrance mainly for the purpose of proving to themselves that they have distanced themselves from the crimes of the National Socialist period. In this stylized process, Jews have a 'kind of ideological work' of reassuring the Germans of their own good intentions manifested in the ritualized act of remembering. It is a form of 'theatre', he argues, because the supposed reconciliation is on a public stage in which the relationship to the audience is more important than the relationship to reality.[122]

Elsewhere, Czollek explains that the 'German collective' is constructed through a shared desire for normality and positive national pride, citing Max Horkheimer's observation from the 1960s:

[118] Edna Bonhomme, 'Germany's Anti-vaccination History Is Riddled With Anti-Semitism' (*The Atlantic*, 2 May 2021) <https://www.theatlantic.com/health/archive/2021/05/anti-vaccination-germany-anti-semitism/618777/> accessed 16 April 2023.

[119] See Jewish World Congress, 'Jeder vierte Deutsche denkt antisemitisch' (*Süddeutsche Zietung*, 23 October 2019) <https://www.sueddeutsche.de/politik/antisemitismus-deutschland-juedischer-weltkongress-1.4652536> accessed 30 May 2023.

[120] Theodor Adorno, 'Schuld und Abwehr' in Theodor Adorno, *Soziologische Schriften II.2* (Suhrkamp 2003); see also Michael Höttemann, 'Die Abwehr der Antisemitismuskritik: Zur Logik, Form und Intention der Solidarisierung mit Günter Grass' in Marc Grimm and Bodo Kahmann (eds), *Antisemitismus im 21. Jahrhundert: Virulenz einer alten Feindschaft in Zeiten von Islamismus und Terror* (De Gruyter 2018) (hereafter Höttemann, 'Die Abwehr der Antisemitismuskritik').

[121] Theodor W Adorno, *Minima Moralia. Reflexionen aus dem be schädigten Leben* (Subricamp 1951) 53 cited in Imke Meyer, '"Ein Schandgesetz erkennt man, nach dem alles angerichtet ist": Täter-Opfer-Konstellationen in Ingeborg Bachmanns Erzählung "Unter Mördern und Irren"' (1998) 31(1) Modern Austrian Literature 39, 39.

[122] Max Czollek, *Versöhnungstheater* (Carl Hanser Verlag 2023) 5 (translation my own). In another essay, Czollek refers to Michal Bodemann's idea of the 'theatre of memory': see Michal Bodemann, *Gedächtnistheater. Die jüdische Gemeinschaft und ihre deutsche Erfindung* (Rotbuch 1996); Max Czollek (Jon Cho-Polizzi tr.), 'Overcoming the Present [*Gegenwärtsbewältigung*]' (2020) 12(2) *TRANSIT* 144 (hereafter Czollek, 'Overcoming the Present').

> [T]he Germans' recognition of guilt after the defeat of National Socialism was a splendid process for preserving a *völkisch* feeling of commonality in the postwar period. The main thing was to preserve the We.[123]

Early on in the history of West Germany, in particular, Jewish people were given a role to confirm this national catharsis. But it is a passive role that is fundamentally altruistic. Further, their mere presence suffices: if Jews exist in Germany, National Socialism *must* be a thing of the past.[124] There is no need to engage with Jewish life on its own terms at all.

There is, in my experience, a clear disconnect between the public discourse and the private conversations held in German-speaking Europe. What we are seeing now is nothing but people speaking their private minds in public. This realization has been shocking to me, as I believe it has been to many others. My relationship with Germany began with a school exchange in 2001—in what Alan Posener describes as the high point of German philosemitism. The *68er* generation was ascendant and could now begin the work of *Aufklärung* in earnest. According to Posener, the Jewish Museum in Berlin seemed the ideal flagship for the message:[125]

> The permanent exhibition at the Jewish Museum celebrated '2,000 years of German-Jewish history' and the essential message ... was reassuring: the Jews aren't threatening anybody ... [A]part from a few dietary quirks and strange rituals ... Jews are just like ordinary Germans and always have been. The exhibition said a lot about the contribution of individual Jews to German society—as businesspeople, scientists, politicians, intellectuals, and artists—and almost nothing about Judaism as a religion, or anti-Judaism as a driving force of Western civilization since the earliest days of Christianity. It also said next to nothing about Zionism or about Israel, where German-Jewish life continued after 1933 and German Jews played a key role in the formation of the Jewish state.[126]

[123] Czollek, 'Overcoming the Present' (n 122) 146, citing Max Horkheimer, *Notizen 1950–1969 und Dämmerung. Notizen in Deutschland* (Fischer 1974) 200. Translation in original.

[124] Czollek, 'Overcoming the Present' (n 122) 146.

[125] I visited this museum as a 17-year-old exchange student. It was a formative experience for me, both in terms of its presentation of Jewish life in Europe and the modern German response to it. I visited with my host mother (a trained historian and *68er*) during a visit to Berlin in 2001. For an exploration of the Jewish Museum, which is run mainly by non-Jews and is an institution of the German state rather than a Jewish organization, see Michal Friedländer, 'From Object to Subject: Representing Jews and Jewishness at the Jewish Museum Berlin' in Reuveni and Franklin (eds), *The German-Jewish Past* (n 7) 42. Friedländer was behind the controversial, but in my view ingenious, exhibition labelled as a 'Jew in a Box' whereby contemporary German Jews volunteered to sit in the museum and answer questions as an inversion (and subversion) of the traditional objectification of Jews in the German museum tradition.

[126] Alan Posener, 'No More Mister Nice Guy: Questioning the Ideal of Assimilation' in Reuveni and Franklin (eds), *The German-Jewish Past* (n 7) 8.

Posener describes the subsequent phase of the Museum, and the controversies under its second (non-Jewish) director, ultimately leading to his resignation.[127] Posener also tables the very serious proposition that German philosemitism can be, and often is, a kind of 'reverse antisemitism'. The negative aspects of 'Jewishness' are attributed to Israel, while the 'model minority' Western European Jew is idealized as intelligent, industrious, secular, etc.—'a better sort of "other" as portrayed by the Jewish Museum'.[128] This ideal is the same one that is weaponized against other groups (such as Turks and Arabs). As Lisa Silverman writes, antisemitism and philosemitism are components of a larger ordering system of Jewish difference that continues to operate in modern Central Europe.[129]

The evolution of popular culture is equally disheartening. In recent decades, a spate of German-language media has been produced which presents a hackneyed view of the past that both emphasizes German victimhood and either ignores or glosses over the presence of Jews in Germany and their position in German society.[130] In a modern Europe, in which large proportions of youth are totally unaware of what really happened, these otherwise hyper-realistic historical dramas play an important didactic function.

Notably, young German Jews like Czollek have different Jewish histories and backgrounds, and (like myself) engage with German-speaking Europe on a different basis to German-Jewish émigrés and their descendants. Many of today's German Jews have grandparents, for example, who fought with the Red Army, which changes their perspective considerably. Posener describes their approach as 'No More Mr Nice Guy', and questions the ideal of assimilation fundamentally:

> Instead of papering over cultural differences, a Jewish view of Jewish history needs to stress them; needs to stress the strangeness of being Jewish, of being the archetypal Other not only in Christian, but also in Enlightenment thought ... Jewish assimilation was a noble enterprise, but it was doomed and, in certain moments, even my father knew that. Writing to his mother from France in February 1935, he says he intends to go to Palestine, because he 'can't always be the little man who apologises for his existence' and that he 'cannot imagine passing this fate onto a child—again to love, where he is hated, and to live where he is only tolerated'.[131]

[127] ibid. *Inter alia*, the Central Council of Jews in Germany called for the removal of the word 'Jewish' in the museum's title: <https://twitter.com/zentralratjuden/status/1138364310294540288> accessed 5 June 2023.

[128] Alan Posener, 'No More Mister Nice Guy: Questioning the Ideal of Assimilation' in Reuveni and Franklin (eds), *The German-Jewish Past* (n 7) 8.

[129] Lisa Silverman, 'Rethinking Jews, Antisemitism and Jewish Difference in Post-War Germany' in Reuveni and Franklin (eds), *The German-Jewish Past* (n 7) 136.

[130] For example, see this op-ed on *Babylon Berlin*: Alan Posener, 'German TV Is Sanitizing History: A New Wave of Historical Dramas is Telling the Wrong Stories About the Country's Past' (*Foreign Policy*, 9 April 2018) <https://foreignpolicy.com/2018/04/09/dont-mention-the-war-germany-television-holocaust-anti-semitism-babylon-berlin-europe/> accessed 5 June 2023.

[131] Alan Posener, 'No More Mister Nice Guy: Questioning the Ideal of Assimilation' in Reuveni and Franklin (eds), *The German-Jewish Past* (n 7) 9.

On the German side, too, a new generation is engaging with the past and critically reassessing the whole mess. König's biographical work on Mann is exemplary of this.[132] It remains to be seen how this next generation discharges its stewardship of the *Erinnerungskultur*. On the one hand, they may feel distant enough from the events of 1933–1945 to approach the matter more objectively: paradoxically, perhaps, *because* they do not feel as burdened by collective guilt, they may be less invested in collective *Schuldabwehr*. Alternatively, they may wish to achieve the *Schlussstrich* sought in the 1950s, and finally succeed.[133]

B. Israel and Modern European Anti-Semitism

Israel itself is not a major theme in our treatment of Mann or his legacy. There are a few mentions of the State of Israel in his letters; Mann maintained familial and professional connections with people in the country, but was no Zionist. He wrote in 1946 about the position taken by the Jewish Agency vis-à-vis the actions of the paramilitary group the Irgun:[134]

> No papers have arrived here since Friday. I hope very much that they will be here this morning. I read the Palestine Debate in *The Times*, but could not find that part of Churchill's speech which Päps mentions in his letter. I share most of the excitement about Palestine, but not all of it. It is quite obvious to my mind that the Jewish Agency has instigated and supports and shields this terrorism which I condemn as severely as I condemned the horrors of the Nazis. So long as this continues, the Jewish Agency, representing terrorism, must share the blame. It is essential to stick to moral values, and if one fails, as the Jewish Agency has done, one forfeits the right to complain.[135]

Elsewhere he wrote of Irgun's bombing of the British military headquarters in Jerusalem at the King David Hotel: 'This is very bad indeed. I only hope the Jewish authorities will not try to explain or court sympathy for such a shocking thing.'[136] At the time, of course, Mann himself was a uniformed officer in British Army

[132] In addition to his chapter in this volume—Chapter 3, 'Pragmatism Meets *Praxisorientierung*: FA Mann and a Transnational Biography in Law'—König is writing a more comprehensive legal biography of Mann as an output of this project.

[133] On the half-life of collective memory and attention, see Cristian Candia and others, 'The Universal Decay of Collective Memory and Attention' (2019) 3(1) Nature Human Behaviour 82. Biographies seem to survive longest—20–30 years—and music has the shortest shelf-life. Remembering interacts with technologies of recording in interesting ways.

[134] The official position of the Jewish Agency for Palestine was ultimately more nuanced than this; see, e.g., *The Jewish Plan for Palestine: Memoranda and Statements Presented to the United Nations Special Committee on Palestine* (United Nations 1947) 32, 41, 264.

[135] Letter from FA Mann to Lore Mann (Mann estate, RS1000_NLMann_0984, undated 1946).

[136] ibid.

headquarters in Berlin. Perhaps here, again, he felt the two halves of his identity—and status—in tension.

Even though we might like to avoid it, it is necessary to briefly touch on Israel in our present undertaking. This is because Israel provides the ultimate context for Adorno's victim–perpetrator reversal, such that questions of 20th-century German-Jewish identification and identity interact with modern narratives around the 'Israel Question' in complex ways. In particular, because Israel gives critics a plausible basis on which to make arguments about Jews (for example, taking the above, an equivalency between the crimes of the Nazi state and the crimes of paramilitary organizations that led to the creation of the Jewish state), it provides an ideal rhetorical standpoint from which to make cloaked antisemitic arguments and, simultaneously, criticize those who seek to point out contemporary antisemitism.[137]

At the outset some basic facts must be stated: First, there is room for Europeans of all backgrounds, including Germans, to criticize the actions of the Israeli government—and indeed Israeli society, just as they might criticize Jordanian or Costa Rican society. Secondly, many Jews of Mann's generation were critical of Israel and many Jews today are anti-Zionist. It is *per se* legitimate to take their views into consideration and even marshal them in support of a genuine and principled objection to some feature of Israeli government and society. Thirdly, however, the way that many Europeans choose to engage with the complex situation of Israel and Palestine is a manifestation of latent antisemitism rather than legitimate engagement with the issues.

About a decade ago, Monika Schwarz-Friesel and Jehuda Reinharz analysed some 14,000 letters sent (unsolicited) to the *Zentralrat der Juden in Deutschland* and the Israeli Embassy in Berlin.[138] Their book 'meticulously dissects' the components of current German debate and identifies the way that modern criticism of Israel plays out ancient tropes: Jews as parasites, as quintessential 'Others', as Christ-murderers, and (surprisingly often) as child murderers in a modern twist on the medieval blood libel.[139] Thomas Kühne summarizes:

> Traditional clichés ... gain traction only through assimilation into current politics, most prominently condemnation of Israel. The conflation of traditional antisemitism (or anti-Judaism) and current anti-Israel expressions is crucial: instead of criticizing aspects of Israeli political behavior, writers deny the legitimacy of Israel altogether, simultaneously holding all Jews (or those in Germany) responsible for Israel's alleged evil-doing.[140]

[137] See Höttemann, 'Die Abwehr der Antisemitismuskritik' (n 120).
[138] Monika Schwarz-Friesel and Jehuda Reinharz, *Die Sprache der Judenfeindschaft im 21. Jahrhundert* (Walter de Gruyter 2013).
[139] Thomas Kühne, 'Monika Schwarz-Friesel and Jehuda Reinharz, *Die Sprache der Judenfeindschaft im 21. Jahrhundert*' (2015) 29(2) Holocaust and Genocide Studies 301.
[140] ibid.

My anecdotal experience, sadly, supports this: I have been accused of supporting 'child murderers and land thieves' because I was wearing a *kippah* on a Berlin street, by a well-dressed middle-aged German man.[141] (Recall Mann's fellow theatre-goers). I do not usually wear a *kippah*; I did so for a time in Berlin because the German Government Commissioner on Antisemitism, Felix Klein, had in May 2019 advised Jewish men not to wear them in public in light of a recent spike in antisemitic violence—a suggestion I found unacceptable at the time.[142]

The currency of problematic attitudes towards Jews in the educated middle has been well-documented.[143] The same, tired old antisemitic tropes are dressed up as progressive criticism of Israel in ways that blur lines between what it means to be 'German', 'Jewish', 'Zionist', and 'Israeli'. Again, recent data from a sample of European countries illustrates the predicament: (i) nearly one in five polled said that antisemitism in their countries was a response to the everyday behaviour of Jewish people; (ii) one in three said that Israel uses the Holocaust to justify its actions (only one in five disagreed with this proposition); (iii) one in three said that supporters of Israel use accusations of antisemitism to shut down criticism of Israel, while only one in 10 said that was not true.[144] Within these poll results lies evidence of a 'perfidious perpetrator–victim reversal' that places the blame for antisemitism on Jews themselves.[145] It is deployed to give European antisemites a veneer of respectability and helps to square their antisemitism with their professed liberal or progressive world view. As this manuscript was being finalized for publication, with violence again flaring in the Middle East, the Israel question has rightly been observed to 'cut deep' into Germany's post-war soul.[146]

[141] I was asked what the 'rag' [*Lappen*] on my head meant, to which I answered 'that I am a Jew'. In response, the man told me it meant that I 'supported land thieves and child murderers'.

[142] Shaun Walker, 'Jews in Germany Warned of Risks of Wearing Kippah Cap in Public' *The Guardian* (26 May 2019) <https://www.theguardian.com/world/2019/may/26/jews-in-germany-warned-of-risks-of-wearing-kippah-cap-in-public> accessed 26 April 2023; 'German Official Warns Jews against Wearing Yarmulkes' (*DW*, 25 May 2019) <https://www.dw.com/en/german-official-warns-jews-against-wearing-kippahs-in-public/a-48874433? accessed 16 April 2023 .

[143] Monika Schwarz-Friesel, '"Antisemitism 2.0"—The Spreading of Jew-Hatred on the World Wide Web' in Armin Lange and others, *Comprehending and Confronting Antisemitism: A Multi-faceted Approach* (De Gruyter 2020); see also Werner Bergmann, *Antisemitism In Europe Today: The Phenomena, The Conflicts* (Jewish Museum Berlin) <https://www.jmberlin.de/en/online-publication-antisemitism-europe-today> accessed 26 April 2023.

[144] Greene, 'A Shadow Over Europe' (n 111).

[145] See Hannah Project, 'Without Israel There Would Be No Antisemitism' <https://hannah-project.eu/without-israel-there-would-be-no-antisemitism/> accessed 5 June 2023.

[146] See, e.g., James Angelos, 'Israel-Hamas War Cuts Deep into Germany's Soul' (*POLITICO*, 21 October 2023), <https://www.politico.eu/article/israel-hamas-war-germany-germany-berlin/> accessed 3 November 2023. Amidst the chaos and confusion, Vice-Chancellor Robert Habeck recorded what will be considered, in my view, one of the great speeches of post-war Germany: <https://www.youtube.com/watch?v=MdZvkkpJaVI> accessed 20 November 2023. The speech has been widely praised for its ability to disentangle complex issues in contemporary German politics (including Islamic, right-wing, and left-wing antisemitism), state clearly Germany's historical responsibility towards Israel and the Jews, and communicate a compelling empathy for Palestinians in Gaza.

This makes it imperative that we guard against the 'weaponization' of Jewish voices (such as Mann's) in ways that could play into an antisemitic agenda—or, more saliently, in ways that could play into the *Schuldabwehr* tendencies of Germans or the tendency to divide the world into 'good' Jews (those that criticize Israel—best of all those who equiparate Zionism to Nazism) and 'bad' Jews (Zionists). Being alert to this does not preclude any legitimate avenue of critical engagement with the situation in the Middle East.

VII. Conclusion

Max Fürst, a German writer and Holocaust survivor, wrote: 'The role Jewishness plays in my life today can only be attributed to the way it was imposed upon me through Hitler.'[147] The same could be said of many German-Jewish lives, especially those with identities we might label 'assimilated', 'secular', 'atheist', or who converted to another religion. Despite this fact, when writing about these lives today, it is important to explore the 'Jewish dimension' with open curiosity.

If we do so in the right manner, it does not reinforce the National Socialist categories. It unlocks the oft-obscured contribution of Jewish people and culture to German-speaking culture and civilization. This is at very real risk of being forgotten. If we write about Mann as an 'undifferentiated' German, we push that memory a further inch towards oblivion. More subtly, but just as importantly, if we fail to explore what is *Jewish* about Mann's 'bourgeois German Jewish milieu', we fail to understand the *German* culture and civilization to which it made outsized contributions. Mann had good prudential and intimate psychological reasons to stress that he and his family had a 'wholly and firmly German' 'cultural status'. To us, in the present day, however, his claim may have to be interpreted in a way that would have surprised Mann and his contemporaries.

It is our job to enquire, because the enquiry itself is the major contribution we can make towards the project of the *Erinnerungskultur*—a project which is for the benefit of Jews generally and of non-Jewish Germans. That project is in a state of transition, and its success is by no means assured. Its demise takes the form of a ritualized theatre in which truths are inverted and narratives are manipulated to serve the psychological needs of those Germans who prefer not to face the difficult historical truth head-on. Unfortunately, evidence is not encouraging that things are developing in a positive direction.

Not only projects with an explicit Holocaust focus are relevant to countering these trends. In fact, the ones that only incidentally touch on the historiography of the Holocaust may be even more important to the production of a healthy culture

[147] Cited in Zipes, 'The Holocaust and the Vicissitudes of Jewish Identity' (n 66) 163.

today. This project saw us talk about a German Jew. That forced us to talk about, and indeed argue about, what being a 'German Jew' meant then and means now, and whether asking this multi-layered question is even appropriate in a project like this. Our discussions convinced me that this chapter was an important one to write.

In closing, I would like to thank my fellow project members and affiliates, who were exemplary in our discussions on this difficult topic. As foreshadowed earlier, there was a diversity of opinion in our large group—and, as one might expect, some of the starkest differences of opinion were in fact between members of our group who identify as Jewish. It is a small achievement in itself that these debates could be held under the auspices of the Humboldt-Universität zu Berlin and supported by the *Deutsche Forschungsgemeinschaft*.[148] May there be many more in years to come.

Bibliography

Adorno T, *Minima Moralia. Reflexionen aus dem beschädigten Leben* (Subricamp 1951)

Adorno T, 'Schuld und Abwehr' in *Soziologische Schriften II.2* (Suhrkamp 2003)

Allen JG, 'Group Consent and the Nature of Group Belonging: Genomics, Race, and Indigenous Rights' (2010) 20(2) Journal of Law, Information and Science 28

Beatson J and Zimmermann R (eds), *Jurists Uprooted: German-Speaking Emigré Lawyers in Twentieth Century Britain* (OUP 2006)

Bilsky L and Weinke A, *Jewish-European Émigré Lawyers: Twentieth Century International Humanitarian Law as Idea and Profession* (Wallstein 2021)

Blach F and Alexander JC, *The Civil Sphere* (OUP 2006)

Bodemann M, *Gedächtnistheater. Die jüdische Gemeinschaft und ihre deutsche Erfindung* (Rotbuch 1996)

Born J, *Franz Kafka: Kritik und Rezensionen zu seinem Lebzeiten 1912–1924* (Fischer Verlag 1979)

Broszat M and Friedländer S, 'Um die Historisierung des Nationalsozialismus. Ein Briefwechsel' (1988) 36 Vierteljahresheft für Zeitgeschichte 339

Candia C and others, 'The Universal Decay of Collective Memory and Attention' (2019) 3(1) Nature Human Behaviour 82

Cooney TA, 'New York Intellectuals and the Question of Jewish Identity' (1991) 80(3) American Jewish History 344

Czollek M, *Versöhnungstheater* (Carl Hanser Verlag 2023)

Czollek M (Jon Cho-Polizzi tr.), 'Overcoming the Present [Gegenwärtsbewältigung]' (2020) 12(2) TRANSIT 144

Deutscher I, *The Non-Jewish Jew and Other Essays* (Verso Books 2017)

Dreßen W, *Deutsche verwerten jüdische Nachbarn. Dokumente zur Arisierung* (Aufbau Verlag 1998)

Dyzenhaus D, 'Reviewed Work: A Life of HLA Hart: The Nightmare and the Noble Dream by Nicola Lacey' (2005) 55(4) Journal of Legal Education 606

[148] On the history of the DFG, including its support of various projects on racial pseudo-science and the ethnographic research that supported the Eastern expansion, see: <https://www.dfg.de/dfg_magazin/aus_der_dfg/geschichte/zeit_des_nationalsozialismus/index.html>; <https://www.gepris-historisch.dfg.de/> accessed 5 June 2023.

Einstein A, 'Was ist Relativitäts-Theorie?' (28 November 1919) in Albert Einstein, *Mein Weltbild* (Querido Verlag 1934)

Elias P, *A Few from Afar: Jewish Lives in Tasmania from 1804* (Hobart Hebrew Congregation 2003)

Farber S, 'Deutscher and the Jews: On the Non-Jewish Jew – An Analysis and Personal Reflection' in J Jacobs (ed), *Jews and Leftist Politics: Judaism, Israel, Anti-Semitism and Gender* (Cambridge University Press 2017)

Feesche H, 'Warum erst jetzt?' (Göttinger Institut für Demokratieforschung, 22 September 2014) <https://www.ifdem.de/beitraege/warum-erst-jetzt/> accessed November 2022

Fingerhut K, '"Manchmal nur, in dunkeln Zeiten": Heine, Kafka, Celan—Schreibweisen jüdischer Selbstreflexion' in JA Kruse (ed), *Heine-Jahrbuch 2002* (Springer 2002)

Frei Norbert, *Adenauer's Germany and the Nazi Past* (Joel Golb tr., Columbia University Press 2003)

Reuveni G and D Franklin (eds), *The Future of the German-Jewish Past* (Purdue University Press 2021)

Friedländer S, *Nazi Germany and the Jews: The Years of Persecution, 1933–1939* (Harper Collins 1997)

Friedländer S, *Nazi Germany and the Jews: The Years of Extermination, 1939–1945* (Harper Collins 2007)

Geller J, *Bestarium Judaicum: Unnatural Histories of the Jews* (Fordham University Press 2018)

Glahé P, 'The Heidelberg Circle of Jurists and Its Struggle against Allied Jurisdiction: Amnesty-Lobbyism and Impunity-Demands for National Socialist War Criminals (1949–1955)' (2019) 22(1) Journal of the History of International Law / Revue d'histoire du droit international 1.

Gödecke P, 'Criminal Law after National Socialism: The Renaissance of Natural Law and the Beginnings of Penal Reform in West Germany' in RF Wetzell (ed), *Crime and Criminal Justice in Modern Germany* (Berghahn Books 2014)

Grefrath M, *Zerstörung einer Zukunft: Gespräche mit emigrierten Sozialwissenschaftlern* (Rohwolt Taschenbuch 1979)

Harrisville DA, *The Virtuous Wehrmacht: Crafting the Myth of the German Solider on the Eastern Front, 1941–1944* (Cornell University Press 2021)

Heer H and others (eds), *The Discursive Construction of History: Remembering the Wehrmacht's War of Annihilation* (Palgrave-Macmillan 2008)

Hödl K, 'Jewish Studies without the "Other"' in Gideon Reuveni and Diana Franklin (eds), *The Future of the German-Jewish Past* (Purdue University Press 2021)

Horkeimer M, *Notizen 1950–1969 und Dämmerung. Notizen in Deutschland* (Fischer 1974)

Höttemann M, 'Die Abwehr der Antisemitismuskritik Zur Logik, Form und Intention der Solidarisierung mit Günter Grass' in M Grimm and B Kahmann (eds), *Antisemitismus im 21. Jahrhundert: Virulenz einer alten Feindschaft in Zeiten von Islamismus und Terror* (De Gruyter 2018)

Howse R, 'Review of Reut Yael Paz, A Gateway between a Distant God and a Cruel World: The Contribution of Jewish German-Speaking Scholars to International Law' (2015) 26 European Journal of International Law 2

Jung O, 'Der literarische Judenstern: Die Indizierung der "jüdischen" Rechtsliteratur im nationalsozialistisschen Deutschland' (2006) 54(1) Vierteljahreshefte für Zeitgeschichte 25

Kadushin C, 'Social Networks and Jews' (2011) 31 Contemporary Jewry 55

Kafka F, 'Ein Bericht für eine Akademie' (1917) 2(8) Der Jude 559

Vormbaum T, 'Eduard Kohlrausch (1874–1948) Opportunismus oder Kontinuität?' in S Grundmann and others (eds), *Festschrift 200 Jahre Juristische Fakultät der Humboldt-Universität zu Berlin: Geschichte, Gegenwart und Zukunft* (De Gruyter 2010)

Kühne T and others, 'Die Sprache der Judenfeindschaft im Jahrhundert' (2015) 29(2) Holocaust and Genocide Studies 301

Lenard P, *Deutsche Physik in 4 Bänden* (JF Lehmann 1936)

Lessing T, *Jewish Self-Hate* (PC Appelbaum tr., Berghahn Books 2021 [1930])

Lewis G, *F.A. Mann: A Memoir* (Hart 2013)

Lindemann T, 'Es kommt spat, aber zur rechten Zeit' *Die Welt* (8 May 2005)

Mann FA, *Life and Cases: Manuscript of an Autobiography* (Wolfgang Ernst ed., Bonn University Press 2022)

Mecklenburg F, 'Jewish and German: The Leo Baeck Institute Archives and Library' in Gideon Reuveni and Diana Franklin (eds), *The Future of the German-Jewish Past* (Purdue University Press 2021)

Meyer I, '"Ein Schandgesetz erkennt man, nach dem alles angerichtet ist": Täter-Opfer-Konstellationen in Ingeborg Bachmanns Erzählung "Unter Mördern und Irren"' (1998) 31(1) Modern Austrian Literature 39

Mommsen T, 'Auch ein Wort über unser Judentum' in Walter Boehlich (ed), *Der Berliner Antisemitismusstreit* (Frankfurt 1965)

Moses D, 'The Non-German German and the German German: Dilemmas of Identity after the Holocaust' (2007) 101 New German Critique 45

Mounk Y, *Stranger in My Own Country: A Jewish Family in Modern Germany* (Macmillan 2014)

Paz RY, *A Gateway Between a Distant God and a Cruel World* (Brill 2013)

Pearlman W, 'How Homeland Experiences Shape Refugee Belonging: Rethinking Exile, Home, and Integration in the Syrian Case' (2023) 57(1) International Migration Review 160

Reitter P, *On the Origins of Jewish Self-Hatred* (Princeton University Press 2012)

Roberston R, *The 'Jewish Question' in German Literature 1749–1939* (OUP 2001)

Rosenberg H, 'Is There a Jewish Art?' in Harold Rosenberg, *Discovering the Present: Three Decades in Art, Culture, and Politics* (Chicago 1973)

Roth P, *Portnoy's Complaint* (Random House 1969)

Rubinstein WC, 'Franz Kafka's "A Report to an Academy"' (1954) 55 MLQ 359

Rürup R, 'The Torturous and Thorny Path to Equality. "Jew Laws" and Emancipatory Legislation in Germany from the late 18th Century' (1986) 31 Leo Baeck Institute Yearbook 24

Salzborn S, *Kollektive Unschuld: Die Abwehr der Shoah im deutschen Erinnern* (Hentrich und Hentrich Verlag Berlin 2020)

Sartre JP, *Anti-Semite and Jew: An Exploration of the Etiology of Hate* (George Becker tr., Schoken Books 1944)

Schama S, *The Story of the Jews: Finding the Words (1000 BCE—1492 CE)* (The Bodley Head 2013)

Schama S, *The Story of the Jews: Belonging (1492 CE—1900 CE)* (The Bodley Head 2017)

Schmitt C, 'Die deutsche Rechtswissenschaft im Kampf gegen den jüdischen Geist: Schlusswort auf der Tagung der Reichsgruppe Hochschullehrer des NSRB vom 3. und 4. Oktober 1936' (1936) 41(2) Deutsche Juristenzeitung 1194

Schmitt C, 'Schlußwort des Reichsgruppenwalters Staatsrat Prof. Dr. Carl Schmitt' (1936) 41(20) Deutsche Juristenzeitung 1194

Schulz-Behrend G, 'Kafka's "Ein Bericht für eine Akademie": An Interpretation' (1963) 55(1) Monatshefte für Deutschen Unterricht, Deutsche Sprache und Literatur 1

Schwarz-Friesel M and others, *Aktueller Antisemitismus – ein Phänomen der Mitte* (De Gruyter 2010)

Schwarz-Friesel M and others, *Die Sprache der Judenfeindschaft im 21. Jahrhundert* (Walter de Gruyter 2013)

Schwarz-Friesel M, '"Antisemitism 2.0"—The Spreading of Jew-Hatred on the World Wide Web' in A Lange and others, *Comprehending and Confronting Antisemitism: A Multi-faceted Approach* (De Gruyter 2020)

Sefcovic EMI, 'Toward a Conception of "Gonzo" Ethnography' (1995) 19(1) Journal of Communication Enquiry 20

Sokel W, 'Kafka as a Jew' (1999) 30(4) New Literary History 837

Trebers L, *Mythos Trümmerfrauen: Von der Trümmerbeseitigung in der Kriegs- und Nachkriegszeit und der Enstehung eines deutschen Erinnerungsortes* (Klartext Verlag 2015)

Volkov S, *Germans, Jews, and Antisemites: Trials in Emancipation* (Cambridge University Press 2006)

von Lösch AM, *Der nackte Geist: Die juristische Fakultät der Berliner* (Mohr Seibeck 1999)

Wassermann J, *Mein Weg als Deutscher und Jude* (Suhrkamp Jüdischer Verlag 2005)

Zipes J, 'The Holocaust and the Vicissitudes of Jewish Identity' (1980) 20(2) New German Critique 155

2

On Being a German Jew in the 'Golden Years'

Frank Mecklenburg

I. Introduction

Presenting a critical appraisal of FA Mann's influence on German, English, European, and international law requires a look beyond the legal considerations, an understanding of the person and his background. This essay will shine a light on his family background, his upbringing, and his education to see what intellectual and cultural capital he brought to become the eminent expert that he was.

Frederick (Francis) Alexander Mann, 'one of the most influential British legal scholars of his generation',[1] was born in August of 1907, seven years before the start of World War I, in the small south-western German town of Frankenthal. In his childhood, youth, and early adulthood, he lived through formative political changes including the German Empire, World War I, the end of the German Empire, and the beginning of the first German Republic, through a period of massive inflation, through the French occupation of the lands around him, and through an exceptionally creative period of renewal until the collapse of the democratic system and the beginning of one of the darkest periods in history that forced him and his wife to leave Germany for the United Kingdom in 1933.

His personal circumstances, however, were in many ways not typical; for instance, he stated in his autobiography that, as a Jew, 'I did not ever or anywhere

[1] 'FA Mann', *Wikipedia* <https://en.wikipedia.org/wiki/F._A._Mann> accessed 20 June 2020.

Frank Mecklenburg, *On Being a German Jew in the 'Golden Years'* In: *FA Mann*. Edited by: Jason Grant Allen and Gerhard Dannemann, Oxford University Press. © Frank Mecklenburg 2024. DOI: 10.1093/oso/9780198881452.003.0003

have any experience of antisemitism directed against myself',[2] and that he was already the third generation in his family to become a lawyer. His father, Richard Mann, was a highly accomplished lawyer in Frankenthal,[3] and his maternal grandfather, Nathaniel August Oppenheim, had already been a lawyer one generation earlier.[4] Frankenthal, although a small town in comparison to the neighbouring cities of Ludwigshafen and Mannheim, was the seat of the district court (*Landgericht*) and had a high concentration of lawyers with a considerable number of Jews among them.[5]

The task of my contribution to this volume is to capture the German-Jewish aspects of Mann's story and particularly his background. As the overview in my earlier project states: 'Mann is significant for the German-Jewish studies in two respects. First, he is an important person in his own right and the study of his life as a "jurist uprooted" is a significant object of historical study. In this respect, his experience at the (then) Friedrich-Wilhelm University of Berlin is important, as is his reception (and perceived reception) in war-time England, and indeed his work on the de-Nazification of law in Germany after the end of WWII. Through studying Mann's biography, we can understand a little more of the vibrant German-Jewish world that was so effectively destroyed in Germany in the 1930s.'[6] Or as Mann writes in his introduction to his autobiography: 'It is my duty to tell the story of a world that has disappeared, but should not be forgotten.'[7] And he continued, in great modesty, to outline the impact of that history on his own life as well as the significance of an entire historical period: 'I write, because the survival of that social group in the countries of refuge, particularly in England is equally lacking in illustration. The German Jewish immigration of the 1930's is a phenomenon which in many fields has led to remarkable achievements. Mine has not been remarkable, is somewhere in the middle, it is average and, therefore, less untypical than the work of many famous men, yet more vivid than that of the majority. Hence it is a contribution to a history which, again, has not yet been written.'[8]

As much as Mann characterized his own life and achievements as 'not remarkable', this characterization is not true even in view of and in comparison to the hundreds of thousands of Jewish refugees from Central Europe including subsequent generations. The impact is noted, and felt, and not so hidden. The distribution of Jews from Central Europe around the world after 1933 resulted in contributions

[2] FA Mann, *Life and Cases. Manuscript of an Autobiography* (Wolfgang Ernst ed., V&R Unipress 2021) 31 (hereafter Mann, *Life and Cases*).

[3] Paul Theobald, *Juedische Juristen in Frankenthal* (Edition Winterwork 2017) 15 (hereafter Theobald, *Juedische Juristen*).

[4] Jost Pietzcker, *In Memoriam* (Mann estate, NL Mann 0999, 1992) 24 (hereafter Pietzcker, *In Memoriam*).

[5] Theobald, *Juedische Juristen* (n 3).

[6] Overview of the DFG-Project on FA Mann <https://rs.cms.hu-berlin.de/fa_mann_1907-1991> accessed 31 October 2023.

[7] Mann, *Life and Cases* (n 2).

[8] ibid 13.

to many political, social, scientific, and cultural areas. It has remained a puzzle to understand how FA Mann was provided with the significant professional, intellectual, and cultural capital, as is true of many other refugees, that enabled him to make his mark as a lawyer in a foreign country with a different legal system, indeed one of the major global powers, given that he came from a modest regional territory in Germany. To understand his role and importance, it will be helpful to provide a broader context about the German-Jewish world before its destruction, and maybe also to understand what the 'brain drain' meant for Germany and the 'brain gain' for Britain, that is, the impoverishment of Germany and the import of intellectual and professional gain for his country of refuge.

One of the key documents is Mann's autobiography, which has become available only recently. The text provides insight into a number of questions and topics that only he could tell, plus it also gives details of some of the general circumstances.

II. German Jews

Being German and being Jewish, being German first, and then being German of Jewish faith, the topic has over the years found many expressions and many answers, but for the majority of Jews in German lands, this was where they and their ancestors had lived for hundreds of years, especially in the areas along the Rhine River.[9] It can even be said that the history of Jews in this area reaches back more than 1700 years, although not necessarily on a continuous basis since acceptance and expulsion, toleration and persecution had been part of Jewish life in Central Europe throughout the ages.[10] In Germany, this question has taken on special meaning following the Holocaust, which differs from that in comparison to the world before 1933.

Until 1871, there was no political entity called Germany, but rather a multitude of territories with an ever-changing variety of conditions and situations for Jews. Mann dedicated a whole chapter of his autobiography to his family background before starting to talk about his father. There was a clear sense of belonging and pride having been settled in this part of Central Europe for a long time, and the family history providing a proof of that. He remembered that his father had collected 'some family trees',[11] which he could no longer find and needed to reconstruct. Going back to the middle of the 18th century, the family narrative shows the embeddedness of his ancestors within the local society, and the interconnectedness of Jewish families in the social and commercial environment of the Palatinate region.

9 The migration of Jews from Central Europe to Eastern Europe, and vice versa, over hundreds of years, is an inseparable part of the history, but it cannot be explicated in this chapter.

10 Hermann Arnold, *Von den Juden in der Pfalz* (Verlag der Pfaelzischen Gesellschaft zur Foerderung der Wissenschaften 1967).

11 Mann, *Life and Cases* (n 2) 19.

Coming from the small village of Wattenheim, the history of which can be traced back to a settlement established by the Romans, Mann's great-grandfather moved some 20 km to the town of Frankenthal, approximately halfway between the cities of Worms and Mannheim, with Worms being one of the places where Jews had lived for more than 1,000 years. Practically every town and village in the south-west of Germany had a sizeable Jewish population with their own synagogues and cemeteries. The Mann family moved during a period of increasing toleration and integration of Jews. The French rule since 1797 had brought them equal rights. And by the mid-18th century, Frankenthal had already developed as a centre of commerce and industry. When the Palatinate came under Bavarian rule in 1816, many of the legal and administrative regulations from the French era remained. Frankenthal became the seat of the district court,[12] which moved from the regional capital Speyer after complex redistribution of the territory between Prussia and Bavaria following the conclusion of the Congress of Vienna in 1815. The French Civil Code was in place until 1900, only then replaced by the German Civil Code (*Buergerliches Gesetzbuch*, BGB). Frankenthal has continued to be the seat of the court throughout all subsequent periods and territorial changes until today. The Mann family engaged in banking and the law became part of the urban middle class, though we have no exact date for this. Mann mentions that the 'banking firm of Mann & Loeb' was listed in the Commercial Register at Frankenthal as of 1863.[13] Moreover, from his mother's side he was connected to an old Jewish family from Bonn, the Oppenheim family, down the Rhine River where his father had studied law. Mann, in his autobiography, goes into great detail displaying his pride and strong identity as a German Jew.

The Jews within the legal profession in the town of Frankenthal, FA Mann's birthplace, are well documented by local historian Paul Theobald. The Archives of the Leo Baeck Institute hold a number of collections of families from Frankenthal. To name one of its most prominent citizens, Ludwig Marum, born in 1885, was also a lawyer, member of the Social Democratic Party, Minister of Justice after World War I, member of the Reichstag from 1928 until 1933, arrested a few months after the end of the Weimar Republic, and killed in March of 1934 in the local Kislau concentration camp.[14]

The period between 1871 and 1933 has a special place in German-Jewish history, when Jews had for the first time received full civil rights, and when Germany was considered among Jews worldwide one of the least offensive places to live. This is especially the case for the time between the start of the German nation state in 1871 and halfway through the First World War. One of the first major offences occurred

[12] Bavaria had 34 district courts (*Bezirksgericht*, today *Landgericht*); four of them were in Bavarian Palatinate along with Frankenthal in Kaiserslautern, Landau, and Zweibruecken.

[13] Mann, *Life and Cases* (n 2) 19.

[14] Ludwig Marum Collection, Leo Baeck Institute Archives, AR 4969.

in 1916 when Jews were blamed for the failure of the war campaign, and again after the end of the war. 'German Citizens of Jewish Faith' was how the vast majority proudly characterized their citizenship and relationship to the nation. In the 1890s, the *Central-Verein deutscher Staatsbuerger juedischen Glaubens*, the Central Association of German Citizens of Jewish Faith, formed as a successfully organized nationwide network to combat attacks against Jews. At the same time, Jews in Germany found opportunities never seen before, and a new anti-Jewish movement developed. It should also be noted that the new Zionist movement emerged, to a large part within a larger transnational German-Jewish cultural context. Thus, new conflicts were emerging but within an atmosphere where, for a large section of German speaking Jews, there was no contradiction between German first and Jewish second. And even as this emancipated position of Jews was challenged by new forms of antisemitism, the situation in Germany was unlike the hostility against Jews common in Russia and Poland, or to a different degree in France with the Dreyfus Affair.[15] The rather sudden opening of opportunities with the unification of 1871 found many takers, in all sorts of businesses, large and small. Jews had been traditionally involved in the rural economy as wine, grain, cattle, and horse traders. By the mid-19th century, Jews had entered increasingly into the professions (law, medicine, science, etc.), though the opening to civil service positions only took place in the German Republic after the end of the monarchy in 1918. Until then, Jews who refused to convert to Christianity were largely barred from entry into national, regional, and local governmental and public positions.[16]

III. The Jewish Community

Jewish communal life in Central Europe had existed since the Romans had occupied the lands along the Rhine River and beyond. Jewish life in Cologne goes back at least to the 4th century. The area between the cities of Speyer, Worms, and Mainz were centres of Jewish life and learning from the 9th century. Jewish communities had existed in southern Germany for hundreds of years, though often in discontinuous ways, with expulsions, pogroms, and dispossession interrupting the lives of Jews, and therefore resettlement was not uncommon. The majority of Jews lived in rural areas, villages, and small towns. By the 19th century, there were several thousand Jewish communities in German lands, and, in areas of the south-west,

[15] Shulamit Volkov, *Deutschland aus Juedischer Sicht: Eine andere Geschichte* (CH Beck 2022) (hereinafter Volkov, *Deutschland aus Juedischer Sicht*); see also her lecture on *Rewriting German History: Jewish Experience as a Corrective* (The Leo Baeck Memorial Lecture, 63, New York 2022) 15.

[16] See Till van Rahden, *Jews and other Germans: Civil Society, Religious Diversity and Urban Politics in Breslau, 1860–1925* (The University of Wisconsin Press 2008); see also Elisabeth Kraus, *Die Familie Mosse. Deutsch-juedisches Buergertum im 19. und 20. Jahrhundert* (CH Beck 1999) about the meteoric rise of a Jewish family essentially coming from a similar background in the eastern parts of Prussia (hereafter Kraus, *Die Familie Mosse*).

practically every village, town, and city had their own congregations with synagogues and cemeteries.

Life in the Jewish community meant more than religion. Many institutions formed a network of mutual support, in part forced by exclusion but mainly guided by tradition, and the financial support of and personal involvement in those institutions was the common commitment to Judaism beyond religious piety. Pride in the history and the traditions played an important role in the Mann and Oppenheim (FA Mann's maternal family) families.

Even before the time of the German Reich of 1871, religious observance had begun to fade for Jews, as was the case in German-speaking lands in general among all religious denominations. For Jews, citizenship had become a defining factor, along with religion and ethnicity. FA Mann's father, born in the early years of the *Kaiserreich*, who started his law studies in 1891 and was a second-generation member of the legal profession, remained engaged in the Jewish community of his hometown Frankenthal, where he served as the head of the board of the Jewish community during the second half of the 1920s. 'We left Germany [in 1933], because we were Jews and as such the victims of attack ... We were not, we are not practicing Jews. But we felt as Jews by background, history, tradition ...'[17]

However, from his mother's side, FA Mann was connected to a different Jewish world. His maternal grandfather, Nathaniel August Oppenheim, born 1847, a lawyer one generation earlier than Mann's father, was a member of the Oppenheim family of Bonn and Cologne, originally from Worms. The family is known in the business world for the biggest private bank in Europe, Sal. Oppenheim Jr & Cie,[18] and less known for its far-reaching Jewish traditional connections. The Oppenheim family has a long line of rabbis and businesspeople; in the early days business was mainly conducted by women since traditionally men were to study. During the early modern era, the Oppenheims were intermarried to other influential business and finance families and to Court Jews such as the Wertheimer and Leffman Behrends Cohen families, who rose to prominence and wealth in the early modern period.[19] On the other hand, Nathaniel August Oppenheim's wife, FA Mann's maternal grandmother, was a descendant of the Chief Rabbi of Bonn, Simcha Benjamin Cohen, who died in 1816.[20] A distant cousin from the Vienna branch of the Oppenheim family characterized the transition from the early days of the Court Jews: 'But the downfall of the individual Court Jews did by no means spell the end of their dynastic families. The Oppenheims, the Wertheimers, the Hitzigs, the Leffman Behrends, the Gumbels, and the many others had by now intermarried and formed a close-knit community which had spread over most of Europe.

[17] Mann, *Life and Cases* (n 2) 49.

[18] ibid 20f.

[19] See Selma Stern, *The Court Jew: A Contribution to the History of the Period of Absolutism in Central Europe* (Jewish Publication Society of America 1950).

[20] Mann, *Life and Cases* (n 2) 21.

Now they were not only connected with each other by sharing the same spheres of interest whether they were commercial, intellectual or religious, but they were bound together by family bonds, they had formed a kinship. Though they had become worldly and had eagerly accepted the lifestyle of the gentile aristocracy, they were still religious Jews.'[21]

IV. Education

Bildung, in the sense of education, was the requisite entry ticket to the professional middle class. Jews put a high value on schooling and academic achievement. However, the German concept of *Bildung* implied education in a broad sense; schooling was an important part of it, but it also meant character formation. The German genre of *Bildungsroman* as a roadmap and the *Bildungsbuerger* as the civic ideal became the stereotype of the mature cultured person and their formation. Probably the best perspective of the concept in regard to German Jews as emancipated citizens is outlined in George Mosse's *German Jews Beyond Judaism*, a collection of a series of lectures Mosse gave at Hebrew Union College in 1983.[22] This is, of course, a contested concept—Shulamit Volkov does not believe 'that they were—as a whole—truer to the ideas of *Bildung* and Enlightenment than other Germans'[23]—but given that middle class Jews during the *Kaiserreich* and also during the Republic were mostly liberal politically and culturally, there is an argument to be made that Jews managed to take advantage of the new opportunities in the realm of culture and education as well. It was certainly true for Richard Mann who, for instance, met in high school the future president of the German Central Bank, and then studied, as was common in German law school training, at various universities around the country: Munich, Berlin, Bonn, and Erlangen. After his Doctor of Law degree and passing the required exams to be admitted to the bar, he opened his law office in 1898 in Frankenthal.[24] He settled in Frankenthal 'and in due course my father built up a very considerable, profitable and remarkably distinguished practice in commercial and civil litigation. He acted for many of the industrial undertakings, for all public authorities (Reich and Bavarian Government, Post Office, Railway Administration) and for many of the wine producers; in fact he acquired a reputation far beyond the Palatinate in the law relating to wine production and frequently was called upon to assist in cases arising from it in other parts of Germany.'[25] And FA Mann further remarks in his memoirs: 'The special

[21] Unpublished manuscript by Doris Oppenheim-Liffman and Herbert Liffman, 'The Jew in European Society' in *The Oppenheim Family*, Leo Baeck Institute Archives, AR 5166, 3f.

[22] George Mosse, *German Jews beyond Judaism* (Bloomington 1985).

[23] Volkov, *Deutschland aus Juedischer Sicht* (n 15).

[24] Mann, *Life and Cases* (n 2) 23.

[25] ibid 24.

luck which invariably, professional men need for their success, came to my father in the oddest possible way.'[26] He continues by mentioning a case that arrived by way of mixed-up addresses, which gave Richard Mann a big and important case to start his career. And obviously he was able to take advantage of the opportunity despite being a freshly minted lawyer. But we do not learn more about the larger circumstances and properties he brought to the job, i.e. his cultural, intellectual, and professional capital, which came not so much from his father's family, and we can only speculate what part his wife's family played. We do learn, however, that the opposing lawyer in that first big case was Max Hachenburg, legendary Jewish attorney of the first generation, who had started to study law at the time when Richard Mann entered elementary school. In this case, Richard Mann's luck was to oppose Hachenburg and thus build his reputation early in his career. And to drop more names, FA Mann recounts, 'At an early age I met famous lawyers coming to Frankenthal to argue cases with or against my father. I remember ... in particular criminal lawyers, Max Alsberg (a university friend of my father's) above all.'[27] Alsberg was a prominent criminal defence lawyer who defended Carl von Ossietzky in 1931.

It is safe to assume that *Bildung* and family background were the capital that FA Mann brought to his career; the accumulated knowledge and sense of achievement over several generations. Such knowledge and sense of achievement is mirrored in this recollection of how his father shaped him: 'I owe him more than I can realize. I owe him the standards which have decisively influenced my own life and my attitude towards people and things. I owe him the unbending professional integrity which, frequently quite unconsciously and incidentally he taught and impressed upon me. It was the little things I learned from him, yet they are so great.'[28] In Mann's case, he benefitted from the multi-generational line in the legal profession, which was rare due to the late opportunities for Jews to enter the professions, emphasized by the town of Frankenthal, small but significant as the seat of the regional courts.

To mention an example of another Jewish family, the Mosse family had modest beginnings in the eastern provinces of Prussia. The children, 14 altogether, moved to Berlin, starting in the 1860s. There were several lines of lawyers, most prominently Albert Mosse, who became a high-ranking judge in East Prussia in the 1890s without having to convert. Three of his five children in Richard Mann's generation became lawyers as well.[29] Also significant is the story of Hermann Makower, whose father had come from Russia to be a tutor in a small town in Posen, Prussia, in the 1820s.[30] Hermann Makower went to school in Berlin, studied law, and became the

[26] ibid.
[27] ibid 25.
[28] ibid.
[29] Kraus, *Die Familie Mosse* (n 16).
[30] The connection and exchange of Jewish professionals between Central Europe and Russia is described in Yuri Slezkine, *The Jewish Century* (Princeton University Press 2004).

first Jewish notar in Imperial Germany. He served on the board of governors of the Berlin Jewish community between 1866 and 1892. His granddaughter married into one of the branches of the Mosse family.[31]

V. Jews in the Legal Professions

Only the Napoleonic occupation of German territories brought about changes that began to give Jews civic rights on an equal basis. Although many of those achievements were reversed after the defeat of Napoleon and restoration, it did mean the beginning of public careers for Jews. There are various accounts about the first Jewish lawyers in German lands. Gabriel Riesser, born 1806 in Hamburg, at that time under French rule, had studied law in the mid-1820s but couldn't practice as an attorney until 1840. Adolf Aronheim, born 1818 and the first Jewish lawyer in Braunschweig, was also admitted to the bar in the early 1840s but could not practice as a notar since Jews could not administer the oath of a Christian. Prior to the first German Republic of 1918, it was very difficult if not impossible for Jews to be admitted to the civil service; although with the start of the German national state in 1871 this was theoretically no longer a problem, in reality it remained an obstacle. Among the rare cases was aforementioned Albert Mosse (1846–1925), who passed his first exam in 1868 and was appointed judge in 1876. He was the younger brother of Berlin-based publisher Rudolf Mosse. In the 1890s, Albert Mosse was a legal consultant to the Japanese Empire involved in drafting the new Japanese Constitution, and who upon return to Prussia was appointed a supreme court judge in Koenigsberg, East Prussia, as a rare exception without having to convert. But this was only possible by way of extraordinary achievement and privilege. And another rare occurrence was Jewish lawyers being made partners in non-Jewish law firms; for instance, Siegfried Guggenheim, born 1873 in Worms, became junior partner in 1900 at the law firm of Otto von Brentano, who would serve as the Minister of the Interior in Hesse between 1918 and 1927, and whose son Heinrich von Brentano was the Foreign Minister in the government of Konrad Adenauer in the new Federal Republic of Germany. Guggenheim's family had been in Worms since at least the middle of the 16th century. He was a major figure in the development of Jewish culture before 1933, deeply engaged in book art and the author of a modern version of the Passover Haggadah, called the Offenbacher Haggadah.[32]

Frankenthal became the seat of the district court (*Landgericht*) in 1816. It was a rather small town in the middle of the 19th century, with less than 5,000 inhabitants, but by the turn of the century the number had more than tripled. Owing to its importance as a judicial centre and, since the middle of the century, as an industrial

[31] Kraus, *Die Familie Mosse* (n 16).

[32] Siegfried Guggenheim Collection, Leo Baeck Institute Archives, AR 180.

and commercial centre, the number of lawyers was disproportionate to the size of the population. The first Jewish lawyer in Frankenthal was Cornelius David, born 1828 in Speyer, who was admitted in 1865.[33] There were some prominent figures such as Ludwig Marum, an example of the next generation of Jewish lawyers, who was born in Frankenthal in 1882, an important politician during the Weimar years, and member of the Social Democratic Party since 1904, and who established his law office in Karlsruhe before World War I. Marum became the Minister of Justice in 1918/19 in Baden, member of the diet of Baden from 1914 until 1928, and member of the national assembly, Reichstag, from 1928 until 1933; he was one of the early victims of Nazi persecution and died in a local concentration camp in 1934.[34] As mentioned earlier, FA Mann's maternal grandfather, Nathaniel August Oppenheim, was a lawyer who practiced in Bonn, though it is not clear when exactly he was admitted to the bar.[35] What had become possible for ordinary Jewish citizens was to be a university student to qualify for admission to the 'free professions', i.e. lawyers and doctors. Entry into the civil service was in reality only possible after being baptized, and even then, people met with many obstacles. FA Mann's father did not convert. Richard Mann, born 1873 in Frankenthal in Baden, studied law from 1891 and passed his first exam in 1896. Two years later he passed his second exam and was admitted as an attorney. His career was marked by service in professional organizations, in the lawyer's association of Frankenthal and later as a member of the bar association of the district court of Zweibruecken, until he was kicked out after the Nazi takeover in 1933. In 1921, in the early years of the Weimar Republic, he received the title of *Justizrat*, an honorary title of distinction within the profession, but whether it in fact did carry any advantages remained an argument between members of the profession. Between 1925 and 1929, Richard Mann served as the head of the Jewish community in Frankenthal. By 1936, he lost his admission as an attorney and two years later he left Germany and went to England, where he died in 1953.[36]

The legal profession during the 1871 to 1933 period provides us with a particular view of the social and political situation in Germany. The debate about the position and the participation of Jews in German society has continued to be controversial since the rupture of the social contract in 1933 and remains an open debate. Were the Jews of Germany truly part of the nation? In their own view, to a large degree, but in the eyes of non-Jews, mostly not? With the dynamics and tensions of civic society since 1871—the rising hostility against Jews, the new antisemitism during the *Kaiserreich*, and yet at the same time unprecedented acceptance—the role of Jewish lawyers deserves closer scrutiny. By the end of the 19th century, alongside

[33] Theobald, *Juedische Juristen* (n 3).
[34] Ludwig Marum Collection, Leo Baeck Institute Archives, AR 4969.
[35] Pietzcker, *In Memoriam* (n 4) 24.
[36] Theobald, *Juedische Juristen* (n 3).

rapid integration grew anti-Jewish sentiments among conservative German non-Jews; the term antisemitism emerged, and so did political parties with explicit antisemitic programmes. At the same time, in 1896, the Central Association of German Citizens of Jewish Faith (CV) was founded. As the title of the organization indicated, being German and being Jewish was no longer seen as a contradiction by the members of this organization, the largest Jewish membership organization in Germany. Aside from publications and events, it was a legal defence organization for fighting antisemitic attacks, at times with 15,000 court cases per year, litigated by Jewish lawyers. Research into the details of that organization has taken off only in recent years with a new generation of historians.[37] One particular aspect of the work of the CV has only recently become a research topic, that is, its transnational activities, especially with American organizations, during the last 10 years before the end of the CV in 1938.[38] And another indication of the dynamic developments and the rupture in civic society most visible in the legal profession is the role of women in society. Very few women were able to study law during the later years of the *Kaiserreich*, among them a disproportionately high number of Jews, and only in the early years of the Weimar Republic, not at the onset, were women admitted to the bar and slowly allowed to enter the ranks. As of 1933, however, for Jewish women lawyers, their careers were finished in Germany.[39]

VI. Conclusion: Refugee Lawyers in the War and Post-War Efforts

The Nazi takeover in 1933 ended the careers of young Jewish lawyers almost immediately. Only veterans of World War I were permitted to practice with increasing limitations until *Kristallnacht*. Many of the young lawyers counted among the earliest refugees from Germany, among them FA Mann. Those who went to England and the United States found a difficult environment, largely due to the Great Depression and the different legal system, but they had a chance to retool, unlike later arrivals when the countries of refuge put up barriers against professionals, lawyers and doctors, and forced them to pass exams for which they had to study again. And most of them could not afford a re-education and needed to change professions. At the beginning of the war, early arrivals had mostly acquired citizenship, and refugees, particularly refugee lawyers, had become crucial participants in the efforts to fight Germany, to prepare for the occupation of Germany after the defeat, and to institute new regulations and reform of the law in post-war

[37] See Centralverein, <Centralverein.net> accessed 29 December 2022.

[38] Hendrik Schemann at the University Duisburg-Essen.

[39] For a summary, see Frank Mecklenburg, *Juristinnen in der Weimarer Republik* (Lemo. Lebendiges Museum Online, 10 December 2019) <https://www.dhm.de/lemo/kapitel/weimarer-republik/alltagsleben/juristinnen-in-der-weimarer-republik.html> accessed 28 December 2022.

Germany. FA Mann participated in the latter and, during his work as the British delegate in the Allied Control Council situated in Berlin, he met his old friends from Germany performing the American share of the work. For instance, he mentioned Max Rheinstein, who had assumed a position at the University of Chicago Law School and participated in the war crimes trial held before the International Military Tribunal, Nuremberg.

There were many differences between the Allies when it came to dealing with the Nazi past and the reconstitution of a democratic society. Mann's memoirs are full of examples of such differences and resulting difficulties. One of the issues discussed in the Control Council was the problem of restitution of property to victims of Nazi persecution. Mann mentioned that his British superiors were 'violently opposed to any measure of restitution … which might make life uncomfortable for the occupation authorities'.[40] The American authorities took a different approach, in part by being better informed about the situation on the ground due to the massive participation of refugees, especially legal professionals and political scientists but also art historians, health professionals, social work specialists, etc. German-Jewish refugee lawyers contributed with their intellectual and cultural knowledge and experience to the job of helping in the war effort, being a source of major importance regarding the German legal and political system as well as the social fabric of German society.

It is a matter of historical irony that Nazi Germany kicked out a large section of valuable professionals in law, medicine, science, business, the arts, etc., who would become instrumental in defeating the Nazi regime. Especially in the United States, knowledge about German society and state affairs was poor, and the recruitment of legal experts, along with experts in many other fields, was an essential element of strategic military planning, of intelligence gathering, and in considerations for the reconstruction of a functional state and society after the defeat of the Nazi regime. To name a few, who came with qualifications similar to what FA Mann was able to contribute, there was Fritz Oppenheimer, born 1898, son of a Berlin lawyer, who worked in Supreme Headquarters, SHAEF, and who became a consultant to the US Commissioner John McCloy; Karl Loewenstein, born 1891, a lawyer from Munich, who then taught at Amherst College and worked in the Legal Division of the US Military Government, OMGUS; and Joachim von Elbe, born 1902, whose father (a descendant of the Moses Mendelssohn) had been a *Landrat* in Hamm in Westfalia and who went through counterintelligence training at Camp Ritchie, along with many other refugees. Some 1,500 German-Jewish refugees in the US Army were trained there, among some 20,000 recruits with language expertise of other enemy countries in the European and Pacific theatres of war. Von Elbe then worked in OMGUS and subsequently was in the US diplomatic service in Germany for many

[40] Mann, *Life and Cases* (n 2) 71.

years. John Herz, born 1908, a graduate of the Geneva Institute of International and Development Studies, worked in the wartime intelligence service (Office of Strategic Services, OSS, precursor of the CIA) and later was the author of *From Dictatorship to Democracy* (1982), a study comparing efforts in Germany with other countries. Ernst Stiefel, born 1907 in Mannheim, worked first for the Office of Economic Warfare and then for OSS, and was one of the authors of the Civil Affairs Information Guide on Civil Law and a specialist in insurance questions.[41]

A few of them 'returned' to Germany, like Ernst Cramer, who was instrumental in re-establishing newspapers in Germany and who stayed with the Axel Springer company. However, for most of the refugees, after settling in their new country with their families, re-establishing their careers, and making a new home, and, more so, after slowly learning what had happened to their families, relatives, and the country of their former homes, it became unimaginable for them to 'return', because there was nothing to return to, it was all gone, destroyed, betrayed, vanished. Many refugees would not even set foot in Germany ever again. And even if they were willing to return, it was made rather clear to them that they were not welcome in Germany.

What does this story tell us today, looking back at the collective experience beyond the biography of one person? The larger issue to be considered revolves around questions of whether the German-Jewish experience was an experiment, sometimes called symbiosis, and whether it failed or never existed or was only a one-sided and blind-sided illusion of wishful thinking or was rather a negative symbiosis. But does it invalidate what happened before the breakdown? And how does this story play within the context of a reality that turned out to be the breakdown of civilization as we knew it, when, so to speak, a black hole opened up in history that swallowed all achievements of humanity and enlightenment?[42] The search for an acceptable model for historiography, for philosophy, for a paradigm to work with for the future, all these attempts are still in the works and no meaningful or acceptable conclusion has been found. The debates about the singularity of the Holocaust, which continue to produce new models of comparability, for instance by way of the study of genocides in general, recently with a new 600-page volume,[43] do not satisfy the need for a model of human behaviour that would explain what happened and alert us to the possibility of its repetition and its consequences.

Hannah Arendt's provocative post-Holocaust statement about the 'banality of evil'[44] has been widely interpreted as a banalization of evil, whereas her idea was

[41] See also Ernst Stiefel and Frank Mecklenburg, *Deutsche Juristen im amerikanischen Exil (1933–1945)* (Mohr Siebeck 1991).

[42] Or to use another metaphor, not as cosmic as a black hole but rather from considerations of climate change: when a house gets destroyed in a hurricane, does it mean that the house was badly built? Not necessarily.

[43] A Dirk Moses, *The Problems of Genocide: Permanent Security and the Language of Transgression* (Cambridge University Press 2022).

[44] See Hannah Arendt, *Eichmann in Jerusalem: A Report on the Banality of Evil* (Viking Press 1963).

to characterize radical evil as of no depth other than violence and destruction, without any positive constructive intentions or outcome. This is also expressed in the mid-1930s, at the beginning of the Nazi era, in a way that to imagine what was to come was not possible. Ismar Elbogen's book about the more than one thousand years of the history of Jews in Germany, published in 1935, the manuscript finished in 1934, opened with the prophetic sentence, 'Since their settlement during the Roman times Jews have always lived in Germany, they went through evil and good days, . . .' ('*Seit ihrer Niederlassung in der Römerzeit haben immer Juden in Deutschland gewohnt, sie haben böse und gute Tage durchgemacht, . . .*') and then finished the book with, 'Once again, German Jews are confronted with the question of testing our resilience, to prove ourselves worthy.'[45] Elbogen was aware of all the ups and downs of the history of Jews in Central Europe, he had studied all the atrocities of the past thousand years, and when he left Germany in 1938, entered the United States in late October of that year, he was not witness to a level of violence and destruction that was familiar. And when he died in 1943, little was known of what had turned into radical evil and would escalate in subsequent years. We don't know how he would have looked at his statements from the mid-1930s in a postwar world had he lived to tell.

I want to suggest that we have not yet arrived at a valid and acceptable model for what happened in Germany during the 1930s and 1940s, and that therefore the answer to the question whether the 'German-Jewish symbiosis' failed, never existed, or was a 'negative' one, whatever that may mean, is still out for debate.

Bibliography

Arendt H, *Eichmann in Jerusalem: A Report on the Banality of Evil* (Viking Press 1963)
Arnold H, *Von den Juden in der Pfalz* (Verlag der Pfaelzischen Gesellschaft zur Foerderung der Wissenschaften 1967)
Elbogen I, *Geschichte der Juden in Deutschland* (Jüdische Buch-Vereinigung 1935)
Kraus E, *Die Familie Mosse. Deutsch-juedisches Buergertum im 19. und 20. Jahrhundert* (CH Beck 1999)
Mann FA, *Life and Cases. Manuscript of an Autobiography* (Wolfgang Ernst ed., V&R Unipress 2021)
Mecklenburg F, *Juristinnen in der Weimarer Republik* (Lemo. Lebendiges Museum Online) <https://www.dhm.de/lemo/kapitel/weimarer-republik/alltagsleben/juristinnen-in-der-weimarer-republik.html> accessed 28 December 2022.
Moses DA, *The Problems of Genocide: Permanent Security and the Language of Transgression* (Cambridge University Press 2022)
Mosse G, *German Jews beyond Judaism* (Bloomington 1985)
Oppenheim-Liffman D and Liffman H, 'The Jew in European Society' in *The Oppenheim Family*, Leo Baeck Institute Archives, AR 5166 (unpublished manuscript)

45 Ismar Elbogen, *Geschichte der Juden in Deutschland* (Jüdische Buch-Vereinigung 1935).

Slezkine Y, *The Jewish Century* (Princeton University Press 2004)
Stern S, *The Court Jew: A Contribution to the History of the Period of Absolutism in Central Europe* (Jewish Publication Society of America 1950)
Stiefel E and Mecklenburg F, *Deutsche Juristen im amerikanischen Exil (1933–1945)* (Mohr Siebeck 1991)
Theobald P, *Juedische Juristen in Frankenthal* (Edition Winterwork 2017)
van Rahden T, *Jews and other Germans. Civil Society, Religious Diversity and Urban Politics in Breslau, 1860–1925* (The University of Wisconsin Press 2008)
Volkov S, *Deutschland aus juedischer Sicht: Eine andere Geschichte* (CH Beck 2022)
Volkov S, *Rewriting German History: Jewish Experience as a Corrective* (The Leo Baeck Memorial Lecture, 63, New York 2022)

3

Pragmatism Meets *Praxisorientierung*

FA Mann and a Transnational Biography in Law

Christoph König

I. Introduction: What is a Transnational Biography?

A transnational biography could simply mean that the person or institution that is being studied has crossed political borders with his, her, or its physical presence. It means a life's work plays out on multiple theatres. It could also be understood as the study of a person or institution that crosses political borders in thought. Where it becomes interesting is when the crossing of political borders physically or in thought leads to a transcendence from an individual's point of origin and terminus. As a result, something new is created that goes beyond the sum of its elements.

In jurisprudence, the crossing of national borders holds special significance. For the study of law and jurisprudence, perspective is very much dominated by nations and their legal systems. Legal systems are closely linked to nation states. In a world where often only the nation state is vested with real power over laws, crossing national borders and moving betwixt them brings the traveller outside that traditional perspective. The quitting of this national franchise can render the traveller a foreign entity; at best, a visitor, or in the worst case, a 'barbarian'.[1] It can also mark the traveller as a challenger to the nation state, as those who inhabit the

[1] Teemu Ruskola, *Legal Orientalism* (Harvard University Press 2013); Bonilla Maldonado, *Legal Barbarians* (Cambridge University Press 2021).

Christoph König, *Pragmatism Meets* Praxisorientierung In: *FA Mann*. Edited by: Jason Grant Allen and Gerhard Dannemann, Oxford University Press. © Christoph König 2024. DOI: 10.1093/oso/9780198881452.003.0004

space between the nations may serve as a tacit challenge to established order (and vested power).

Studying a person or institution that transcends national borders in this way first of all means investigating how that person or institution reacts in the new environment. That can of course refer to the political, cultural, historical, etc. environment. For the purpose of this chapter, it is, however, the legal environment that is of most interest. How does the traveller comprehend the assumptions, procedures, and traditions of a different legal system? How does their (institutions can also be 'foreigners' in this sense) socialization translate into the different legal system? How is that translation perceived by the persons or institutions of the different legal system?

Studying a person or institution that transcends national borders can also mean investigating the outcomes of these processes of communication. Where a person or institution has come into contact with a different legal system, the interaction can have an impact on the person or institution just as much as on the system itself.

Understanding transnational biographies in legal history as the study of interacting systems and influences means describing the thinking and actions of persons or institutions as an amalgamation; a meeting of sorts. In this, it is an amalgamation that is not only limited to the sum of the influences described. Instead, it creates something new from the elements it combines.

For FA Mann, this interaction could be described as the amalgamation of *Praxisorientierung* and pragmatism. These two narratives can be used to contextualize both FA Mann's thinking and his impact on the law. *Praxisorientierung* refers to the practical approach to jurisprudence and its uses as FA Mann learned them in the Berlin law faculty between the world wars (Section II); pragmatism is the central—somewhat undeclared—principle in the liberal cosmopolitan tradition of especially international law as FA Mann found it after moving to London in 1933 (Section III).

II. *Praxisorientierung*

> Berlin at the time was by no means that centre of sin, corruption, and crime which many people, impressed by isolated incidents, Nazi propaganda or fiction believe it to have been. On the contrary, it was a centre of research, art, and academic and cultural activity such as the world has rarely seen, and we participated in and profited from it to the fullest extent.[2]

[2] FA Mann, *Life and Cases: Manuscript of an Autobiography* (Wolfgang Ernst ed., Bonn University Press 2021) 38 (hereafter Mann, *Life and Cases*).

The Faculty of Law at the Friedrich-Wilhelm Universität—today continued as the Humboldt-Universität in former East-Berlin and to some extent as the Freie Universität in former West-Berlin—held a special place in Berlin in the time between the world wars, and not just for FA Mann. He started his legal education in Geneva in the spring of 1926. After a first semester in Berlin, he took to Munich for another, after which he returned to Berlin to finish his degree.[3]

The Berlin faculty assembled an ever-growing cast of influential legal minds. As Mann puts it:

> My prime recollection is that we were hard working and that standards in every sphere of life were high. The standard of teaching in the Faculty [sic] of law were incredibly high. The Faculty comprised not only the leading lights in German legal science, but also men who were splendid teachers. [Viktor] Bruns,[4] [Heinrich] Triepel,[5] [Rudolf] Smend[6] and Erich Kaufmann[7] for public international and constitutional law, [Eduard] Kohlrausch[8] for criminal law, [Ernst] Heymann,[9] Theodor Kipp,[10] [Hans] Lewald,[11] [Ernst] Ra[b]el,[12] [Arthur] Nussbaum,[13] Martin Wolff,[14] [Julius] Flechtheim[15] for civil and commercial law,

[3] ibid 34–35.

[4] Viktor Bruns (1884–1943): Edwin Borchard, 'Viktor Bruns (1884–1943)'(1943) 37(4) American Journal of International Law 658–60 (hereafter Borchard, 'Viktor Bruns').

[5] Heinrich Triepel (1868–1946): Charles Kruszewski, 'Hegemony and International Law' (1941) 35(6) American Political Science Review 1127–44.

[6] Rudolf Smend (1882–1975): Helmuth Schulze-Fielitz, 'Rudolf Smend' in Peter Häberle, Michael Kilian, and Heinrich Amadeus Wolff (eds), *Staatsrechtslehrer des 20. Jahrhunderts. Deutschland, Österreich, Schweiz* (2nd edn, De Gruyter 2018) 317–33.

[7] Erich Kaufmann (1880–1972): Frank Degenhardt, *Zwischen Machtstaat und Völkerbund. Erich Kaufmann (1880–1972)* (Nomos 2008).

[8] Eduard Kohlrausch (1874–1948): Holger Karitzky, *Eduard Kohlrausch, Kriminalpolitik in vier Systemen. Eine strafrechtshistorische Biographie* (Berlin Verlag A Spitz 2002).

[9] Ernst Heymann (1870–1946): Heinrich Mitteis, 'Nachruf Ernst Heymann' (Deutsches Archiv für Erforschung des Mittelalters 8, 1951) 256.

[10] Theodor Kipp (1862–1931): Ernst Levy, 'In memoriam [Theodor Kipp]' (1931) 51 Zeitschrift der Savigny-Stiftung für Rechtsgeschichte. Romanistische Abteilung 609.

[11] Hans Karl Ernst Albert Wilhelm Lewald (1883–1963): Leonie Breunung and Manfred Walther, *Die Emigration deutscher Rechtswissenschaftler ab 1933 – Ein bio-bibliographisches Handbuch* (De Gruyter Saur 2012) 275–90.

[12] Ernst Rabel (1874–1955): Rolf-Ulrich Kunze, *Ernst Rabel und das Kaiser-Wilhelm-Institut für ausländisches und internationales Privatrecht 1926–1945* (Wallstein Verlag 2004) (hereafter Kunze, *Ernst Rabel*); Timo Utermark, *Rechtsgeschichte und Rechtsvergleichung bei Ernst Rabel* (Lang 2005).

[13] Arthur Nussbaum (1877–1964): Martin Domke, 'Arthur Nussbaum: The Pioneer of International Commercial Arbitration' (1957) 57 Columbia Law Review 1, 8–10.

[14] Martin Wolff (1872–1953): Gerhard Dannemann, 'Martin Wolff (1872–1953)' in Jack Beatson and Rheinhard Zimmermann (eds), *Jurists Uprooted: German-Speaking Émigré Lawyers in Twentieth-Century Britain* (OUP 2004) (hereafter Beatson and Zimmerman (eds), *Jurists Uprooted*).

[15] Julius Flechtheim (1876–1940): Annegret Heymann, *Der Jurist Julius Flechtheim: Leben und Werk* (Heymanns 1990) (hereafter Heymann, *Der Jurist Julius Flechtheim*).

> [James] Goldschmidt[16] for civil procedure,—these are some outstanding representatives of a Faculty which in those years constituted the best Germany had to offer.[17]

One might feel the need to amend FA Mann's list by adding Fritz Schulz[18] and Walter Hallstein.[19] FA Mann writes this list from his perspective as a student when arriving in 1928. Fritz Schulz only joined the faculty in October 1931 after FA Mann would have heard most of his lectures.[20] Walter Hallstein on the other hand had completed his *Habilitation* in 1929 and subsequently accepted an offer for a chair in Rostock. FA Mann therefore probably also never personally experienced him as a teacher.[21]

What most names in his list have in common is their intertwinement with the *Kaiser-Wilhelm Institutes* (KWIs). The KWIs were a group of research institutes in Germany that were first established in 1911. They were located in several cities across Germany and focused on a wide range of scientific and technological fields, including biology, physics, chemistry, and medicine. In terms of jurisprudence, they played a significant role in the development of legal scholarship in Germany. They started off in the *Stadtschloss*—the old palace that has recently been reconstructed—close to the 'political pulse, in the centre of the capital of the Weimar Republic and in walking distance to the [University]'.[22] Today the *Kaiser-Wilhelm Institutes* continue as *Max-Planck Institutes* (MPIs).[23]

Institutionally, the two KWIs which were founded after WWI—the *Kaiser Wilhelm Institut für ausländisches Recht und Völkerrecht*[24]—for foreign and international law (1924)—and the *Kaiser Wilhelm Institut für ausländisches und*

[16] James Paul Goldschmidt (1874–1940): Wolfgang Sellert, 'James Paul Goldschmidt (1874–1940)' in Helmut Heinrichs and others (eds), *Deutsche Juristen jüdischer Herkunft* (München 1993) 595–613.

[17] Mann, *Life and Cases* (n 2) 37.

[18] Fritz Schulz (1879–1957): Wolfgang Ernst, 'Fritz Schulz (1879–1957)' in Beatson and Zimmerman (eds), *Jurists Uprooted* (n 14).

[19] Walter Hallstein (1901–1982): Ingrid Piela, *Walter Hallstein – Jurist und gestaltender Europapolitiker der ersten Stunde. Politische und institutionelle Visionen des ersten Präsidenten der EWG-Kommission (1958–1967)* (Berliner Wissenschaftsverlag 2012); Michael Killian, 'Walter Hallstein. Jurist und Europäer' (2005) 53 Jahrbuch des öffentlichen Rechts der Gegenwart 369–89.

[20] Anna M von Lösch, *Der nackte Geist, Die Juristische Fakultät der Berliner Universität im Umbruch von 1933* (Mohr Siebeck 1999) 184 (hereafter Lösch, *Der nackte Geist*).

[21] ibid 62.

[22] Jasper Kunstreich, 'Die Rechtswissenschaft in der MPG: Versuch einer Vogelperspektive' in Thomas Duve, Jasper Kunstreich, and Stefan Vogenauer (eds), *Rechtswissenschaft in der Max-Planck-Gesellschaft, 1948–2002* (Vandenhoeck & Ruprecht 2023) 15 (hereafter Kunstereich, 'Rechtswissenschaft in der MPG').

[23] For the history of the Institutes mainly but not limited to after 1945 see: ibid.

[24] Today: *Max-Planck-Institut für ausländisches öffentliches Recht und Völkerrecht* in Heidelberg. See Felix Lange, 'Zwischen völkerrechtlicher Systembildung und Begleitung der deutschen Außenpolitik: Das Max-Planck-Institut für ausländisches öffentliches Recht und Völkerrecht, 1945–2002' in Thomas Duve, Jasper Kunstreich, and Stefan Vogenauer (eds), *Rechtswissenschaft in der Max-Planck-Gesellschaft, 1948–2002* (Vandenhoeck & Ruprecht 2023).

internationales Privatrecht[25]—for foreign and international private law (1926)—stood for the proximity between the state and the academic advisory. Closely intertwined not just in personnel but also in thought,[26] they were intended to allow for foundational study of the basic structures of jurisprudence but also to inform and advise the German government on its legal options and responsibilities in the interwar period on the global stage.[27] They were to study the law of other countries and observe their developments, on the basis of which they would advise Germany on best practices and potential improvements and even be asked to give expert opinion on practical legal matters.[28]

FA Mann's recollections of Berlin are about art and music, academic and cultural activity in the city. The careless 'Golden Twenties' were full of opportunity and expression. At the same time Berlin was the capital of the Weimar Republic. The young republic was concerned with other political and economic problems and faced many challenges while trying to find its place on the world stage. The legal intellectuals of the Berlin faculty and the KWIs were able and willing to provide expertise on some of these pressing concerns. The Treaty of Versailles did not just squarely place the responsibility for the war on Germany but also engulfed the republic in a broad set of duties, responsibilities, and limitations with regard to its neighbours and the League of Nations. The Treaty of Rapallo (1922), which legally ended the state of war between Germany and Italy; the Treaties of Locarno (1925), which settled Germany's western borders in exchange for readmittance into the international community; the Kellog-Briand Pact (1928), which intended for the member countries to renounce the right to use warfare as an instrument of national policy; The Hague Conference of Reparations (1929–1930) on the application of the Young Plan to resettle, lower, and commercialize Germany's debt on war reparations;[29] and other treaties and conferences needed interpretation and consultation to defend Germany's interests.[30]

Viktor Bruns was the founding director of the *Kaiser Wilhelm Institut für ausländisches öffentliches Recht und Völkerrecht*.[31] His influence was so great that

[25] Today: *Max-Planck-Institut für ausländisches und internationales Privatrecht* in Hamburg. Ulrich Magnus, 'Geschichte des Max-Planck-Instituts für ausländisches und internationales Privatrecht, 1949–2000' in Thomas Duve, Jasper Kunstreich, and Stefan Vogenauer (eds), *Rechtswissenschaft in der Max-Planck-Gesellschaft, 1948–2002* (Vandenhoeck & Ruprecht 2023) (hereafter Magnus, 'Geschichte des MPIs')

[26] Lösch, *Der nackte Geist* (n 20) 53.

[27] Kunstreich, 'Rechtswissenschaft in der MPG' (n 22) 15.

[28] Magnus, 'Geschichte des MPIs' (n 25) 91.

[29] Bank für Internationalen Zahlungsausgleich, *Die Bank für Internationalen Zahlungsausgleich und die Basler Zusammenkünfte: Herausgegeben zum fünfzigjährigen Bestehen der Bank 1930–1980* (Bank für Internationalen Zahlungsausgleich 1980) 88.

[30] Felix Lange, 'Praxisorientierung und Gemeinschaftskonzeption' (Dissertation) 27. In 1979 FA Mann would become legal counsel for Germany in the Young Loan Arbitration that sought to revalue the remaining debt in the terms of the London Debt Agreement of 1952.

[31] Heinrich Triepel, 'Viktor Bruns' (1942/43) 11 Zeitschrift für ausländisches öffentliches Recht und Völkerrecht 324c.

it was unofficially frequently referred to as the 'Bruns Institute'.[32] In Bruns' view the scholarship of international law had to be focused solely on the practice of international law,[33] a view that even gave rise to a notion of 'International Law as a German Discipline'.[34] While Heinrich Triepel[35] was considered the expert on international law, it remains unclear why Bruns became the leading figure for the institute instead.[36] Erich Kaufmann was not just at the institute but also represented the new German republic before the Permanent Court of International Justice (PCIJ) in The Hague.[37] The other *Kaiser Wilhelm Institut für ausländisches und internationals Privatrecht* is mostly associated with Ernst Rabel.[38] Ernst Heymann, Hans Lewald, and Walter Hallstein also worked there before the war.[39] Ernst Rabel served as appointed German judge at the new Permanent International Court of Justice in the important reparations case of *The Factory at Chorzów*.[40]

It was, however, not the sole privilege of the KWIs to be in close physical and intellectual proximity to Germany's highest executive and legislative authorities. From its founding during the German struggle against Napoleon, the law faculty of Berlin's Friedrich-Wilhelm Universität constituted its purpose in its statues as the 'comprehensive teaching of jurisprudence with eminent concern for the needs of the Prussian state'.[41] Earlier members of the faculty had already been members of the legislative bodies of Prussia that existed before WWI.[42] During FA Mann's time they also helped advise the new republic with its ever-changing governments through the legal and political turmoil of inter-war Europe.

While at the Berlin faculty FA Mann remembers having mostly worked for Julius Flechtheim, Fritz Schulz, Walter Hallstein, and Martin Wolff. He does not specify what his contractual situation was. We know that he was employed by the

[32] Borchard, 'Viktor Bruns' (n 4) 658.

[33] Felix Lange, 'Between Systematization and Expertise for Foreign Policy: The Practice-Oriented Approach in Germany's International Legal Scholarship (1920–1980)' (2017) 28(2) European Journal of International Law 535, 537 (hereafter Lange, 'Between Systematization and Expertise for Foreign Policy').

[34] Martti Koskenniemi, 'Between Coordination and Constitution: International Law as a German Discipline' (2011) 15 Redescriptions 45.

[35] Carl Bilfinger, 'In Memoriam Heinrich Triepel' (1950/51) 13 Zeitschrift für ausländisches öffentliches Recht und Völkerrecht 1.

[36] Lange, 'Between Systematization and Expertise for Foreign Policy' (n 33) 540.

[37] Hermann Schäfer and Oliver Werner, 'Erich Felix Kaufmann' in Rotary unter dem Nationalsozialismus. Digitales Gedenkbuch diskriminierter Rotarier <https://memorial-rotary.de/members/1046> accessed 12 January 2023.

[38] Kunze, *Ernst Rabel* (n 12) 54.

[39] Leonie Breunung and Martin Walther, *Die Emigration deutscher Rechtswissenschaftler ab 1933 – Ein bio-bibliographisches Handbuch* (De Gruyter 2012) 278.

[40] PCIJ 13.9.1928, *Factory at Chorzów*, Pub. PCIJ Ser. A No. 17.

[41] '*die Lehre der gesamten Rechtswissenschaft mit vorzüglicher Rücksicht auf die Bedürfnisse des preussischen Staates*', cited in Martin Wolff, 'Die Juristische Fakultät der Kgl. Friedrich-Wilhelms-Universität' in Friedrich Holtze, *Aus dem Berliner Rechtsleben: Festgabe zum XXVI. Deutschen Juristentage. Ueberreicht vom Ortsausschusse. Berlin, im September 1902* (Franz Vahlen 1902) 113 (hereafter Wolff, 'Die Juristische Fakultät').

[42] ibid 124.

Berlin faculty as an assistant.[43] It is unclear if FA Mann also worked for the KWIs when engaged with some of these professors that were also connected to KWIs. It is not unlikely that his contractual connection was just with the Berlin faculty and he was merely allowed to use the facilities like the specialized libraries when working for the professors that were also connected to the KWIs.

FA Mann remembers from his time in Berlin that he 'spent much time at the Institute [for foreign and private international law], not only because [he] had to do some comparative research for [his] own work, but also in order to write two articles [he] was invited to contribute to the Encyclopedia of Comparative Law[44] and to assist Walter Hallstein in producing his work on Die Aktienrechte der Gegenwart'.[45]

In *Die Aktienrechte der Gegenwart*,[46] Walter Hallstein was tasked with supporting the preparations for a planned reform of the German stock company.[47] This task came from *Reichsjustizministerium*[48]—the Reich Ministry of Justice—under the auspices of the *Kaiser Wilhelm Institute für ausländisches und internationales Privatrecht*, which also functioned as publishers for the work. In this work Walter Hallstein collects the 'conceptions and reform ideas of the non-German world'[49] in a systematic way and 'compares amongst themselves and with the German solutions'.[50]

Walter Hallstein follows a systematization typical of a German textbook.[51] He first divides the stock company into its relevant functions, procedures, and problems. Each of these is then given an individual chapter: legal existence, capital, shares and bonds, membership, shareholder meetings, etc. Within these chapters Hallstein then compares and contrasts the national legal frameworks regarding these functions and procedures and reviews them for their merits for the German reform.[52] The book is considered a 'gigantic task, upon which only a German

43 Lösch, *Der nackte Geist* (n 20) 490; Humboldt-Universität zu Berlin Archive, HUB-A Jur. Fak Nr. 579 and HUB-A UK Nr. 808.

44 FA Mann's contributions to the *Encyclopedia* have not yet been recovered. It is likely that they were not finished or never published.

45 Mann, *Life and Cases* (n 2) 38.

46 Walter Hallstein, *Die Aktienrechte Der Gegenwart: Gesetze Und Entwürfe in Rechtsvergleichender Darstellung* (Franz Vahlen 1931) (hereafter Hallstein, *Die Aktienrechte Der Gegenwart*).

47 Walter Hallstein, 'Die Aktienrechte der Gegenwart Gesetze und Entwürfe in rechtsvergleichender Darstellung' (1931) 5 Rabels Zeitschrift für ausländisches und internationales Privatrecht / The Rabel Journal of Comparative and International Private Law 742.

48 See Manfred Görtemaker (ed.), *Die Rosenburg: Das Bundesministerium der Justiz und die NS-Vergangenheit—eine Bestandsaufnahme* (Vandenhoeck & Ruprecht 2013).

49 Hallstein, *Die Aktienrechte der Gegenwart* (n 46) Foreword: '*Anschauungen und Reformgedanken der außerdeutschen Welt auffängt und untereinander und mit den deutschen Lösungen vergleicht.*'

50 ibid.

51 Walter Hug, 'The History of Comparative Law' (1932) 45 Harvard Law Review 1281, 1283 (hereafter Hug, 'Comparative Law').

52 H. C. G., 'Review of Trading Corporations, by Walter Hallstein' (1932) 14 Journal of Comparative Legislation and International Law307, 308.

scholar would venture, and executed with rare skill and judgement',[53] but to others it evoked the French maxim: '*Qui trop embrasse mal étreint*.'[54]

In his introduction, Hallstein thanks 'younger forces' at the KWI for their continuous support.[55] Some of these 'young forces' are then additionally mentioned by name: Anne-Gudrun Meier-Scherling,[56] Ernst von Caemmerer,[57] Konrad Wolff,[58] and [FA] Mann. While Ernst von Caemmerer is righty identified by Hallstein as an assistant at the KWI, the affiliation of Konrad Wolff and FA Mann is left vague. It appears that FA Mann had no formal role at the institute. Yet he was nonetheless involved in projects that were facilitated by the institute and featured academics from the Berlin faculty. He furthermore does not seem to be the only academic that the professors from the Berlin faculty brought to the institute to assist them with the projects hosted there. With that in mind the association with the KWI should be understood beyond just formal roles and titles. It might be better understood as a place of academic and intellectual socialization and a place where networks were formed.

During his time at the KWI working on the project, he tried to avoid the director of the *Kaiser Wilhelm Institut für Ausländisches und Internationales Privatrecht*, Ernst Rabel. He was a man who FA Mann considered 'one of the least pleasant men [he] ever met, who in [his] view (no doubt influenced by Martin Wolff) was very much overrated, and [whose] whole principal merit lay in his ability to promote new fields of research'.[59] His 'completely unjustified hero worship in Germany'[60] shocked FA Mann. Others formulated Ernst Rabel's appeal slightly differently: 'Unlike his British counterparts, Rabel consciously chose (mostly) not to link his comparative studies to history or philosophy but to the interests and needs of the practitioners of his time; and he saw to it that his disciples did the same.'[61]

[53] The Yale Law Journal, 'Book Note: Die Aktienrechte der Gegenwart: Gesetze und Entwürfe in rechtsvergleichender Darstellung by Walter Hallstein' (1932) 42 The Yale Law Journal 159.

[54] Hug, 'Comparative Law' (n 51) 1283f.: 'grasp all, lose all'.

[55] Hallstein, *Die Aktienrechte der Gegenwart* (n 46) Vorwort.

[56] Anne-Gudrun Meier-Scherling would later become the first female judge at the German Federal Labour Court (*Bundesarbeitsgericht*) in 1955; see M Röwekamp (ed.), *Juristinnen: Lexikon zu Leben und Werk* (Nomos 2005).

[57] Ernst von Caemmerer (1908–1985): Günter Hager, *Ernst von Caemmerer (1908–1985)* (ZEuP 2005) 506; Hans G Leser, 'Nachruf' *Juristenzeitung* (1985) 735; Wolfram Müller-Freienfels, 'Ernst von Caemmerer' (1986) 50 RabelsZ 339. In a letter to Werner Flume from 22 February 1978, FA Mann disparagingly refers to Caemmerer as '*Meister*', i.e. 'master', put in quotation marks: FA Mann to Werner Flume (Mann estate, NLMann_0250, 22 February 1978).

[58] Konrad Martin Wolff (1907–1989): the son of Martin Wolff. After his doctorate in law he became a concert pianist. Ruth Gillen (ed.) *The Writings and Letters of Konrad Wolff* (Indiana University Press 2006).

[59] Man, *Life and Cases* (n 2) 38.

[60] FA Mann to Werner Flume (Mann estate, NLMann_0250, 22 February 1978): '*Dabei bin ich immer wieder betroffen über die vollkommen unberechtigte Heldenverehrung, die in Deutschland Rabel zuteil wird.*'

[61] Basileios S Markezinēs, *Comparative Law in the Courtroom and Classroom: The Story of the Last Thirty-Five Years* (Hart 2003) 13.

FA Mann also worked for Julius Flechtheim, who started his career as a practising commercial lawyer in Cologne and only later found his way to academia. FA Mann would consider him 'one of the greatest German jurists', whom he shared a strong personal friendship with.[62] Although often understood as a cartel lawyer,[63] FA Mann insisted that his capacity in commercial law, especially the law of stock companies, was greater still.[64]

In FA Mann's words:

> Another great figure I must mention was Julius Flechtheim. He came from Cologne where as a young man he started to practice at the Court of Appeal, one of the most important ones in Germany at the time, and had a success widely regarded as phenomenal. In his early years he wrote the first and fundamental book on the law of Cartels,—then a new subject. Later he moved to Berlin where he became the legal advisor to one of the banks, a leading authority on company law, the author of a work on the subject, which to this day is in many aspects still authoritative, and a professor at the University. It was in this capacity that I met and respected him and for some terms I worked for him as Faculty Assistant. He inspired some of my early publications and showed much kindness to me.[65]

It is unclear which publications or projects FA Mann specifically supported Fritz Schulz with while in Berlin. FA Mann admired Fritz Schulz's lectures on Roman law that he held when the Nazis were already in power. FA Mann himself cannot have attended any of these as his student or assistant.

> Fritz Schulz was an entirely different personality. A Roman lawyer, a legal historian of great distinction, but also a man imbued with the most broadly based general culture, a fighter by nature [. . .] His last achievement in Germany had been a course of lectures on Principles of Roman Law, which in truth and substance was nothing but a veiled attack on Nazi despotism and lawlessness.[66]

FA Mann considers him to be the 'most outstanding among all refugee lawyers'[67] next to Martin Wolff. FA Mann was impressed with Schulz's later writings on Bracton that he produced during his exile in Oxford. After Schulz's death, FA Mann

[62] FA Mann to Annegret Heymann (Mann estate, NLMann_0356, 23 June1989): '*Er war einer der größten deutschen Juristen. Ich war viele Jahre lang sein Assistent und auch persönlich mit ihm sehr befreundet.*'

[63] See Heymann, *Der Jurist Julius Flechtheim* (n 15).

[64] FA Mann to Annegret Heymann (Mann estate, NLMann_0356, 18 October 1990): '*Ich verstehe gut, dass Sie ihn insbesondere im Rahmen des Kartellrechts gewürdigt haben. Aber sein Einfluss aus dem Gebiet des Handelsrechts, einschließlich des Aktienrechts ist selbst heute noch größer. Man stößt immer wieder darauf, dass er Dinge gesehen hat, die sonst niemand sehen konnte.*'

[65] Mann, *Life and Cases* (n 2) 39.

[66] Mann, *Life and Cases* (n 2) 64.

[67] FA Mann to Christian Tyler (Mann estate, NLMann_0814, 26 September 1988).

claims to have unsuccessfully tried to convince Oxford University Press to publish an edited volume in his honour.[68] It is unclear how strong a friendship they actually developed during FA Mann's time in Berlin. What we do know, for example from the excerpt below, is that the Schulz family used FA Mann to circumvent the growing restrictions on foreign exchange and to ensure that their children, who were already in England, were financially secure. It is also the door of the Manns in London that Fritz Schulz and his wife knocked on when they made their secret escape to England.

> [Fritz Schulz] had first gone to Holland, where the University of Utrecht had offered him some opportunity for research, but on 2 September 1939 he and his wife suddenly appeared at our house in London and after a few days went to Oxford where Clarendon Press under Kenneth Sisam[69] provided Schulz with £300 p.a. on account of books he was to write and did write. Before leaving Germany, Mrs. Schulz had taken numerous foreign students as paying guests into their beautiful house in Berlin on the understanding that payment would be made to me. By this means, naturally illegal under German law, she could ensure the education of her four children in England. All of them made good. But how often did they come to us to collect a few shillings for cleaning a pair of trousers or similar purposes! It was a continuous battle and frequently I had to advance a little money to bridge a gap.[70]

His closest relationship at the Berlin faculty, however, was with Martin Wolff, who is often proclaimed to be one of the greatest German law teachers of the 20th century.[71] His lectures were so sought after that he became the top earner among the professors at the Berlin faculty, where students during this time had to pay fees to attend lectures.[72] His practical approach to legal argumentation rested on a simple attitude: logic and clarity trump disorder and *Dummheit*.[73] Martin Wolff is praised for his ability to command a lecture hall full of students distinctly not by his rhetoric or charisma but by the mere authority of his argument.[74] He presented a well-structured argument, always based on history and systematic contextualization:

[68] FA Mann to Horst Heinrich Jakobs (Mann estate, NLMann_0400, 28 March 1990).

[69] Kenneth Sisam (1887–1971): Christopher Stray, 'Sisam, Kenneth (1887–1971), Anglo-Saxon Scholar and Publisher' in *Oxford Dictionary of National Biography* (OUP 2016).

[70] Mann, *Life and Cases* (n 2) 64.

[71] Gerhard Dannemann, 'Martin Wolff (1872–1953)' in Beatson and Zimmerman (eds), *Jurists Uprooted* (n 14) 441.

[72] Wolff reported a base salary of 15.000 RM per year but earned another 35.000 RM in fees from students. Lösch, *Der nackte Geist* (n 20) 106.

[73] Dieter Medicus, 'Martin Wolff (1872–1953)' in Helmut Heinrichs (ed.), *Deutsche Juristen Jüdischer Herkunft* (CH Beck 1993) 543–53. *Dummheit* could be translated as stupidity.

[74] Mann, *Life and Cases* (n 2) 41; Geoffrey Lewis, *FA Mann: A Memoir* (Hart Publishing 2013) 13.

> His strength was the systematic, logical, coherent exposition of the law. Legal policy or the functional explanation, though by no means alien to his method of approach, were not allowed that supreme role which has led to so much misuse and to a distortion of the true judicial role.[75]

Martin Wolff approached law in a historical fashion. Martin Wolff was, however, not an actual member of *Historische Rechtsschule*: the historical school of jurisprudence that Friedrich Carl von Savigny had envisioned. He was not interested in the study of *heutiges römisches Recht* (the system of true Roman law as was allegedly still reigning supreme over Germany). Martin Wolff did not summon the *Volksgeist*—the spirit of the people, expressed through this storied roman legal system and manifested by the jurists of their time through historiographical exploration of this system—to inform him how to solve contractual conflicts. He had limited interest in legal sociology or philosophy: according to FA Mann, Martin Wollf's strength was the 'systematic, logical, coherent expression of the law. Legal policy or the functional explanation, though by no means alien to his method of approach, were not allowed that supreme role which has led to so much misuse and to a distortion of the true judicial role.'[76] Recalled by one of his other students, Martin Wolff's passion was not with legal history in itself but with *Rechtsdogmatik* (the systematic digestion of positive law with a self-declared scientific method).[77] Martin Wolff's law of the land was not the *Ius Commune* but *Bürgerliches Gesetzbuch*. As Wolfgang Ernst traces in his chapter, he might even have had a prominent role in introducing FA Mann to the legal treatment of money.[78]

Martin Wolff's jurisprudence was nonetheless historical.[79] This historical jurisprudence was not intended to procure a hierarchy of thinking, branding sociology and philosophy of law as lesser, but was in fact a practical decision to focus one's effort of thinking on a specific chosen issue at hand; something critics have called 'distinctly tedious *Fleißarbeit*'.[80] What a jurist can achieve by making an intellectual effort in this way is finding an informed and educated solution to an issue at hand, be it identifying the central question of a specific case or systematizing the German tradition of family law. For that, a deep historical and comparative contextual analysis is not just sufficient but necessary. Lack of focus and effort is what leads to disorder and *Dummheit*.

75 Mann, *Life and Cases* (n 2) 42.

76 ibid.

77 Ludwig Raiser, 'Martin Wolff 26.9.1872–20.7.1953' (1972) 172 AcP 489, 491.

78 See Chapter 8 in this volume by Wolfgang Ernst, 'Before FA Mann: Martin Wolff on Money'.

79 Reinhard Zimmermann, 'Juristische Bücher des Jahres: Eine Leseempfehlung' (2011) Neue Juristische Wochenschrift 3561–62 (hereafter Zimmermann, 'Juristische Bücher').

80 A quite German term referring—not necessarily with good intentions—to a task requiring great diligence. Jan Thiessen, 'Statt eines Diskussionsberichts' in Stefan Grundmann and Karl Riesenhuber (eds), *Deutschsprachige Zivilrechtslehrer des 20. Jahrhunderts in Berichten ihrer Schüler* (Vol. 2, De Gruyter 2007) 408 (hereafter Grundmann and Riesenhuber, *Deutschsprachige Zivilrechtslehrer*).

Martin Wolff stands in this practical tradition of the *Historische Rechtsschule*—their *Arbeitsweise* and habitus. In understanding that their treatment of the law is based on *topoi* around economical liberalism and practicality, Roman law here only ever really functioned as a structural starting point from which to begin the doctrinal work.[81] When Martin Wolff talks about the 'spirit of the historical school'[82] that remains within the Berlin faculty, he refers to a 'wide historical view' and an 'affectionate dedication to the sources'.[83] It is the 'lesser minds'[84] that *Historische Rechtsschule* 'seduced to only thoroughly study the law as it developed so far';[85] closing one's mind to the 'further becoming of law [. . .] and with that fall for unnecessary emphasis on historical details and an unhealthy quietism'.[86]

The apocryphal programme of the *Historische Rechtsschule* has always rather been the *Verwissenschaftlichung der gerichtlichen Praxis* (literally, the scientification of the judicial practice). If court decisions are a source of law, then courts and their cases are part of the jurisprudential dialogue.[87] Earlier manifestations of this *Historische Schule* understood that programme as a '*Belehrung des Richters*'[88] (instruction of the judges). Later, courts were more or less accepted as equal partners in order to enshrine a 'productive private law in legal reality'.[89] For that to happen, there had to be a productive dialogue between judges and professors[90] driving the development and progression of law—distinctly not with parliament.[91] This is the turn to judicial practice: *Praxisorientierung.*

For FA Mann, *Praxisorientierung* means making an intellectual effort that creates something new:

> As a firm general rule, lawyers should never publish anything, unless they have something new to say. Mere repetition or the mere compilation of known material merits publication only in the most exceptional case. The observation of the

[81] Hans-Peter Haferkamp, *Die Historische Rechtsschule* (Studien zur europäischen Rechtsgeschichte 310, Klostermann 2018) 329 (hereafter Haferkamp, *Historische Rechtsschule*).

[82] Wolff, 'Die Juristische Fakultät' (n 41) 115: '*Der Geist der historischen Rechtsschule bleibt ihr unverloren.*'

[83] ibid: '*Der weite historische Blick, die liebevolle Versenkung in die Quellen.*'

[84] ibid 115–16: '*schwächere Köpfe.*'

[85] ibid: '*dazu verführte, nur das bis dahin gewordene Recht gründlich zu erforschen.*'

[86] ibid: '*aber dem weiteren Werden des Rechts zu verschliessen und damit einer allzugrossen Betonung geschichtlicher Einzelheiten und einem ungesunden Quietismus zu verfallen.*'

[87] Haferkamp, *Historische Rechtsschule* (n 81) 299: '*Wenn Richtersprüche eine Rechtsquelle sein konnten, deren Geltung ständiger rechtswissenschaftlicher Überprüfung bedufte, dann mussten die Gerichte Teil eines rechtswissenschaftlichen Gesprächs sein.*'

[88] *Staatsratsgutachten* from 7 March 1823 as quoted in Haferkamp, *Die Historische Rechtsschule* (n 81) 301.

[89] ibid 312.

[90] ibid 329.

[91] Dieter Grimm, 'Methode als Machtfaktor' in Norbert Horn (ed.), *Europäisches Rechtsdenken in Geschichte und Gegenwart: Festschrift für Helmut Coing zum 70. Geburtstag* (Beck 1982).

> rule presupposes that before publication every conceivable effort has been made to ensure that everything published on the subject has been read and that every relevant contribution has been cited.[92]

This legacy of *Praxisorientierung* not just by Martin Wolff but also Fritz Schulz is carried on after World War II by FA Mann, Werner Flume,[93] and Brigitte Knobbe-Keuk[94] at the law faculty in Bonn: they promoted a 'mindset grounded in historical and academic thought encompassing current law'.[95] As Reinhard Zimmerman succinctly explains:

> [The style of] academia that is not unilaterally missed. It is not about finding trends, not about weighing pros and cons of arguments. It is more the practicing of the out of fashion art of polemic with temperament and certainty in correctness, sometimes intimidating in tone, yet always mindful of the continuation of a certain legal culture. Today this form of 'historic jurisprudence' is probably historic itself.[96]

Praxisorientierung is FA Mann's academic upbringing in Berlin. It is based on an elite education by some of the most influential German legal intellectuals of the time. Legal intellectuals that put their minds in the service of the young republic. It encourages engagement with the grand challenges faced by the young republic trying to negotiate its way back onto the international stage with meticulous work on the details. *Praxisorientierung* values a clear rhetoric in its argumentation. It is a rhetoric whose goal is not intellectual compromise but the induction of confidence into the argument that is grounded in history and comparativism. FA Mann took that intellectual self-confidence with him when he and his now wife Eleonore left Germany for England. Here, FA Mann encountered another narrative originating in the study of international law.

[92] Mann, *Life and Cases* (n 2) 85–86.

[93] Werner Flume (1908–2009): Jan Wilhelm, 'Werner Flume zum 95. Geburtstag' (2003) 37 Zeitschrift für Wirtschaftsrecht 1691; Gerhard Wagner, 'Vorwort: Zum 100. Geburtstag von Werner Flume' (2009) Archiv für die civilistische Praxis 141f.

[94] Brigitte Knobbe-Keuk (1940–1995): Wolfgang Schön, 'Nachruf für Brigitte Knobbe-Keuk' (1995) NJW 1729f.

[95] Zimmermann, 'Juristische Bücher' (n 79) 3561–62.

[96] ibid: '*Auch dem wissenschaftlichen Stil der drei Gelehrten wird nicht jeder nachtrauern. Da werden nicht Trends aufgespürt, nicht Argumente des Einerseits-Andererseits abgewogen. Da wird vielmehr mit Temperament und Richtigkeitsgewissheit die aus der Mode geratene Kunst der Polemik geübt, gelegentlich in einschüchterndem Tonfall, aber stets eingedenk einer fortlebenden Rechtskultur. Heute ist diese Form "historischer Rechtswissenschaft" möglicherweise selbst historisch geworden.*'

III. Pragmatism

What actually is international law and how is it made? According to Phillip Sands, this is how international law works in simple terms: 'someone develops an idea, puts it into writing (in an article or a book, perhaps), it germinates into an agreed legal text, migrates into another legal text, and then develops a life of its own as judges interpret it and apply the words. [It is] cross-fertilised, percolated elsewhere and, eventually would reach the judges.'[97] Martti Koskenniemi gives a slightly more sophisticated answer: 'The way we think about international law today is the effect of the imagination of a small number of academic and practising lawyers during the "twenty-years' crisis" of 1919–1939.'[98] What both the responses have in common is the idea that the origin of international law is an argument. An argument put into writing by a (legal) intellectual. Of course, that practice did not start with the crisis of 1919–1939. This crisis did, however, serve as a catalyst for the escalation of the practice. Developing that thought further, one way of understanding international law and its evolution in the last century is as the reaction of an enlightened cast of international lawyers to the crises of inter-war Europe.

These crises brought to light a new problem: how can nation states—meaning European nation states—be tamed in their treatment of the people that live within their borders?[99] With the end of World War I many new nation states emerged in Europe with many new or old peoples residing within their territories. Some borders were drawn to encapsulate nationhood for a specific people. Other borders sought to manifest imperial ambitions. There were little to no rules regarding the treatment of new and old citizens and residents of these nations. That holds especially true for those new and old citizens and residents that did not align with the new affiliation of their abode. The rules that could be argued to have existed lacked enforcement.

The answer to this conundrum was to imagine international law as a legal order 'on a par with domestic law, [with] judicial activity as its centre, together with the ideas of peace as a legal postulate, human beings as the law's ultimate subjects, as well as of diplomacy as the administration of the rule of law'.[100] The nation states were to be bound by a system of rules and boundaries that entitled the citizens and residents of these nation states to the same level of protection as they were in allegedly more enlightened parts of the world.

[97] Philippe Sands and Martin Rowson, *The Last Colony: A Tale of Exile, Justice and Britain's Colonial Legacy* (Weidenfeld & Nicolson 2022) 20.

[98] Martti Koskenniemi, 'Hersch Lauterpacht (1897–1960)' in Beatson and Zimmermann, *Jurists Uprooted* (n 14) 601.

[99] Phillipe Sands, *East West Street* (Vintage 2017) 70 (hereafter Sands, *East West Street*).

[100] Martti Koskenniemi, 'Hersch Lauterpacht (1897–1960)' in Beatson and Zimmermann, *Jurists Uprooted* (n 14) 601.

This imagination emerged from 'liberal universalism that reached its peak during that period through its odd combination of utopian determination and a flight from what critical thought at the time learned to call "technological reason"'.[101] This was a cosmopolitan liberal idealism that sought nothing less than peace on earth.

This cosmopolitan liberal idealism was fostered by *avant-garde* elite jurists of that time: an 'invisible college of international lawyers'.[102] The college was made up of leading intellectuals who formed a non-official community that would meet in the committee rooms and conferences of international organizations such as the *Institut de Droit International* or the International Law Association (ILA). Here they would draft resolutions, produce reports, and make proposals on questions of international law.[103]

Membership of this fraternity was based on acceptance by peers linked to each other by a similar mindset, an intellectual motive underpinned by the same values, and an intellectualism best described—though not about international law specifically—by Ville Erkkilä in his biography on Franz Wieacker[104] as *Rechtsgewissen* (legal conscience): 'a mental tool for the more informed, capable and aware experts, who by means of this skill were able to give judgements in a way which benefitted the whole social constellation and brought about social change.'[105]

The college would form a bridge between legal practitioners and pure academics.[106] It is in these international boards and bodies that the practice of law and the study of law came together: a 'legal activism'[107] practised by the academics, manifesting a more elevated form of patriotism.[108]

The person this admittedly abbreviated programme of the invisible college can be most identified with is Hersch Lauterpacht:[109] himself of Jewish extraction and

[101] ibid.

[102] Oscar Schachter, 'The Invisible College of International Lawyers' (1977) 72(2) Northwestern University Law Review 217 (hereafter Schachter, 'The Invisible College').

[103] ibid 225f.

[104] Joseph G Wolf, 'Franz Wieacker (5. August 1908–17. February 1994)' in Grundmann and Riesenhuber, *Deutschsprachige Zivilrechtslehrer* (n 80) 73; RC van Caenegem, 'Legal Historians I Have Known: A Personal Memoir' (2010) 17 Zeitschrift des Max-Planck-Instituts für europäische Rechtsgeschichte 253–99.

[105] Ville Erkkilä, *The Conceptual Change of Conscience: Franz Wieacker and German Legal Historiography 1933–1968* (Mohr Siebeck 2019) 177. For a critique of the work see Christoph König, 'Book Review: Erkkilä, Ville: The Conceptual Change of Conscience' (*H-Soz-Kult*, 29 March 2023) <https://www.hsozkult.de/publicationreview/id/reb-29729> accessed 15 May 2023.

[106] Schachter, 'The Invisible College' (n 102) 217.

[107] Martti Koskenniemi, *The Gentle Civiliser of Nations* (Cambridge University Press 2009) 399 (hereafter Koskenniemi, *Gentle Civilizer*).

[108] Martti Koskenniemi and Ville Kari, 'A More Elevated Patriotism: The Emergence of International and Comparative Law (Nineteenth Century)' in Heikki Pihlajamäki, Markus D Dubber, and Mark Godfrey (eds), *Oxford Handbook of European Legal History* (OUP 2018).

[109] Hersch Lauterpacht (1897–1960): Sands, *East West Street* (n 99); Koskenniemi, 'Hersch Lauterpacht (1897–1960)' in Beatson and Zimmermann, *Jurists Uprooted* (n 14) 601–61; James B Loeffler, *Rooted Cosmopolitans, Jews and Human Rights in the Twentieth Century* (Yale University Press 2018) 7 (hereafter Loeffler, *Rooted Cosmopolitans*).

from Lemberg, the capital city of the Austro-Hungarian province of Galicia; Lviv in modern day Ukraine, who experienced the above-mentioned impact of the absence of international law first hand.[110] He 'aimed to grasp the problem of world peace—always a problem of legal order to Lauterpacht—from two sides: the postulation of a cosmopolitan ethic and a stress on legal activism'.[111]

In this understanding, in the optimal case the world is 'ruled by lawyers'.[112] In this rule, however, the lawyers are sometimes required to compromise between conception and practice. As lawyers 'can—and should—decide the issues brought before them'[113] they need to be pragmatic. This pragmatism might be best exemplified by some of Lauterpacht's thoughts on Israel, as observed by Martti Koskenniemi.

> The oscillation between a critique of sovereignty and reliance upon (Israeli) sovereignty reveals an important aspect of Lauterpacht's pragmatism. Lauterpacht had [. . .] internalized a critique of formal rules and institutions, highlighting the need for their morally enlightened application. This meant that he could not really believe that international progress would be the automatic consequence of any particular institutional solution. Thus, in a talk in 1940, when the time for institutional innovation was at hand, he showed himself remarkably flexible.[114]

At the time FA Mann was obtaining his LLM at the London School of Economics, Hersch Lauterpacht was lecturing there. It is not unlikely that FA Mann sat in his lectures, considering the life-long admiration he developed for Hersch Lauterpacht and his writing—a rare compliment from FA Mann—which was even carried on to the next generation in the form of a close friendship with Hersch's son Elihu Lauterpacht.[115] In FA Mann's own words:

> No week passed when we did not exchange one or two letters or met for lunch at the Athenaeum. He was the kindest of men, the warmest of friends, the greatest of idealists and at the same time the sharpest of lawyers. And he had an uncanny ability to stimulate, suggest and provoke. In so far as I am concerned it is due to him alone that I have become interested in public international law and can no[w] with some humility, describe myself as a student of and, perhaps, as an expert in public international law. [. . .] What is ever more important is that Hersch

[110] See Sands, *East West Street* (n 99).
[111] Koskenniemi, *Gentle Civilizer* (n 107) 399.
[112] ibid 404.
[113] Koskenniemi, 'Hersch Lauterpacht (1897–1960)' in Beatson and Zimmermann, *Jurists Uprooted* (n 14) 658.
[114] ibid.
[115] The Humboldt-Universität zu Berlin archive has extensive correspondence between FA Mann and Hersch Lauterpacht just as between FA Mann and Elihu Lauterpacht: NLMann_0482, NLMann_0483, NLMann_0484.

> Lauterpacht has determined my attitude towards international law, its character and limits.[116]

A global legal order aimed at overcoming whatever challenges the world faces, fuelled by the intellect of the great legal thinkers and their liberal cosmopolitan ethics: that is the remarkable programme of Hersch Lauterpacht. A programme that nonetheless requires a great deal of intuitiveness and pragmatism to operate. A programme that demands legal academics to step out of their universities and put their minds to work. That programme resonated with FA Mann.

IV. The Meeting

FA Mann's writing and way of arguing might be best understood as the meeting of *Praxisorientierung* and pragmatism: the intellectual confidence of an academic upbringing in inter-war Berlin meeting the pragmatism and cosmopolitan zeal of Hersch Lauterpacht. This meeting might be best exemplified in FA Mann's *The Legal Aspect of Money*.[117] It can broadly be described as a traditional systematic approach structuring specific legal questions surrounding money in English law. Such an elaborate undertaking, collecting and cross-referencing the vast English legal sources could—from the perspective of a student of Martin Wolff and very much informed by FA Mann's experience supporting Walter Hallstein's *Aktienrechte der Gegenwart*—only be done in a comparativist fashion with a broad global outlook and deep dives into the respective context.

In this tradition, *The Legal Aspect of Money* in its original edition opens with a chapter on the nature of money. Here, FA Mann comes to a conclusion that might appear banal: 'it is the intrinsic nature of money to represent purchasing power.'[118] Money can be used to dispel debt; nothing less, nothing more. For someone who is sometimes considered to even have started the study of money as a concept of law—at least in English law—that might appear as an underwhelming conclusion. Which misses the way FA Mann structures his argument to come to that conclusion.

It opens up with a long list of all the things money is not. While FA Mann never denies that money is a category of economics,[119] he argues that it is much more:

> debt, damages, value, payment, price, capital, interest, pecuniary legality. Money is a term so frequently used and of such importance that one is apt to overlook

[116] Mann, *Life and Cases* (n 2) 81–82.
[117] FA Mann, *The Legal Aspect of Money with Special Reference to Comparative and Private International Law* (OUP 1938) (hereafter Mann, *Legal Aspect*).
[118] ibid 22.
[119] ibid 3.

> its inherent difficulties, and to forget that its multitude of functions has led to a multitude of meanings.[120]

According to FA Mann, money is complicated and has many functions, procedures, and problems. Economics are merely one of many. The real question is which of these functions is the relevant one for his undertaking. Trying to just pin down FA Mann on his beliefs about money—as a nominalist, or a chartalist, or merely eccentric—misses the point of how he structures his argument. Joseph Sommer has masterfully outlined in Chapter 10 how FA Mann's understanding of money falls between these categories, and how it has held up against the development of finance and economics.[121] Christian Hofmann takes it even further and shows us the (ir)relevance of this line of argument on current issues like the treatment of Central Bank Digital Currency (CBDC).[122]

In that way one might expect a book about money to start with a working definition of what money is and, from there, to develop its legal aspects. In *The Legal Aspect of Money*, however, FA Mann is not interested in what money is. What he does is define the function of money that is relevant to his question. Instead of defining the thing itself, he defines the function of it that is relevant for his study. The practical result of the study is at the same time its starting point: what does a lawyer need to know to be able to make a convincing argument when questions of money are raised in a court of law? That indeed is 'the great value of his work'.[123]

> What are the characteristics in virtue of which a thing is called money? [. . .] What is the intrinsic nature of the phenomenon described by the word 'money'? These two questions will have to be answered separately. In both connexions, it should be noted, results reached by economic theory are of no direct assistance to a lawyer. In the first place, economic theory is concerned with the question of sound and unsound money. [. . .] Such postulates are important from the point of view of monetary policy, but they do not help to solve monetary problems in law.[124]

In *The Legal Aspect of Money*, FA Mann seeks to identify and structure the practical and relevant problems courts have when dealing with money due to pending proceedings at English courts. He did that because when he arrived in England in 1933

[120] ibid.

[121] See Chapter 10 of this volume by Joseph Sommer, 'FA Mann's Conservative Revolution'.

[122] See Chapter 14 of this volume by Christian Hofmann, 'A New and Unsolved Riddle in Monetary Law: The Complex Case of Central Bank Digital Currency'.

[123] See Chapter 9 of this volume by David Fox, 'Gold Clauses in the Capital Markets of the Early 20th Century'.

[124] Mann, *Legal Aspect* (n 117) 5.

he could find no such resource to be available, even though its use and need were obvious, at least to him.

> By that time I had decided to write a book on the law of money: a number of cases which were before the courts in those years appeared to make a systematic investigation and presentation of the subject necessary, particularly since no work in the English language was available.[125]

These problems and conflicts are what defines the field of monetary law. That is, as Horst Heinrich Jakobs puts it, the 'one characteristic of the book': the cases are not used to 'elaborate the existing rules, but are the very material in which the rule resides and has to be found'.[126] Which problems are relevant is self-evident for FA Mann: relevant is what made it into his book, what made it into his book is what is relevant.[127] That again might sound paradoxical: the outset of the argument is not just set by its anticipated result; the content selected to argue the connection between these two points is also self-evident. What qualifies the material to be relevant to answer the question is the fact that the author, with all his intellect and academic self-confidence, has deemed it to be so.

In this, a brief survey of what makes it in and what does not is convenient. The state makes it in: the state is the central actor on making money a legal question for FA Mann:

> Whatever one may be inclined to think of these doctrines in theory, it cannot be denied that in this country the State theory rules.[128]

Discarded under this programme is *commodity money*, i.e. the notion of valuable materials as a form of payment. Market economics dictate the function of commodity money. They are therefore not relevant for legal questions in courts.[129] Also discarded are bank notes, at least originally: while originally purely private, the English state declared them legal tender in the mid-19th century.[130]

Discarded is also the question of the value of money. A court renders a decision on a specific sum denominated in a currency. This is with one exception: the

[125] Mann, *Life and Cases* (n 2) 53.

[126] '*Der eine Charakter des Buches ist diese sein Ausrichtung auf die Praxis der entschiedenen Fälle, und in dieser Ausrichtung kennt es, indem die Fälle nicht der Verdeutlichung der vorhandenen Regel dienen, sondern das Material sind, in dem die Regel ist und gefunden werden muß, keine Beschränkung.*' Horst H Jakobs, 'In Memoriam Frederick Alexander Mann' in Jost Pietzker (ed.), *In memoriam Frederick Alexander Mann: Reden gehalten am 8. Februar 1992 bei den Gedenkfeier der Rechts- und Staatswissenschaftlichen Fakultät der Rheinischen Friedrich-Wilhelms-Universität Bonn* (Bouvier 1992) 13–14.

[127] Mann, *Legal Aspect* (n 117) vi–vii

[128] ibid 12.

[129] ibid 7.

[130] ibid 14–15.

Aufwertungsrechtsprechung of the *Reichsgericht* in response to hyperinflation in 1923.[131] Yet here, too, FA Mann manages to argue in his characteristic fashion, portraying a great deal of pragmatism, that even this decision does not break nominalism. At least not the practical spirit of it, though maybe its formal characteristics: the *Reichsgericht* has not actually rendered a judgement for or against nominalism, not even on the intrinsic value of money. It is merely a decision about 'equity and the law of contracts'.[132]

> As has been indicated above, in some countries, notably Germany, the complete collapse of a currency led to a practice of revalorization, as follows. According to s. 242 of the German Civil Code (which binds together the debtor to effect the performance of his obligation according to the requirements of good faith, ordinary usage being taken into consideration) the whole of the circumstances, including the financial position of both parties, are to be reviewed in order to translate a sum of marks into reichsmarks; it is therefore necessary and possible to investigate whether and to what extent the creditor would have been able to protect the owed sum of money from the effects of inflation, and to consider [. . .] the general reduction of the national wealth.[133]

Money is not just governed by law; it is created by law. When facing questions about how money is to be treated one has to engage in legal argumentation. That is the result of his study, based on the many materials FA Mann encountered, weighed for relevance, and digested into his treaties. It takes the intellectual confidence and conviction of someone who has been brought up under Martin Wolff at the interwar Berlin law faculty to approach a topic in this manner.

As a disciple of Hersch Lauterpacht, this academic undertaking, however, is not the end but only the beginning of his duty to the global legal order. FA Mann also made his expertise available to the world as an active member of the invisible college.[134] For instance, on questions of money his most prominent role was his active and prolonged engagement with the Committee on International Monetary Law of the International Law Association (MOCOMILA).

V. Forced Migration and Transnational Biographies

Crossing national borders is not always voluntary. It is not always cosmopolitan zeal that brings a person or institution from one national system to another,

[131] Instead of many others: Jan Thiessen, 'The German Hyperinflation of the 1920s' in David Fox and Wolfgang Ernst (eds), *Money in the Western Legal Tradition: Middle Ages to Bretton Woods* (OUP 2016).
[132] Mann, *Legal Aspect* (n 117) 75.
[133] ibid 76–77.
[134] For instance, Mann, *Life and Cases* (n 2) 1, 58–59, 60, 62.

physically or intellectually. Crossing a border can also mean experiences of expulsion, violence, or refuge. Being forced out of one's home country automatically drafts a biography of crossing borders and often comes hand in hand with statelessness, discrimination, and violence.[135]

Frank Mecklenburg outlines in his chapter the reference frame for the Jewish experience that FA Mann falls into. He rightly points out that the story of the 'German-Jewish symbiosis'[136] is not yet written. With that in mind any thoughts on FA Mann's Jewish identity and its influence should be understood as a temporary theory subject to changing interpretations. What should be avoided, however, is to follow a trend in historiography that circumvents any effort on the topic by ruling out the Jewish context of a person. Thereby implying the existence of a concrete definition of what being Jewish means. A 'real' Jew in this rationale can only be an observing, practising Jew; a stand-in for organized Jewry.[137] That reductive view inevitably will pass over the group of assimilated Jews that FA Mann considered himself to be a part of. Reut Paz is able to trace this modern 'iron cage' of Jewish cosmopolitanism in FA Mann's writing. She argues how FA Mann is not just a 'German conservative lawyer *avant la lettre*' but also 'a child, if not grandchild, of Jewish German cosmopolitanism' and how illuminating this context can support the understanding of FA Mann's writing and thinking without supplanting the other facets that can inform the study of FA Mann.[138]

FA Mann would describe himself to be of 'Jewish extraction',[139] 'Jewish by background, history and tradition, [but] wholly and firmly German'.[140] When on 11 September 1978 a piece on Werner Flume appeared in the *Frankfurter Allgemeine Zeitung*, Martin Wolff was mentioned. There Wolff was referred to as the 'great Jewish legal scholar'.[141] It prompted FA Mann to write a furious response: 'referring to Martin Wolff (with whom [Werner] Flume had nothing to do whatsoever) as a "great Jewish legal scholar" is unworthy of the [*Frankfurter Allgemeine Zeitung*].'[142] FA Mann's reaction is to what has been coined *Überbemerktheit*: an 'overwhelming

[135] Miriam Rürup, 'Legal Expertise and Biographical Experience – Statelessness, Migrants, and the Shaping of New Legal Knowledge in the Postwar World' (2017) 43 Geschichte und Gesellschaft 438, 463.

[136] See Chapter 2 in this volume by Frank Mecklenburg, 'On Being a German Jew in the "Golden Years"'.

[137] See Loeffler, *Rooted Cosmopolitans* (n 109) xiii–xiv.

[138] See Chapter 4 in this volume by Reut Yael Paz, '"Out of Harm's Way": FA Mann's Attempts to Demystify Money, Law, and Judaism'.

[139] FA Mann to Stephan Duggan (Mann estate, NLMann_0970, 01 July 1933).

[140] Mann, *Life and Cases* (n 2) 49.

[141] Fernando Wassner, 'Werner Flume 70 Jahre' *Frankfurter Allgemeine Zeitung* (11 September 1978).

[142] FA Mann to Friedrich Fromme (Mann estate, NLMann_0260, 20 September 1978): '*Das bedauerliche ist nur, dass der Artikel von Herrn F.W. voll von Unrichtigkeiten ist, Wesentliches weglässt und eine Reihe von groben Geschmacklosigkeiten enthält. Dass man Martin Wolff (mit dem Flume übrigens nicht das mindeste zu tun hatte) einen "großen jüdischen Rechtsgelehrten" nennt, ist der FAZ nicht würdig.*'

tradition of the tracing and demerging gaze'.[143] As JG Allen points out in his chapter, this must be seen against the backdrop of the Nazi period of mandating Jews to be identified as Jews.[144] It is not farfetched to assume he would have similar reservations if we described him in what might have sounded to him like: another accomplished Jewish lawyer.

When talking about FA Mann's biography as a transnational one it must, however, be accentuated that it was for being Jewish that he was forced to cross borders. FA Mann's transnational biography and everything that has so far been said about the meeting of pragmatism and *Praxisorientierung* was not voluntary. His intentions were initially different:

> I had the intention and the possibility of becoming a professor, and I had already begun to write a book on the own stock of companies. Besides lecturing at a university[,] I had intended to go to the bar, and probably I would have achieved both aims during the following winter. I am 26 years old.[145]

VI. Conclusion: *dogmatische Rechtswissenschaften*

FA Mann's style of arguing can be described as an amalgamation of *Praxisorientierung* and pragmatism. The influence of his academic upbringing in Berlin and his instruction with Martin Wolff in particular proved fruitful when integrating into the pragmatism of cosmopolitan England. This can be exemplified by the manner in which he introduces money into *The Legal Aspect of Money*, just as much as by his legal activism on the boards and committees of international organizations.

This understanding of the life and work of FA Mann is open to another branch of interpretation. FA Mann's understanding of legal practice and academia, and their interaction, shaped in this specific amalgamation of his upbringing and crossing of national boundaries, could bring insight into the ongoing debate on what is continental *Rechtswissenschaft* (jurisprudence).

Rechtswissenschaft is dead: ever since but no later than 1 January 1900 when the German *Bürgerliches Gesetzbuch* (civil code) came into force and allegedly severed the connection of the historical and non-statutory tradition of the formation of law from the current law argued in courts; with it died its science for the formation of law, *Rechtsdogmatik* (doctrinal studies of law).[146] Long live

[143] Volkhard Knigge, 'Mit den Augen der Eskimos: Können Deutsche Juden sehen?' in Volker Knigge and Axel Doßmann (eds), *Geschichte als Verunsicherung* (Wallstein 2020) 57: '*[übermächtige] Tradition des fahndenden aussondernden Blicks.*'

[144] See Chapter 1 of this volume by Jason Grant Allen, '*Ein Bericht aus einer Akademie*: Writing About Germany's Lost Jewish Scholars, 80 Years On'.

[145] FA Mann to Stephan Duggan (Mann estate, NLMann_0970, 01 August 1933).

[146] Rainer M Kiesow, 'Rechtswissenschaft—was ist das?' (2010) 65(12) JuristenZeitung 585, 588–89.

Rechtswissenschaft: most law faculties have still not been disbanded and to this day are branded *Rechtswissenschaftlich*. That holds true at least in Germany. Much has been written about how *Rechtsdogmatik* works today and what its logic and purpose is.[147] Is it maybe itself a methodology of legal interpretation and legal argument?[148] Is it a German or continental singularity or does it exist in England or elsewhere?[149]

At the core of these thoughts lies the observation that the gravitational centre of law has shifted away from the lecture halls—if it ever really was there—towards the courtrooms, even in Germany: 'if you want to orientate yourself in the law, you ask for judicature, not for the current state of scientific knowledge.'[150] In this struggle for the prerogative of interpretation, jurisprudence has lost much of its *Selbstbewusstsein* (self-confidence).[151] So much so, in fact, that much of the intellectual work at the faculties is now weighed up solely in terms of whether the courts will follow it or not.[152] The professors' burden now seems to be to anticipate what the judges will rule to be just.

The development of English law only appears to drift towards the old continental ways of *Rechtswissenschaft*: English law has gone through a rigorous process of academic dogmatization.[153] As Martin Flohr showed, however, English *Rechtsdogmatik* does not take inspiration from 19th-century Germany: rather it created something new, a 'transformation in difference',[154] but in the 20th century this was not infrequently with the support of the intellect of German-Jewish émigrés.[155]

This is where the study of FA Mann's monographs and papers becomes interesting beyond the legal arguments laid out in them: what FA Mann practises can be described as a case study in the evolution of English *Rechtswissenschaften*, and perhaps suggests how German legal academia might regain some of its self-confidence. The meeting of pragmatism and *Praxisorientierung* is indicative for how academic *Rechtsdogmatik* can work: confidence in one's *Judiz* (a jurist's feeling for the right legal decision), based on meticulous intellectual effort, and with the

[147] See, e.g., Wolfgang Finkentscher, *Methoden des Rechts in vergleichender Darstellung* (Mohr Siebeck 1977); Christian Bumke, *Rechtsdogmatik* (Mohr Siebeck 2017); Josef Esser, 'Möglichkeiten und Grenzen des dogmatischen Denkens im modernen Zivilrecht' (1972) 172 AcP 97–130; Gregor Kirchhof, Stefan Magen, and Karsten Schneider (eds), *Was weiß Dogmatik?: Was leistet und wie steuert die Dogmatik des Öffentlichen Rechts?* (Mohr Siebeck 2012).

[148] Jannis Lennartz, *Dogmatik als Methode* (Mohr Siebeck 2017).

[149] Martin Flohr, *Rechtsdogmatik in England* (Mohr Siebeck 2017) (hereafter Flohr, *Rechtsdogmatik*).

[150] Nils Jansen, 'Rechtsdogmatik, Rechtswissenschaft und juristische Praxis: Zum gesellschaftlichen Ort wissenschaftlichen Sebstverständnis universitärer Rechtsdogmatik' (2018) 143 AcP 623, 627 (hereafter Jansen, 'Rechtsdogmatik, Rechtswissenschaft und juristische Praxis').

[151] ibid 629.

[152] ibid.

[153] ibid 631.

[154] Flohr, *Rechtsdogmatik* (n 149) 296.

[155] Beatson and Zimmermann, *Jurists Uprooted* (n 14).

confidence that such arguments hold value beyond the question of whether the courts would have reached the same decision.

FA Mann has reflected on not just his personal role, but the role of *Rechtsdogmatik* and legal academia in the practice of law.

> I owe it to my practical experience that I knew what to do. This is a lesson for many academics. Purely academic law is liable to become sterile. The demands of an extensive practice are such that they always lead to some fruitful starting point for research. It is rare that practice directly brings up the wish to explore a particular problem. What arises in practice is usually on the fringe of some central topic. Or when reading something up for the purpose of solving a specific, probably very narrow problem, one suddenly comes across or sees a much wider subject worthy of exploration. But it is life in practice that provides the fertile ground for work which, the author feels and some believe serves a useful purpose.[156]

It is not just that FA Mann is immersed in both legal practice and legal academia. It is the way in which he can utilize both his 'knowledge of the practice and scientific distance'[157] in his argument. This self-image, which incorporates both the contextual knowledge of legal practice and the intellectual confidence of academia to procure answers to legal problems beyond the anticipation of judicial approval, is what is brought forth today as the way *Rechtswissenschaften* should be conducted in the 21st century.[158] For that alone, it is worth studying and taking inspiration from FA Mann's biography and works.

Bibliography

Bank für Internationalen Zahlungsausgleich, *Die Bank für Internationalen Zahlungsausgleich und die Basler Zusammenkünfte: Herausgegeben zum fünfzigjährigen Bestehen der Bank 1930–1980* (Bank für Internationalen Zahlungsausgleich 1980)

Beatson J and Zimmermann R (eds), *Jurists Uprooted: German-Speaking Émigré Lawyers in Twentieth-Century Britain* (OUP 2004)

Böckstiegel K-H, 'F. A. Mann 11. 8. 1907–17. 9. 1991' (1992) 56(3) Rabels Zeitschrift für ausländisches und internationales Privatrecht / The Rabel Journal of Comparative and International Private Law 407

[156] Mann, *Life and Cases* (n 2) 85.

[157] Karl-Heinz Böckstiegel, 'F. A. Mann 11. 8. 1907–17. 9. 1991' (1992) 56(3) Rabels Zeitschrift für ausländisches und internationales Privatrecht / The Rabel Journal of Comparative and International Private Law 407, 408 <http://www.jstor.org/stable/27877543> accessed 15 May 2023: '*Kenntnis der Praxis und wissenschaftlichem Abstand.*'

[158] Jansen, 'Rechtsdogmatik, Rechtswissenschaft und juristische Praxis' (n 150) 632; Christoph Schönberger, 'Der "German Approach": Die deutsche Staatsrechtslehre im Wissenschaftsvergleich' in Christoph Schönberger, Atsushi Takada, and András Jakab (eds), *Der 'German Approach': Die deutsche Staatsrechtslehre im Wissenschaftsvergleich* (Mohr Siebeck 2015) 1–51.

Erkkilä V, *The Conceptual Change of Conscience: Franz Wieacker and German Legal Historiography 1933–1968* (Mohr Siebeck 2019)

Ernst W, 'Fritz Schulz (1879–1957)' in Jack Beatson and Reinhard Zimmermann (eds), *Jurists Uprooted: German-Speaking Émigré Lawyers in Twentieth-Century Britain* (OUP 2004)

Mann FA, *Life and Cases: Manuscript of an Autobiography* (Wolfgang Ernst ed., Bonn University Press 2021)

Fernando Wassner, 'Werner Flume 70 Jahre' *Frankfurter Allgemeine Zeitung* (11 September 1978)

Flohr M, *Rechtsdogmatik in England* (Mohr Siebeck 2017)

Görtemaker M (ed.), *Die Rosenburg: Das Bundesministerium der Justiz und die NS-Vergangenheit—eine Bestandsaufnahme [Symposium, April 2012]* (Vandenhoeck & Ruprecht 2013)

Grimm D, 'Methode als Machtfaktor' in Norbert Horn (ed.), *Europäisches Rechtsdenken in Geschichte und Gegenwart: Festschrift für Helmut Coing zum 70. Geburtstag* (Beck 1982)

Heymann A, *Der Jurist Julius Flechtheim: Leben und Werk* (Julius Flechtheim tr., Heymanns 1990)

Jakobs HH, 'In Memoriam Frederick Alexander Mann' in Jost Pietzker (ed.), *In memoriam Frederick Alexander Mann: Reden gehalten am 8. Februar 1992 bei den Gedenkfeier der Rechts- und Staatswissenschaftlichen Fakultät der Rheinischen Friedrich-Wilhelms-Universität Bonn* (Bouvier 1992)

Jansen N, 'Rechtsdogmatik, Rechtswissenschaft und juristische Praxis: Zum gesellschaftlichen Ort wissenschaftlichen Sebstverständnis universitärer Rechtsdogmatik' (2018) 143 AcP 623

Kiesow RM, 'Rechtswissenschaft—was ist das?' (2010) 65(12) JuristenZeitung 585

Kirchhof G, Magen S, and Schneider K (eds), *Was weiß Dogmatik?: Was leistet und wie steuert die Dogmatik des Öffentlichen Rechts?* (Mohr Siebeck 2012)

Volkhard Knigge, 'Mit den Augen der Eskimos: Können Deutsche Juden sehen?' in Volker Knigge and Axel Doßmann (eds), *Geschichte als Verunsicherung* (Wallstein 2020)

Koskenniemi M, 'Hersch Lauterpacht (1897–1960)' in Jack Beatson and Reinhard Zimmermann (eds), *Jurists Uprooted: German-Speaking Émigré Lawyers in Twentieth-Century Britain* (OUP 2004)

Koskenniemi M, *The Gentle Civilizer of Nations* (Cambridge University Press 2009)

Koskenniemi M and Kari V, 'A More Elevated Patriotism: The Emergence of International and Comparative Law (Nineteenth Century)' in Heikki Pihlajamäki, Markus D Dubber, and Mark Godfrey (eds), *Oxford Handbook of European Legal History* (OUP 2018)

Kunstreich J, 'Die Rechtswissenschaft in der MPG: Versuch einer Vogelperspektive' in Thomas Duve, Jasper Kunstreich, and Stefan Vogenauer (eds), *Rechtswissenschaft in der Max-Planck-Gesellschaft, 1948–2002* (Vandenhoeck & Ruprecht 2023)

Lange F, 'Praxisorientierung und Gemeinschaftskonzeption' (Dissertation, Springer 2017)

Lange F, 'Between Systematization and Expertise for Foreign Policy: The Practice-Oriented Approach in Germany's International Legal Scholarship (1920–1980)' (2017) 28(2) European Journal of International Law 535

Langer F, 'Zwischen völkerrechtlicher Systembildung und Begleitung der deutschen Außenpolitik: Das Max-Planck-Institut für ausländisches öffentliches Recht und Völkerrecht, 1945–2002' in Thomas Duve, Jasper Kunstreich, and Stefan Vogenauer (eds), *Rechtswissenschaft in der Max-Planck-Gesellschaft, 1948–2002* (Vandenhoeck & Ruprecht 2023)

Lewis G, *FA Mann: A Memoir* (Hart Publishing 2013)

Loeffler JB, *Rooted Cosmopolitans, Jews and Human Rights in the Twentieth Century* (Yale University Press 2018)
Lösch A-Mv, *Der nackte Geist: Die Juristische Fakultät der Berliner Universität im Umbruch von 1933* (Mohr Siebeck 1999)
Magnus U, 'Geschichte des Max-Planck-Instituts für ausländisches und internationales Privatrecht, 1949–2000' in Thomas Duve, Jasper Kunstreich, and Stefan Vogenauer (eds), *Rechtswissenschaft in der Max-Planck-Gesellschaft, 1948–2002* (Vandenhoeck & Ruprecht 2023)
Mann FA, *The Legal Aspect of Money with Special Reference to Comparative and Private International Law* (OUP 1938)
Markezinēs BS, *Comparative Law in the Courtroom and Classroom: The Story of the Last Thirty-Five Years* (Hart 2003)
Sands P and Rowson M, *The Last Colony: A Tale of Exile, Justice and Britain's Colonial Legacy* (Weidenfeld & Nicolson 2022)
Schachter O, 'The Invisible College of International Lawyers' (1977) 72(2) Northwestern University Law Review 217
Schönberger C, 'Der "German Approach": Die deutsche Staatsrechtslehre im Wissenschaftsvergleich' in Christoph Schönberger, Atsushi Takada, and András Jakab (eds), *Der 'German Approach': Die deutsche Staatsrechtslehre im Wissenschaftsvergleich* (Mohr Siebeck 2015)
Stray C, 'Sisam, Kenneth (1887–1971), Anglo-Saxon Scholar and Publisher', *Oxford Dictionary of National Biography* (OUP 2016)
Thiessen J, 'The German Hyperinflation of the 1920s' in David Fox and Wolfgang Ernst (eds), *Money in the Western Legal Tradition: Middle Ages to Bretton Woods* (OUP 2016)
Utermark T, *Rechtsgeschichte und Rechtsvergleichung bei Ernst Rabel* (Lang 2005)
Wolff M, 'Die juristische Fakultät der Kgl. Friedrich-Wilhelms-Universität', *Aus dem Berliner Rechtsleben: Festgabe zum XXVI. Deutschen Juristentage. Ueberreicht vom Ortsausschusse. Berlin, im September 1902* (F. Vahlen 1902)

4

'Out of Harm's Way'

FA Mann's Attempts to Demystify Money, Law, and Judaism

Reut Yael Paz

I. Introduction

This chapter explores the relevance of FA Mann's Jewish-German background to his legal approach, which weaves public international law and private international law in a unique and unprecedented way. Mann's approach is all the more interesting because of its focus on money. Indeed, his treatise on *The Legal Aspect of Money* (first published in 1938) remains the foremost authority on the law of money today. Contextualizing his approach, and its success, is all the more insightful because it impacted our contemporary understanding of international law and money in a non-Christian manner. After all, the Christian character of international law remains a tool of subjugation and liberation of the 'Other' to date and hence,[1] albeit

[1] As discussed in more detail below, the structure of the legal argument is ultimately conceived as 'empty', 'formal', and/or value-less; it inherently permeates dichotomous ideologies. As 'Third World Approaches to International Law' scholarship clearly shows, while international law was used in the past to legitimize colonialism and acts of exploitation in developing countries by white Christian, Western men, today the discipline is predominantly used to protect, project, and promote the interest of the Westerners. See more in Brian-Vincent Ikejiak, 'International Law is Western Made Global Law: The Perception of Third-World Category' (2014) 6(2–3) African Journal of Legal Studies 337–56.

Reut Yael Paz, *'Out of Harm's Way'* In: *FA Mann*. Edited by: Jason Grant Allen and Gerhard Dannemann, Oxford University Press. © Reut Yael Paz 2024. DOI: 10.1093/oso/9780198881452.003.0005

with historical and circumstantial differences, continues to be a kind of Achilles' heel for the discipline.

The specific goal of this chapter is to explore whether FA Mann's relationship to Judaism, and to the Jewish cosmopolitan tradition in particular, informed his legalistic approach to money. As a highly assimilated and emancipated German Jew in the early 20th century, Mann inherited a certain Jewish-German cosmopolitan *Denkstil* ('style of thinking'), which could also be described as being part of a *Denkkollektiv* ('thought collective'), that I argue is part and parcel of his approach. I ask if and how this *Denkstil*, similarly to Max Weber's metaphor of an 'iron-cage',[2] interacted in structuring, forming, and shaping his general legal methodology. Did this inherited intellectual framework motivate (or even compel?) Mann to explore the intersection of law and money? While there is no evidence that it did so intentionally, there is a phenomenon in search of an explanation to the extent that so many German-speaking theorists of law but also money and capitalism were Jewish (*sensu lato*, including the children of more and less willing converts). Whereas most of my research unpacks the interaction between such *Denkstil/Denkkollektiv* and international law,[3] here the intention is to add the feature of money more specifically.

Apart from the Jewish Polish/German Rosa Luxemburg (1871–1919), who was one of the first women to earn a Doctor of Law degree and later published *Accumulation of Capital* (1913), which is the most important advance on Marx's political economy to date,[4] we can draw some parallels to two other German-Jewish thinkers—Karl Marx and Georg Simmel. While Marx cannot be called a 'Jewish thinker' straightforwardly, his family experience of emancipation under Napoleonic rule and its loss under Prussian rule has been argued to inform Marx's philosophical interests and outlook in various ways, including his ambiguous and problematic critique of capitalism/Judaism.[5] Simmel was born into a Jewish

[2] Max Weber's metaphor of an 'iron cage' describes the increased rationalization of modern social life; this 'iron cage' holds individuals in systems based purely on teleological efficiency, rational calculation, and control.

[3] See for instance Reut Yael Paz, *A Gateway Between a Distant God and a Cruel World: The Contribution of Jewish German Scholars to International Law* (Brill 2012) (hereafter Paz, *A Gateway*); Reut Yael Paz, 'Kelsen's *Pure Theory of Law* as "a Hole in Time"' / '*La Théorie pure du droit* de Hans Kelsen comme "un trou dans le temps"' (2015) 1(7) Monde(s) 75; Reut Yael Paz, 'A Forgotten Kelsenian? The Story of Helen Silving-Ryu (1906–1993)' (2014) 25 The European Journal of International Law 4; Reut Yael Paz, 'Making it Whole: Hersch Lauterpacht and the Rabbinical Approach to International Law' (2012) 4(2) Gottingen Journal of International Law 417–45; Reut Yael Paz, 'Review Essay – Erich K. *Before the Law: Reflections on Degenhardt's Study of Erich Kaufmann*' (2010) 11 German Law Journal 439–56).

[4] See more in Reut Yael Paz, 'From Rosa Luxemburg to Hersch Lauterpacht: An *Ostjüdische* Heritage in International Law?' in Alberto Puppo and Dawid Bunikowski (eds), *On a Critical Philosophy of Law, Peace and Religion* (Springer 2019).

[5] Although Marx's father converted into Christianity, that he was a grandchild of two rabbis never escaped anyone. See in particular Sholom Avineri, *Karl Marx: Philosophy and Revolution* (Yale University Press 2019) (hereafter Avineri, *Karl Marx*); Avineri interprets Marx's essay in the context of his debate with other (obviously antisemitic) neo-Hegelians, and presents some compelling arguments that Marx's

family and had Jewish ancestry, but as many others of his Jewish-German milieu he was not a religiously observant person and did not identify as a Jewish thinker in the traditional sense. Be that as it may, his experiences as a member of a minority group in German society and his understanding of the social dynamics of exclusion and marginalization impacted his singular approach to the role of social differentiation and conflict in shaping modern society and the experiences of individuals within it. Arguably, his attempt to rehabilitate the negative implications of the Jewish moneylender is part and parcel of his personal experiences.

A disclaimer is in place: Contextualizing Mann's work against the backdrop of other Jewish-German scholars, such as Marx and Simmel and their shared socio-economic cosmopolitan context, leads us into the 'messiness' of identity politics.[6] Writing about Jewish identities—which necessarily implicates antisemitism, negative Jewish stereotypical tropes, and other conspiratorial thinking—intensifies anxieties by Jews and non-Jews alike. Once, however, it is accepted that our identity is transient and encompasses alternate intersectionalities, much can be gained by relying on this methodology. Social movements based on shared identities, such as race, gender, sexuality, religion, or nationality, enable important criticism and the space to negotiate social justice and equality. Whereas acknowledging the centrality and indeed the intersectionality between social justice and equality to both Jewish traditions and international law is discussed elsewhere,[7] here I focus on if and how Mann's Jewish identity together with his German-speaking legal education relates to his *Weltanschauung* in general and to his scientific approach more specifically.[8]

My overarching hypothesis is that Mann was both a German conservative lawyer *avant la lettre* and a child, if not a grandchild, of Jewish/German cosmopolitanism. The way he wove together *money and law* remains very Jewish, German, and cosmopolitan. *Ergo*, however conservative he may have been, his approach mirrors a global sense of being without boundaries: 'An everyday, historically alert, reflexive awareness of ambivalences [which] reveals not just the "anguish" but also the possibility of shaping one's life and social relations under conditions of cultural mixture [that is] simultaneously a sceptical, disillusioned, self-critical outlook.'[9]

Jewish background, although complex and ambivalent, was a 'lost paradise' that helped shape his critiques of capitalist society and his vision of a more just and egalitarian social order.

[6] For more on identity politics see Bobby Gentry, 'Political Identity: Meaning, Measures, and Evidence' in *Why Youth Vote* (Springer 2018).

[7] See more in Paz, *A Gateway* (n 3) 93.

[8] For more on how law impacts its practitioner and vice versa see Pierre Bourdieu, 'The Force of Law: Towards a Sociology of Juridical Field' (1987) 38 Hastings LJ 814.

[9] Ulrich Beck, *Cosmopolitan Vision* (Polity Press 2006) (hereafter Beck, *Cosmopolitan Vision*).

Put simply, if more provocatively, I argue that Mann's legal approach attempts to rehabilitate both 'money' and 'the Jew' through law.[10]

II. Mann's Professional Trajectory Between Scholarship and Practice

FA Mann wrote his magnum opus at the age of 31. *The Legal Aspect of Money* was actually his second attempt to be published in English since arriving in London in October 1933.[11] Despite the difficulties of his position—having been ejected from 'the trinity of state–people–territory', as Hannah Arendt phrased it—Mann was both industrious and productive after leaving Germany.[12] Notwithstanding his eagerness, obvious commitment, and sophistication, however, Mann's foreignness seems not to have been ignored in England. Indeed, one of the first reservations made about *The Legal Aspect of Money* was that its construction had 'an alien character'.[13] And yet, because the book was 'a monument of erudition', it was accepted and published in 1938.[14] In a review of the fifth edition—the last edition that Mann wrote personally—Mann is described as 'one of the finest British lawyers of this century; and the book had become the leading work on the law of money in the world and had been translated into German and Spanish'.[15]

Apart from these broad acknowledgements, it is said that Mann's contribution paved a way through 'an unworked field'; his work has been resorted to by both legal theorists and practitioners and was even cited in the House of Lords.[16] Despite Mann's academic predispositions and clear ambition, however, he never became an English law professor. The reasons for these seem to be layered. Though he was offered a position at the University of Oxford, Mann did not take it up for apparently financial reasons.[17] In 1949, with the support of a few colleagues and friends (Sir Hersch Lauterpacht and Sir Valentine Holmes among others), Mann

[10] Here I borrow and play with Amos Morris-Reich's title to his contribution on Georg Simmel: 'The Beautiful Jew is a Moneylender: Money and Individuality in Simmel's Rehabilitation of the "Jew"' (2003) 20(4) Theory, Culture & Society 127–42 (hereafter Morris-Reich, 'The Beautiful Jew is a Moneylender').

[11] The Clarendon Press accepted Mann's book after it 'declined a proposal from him as early as 1934 (less than six months after he had arrived in England as a refugee) to produce a translation of the new German Company Law with a commentary'. See Geoffrey Lewis, *F. A. Mann: A Memoir* (Hart Publishing 2013) 54.

[12] Hannah Arendt, 'Nation State and Democracy' in J Kohn (ed.), *Thinking Without A Banister: Essays in Understanding, 1953–1975* (Schocken Books 2018) 255–61.

[13] Llewellyn Davis quoted in ibid 255.

[14] Professor HC Gutteridge quoted in ibid 257.

[15] ibid. On the Spanish translation, see Chapter 12 in this volume by María Emilia Buccella, Rosa Maria Lastra, and Jason Grant Allen, '*El Aspecto Legal del Dinero*: FA Mann's Impact in Latin America'.

[16] JG Merrills, 'Oppenheimer v. Cattermole—The Curtain Falls' (1975) 24(4) The International and Comparative Law Quarterly 619.

[17] FA Mann, *Life and Cases: Manuscript of an Autobiography* (Wolfgang Ernst ed., Unipress 2021) 78 (hereafter Mann, *Life and Cases*).

unsuccessfully applied for the professorship in international law at the University of London. This position, as Mann learned later, was not filled for a decade: as Mann interprets this event in his autobiography, the university 'did not wish to appoint a lawyer of foreign origin' but it would have been awkward to appoint anyone but Mann. Apparently, 'therefore one preferred not to make any appointment at all'. Despite having worked tirelessly to earn his 'entry ticket' to English bourgeois society,[18] Mann may have felt a little like Moses on Mount Nebo, looking into the promised land.[19]

Despite the challenges of dislocation to a new and very different scholarly and professional environment, Mann became an influential and productive practitioner and scholar. While being a full-time lawyer, he remained an independent and noteworthy academic writer whose work impacted the evolving interplay of law and money, among other things.[20] Phrased differently, Mann's focus on law and money—on the *law of money*—turned into a source of stability and security, as explained in Joseph Sommer's contribution to this volume. Mann's constant insistence to start his approach from the level of nation state—instead of the international universal—helps him stay within the 'conservative revolutionary' paradigm. It also assists Mann's legalistic concept of money to become the foremost authority on the law of money, despite some substantial questions.

This chapter does not explore the substance of Mann's concept of money, or work in monetary law, which is treated at length in Part III of this volume. Instead, it looks at whether, and if so how, Mann's Jewish-German background may have informed his work on money. Like Shlomo Avineri's recent biography of Marx, this chapter explores some of the possible intersections of money and Jewishness in Mann's scholarship and attempts to put his Jewish-German background in its proper and balanced perspective within Mann's intellectual historical context.[21]

Therefore, the goal here is limited to unpacking if, and more importantly how, the fragility of his specific Jewish-German *situationality* may have impelled him to

[18] As I discuss elsewhere, for Heinrich Heine the 'entry ticket to the bourgeois society' was either through Baptism or proof of indispensable intellectual qualities. (See more in Paz, *A Gateway* (n 3) 93.) In the German context, 'bourgeois' [*Bürgerlich*] means something more like 'civil' than the connotation that word has in English. See also Frank Mecklenburg's chapter in this volume on the *Bildungsbürger*, i.e. those who gain their entry ticket to civil society through *Bildung* or education.

[19] Indeed, the sense of being an 'outsider on the inside' is common to many Jewish biographies, including those without a history of dislocation and migration. See, for example, Nicola Lacey, *A Life of HLA Hart: The Nightmare and the Noble Dream* (OUP 2006).

[20] Apart from writing numerous reports and opinions, Mann acted as the rapporteur of the Monetary Law Committee of the International Law Association for 21 years and was also a member of the Lord Chancellor's Private International Law Committee.

[21] See Avineri, *Karl Marx* (n 5). The first chapter of Avineri's biography—with the apt title 'Jew? Of Jewish Origin? A Converted Jew?'—explores the Franco-Prussian history of the Rhineland and the particular experience of Marx's father (also a lawyer) as a beneficiary of early emancipation. The reversal of the civil and economic benefits of French rule was, according to Avineri, a source of radicalization among many young assimilated Jews of Marx's generation. The Rhenish history of Mann's family (his father also a lawyer) is explored in Frank Mecklenburg's chapter to this volume.

link law to money for the sake of stability, in England and beyond.[22] After all, and as Mann notes in his autobiography, it was the 1923 inflation and its direct effect on the creation of 'emergency money' that troubled him 'on account of the definition of their legal character'.[23] The silver lining here is the link between the uncertainty implicated in his Jewish alienness, on the one hand, and his German (and hence necessarily conservative, if not reactionary) legal training, on the other hand. Ultimately, it is Mann's motivation that interests me here. In this chapter I ask, *what is it that he tried to do with his legal(istic) approach to money?*

III. Influence of German Education on Mann as a Lawyer

These questions require two preliminary caveats: Mann's Jewishness and his learnedness, or rather how he understood these two aspects to have been interlaced through antisemitism, certainly stimulated his *Weltanschauung* by and large. Tellingly, in his autobiography he weaves the two in the following paragraph:

> At school I was, I believe, always top or near the top of my form. We were very hardworking, studying not only German, but also French, Latin, Greek and old-fashioned mathematics, also some chemistry and physics. My knowledge of French and Latin lasted me a life-time, Greek and mathematics I have completely forgotten. The standard of the form was not only high, but I believe that the teaching was excellent,—intensive, liberal and broad-minded. I have no recollection of any political or antisemitic unpleasantness; indeed I must say that in so far as I personally am concerned I did not ever or anywhere have any experience of antisemitism directed against myself—a qualification by which I intend to exclude discussions of a general character which, of course, in later years were inevitable. We worked very hard ... On one occasion I gave a lecture about Frederick the Great based on the most remarkable book by Franz Mehring *Die Lessinglegende*. On another occasion I spoke about the reception of Roman law in Germany,—a topic that resulted from my talks with my father. I had, of course, no legal knowledge at all, but I read a good deal of general literature for the purpose, though I seem to remember that I also looked into my father's original edition of Jhering's *System of Roman Law* which I still possess.[24]

[22] Situationality assumes that the social characteristics of the people involved in each instance determine its outcome at least as much as historically socially based legal principles, rules, doctrines, interpretations, etc. '[T]he situation comprises the interplay between the social, biological, cultural, etc. constraints on the human freedom, the effort towards objective justice, and self-expression, and the diverse potentials to manage the maximum amount of freedom from these constraints.' Outi Korhonen, *International Law Situated; An Analysis of the Lawyers Stance Towards Culture, History and Community* (Kluwer Law International 2000) 8.

[23] Mann, *Life and Cases* (n 17) 30.

[24] ibid 31.

One's early socialization of knowledge, as Peter Berger and Thomas Luckmann argue, impacts the individual's internalization of reality.[25] For Mann, and for every child born in a family that had, for one reason or another, refused to convert to Christianity to avoid civil and political exclusions, this included an explicit Jewish self-awareness.[26] But what would this self-awareness have entailed?

Specifically, the primary level of socialization is 'homebound': an emotionally charged process of cognitive learning through family and early childhood impressions. It is on this level that the individual is assigned an identity. This is the significance of the 'highly cultured German Jewish bourgeois *milieu*' that Mann describes in his autobiography.[27] The secondary level of socialization—which we might call *Denkstil* following Ludwik Fleck—is the subsequent process that introduces the already-socialized person into new sectors of the 'objective world' or 'sub-worlds' of the relevant society.

The second phase of socialization presupposes the preceding primary process of socialization. It normally carries high degrees of anonymity, objectivity, and detachment from the socializing individual. Evidently, Mann was capable to internalize his homebound level of socialization of knowledge together with his external circumstances, even as these worsened over time.[28] I will elaborate on this point below; for now, it suffices to note that Mann's ambitious liberal education fits perfectly with his close relationship to his Jewish heritage of learnedness, which in its turn is coupled with a specific socio-economic bourgeois background later connected to the renaissance of Enlightened European cosmopolitanism—and also Jewish cosmopolitanism. As I have written elsewhere, one important aspect of Jewish cosmopolitanism is how it historically interacted with the creation of a class (Mann's '*milieu*') which linked traditional focuses on learning to wealth:

> As a matter of course, in Jewish communities wealth and learning supported each other and defined the rank order in society: the sons of the rich and the learned had a better chance to become both learned and rich through better educational facilities and through marriages. What is so significant in this is that both wealth and learning are attainable qualities creating a situation where even the highest ranks of societies were—at least in theory—open to everyone. Although the basis for these traditions was religious to begin with, they were just as helpful for Jewish

[25] Peter L Berger and Thomas Luckmann, *The Social Construction of Reality: A Treatise in the Sociology of Knowledge* (Doubleday & Company Inc. 1967) 129–80.

[26] See Chapter 1 in this volume by Jason Grant Allen, '*Ein Bericht aus einer Akademie*: Writing About Germany's Lost Jewish Scholars, 80 Years On'.

[27] Mann, *Life and Cases* (n 17) 93.

[28] ibid. There are different reasons for the failure of socialization of knowledge. For example, complex heterogeneity during childhood, socially concealed asymmetry between public and private biography, dominant and invasive ideologies in the secondary level of socialization, and the lack of authentic socialization on the primary or secondary level are equally dangerous.

> communities to cope with modernity's demands, particularly with the decline of religious cohesion.[29]

Evaluating Mann professionally requires us to go beyond this relationship between identity and context, however. After all, law is a 'tool' to accomplish a variety of objectives, depending on the particular context and circumstances. This entails a twofold appreciation of law's possibilities and limitations: on the one hand, law is constantly negotiated by legal agents' intentions and desires, by what it is that we do with law, which requires us to appreciate legal words to mean 'what "we" want them to mean'.[30] On the other hand, we must accept that the law has a 'deep structure',[31] which in its turn implicates a specific and rigid legal identity. Law is hardly an empty, objective, and value-neutral tool. Within its structure remains an essential ideology 'posited [as] structuring category, rather than an expression of an underlying logic'.[32] It is this covert ideological logic that remains (one of) the discipline's Achilles' Heels.

Thus conceived, international law subsists and collapses into the 'grey' gap between the law on the books and the law in action.[33] Different conceptions of global consciousness/intuition—carried to varying degrees both by laymen and legal professionals—connect the (legal) text and practice. Here, I draw on Martti Koskenniemi's description of the legal profession as an insoluble 'ascending/descending' liberal dyad structured between theory and practice, concreteness and normativity, law and politics, apology and utopia, public and private, etc.[34] What we understand the law to mean comes to life within the limits of this deep structure.

In Germany, at least since the 19th-century work on Roman law and private international law by Friedrich Carl von Savigny (1779–1861)—one of Mann's legal 'doctor-grandfathers' and the Goethe of German jurisprudence—the Christian state 'offered a progressive modern-day nationalistic alternative that reacted against and reversed the French Revolution'.[35] In other words, unlike the radical alternative

[29] Paz, *A Gateway* (n 3) 70.

[30] See Martti Koskenniemi, 'Between Empire and Legal Formalism', Speech in Recife, Brazil (on file with author).

[31] Law's deep structure, *à la* Martti Koskenniemi, 'refers to a set of assumptions which, when explicated, most lawyers would probably recognize as very basic to the identity of their "legal" profession'. See Martti Koskenniemi, *From Apology to Utopia. The Structure of International Legal Argument, Reissue with New Epilogue* (Cambridge University Press 2005) 3, fn 8 (hereafter Koskenniemi, *Apology to Utopia*).

[32] China Miéville, *Between Equal Rights: A Marxist Theory of International Law* (Brill 2005) 81.

[33] See Susan Silbey, 'After Legal Consciousness' (2005) 1 Annual Review of Law and Social Science 323–68.

[34] As Martti Koskenniemi phrases this: 'Doctrine is forced to maintain itself in constant movement from emphasizing concreteness to emphasizing normativity and vice versa, without ever being able to establish itself permanently in either position.... [Ultimately this is] explained by the contradictory nature of the liberal doctrine of politics.' See Koskenniemi, *Apology to Utopia* (n 31) 46–47.

[35] See more in Reut Yael Paz, 'Legalizing Antisemitism? The Legacy of Savigny's Roman(tic) Law' in Pamela Slotte and John D Haskell (eds), *Christianity and International Law*, edited by (Cambridge University Press 2021) 177–98.

that France became, Germany remained openly conservative and Christian even if arguably 'secular' *inter alia* because of its counterrevolutionary sentiment. The failure of Germany's already belated revolution in 1848 is equally informative: not only is it a cornerstone in Germany's *Sonderweg* thesis, it also assisted in the emergence of popular conservatism.[36] In brief, whereas secularism remains a mutation of Western Christianities in Germany—where religion and religious actors actually played crucial roles in the history of secularism and the establishment of the modern nation state and judiciary, which were made to control and limit but not extinguish institutionalized religion—post-revolutionary France becomes the embodiment of enlightened cosmopolitanism by enhancing a Christian-based defence of universal human rights.[37] Whatever the divergences, both Germany and France—also because secularism cut through a common political and religious heritage—remained locked in the structural and Christian and universal biases. These, as I argue elsewhere, go back to a specific European imagination of what the Roman Empire and its private–public divide were about, which was reinvigorated by the 15th-century clergies/jurists of the Spanish School of Salamanca.[38] Ergo, although 'the history of international law is frequently explicated as an overly secular project with several feeble inheritances from Europe's Christian past, the specific examination of the Jewish identity against international law opens the discipline for a closer religious scrutiny'.[39]

Mann's scholarship, like that of all legal practitioners, expresses law's deep structure and reveals how the tropes that determine apparently value-free arguments are linked and tied together with the sentiments, sensibilities, habits, and even forced choices of legal agents. Thus, just as certain assumptions identify the legal profession, they also ascertain the lawyer's subjective convictions: what is right and what is wrong, what is true and what is not, can be read from the lawyer's legal formulations that are presented as 'public', 'objective', 'empty', and 'value-free' argumentations. Recapping what Mann sought to do with the law, his motivation implicates his Jewish-German identity and his cosmopolitanism—as well as the unprecedented impact of German legal science [*Rechtswissenschaft*] on international law by and large.[40] My overarching hypothesis is that Mann was both

[36] James F Harris, 'Rethinking the Categories of the German Revolution of 1848: The Emergence of Popular Conservatism in Bavaria' (1992) 25(2) Central European History 123–48. The *Sonderweg* thesis is that German-speaking Europe followed a 'special path' to democratic modernity.

[37] Suzanne Desan, 'Foreigners, Cosmopolitanism, and French Revolutionary Universalism' in Suzanne Desan, Lynn Hunt, and William Max Nelson (eds), *The French Revolution in Global Perspective* (Cornell University Press 2013) 86–100.

[38] See more in Reut Yael Paz, 'Religion, Secularism and International Law' in Anne Orford and Florian Hofmann (eds), *Oxford Handbook of International Legal Theory* (OUP 2016) 923–38 (hereafter Paz, 'Religion, Secularism and IL')

[39] Paz, *A Gateway* (n 3) 4.

[40] As Martti Koskenniemi argues: '(M)uch of the way we speak about international law has been received from German Public law as it developed from constitutional commentaries about the nature of the Holy Roman Empire in the seventeenth century to the natural law of the eighteenth and public law formalism of the nineteenth centuries. No legal tradition in this period compares with the German

a German conservative lawyer *avant la lettre* and a child, if not a grandchild, of Jewish-German cosmopolitanism. Moreover, his preference of the private over the public, and the national over the international, 'lives' within the liberal demands of the profession. The way Mann wove together 'money' and 'law' (as set out in further detail in Joseph Sommer's chapter) remains distinctively Jewish, German, and cosmopolitan.

IV. More about Cosmopolitanism(s)

The argument that Mann's work reflects a Jewish-German cosmopolitan outlook should not be overly controversial. Despite his German conservatism, his approach mirrors a 'global' way of 'being without boundaries'. As Ulrich Beck describes it, this sense manifests as '[a]n everyday, historically alert, reflexive awareness of ambivalences [that] reveals not just the "anguish" but also the possibility of shaping one's life and social relations under conditions of cultural mixture'.[41] This outlook is simultaneously sceptical, disillusioned, and self-critical.

In more provocative terms, I argue that Mann's legal approach attempts to rehabilitate, *through law*, two categories that are much maligned, and often connected, in European thought: 'money' and 'the Jew'. The first step in this argument is to connect Mann to the history of a Jewish-German cosmopolitanism, which motivated and necessarily implicated Mann's legal *and* fiscal approach.[42]

A. Cosmopolitanism

Kosmopolites literally refers to a 'world (*kosmos*) citizen (*polites*)' and was translated by RD Hicks as 'citizen of the world'.[43] This term and the idea it represents, however, need to be contextualized—especially today, when any reference to

in the depth, complexity, or sense of urgency of its questions.' Martti Koskenniemi, 'Introduction' to Hersch Lauterpacht, *The Function of Law in the International Community* (OUP 2011) xxxiv.

[41] Beck, *Cosmopolitan Vision* (n 9).

[42] Reinhard Zimmermann similarly asks the following set of questions about the manner in which Jewish German-speaking scholars approached the law with such unprecedented erudition: 'Was it the striking affinity between two cultures that held reason and knowledge in high esteem? Was it a specific "single-mindedness and relentless moral seriousness", or a highly developed work ethic and a propensity to legal positivism and abstract thinking which both cultures shared? Did the Jews find the philosophical idealism of a Kant congenial, or were they attracted by the writing of Goethe, Schiller and Lessing? Or was that affinity to be explained by the fact that both Jews and Germans, being a people without a nation, shared a basic insecurity and a craving for recognition, a mixture of arrogance and angst?' See Reinhard Zimmermann, 'Was Heimat Hiess, nun heist es Hölle' in Jack Beatson and Reinhard Zimmermann (eds), *Jurists Uprooted: German-Speaking Emigré Lawyers in Twentieth-Century Britain* (OUP 2004) 12–13.

[43] Diogenes Laertius, *Lives of the Eminent Philosophers* (Harvard University Press 2005) 64–65.

cosmopolitanism describes everything and therefore hardly anything, especially as its meaning is branded as obvious.[44] Viewed critically, cosmopolitanism refers to the 'world as a kind of giant supermarket, where place of residence is to be decided by the particular basket of goods (jobs, amenities, climate, etc.) available there'.[45]

But cosmopolitanism—also because it is an identity category that oftentimes assumes voluntarism—is not an ephemeral doctrine.[46] Nor is it a new philosophical viewpoint. The earliest records of the cosmopolitan idea—wrapped by universalistic monotheism—date back to the 13th century BCE. It expanded further together with Hellenistic contributions and biblical literature.[47] During the Alexandrian age, with the foundation of the Stoic school, which did not see the city-state as the only order to be served,[48] the notion of cosmopolitanism was promoted even further to include vocation.[49] The focus for the Stoic cosmopolitans lay in a personal and political commitment to serve justice, which may entail departing from the comfort of patriotism.[50] Although the concept of cosmopolitanism resembles monotheism because it, too, meets the universal, as a 'metaphysical fixed idea', cosmopolitan doctrines advocate a more rational and normative approach for how we as people relate to other people. Arguably, to date, such monotheistic images inform and construct our cosmopolitan approaches. It has certainly loomed

[44] See a more detailed description of this in Timothy Brennan, *At Home in the World* (Harvard University Press 1997).

[45] David Miller, *On Nationality* (Clarendon Press 1995) 14.

[46] This comes very close to David Hollinger's definition of *postethnicity*, which 'prefers voluntary to prescribed affiliations, appreciates multiple identities, pushes for communities of wide scope, recognizes the constructed character of ethno-racial groups, and accepts the formation of new groups as part of the normal life of a democratic society'. See more in David Hollinger, *Postethnic America: Beyond Multiculturalism* (Hachette 2006)

[47] Hugh Harris, 'The Greek Origin of the Idea of Cosmopolitanism' (1927) XXXVIII The International Journal of Ethics 1–10.

[48] For the Stoic cosmopolitans beyond the city-state were concentric circles culminating in humanity as a whole. The first concentric circle 'is drawn around the self; the next takes in one's immediate family; then, in order, one's neighbours or local group, one's fellow city-dwellers, one's fellow countrymen—and we can easily add to this list of groupings based on ethnic, linguistic, historical, professional, gender and sexual identities. Outside all these circles is the largest. One that of humanity as a whole.' Martha Nussbaum, 'Patriotism and Cosmopolitanism' (1994) 19 Boston Review 5.

[49] Harris argues that enlightened Greeks arrived at the cosmopolitan idea through four notions: the poetic (i.e. Homeric tradition of wandering that helped spread a common culture between the different Greek city-states); the scientific (i.e. based on Solon's travels 'through many lands from love of knowledge and a desire to see the world': Anaximander of Miletus shows human solidarity by drawing the first world map); the philosophical (i.e. the synoptic attitude led towards the universal); and the religious (i.e. insufficiency of the particularistic type of religion escalated the need for a universalism, distinguished by Zeus, for example, who was the universal father/king of gods and men).

[50] Essentially this was the mechanism that made Romanization possible, a process that transformed the empire from an imperium, a collection of conquered provinces, into a patria, a focus for the patriotic loyalties of its subjects. With such added twists, Stoic cosmopolitanism grew substantially due to the rise of the Roman Empire. The later Roman Stoics, in contrast, were less strict and extended citizenship to all human beings by virtue of their rationality. Eventually, Romans requested less philosophical honesty so that the cosmopolitan programme drew more people across the empire while local citizenship became more demanding. (See for example AA Long, *The Hellenistic Philosophers, Volume One: Translations of the Principal Sources, with Philosophical Commentary* (DN Sedley tr., Cambridge University Press 1987).

large in the consciousness (which is also often referred to as sensibility, imagination, and/or intuition) of the white European and Christian men who launched the international legal project at the end of the 19th century.[51]

It is neither a coincidence that the birth of modern international law—as a cosmopolitan project—happened when liberal empires formalized *de jure* their *de facto* colonialist projects. Nor is it surprising that the promotion of a professional 'international consciousness' coincided with the peak of Jewish emancipation, especially in Germany.[52] Over time, this 'international consciousness' became embedded in the 'civilized consciousness' mentioned in Article 38 of the Statute of the International Court of Justice. That question is discussed elsewhere;[53] for now, it is enough to keep in mind that the process of professionalizing international law, including around the abstract understanding of 19th-century cosmopolitanism, guaranteed its exclusive, elitist, and Christian nature.

However much the notion of cosmopolitanism changed over the centuries (the Stoic's cosmopolitanism is certainly different to contemporary cosmopolitanism), most versions are less about (a) God *per se* and more about intellectual and factual interpretations of an imagined correlation between some 'We' and the 'Other'. As the word itself suggests, it is about 'political' relationships. Yet there is an aspect of the transcendental: because the category of the Other is essentially ahistorical, the specifics of time and place in its creation can easily be linked to monotheistic religions and/or God.[54] A thorough analysis of how God and/or his religious

[51] The notion of global consciousness goes back, in different forms and shapes, to the first institute of international lawyers, *Institut de Droit International*, which held its first session in Geneva in 1874. Article 1 of the Institute's Statute proclaims that: 'It's [the institute's] purpose to promote the progress of international law by striving to formulate the general principles of the subject, in such a way as to correspond to the legal consciousness of the civilised world.' As Martti Koskenniemi argues, it was then that 11 European men defined themselves as 'the juridical conscience of the civilized world'. Martti Koskenniemi, 'International Law in Europe: Between Tradition and Renewal' (2005) 16(1) European Journal of International Law 113–24. See also Irwin Abrams, 'The Emergence of the International Law Societies' (1957) Review of Politics 19, 361–80. As I argue elsewhere, it was with the development of modernity that a clear need for a *modus operandi* to protect certain achievements of enlightened and liberal ideas from potential instability emerged. We see how social circumstances shaped an elitist group that gradually internalized the need to answer modernity's call with a cosmopolitan mentality or as they termed it, 'international consciousness'. The establishment of associations, conferences, publications, and university chairs creates the formal framework which guarantees the exclusive mentality of international lawyers. For more on the notion of international law as an intuition and as an academic sensibility. See Martti Koskenniemi, *The Gentle Civilizer of Nations* (Cambridge University Press 2001). For more on the success of Jewish protagonists in German-speaking law faculties see Paz, *A Gateway* (n 3).

[52] Mann, *Life and Cases* (n 17) 93.

[53] Article 28 lists among the sources of international law '*the general principles of law recognized by civilized nations*'. See ICJ Statute.

[54] In brief, the critique of religion and God initiated by Baruch Spinoza and continued by Ludwig Feuerbach and Karl Marx unpacks these issues but this exceeds the scope of this chapter. Suffice it here to note that the claim that monotheistic religions are conceptual and egoistic illusions invented by humanity for the sake of self-preservation (an invention that might, as Feuerbach and Marx later argue, turn harmful in its ability to generate alienation) depends on our understanding of ourselves as individuals, a *sine qua non* of the Other and/or God. Ergo, regardless of the differences between monotheistic religions, negotiating human differences remains related to how humanity confronts the 'metaphysical fixed idea' or indeed the otherness of God. Feuerbach, similarly to other 'young Hegelians', directed his critique against 19th century academic philosophy, and hence saw himself as a reformer and even a

conceptualization impacts the 'We' versus 'Other' dichotomy is beyond the aims of this chapter.[55] Here, it is sufficient to note that early Christians, who divided the civil from the holy, added the local ruler/state as an important twist to the philosophy of cosmopolitanism.[56]

There were a few 'cosmopolitan moments' during the Middle Ages.[57] Jews had an important role to play in these moments, serving as the archetypal Other who, according to the Christian majorities, were often at best 'coin clippers and money lenders in league with the Devil'.[58] This relationship was hardly hermetical: European Jews and Christians exchanged religious symbols and images to construct and mirror positive and negative self-images of each other.[59] The constant is that Jews remained central for the formation of modern European national identities. This relationship becomes all the more significant with the renewed interest in cosmopolitanism during the 18th century together with the French Revolution and the rise of Enlightenments in Europe.[60]

A 'Jewish Enlightenment' movement, called the *Haskalah* ('knowledge/wisdom' in Hebrew), was a corresponding cultural and intellectual movement that emerged in Eastern and Central Europe. The *Haskalah* sought to square the circle—to integrate Jews into European society and culture while preserving their Jewish religion and identity. We could say that *Haskalah* was inaugurated when Moses Mendelsohn (1728–1786) entered Berlin as a penniless Jew.

'human' prophet of a new culture that was to take the place of religion and religious belief. It is therefore not surprising that he downplays differences and considers the Christian religion to be 'the Jewish religion purified of national egoism'. See Ludwig Feuerbach, *The Essence of Christianity* (Barnes and Noble 2004 [1841]) 75 (hereafter Feuerbach, *The Essence of Christianity*); see also Kelan Malik, 'Universalism and Difference in Discourses of Race' (2000) 26 Review of International Studies 155–77 (hereafter Malik, 'Universalism and Difference').

55 For more on the importance of God/Monotheism to cosmopolitanism see Paz, *A Gateway* (n 3) 23.

56 As stated in the book of Matthew (22:21): 'Render therefore unto Caesar the things which are Caesar's; and unto God the things that are God's.' Apart for the otherness of God to humanity, and the differences between monotheistic religions, now there is also another division between civil/secular organizations.

57 Some examples of early modernist cosmopolitans include: Erasmus of Rotterdam (1466–1536), who advocated for national and religious tolerance on the basis of his knowledge of ancient Stoic texts, and the 16th-century School of Salamanca cosmopolitan development by theologians and jurists such as Francisco de Vitoria and Francisco Suarez, who advanced theories of natural law and morality drawing primarily from the works of Thomas Aquinas. The School of Salamanca, driven by the rise of Protestant humanism and by the new geographical discoveries, represented the end of medieval juridical doctrine. See James D Tracy, *Erasmus: The Growth of a Mind, Travaux D'humanisme et Renaissance* (1972); Erika Rummel (ed.), The Erasmus Reader (University of Toronto Press 1990); and Paz, 'Religion, Secularism and IL' (n 38).

58 Frank Felsenstein, 'Jews and Devils: Antisemitic Stereotypes of Late Medieval and Renaissance England' (1990) 4(1) Literature and Theology 15, 17.

59 See more in Ivan G Marcus, 'Jews and Christians Imagining the Other in Medieval Europe' (1995) 15(3) Prooftexts 209, 210.

60 Franz Rosenzweig has argued that there are multiple Enlightenments. See Franz Rosenzweig, *The Star of Redemption* (Barbara Galli tr., University of Wisconsin Press 2005) 107. Additionally, David Nirenberg has posited that Jews served as the archetypal Other for European Enlightenment thought (see David Nirenberg, *Anti-Judaism: The Western Tradition* (WW Norton 2013)).

B. Jewish cosmopolitanism

A Jewish cosmopolitan movement emerged during the 18th and early 19th century. Although a detailed exploration of Jewish-German cosmopolitanism is not necessary here,[61] a brief detour in the history of the powerful concept is important for our present purposes. Together with the 'birth' of modern nation-statism—later invigorated by the French Revolution—the *Haskalah* movement and Jewish cosmopolitanism responded to Jewish socio-economic marginalization in Germany shifted its religious-basis, but remained intact. Whereas some Jews embraced extreme German patriotism, with the hope of complete assimilation, enlightened cosmopolitanism remained the more natural path.[62]

In brief, as a movement, the *Haskalah* modernized and secularized Jewish society through a fragile and unofficial *quid pro quo*-based socio-cultural, religious, and economical interaction with Christian men of the Enlightenment.[63] Judaism's history and traditions concurrently boosted a particularistic *and* a universalistic model of being both Jewish *and* cosmopolitan. In more than one-way, Jewish *Maskilim*—Jewish emancipators/enlightened men—wore at least two Enlightenment hats: On the one hand, they remained loyal to Jewish education, while on the other, they integrated more critical thinking and the use of reason in interpreting Jewish texts and tradition, while intermingling with their Christian and German counterparts in forming a more general and universal approach.

One important and relevant consequence of this movement was a specific *Denkstil/Denkkollektiv* made paradigmatic by *Maskilic* Jewish Germans.[64] This *Denkstil/Denkkollektiv* was part and parcel of Jewish-German cosmopolitanism, which was promoted by numerous German-speaking Jewish protagonists, who necessarily played a key role—both nationally and internationally. A Jewish

[61] For more see Cath Gelbin and Sander Gilman, *Cosmopolitanisms and the Jews* (University of Michigan Press 2017).

[62] Patriotic Jewish Germans as exemplified for instance by *Der Verband nationaldeutscher Juden* (an organization that was established during the Weimar Republic in 1921 and later came out in support of Adolf Hitler. For more on Jewish patriotism in different European countries see David Aberbach, *The European Jews, Patriotism and the Liberal State 1789–1933* (Routledge 2013).

[63] Indeed, during the 19th and 20th centuries, the German notions of *Kultur, Bildung, Aufklärung*, and emancipation share common features with both Jewish cosmopolitanism and the *Haskalah/Maskilim* (Jewish version of *Aufklärung/Aufklärer*). For a more thorough take on the development of cosmopolitanism, especially Jewish cosmopolitanism, see Paz, *A Gateway* (n 3) 23.

[64] To define *Denkstil/Denkkollektiv* I draw from Ludwik Fleck's approach, especially because he referred to 'collective homes' of thought styles too. Fleck termed nonempirical elements affecting scientific facts—the subjective fictions of the mind—'thought-style' and 'thought-collective' (*Denkstil/Denkkollektiv*). Accordingly, a *Denkstil* is a collective phenomenon (i.e. each *Denkkollektiv* has its own *Denkstil*) that results from the socialization process of closed communities. These *Denkstile* are not necessarily visible to members of such communities. Moreover, one *Denkstil* does not exclude others. The individual is intertwined in many such *Denkstile* that together create the individuality of the particular. Even if sharing a *Denkstil* implies understanding others in closed communities, it must also mean the misunderstanding of others. This also assures the uniqueness of each member of the *Denkstil* community. (See more in Robert Cohen and others (eds), *Cognition and Fact – Materials on Ludwig Fleck* (Dordrecht Reidel Publishing Company 1986) ix–xxxiii.

cosmopolitan *Denkstil/Denkkollektiv* interlaced with a specific socio-economic development of mainstream culture became very influential. As I argue elsewhere, it may have been the constant dialogue between these cosmopolitanisms—between the *Maskilim* and *Gebildeten* (German Christian Enlighteners)— that promoted the ideological intensification of cosmopolitan ideas for both Jews and non-Jews. Significantly, with the rise of German romanticism, it seems that the cosmopolitan burden was left for the Jews to carry. 'This in turn made cosmopolitanism part and parcel of a Jewish-German "survival strategy" that necessarily turned on a stronger subcultural framework that was inherited by generations of Jewish-Germans.'[65] This is what makes Jewish cosmopolitanism a useful conceptual framework for approaching our study of Mann, because Mann inherited this legacy and it may have been a factor motivating him to approach the legal study of money in the first place as well as informing the way in which he approached it.

C. Jewish-German cosmopolitan protagonist personae

To date, Europe is associated with a certain cosmopolitan construction envisioned by Immanuel Kant,[66] who was Moses Mendelssohn's contemporary and an important disputant.[67] Be that as it may, under the guise of cosmopolitanism as a means of cultural exchange, technologies, and the spread of ideas about reason, tolerance, and universal human values, European cosmopolitanism also enabled European expansion and dominance in international trade. The new 'division of labour' between Caesar and God propounded by early cosmopolitans provided new opportunities for modern promoters of the nation state and its legal order. It is therefore hardly a coincidence that the European nation state grew side-by-side with 'the birth of the liberal creed',[68] colonialism, and the modern antisemitism that culminated with the Holocaust.[69]

Jewish cosmopolitanism, which is dialectically intertwined with the numerous characterizations of the 'Jewish condition', arguably personified a more authentic

[65] Paz, *A Gateway* (n 3) 28.

[66] See for instance David Harvey, *Cosmopolitanism and the Geographies of Freedom* (Columbia University Press 2009) 83.

[67] For more on this debate see more in Paz, *A Gateway* (n 3).

[68] See Karl Polany, *The Great Transformation: The Political and Economic Origins of our Time* (Beacon Press 2001)141–55.

[69] As Eric Gans argues: 'The Holocaust is the ultimate form of the modern anti-Semitism that evolved step by step with European embourgeoisement: the Jews, the archetypal stateless nation, were made the fantastic Subject of the subjectless, transnational marketplace.' (Eric Gans, 'Who are We?' *Chronicles of Love and Resentment No. 265* (20 July 2002) <http://www.anthropoetics.ucla.edu/views/vw265.htm> accessed 23 May 2023. Lassa Oppenheim, in his book *International Law Vol I: Peace* (2nd edn, Longman Greens & Co 1912) § 28, categorizes the Family of Nations into original Christian states of Western Europe, Christian states outside Europe, and non-Christian states like Turkey and Japan, while noting that the status of states such as Persia, Siam, China, Morocco, and Abyssinia remains uncertain due to their level of civilization.

ethnocentricity,[70] and hence dangerously challenged its Christian counterpart. It posed an implicit challenge because the latter remains not much more than an ethnocentric projection of the white, Christian, and masculine self-image of the world. This self-image later shaped, among other things, the modern legal distinction between the private and the public sphere, which is essential to an understanding of law as a modern profession.[71] As I discuss elsewhere, the real and almost infinite success of international law's Christianization is evident today:

> [In the] irreconcilable gap between the 'public', that deals with issues of territory, jurisdiction, regulating wars, and so on, and 'private', that covers matters of property, commercial, and contract law ... In other words, together with the European conquests, the more organic experience of the public/private modes as a distinction that does not necessarily admit a separation axiomatically reconstitutes the public and private as categories that are susceptible to separation in both traditional and modern societies. Granted that the very dichotomy between the public and private is synthetic and as such, socially and historically contingent, its very impact stems from the authoritative way it constructed and still constructs our daily routines.[72]

The cosmopolitan project and its multifaceted accomplishments necessarily impacted and implicated Jewish cosmopolitan approaches differently. The modern cosmopolitan project also required new social, political, and legal theories which gave Jewish cosmopolitans a distinctive way to participate in ongoing conceptual and academic debates. It was also thanks to the particularistic/universalist positionality, however precarious that was, of Jewish German-speaking cosmopolitans that propelled them to shape a nuanced and at times more successful approach to globalism, capitalism, and nationalism, also through law.[73] In more ways than one, the Jews' stereotypical attachment to money/the marketplace on the one hand, and the all too natural assumption of their statelessness, on the other hand, help to explain the shifting of cultural boundaries and of the consequences of 'Otherness' during these social and cultural changes.

It is important to keep this history in mind when examining Mann's legal approach to money especially because it goes over and above the antisemitic medieval

[70] Feuerbach, for instance, categorized Jewish monotheism as resilient ethnocentrism: 'The Jews have maintained their peculiarity to this day. Their principle, their God, is the most practical principle in the world,—namely, egoism; and moreover egoism in the form of religion. Egoism is the God who will not let his servants come to shame. Egoism is essentially monotheistic, for it has only one, only self, as its end. Egoism strengthens cohesion, concentrates man on himself, gives him a consistent principle of life.' (Feuerbach, *The Essence of Christianity* (n 54) 78). For more on Sigmund Freud's understanding of the Jewish condition as a result of their constant state of uprootedness see Paz, *A Gateway* (n 3) 20–23.

[71] Malik, 'Universalism and Difference' (n 54) 155–77.

[72] See more in Paz, 'Religion, Secularism and IL' (n 38) 936.

[73] See more in Paz, *A Gateway* (n 3).

Jewish stereotype, and goes through the works of Marx and Simmel.[74] Arguably, these men's understanding of modern society's money-fetishism is necessarily linked to their Jewish-German cosmopolitanism, which in turn is based on a nuanced intellectual and factual interpretation of an imagined correlation between the private *versus* public and the particular *versus* the universal.

V. German-Jewish Cosmopolitan Tradition and the Theory of Money

In the following section therefore, instead of unpacking if and how Mann's legal work interacts with his Judaism, I show through Marx and Simmel a longer tradition of Jewish-German cosmopolitan challengers and/or enablers of the way money is socially constructed. The argument remains that, regardless of their circumstantial differences, they shared a sense of universality that went over and above both their German and Jewish identities. To stay within the obvious limits of this contribution, I mention several biographical similarities and differences and move to examine how their general approach implicates money.

A. Jewish-German cosmopolitan *Denkstil/Denkkollektiv* between law and money

Whereas Marx also studied law in Berlin (and Bonn), Simmel remained a sociologist and a very close friend and collaborator of Max Weber. All three of Marx, Simmel, and Mann were raised in secular and assimilationist Prussian families (Marx was already born out of the Jewish faith). Arguably, all three drew on money also in order to 'normalize' if not to bring Jews and Judaism to the mainstream on the one hand, while seeking a fiscal and social stability on the other hand. All three were well-educated, were fluent in several languages, and had a deep understanding of European culture, literature, and history. Despite slight generational differences, all three experienced antisemitism and discrimination which also impacted their career prospects, in spite of their clear qualifications. (As Avineri argues compellingly, Marx experienced this vicariously through his father who lost the right to practice law upon the assumption of Prussian rule in the Rhineland.) Simmel's parents also converted before he was born in Berlin. Whereas his father embraced Roman Catholicism, his mother converted into the Lutheran faith before Simmel himself was baptized as a Protestant in his early childhood. Arguably, the fact that Simmel inherited significant money, first from his father and later

[74] See more in Robert Chazan, *Medieval Stereotypes and Modern Antisemitism* (University of California Press 1997).

from his adopting father, brought him closer to both antisemitism and money as research avenues, too.[75] Mann, for his part, claims to have experienced little or no antisemitism in his early years but experienced the Nuremberg Race Laws' passage as a young man about to enter his chosen profession.

Importantly, while all three never felt limited by their ethnic religious affiliation or their early Jewish/German socialization of knowledge, they all shared a commitment to change, even if it was—as in Mann's German conservative case—only to strengthen and enable stability linked to Germany's counterrevolutionary (or failed revolutionary) *Sonderweg*.

Without having to go through Marx's unbelievable *oeuvre*, it serves to note his 1843 essay titled 'On the Jewish Question'. Written when he was 25 years old, this essay answers Bruno Bauer's earlier publication 'The Jewish Question', which argued that removal of *all* religious and social barriers needs to precede the completion of Jewish political emancipation. It is significant to note that Jewish emancipation was still very much an ongoing political project more than a century after Moses Mendelssohn launched the *Haskalah*. Although Marx's criticism of Bauer's text was considered controversial and even antisemitic itself, it remains within the Marxist critique of capitalism because he primarily argued that political emancipation alone was not enough to address the social and economic problems facing the Jews. According to Marx, Bauer's call for political emancipation would only result in the assimilation of Jews into Christian society, rather than their true liberation. In Marx's words:

> The Jew emancipated himself in a Jewish way not only by acquiring financial power but also because through him and apart from him money has become a world power and the practical Jewish spirit has become the practical spirit of the Christian people. The Jews have emancipated themselves in so far as the Christians have become Jews.[76]

Incidentally, *pace* Marx the Jews played a major role in the construction, strengthening, and/or the universalization of the European middle class, a new modern phenomenon. Indeed, as Yuri Slezkine phrases it: 'the statistical connection between "the Jewish question" and the hope for a new species of mankind seems fairly strong.'[77] As I argue elsewhere: 'This is ultimately exemplified by the force of

[75] Lewis A Coser, 'Georg Simmel: Biographic Information' in *Masters of Sociological Thought: Ideas in Historical and Social Context* (2nd edn, Harcourt Brace Jovanovich 1977) <https://socio.ch/sim/bio.htm> 6 June 2023.

[76] Karl Marx, 'On the Jewish Question' in Early Writings (Alfred A. Knopf 1980) 236, 237, 241.

[77] Slezkine mentions the following:

> Some of the most important theorists of German Social Democracy were Jews (Ferdinand Lassalle, Eduard Bernstein, Hugo Haase, Otto Landsberg), as were virtually all 'Austro-Marxists' with the exception of Karl Renner (Rudolf Hilferding, Otto Bauer, Max Adler, Gustav Eckstein, Friedrich Adler). Socialists of Jewish descent—among them the creator

Marxism and Freudianism, largely Jewish in their origins, as cosmopolitan, universal and most importantly competitive "religions" to the mainstream "cosmopolitan nationalism".[78]

But such reading needs to be complimented with Marx's more nuanced understanding of Jews—one that is often misread as antisemitic, if only because he callously repeats Bauer's claims against Jews that go beyond their incidental and unfortunate role in the failures of liberal politics.[79] Instead, for Marx it is all about real emancipation, that is to say, freedom of and for the Jews means complete emancipation from all gods, religious gods or otherwise. In this as in other writings, a society's treatment of its Jews is indicative of its stage of political development:[80] And the clingiest of all gods remains: Money. 'What is the profane basis of Judaism? *Practical* need, *self-interest*. ... Money is the jealous god of Israel.'[81] The Jew therefore becomes a symbol for Marx who speaks of the growing power of money over politics by pushing Jewish symbolism to its cynical limits: society as a whole is now 'Jewish'.[82]

Unlike Bauer, who follows the Hegelian idea of the state as the highest political sphere of universality, Marx sees clearly the state's failure, especially because it preserves religion, but also property, as private duties. Here, Marx even seems to warn the Jews from buying into the political emancipation argument and urges them to stay Jews until the dawn of true human emancipation. And it is in his brief

> of the Weimar constitution, Hugo Preuss, and the prime ministers of Bavaria (Kurt Eisner, 1918–19), Prussia (Paul Hirsch, 1918–19), and Saxony (Georg Gradnauer, 1919–21)—were well represented in various governments established in Germany in the wake of the imperial defeat in World War I. The same was true of the Communist uprisings of 1919: Spartacist leaders in Berlin included Rosa Luxemburg, Leo Jogisches, and Paul Levi; the Bavarian 'Soviet republic' was headed (after April 13) by Eugen Leviné and at least seven other Jewish Commissars ... ; and Béla Kun's revolutionary regime in Hungary consisted almost entirely of young Jews. ... Probably the most influential (in the long run) left-wing intellectuals in Weimar Germany belonged to the so-called Frankfurt School, all of whose principal members (Theodor W. Adorno, Walter Benjamin, Erich Fromm, Max Horkheimer, Leo Löwenthal, and Herbert Marcuse, among others) came from middle-class Jewish homes. In Hungary, first—or second—generation Magyars of Jewish descent were overrepresented not only among socialist intellectuals but also among communist militants. In Poland, 'ethnic' Jews composed the majority of the original Communist leadership. ... In the United States in the same period, Jews (most of them immigrants from Eastern Europe) accounted for about 40 to 50 percent of the Communist Party membership and at least a comparable proportion of the Party's leaders, journalists, theorists, and organizers.

(Yuri Slezkine, *The Jewish Century* (Princeton University Press 2004) 85–86.)

[78] Paz, *A Gateway* (n 3) 27–28.

[79] Here I have in mind Marx's quoting of Bauer's claim: 'The Jew, by his very nature, cannot be emancipated ... since he opposes his illusory nationality to actual nationality, his illusory law to actual law.' (Karl Marx, 'On the Jewish Question' in Robert C Tucker (ed.), *The Marx-Engels Reader* (2nd edn, WW Norton and Co. 1978) 27.

[80] Avineri, *Karl Marx* (n 5) 53, citing Marx's essays 'On the Jewish Question' in his 1845 *Die heilige Familie*: 'The states which cannot yet emancipate the Jews politically have to be judged against the fully-developed political states—and be found wanting.'

[81] ibid 48.

[82] See more in Dennis Fischman, 'The Jewish Question about Marx' (1989) 21(4) Polity 755.

definition of human emancipation, when social and political powers become one and the same,[83] that we can see a nuanced Jewish cosmopolitanism—if only because it challenges the normative assumption behind the Christian division between private and public statism.

While recognizing that Marx's essay is problematic viewed in light of modern European history, Avineri likewise stresses a contextual reading. This includes (i) Marx's even harsher indictment of Christianity in the same essay, (ii) the possible use of the concept of *Judentum* as a kind of code or heuristic for behaviours such as 'huckstering' typically associated with Jews, and (iii) his likely borrowing from Moses Hess's essay 'On Money' in which the connection between Jews and money was examined from a critical but very Jewish perspective.[84] Most importantly, however, Avineri points to Marx's other writings on the same question (and *contra* Bauer), which are decidedly more sympathetic to Jews (and even, incidentally, to *Judaism* as a religion).[85] On the whole, Marx demands a subtle reading on this point. One cannot square the circle between Marx's rebuttal of Bauer and his own hyperbolic attack on '*Judentum*'; Avineri speculates that it could hint at a desire to avoid being accused of sympathy for the Jews owing to Marx's own family background, or a kind of defensive reflex to avoid guilt by association. In any case, it may well be the expression of a double burden:

> [T]hat of his Jewish background as well as that of his family's conversion to Christianity, which lacked any spiritual or religious conviction but was ultimately motivated by purely professional if not pecuniary considerations [i.e. because Marx's father lost the right to practice law after the assumption of Prussian rule in the Rhineland]. We do not know, but it would be wrong to divorce the complexity of Marx's arguments in his essay from his own family history, despite the fact that it was never acknowledged publicly.[86]

Georg Simmel's approach to money also attempted to rehabilitate the figure of the Jew from negative money-related stereotypes. For Simmel (in contrast to Marx), money was more than just a means of circulation/exchange.[87] For Simmel,

[83] 'Human emancipation will only be complete when the real individual man has absorbed into himself the abstract citizen; when as an individual man, in his everyday life, in his work, and in his relationships, he has become a *species-being*; and when he has recognized and organized his own powers (*foces propres*) as social powers so that he no longer separates this social power from himself as *political* power.' (ibid.)

[84] Avineri, *Karl Marx* (n 5) 46–47.

[85] ibid 50–53. For example, countering calls that Jews in France should respect the Sunday sabbath with a rhetorical question why Jews, as equal French citizens, should not have *their* sabbath recognized equally.

[86] ibid 49.

[87] As Marx writes in his *Capital*: 'It is not money that renders commodities commensurable. Just the contrary. It is all because all commodities as values are realized human labour and therefore commensurable, that their values can be measured by one and the same special commodity, and the latter can be converted into the common measure of their values, i.e. money. Money as a measure of value, is the

money was a means to understand the essence of modernity: 'an example for the presentation of relations that exist between the most superficial, "realistic" and fortuitous phenomena and the most idealized powers of existence, the most profound currents of individual life and history.'[88] As Amos Morris-Reich argues: Simmel chose money because he 'was well aware that money was considered the basest of all things (and not only in his time), but also that in the Christian, Western world Jews and money were closely associated'.[89] Money is the stable point of triviality: it represents the general contingency of worth, but in fact establishes it by connecting widely diverse objects into a single economic life.[90] But Simmel did not wish to only say something about Jews, modernity, and the negative reputation attached to Jews because of money. Rather, Simmel chose to rehabilitate the Jewish stereotype in a 'unique way'.[91]

In brief and general terms, Simmel sought to transform the negative characteristics of money into a positive epitome of modernity. As Morris-Reich argues, this is sufficient to 'enable sensitive readers to conclude that Simmel rehabilitates those who make their living from money'.[92] Importantly, although the Jew is the ultimate Other/stranger oriented towards money and merchantry, he remains, to Simmel, as permanent a resident as any other members of society, not a nomadic stranger. Here 'Simmel's insistence on the *permanence of the stranger* aims at confronting another aspect of the stereotype of the Jew—the medieval Christian myth of the wandering Jew'.[93] Simmel's insistence on the permanency of the stranger proves his commitment to modernity and Jews.

Evidently, both Marx and Simmel, in spite of their clear disciplinary divergences, draw on money and its vicinity to the 'Jewish question' in order to salvage a clearer and more secure approach to both money and the Jews. What can be said in this regard of Mann?[94] First, in contrast to Marx and Simmel, Mann does not expressly mention Jews in his treatise on money. This should be unsurprising, as

phenomenal form that must of necessity be assumed by that measure of value which is immanent in commodities, labour time.' (Karl Marx, *Capital: A Critical Analysis of Capitalist Production* (Random House 1936) 106.)

[88] Georg Simmel, *The Philosophy of Money* ([1900] 2004) 55 (hereafter Simmel, *The Philosophy of Money*).

[89] As a tangible item, money is the most ephemeral thing in the external-practical world; yet in its content it is the most stable, since it stands at the point of indifference and balance between all other phenomena in the world. Morris-Reich, 'The Beautiful Jew is a Moneylender' (n 10) 128.

[90] Money is nothing but the vehicle for a movement in which everything else that is not in motion is completely extinguished. It is, as it were, an *actus purus*; it lives in continuous self-alienation from any given point and thus forms the counterpart and direct negation of all being in itself (Simmel, *The Philosophy of Money* (n 88) 510–11).

[91] ibid.

[92] Morris-Reich, 'The Beautiful Jew is a Moneylender' (n 10) 133.

[93] ibid. Emphasis added.

[94] On the relationship between Simmel and Mann see further Chapter 10 in this volume by Joseph Sommer, 'FA Mann's Conservative Revolution'.

it was written and presented as a book on the *law* of money, within a fairly conservative view of what such a book must look like.[95] While it cannot be conclusively stated that Mann's work on the law of money was motivated by a desire to make the subject more respectable or to improve the reputation of those associated with it, it is possible that such factors played a role in his scholarly pursuits.[96]

Like Marx and Simmel, Mann considers money in its abstract and international perspective. He appears to use a conservative legal approach as an effective veil: it is just money, law, and the state. 'There is, accordingly, no room in a book on the law of money for a discussion of such problems as bank accounts, deposits ... or negotiable instruments.'[97] Money is 'all chattels which, issued by the authority of the law and denominated with reference to a unit of account, are meant to serve as universal means of exchange in the State of issue'.[98] As Sommer explains, 'Mann's argument seemed to be mostly from tradition, not necessity ... [He] demanded chattel money. Bank money would not do ... [his] definition did not require legal tender: just state authority.'[99] Significantly, and with complete disregard to the shifts between what 'civilized' and 'uncivilized' may mean in his own personal context, Mann constructed this apparatus on the international legal differentiation between civilized and primitive countries.[100] Linking this together with the important blind spot of 'the juridical consciousness of the civilized world', embraced by modern, white Christian and European international lawyers, proves Mann's own oversight and conservative approach, albeit with possible inconsistencies.[101]

Mann remains in the Jewish cosmopolitan tradition, even if his methodology is more traditionalist than that of Marx and Simmel, who had an unprecedented influence on socialist-left and cosmopolitan scholarship. As Sommer argues, revolutionary conservatism in Mann's approach demystifies gold and replaces it with

[95] See further Chapter 3 in this volume by Christoph König, 'Pragmatism Meets *Praxisorientierung*: FA Mann and a Transnational Biography in Law'.

[96] Collins notes that Mann's interest in money law may have been influenced by personal factors, including his family connection to banking and his experience with the German inflation of 1923, which made a deep impression on him. Lawrence Collins, 'F.A. Mann (1907–1991)' in Jack Beatson and Rheinhard Zimmermann (eds), *Jurists Uprooted. German-Speaking Émigré Lawyers in Twentieth-Century Britain* (OUP 2004) 398–99.

[97] FA Mann, *Legal Aspect of Money* (5th edn, Clarendon Press 1992) 271–310. This language was missing in the first edition.

[98] ibid. The words 'in the State of issue' were missing from the first edition. See FA Mann, *Legal Aspect of Money* (Clarendon Press 1938).

[99] FA Mann, *Legal Aspect of Money* (5th edn, Clarendon Press 1992) 42–43.

[100] 'Although at times money was not expressed by any corporeal symbols but was represented by accounts with a bank, which, for the purpose of effecting payments, were credited or debited (bank money), yet from primitive periods until the present day men have been accustomed to connect the idea of money with definite symbols, whether these were animals, commodities, quantities of metal, or coins and bank notes, as we today find them in all civilized countries. Money is a chattel personal.' (ibid 8.)

[101] Here one should nevertheless mention Mann's wife, Eleonore (née Ehrlich), who was one of the first women to finish a doctorate in law at the Friedrich-Wilhelm University, Berlin. Eleonore was an outspoken and committed socialist. For more on Lore Ehrlich Mann see Mann, *Life and Cases* (n 17) 93–98.

state sovereignty by law. In other words, since the value of money for Mann has no external standard by which to measure it, it can only be measured by reference to law, or nominalism, as he calls it.

To be sure, Mann sees the state as being able to introduce a currency as money not in its role as legislator but due to the fact that the state has enormous legitimating and transactional power and can thereby determine money.[102] Here, too, it is evident that Mann ascribes a superior role to the state, even as he limits it in its power as a legislator. The impression is that Mann, on the one hand, takes a conservative approach to monetary theory, which can be attributed to his German upbringing, and, on the other hand, relativizes this conservative approach by ascribing less influence to the legislature, which again can be attributed to his Jewish cosmopolitan upbringing.

Apart from that, Mann changed as little as possible: 'Mann's approach was conservative even by the standards of his time. And now he is showing his age. Mann's god of legal tender is losing its believers.'[103] In short, even though his legal approach begins with the state—which precedes the international (international relations, law, and economics) because, in his view, the state secures more protections and guarantees for both the individual and the international community—it is a certain universality that links law, politics, and economics that he seeks to capture and secure. Although Mann was shaped by his conservative German upbringing, it can be seen in some parts of his work that Jewish cosmopolitanism was a major influence on his work and his views.

VI. Conclusion

Mann's contribution to money and law paved 'an unworked field', especially in England, his new home. Although it cannot be said with certainty whether his approach to money law was truly new, his work was nonetheless more influential than any other work in the same field.

Without obtaining a permanent academic appointment, his work was nevertheless helpful to, cited by, and resorted to by jurists and politicians alike. This contribution shows the extent to which his *Weltanschauung*, encapsulating Jewish cosmopolitanism with conservative German legalism, had a lasting affect and thus continues to have a non-Christian influence on our understanding of international law and money today.

Whatever reservations one may have against relying on identity politics as an instructive methodology, it is impossible to eradicate the importance of Mann's Jewish heritage, which, as this chapter unpacks, combines his liberal upbringing

[102] See further Chapter 10 in this volume by Joseph Sommer, 'FA Mann's Conservative Revolution'.
[103] See further Chapter 10 in this volume by Joseph Sommer, 'FA Mann's Conservative Revolution'.

to produce a deep attachment to the Jewish cosmopolitan *Denkstil/Denkkollektiv* that can be seen through his legal approach. Moreover, his early encounter with the devaluation of money during the inflationary period left an indelible impression on his life. Arguably, it was this personal experience made him appear as a 'conservative revolutionary'. Whereas the conservative part stems from the German legal education that propelled his bottom (state)-up (international realm) perspective, the revolutionary part can be seen to describe his commitment to the liberal, cosmopolitan, and international apparatus from the beginning.

Contextualizing Mann's intellectual foundations within Jewish cosmopolitanism is helpful in clarifying why he eventually turned to the fields of money and law. In this contribution I attempt to make it plausible to argue that although Marx and Simmel were more cosmopolitan, left-leaning, and radical in their approach to money, Mann's intellectual motivations and goals overlapped with theirs. This can, at least in part, be explained by their shared Jewish-German backgrounds and experiences with Jewish cosmopolitanism and antisemitism. While Marx and Simmel explicitly refer to Judaism in their works, Mann's conservative approach is evident from the fact that he does not directly address the Jewish aspect in his remarks on questions of law and money. Nevertheless, it can be surmised that he, too, harboured a desire to cultivate a more dignified and appreciative perception of the subject. A notable commonality shared by all three is their inherent dependence on financial resources to realize their aspirations and achieve social stability, even though they were prevented from doing so by recurring obstacles due to antisemitic prejudices prevalent in their respective societies. Although Mann's work focused more on the state apparatus, his quest to emphasize his universal approach to money across national boundaries highlights the interconnectedness of business and society.

In sum, Mann's deep exploration of the intricate interplay of Jewish cosmopolitanism, money, and law has produced a compelling discourse that transcends his personal experiences. The confluence of his Jewish heritage and his liberal education, which brought him to the Jewish cosmopolitan style of thinking, gave his scholarly endeavours a distinctive impetus. These multilayered and diverse influences suggest that Mann's approach was precisely that money and law were universally connected, even if he never explicitly mentioned this in his conservative manner.

Bibliography

Aberbach D, *The European Jews, Patriotism and the Liberal State 1789–1933* (Routledge 2013)

Abrams I, 'The Emergence of the International Law Societies' (1957) 19 Review of Politics 361

Arendt H, 'Nation State and Democracy' in J Kohn (ed.), *Thinking Without A Banister: Essays in Understanding, 1953–1975* (Schocken Books 2018)

Avineri S, *Karl Marx: Philosophy and Revolution* (Yale University Press 2019)
Beck U, *Cosmopolitan Vision* (Polity Press 2006)
Berger PL and Luckmann T, *The Social Construction of Reality: A Treatise in the Sociology of Knowledge* (Doubleday & Company Inc. 1967)
Bourdieu P, 'The Force of Law: Towards a Sociology of Juridical Field' (1987) 38 Hastings LJ 814
Chazan R, *Medieval Stereotypes and Modern Antisemitism* (University of California Press 1997)
Cohen R and others (eds), *Cognition and Fact – Materials on Ludwig Fleck* (Dordrecht Reidel Publishing Company 1986)
Collins L, 'F.A. Mann (1907–1991)' in Jack Beatson and Reinhard Zimmermann (eds), *Jurists Uprooted. German-Speaking Émigré Lawyers in Twentieth-Century Britain* (OUP 2004)
Coser LA, 'Georg Simmel: Biographic Information' in *Masters of Sociological Thought: Ideas in Historical and Social Context* (2nd edn, Harcourt Brace Jovanovich 1977) available at <https://socio.ch/sim/bio.htm> accessed 7 June 2023.
Desan S, 'Foreigners, Cosmopolitanism, and French Revolutionary Universalism' in S Desan and others (eds), *The French Revolution in Global Perspective* (Cornell University Press 2013)
Felsenstein F, 'Jews and Devils: Antisemitic Stereotypes of Late Medieval and Renaissance England' (1990) 4(1) Literature and Theology 15
Feuerbach L, *The Essence of Christianity* (Barnes and Noble 2004 [1841])
Fischman D, 'The Jewish Question about Marx' (1989) 21(4) Polity 755
Gans E, 'Who are We?' *Chronicles of Love and Resentment No. 265* (20 July 2002) <http://www.anthropoetics.ucla.edu/views/vw265.htm> accessed 23 May 2023
Gelbin C and Gilman S, *Cosmopolitanisms and the Jews* (University of Michigan Press 2017)
Gentry B, 'Political Identity: Meaning, Measures, and Evidence' in *Why Youth Vote* (Springer 2018)
Harris JF, 'Rethinking the Categories of the German Revolution of 1848: The Emergence of Popular Conservatism in Bavaria' (1992) 25(2) Central European History 123
Harris H, 'The Greek Origin of the Idea of Cosmopolitanism' (1927) XXXVIII The International Journal of Ethics 1
Harvey D, *Cosmopolitanism and the Geographies of Freedom* (Columbia University Press 2009)
Hollinger D, *Postethnic America: Beyond Multiculturalism* (Hachette 2006)
Ikejiak BV, 'International Law is Western Made Global Law: The Perception of Third-World Category' (2014) 6(2–3) African Journal of Legal Studies 337
Korhonen O, *International Law Situated; An Analysis of the Lawyers Stance Towards Culture, History and Community* (Kluwer Law International 2000)
Koskenniemi M, *The Gentle Civilizer of Nations* (Cambridge University Press 2001)
Koskenniemi M, *From Apology to Utopia. The Structure of International Legal Argument, Reissue with New Epilogue* (Cambridge University Press 2005)
Koskenniemi M, 'International Law in Europe: Between Tradition and Renewal' (2005) 16(1) European Journal of International Law 113
Koskenniemi M, 'Introduction' in Hersch Lauterpacht, *The Function of Law in the International Community* (OUP 2011)
Koskenniemi M, 'Between Empire and Legal Formalism', Speech in Recife, Brazil (on file with author)
Lacey N, *A Life of HLA Hart: The Nightmare and the Noble Dream* (OUP 2006)
Laertius D, *Lives of the Eminent Philosophers* (Harvard University Press 2005)

Lewis G, *FA Mann: A Memoir* (Hart Publishing 2013)
Long AA, *The Hellenistic Philosophers, Volume One: Translations of the Principal Sources, with Philosophical Commentary* (DN Sedley tr., Cambridge University Press 1987)
Malik K, 'Universalism and Difference in Discourses of Race' (2000) 26 Review of International Studies 155
Mann FA, *Legal Aspect of Money* (Clarendon Press 1938)
Mann FA, *Legal Aspect of Money* (5th edn, Clarendon Press 1992)
Mann FA, *Life and Cases: Manuscript of an Autobiography* (Wolfgang Ernst ed., Unipress 2021)
Marcus IG, 'Jews and Christians Imagining the Other in Medieval Europe' (1995) 15(3) Prooftexts 209
Marx K, *Capital: A Critical Analysis of Capitalist Production* (Random House 1936)
Marx K, 'On the Jewish Question' in Robert C Tucker (ed.), *The Marx-Engels Reader* (2nd edn, WW Norton and Co. 1978)
Marx K, 'On the Jewish Question' in *Early Writings* (Alfred A. Knopf 1980)
Merrills JG, 'Oppenheimer v. Cattermole—The Curtain Falls' (1975) 24(4) The International and Comparative Law Quarterly 619
Miéville C, *Between Equal Rights: A Marxist Theory of International Law* (Brill 2005)
Miller, David, *On Nationality* (Clarendon Press 1995)
Nirenberg D, *Anti-Judaism: The Western Tradition* (WW Norton 2013)
Nussbaum M, 'Patriotism and Cosmopolitanism' (1994) 19 Boston Review 5
Oppenheim L, *International Law Vol I: Peace* (2nd edn, Longman Greens & Co 1912)
Paz RY, 'Review Essay – Erich K. *Before the Law: Reflections on Degenhardt's Study of Erich Kaufmann*' (2010) 11 German Law Journal 439
Paz RY, *A Gateway Between a Distant God and a Cruel World: The Contribution of Jewish German Scholars to International Law* (Brill 2012)
Paz RY, 'Making it Whole: Hersch Lauterpacht and the Rabbinical Approach to International Law' (2012) 2 Gottingen Journal of International Law 417
Paz RY, 'A Forgotten Kelsenian? The Story of Helen Silving-Ryu (1906–1993)' (2014) 25 The European Journal of International Law 4
Paz RY, 'Kelsen's *Pure Theory of Law* as "a Hole in Time"' / '*La Théorie pure du droit* de Hans Kelsen comme "un trou dans le temps"' (2015) 1(7) Monde(s) 75
Paz RY, 'Religion, Secularism and International Law' in Anne Orford and Florian Hofmann (eds), *Oxford Handbook of International Legal Theory* (OUP 2016)
Paz RY, 'From Rosa Luxemburg to Hersch Lauterpacht: An *Ostjüdische* Heritage in International Law?' in Alberto Puppo and Dawid Bunikowski (eds), *On a Critical Philosophy of Law, Peace and Religion* (Springer 2019)
Paz RY, 'Legalizing Antisemitism? The Legacy of Savigny's Roman (Tic) Law' in Pamela Slotte and JD Haskell (eds), *Christianity and International Law* (Cambridge University Press 2021)
Polany K, *The Great Transformation: The Political and Economic Origins of our Time* (Beacon Press 2001)
Rosenzweig F, *The Star of Redemption* (Barbara Galli tr., University of Wisconsin Press 2005)
Rummel E (ed.), *The Erasmus Reader* (University of Toronto Press 1990)
Silbey S, 'After Legal Consciousness' (2005) 1 Annual Review of Law and Social Science 323
Simmel G, 'The Beautiful Jew is a Moneylender: Money and Individuality in Simmel's Rehabilitation of the "Jew"' (2003) 20(4) Theory, Culture & Society 127

Simmel G, *The Philosophy of Money* (Routledge [1900], 2004)
Slezkine Y, *The Jewish Century* (Princeton University Press 2004)
Tracy JD, *Erasmus: The Growth of a Mind, Travaux D'humanisme et Renaissance* (Librairie Droz 1972)
Zimmermann R, 'Was Heimat Hiess, nun heist es Hölle' in Jack Beatson and Reinhard Zimmermann (eds), *Jurists Uprooted: German-Speaking Emigré Lawyers in Twentieth-Century Britain* (OUP 2004)

PART II

'A WEALTH OF LEGAL KNOWLEDGE'

The International Lawyer

5

The Influence of FA Mann on English Case Law

The Validity of Acts of State Contrary to Human Rights and International Law and the Enforcement of Foreign Public Law

Lawrence Collins

I. Introduction

This contribution is intended to highlight two areas of law in which Francis Mann's writing had an important effect on the decisions of English courts (and also of the High Court of Australia), and, in at least one case, a decisive effect.[1] The two areas are (1) the application of the act of state doctrine to acts of state[2] which are contrary

[1] This piece draws on Lawrence Collins, 'Dr F.A. Mann: His Work and Influence' (1993) 64 BYIL 55 and Lawrence Collins, 'F.A. Mann (1907–1991) in Jack Beatson and Reinhard Zimmerman (eds), *Jurists Uprooted* (OUP 2004).

[2] There has also been extensive discussion of, and use of, Mann's work on 'acts of state', i.e. issues concerning recognition of governments and states, and the conclusiveness of executive statements, which are outside the scope of this paper: see *Emin v Yeldag* [2002] 1 FLR 956; *M v NA (Declaration of Marital Status: Unrecognised State)* [2020] EWHC 93 (Fam), [2020] 1 FLR 967; *High Commissioner for Pakistan in the United Kingdom v Prince Muffakham Jah* [2019] EWHC 2551 (Ch), [2020] Ch 421; and especially *Maduro Board of the Central Bank of Venezuela v Guaido Board of the Central Bank of Venezuela* [2021] UKSC 57, [2023] AC 156, *per* Lord Lloyd-Jones, at [91], [112]. See especially FA Mann, *Foreign Affairs in English Courts* (OUP 1986) ch. 2.

Lawrence Collins, *The Influence of FA Mann on English Case Law* In: *FA Mann*. Edited by: Jason Grant Allen and Gerhard Dannemann, Oxford University Press. © Lawrence Collins 2024. DOI: 10.1093/oso/9780198881452.003.0006

to fundamental principles of human rights or to international law; and (2) the limits of the principle that a court will not enforce foreign public law.[3]

II. Acts of State

A. *Oppenheimer v Cattermole*

It is appropriate to begin by a wholly remarkable and dramatic example of Francis Mann's influence on the case law. The extraordinary case of *Oppenheimer v Cattermole*[4] concerned the question of whether a taxpayer, who was born in Germany in 1896 and, therefore, a German national by birth, was entitled to exemption from United Kingdom tax in respect of pensions paid to him by the German government for the years 1953 to 1968. Under the Double Taxation Conventions the pensions were exempt from United Kingdom income tax if during the relevant years the taxpayer was a 'national' both of the United Kingdom and of Germany, and they were not exempt if he was a national of the United Kingdom only. Consequently, the taxpayer was concerned to establish that he retained his German nationality. It is notorious that Nazi decrees deprived Jews living abroad of their German nationality and of their property, and the case appeared to raise the question whether the English courts would recognize these disgraceful laws, and indeed whether they were to be regarded as 'laws' at all.

The taxpayer's argument involved the curious position that for certain purposes the Nazi nationality law was entitled to recognition in England. The taxpayer was a Jew; he was born in Germany in 1896 and was for many years a teacher at a Jewish orphanage in Bavaria. In 1939, after a period of detention in the Dachau concentration camp, he came to live in England, where he remained during the war.

The German Nationality Act of 1913 provided that a German who had neither his habitual residence nor his permanent abode in Germany lost his nationality when he acquired a foreign nationality. By a Nazi decree of 1941 a Jew lost his German citizenship if he lived abroad, and the decree also provided for confiscation of the property of Jews thus deprived of their nationality and for the use of that property 'to further aims connected with the solution of the Jewish problem'.[5]

After the war Mr Oppenheimer became, in 1948, a British subject by naturalization. In May 1949, on the founding of the Federal Republic of Germany, the Basic Law was enacted which provided that former German citizens who had been

[3] See also his contribution to the debate on the meaning of 'any civil or commercial matter' in relation to *Re State of Norway's Application (No 1)* [1990] 1 AC 723: (1986) 102 LQR 346 and (1989) 105 LQR 341 in FA Mann, *Notes and Comments on Cases in International Law, Commercial Law, and Arbitration* (OUP 1992) 140 and 253 (hereafter Mann, *Notes and Comments*).

[4] [1974] Ch 585, revd [1973] Ch 264 (CA), affd on different grounds [1976] AC 249.

[5] §§ 1, 3 Elfte Verordnung zum Reichsbürgergesetz, 25.11.1941, RGBl 1941, 722.

deprived of their German nationality during the period 1933 to 1945 were to be 're-naturalized' on application and were to be considered as not having been deprived of their nationality if they took up residence in Germany after 8 May 1945 and did not express any wish to the contrary. But Mr Oppenheimer remained resident in the United Kingdom.

The uncontested evidence of Dr EJ Cohn, for the Inland Revenue, before the Special Commissioners was that a decision of the German Federal Constitutional Court in 1968 had declared that the 1941 decree was void *ab initio* (but without retrospective effect), and that the 1913 Act was unaffected by the decision; and consequently the taxpayer, if he had not lost German nationality in 1941, had lost it in 1948, as a consequence of the 1913 Act, when he became a naturalized British subject. The taxpayer's argument was that under German law he lost his nationality in 1941; and, consequently, he was not a German national in 1948 and the 1913 Act had no effect on him. Nonetheless, it would be contrary to public policy (on a variety of grounds) to recognize the 1941 decree, and consequently he should be treated as a German national. The Special Commissioners decided that the taxpayer ceased to be a German national not later than the date in 1948 when he became a British subject, and was not therefore entitled to relief from income tax under the double taxation relief provision.

At first instance, on appeal from the Special Commissioners, Goulding J recognized that the decree was made on racial grounds, but held that:

> the English courts cannot properly or efficaciously undertake the censorship on grounds of humanity or morality of foreign legislation dealing with nationality. Nationality is a fundamental and intimate matter in the constitution of any state, and one essentially under its own exclusive jurisdiction.[6]

Accordingly, he declined to disregard the 1941 decree on the sole ground that it was penal or confiscatory. But he was prepared to disregard it on the basis of the principle of non-recognition of laws altering the nationality of enemy aliens in wartime.[7] Goulding J then concluded (in reasoning which is very hard to follow) that Mr Oppenheimer was entitled to assert his German nationality, on the basis that it was not open to the Crown to say he lost it by German law in 1948, because he had lost it long before (i.e. in 1941) under a law upon which the Crown could not rely.

In the Court of Appeal Mr Oppenheimer's case was heard with the similar case of Miss Nothman.[8] The appeal was allowed, but for somewhat different reasons.

[6] [1972] Ch at 592–93.

[7] *R v Home Secretary, ex parte L* [1945] 1 KB 7; *Lowenthal v Attorney-General* [1948] 1 All ER 295.

[8] Who appeared in person in this and other cases. She came to England in 1939 and had a career as a teacher. She was 'a woman of intellect': *Nothman v Barnet London Borough Council* [1978] 1 WLR 220, 226, *per* Lord Denning MR (affd [1979] 1 WLR 67 (HL)). See also *Nothman v Hartigan* [1980] 10 WLUK 247.

Buckley and Orr LJJ were prepared to recognize the 1941 decree. In the words of Buckley LJ:[9]

> The law may be as oppressive as can be; nevertheless within the country whose domestic law it is, it is effective to deprive the person concerned of whatever that law affects—in this case, citizenship. The question being whether by the domestic law of that country the person is or is not a citizen of the country, it is of no avail to say that the law is one which the courts of this country should not recognise: that does not alter the fact that the answer to the question whether or not the person is a national or citizen of the country must be answered in the light of the law of that country however inequitable, oppressive or objectionable it may be.

Orr LJ agreed with Buckley LJ that the 1941 decree should be recognized 'however offensive its character'.[10] Lord Denning MR held that the 1941 decree was not entitled to recognition: 'Not only was it an objectionable and atrocious law', but also (agreeing with Goulding J) English law would not recognize an enemy decree which deprived its citizens of enemy nationality in time of war. But he considered that the taxpayers were not to be regarded as German nationals, since they had become British subjects by naturalization at a time when a state of war still existed between the United Kingdom and Germany. By applying for nationality in the United Kingdom in 1948, Mr Oppenheimer had renounced his German nationality, and by taking the oath of allegiance in the United Kingdom he had accepted the repudiation of the protection of German nationality which had been effected by the 1941 decree.

In the Court of Appeal the majority therefore considered that recognition of the 1941 decree was decisive. In late March 1973 the House of Lords heard an appeal from the decision of the Court of Appeal. In the April 1973 issue of the Law Quarterly Review, Mann published an article entitled 'The Present Validity of Nazi Nationality Laws', in which he suggested that by German law the taxpayer had undoubtedly lost his German nationality not later than the date of his naturalization in 1948 because of the German Act of 1913. But he also drew attention to the potential relevance of the Basic Law of 1949 and the decisions of the Federal Supreme Court and Constitutional Court. He said:[11]

> When the Federal Republic came into existence in 1949 it did not enact any further legislation on the subject except that its Constitution included the important Art. 116(2):

9 [1973] Ch at 273.
10 ibid para 274.
11 (1973) 89 LQR at 198–200.

> Former German citizens who, between 30 January 1933 and 8 May 1945, were deprived of their citizenship on political, racial or religious grounds, and their descendants, shall be regranted German citizenship on application. They shall be considered as not having been deprived of their German citizenship if they have established their domicile [*Wohnsitz*] in Germany after 8 May 1945 and have not expressed a contrary intention.

The first of these sentences enabled persons such as Mr Oppenheimer to obtain German nationality by a simple application (a fact which is bound to render his claim against the Inland Revenue even less attractive). From this it was concluded for a long time and by many that Art. 116(2) [of the German Constitution] had impliedly recognized the effectiveness of the 1941 decree. But such an inference ignored the teachings of the natural law philosophy which, to their ever-lasting credit, the supreme tribunals of the Federal Republic adopted after the Second World War. Thus the Federal Supreme Court held since 1952 that the confiscations, and since 1962 that the expatriations brought about by the decree of 1941 were null and void *ab initio*. The reason was that, in view of its arbitrary character and the *abus de droit* inherent in it, the decree of 1941 lacked the quality of law, was a 'non-law'. It may have been lex, but it was not *jus*. It was *injuria*, *Unrecht*, or, in the words of a German author (von Hippel) a perversion of law. Finally in 1968 the Federal Constitutional Court was confronted by the following case: Shortly before the outbreak of war, the deceased, a German lawyer, escaped to Amsterdam whence he was deported to the East in 1942. He was presumed to have died on May 8, 1945. He died intestate. He left surviving him two brothers and the children of two other brothers who had predeceased him. Under Dutch law the surviving brothers were the only persons entitled to the estate. Under German law the nephews and nieces shared it. If the deceased was, by virtue of the 1941 decree, stateless, Dutch law applied. If he was a German national, German law applied. The County Court, the District Court and the Court of Appeal at Frankfurt held that the deceased was stateless. In a most inspiring and enlightened decision the Federal Constitutional Court held that he had remained a German national. The decree of 1941 'violated fundamental principles. It is to so intolerable a degree irreconcilable with justice that it must be considered to have been null and void ex tunc.' This did not necessarily mean that, contrary to his intentions, German nationality was imposed upon every person who believed he had lost it. Certain distinctions were required, in particular between people who had survived and could avail themselves of Art. 116(2), and others who had died. The latter are German nationals, 'unless they displayed the intention not to retain German nationality.' As to the former, 'notwithstanding the fact that they have not lost German nationality by expatriation, the German State does not treat them as Germans except under the conditions of Art. 116(2); the contrast

> between having, and being treated as having, German nationality is certainly difficult to understand or apply, and is in fact likely to be unrealistic.
>
> Another special and in the present context most significant case is that of persons who meanwhile had become naturalised in a foreign country. By virtue of section 25 of the German Nationality Act of 1913 they had lost their German nationality on naturalisation; as the Court put it, 'the victims of persecution have never lost their German nationality in consequence of their expatriation. They may, however, have lost it on another legal ground, in particular as a result of the acquisition of a foreign nationality.'

But Mann emphasized that German victims of persecution could have lost their German nationality in consequence of the acquisition of a foreign nationality under the German Nationality Act of 1913. On this basis Mr Oppenheimer's case was without foundation in German law, and yet the decision of the Court of Appeal (particularly Buckley and Orr LJJ) had disregarded that decision and the unchallenged evidence of Dr Cohn. Accordingly, the character of the 1941 decree or its recognition by English courts was not a necessary part of the decision. If it was recognized, he had lost his German nationality in 1941, and if it was not recognized he ceased to be a German national in 1948.

Mann met Lord Hodson, one of the Law Lords sitting on the case, at a reception shortly before publication of the article, and Lord Hodson told him that he had already written a speech to reverse the decision of the Court of Appeal. Mann told Lord Hodson that he had written an article on the decision of the Court of Appeal.

On 23 May 1973 the Principal Clerk in the Judicial Office of the House of Lords wrote on behalf of the Lord Chancellor to inform the parties that the attention of the Lords of Appeal who had heard the appeal had been drawn to Mann's article,[12] and that they were minded to hear further argument in the appeal on the relevance of Article 116 of the German Basic Law. After further argument on 5 November 1973, the matter was remitted back to the Special Commissioners for further consideration. Lord Cross said on that occasion:[13]

> before we reported our views to the House we became aware that there were grounds for thinking that the findings of the Commissioners as to the relevant German law might have been based on inadequate material and that, in particular, Article 116(2) of the Constitution of the Federal Republic enacted in 1949 before the years of assessment might have a bearing on the point to be decided.

[12] Mann understood that Lord Salmon had read the article on publication and had advocated a re-hearing.

[13] [1976] AC 254.

Further argument then took place in the House almost a year later in November 1974, and on 5 February 1975 the House of Lords affirmed the result of the decision of the Court of Appeal, but on entirely different grounds. Lord Hailsham referred to Mann's article and said that it led, directly or indirectly, to the remission of the case to the Commissioners,[14] and Lord Cross said:

> before we reported our views to the House we became aware from an article by Dr. F.A. Mann on 'The Present Validity of Nazi Nationality Laws' in the Law Quarterly Review, vol. 89, p. 194, that the findings of the Commissioners as to the relevant German law were almost certainly based on inadequate material. We therefore put the appeal back into the list for further argument and, as a result of the discussion which then ensued, it became clear—and was accepted by counsel on both sides—that the case ought to be sent back to the commissioners for further findings as to the relevant German law.[15]

The Special Commissioners heard the matter in April and May 1974, in which expert evidence was given, not only with regard to the 1941 decree and the 1913 law, but also in relation to Article 116 of the Basic Law and various decisions of German courts, including decisions of 1958 and 1968 of the Federal Constitutional Court. Article 116(2) was held to be decisive. Lord Cross said that the ordinary meaning of Article 116(2) suggested that the Nazi legislation must be taken as having effectively deprived those falling within its terms of their German nationality unless they had returned to live in Germany after the war, and had not expressed a wish not to be German nationals. But those still abroad could regain German nationality which they had lost whenever they wished by applying for it to the appropriate authority. But the effect of the 1968 decision of the Federal Constitutional Court was that it was wrong to interpret Article 116(2) as saying, expressly or by implication, that the Nazi legislation had deprived anyone of his German nationality. The effect of the decision was that up to 1949 people who fell within the scope of the 1941 decree retained their German nationality unless they had given some positive indication that they rejected it; but after the date of the coming into force of the new constitution it was up to the persons concerned to give some positive indication that they wished to be nationals of the new Germany either by living there or by applying for German nationality. The consequence of this was that the House of Lords held that on the true construction of Article 116(2) the taxpayers had, on the enactment of the Basic Law, ceased to be German nationals unless and until they applied to be such, which they had not done, and therefore there was no reason

[14] This writer asked Lord Hailsham whether he would expand on the circumstances in which this came about, but Lord Hailsham refused to do so, on the basis that deliberations of the House were confidential. His letter is Figure 5.1 in the appendix to this chapter.

[15] [1976] AC 254, [268].

to attribute German nationality to them for the purposes of the double taxation legislation.

It was, therefore, Mann's article, and his treatment of Article 116(2) and the subsequent cases, which had a decisive effect, although Mann himself thought that the decision should have been based upon the continuing effect of the 1913 law, which had throughout been the expert evidence of Dr Cohn.

With regard to the very regrettable suggestions by Buckley and Orr LJ J that the 1941 decree should be recognized, however oppressive it was, a majority of the House of Lords refused to accept the approach of the majority in the Court of Appeal. Lord Cross expressly dissented from the view of Buckley LJ that the question of nationality must be answered in the light of the law of the foreign country 'however inequitable, oppressive or objectionable it may be'. Lord Cross said:

> if the decree had simply provided that all Germans who had left Germany since Hitler's advent to power with the intention of making their homes elsewhere should cease to be German nationals it may be that our courts would have had to recognise it even though many of those concerned were not in truth voluntary emigrants but had been driven from their native land. But the 1941 decree did not deprive *all* 'emigrés' of their status as German nationals. It only deprived *Jewish* emigrés of their citizenship. Further, as the later paragraphs of the decree show, this discriminatory withdrawal of their rights of citizenship was used as a peg upon which to hang a discriminatory confiscation of their property.... But what we are concerned with here is legislation which takes away without compensation from a section of the citizen body singled out on racial grounds all their property on which the state passing the legislation can lay its hands and, in addition, deprives them of their citizenship. To my mind a law of this sort constitutes so grave an infringement of human rights that the courts of this country ought to refuse to recognise it as a law at all.[16]

Lord Salmon said:

> Whilst there are many examples in the books of penal or confiscatory legislation which according to our views is unjust, the barbarity of much of the Nazi legislation, of which this decree is but an example, is happily unique. I do not consider that any of the principles laid down in any of the existing authorities require our courts to recognise such a decree and I have no doubt that on the grounds of public policy they should refuse to do so.[17]

[16] ibid para 277–78.
[17] ibid para 282.

Lord Hodson agreed with Lord Cross. Lord Hailsham preferred to treat the 1941 decree as invalid because it had been treated as 'non-law' by the Federal Constitutional Court, although he seemed to be unhappy about not recognizing it on broader grounds. Only Lord Pearson dissented on this aspect. In a short dissenting speech he said:

> When a government, however wicked, has been holding and exercising full and exclusive sovereign power in a foreign country for a number of years, and has been recognised throughout by our government as the government of that country, and some legislative or executive act of that government, however unjust and discriminatory and unfair, has changed the status of an individual by depriving him of his nationality of that country, he does in my opinion effectively cease to be a national of that country and becomes a stateless person unless and until he has acquired some other nationality.[18]

As Mann noted in the Law Quarterly Review in 1981,[19] the Federal Constitutional Court, by majority of six to one, reached in 1980 the same conclusion as the House of Lords without, apparently, having been made aware of the decision of the House of Lords. Mann said that the Federal Constitutional Court did not state in terms (as the House of Lords had done) that Oppenheimer had lost his German nationality, but he considered that the conclusion was implicit in its decision or its effect:

> It is the principal point which renders the decisions of both tribunals open to doubt. Is it reasonable to assume that a legislator who regards the expatriation as null and void and desires to undo a grave injustice commits the very act which he condemns, though admittedly he renders a remedy available for future use only?

B. *Kuwait Airways Corp v Iraqi Airways Co*

In 1943, Mann's article 'The Sacrosanctity of Foreign Act of State'[20] touched on a question to which he was to return often in later years, namely whether a foreign law which was applicable by the normal rules of private international law could (or should) be disregarded because it was contrary to public international law. In 1943 he said:

[18] ibid para 265.

[19] FA Mann, '*Oppenheimer v Cattermole* Revisited' (1981) 97 LQR 220, reprinted in Mann, *Notes and Comments* (n 3) 203.

[20] (1943) 59 LQR 42 and 155; FA Mann, *Studies in International Law* (OUP 1972) 420 (hereafter Mann, *Studies*).

> it is perhaps a principle of international law that no State may confiscate a foreigner's property unless compensation is paid. A State violating this rule is said to commit an international delinquency. It is, of course, possible that, although the Government of the forum may be entitled to treat an act of State as unlawful according to international law, a court may yet have to regard it as sacrosanct and valid. There may be some, however, to whom such a result will appear paradoxical.[21]

A decade or so later he developed the thesis, in 'International Delinquencies before Municipal Courts',[22] that where the conflict rule of the forum refers the court to a foreign law, the court should not apply the foreign law if and in so far as it expresses or results from an international delinquency; since it was international law itself which in the event of an international delinquency superseded the *lex causae*, the refusal to recognize or give effect to an international delinquency arose as a matter not of right but of duty. After another 20 years he returned to the issue in his article 'The Consequences of an International Wrong in International and National Law',[23] where he said, in the context of the question whether public international law should be applied as such or simply as a discretionary element in the application of public policy:

> To suggest public international law as a directly applicable test implies its obligatory character so as to deprive the judge of any discretion. Yet there is no need to shrink from such a conclusion: it has the advantage of being progressive, of facilitating both the reasoning and the decision of the judge and of protecting him against participating in the consummation of an international wrong.[24]

Consequently he was among those who were bitterly disappointed by the decision of the United States Supreme Court in *Banco Nacional de Cuba v Sabbatino*[25] in which the Supreme Court held that the court was bound to recognize the confiscation of sugar belonging to a US citizen by the Cuban government, even though the United States government took the view in its international relations that the confiscatory nature of the taking was manifestly in violation of those principles of international law which had long been accepted by the free countries of the West—it was in essence discriminatory, arbitrary, and confiscatory. The court decided that:

[21] Mann, *Studies* (n 20) 464–65.
[22] (1954) 70 LQR 181; Mann, *Studies* (n 20) 366.
[23] (1975–6) 49 BYIL 1, in FA Mann, *Further Studies in International Law* (OUP 1990)124 (hereafter Mann, *Further Studies*) especially at 155–88. See also (1956) 19 MLR 301, in Mann, *Notes and Comments* (n 3) 140.
[24] Mann, *Further Studies* (n 23) 156–57.
[25] 376 US 398 (1964).

> the Judicial Branch will not examine the validity of a taking of property within its own territory by a foreign sovereign government, extant and recognized by this country at the time of suit, in the absence of a treaty or other unambiguous agreement regarding controlling legal principles, even if the complaint alleges that the taking violates customary international law.[26]

As a result of this holding, said Mann (in a rare case of exaggeration), 'Jubilation on the other side of the Iron Curtain was as emphatic as the grief and consternation among the majority of lawyers in the West'.[27] He concluded his first critique (of several) by recalling the question raised by Philip Jessup[28] in relation to *Republic of Mexico v Hoffmann*:[29] Has the Supreme Court abdicated one of its functions? Mann answered: 'It seems that an affirmative answer has now been given.'[30]

The point arose for decision in England in the extensive litigation in England following the Iraqi invasion of Kuwait in 1990. Following the invasion, Iraq removed 10 aircraft belonging to Kuwait Airways from Kuwait to Iraq. Iraqi legislation purported to dissolve Kuwait Airways and to transfer all its property to Iraqi Airways. The aircraft were then repainted and prepared for commercial operations in Iraq.

It was held that, even though the aircraft were in Iraq at the time of the confiscatory legislation, the act of state doctrine did not require its recognition because (1) in appropriate circumstances where the standard being applied by the court was clear and manageable it was legitimate for an English court to have regard to the content of international law in deciding whether to recognize a foreign law; (2) the expropriatory decree made in the circumstances of Iraq's invasion of Kuwait, seizure of Kuwait's asset, and attempt to extinguish Kuwait's existence as a separate state was a gross breach of established rules of international law and unacceptable by contemporary standards; and (3) enforcement or recognition of the Iraqi decree would be contrary to the United Kingdom's obligations under the United Nations Charter and manifestly contrary to the public policy of English law.

Mann's work was referred to at all stages of this part of the litigation. At first instance, Mance J (now Lord Mance) said:[31]

> As to embarrassment or sensitivity, in clearcut cases it may involve a far greater affront to comity with other innocent sovereign states (not to mention elementary conceptions of justice and sound policy) if domestic courts refuse to address

[26] ibid para 428.
[27] 'The Legal Consequences of *Sabbatino*' (1965) 51 Virg Law Review 604, in Mann, *Studies* (n 20) 466.
[28] Phillip Jessup, 'Has the Court Abdicated One of Its Functions' (1946) 40 AJIL 168.
[29] 324 US 30 (1945).
[30] Mann, *Studies* (n 20) 491.
[31] [1999] CLC 31, 62.

> the reality, than if they do so squarely. Dr Mann expressed this consideration with clarity and force—whether or not one goes as far as his last 15 words—when, writing of the significance of international delinquencies, he said that ((1954) 70 LQR 181, 198): 'if a State commits an international wrong and the court of another State, the forum, refuses recognition to that wrong, the latter does what international law expects it to do and what it must do in order not to become an accessory to the delinquency'.

In the Court of Appeal[32] Rix LJ said (without specifically endorsing Mann's views):

> Dr. F A Mann was not deterred by controversy from arguing in favour of the recognition of international law in this area. His article 'International Delinquencies before Municipal Courts' (1954) 70 LQR 181, reprinted in *Studies in International Law* (1973), p 366, is a well known milestone. He ended the article, at pp 201–202, by advancing the following conclusions, among others, as his contribution to a 'broad and still fertile subject of inquiry':
>
> 1. When the conflict rule of the forum refers the court to a foreign law (lex causae), the court will not apply the latter if and in so far as it expresses or results from an international delinquency. . . .
> 5. The question whether an international delinquency has been committed is to be answered according to the generally accepted principles of international law, but a municipal court will not answer it affirmatively except where both the law and the facts are clearly established.
>
> Dr Mann returned to this topic in later publications: see Foreign Affairs in English Courts (1986), in particular at pp 148–182, and 'The Consequences of an International Wrong in International and National Law' in Further Studies in International Law (1990), pp 175–188. It is fair to say that his thesis as to the extent to which international law should guide national courts goes further than has so far been adopted in English jurisprudence. But it is also clear that since his 1954 article English law has developed in its willingness to recognise international law as relevant to its reasoning.

But in the House of Lords there was specific endorsement of Mann's position. Lord Hope said:[33]

> For these reasons I would hold that a legislative act by a foreign state which is in flagrant breach of clearly established rules of international law ought not to be

[32] [2002] UKHL 19, [2002] 2 AC 283, paras 311–12 in the Court of Appeal judgment.
[33] ibid paras 148–49 in the House of Lords.

recognised by the courts of this country as forming part of the lex situs of that state. This was the conclusion that Dr. F A Mann advocated in his article *International Delinquencies before Municipal Courts (1954) 70 LQR 181*; see also his *Further Studies in International Law*, pp 177–183. At p 202 of the article he said:

> 1. When the conflict rule of the forum refers the court to a foreign law (lex causae), the court will not apply the latter if and in so far as it expresses or results from an international delinquency. . . .
> 5. The question whether an international delinquency has been committed is to be answered according to the generally accepted principles of international law, but a municipal court will not answer it affirmatively except where both the law and the facts are clearly established.
>
> 149. I would endorse everything that is said in that passage, and I would apply it to this case.

C. *Moti v R*

In *Moti v R*[34] Mr Moti claimed that he had been deported by officials of the Solomon Islands government from the Solomon Islands to Australia, where he was wanted for trial. The deportation occurred after the High Commissioner had issued a travel document for Mr Moti and visas for the Solomon Islands officials who were to accompany him on the aircraft bound for Australia, knowing that Solomon Islands law was going to be breached by deporting Mr Moti on the same day without giving him a seven-day opportunity to challenge deportation.

The majority judgment of the High Court of Australia, given by French CJ for six out of the seven members of the High Court, held that there was no 'general and universally applicable rule that Australian courts may not be required (or do not have or may not exercise jurisdiction) to form a view about the lawfulness of conduct that occurred outside Australia by reference to foreign law' ([50]) and that ([52]):

> Rather, as Mann has correctly said,[35] 'the Courts are free to consider and pronounce an opinion upon the exercises of sovereign power by a foreign Government, if the consideration of those acts of a foreign Government only constitutes a preliminary to the decision of a question . . . which in itself is subject to the competency of the Court of law'. The fact that the decision of a foreign official is called into question does not of itself prevent the courts from considering

[34] [2011] HCA 50, (2011) 245 CLR 456.
[35] Citing Mann's article 'The Sacrosanctity of the Foreign Act of State' in Mann, *Studies* (n 20) 433–34.

> the issue. Here, the question of the lawfulness of the appellant's removal from Solomon Islands, although effected by the Solomon Islands Government, was 'a preliminary' to the decision whether a stay should be granted. The primary judge was not right to conclude that '[i]t is not for this court to express an opinion on these decisions made by the Solomon Islands government'.

This was subjected to criticism by Lord Sumption in the UK Supreme Court in *Belhaj v Straw*.[36] In these cases, actions were brought against the British government by claimants who alleged that that they had been abducted and tortured by agents of foreign governments with the collusion and participation of the British government. The decision contains a very extensive discussion of various aspects of the act of state doctrine which are outside the scope of this chapter. So far as relevant to this chapter, the overall effect of the extensive discussion in the judgments is that the act of state doctrine has the effect that the court will recognize, and will not question, the effect of a foreign state's legislation or other laws in relation to any acts which take place or take effect within the territory of that state; the court will recognize, and will not question, the effect of an act of a foreign state's executive in relation to acts which take place or take effect within the territory of that state if the acts relate to property (and not personal injuries or death) within that state and are lawful under the law of that state; and an English court will refrain from resolving issues which are inappropriate for the court to resolve because they involve a challenge to the lawfulness of the act of a foreign state which is of such a nature that a municipal court cannot or ought not to rule on them (such as dealings between sovereign states, including making war and peace, making treaties with foreign sovereigns, and annexation and cession), and whether an issue is non-justiciable for this purpose falls to be considered on a case-by-case basis, having regard to the separation of powers and the sovereign nature of the activities concerned, based on factors including the existence of judicial or manageable standards, the consequences for international relations or security interests of a judicial determination of sensitive issues, the availability of alternative fora, and whether issues of fundamental rights are engaged, in particular, issues of liberty, access to justice, and freedom from torture.

Lord Sumption's criticism of the decision of the High Court of Australia was that the short answer to the foreign act of state defence would have been that the unlawfulness of the Australian officials' conduct was enough to justify staying the proceedings against Mr Moti, and that the court should not have relied on 'that great scholar' Dr Mann. He said that the unlawfulness of the acts of their foreign collaborators was incidental and irrelevant, and went on:[37]

[36] [2017] UKSC 3, [2017] AC 964.

[37] ibid paras 246–47. Mann was cited with approval in several passages of the judgment of Lord Mance, paras 33, 40, 47, 66.

But in rejecting the argument, the court adopted the view of Dr F A Mann, a long-standing critic of the act of state doctrine, that there was no bar to adjudication of the lawfulness of a foreign governmental act if it was necessary to the resolution of an issue within the jurisdiction and competence of the forum: see paras 50–52. In my view this was too wide and certainly wider than anything that was required for the decision of the case.

The proposition which the High Court of Australia accepted from Dr Mann is tantamount to the abolition of the foreign act of state doctrine. This was indeed a consummation devoutly wished by that great scholar. He regarded the whole doctrine as incoherent. Properly understood, I do not think that it is incoherent. What is clear, however, is that to arrive at the view held by Dr Mann it would be necessary to throw over a substantial body of jurisprudence, much of it recent and much of it not considered by the High Court of Australia.

III. Enforcement of Foreign Public Law

In 1955 Mann published a short but influential article, 'Prerogative Rights of Foreign States and the Conflict of Laws'.[38] Mann argued forcefully that the familiar rule that revenue claims and penal claims by foreign states could not be pursued in the English court was part of a wider principle that a state could not enforce its 'prerogative rights' in a foreign court. The essence of the thesis was (echoing the words of Lord Watson in *Huntington v Attrill*[39]) that certain claims by states are unenforceable in foreign courts because those claims 'by the law of nations are exclusively assigned to their domestic forum'. Mann suggested that the claims which were so assigned were those which were based upon the *jus imperii* of the state, since their exercise is inherently limited to the state's territory.

The first edition of Dicey's *Conflict of Laws* suggested that the English court had no jurisdiction to entertain an action for the enforcement, either directly or indirectly, of a penal law of a foreign country, and in the third edition the rule was expanded to cover revenue law, as well as penal law (after a number of cases on revenue claims in the early part of the 20th century). In the fourth edition in 1927, Professor Berriedale Keith expanded the rule to add 'political law'.[40] This remained the formula in Dicey until the eighth edition in 1958, where the expression 'political law' was changed to 'public law'.[41] But there was no clear authority for this

[38] FA Mann, 'Prerogative Rights of Foreign States and the Conflict of Laws' (1955) 40 Tr Grot Soc 25; Mann, *Studies* (n 20) 492. See also *Conflict of Laws and Public Law* (1971) 132 Recueil des cours 107; 'The International Enforcement of Public Rights' in Mann, *Further Studies* (n 23) 355, first published in 1987 in a version edited in a manner unsatisfactory to Mann: (1987) 19 Journal of International Law and Policy 603.

[39] [1893] AC 150, 156.

[40] ibid para 224, citing *Emperor of Austria v Day and Kossuth* (1861) 3 De G F & J 217.

[41] ibid para 160.

residual category of 'political law' or 'public law' in England, although the principle was well established in continental countries.

A. *Attorney-General of New Zealand v Ortiz*

In *Attorney-General of New Zealand v Ortiz*,[42] the government of New Zealand sought to recover an antique Maori carving which (it claimed) had been illegally exported from New Zealand by George Ortiz and put up for sale at Sotheby's at auction.

The background was that George Ortiz was a collector who had formed one of the world's greatest collections of ancient and tribal art. He needed money to fund the reported US$2 million which he had paid in 1977 as ransom when his daughter had been kidnapped. Under the Historic Articles Act 1962 of New Zealand, an historic article knowingly exported in breach of the Act was forfeited to the Crown. There were two principal issues in the litigation in England. The first was whether forfeiture under the New Zealand legislation took effect only when an historic article was seized by the New Zealand customs or police, or whether it took place automatically when the article was exported. The distinction was crucial since no actual seizure had taken place: if actual seizure was required, there was no basis for an assertion of title by the New Zealand government. The second question was whether the claim was unenforceable in England in any event as being brought to enforce a foreign penal, revenue, and/or public law. These issues were tried as preliminary issues. On the first issue, Staughton J (as he then was) held that the Crown had title automatically when the goods were exported or attempted to be exported, and that the claim was enforceable in England. The Court of Appeal allowed an appeal from this decision, and held that forfeiture was not automatic, and that the claim was unenforceable. The House of Lords dismissed the appeal, affirming that the forfeiture was not automatic. On the second issue, at first instance Staughton J referred to what he described as the most difficult issue in the whole case: whether there was a third category of foreign law which the courts would not enforce, namely, public law. He noted that 'in finding the point difficult I am in good company'[43] and then referred to Mann's article. He said that Mann described the class of claims which would not be enforced as foreign prerogative rights, or claims *jure imperii*, as those 'which are enforced as an assertion of the authority of central or local government'. Staughton J said:

> With the greatest respect, I do not accept that any such general principle exists in English law nor do I consider that it would be right for me to establish it. The

[42] [1982] QB 349, affd [1984] AC 1 (CA and HL).
[43] [1982] QB, para 367.

> kinds of law which would be comprised in such a wide class are so many and so various, that some should properly be enforced in this country while others perhaps should not. The right of a state to succeed to heirless property as bona vacantia, mentioned by Dr Mann, may be one instance where public policy provides no easy answer. It is a better solution, in my judgment, to follow the treatment of Halsbury, Cheshire and North: and the Restatement, considering in each individual case whether there is any special ground of public policy which requires the law in question not to be enforced here.[44]

The Court of Appeal unanimously reversed Staughton J on both issues, but differed on the reasons for holding that, even if by New Zealand law the government had title, that title would not be recognized. Lord Denning MR held that the claim was unenforceable because it was based on foreign public law, and expressly approved Mann's article. He said:[45]

> No one has ever doubted that our courts will not entertain a suit brought by a foreign sovereign, directly or indirectly, to enforce the penal or revenue laws of that foreign state. We do not sit to collect taxes for another country or to inflict punishments for it. Now the question arises whether this rule extends to 'other public laws'. Dicey & Morris, *The Conflict of Laws*, 10th ed. (1980), vol. 1, p. 90, rule 3 say it does. I agree with them. The term 'other public laws' is very uncertain. But so are the terms 'penal' and 'revenue'. The meaning of 'penal' was discussed in *Huntington v. Attrill* [1893] AC 150 and *Loucks v Standard Oil Co of New York* (1918) 120o NE 198. The meaning of 'revenue' was discussed in *Government of India v Taylor* [1955] AC 491. But what are 'other public laws'? I think they are laws which are eiusdem generis with 'penal' or 'revenue' laws.
>
> Then what is the genus? Or, in English, what is the general concept which embraces 'penal' and 'revenue' laws and others like them? It is to be found, I think, by going back to the classification of acts taken in international law. One class comprises those acts which are done by a sovereign 'jure imperii', that is, by virtue of his sovereign authority. The others are those which are done by him 'jure gestionis', that is, which obtain their validity by virtue of his performance of them. The application of this distinction to our present problem was well drawn by Dr F.A. Mann 28 years ago in an article 'Prerogative Rights of Foreign States and the Conflict of Laws', in *Transactions of the Grotius Society* (1954) 40 Tr. Gr. Soc. 25, reprinted in his *Studies in International Law* (1973), pp. 492 to 514.

[44] ibid para 371.
[45] [1984] AC 1, at 20–21.

> Applied to our present problem the class of laws which will be enforced are those laws which are an exercise by the sovereign government of its sovereign authority over property within its territory or over its subjects wherever they may be. But other laws will not be enforced. By international law every sovereign state has no sovereignty beyond its own frontiers. The courts of other countries will not allow it to go beyond the bounds. They will not enforce any of its laws which purport to exercise sovereignty beyond the limits of its authority.

But Ackner LJ (with whom O'Connor LJ agreed) thought that the New Zealand law was unenforceable because it was a 'penal' law:[46]

> It seems to me to be wholly unreal to suggest that when a foreign state seeks to enforce these forfeiture provisions in another country, it is not seeking to enforce a foreign penal statute. . . .
>
> In these circumstances it is unnecessary for me to consider the question of whether there is a third category of foreign laws which our courts do not enforce, namely public law, and if so, what it comprises. Without reaching any firm conclusion, I am impressed by the reasoning of the judge that there is no such vague general residual category.

In the House of Lords the appeal was dealt with solely on the question whether the New Zealand forfeiture law took effect without actual seizure, and the House did not call for argument on the public law issue. Lord Brightman (with whom all the other members agreed) expressed the view that the opinions expressed in the Court of Appeal on the second issue were *obiter*, and suggested that the House of Lords would 'not wish to be taken as expressing any conclusion on the correctness or otherwise of the opinions' expressed in the Court of Appeal.[47]

B. The Equatorial Guinea cases

The Republic of Equatorial Guinea has a population of not much more than 1,500,000, but it is rich in oil and gas. It is the sixth-largest producer in sub-Saharan Africa after Nigeria, Angola, Republic of Congo, Gabon, and South Sudan.[48] President Obiang has been the President of Equatorial Guinea since 1979.

The United States Department of Energy reported in 2004 that there was strong evidence that oil revenues had been misappropriated by the government, and a

[46] ibid para 34.
[47] ibid para 46.
[48] See oil production in Africa as of 2021, by country, at <https://www.statista.com/statistics/1178514/main-oil-producing-countries-in-africa/> accessed 3 April 2023.

United States Senate investigation in 2004 claimed the misappropriation of at least $35 billion of oil revenues from foreign oil companies by President Obiang, his family, and other senior government officials through foreign bank accounts since the country started exporting oil in the mid-1990s.

1. In March 2004, Zimbabwean police in Harare impounded a plane from South Africa with 64 alleged mercenaries on board, including Simon Mann. The following day others were arrested in Equatorial Guinea. President Obiang announced that there had been a plot to overthrow him, which allegedly involved the intelligence services of the United States, United Kingdom, and Spain, together with Mark Thatcher (the son of the former Prime Minister) and Simon Mann. The government alleged that the individuals arrested were involved in an attempt to overthrow the Government of Equatorial Guinea by means of a privately hired force of mercenaries armed with weapons (including machine guns, rocket grenade launchers, mortars, mortar bombs, and hand grenades acquired in Zimbabwe) and to seize control of the state and its assets, in particular its substantial oil and gas reserves, to kill, severely injure or abduct the President, and to install Mr Severo Moto, who was in exile in Spain, as President. They alleged that this was pursuant to a conspiracy plotted and financed in England and elsewhere.
2. Simon Mann was convicted in Zimbabwe of offences relating to unlawful procurement of munitions and, on 10 September 2004, sentenced to seven years' imprisonment, reduced on appeal to four years. The main body of mercenaries received lesser sentences for immigration offences. At the end of 2004 and beginning of 2005, others, including Sir Mark Thatcher, pleaded guilty and were convicted of offences contrary to the South African Regulation of Foreign Military Assistance Act 1998. Those arrested in Equatorial Guinea, as members of the advance group, were prosecuted and convicted in October 2004 of offences relating to the coup attempt. They were given long prison sentences.
3. The President of Equatorial Guinea then sued Simon Mann and his companies in England for damage caused by the unsuccessful attempt at revolution, and obtained orders in Guernsey for a bank to give information about the ownership of various companies and bank accounts which the government had traced.
4. The litigation in Guernsey concerned attempts by the government to obtain information about bank accounts in Guernsey in support of proceedings abroad. The court gave the government permission to use the information supplied to them to pursue others in Guernsey, Equatorial Guinea, Spain, Jersey, and England. The government gave an undertaking to use the information only for the purposes of civil legal action in the jurisdictions mentioned and specifically not to use it in any criminal proceedings. The Privy

Council, sitting on appeal from the Court of Appeal of Guernsey, decided that the order should be upheld, but (in an opinion written by Lord Bingham and Lord Hoffmann) it expressed disquiet at the fact that no argument was addressed, whether to the courts in Guernsey or to the Privy Council, on the question of whether the Guernsey court lacked jurisdiction to make the order which it made, on the ground that it could be regarded as the enforcement, direct or indirect, of the public law of a foreign state. There was no direct reference to the work of Mann in this field.

But in the English litigation the claim was by the President and by the Republic for, inter alia, conspiracy and intentional infliction of harm by unlawful means, alleging that the defendants had conspired in England and elsewhere to overthrow the state's government and seize power by means of a coup which ultimately failed. In *Mbasogo v Logo Ltd*,[49] the Court of Appeal decided that most of the claims were in respect of losses which arose as a result of decisions taken by the claimants to protect the state and its citizens, which could only have been suffered by the governing body of the state. An action which amounted to the exercise of sovereign authority in the territory of a foreign state was not justiciable in the English courts.

In the course of the judgment, there was extensive reference to Mann's views. The Court of Appeal expressly approved[50] the distinction made by Mann between an action which amounts to the exercise of sovereign authority in the territory of another and an action brought to protect property rights, such as might be brought by an individual. The court agreed with formulations of the principle in Mann's article on prerogative rights. It said:[51]

> As Lord Denning MR made clear in the Ortiz case, his judgment was influenced by the article by Dr F A Mann, 'Prerogative Rights of Foreign States and the Conflict of Laws' 40 Tr Gro Soc 25, to which we have referred at para 26 above. Dr Mann said, at p 34:
>
> Where the foreign state pursues a right that by its nature could equally well belong to an individual, no question of a prerogative claim arises and the state's access to the courts is unrestricted. Thus a state whose property is in the defendant's possession can recover it by an action in detinue. A state which has a contractual claim against the defendant is at liberty to recover the money due to it. If a state's ship has been damaged in a collision, an action for damages undoubtedly lies. On the other hand, a foreign state cannot enforce in England such rights as are

[49] [2006] EWCA Civ 1370, [2007] QB 846.
[50] ibid para 27.
[51] ibid paras 42, 43, 44, 51, 53. See also *Iran v Barakat Galleries Ltd* [2007] EWCA Civ 1374, [2009] QB 22, paras 113–14.

founded upon its peculiar powers of prerogative. Claims for the payment of penalties, for the recovery of customs duties or the satisfaction of tax liabilities are, of course, the most firmly established examples of this principle.

We agree.

In a later article on 'The International Enforcement of Public Rights' (1987) 19 New York University of International Law and Politics 603, 629–630 Dr Mann said that the decisive question is whether the plaintiff asserts a claim that, by its nature, involves the assertion of a sovereign right. Quoting Grotius, he suggested that claims are capable of international enforcement if they arise from acts that may be done not only by the King, but also by anyone else: '*actus qui a rege sed ut a quovis alio fiant*.' Again, we agree.

This part of Dr Mann's article was cited with apparent approval by Sir Robin Cooke P in *Attorney General for the United Kingdom v Wellington Newspapers Ltd* [1988] 1 NZLR 129, 174 (the New Zealand *Spycatcher* case).

. . .

. . . Like Lord Denning MR in the *Ortiz* case [1984] AC 1, we have found the analyses by Dr Mann illuminating. As we understand Dr Mann, his criticism of the *Emperor of Austria* case 3 De GF & J 217 was not of the principles stated but of the application of those principles to the facts.

. . .

The facts of this case are a far cry from any other authority to which our attention has been drawn. The nearest is the *Emperor of Austria* case 3 De GF & J 217. We find compelling the criticism by Dr Mann of that decision on its facts.

C. The Danish tax recovery case

The case *Skatteforvaltningen (the Danish Customs and Tax Administration) v Solo Capital Partners LLP*[52] (also known as the Danish tax recovery case) concerned Danish tax, totalling £1.44 billion, which had been refunded to the defendants. The basis of the claims by the Danish tax authority was not the recovery of tax, but the recovery of sums which had been wrongfully extracted from it by fraudulent misrepresentations. The defendants were individuals and corporate entities who had procured the refund applications and received the bulk of the sums; they had never paid, or been liable to pay, the tax themselves. The principal question was whether the claims were barred by the principle set out in Dicey's Rule 3 that English courts

[52] [2021] EWHC 974 (Comm), revd [2022] EWCA Civ 234, [2022] QB 772. Since this contribution went to press, the decision of the Court of Appeal has been affirmed by the UK Supreme Court: [2023[UKSC 40, citing Mann's work at paras 56–57.

had no jurisdiction to entertain an action for the enforcement, either directly or indirectly, of a penal, revenue, or other public law of a foreign state.

At first instance, the Commercial Court decided that the tax authority's claims fell within the scope of the Rule. Although the claims were framed as private law causes of action, they were, in substance, claims to enforce Denmark's sovereign right to the tax. The judge, relying on Mann, said:[53]

> That is not to say a foreign sovereign tax authority cannot bring a fraud claim here. Not every fraud against a foreign sovereign tax authority will be a fraud on the foreign revenue for which it is responsible. It will depend on the nature and subject matter of the fraud. A claim by SKAT alleging against a contractor that it had dishonestly overcharged SKAT for work done or services supplied, using inflated invoices overstating what was done or the time spent, would be governed by the ordinary rules of the law of contract, tort/delict, restitution, or as the case may be depending on the cause of action pursued, of the system of law that applied under ordinary choice of law rules; that would not be 'a claim that, by its nature, involves the assertion of a sovereign right', but a claim arising 'from acts that may be done not only by the King, but also by anyone else: "*actus qui a rege sed ut a quovis alio fiant*"', to quote *Mbasogo v Logo* ... at [43], adopting an articulation of the essential nature of a patrimonial claim that may be brought by a foreign sovereign as much as by a private party in an article by Dr Mann, 'The International Enforcement of Public Rights' (1987) 19 New York University Journal of International Law and Politics 603, at 629–630. Dr Mann there concluded that 'Careful assessment and delimitation is required. The decision will not always be an easy one. Nor will the results always be universally approved, for in many cases they will depend upon legal judgment or instinct. What should not be open to dispute is the starting point and the purpose of the reasoning. ... The true question is whether in substance the claim asserts a public right.'

But the Court of Appeal,[54] also relying on Mann, reversed the judge's decision and decided that in determining whether a claim was inadmissible, the court had to examine the substance of the claim to see whether it really was a claim to recover foreign revenue. In this case, it was not such a claim. The tax had been legitimately paid and the refunds had not been refunds of tax, but an abstraction of the tax authority's general funds, just as if the defendants had broken into its safe and stolen its money. As there was no unsatisfied claim to tax, the

[53] ibid para 35.
[54] [2022] EWCA Civ 234, [2022] QB 772.

revenue rule did not apply. The defendant's argument that the claim was precluded by wider sovereign powers was misconceived. In bringing a claim to recover the monies of which it was defrauded, the tax authority was not performing an act of sovereign character or enforcing a sovereign right, nor was it seeking to vindicate a sovereign power: it was merely making a claim, as the victim of fraud, for the restitution of monies. The fact that, at trial, there would be a detailed examination of the Danish tax regime and possible criticism of the authority's systems did not convert the claims into ones to enforce a tax regime.

The Court of Appeal said:[55]

> Although there is no English authority directly on point which decides that a claim such as the present one is not a sovereign act or the vindication of a sovereign act, that was clearly the view of Dr Mann in the articles which were expressly approved by this Court in *Mbasogo*. Thus, in his 1954 article quoted at [42] of the judgment in *Mbasogo*, Dr Mann said:
>
> Where the foreign state pursues a right that by its nature could equally well belong to an individual, no question of a prerogative claim arises and the state's access to the courts is unrestricted. Thus a state whose property is in the defendant's possession can recover it by an action in detinue. A state which has a contractual claim against the defendant is at liberty to recover the money due to it. If a state's ship has been damaged in a collision, an action for damages undoubtedly lies.
>
> In the conclusion to his 1987 article, also approved by this Court at [43] of the judgment in *Mbasogo*, Dr Mann said:
>
> The decisive question is whether the plaintiff asserts a claim that, by its nature, involves the assertion of a sovereign right. Where the state's claims arise from '*actus qui a rege sed ut a quovis alio fiant*' [the quotation from Grotius, which roughly translates as 'acts which may be done not only by the king but by anyone else'], then they are capable of international enforcement.
>
> . . . [C]laims by a state which will be categorised as ones which could just as well be brought by a private citizen and thus outside Dicey Rule 3, are not limited to 'patrimonial' claims, that is claims in respect of rights in real or personal property. This is clear from the examples which Dr. Mann gives.

55 ibid paras 131–33.

IV. Conclusion

Formal conclusions are unnecessary in a piece which has said enough about the areas of law with which it is concerned.

Francis Mann had a busy legal practice, but in the evenings he would work at home on his ancient typewriter and on many Saturday mornings he would go the Institute of Advanced Legal Studies of the University of London to conduct research.

At this stage it is not necessary to do more than signal that the reason for his influence on the judiciary was not only his outstanding scholarship but also the fact that he had won the respect of senior members of judiciary through his interaction with many of them when they were at the bar or when he sat on legal committees with them.

He was not a mere collector of data or names of cases. He only wrote when he had something to say, and particularly when he thought that the law or academic opinion had taken a wrong turning. It was the ability to see where others had gone wrong or had missed the underlying principles which was the secret to his academic distinction, coupled with a distinctive style which was wholly remarkable in one whose native language was not English.

His influence on the case law was a remarkable achievement in a legal system which traditionally had little respect for the views of academic authors, especially living authors, and those who were not barristers.

Appendix

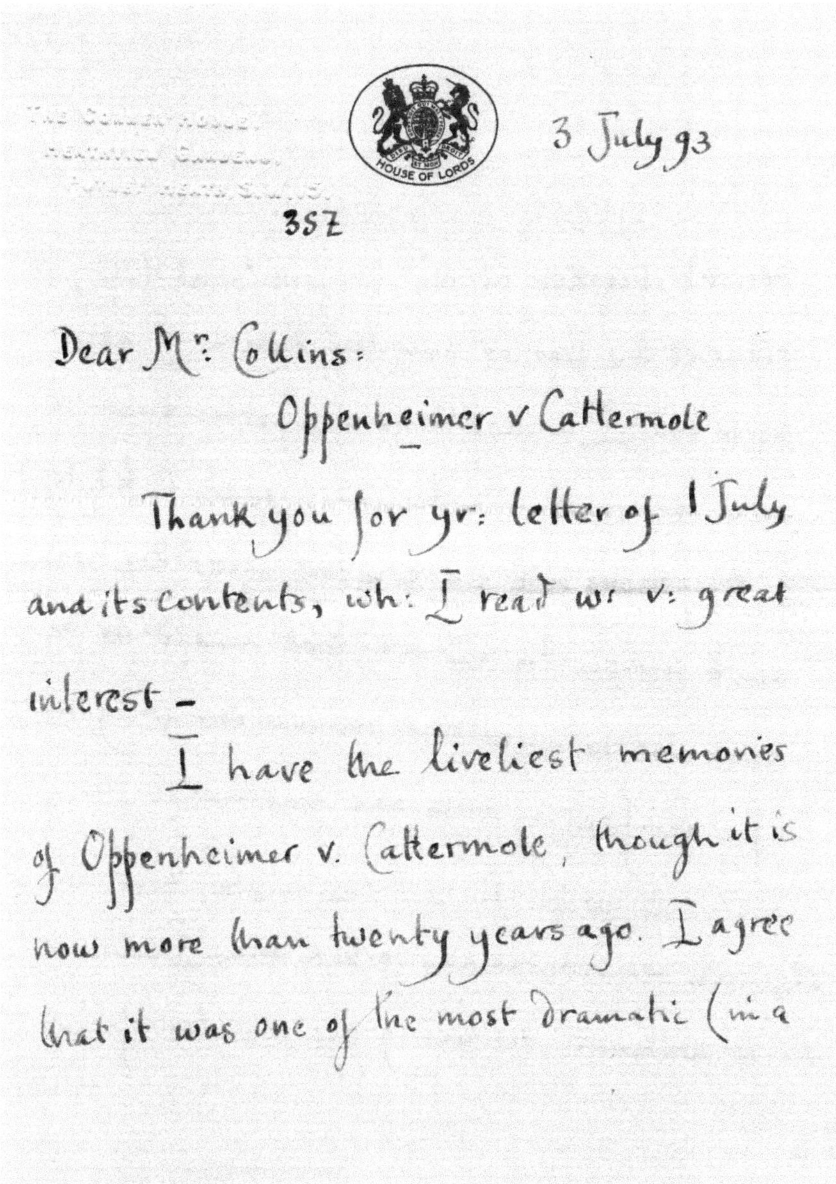

HOUSE OF LORDS

3 July 93

357

Dear Mr: Collins:

Oppenheimer v Cattermole

Thank you for yr: letter of 1 July and its contents, wh: I read w: v: great interest -

I have the liveliest memories of Oppenheimer v. Cattermole, though it is now more than twenty years ago. I agree that it was one of the most dramatic (in a

Figure 5.1 Letter from Quintin Hogg, Lord Hailsham of St Marylebone, to Lawrence (now Lord) Collins, relating to FA Mann's role in *Oppenheimer v Cattermole* [1976] AC 249

Source: Letter from Lord Hailsham to the author, 3 July 1993, reproduced with permission from Lord Hailsham's estate.

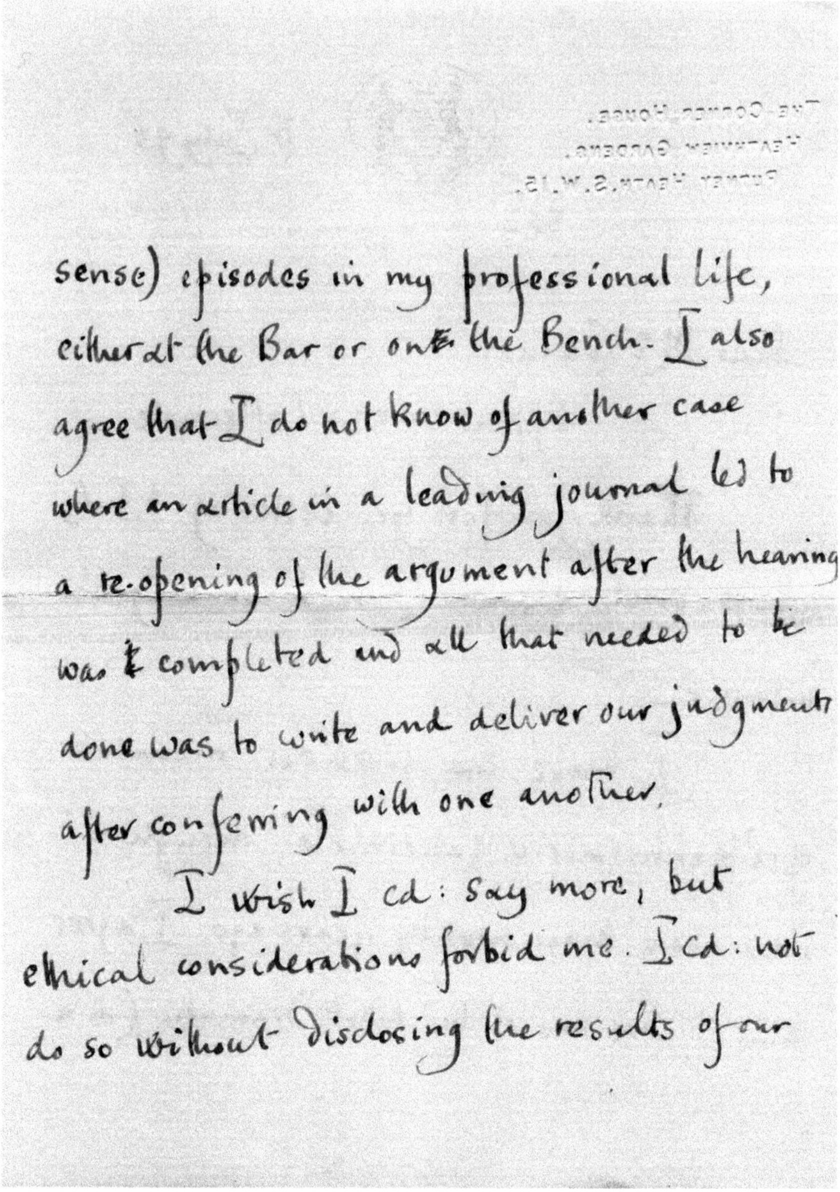

sense) episodes in my professional life, either at the Bar or on the Bench. I also agree that I do not know of another case where an article in a leading journal led to a re-opening of the argument after the hearing was completed and all that needed to be done was to write and deliver our judgments after conferring with one another.

I wish I cd: say more, but ethical considerations forbid me. I cd: not do so without disclosing the results of our

Figure 5.1b Continued

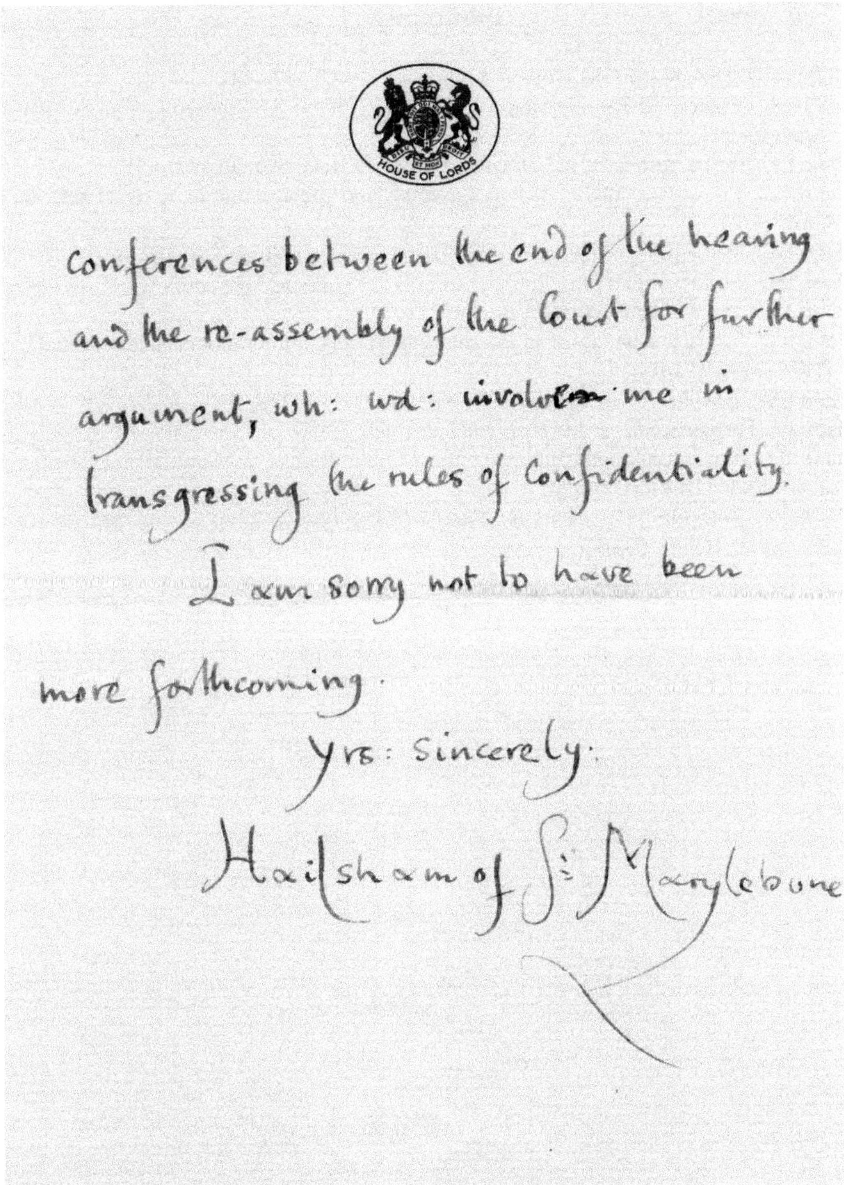

HOUSE OF LORDS

conferences between the end of the hearing and the re-assembly of the Court for further argument, wh: wd: involve me in transgressing the rules of Confidentiality.

I am sorry not to have been more forthcoming.

Yrs: sincerely.

Hailsham of St Marylebone

Figure 5.1c Continued

Bibliography

Collins L, 'Dr F.A. Mann: His Work and Influence' (1993) 64 BYBIL 55

Collins L, 'Francis Alexander Mann, 1907–1991' (1993) 84 Proceedings of the British Academy 393

Mann FA, 'The Sacrosanctity of Foreign Act of State' (1943) 59 LQR 42 and 155

Mann FA, 'Prerogative Rights of Foreign States and the Conflict of Laws' (1955) 40 Tr Grot Soc 25

Mann FA, 'The Legal Consequences of Sabbatino' (1965) 51 Virg L Rev 604

Mann FA, 'Conflict of Laws and Public Law' (1971) 132 Recueil des cours 107

Mann FA, *Studies in International Law* (OUP 1973)

Mann FA, 'The Consequences of an International Wrong in International and National Law' (1975–6) 49 BYBIL 1

Mann FA, '*Oppenheimer v Cattermole* Revisited' (1981) 97 LQR 220

Mann FA, *Further Studies in International Law* (OUP 1990)

Mann FA, 'The International Enforcement of Public Rights' in Mann, *Further Studies in International Law* (OUP 1990)

Mann FA, *Notes and Comments on Cases in International Law, Commercial Law, and Arbitration* (OUP 1992)

6

Jurisdiction and Private International Law

FA Mann's *Unvollendete*?

Gerhard Dannemann

I. Introduction

The Legal Aspect of Money is without doubt Francis Mann's most influential scholarly work. Lawrence Collins has suggested, for good reason, that pride of second place should go to Mann's two Hague lectures on the doctrine of jurisdiction in international law.[1] These lectures in general and the topic of jurisdiction in particular provide a linchpin between two of his other main research interests, namely public and private international law.

The Legal Aspect of Money offers a comprehensive and systematic treatment of an entire area of law, and to this effect follows the style of the teacher whom Mann revered, Martin Wolff. Wolff's textbooks on German property law, and also his two very different textbooks on German and on English private international law, are rare masterpieces in their dogmatically clear, practically relevant, comprehensive,

[1] Lawrence Collins, 'F. A. Mann (1907–1991)' in Jack Beatson and Reinhard Zimmermann (eds), *Jurists Uprooted. German-Speaking Émigré Lawyers in Twentieth-Century Britain* (OUP 2003) 408 (hereafter Beatson and Zimmermann, *Jurists Uprooted*); FA Mann, 'The Doctrine of Jurisdiction in International Law' (1963) 111 Recueil des Cours 1 (hereafter Mann, 'Jurisdiction in International Law'); FA Mann, 'The Doctrine of Jurisdiction in International Law Revisited After Twenty Years' (1984) 186 Recueil des Cours 9 (hereafter Mann, 'Jurisdiction Revisited After Twenty Years').

Gerhard Dannemann, *Jurisdiction and Private International Law* In: *FA Mann*. Edited by: Jason Grant Allen and Gerhard Dannemann, Oxford University Press. © Gerhard Dannemann 2024. DOI: 10.1093/oso/9780198881452.003.0007

systematic, and highly lucid treatment of a subject,[2] in what Mann described as 'the systematic, logical, coherent exposition of the law'.[3] Mann would have been well suited to write similarly influential textbooks on public or on private international law. While Mann toyed for some time with the idea of writing an entire book on 'Jurisdiction', in which Oxford University Press expressed a firm interest,[4] there is, however, no indication that he ever started any serious work on a textbook on either public or private international law.

He might indeed have written a textbook on public international law if his application for a vacant chair in public international law at the University of London in 1949 had been successful. The fact that the University left the chair vacant for several years rather than appointing him remained a source of lasting resentment for him.[5] Remaining in legal practice left him presumably little time or appetite for those parts of public international law which have nothing to do with economic aspects. That would explain why there is no 'Mann on Public International Law'.

As concerns private international law, his writing also had a strong focus on business-related aspects. But there is a difference: he wrote on a wide range of areas of private international law, including general questions such as habitual residence, the 'citizenship' of legal persons, the borderline between conflicts norms and substantive norms with limited territorial application, or overriding mandatory norms.[6]

Was he ever tempted to write a general treatise on private international law? We know that the answer is positive: he would indeed have given much for being allowed to continue Wolff's *Private International Law* after the author's death. He could forgive neither Wolff's widow Marguerite for preferring Kurt Lipstein instead, nor Lipstein for never producing the third edition.[7] But that further disappointment would not necessarily have precluded him from writing his own book on private international law.

The title of the present contribution suggests, perhaps somewhat luridly, that such a conflicts law textbook was on the cards. Those who are familiar with Mann

[2] Martin Wolff, *Das Sachenrecht* (Elwert 1910) to (9th edn, Elwert 1932); Martin Wolff, *Internationales Privatrecht* (Springer 1933) to *Das Internationale Privatrecht Deutschlands* (3rd edn, Springer 1954); Martin Wolff, *Private International Law* (OUP 1945) and (2nd edn, OUP 1950).

[3] FA Mann, *Life and Cases. Manuscript of an Autobiography* (Wolfgang Ernst ed., V&R unipress 2021) 42 (hereafter Mann, *Life and Cases*).

[4] Adam Hodgkin (OUP) to FA Mann (Mann estate, NLMann_0832, 20 October 1981) ('I do hope you will write the book'); FA Mann to Adam Hodgkin (Mann estate, NLMann_0832, 13 October 1981) ('Please don't take the book on jurisdiction too seriously. I hope to be able to do it, but in view of my general position, I can't commit to it.')

[5] Mann, *Life and Cases* (n 3) 79.

[6] A collection of his German language articles on private international law involving these and other topics appeared as FA Mann, *Beiträge zum Internationalen Privatrecht* (Duncker & Humblot 1976) (hereafter *Beiträge zum Internationalen Privatrecht*).

[7] Mann, *Life and Cases* (n 3) 63.

will also know that he greatly admired the composer Franz Schubert, above all the string quintet in C major, which was played at his own request at his funeral.[8] Schubert is also known for an unfinished sinfonia in B minor, called in German 'Die Unvollendete'. In the following, I will try to explore, with the help of archival material and Mann's publications, what such an *Unvollendete* might have looked like in his case.

II. International Lawyers Talking at Cross-Purposes

Such a book would have had an enormous potential for enriching scholarly debate and guiding practitioners alike. Mann was the rare case not only of a lawyer who was equally versed in academia and in practice, but also of an international lawyer who was equally at home in public international law and in private international law. As Mann writes in his autobiography, in a mixture of amusement and desperation:[9]

> It is ... fascinating to observe how great the cleavage is between public and private international lawyers. When they discuss these particular questions (as the elite of international lawyers did in the course of the sessions of the Institut de Droit International ... in Oslo in 1977 and Athens in 1979) it becomes apparent how difficult it is for them to understand each other. In Athens I had to intervene to save the discussion from becoming completely confused and subsequent speakers made it clear that up to my intervention they had hardly understood whether people were talking about public or private international law or about both.
>
> The reason, of course, is that these subjects are everywhere taught and studied by different scholars, hardly ever by the same. ... This is the real cause of the enormous amount of misunderstanding which is peculiar to discussions on the borderline problems and which I have done my best to clear away.

A textbook on private international law written by Mann could have done so much more to reduce such misunderstandings. It could easily have become a leading authority on the relationship between those two areas of law.

[8] FA Mann (Mann estate, NLMann_1002, two undated versions).

[9] Mann, *Life and Cases* (n 3) 241–42. See also Chapter 7 by Giuditta Cordero-Moss in this volume, 'Delocalization and Re-localization in Commercial Law and the Law of Arbitration: The Continued Relevance of FA Mann's Thought', at Section IV.

III. Public International Law Influences on Private International Law

Mann's Hague jurisdiction lectures and numerous articles on private international law give us many clues. Even better insights of what such a book might have looked like can be gleaned from a somewhat neglected source which gives further proof that Mann attempted to re-conceptualize private international law in such a way that public international law influences were given considerably more prominence. This source is Mann's own address on the occasion of the 50th anniversary of his doctoral degree, which he had completed in Berlin in 1931, an event which the University of Bonn celebrated accordingly in 1981. This address was published in the German original.[10] We have on file an English translation which was produced by Yvonne Podbielski in 1998,[11] seven years after the death of Mann, most likely at the behest of his son, David Mann. Apparently, this English translation was never published. I will quote from this translation and start with the last three sentences:

> A large area of unsolved problems calls for clarification. I will not be able to contribute much to it any more. It is left to the next generation to fulfil this task.

So this is definitely *unvollendet.*

Mann's 1981 address reiterates many points he has made elsewhere, and many cases in which he was intimately involved or on which he has commented. But it also explains the historical trajectory of his approach towards private international law. It begins, unsurprisingly, with Martin Wolff. Mann attended Wolff's seminars on private international law in Berlin, which preceded Wolff's volumes *German Private International Law* (first published in 1933) and *English Private International Law* (first published in 1945).[12] Mann normally treats Wolff in nothing but the most deferential terms, but on this point he notes that in Wolff's 1933 book:

> there is no extensive discussion of public international law, of public law of conflicts ... and of the territoriality of laws. In particular, the relationship between private international law and public international laws is discussed in a very traditional manner.[13]

[10] Hans-Heinrich Jacobs, Gerhard Kegel, and Frederick Alexander Mann, *Reden zum 50. Doktorjubiläum von Frederick Alexander Mann* (Bouvier 1982).

[11] Hans-Heinrich Jacobs, Gerhard Kegel, and Frederick Alexander Mann, *Speeches Celebrating the 50th Anniversary of Frederick Alexander Mann's Doctorate Degree, 4 July 1981* (Mann estate, NLMann_1010) (hereafter Jacobs, Kegel, and Mann, *Speeches*).

[12] See n 2.

[13] Jacobs, Kegel, and Mann, *Speeches* (n 11).

By this Mann refers to Savigny's concept of *comitas* and a mutual quest for harmonious decisions.

Mann's emigration to London in 1933 also marks a turning point in his approach towards private international law. The person who is to bring about this change is Hersch Lauterpacht, in particular his books *Private Law Sources and Analogies of International Law* and *The Function of Law in the International Community.*[14] Mann writes:[15]

> Soon I became an intimate friend not only of the books, but also of their author. This eminent scholar and exceptional man influenced me as much as his teachings did.

And that applied in particular to Lauterpacht's use of 'comparative law as a source of legal principles'. Mann conversely became interested in:

> the influence of public international law on private law … and of how the doctrine of state sovereignty, that is the doctrine of jurisdiction which is part of public international law, limited national legal provisions. … It is easily neglected by both those who are concerned either with public international law of with public law, and those who are concerned solely with private law.[16]

We can see that for Mann, jurisdiction and state sovereignty provide the bridge between public and private international law. This bridging function also corresponds with Mann's views on the rule of law.

He was far from sharing Zitelmann's somewhat naïve or at least very optimistic view that an entire system of private international law rules can and should be generated from public international law rules.[17] Mann's publications, and also the 50th anniversary address, rather demonstrate a careful exploration as to how far such public international law influences should go. The starting point, as expressed in the 1963 Hague Lecture, is that civil law jurisdiction must be connected to jurisdiction for legislative or administrative action under public international law:[18]

> A judgment, viz. a command conveyed through the courts, is not essentially different from a command expressed by legislative or administrative action. It

[14] Hersch Lauterpacht, *Private Law Sources and Analogies in International Law* (with special reference to international arbitration) (Longmans, Green and Co 1927); Hersch Lauterpacht, *The Function of Law in the International Community* (Clarendon 1933).

[15] Jacobs, Kegel, and Mann, *Speeches* (n 11).

[16] ibid.

[17] Ernst Zitelmann, *Internationales Privatrecht, Erster Band* (Duncker & Humblot 1897) 71–82.

[18] Mann, 'Jurisdiction in International Law' (n 1) 61.

cannot claim international validity except if and in so far as it keeps within the limits which public international law imposes.

IV. Integration of Some Particular Views

These explorations are shaped by two factors in particular. The first is his practical experience as a solicitor, on which more will be said below (Section V). The second factor is some very firm views in particular about what he saw as courts claiming excessive jurisdiction, international overreach of economic policies and sanctions, excessive expropriation or violations of territorial integrity, and generally violations of the rule of law.

The 50th anniversary address shows us how Mann integrates these views into a systematic approach which encompasses public and private international law. He explains:

> The question as to the scope of laws is . . . a common element of private and public international law. It is, in fact, the starting point which limits in both areas of law the extent of the sovereignty of states according to suitability, public international law and practical needs.[19]

Mann's starting point for defining the extent of sovereignty is '[t]he century-old concept of territorial and personal sovereignty in public international law'.[20] For him, it makes no difference whether Nazi Germany abducts Jacob Salomon in Switzerland, or France abducts Antoine Argoud in West Germany, or Israel abducts Adolf Eichmann in Argentina. These are clear violations of public international law. When such events surface in a civil lawsuit, private international law rules must neither recognize nor tolerate such illegal state activity. But Mann goes much further. He believes that private international law rules must likewise neither recognize nor tolerate when a state is violating the territorial sovereignty of another state by 'issuing documents, collecting evidence or making tax enquiries' in a foreign country. He even refuses to recognize notarial documentations undertaken on foreign soil.[21]

19 Jacobs, Kegel, and Mann, *Speeches* (n 11).
20 ibid.
21 ibid.

A. Excessive jurisdiction

Mann led a passionate fight against courts claiming excessive jurisdiction in international cases which have very weak or no genuine links to the forum, such as a peripheral commercial interest in the United States, a negligible amount of assets such as a pair of slippers left in a hotel in Germany, French citizenship of one party in a commercial case, or the serving of documents on a passenger in international transit at Heathrow Airport. Indeed, most of what Mann writes about civil jurisdiction in his 1963 Hague Lecture is a critical review of such excessive jurisdiction, for which he sees no basis in public international law.[22] His late work, 'The Extremism of American Extraterritorial Jurisdiction', carries this distaste in its title.[23] It is a case note on a US court ruling on the merger of two foreign companies where jurisdiction is based on a very small proportion of shares in US ownership.

Mann's 50th anniversary address links this rejection of excessive jurisdiction to the Lauterpacht-inspired influence of public on private international law, as developed in Mann's Hague Lectures: jurisdiction to adjudicate must be linked to jurisdiction to legislate, and any jurisdiction which cannot reasonably be linked to sovereignty is to be rejected. As Mann also states: 'We have to accept this theory of the extent of sovereignty as a dominant theme, and indeed, as a fundamental basis of our legal system.'[24]

B. Overriding mandatory provisions

Mann was also highly critical of jurisdiction-based rules which seek to impede economic activities abroad on the basis of similarly weak links, surfacing in various private and economic law situations, often in the form of what the Rome I Regulation now calls 'overriding mandatory provisions', or *Eingriffsnormen* in German, or *lois de police* in French.[25] As early as 1937, Mann expressed reservations about contracts being declared invalid on account of a law which is not the proper law of the contract.[26] His later work links this to public international law notions of jurisdiction. Sovereignty, and in particular territorial sovereignty, Mann tells us in his 50th anniversary address, is the principle on which a solution must be based for whether a state can 'prescribe conduct which either violates, or is at least not accepted, by the laws of foreign countries'.[27]

22 Mann, 'Jurisdiction in International Law' (n 1) 62–68.

23 FA Mann, 'The Extremism of American Extraterritorial Jurisdiction' (1990) 39 ICLQ 410.

24 Mann Nachlass, NLMann_1010.

25 Art. 9 Regulation (EC) No 593/2008 of the European Parliament and of the Council of 17 June 2008 on the law applicable to contractual obligations (Rome I).

26 FA Mann, 'Proper Law and Illegality in Private International Law' (1937) 18 Brit YB Int'l L 97; see also FA Mann, 'Illegality and the Conflict of Laws' (1958) 21 Mod L Rev 180.

27 Mann estate, NLMann_1010.

C. Expropriations

Public international law notions were likewise used by Mann to limit the effect of expropriations. Mann developed his views over a series of articles. His 1943 article 'The Sacrosanctity of the Foreign Act of State' suggested in the ultimate paragraph that domestic courts might, but would not necessarily have to, refuse to recognize a foreign expropriation unless compensation had been paid.[28] He went further in a 1954 article, 'International Delinquencies Before Municipal Courts', suggesting that domestic courts should quite generally not apply an otherwise applicable foreign law 'if and in so far as it expresses or results from an international delinquency', i.e. a violation of public international law.[29] And while an article published in 1950, 'Völkerrecht im Prozeßrecht' ('Public International Law in Procedural Law'), confirms that the effectiveness of expropriations is to be decided in accordance with the law at the place where the expropriated property is located,[30] his 1961 article 'Völkerrechtswidrige Enteignungen vor nationalen Gerichten' ('Expropriations in Violation of Public International Law Before Domestic Courts') goes very specifically beyond the traditional notion that the effects of expropriations are both governed by and limited to the territory of the expropriating state. He urges courts to deny giving any international effect to expropriations which violate public international law rules, even if they occurred exclusively on the territory of the expropriating state.[31]

V. Challenges

While many of Mann's preoccupations could thus be easily integrated into a systematic, coherent, and concise treatise on private international law which would give prominence to public international law influences, there are other aspects which would have made this task more challenging.

[28] FA Mann, 'The Sacrosanctity of the Foreign Act of State' (1943) 42 LQR 155, reproduced in FA Mann, *Studies in International Law* (Clarendon 1973) 420.

[29] FA Mann, 'International Delinquencies Before Domestic Courts' (1954) 70 LQR 181, reproduced in *Studies in International Law* (n 28) 366, 389. This aspect is further explored in the contribution by Lawrence Collins to the present volume (at Section II.B).

[30] FA Mann, 'Völkerrecht im Prozeßrecht' (1950) 5 Süddeutsche Juristen-Zeitung col. 545, 557, reproduced in *Beiträge zum Internationalen Privatrecht* (n 6).

[31] FA Mann, 'Völkerrechtswidrige Enteignungen vor nationalen Gerichten' (1961) 14 Neue Juristische Wochenschrift 705.

A. From territoriality to contact

Some of Mann's correspondence conveys the impression that Mann's enthusiasm for deriving private international law jurisdiction rules from public international law may have peaked between 1981 (his 50th doctoral anniversary address) and 1984 (his second Hague Lecture on jurisdiction).

Arthur Taylor von Mehren wrote to Mann in March 1984 on Mann's forthcoming Hague Lecture:[32]

> Among the several possible subjects that you might treat in your remaining lecture, civil jurisdiction seems to me by far the most interesting and important.

Mann responded on 14 March:[33]

> Thank you so much for your helpful letter of 9th March which I find very encouraging. It has persuaded me to look more closely at civil jurisdiction. I had great reluctance to touch a subject which is so much in a state of flux, and about which it is difficult to say something that will stand the test of time, but I shall see how I get on.

The 1984 lecture repeats that jurisdiction to adjudicate must follow jurisdiction to legislate and postulates that where public international law rules meet private international rules, the latter should be based more on contact than on territoriality.[34] He laments at the same time the questionable results which US courts had achieved when replacing territorial connection with reasonable contact.[35] We learn more about this in a letter which Mann wrote to Peter Hay:[36]

> It is very easy for academic writers like myself to suggest the test of reasonableness, but if you have an immense country like the United States with innumerable litigious lawyers and a contingent fee system, the practical difficulties for foreign traders who directly or indirectly sell goods to the American market are formidable, and the uncertainties are so great that one is bound to ask oneself whether a simpler and stricter test would not in practice be more preferable.

[32] Arthur Taylor von Mehren to FA Mann (Mann estate, NLMann_0504, 9 March 1984).
[33] FA Mann to Arthur Taylor von Mehren (Mann estate, NLMann_0504, 14 March 1984).
[34] Mann, 'Jurisdiction Revisited After Twenty Years' (n 1) 67.
[35] ibid 70–72. Mann also welcomed the abolishment of excessive jurisdiction under German, French, and English law by the Brussels Convention on Jurisdiction and the Enforcement of Judgments in Civil and Commercial Matters of 1968, now Regulation (EU) No 1215/2012 of the European Parliament and of the Council of 12 December 2012 on jurisdiction and the recognition and enforcement of judgments in civil and commercial matters (recast).
[36] FA Mann to Peter Hay (Mann estate, NLMann_0846, 5 March 1986).

The in-built vagueness of what amounts to a sufficient contact (which according to Mann's 1984 Hague Lecture is to replace territoriality as a jurisdiction-generating principle in private international law) may explain some of his 'great reluctance to touch a subject which is so much in a state of flux'. Rather than developing in more detail how civil jurisdiction rules which are defined by contact are to be developed in line with public international law principles which are based on territoriality, Mann spent most of his observations on civil jurisdiction in his 1984 Hague Lecture on an assessment of the 1968 Brussels Convention on the Jurisdiction and Enforcement of Judgments in Civil and Commercial Matters, giving a very cautious and heavily guarded welcome:

> Yet, unwelcome though it is in very many respects, the convention has to be recognized as an important step in the evolution of an international law of civil jurisdiction. However sceptical and even hostile one may be to many of the provisions of the convention, its pervading influence must be acknowledged. In other words the international lawyer has to recognize that what the convention accepts is likely to be consistent with the demands of international law and that what it leaves to the individual States for application in their relations with third parties may not necessarily be inconsistent with international law.[37]

B. A solicitor's need for certainty

This leads us to the point where Mann might have struggled most to reconcile his own views and preoccupations with the task of formulating a treatise on private international law which gives prominence to public international law influences, in particular where public international law demands, suggests, or facilitates greater international harmony of conflict rules.

It is of paramount importance to Mann that rules must produce highly predictable results. Predictability as a desideratum is entirely uncontroversial and certainly helpful for private international law rules. But with Mann as a legal practitioner and, one should add, in particular as an English solicitor, this desire for predictability takes a form which would have curried little favour with his teacher Martin Wolff. For Mann, it is far better to keep known deficiencies in the law than to risk the uncertainty which new or reformulated rules create—as long as a savvy solicitor with a good command of the case law can write around those deficiencies. The potential benefit of replacing deficient and diverse domestic rules with an internationally harmonized new rule which can be applied much more easily and uniformly by lawyers and courts in different countries is no compensation for the

[37] Mann, 'Jurisdiction Revisited After Twenty Years' (n 1) 69.

disadvantage of the uncertainty which a new rule creates. And if such a rule is to be interpreted by international and foreign courts, this is no help but aggravates the problem.

1. The Brussels and Rome conventions

Mann is not alone amongst English lawyers in taking this view, but he may go further than others. While loss of certainty of domestic rules was only among the reasons why his welcome of the Brussels Convention was so heavily guarded,[38] the same loss explains much of his fundamental objection to what is now the Rome I Regulation and then was the Rome Convention on the Law Applicable to Contractual Obligations, which Mann, in one of his last articles, castigated under the heading 'The Proper Law of the Contract—an Obituary'.[39] It was no consolation that this convention enshrined the principle of freedom of choice of law, which Mann supported wholeheartedly. Mann also did not dispute that many of the rules of this convention were based on or at least similar to English conflict law. For Mann, the fundamental problem with the Rome Convention was that it codified case law:[40]

> In the first place the Act substitutes statutory rules for judicially developed experience and thus creates problems of statutory interpretation, where formerly there existed flexible and fruitful judicial practice leading to enlightened development. Statutory interpretation is an entirely different process from judicial evolution based on argument and derived from principles, precedents and experience.

What made the matter worse was that statutory interpretation of the Rome Convention was not left to the discrete jurisdictions of the courts of all (then) twelve Member States. That the European Court of Justice was to provide uniform interpretation, under an accompanying protocol, was, to Mann, a 'feature of the utmost gravity'.[41]

This rejection of internationally harmonized law on the ground that it can disturb a far-from-perfect English law would be difficult to reconcile with Wolff's approach to both law and legal textbooks. Wolff would categorically reject any attempt to defy systematization by muddling through. Indeed, the most serious criticism which reviewers had levelled against Wolff's *Private International Law* was that he suggested that the *ratio decidendi* of a particularly troublesome 19th-century decision of the House of Lords should be interpreted very restrictively,[42]

[38] ibid 69: 'unwelcome though it is in very many respects' and '[h]owever sceptical and even hostile one may be to many of the provisions of the convention'.

[39] FA Mann, 'The Proper Law of Contract – An Obituary' (1991) 107 LQR 353.

[40] ibid.

[41] ibid 354.

[42] Wolff, *Private International Law* (n 2) 395, relating to *Shaw v Gould* (1868) LR 3 HL 55. Critical, John Morris, 'Review of M. Wolff, *Private International Law*' (1946) 62 LQR 88, 90: 'Dr. Wolff is more at

as would indeed happen only three years after the publication of Wolff's book.[43] Mann's strong urge for certainty and predictability was likely to clash with any attempt to present the entire private international law in a systematic, clear, and consistent fashion. Such a desire for certainty and predictability would have been much easier to square with the approach taken by classic, and fortunately no longer fashionable, English law textbooks which made little effort of going beyond a digest of case law, without attempting to place this case law within a structure, system, or concept. But that is a legal writing style which is entirely absent from Mann's work. We can only speculate how Mann would have integrated this particular form of predictability into a general notion of private international law which he would have had to develop if he had been allowed to continue Wolff's treatise, or if he had written a private international law textbook of his own.

2. Domicile and the Hague Convention

Mann's work in the Lord Chancellor's Private International Law Committee can shed further light on how a solicitor's perspective on certainty can complement or collide with Mann's views on public international law influences in private international law. Our archives include Mann's bundle of documents of this committee together with the related correspondence.[44]

In 1952, the Lord Chancellor, Viscount Simonds, invited Mann to join a new Standing Committee on Private International Law. The purpose of this committee was to deal with 'international conferences on this subject which are held at The Hague and elsewhere'.[45] Mann served on this committee until it was eventually dissolved in 1964.

The most immediate task of this committee was to form a view on whether the UK should adopt the Hague Convention Relating to the Settlement of Conflicts Between the Law of Nationality and the Law of Domicile (1955). The purpose of this convention was to reduce frictions which occurred when common law countries would use domicile as a connection point for an applicable law where continental jurisdictions would apply the law of this person's citizenship.

home in discussing unsolved problems than in handling English case law'; similar, Harold Gutteridge, 'Review of Martin Wolff, *Private International Law* (1945)' (1945) 9 Cambridge LJ 268, 269. See Gerhard Dannemann, 'Martin Wolff (1872–1953)' in Beatson and Zimmermann, *Jurists Uprooted* (n 1) 441, 450–52, 455–56.

[43] *In re Bischoffsheim; Cassel v Grant* [1948] Ch 79 (HC).

[44] NLMann_0646 - NLMann_0649, Mann estate. For a fuller account of FA Mann's work in this committee, see Gerhard Dannemann, Christoph König, and Franziska Stamm, 'The Correspondence of Frederick Alexander Mann (1907–1991)' 13–15 <https://www.biicl.org/documents/2054_letters_of_fa_mann.pdf> last accessed 1 June 2023 (hereafter Dannemann, König, and Stamm, 'Correspondence').

[45] Gavin Turnbull (Viscount Simonds) to FA Mann and others (Mann estate, NLMann_0646, 18 September 1952).

The Hague Convention offers a trade-off between the common law preference of domicile and the civilian preference of citizenship as connection points for conflicts rules. Under Article 1, domicile would take precedence over nationality in any clash. However, Article 5 redefined domicile as the place of habitual residence. Effectively, habitual residence was to replace both a common law notion of domicile and a civil law notion of citizenship as connection points. The influential scholar Geoffrey Cheshire saw this as a wonderful opportunity to overcome the 'sentimental and patriotic views of the early 19th century when Englishmen adventured abroad in search of a fortune, but always intended to return some day'.[46]

Mann, who was asked to write a draft bill together with Geoffrey Cross (later Lord Cross), did not embrace this proposed harmonization, taking instead a much more pragmatic and also traditional approach. The Cross–Mann draft essentially sought to codify existing English case law, removing only the disturbing effects of the so-called domicile of origin, which is the father's domicile at the time of birth.[47] The inevitable consequence is that some people will have their domicile of origin in a country in which they have never set foot and to which they are not connected in any other way. It is perhaps telling that this is the only innovation which found Mann's support: if a person has a domicile of birth in Ruritania without ever having set foot in this country, or having any claim to citizenship, there is a complete lack of any territorial or personal sovereignty of Ruritania which could possibly be linked to this domicile. But Cross and Mann would make no similar allowance for the central trade-off of the Hague Convention by moving domicile closer to habitual residence, in spite of the fact that residence has a clearer and generally also stronger link to territorial sovereignty than domicile.[48] The notion of domicile allows persons to reject the territorial connection to the country they live in simply by stating that they do not intend to live there permanently.

The Cross–Mann draft also sought to keep the common law rule according to which a married woman takes the domicile of her husband.[49] That rule was not only becoming outdated as a matter of principle but also capable of causing practical problems, notably in divorce cases.

After long deliberations, the committee recommended that Article 5 of the Hague Convention should not be enacted, thus removing the essential trade-off

[46] Geoffrey Cheshire, Memorandum in preparation of the Second Meeting of the PIL Committee on 18 February 1952 (Mann estate, NLMann_0646).

[47] FA Mann to DW Dobson (Mann estate, NLMann_0646, 13 July 1953).

[48] 'This is a country from which for centuries people have gone out into the world with the intention ultimately to return and without any intention to sever their connexion with the British legal system and the ideas underlying it. It would not be in harmony with the temper of the British people, if those who settle abroad had to be told that there was no method whereby they could regulate their lives according to the familiar British conceptions'. *Draft Code of the Law of Domicile. An Act for modifying and amending the definition of domicile*, prepared by Geoffrey Cross and F.A. Mann (undated), presented to the third meeting of the Private International Law Committee on 10 Jun 1953 (Mann estate, NLMann_0646).

[49] ibid, Section 3.

and the tool for genuine harmonization. As the committee's secretary would later write in a confidential letter to Mann: 'It seems to me, and the Foreign Office agree with me, that it might be better to bring our law into a satisfactory state without paying too much attention to what foreign countries do.'[50] Mann would eventually support a minimal reform which would have created a rebuttable presumption that if a person had their home in the UK they also had the intention to live there. Lack of governmental support led the Lord Chancellor to introduce the required legislation in the form of a Private Member Bill. In spite of Mann's best efforts to shore up support behind the scene, this bill failed due to stiff opposition from businesspeople, in particular from those who were afraid to lose their non-domiciled tax status.[51] The attempt 'to bring our law into a satisfactory state without paying too much attention to what foreign countries do' thus ended in abject failure. The difference between citizenship, domicile, and habitual residence as connecting points in private international law continues to keep courts and scholars alike busy and frequently creates the very opposite of legal certainty.

VI. Conclusion: Further Speculation

While I have not found any specific indication in Mann's writings or correspondence which would support the following proposition, I nevertheless find it likely that Mann, had he written a treatise on private international law, would eventually have discovered that, next to territorial and personal sovereignty, there is also sovereign exercise of state power as a public international law principle which can determine, shape, or limit private international law rules. Perhaps the best example is currency. When more than 20 years ago I needed for my *Habilitationsschrift* a source to confirm that the law which applies to a particular currency is necessarily the law of the country which regulates that currency,[52] I was confident that Mann's *Legal Aspect of Money* would provide the answer. And it did, pointing me to the Permanent Court of International Justice's 1929 judgment in the *Case of Serbian Loans*, where the court stated:[53]

> It is indeed a generally accepted principle that a state is entitled to regulate its own currency.

[50] JM Cartwright-Sharp to FA Mann (Mann estate, NLMann_0647, 3 October 1957).

[51] For further details, see Dannemann, König, and Stamm, 'Correspondence' (n 44) 14–15.

[52] Gerhard Dannemann, *Die ungewollte Diskriminierung in der internationalen Rechtsanwendung. Zur Anwendung, Berücksichtigung und Anpassung von Normen aus unterschiedlichen Rechtsordnungen* (Mohr Siebeck 2004) 70 (hereafter Dannemann, *Die ungewollte Diskriminierung*).

[53] *Case of Serbian Loans* [1929] Pub. PCIJ Ser. A No. 20, 44; FA Mann, *The Legal Aspect of Money* (5th edn, Clarendon 1991) 461.

This rule figures among a limited number of public international law rules which can and probably even must be applied directly in private international law.[54] However, this rule can be grounded in neither territorial nor personal sovereignty. The rule loses none of its force if a payment is to be made outside of that state's territory and between parties who are neither citizens nor otherwise related to the state which controls that currency. I expect that Mann would have agreed if he had set himself the task of writing that textbook for which his 50th anniversary address provides something of a blueprint. He could have linked other private international law rules to the same principle of state power, including the one that if it is questioned whether the judgment or other decision of a foreign state is final and binding, it is the law of that state which must decide. But this is where I will end with my speculations about what 'Mann on Private International Law' could have looked like.

Bibliography

Collins L, 'F. A. Mann (1907–1991)', in Jack Beatson and Reinhard Zimmermann (eds), *Jurists Uprooted. German-Speaking Émigré Lawyers in Twentieth Century Britain* (OUP 2003)

Dannemann G, *Die ungewollte Diskriminierung in der internationalen Rechtsanwendung. Zur Anwendung, Berücksichtigung und Anpassung von Normen aus unterschiedlichen Rechtsordnungen* (Mohr Siebeck 2004)

Dannemann G, 'Martin Wolff (1872–1953)' in Jack Beatson and Reinhard Zimmermann (eds), *Jurists Uprooted. German-Speaking Émigré Lawyers in Twentieth-Century Britain* (OUP 2003)

Gutteridge H, 'Review of Martin Wolff, *Private International Law* (1945)' (1945) 9 Cambridge LJ 268

Jacobs HH, Kegel G, and Mann FA, *Reden zum 50. Doktorjubiläum von Frederick Alexander Mann* (Bouvier 1982)

Lauterpacht H, *Private Law Sources and Analogies in International Law (with Special Reference to International Arbitration)* (Longmans, Green and co. 1927)

Lauterpacht H, *The Function of Law in the International Community* (Clarendon 1933)

Mann FA, *Beiträge zum Internationalen Privatrecht* (Duncker & Humblot 1976)

Mann FA, 'Illegality and the Conflict of Laws' (1958) 21 Mod L Rev 180

Mann FA, *Life and Cases. Manuscript of an Autobiography* (Wolfgang Ernst ed., V&R unipress 2021)

Mann FA, 'Proper Law and Illegality in Private International Law' (1937) 18 BYBIL 97

Mann FA, *Studies in International Law* (Clarendon 1973)

Mann FA, 'The Doctrine of Jurisdiction in International Law' (1963) 111 Recueil des Cours 1

Mann FA, 'The Doctrine of Jurisdiction in International Law Revisited After Twenty Years' (1984) 186 Recueil des Cours 9

Mann FA, 'The Extremism of American Extraterritorial Jurisdiction' (1990) 39 ICLQ 410

Mann FA, 'The Proper Law of Contract – An Obituary' (1991) 107 LQR 353

54 For an overview, see Dannemann, *Die ungewollte Diskriminierung* (n 52) 51–73.

Mann FA, 'The Sacrosanctity of the Foreign Act of State' (1943) 42 LQR 155
Mann FA, 'Völkerrecht im Prozeßrecht' (1950) 5 Süddeutsche Juristen-Zeitung col. 545
Mann FA, 'Völkerrechtswidrige Enteignungen vor nationalen Gerichten' (1961) 14 Neue Juristische Wochenschrift 705
Morris J, 'Review of M. Wolff, *Private International Law*' (1946) 62 LQR 88
Wolff M, *Das Sachenrecht* (Elwert 1910)
Wolff M, *Das Sachenrecht* (9th edn, Elwert 1932)
Wolff M, *Internationales Privatrecht* (Springer 1933)
Wolff M, *Das Internationale Privatrecht Deutschlands* (3rd edn, Springer 1954)
Wolff M, *Private International Law* (OUP 1945)
Wolff M, *Private International Law* (2nd edn, OUP 1950)
Zitelmann E, *Internationales Privatrecht, Erster Band* (Duncker & Humblot 1897)

7

Delocalization and Re-localization in Commercial Law and the Law of Arbitration

The Continued Relevance of FA Mann's Thought

Giuditta Cordero-Moss

I. Introduction

Cross-border contracts and mechanisms for the resolution of international disputes (particularly arbitration) have for decades given rise to an intense doctrinal debate. The starting point for the debate is the observation that these contracts and dispute resolution mechanisms are not connected with only one single state and that therefore they are potentially subject to a plurality of legal systems. Grossly simplified, this prompts two opposite approaches. One consists in choosing which of the connected legal systems is applicable. The other is to apply a uniform legal system.

FA Mann was among the first to recognize the importance of analysing the legal framework for international commercial relations in a systematic way and following the classical legal method, ultimately founded on Roman law. He made use of the traditional categories developed by legal doctrine and argued that the question of the applicable legal source is a question either of choice of the applicable national law (i.e. a question of private international law—also known as conflict of laws) or of application of conventions among states (i.e. a question of public

Giuditta Cordero-Moss, *Delocalization and Re-localization in Commercial Law and the Law of Arbitration* In: *FA Mann.* Edited by: Jason Grant Allen and Gerhard Dannemann, Oxford University Press. © Giuditta Cordero-Moss 2024. DOI: 10.1093/oso/9780198881452.003.0008

international law). The underlying idea was that a legal relationship is either subject to a national law, or it is subject to instruments of public international law (see Section IV below).

In contrast, in the 1960s a theory developed in France proposed a new legal dimension for international commercial relationships—one that is neither national nor international in the sense of public international law. This theory became known under various names, such as delocalization, new *lex mercatoria*, or transnational law. The strongly innovative profile of the theory, coupled with a professed closeness to commercial reality, made it very popular in the field of international business law and influenced the practice of commercial bodies such as the International Chamber of Commerce (ICC)[1] as well as domestic legislation.[2]

Over the decades, numerous sources of soft law have been developed in this field. Soft law is not binding and is not the emanation of legislative authority but rather is derived from business practice and generally laid down in instruments issued by commercial organizations or international bodies. In the logic of delocalization, these sources are deemed to be the only appropriate sources to be applied in international relationships, in addition to the will of the parties and trade usages. However, critics highlight that these sources are not a self-sufficient, complete set of rules and it is necessary to rely on the traditional legal system to enforce, integrate, and even interpret their provisions and principles.

For decades, the ideal of delocalization went hand in hand with the increased internationalization of business first, and globalization later.

However, globalization is now giving way to regionalization and a certain relocalization. This development emerged years before national borders unexpectedly took a prominent role as a consequence of pandemics, wars, and sanctions. In the field of commercial law, this is reflected in a new development: after decades of asserting delocalization, the attention is increasingly shifting from the necessity that national laws do not interfere with the parties' will, to the advisability that arbitration ensures an accurate application of the most important policies protected by national laws.

In this landscape, FA Mann's approach, based as it is on a sound legal method, is a precious guideline for how to address the issue.

[1] The ICC was the first arbitration institution to introduce in its arbitration rules the so-called *voie directe*, permitting the arbitral tribunal to determine the rules applicable to the dispute without applying any conflict rules: see Art. 17 (1) of the 1998 Arbitration Rules (Art. 21 (1) in the 2021 version).

[2] The *voie directe* (see previous footnote) has also been introduced, e.g., in the French Code of Civil Procedure, Art. 1511.

II. The Background: Contract Law

In the decades that followed the Second World War, international business underwent a remarkable development that gradually but consistently led to the globalization of commercial relationships and consequently of the contracts that regulated them. As we will see in Section V.C, during the last few years this trend has started showing signs of reversal. As long as FA Mann was active in legal practice, however, the trend was unequivocally one of internationalization.

The apparently unstoppable internationalization of business, together with the increasing importance of foreign investor–state disputes (see Section III below), inspired scholars to consider the traditional approach as inadequate.

Indeed, the traditional approach is somewhat asymmetrical. Domestic contracts regulate domestic legal relationships; international contracts regulate international legal relationships. Domestic contracts are subject to domestic law (national law); and for the sake of symmetry, international contracts should be subject to international law. However, with some important exceptions such as the 1980 Vienna Convention on International Contracts for the Sale of Goods (CISG), in contract law there are few treaties or conventions. Hence, according to the traditional approach, international contracts are subject to national law: a branch of each national law, known as private international law or conflict of laws, provides mechanisms to choose the applicable law from the various potentially applicable national laws. Many private international law rules have been harmonized or even unified at a supra-national level, but this does not change the result of their application: international contracts will be subject to a national law.

Those who found this asymmetry to be unsatisfactory advocated for a third system, detached from national law and yet not entirely international law, i.e. not formally based on treaties or conventions. The delocalization theory was launched by renowned scholars, such as Goldmann[3] and Schmitthoff,[4] and has received considerable support.[5] It posits a uniform regulation for international contracts, applicable equally all over the world and irrespective of the involved national legal

[3] Berthold Goldman, 'Frontières du droit et lex mercatoria' (1964) 9 Archives de philosophie du droit 177; Berthold Goldman, 'La lex mercatoria dans les contrats et l'arbitrage internationaux: réalité et perspectives' (1979) 2 Travaux du Comité français de droit international privé 221; Berthold Goldman, 'Lex Mercatoria' (1983) 3 Forum Internationale 3; Berthold Goldman, 'The Applicable Law: General Principles of Law – The Lex Mercatoria' in JDM Lew (ed.), *Contemporary Problems in International Arbitration* (Springer 1986) 113; Berthold Goldman, 'Nouvelles réflexions sur la Lex Mercatoria' in Christian Dominicé, Robert Patry, and Claude Reymond (eds), *Etudes de droit international en l'honneur de Pierre Lalive* (Helbing & Lichtenhahn 1993) 241.

[4] Clive M Schmitthoff, 'The Unification of the Law of International Trade' (1968) Journal of Business Law 105.

[5] Literature on the subject matter is vast. Among the more recent works, the most frequently referred to are F De Ly, *International Business Law and* Lex Mercatoria (Emerald Publishing1992); KP Berger, *The Creeping Codification of the Lex Mercatoria* (2nd edn, Kluwer Law International 2010); Ole Lando, 'The *Lex Mercatoria* in International Commercial Arbitration' (1985) 34 International and Comparative Law Quarterly 747 (hereafter Lando, 'The *Lex Mercatoria*').

systems. This regulation would stem from a body of rules spontaneously emerging from the international business community, and its most prominent principle would be the primacy of the parties' will.

This third system, which goes under a variety of names (such as *lex mercatoria*, transnational law, or soft law), is based on a variety of sources, such as generally accepted principles, trade usages, contract practice, arbitration practice, or publications by trade or branch associations such as the ICC or the International Bar Association (IBA). This results in a fragmentary system, the content of which is not easily accessible.

To achieve a more systematic and accessible transnational law, distillates of the soft law found their way in collections of principles, such as the International Institute for the Unification of Private Law (UNIDROIT) Principles of International Commercial Contracts (UPICC).[6] The UPICC are a collection of principles in the area of contract law, based in part on a comparative analysis of several legal systems, in part on the collection of trade usages and soft sources, and in part on provisions suggested by the drafters as best rules. They are systematic and have a high level of quality. In my opinion, however, they do not achieve the aim of replacing the applicable law, see Section V.B below.

The development of international contract practice must be considered, too. It is now an established fact[7] that contracts are written in the common law style, irrespective of whether there is a connection with English law or another law belonging to the same family. This style is based on the primacy of the parties' will and assumes that all rights and obligations be spelled out in the contract, rather than being implied by the adjudicator or read into the contract by operation of the applicable law. This leads to extensive and detailed contracts which are meant to be self-sufficient and not needing integration with default rules of the applicable law. Furthermore, contracts are often standardized and contain the same wording irrespective of which law governs them. Model contracts are published as soft law and offered for use in any country of the world.

An exhaustive and standardized contract does not invite a consideration of the applicable law. Contract practice may therefore give the impression that contracts are intended to be subject only to the will of the parties and spontaneous, transnational sources of soft law. In my opinion, however, this conclusion is not justified (see Section V.A below).

Often, the preference for transnational law is explained by reference to the widespread use of arbitration for solving international contract disputes. The

[6] See UNIDROIT Principles 2016 (4th edn) at <https://www.unidroit.org/instruments/commercial-contracts/unidroit-principles-2016/> accessed 18 January 2023.

[7] More extensively, see Giuditta Cordero-Moss (ed.), *Boilerplate Clauses, International Commercial Contracts and the Applicable Law* (Cambridge University Press 2011) (hereafter Cordero-Moss (ed.), *Boilerplate Clauses*); Giuditta Cordero-Moss, *International Commercial Contracts* (2nd edn, Cambridge University Press, forthcoming) (hereafter Cordero-Moss, *International Commercial Contracts*).

assumption is that international arbitration is detached from any national law and that consequently arbitrators follow the will of the parties rather than a national law. Transnational law being an emanation of usages, practices, and generally recognized principles, it is believed to be more suitable for application in arbitration than national law. In my opinion, this conclusion is also not justified (see Section III).

III. The Background: Arbitration

The understanding of arbitration as delocalized is the result of an evolution, as illustrated by some resolutions of the Institute of International Law.

The XIV Commission in 1957 clearly stated that arbitration was subject to the law of the country where the arbitral tribunal had its seat, and that the private international law of the seat identified the national law applicable to the merits of the dispute.[8]

The XVIII Commission in 1989 expressly criticized the assumption that arbitration necessarily took place within the framework of a national law.[9] The General Report emphasized the detachment of arbitration from any national law: It proclaimed the 'jurisdictional theory's decline', and that 'party agreement became the only source' for international arbitration to be 'reliable and legitimate'.

The XVIII Commission dealt with disputes between foreign investors and host states, and was a step in the process of enhancing investment protection. Foreign investment needs a legal framework that is wider than the legal system of the host state—to avoid abuses of sovereignty, such as the host state changing the rules of the game to the investor's detriment. The need to be free from national laws in purely commercial contracts is less evident, however. Nevertheless, the delocalization theory has quickly expanded to also cover commercial arbitration.

Commercial arbitration is a method for dispute settlement that provides an alternative to courts. It relies on the will of the parties: they choose to subject the dispute to arbitration, they appoint the arbitral tribunal, they determine the scope of the dispute and thus the tribunal's jurisdiction, they decide the procedure to be followed (usually by making reference to institutional or ad hoc arbitration rules), and they decide which law shall be applied to the merits of the dispute. The remarkable step from a merely contractual regime (fully based on the will of the parties) to

[8] Article 11 of the Resolution on 'Arbitration in private international law', *Yearbook – Institute of International Law* (Vol II, 1957) 491; the XIVth Commission had already prepared a report on this subject in 1952 (*Yearbook – Institute of International Law* (Vol I, 1952) 469–609, but a resolution could not be adopted because of the death of some members of the commission. In 1957, a new XIVth Commission adopted a resolution largely based on the 1952 Report.

[9] Resolution on 'Arbitration between states, state enterprises, or state entities, and foreign enterprises', *Yearbook – Institute of International Law* (Vol II, 1989) 324.

the judicial regime is mainly due to the 1958 New York Convention on Recognition and Enforcement of Foreign Arbitral Awards, ratified by 170 states so far, which remains the most important instrument regulating arbitration. Under the New York Convention, courts must dismiss a claim and refer the parties to arbitration if the claim is covered by an arbitration agreement, and arbitral awards are enforceable. To a large extent this makes arbitration an autonomous system based on the will of the parties. This contributes to validating the theories according to which arbitration is detached from national laws.

However, arbitration is not completely autonomous. There is restricted, but not insignificant, court control. Arbitral awards are final and enforceable, and they are not subject to any appeal before the courts. However, under certain conditions, courts may set aside an award and can refuse its enforcement. To the extent that the conditions for annulling and refusing enforcement are linked to the application of a certain law, therefore, the arbitration is not autonomous or delocalized.

The *validity* of an award is controlled under the law of the arbitration's seat. Arbitration law has been harmonized, in 85 countries, by the United Nations Commission on International Trade Law (UNCITRAL) Model Law on International Commercial Arbitration. The Model Law is a good example of successful soft law: it is used for inspiration by national legislators, and has thus achieved harmonization of arbitration law in the countries that have adopted it. Admittedly, countries such as England, France, Switzerland, and Sweden, where international arbitration mostly takes place, have not adopted the Model Law. Furthermore, harmonization is not absolute even among the countries which have adopted the Model Law, as the legislator is free to interpret, adjust, or modify the Model Law when it adopts it as its own arbitration law. Nevertheless, the level of harmonization of arbitration law is significant.

For investment arbitration, the 1965 Washington Convention on the Settlement of Investment Disputes between States and Nationals of Other States (ICSID) established a special dispute resolution mechanism, without reference to national law, for annulment of the awards. However, a relatively large proportion of investment disputes are carried out under commercial arbitration rules, and they will be subject to the regime applicable to commercial arbitration.

Enforcement is carried out under the New York Convention. For investment arbitration that is carried out under the ICSID Convention, Article 54 requires the award to be enforced as if it were a final court decision rendered in that state.

The New York Convention and the Model Law have similar criteria, which make various references to national law—among others, regarding the court's public policy. In this context, an excessive transnational enthusiasm may lead to misunderstanding French courts' terminology. French courts introduced the delocalization doctrine and firmly support it. They have the power to annul an award or refuse its enforcement when it violates 'international public policy'. This if often interpreted as a reference to a public policy stemming from international sources, thus restricting the courts' possibility to apply their own public policy. Quite apart from the fact that it seems unrealistic to expect a court to be so delocalized that it disregards its own public policy, this interpretation misunderstands French terminology. The adjective 'international' defines the scope of application of the public policy (international disputes), not the source of the public policy.[10] It is, therefore, French (national) international public policy that is applied, not a delocalized public policy.

The autonomy of arbitration, therefore, is not absolute.

IV. FA Mann's Position on Delocalization

In the abovementioned Institute of International Law's XVIII Commission, FA Mann strongly criticized the delocalized approach. He affirmed:[11]

> I confess that I simply do not know what this means. Arbitrations take place on earth, in territories, in localities. They do not take place in a vacuum. [. . .] I fear that, when you speak of 'delocalization' you mean something like 'delegalization', the rejection of the control of law. If, as I fear, this is a correct interpretation, the disagreement is fundamental and almost of a philosophical character. [. . .] More than 50 years of very intensive and extensive practical experience have taught me that, when parties embark upon arbitration proceedings [. . .], they want to win and want to be told with what degree of likelihood they will win. In other words, they want to know the *law*. They are not in the least bit interested in what you seem to understand by 'delocalization'. Nor are they interested in compromise solutions. On the contrary, they regard any tendency on the part of the arbitrators to adopt such solutions as a sign of weakness. In other words, they expect a judicial decision arrived at after a judicial process.

In numerous writings he confirmed his view: arbitration is a legal institution subject to the law of the arbitration's seat. We actually owe the expression '*lex arbitri*' to him.[12] The disputed issues may be international, but the procedure is subject to the law of the seat (including any international conventions), and the merits are subject to the law determined by conflict rules. For investment contracts between a foreign investor and the host state, he was the first[13] to explain that the

[10] See, for example, Cour d'appel de Paris, 5 October 2021, nr. 18/18708. For further references, see Cordero-Moss, *International Commercial Contracts* (n 7), section 5.4.9(b).

[11] *Yearbook – Institute of International Law* (Vol I, 1989) 173.

[12] FA Mann, 'Lex facit arbitrum', in Pieter Sanders (ed.), *Liber Amicorum for Martin Domke* (Martinus Nijhoff 1967) 157.

[13] FA Mann, *Life and Cases. Manuscript of an Autobiography* (Bonn University Press 2021) 241 (hereafter FA Mann, *Life and Cases*).

parties could choose the public international law to govern their relationship.[14] The applicable law is determined by rules of private international law (conflict rules), including party autonomy.[15] Within their freedom of contract, the parties may regulate their interests as they deem fit, including by making reference to sources of soft law.

The parties' wide freedom to regulate their interests and to choose the applicable law does not affect the legal framework's structure. That arbitration or contracts shall enter into a third dimension whenever the dispute or the legal relationship is international was considered by FA Mann to be legal anarchy and heresy.[16]

In a review of a book on arbitration, he comments on the book's references to a transnational setting:[17]

> This phrase [. . .] once again raises the question what the word 'transnational' is intended to mean. There is a very strong reason to fear that it means nothing and is incapable of definition. A contract, a dispute, an arbitration, a problem, a conception is either national or international. The word 'transnational' is confusing and indicates a regrettable lack of precision of thought and language such as lawyers must be expected to eschew.[18]

According to FA Mann, regulation is rooted either in public international law or in the national law designated by the private international law. However, often lawyers specialize in only one of these three fields. Therefore, when faced with complex issues requiring insight in all of them, lawyers run the risk of not mastering all implications. It is then tempting to suggest new approaches or develop ad hoc categories to deal with issues that do not squarely fit in their field of specialization. FA Mann was an expert in the fields of, inter alia, public international law, private international law, and financial law. His holistic understanding of the law permitted him to fit all issues into the system and consistently apply the legal method, without the need to invent new approaches—a need that derives from a lack of knowledge across the different fields of law.[19] It may be worth quoting his words in this context:

[14] FA Mann, 'The Law Governing State Contracts' (1944) British Yearbook of International Law 11.

[15] FA Mann, 'The Proper Law of the Contract' (1950) 3 The International Law Quarterly 1, 60–73.

[16] FA Mann to Pierre Lalive (Mann estate, NLMann_0471, 4 July 1977). See also Gerhard Dannemann, Christoph König, and Franziska Stamm, 'The Correspondence of Frederick Alexander Mann (1907–1991)' fn 125 <https://www.biicl.org/documents/2054_letters_of_fa_mann.pdf> last accessed 1 June 2023.

[17] FA Mann, '*Resolving Transnational Disputes Through International Arbitration. Sixth Sokol Colloquium*. Edited by Thomas Carbonneau' (1986) 2(4) Arbitration International 378 (hereafter Mann, 'Resolving Transnational Disputes').

[18] ibid.

[19] Mann, *Life and Cases* (n 13) 244, remembering his 'astonishment at the fact that among these experts in comparative law [at the Max Planck Institute of Foreign and Comparative Law in Hamburg] Lauterpacht's work was completely unknown. It was the work of a public international lawyer and

> It is [. . .] fascinating to observe how great the cleavage is between public and private international lawyers. When they discuss the particular questions [concerning contracts between States and private persons] (as the elite of international lawyers did in the course of the sessions of the Institut de Droit International in Oslo in 1977 and Athens in 1979) it becomes apparent how difficult it is for them to understand each other. In Athens I had to intervene to save the discussion from becoming completely confused and subsequent speakers made it clear that up to my intervention they had hardly understood whether people were talking about public or private international law or about both.[20]

FA Mann supported a strict legal reasoning[21] and had contempt for what he defined as 'socio-legal thought'.[22] His scientific method, however, was not a dogmatic exercise of merely abstract interest. It was structured and rigorously scientific, but in no way detached from practice. Throughout his career, FA Mann exercised the legal profession, and it is in the legal practice that he found the inspiration for his academic work, see Section V below. His attention to the needs of reality may be exemplified by his approach to what he defines as the 'philosophy of merits'. He observes that particularly (but not only) English judges tend to form an intuitive conclusion about the outcome that a case should have ('Who deserves to win? Who has the merits?')[23] and then develop a legal reasoning supporting this conclusion. In his opinion, this is not an acceptable method: 'If this is correct then law is largely a lie: it is no more than words made to support a result extraneously reached.'[24] FA Mann regrets this development, but does not pretend it did not exist—to the contrary, he accepts it 'as a fact of legal life'.[25]

Furthermore, FA Mann insisted on the objective and neutral nature of the law[26] and did not approve of using it for political purposes.[27] However, he was not prone to positivism and literalism and approved of the law being subject to an ultimate control to avoid absolute injustice, which led him to favour the enactment of human rights.[28]

The picture deriving from the above shows FA Mann's scientific approach to the law. Transposed to the field of international commercial law, this implies that there

private lawyers, so the theory goes on the Continent, are not supposed to be familiar with so strange and remote a subject.'

[20] Mann, *Life and Cases* (n 13) 241f.
[21] ibid 82.
[22] ibid 79.
[23] ibid 226.
[24] ibid.
[25] ibid 227.
[26] ibid 42f., 63, 190.
[27] ibid 59, 68f, 81, 87, 89, 102.
[28] ibid 85, 90, 219, 224, 240. His opinion of the European Court of Human Rights was not very high, see 85.

is no need to invent new approaches to accommodate new phenomena such as international contracts and arbitration: a sound legal method permits to fit them into the system.

V. What FA Mann's Thought can Teach us Today

The delocalization theory is often praised as being more practice oriented than the traditional approach. The traditional approach in turn, including FA Mann's approach, is often accused of being too formalistic and not sufficiently sensitive to the needs of international business. Nothing could be further from reality, as far as FA Mann is concerned.

As known, he was first of all a practitioner. He acted in numerous renowned cases and had a leading position in a prestigious law firm. His academic work was in no way detached from his practice, as he explains in the following: 'Purely academic law is liable to become sterile. The demands of an extensive practice are such that they always lead to some fruitful starting point for research.'[29]

Even before starting law studies, he had been exposed to legal practice in his father's law firm, setting the foundation for his practice-oriented understanding of the law: 'The result was that in matters relating to the practice of law I had a good deal of practical knowledge when I reached the university and thus a considerable advantage over those for whom law was nothing but theory.'[30]

Should there be any doubts about FA Mann's understanding of business, they would be eliminated by looking at what he wrote decades before the financial crisis of 2008. He looked:

> critically at the activities of merchant banks as they have developed since the Second World War. Merchant banks render advice for which they usually charge wholly exorbitant fees and which could just as well, though much more cheaply, be given by stockbrokers, lawyers and accountants. [. . .] One day the courts will be called upon to decide whether and to what extent these advisory activities impose fiduciary duties upon banks. It is to be hoped that the courts will be very strict.[31]

And: 'one day [this] will cause [merchant banks] grave difficulties, the conflict between their own interest and the interest of the client.'[32] It is difficult to define when precisely FA Mann wrote these words—however, it was certainly before 1991, the

[29] ibid 85, 183, 213.
[30] ibid 31.
[31] ibid 229.
[32] ibid 89.

year in which he passed away. About 20 years later these words dramatically proved to be true when the same conflict led to the financial crisis of 2008. His exposure to banking practices and his analytical spirit made him foresee the collapse that would intervene decades later.

There is, therefore, no question that FA Mann's thought is solidly based on legal practice and a deep understanding of business.

The question is rather whether, in the decades since he passed away, the landscape of international business has evolved in such a way that his method and thought are no longer relevant. We will here concentrate on three aspects of this posthumous evolution: contract practice, soft law, and the emerging re-localization of business and arbitration law. As the analysis will show, the question has to be answered in the negative: FA Mann's thought has not lost its relevance.

A. Development of contract practice

Standardization of contract practice is not a new phenomenon, but it has remarkably increased since the 1980s.

The European Commission had even encouraged standard contracts as a tool towards harmonization of the various state contract laws.[33] This plan was, however, soon abandoned.[34] It was soon realized that contracts, even if they are standardized, are subject to a governing law and cannot derogate from its mandatory rules. Therefore, a standard contract, to be effective across the entire territory of the EU, would have to comply with the strictest of the criteria set by the various member states. This would have prevented progress in contract practice, and would not have been desirable.

The question is whether the increasingly standardized contract practice affects FA Mann's position that parties want to know what the law is—they are not interested in delocalized or compromise solutions.[35]

It is often assumed that sufficiently clear and extensive contracts are self-sufficient (see Section II above). As pointed out already, contract practice adopts the common law drafting style, spelling out all assumptions, effects, and eventualities and leaving little or no room for the interpreter to imply terms or be concerned with the parties' hypothetical intentions. National laws are supposed to be irrelevant because the contract offers a solution to any issue that may arise. Furthermore, contracts usually contain an extensive section with so-called boilerplate clauses, regulating the contract's interpretation and operation. Parties aspire

[33] See the Action Plan on a More Coherent European Contract Law, COM(2003) 68 final and European Contract Law and the Revision of the Acquis: The Way Forward, COM(2004) 651 final.

[34] First Annual Progress Report on European Contract Law and the Acquis Review, COM(2005) 456 final.

[35] See Section III.

thus at creating their own general contract law, excluding the need to look at the applicable law for questions of interpretation or of implementation of the contract. Moreover, dealing with standardized contracts, the parties apply the same clauses to interpret contracts that are to be fulfilled in the most disparate parts of the world.

Based on this practice, an observer could question the relevance of national laws that were not considered during contract drafting. Scholarly writings have been proposing a uniform international commercial law as a desirable solution (see Section II above).

This literature presents various arguments to prove that national laws are not adequate sources for governing international contracts. Arguments range from the rather pragmatic (and irrefutable) observation that it is costly and time consuming to analyse, for every contract, all potentially applicable laws, to the not necessarily always appropriate statement that conflict rules are a confusing and complicated mechanism and thus should be avoided, or to the usually unsubstantiated statement that national laws' content is adequate to regulate domestic but not international contracts. This latter argument seems to be less frequently invoked following the publication of principles and rules made specifically for international contracts such as the UPICC. As these rules and principles—tailored to international contracts—show no structural differences to those of national laws, it has become difficult to affirm that national laws are not adequate for governing international contracts.

Certainly, the variety of national laws to which an international contract may be subject requires awareness of the different systems. Many drafters are aware of this and nevertheless draft standardized contracts that are not adjusted to the applicable law—considering this as a calculated legal risk.[36] Standardization is cost-efficient and permits a simpler contract management. However, it does not mean that contract drafters refuse to subject their contracts to national law. It only means that they have evaluated the risk that the contract not be enforced fully in accordance with the terms that contradict the applicable law, have quantified the consequences of that risk materializing, and have measured this against the cost of adjusting every individual contract to the relevant applicable law. The cost/benefit analysis may lead to using standardized contracts clauses, accepting the risk that they may not be enforceable according to their terms. This, however, is not equivalent to refusing the relevance of national law.

So-called transaction lawyers, whose activity mainly consists in negotiating and drafting contracts, will praise efficiency and flexibility. Transaction lawyers

[36] See, more extensively, Cordero-Moss, *International Commercial Contracts* (n 7) ch. 1; David Echenberg, 'Negotiating International Contracts: Does the Process Invite a Review of Standard Contracts from the Point of View of National Legal Requirements?' in Cordero-Moss (ed.), *Boilerplate Clauses* (n 7); Maria Celeste Vettese, 'Multinational Companies and National Contracts' in Cordero-Moss (ed.), *Boilerplate Clauses* (n 7).

are not involved in the performance of the contract and are therefore not concerned with enforceability of the clauses. Their role ceases once the contract is signed. They will consider their work successful if they managed to insert in the contract a wording reflecting their interests. The picture drawn so far could be seen to confirm a delocalized approach. However, there is also a different type of lawyer: the litigation lawyers that take over when a dispute arises. Litigation lawyers are concerned with enforceability. This requires consideration of the applicable law.

When a dispute arises, the parties' assessment is different from what they do when they draft a contract. The parties to a dispute need to evaluate whether it is worth litigating the dispute, or whether they should rather attempt to reach a commercial arrangement. A commercial arrangement's acceptability depends on the probability of success of each party's legal claims—which requires being able to evaluate the legal positions. A party will be more restrictive in making concessions to the other party's requests if its legal position is strong than in the situation where the outcome of the dispute is uncertain.

The support for a delocalized transnational law is based on the misconception that commercial parties always desire a flexible system that can be adapted to their needs. Litigators, however, emphasize the desirability of a predictable legal system that can be objectively applied. This corresponds to FA Mann's experience as quoted in Section IV above. Adapting the contract to the case's specific needs is a task for the contract drafters, not for the adjudicator. What interests litigation lawyers is the enforceability of rights (whether these are based on a contract or on an arbitral award) and the parameters for enforceability. If the criteria upon which the dispute will be decided are uncertain, it will be impossible to assess the risk connected with the dispute. How can a party embark on a costly proceeding that might last for years, without having been able to assess the connected risks?

That contract practice is not meant to displace the applicable law is confirmed by the circumstance that most model contracts contain a clause choosing the applicable law. Furthermore, most model arbitration clauses recommend that the parties choose the law applicable to the merits of the dispute.

Contract practice's massive standardization, therefore, does not restrict the continued relevance of FA Mann's position. While it is true that the standardization of contracts has increased, and that publications with model contracts have proliferated, the interests of the parties to a dispute have not changed: they need to assess the probability of winning the case, and, to do so, they must evaluate their legal position. To evaluate their legal position, the parties must analyse the applicable law. It is highly uncertain that the transnational law allows the opportunity to exercise such analysis with a sufficient degree of predictability and systematicity (see the following section).

B. Development of soft law

In the last few decades there has been a remarkable development in the field of soft law. Codification of usages, best practices, principles, model contracts, model laws, and the like have proliferated—at the initiative of institutions such as the ICC, branch organizations such as the International Swaps and Derivatives Association (ISDA), professional associations such as the IBA, and international organizations such as UNCITRAL or UNIDROIT. This wealth of uniform soft codification has no doubt rendered the transnational law more accessible and systematic than it was when it was necessary to rely on unwritten usages and generally recognized principles. The question remains whether this development has had an impact on the continued relevance of FA Mann's position according to which there is no third dimension beyond public international law and national law.

It has been argued that the open and incomplete character of transnational law is not a disadvantage but a positive characteristic: by not containing specific solutions or clear criteria, the transnational law would permit arbitrators to develop creative solutions, acting as a 'social engineer'.[37] The parties would delegate to the arbitrators the task of developing the decision's parameters. This approach shows deep trust in the arbitrators' capability as private lawmakers. Back in the 1980s, FA Mann considered a similar reliance on trust to indicate 'the naivety' of the 'instigators' of such a theory.[38]

Furthermore, this approach disregards the criterion of predictability. As I explain elsewhere,[39] transnational law lacks a framework within which arbitrators would develop their solutions—this would make the arbitrators' creative work even less predictable. Fascinating as the idea of arbitrators as social engineers may be, the prospect of having to plead in front of a tribunal that develops its own criteria for decision-making alarmingly reminds one of the position of Josef K in Franz Kafka's dystopian novel *Der Prozess*. This is considered by FA Mann to be legal anarchy (see Section IV above).

As a remedy to transnational law's fragmentation and inaccessibility, restatements, systematizations, and standardization have flourished in recent decades, such as the UPICC. The UPICC have been defined as a 'Troika', together with the CISG and the Principles of European Contract Law (PECL):[40] a transnational law body particularly apt for governing commercial contracts.[41]

37 Lando, 'The *Lex Mercatoria*' (n 5) 752; Ole Lando, 'The Law Applicable to the Merits of the Dispute' (1986) 2 Arbitration International 104, 112.

38 Mann, 'Resolving Transnational Disputes' (n 17).

39 Cordero-Moss, *International Commercial Contracts* (n 7) ch. 2.

40 The PECL served as a basis for an extensive work on European contract law, the result of which for the moment consists mainly in the Draft Common Frame of Reference (DCFR), see Christian von Bahr and others (eds), *Principles, Definitions and Model Rules of European Private Law: Draft Common Frame of Reference (DCFR)* (2008).

41 See, for example, Ole Lando, 'CISG and its Followers: A Proposal to Adopt some International Principles of Contract Law' (2005) 53 American Journal of Comparative Law 379–402.

Since the time in which FA Mann was active, restatements of principles and other soft law sources have proliferated—not only in the field of contract law, but in most fields. What does this mean for the continued relevance of FA Mann's position?

Restatements of soft law, compilations of trade usages, and digests of transnational principles and other transnational instruments may be extremely useful for contract drafters. For example, by simply making reference to one of the listed abbreviations in the INCOTERMS (International Commercial Terms, published by the ICC), the contract imports the relevant regulation on passage of risk, organization and cost of insurance, freight, and customs clearance. Drafters save considerable time and resources that they otherwise would have needed to spend in regulating these issues. However, as I explain elsewhere,[42] sources of soft law are no real alternative to a state law. They rather complement the applicable law.

There are, broadly speaking, two types of soft law sources: those that have a specific scope of application and thus assume that other sources will regulate all issues that do not fall within that scope, and those that have a general scope of application and aspire to be the only applicable source.

The INCOTERMS are an example of the former. They are used for the definition of the place of delivery in international sales and thus determine when the risk passes from the seller to the buyer. They do not cover all legal effects relating to the delivery: for example, the moment when the title passes from the buyer to the seller, the contract's validity, or the conditions for and consequences of non-conformity of the goods with the contract.[43] All these aspects will be subject to the applicable law, even though the parties have chosen to apply the INCOTERMS.

An example of sources with the ambition of regulating a whole field of law are the UPICC. The UPICC are meant to systematically formulate the main general principles prevailing in cross-border contracts in a way that may be applied uniformly in all jurisdictions, irrespective of the adjudicator's own legal tradition.

As I explain elsewhere,[44] the UPICC do not, for the moment, provide a sufficiently extensive basis for addressing all issues on a contract's interpretation,

[42] Cordero-Moss, *International Commercial Contracts* (n 7) ch. 2; Cordero-Moss, 'Does the Use of Common Law Contract Models Give Rise to a Tacit Choice of Law or to a Harmonised, Transnational Interpretation?' in Cordero-Moss (ed.), *Boilerplate Clauses* (n 7) 37–61; Giuditta Cordero-Moss, 'Detailed Contract Regulations and the UPICC: Parallels with National Law and Potential for Improvements—The Example of Norwegian Law' in UNIDROIT (ed.), *Eppur si muove: The Age of Uniform Law—Essays in Honour of Michael Joachim Bonell* (UNIDROIT 2016) 1302 (hereafter Cordero-Moss, 'Detailed Contract Regulations and the UPICC').

[43] For a more extensive reasoning, see Cordero-Moss, *International Commercial Contracts* (n 7) section 2.2.6; Maria Celeste Vettese, 'Multinational Companies and National Contracts' in Cordero-Moss (ed.), *Boilerplate Clauses* (n 7) section 2.

[44] Cordero-Moss, *International Commercial Contracts* (n 7) section 2.3; Cordero-Moss, 'Detailed Contract Regulations and the UPICC' (n 42); Cordero-Moss, 'The UNIDROIT Principles of International Commercial Contracts' in Petra Butler (ed.), *International Commercial Contracts* (forthcoming) (hereafter Cordero-Moss, 'The UNIDROIT Principles').

construction, and application. Take a dispute on whether the contract shall be interpreted literally or shall be integrated by purposive considerations, by documents exchanged between the parties during negotiations or by the parties' conduct after the agreement was entered into. The UPICC solve these questions by making extensive reference to the principle of good faith; however, good faith is a legal standard that requires specification, and there is no generally acknowledged legal standard of good faith that is sufficiently precise to be applied uniformly, irrespective of the governing law.[45] It is the applicable contract law that gives guidelines as to the extent to which the adjudicator may or shall disregard the contract wording to ensure a fair balance between the parties' interests, whether the adjudicator shall integrate the contract with obligations that are not explicitly regulated therein, or whether there is a duty on the parties to act loyally towards each other that creates obligations not spelled out in the contract or even contradicting the wording of the contract.

The above shows that soft law may need to be integrated with, or applied in the light of, the applicable law—both when the sources only cover specific issues and when they have a wider scope. It is true that these sources are to be interpreted autonomously, but when there are no underlying principles that may inform an autonomous interpretation, what remains is the applicable law.

Even when it may be sufficient to look at the contract and at the incorporated soft law to solve a dispute, the applicable law is not irrelevant. Admittedly, if no issues fall outside of contract freedom and of what the parties or the soft law regulated, and if this regulation does not require interpretation or construction, there is no need to apply the governing law. The applicable law, however, is in the background, and comes into the foreground whenever there is the need to fill a gap, to construe a rule, or to evaluate issues that do not fall within contract freedom.

Furthermore, the UPICC apply only within the scope of contract freedom: the parties can decide, instead of drafting an original regulation, to refer to the UPICC. However, commercial disputes often also concern issues that do not fall within contract freedom and will be subject to the applicable law. Therefore, even assuming that the soft law does not have any gaps and that it does not need any interpretation or construction (but we know that it does, for example, with respect to the abovementioned principle of good faith), it will be necessary to consider the applicable law. Even disputes arising out of a simple sales contract may require deciding whether or when the title passed from the seller to the buyer (this is a matter of property law and outside of contract freedom); whether the signature is binding (this is a question of legal capacity and outside of contract freedom); whether the agent could bind the principal (this is a question of agency law and may be outside of contract freedom). In more complex legal relationships, even more issues will

45 Cordero-Moss, *International Commercial Contracts* (n 7) section 2.2.5.

fall outside of contract freedom and of soft law—for instance, if the contract creates a security interest, the existence and effects of the security interest are regulated by property law; if the contract relies on a board resolution, the existence and validity of the board resolution is subject to the applicable company law; etc.

Furthermore, soft law cannot derogate from mandatory rules, such as the protection of the weaker party or, for the systems that have it, the principle of good faith.

In my opinion, therefore, the increased availability of systematic sources of soft law can be seen as creating a third layer between the contract and the applicable law, but it does not change the structure of the legal system. This third layer is integrated into the contract when the parties make reference to it, and thus it can be seen as an extension of the contract. The contract and the incorporated soft law will continue being subject to the applicable law for the issues that are not regulated, for the aspects regarding the general operation of the contract, and for the mandatory rules that may exist on the subject matter of the contract. The soft law may be accessible and systematic, but it is a complement of the applicable law, not its replacement—very often an extremely useful and welcome complement, but still subject to the applicable law.

While the structure of the legal system is not affected by the proliferation of soft law sources, it is legitimate to investigate whether the traditional dichotomy between delocalization and the traditional approach may have lost its relevance.

Rather than choosing between one approach or the other, it is useful to concentrate on the two approaches' complementarity.[46]

The soft law cannot be ignored if the parties referred to it. Moreover, soft law's increased accessibility and quality give it a role even when the parties have not referred to it: soft law may be used as an inspiration for interpretating the contract or the applicable law, or as a guideline when exercising the adjudicator's discretion.[47]

Ignoring the applicable law, on the other hand, may lead to unenforceable results. Even where soft law sources enjoy undisputed success, they do not necessarily replace the applicable law. In addition to the considerations made above on the INCOTERMS and the UPICC, another example are the IBA Guidelines on Conflicts of Interest in International Arbitration.[48] They are extremely well received even beyond the area of arbitration and are widely considered to set the

[46] Pointing out the complementarity of the two approaches, as well as the cross-fertilization between them, see Giuditta Cordero-Moss and Diego Fernández Arrojo, 'Introduction to the 2022 Hague Academy Center for Studies and Research on The Law Applicable to International Arbitration' (forthcoming).

[47] These uses of the UPICC are the most widespread. See, for references, Cordero-Moss, 'Detailed Contract Regulations and the UPICC' (n 42); Cordero-Moss, 'The UNIDROIT Principles' (n 44).

[48] IBA Guidelines on Conflicts of Interest in International Arbitration <https://www.ibanet.org/MediaHandler?id=e2fe5e72-eb14-4bba-b10d-d33dafee8918> accessed 5 June 2023.

standard for when an adjudicator is to be considered independent and impartial. Nevertheless, there are examples of court decisions applying a different standard.[49]

The potentially inconsistent application of soft law does not derive exclusively from the interaction with national courts: even arbitrators may be influenced by their own legal tradition and may, consequently, apply soft sources differently. Admittedly, one of the assumptions of the delocalization theory is that arbitration is detached from national laws and thus solves disputes simply on the basis of the contract and of transnational law. This is promoted as a means for avoiding inconsistent results that may flow from the diversity of national laws. This supposed uniform regime for international contracts assumes that arbitration is a homogenous environment. That may or may not have been a realistic assumption decades ago,[50] when the closed circle of arbitrators was composed of a few very recognized professionals, mainly 'male, pale, and stale', with comparable legal backgrounds. But this is certainly not true today. To quote one of the grand old men of arbitration:

> If such days ever existed, they are long gone. Today, new players in the arbitral process include governments, companies, counsel and arbitrators from multiple litigation traditions. [. . .] New entrants come to the arbitral process not only from different geographical regions and legal cultures, but also from varied professional paths. [. . .] In this connection, the impact of diversity in background cannot be overemphasized.[51]

Diversity in arbitration is now promoted by arbitral institutions and looked upon as a desirable development.[52] While this development can only be supported, it contributes to weakening the assumption of harmony and homogeneity of the system upon which the delocalization theory relies.

The development of more accessible and more systematic sources of soft law, therefore, does not limit the continued relevance of FA Mann's position. Soft law needs to be taken into consideration, but it does not replace the applicable law; rather it complements it. The legal systems' structure remains the same: soft law can be seen as an extension of the contract, and the contract is still subject to national law or to international law.

[49] For references, see Cordero-Moss, 'General Report' in Cordero-Moss (ed.), *Independence and Impartiality in International Adjudication*, XXI General Congress of the International Academy of Comparative Law (Intersentia 2023) section 3.1.

[50] The inability of arbitration to generate a uniform regime is not a new phenomenon, see Cordero-Moss, *International Commercial Contracts* (n 7).

[51] William W Park, 'A Fair Fight: Professional Guidelines in International Arbitration' (2014) 30(3) Arbitration International 409, 414f.

[52] For an analysis of today's attention to diversity, see Matteo Winkler and Mikael Schinazi, 'No Longer 'Pale, Male, and Stale'? Approaching Diversity and Inclusiveness in International Arbitration' in Nigel Blackaby and others (eds), *Liber Amicorum Guillermo Aguilar Álvarez* (2021).

C. Emerging re-localization

FA Mann was not enthusiastic about arbitration. Criticizing a book's reference to transnational law, he said:

> [t]hat language, however, leads a most distinguished contributor, a lawyer of the highest quality, Monsieur George A Delaume, to the statement that it 'is generally recognized that, in order to be fully effective, transnational arbitration must be freed from judicial interference.' On the footing of a certain meaning of the word 'transnational' this would be a license, perhaps even an invitation for arbitrariness, a danger which many writers on arbitration are only too prone to ignore and which is liable to bring the whole idea of arbitration into disrepute.[53]

FA Mann is concerned that delocalization may bring arbitration into disrepute. This concern has proven to be justified and it is currently materializing. Arbitration is increasingly criticized for its autonomy from national laws, among others. There is an emerging mistrust, both as far as investment arbitration and as far as commercial arbitration are concerned. This development is threatening to reverse the arbitration-friendly trend of past decades—a trend that had led to, among other things, an ever-growing scope of disputes that could be submitted to arbitration, so-called arbitrability. In a recent ICC conference, this development prompted one speaker to say: 'arbitration is under attack.'[54]

In investment arbitration, concerns are voiced about the ability of arbitrators to understand public interest issues,[55] the consistency of awards, and the lack of appeal.[56] For investment disputes based on intra-EU treaties, the Court of Justice of the EU (CJEU) denied arbitrability, arguing that investment arbitration does not give an effective method to control the uniform application of EU law.[57] The decision was based on an unconvincing distinction between commercial and investment arbitration, which gives reason to fear that the distinction may be abandoned, expanding the non-arbitrability also to commercial disputes.[58] For the moment,

[53] Mann, 'Resolving Transnational Disputes' (n 17).

[54] This was said by Yves Derain at the 39th ICC Institute Annual Conference, 'Explaining Why You Lost – Reasoning in Arbitration', 17 December 2019. For a more extensive reasoning and references, see Giuditta Cordero-Moss, 'The Alleged Failure of Arbitration to Address Due Process Concerns: Is Arbitration under Attack?' (2021) Stockholm Arbitration Yearbook 251.

[55] Report of UNCITRAL Working Group III (Investor–State Dispute Settlement Reform) on the work of its thirty-fifth session (New York, 23–27 April 2017) A/CN.9/935, paras 82–88; Report of UNCITRAL Working Group III (Investor–State Dispute Settlement Reform) on the work of thirty-sixth session (Vienna, 29 October–2 November 2018) A/CN.9/964, paras 64–108.

[56] Report of Working Group III on the work of its thirty-fifth session, A/CN.9/935, paras 35, 38; Report of Working Group III on the work of thirty-sixth session, A/CN.9/964, para 30.

[57] C-284/16 *Achmea* EU:C:2018:158.

[58] For a more extensive analysis and references, see Giuditta Cordero-Moss, '*Achmea*'s Distinction between Investment and Commercial Arbitration' in A Calissendorff (ed.), *The Future of Arbitration in Europe* (Stockholm Centre for Commercial Law Skriftserie No 36, 2020) 17–28.

however, the CJEU, indirectly and as an *obiter dictum*, endorses that commercial disputes regarding the interpretation of EU law may be subject to arbitration, because court control permits the court to review the interpretation of EU law made by the tribunal and, by requesting preliminary rulings, to ensure uniformity of the interpretation of EU law.[59]

For commercial arbitration, there are signs of a more restrictive approach to arbitrability,[60] reversing a liberal approach usually deemed to have been introduced by the US decision in *Mitsubishi*.[61] *Mitsubishi* permitted the arbitrability of disputes relating to competition law—which until that time had been considered to involve too important and general interests to be arbitrable. To justify arbitrability, it emphasized that courts can give a 'second look' at the arbitral tribunal's accurate application of the law—particularly, through the rule on public policy.

A similar opening was made by the CJEU with the *Eco Swiss* case.[62] EU competition law was defined as a matter of public policy; nevertheless, disputes involving competition law are arbitrable. The second look permits courts to review the award's compatibility with public policy.

The second look, therefore, prompted the expansion of arbitrability: recognizing the courts' possibility to assess whether the award was compatible with public policy in the court's system, therefore, is arbitration-friendly. However, the delocalization doctrine advocated for restricting this possibility: it considered any interference by the courts as unacceptable in arbitration. French courts developed the so-called minimalist approach, according to which courts owe deference to the evaluation made by the arbitral tribunal. The arbitral tribunal's assessment of public policy issues, in other words, should be binding on the courts. Elsewhere I have criticized this approach:[63] by preventing the courts from independently evaluating public policy, it basically deprives the second look of any value. By so doing, it prompts a reversal of the liberalization linked to the second look. Therefore, the minimalist approach has only the appearance of being arbitration-friendly—in reality it brings arbitration into disrepute, as FA Mann feared.

[59] *Achmea* (n 57) para 54.

[60] For references, see Giuditta Cordero-Moss, 'Court Control on Arbitral Awards: Public Policy, Uniform Application of EU Law and Arbitrability' in Axel Calissendorff and Patrik Schöldström (eds), *Stockholm Arbitration Yearbook* (2020) 199–217.

[61] *Mitsubishi Motors Corp v Soler Chrysler-Plymouth, Inc* 473 US 614, 628 (1985) (United States). The first Supreme Court judgment recognizing the arbitrability of matters that previously were deemed to be for the exclusive competence of courts of law was *Scherk v Alberto-Culver* 417 US 506 (1974). See, for further references, P Carrington and P Hagen, 'Contract and Jurisdiction' (1997) 8 The Supreme Court Review 331, 362f., and J Sternlight, 'Panacea or Corporate Tool? Debunking the Supreme Court's Preference for Binding Arbitration' (1996) 74 Washington University Law Quarterly 637, 652.

[62] C-126/97 *Eco Swiss China Time Ltd v Benneton Int'l NV* [1999] ECR I-3079.

[63] Giuditta Cordero-Moss, 'Reasons in Arbitral Awards and Court Control' in Antonio Crivellaro and Mélida N Hodgson (eds), *Dossier XVIII: Explaining Why You Lost: Reasoning in Arbitration* (ICC Institute of World Business 2020) 93.

French courts, however, have started to moderate their minimalist approach, as a consequence of what I define as an emerging re-localization.

This is the result of a growing awareness, in the arbitration community,[64] of the necessity to ensure that the award gives due consideration to the law applicable to the merits—at least as far as concerns regulatory norms in areas such as corruption and economic crime.

It has become clear in past decades that a regime simply based on a spontaneous recognition by a homogenous business community is not realistic in these areas. As a consequence, even French courts have abandoned their minimalist approach and have taken a maximalist approach.[65] The courts' possibility of having an independent second look at awards to ensure that fundamental principles are not violated is an incentive for arbitral tribunals to duly consider the applicable law. This should be a sufficient basis to ensure the arbitration-friendly attitude opened by *Mitsubishi*—although the second look does not provide a perfect system.[66]

This reversal of delocalization is particularly evident in the areas of corruption and economic crime. However, there are other areas in which an equivalent development can be expected—for example, human rights' impact on the supply chain, or a parent company's duty of care for its subsidiaries' activity.

Moreover, the dramatic events of the past couple of years—pandemics, wars, sanctions—threaten to put a stopper on the ever-increasing internationalization of business, and consequently on delocalization ambitions.

Those who embraced the delocalization doctrine may find it difficult to justify its reversal. If the assumption is that international contracts and arbitration are detached from national law, it becomes necessary to develop a new basis to explain why certain rules have to be taken into consideration after all, and what the criteria for selecting these rules are.

This difficulty does not arise in the traditional approach, which never professed a detachment from national law. The application or consideration of national law follows from the application of the legal method, and the choice of which law to apply or consider is based on the private international law. There is no need to invent new bases.

64 Luca Radicati di Brozolo, 'Mandatory Rules and International Arbitration' (2012) 23 American Review of International Arbitration 49, 66 ff.

65 This was recently confirmed by the Supreme Court, see Cass Civ 1ère, 23.3.2022, No. 17-17.981 (*Belokon v Kyrgyzstan*). For further references, see Giuditta Cordero-Moss, 'Corruption and Arbitration: Arbitrability, Jurisdiction, Admissibility or Merits?' in *Festschrift Piero Bernardini* (forthcoming); Cordero-Moss, 'Article V (2) (b)' in Herbert Kronke and others (eds), *Recognition and Enforcement of Foreign Arbitral Awards: A Global Commentary on the New York Convention* (2nd edn, forthcoming).

66 Massimo Benedettelli, '"Communitarization" of International Arbitration: A New Spectre Haunting Europe?' (2011) 73 Arbitration International 583, 597; W Park, 'Private Adjudicators and the Public Interest: The Expanding Scope of International Arbitration' (1986) 12 Brooklyn Journal of International Law 642.

The emerging re-localization is a confirmation that FA Mann's fears about delocalization were justified, and it confirms that his approach is more appropriate than ever.

VI. Conclusion

Perhaps the most notable development since FA Mann's last contributions is the proliferation of sources of soft law, their high quality, and the extensive and systematic content of some of them.

As the foregoing showed, this development does not affect the structure of the legal framework for international contracts and arbitration: as soft law generally falls within the area of contract freedom and may be considered to be an extension of the parties' will, the legal framework is still provided by public international law or by national law.

Admittedly, should the scope of soft law be such that its regulation replaced the applicable law, it could be doubted that national law has a significant role to play. However, as was shown above, it is more appropriate to speak of complementarity than of replacement. Soft law is applied and interpreted within the framework of the applicable law; in addition, there may be many issues that do not fall within the scope of the soft law sources, which necessarily are subject to the applicable law.

Another important development is the emerging re-localization. Ensuring an accurate application of important rules has become a significant concern that is threatening the conception of arbitration as a delocalized realm of party autonomy. This development shows that FA Mann's concerns about the credibility of arbitration were correct, and confirms that his approach is still relevant and useful to ensure a sound methodological approach to commercial dispute resolution.

Bibliography

Benedettelli M, 'Communitarization' of International Arbitration: A New Spectre Haunting Europe?' (2011) 73 Arbitration International 583

Berger KP, *The Creeping Codification of the Lex Mercatoria* (2nd edn, Kluwer Law International 2010)

Carrington P and Hagen P, 'Contract and Jurisdiction' (1997) 8 The Supreme Court Review 331

Cordero-Moss G (ed.), *Boilerplate Clauses, International Commercial Contracts and the Applicable Law* (Cambridge University Press 2011)

Cordero-Moss G, 'Does the Use of Common Law Contract Models Give Rise to a Tacit Choice of Law or to a Harmonised, Transnational Interpretation?' in Cordero-Moss (ed.), *Boilerplate Clauses, International Commercial Contracts and the Applicable Law* (Cambridge University Press 2011)

Cordero-Moss G, 'Detailed Contract Regulations and the UPICC: Parallels with National Law and Potential for Improvements—The Example of Norwegian Law' in UNIDROIT (ed.), *Eppur si muove: The Age of Uniform Law—Essays in honour of Michael Joachim Bonell* (UNIDROIT 2016)

Cordero-Moss G, 'Achmea's Distinction between Investment and Commercial Arbitration' in A Calissendorff (ed.), *The Future of Arbitration in Europe* (Stockholm Centre for Commercial Law Skriftserie No 36, 2020)

Cordero-Moss G, 'Court Control on Arbitral Awards: Public Policy, Uniform Application of EU Law and Arbitrability' in Axel Calissendorff and Patrik Schöldström (eds), *Stockholm Arbitration Yearbook* (Wolters Kluwer 2020)

Cordero-Moss G, 'Reasons in Arbitral Awards and Court Control' in Antonio Crivellaro and Mélida N Hodgson (eds), *Dossier XVIII: Explaining Why you Lost: Reasoning in Arbitration* (ICC Institute of World Business 2020)

Cordero-Moss G, 'The Alleged Failure of Arbitration to Address Due Process Concerns: Is Arbitration under Attack?' (2021) Stockholm Arbitration Yearbook 251

Cordero-Moss G, 'Corruption and Arbitration: Arbitrability, Jurisdiction, Admissibility or Merits?' (forthcoming) Festschrift Piero Bernardini

Cordero-Moss G, *International Commercial Contracts* (2nd edn, Cambridge University Press, forthcoming)

Cordero-Moss G, 'The UNIDROIT Principles of International Commercial Contracts' in Petra Butler (ed.), *International Commercial Contracts* (OUP forthcoming)

Cordero-Moss G and Arrojo DE, 'Introduction to the 2022 Hague Academy Center for Studies and Research on The Law Applicable to International Arbitration' (forthcoming)

De Ly F, *International Business Law and Lex Mercatoria* (Emerald Publishing 1992)

Derain Y, 'Explaining Why you Lost—Reasoning in Arbitration' (at the 39th ICC Institute Annual Conference, 17 December 2019)

Echenberg D, 'Negotiating International Contracts: Does the Process Invite a Review of Standard Contracts from the Point of View of National Legal Requirements?' in Giuditta Cordero-Moss (ed.), *Boilerplate Clauses, International Commercial Contracts and the Applicable Law* (Cambridge University Press 2011)

Goldman B, 'Frontières du droit et lex mercatoria'(1964) 9 Archives de philosophie du droit 177

Goldman B, 'La lex mercatoria dans les contrats et l'arbitrage internationaux: réalité et perspectives' (1979) 2 Travaux du Comité français de droit international privé 221

Goldman B, 'Lex Mercatoria' (1983) 3 Forum Internationale 1

Goldman B, 'The Applicable Law: General Principles of Law – The Lex Mercatoria' in JDM Lew (ed.), *Contemporary Problems in International Arbitration* (Springer 1986)

Goldman B, 'Nouvelles réflexions sur la Lex Mercatoria' in Christian Dominicé, Robert Patry, and Claude Reymond (eds), *Etudes de droit international en l'honneur de Pierre Lalive* (Helbing & Lichtenhahn 1993)

Lando O, 'The *Lex Mercatoria* in International Commercial Arbitration' (1985) 34(4) International and Comparative Law Quarterly 747

Lando O, 'The Law Applicable to the Merits of the Dispute' (1986) 2 Arbitration International 104

Lando O, 'CISG and its Followers: A Proposal to Adopt Some International Principles of Contract Law' (2005) 53 American Journal of Comparative Law, 379

Mann FA, 'The Law Governing State Contracts' (1944) 21 BYBIL 11

Mann FA, 'The Proper Law of the Contract' (1950) 3 The International Law Quarterly 60

Mann FA, 'Lex facit arbitrum' in Pieter Sanders (ed.), *Liber Amicorum for Martin Domke* (Martinus Nijhoff 1967)

Mann FA, '*Resolving Transnational Disputes Through International Arbitration. Sixth Sokol Colloquium*. Edited by Thomas Carbonneau' (1986) 2(4) Arbitration International 378

Mann FA, *Life and Cases. Manuscript of an Autobiography* (Wolfgang Ernst ed., Bonn University Press 2021)

Park W, 'Private Adjudicators and the Public Interest: The Expanding Scope of International Arbitration' (1986) 12 Brooklyn Journal of International Law 629

Park WW, 'A Fair Fight; Professional Guidelines in International Arbitration' (2014) 30 Arbitration International 409

Radicati di Brozolo L, 'Mandatory Rules and International Arbitration' (2012) 23 American Review of International Arbitration 49

Schmitthoff CM, 'The Unification of the Law of International Trade' (1968) Journal of Business Law 105

Sternlight J, 'Panacea or Corporate Tool? Debunking the Supreme Court's Preference for Binding Arbitration' (1996) 74 Washington University Law Quarterly 637

Vettese MC, 'Multinational Companies and National Contracts' in Cordero-Moss (ed.), *Boilerplate Clauses, International Commercial Contracts and the Applicable Law* (Cambridge University Press 2011)

von Bahr C and others (eds), *Principles, Definitions and Model Rules of European Private Law: Draft Common Frame of Reference (DCFR)* (Sellier 2008)

Winkler M and Schinazi M, 'No Longer 'Pale, Male, and Stale'? Approaching Diversity and Inclusiveness in International Arbitration' in N Blackaby and others (eds), *Liber Amicorum Guillermo Aguilar Álvarez* (Wolters Kluwer 2021)

PART III

'THE TASK OF THE JURIST TO DEFINE'

The Legal Aspects of Money

8
Before Mann
Martin Wolff on Monetary Law

Wolfgang Ernst

I. Wolff's Money Tract in *Ehrenbergs Handbuch* (1917)

It must have been in or around 1911 that Victor Ehrenberg[1] started a highly ambitious project, an eight-volume handbook of German commercial law.[2] Since the enactment of the German Civil Code (*Bürgerliches Gesetzbuch* or BGB) in 1900, commercial law that had hitherto provided a standalone basis for all dealings of a commercial nature had become ancillary to the German Civil Code. The revised Commercial Code (*Handelsgesetzbuch* or HGB) now supplemented and modified the Civil Code where commercially active parties were in play.

Among many other private law courses, Martin Wolff (1872–1953) taught commercial law. Ehrenberg enlisted Martin Wolff for chapters in the volume that

[1] Victor Ehrenberg (1851–1929), professor of law at the universities of Göttingen and Leipzig, was the son-in-law of Rudolf von Jhering (1818–1892) and the father-in-law of Max Born (1882–1970), the physicist who won the Nobel prize in 1954. His nephew was the ancient historian of the same first name, Victor Ehrenberg (1891–1976). Ehrenberg is best known as a pioneer of academic treatment of insurance law. On Ehrenberg, see Uwe Blaurock, 'Victor Ehrenberg (1851–1929) – "Vater der Versicherungswissenschaft"' in F Loos (ed.), *Rechtswissenschaft in Göttingen. Göttinger Juristen aus 250 Jahren* (Vandenhoeck & Ruprecht 1987) 316–35; Christian Keller (ed.), *Victor Ehrenberg und Georg Jellinek: Briefwechsel 1872–1911* (Klostermann 2005).

[2] Victor Ehrenberg (ed.), *Handbuch des gesamten Handelsrechts mit Einschluss des Wechsel-, Scheck-, See- und Binnenschiffahrtsrechts, des Versicherungsrechts sowie des Post- und Telegraphenrechts* (OR Reisland 1913–1929).

Wolfgang Ernst, *Before Mann* In: *FA Mann.* Edited by: Jason Grant Allen and Gerhard Dannemann, Oxford University Press.
 DOI: 10.1093/oso/9780198881452.003.0009

covered types of assets that were dealt with by commercial law. There was a chapter on negotiable instruments by Ernst Jacobi.[3] The remainder of the volume was written by Wolff, consisting of an introduction, a chapter entitled 'Commodity' (*Die Ware*) and another 'Money' (*Das Geld*).[4] Both chapters are of book length. Wolff, who at that time held a chair at Marburg University, finished his manuscript in 1916. The volume went into print in June 1917, during wartime. The monumental handbook was still unfinished when Ehrenberg died in 1929. The general editorship of the handbook was assigned to Martin Wolff, together with Heinrich Titze (1872–1945);[5] both already cooperated as editors of a Studies in Comparative Law series. No further volumes seem to have come out under their editorship.

Wolff's chapter on money is a first-class piece of German legal academic theory. It is concept-heavy, controlled by the steely ambition to set out the law in a highly systematized, most comprehensive manner, leaving no stone unturned, however small. The subject matter is money in the contemporary German legal system, not just in the Commercial Code. Wolff's chapter explains the place of money in private law in general, and also gives due attention to the German currency framework that might be seen more as a matter of 'public law' than 'commercial law'. Wolff has been praised as a 'master of clarity'.[6] The tract on money confirms this praise. At the time, it was also the most comprehensive exposition ever of the legal aspects of money in the German-speaking legal tradition.[7] The following observations are deliberately selective and cannot reproduce the full impressive granularity of Wolff's exposition.

In two introductory chapters, Wolff discusses money from both an economic and a legal perspective. From an economic point of view, Wolff looks first at the corporeal movables which we call money. They are a general means of exchange, first and foremost. Although, Wolff disagrees with those economists who want to restrict the term 'money' to full-bodied things meant to serve as general means of exchange. One consequence of this metallist view—Karl von Knies[8] is named as a protagonist—is that token money would have needed to be classified as

[3] On Ernst Jacobi (1867–1946), see Gisela Möllenhoff and Rita Schlautmann-Overmeyer, *Jüdische Familien in Münster 1918 bis 1945. Biographisches Lexikon* (Westfälisches Dampfboot 1995) 222.

[4] Martin Wolff, 'Das Geld' in Victor Ehrenberg (ed.), *Handbuch des gesamten Handelsrechts mit Einschluss des Wechsel-, Scheck-, See- und Binnenschiffahrtsrechts, des Versicherungsrechts sowie des Post- und Telegraphenrechts* (Vol IV/section 1, OR Reisland 1917) 563–48 (hereafter Wolff, 'Das Geld').

[5] On Titze, see Hellmut Georg Isele, 'Zur Erinnerung an Heinrich Titze' (1972) 172 Archiv für die Civilistische Praxis 392–95.

[6] Dieter Medicus, 'Martin Wolff (1872–1953): Ein Meister an Klarheit' in Heinrichs and others (eds), *Deutsche Juristen jüdischer Herkunft* (CH Beck 1993) 543–53.

[7] A generation earlier, a considerably shorter chapter by Richard Koch had been devoted to money and money-token ('Geld- und Geldwerthzeichen') in Wilhelm Endemann, *Handbuch des deutschen Handels-, See und Wechselrechts*, vol. 2 (Fues's Verlag 1882) 113–39. On Richard Koch (1834–1910), later president of the Reichsbank, see Manfred Pohl, 'Koch, Richard' in *Neue Deutsche Biographie* (Vol. 12, Historische Kommission bei der Bayerischen Akademie der Wissenschaften 1980) 273–74.

[8] Karl Knies, *Das Geld: Darlegung der Grundlehren von dem Gelde* (2nd edn, Weidmannsche Buchhandlung 1885).

quasi-money (*uneigentliches Geld*). This restriction, Wolff argues, is not called for since trust is the essential element for all general means of exchange. Even full-bodied coins circulate on the basis of the commercial trust placed in their exchangeability for other assets.

Wolff turns to the systematic arrangement of different corporeal items of money. Wolff dubs such a neatly arranged relationship a 'currency' (*Währung*) or 'money-system'. This system backs up the potential use of money as a measure of value. The usability of money is not solely based on the existence of a system of units for expressing monetary values. It also depends, and perhaps even more so, on the use of money as a general means of exchange. It is the circulation of corporeal items of money that allows us to establish the relative value of different commodities. Siding with Simmel, Wolff rejects von Knies's 'error' that in order to fulfil a measurement function the elements of money must have a value content of their own.[9] To round off the commonly attributed functions of money, Wolff looks at the characterization of money as a 'general means of payment'. He does not find this to be a helpful notion. The central use of money rests on its general circulation as a means of exchange. No fundamental insight is added, in Wolff's view, by the observation that money most frequently features as the subject matter of obligations (which then require money as a means of discharge). And nothing follows from the fact that the legal system allows the transformation of commodity obligations into monetary obligations that require the payment of damages.

Wolff engages in a detailed discussion with the 'state theory of money',[10] which was advanced in 1905 by Georg Friedrich Knapp (1842–1926).[11] Since Knapp moved central parts of the analysis of money into the legal field, one would have expected his work to be welcomed by legal scholars. This was not so. For the legal doctrines on money, Knapp's theory was mostly ignored. In this context, Wolff's reply to Knapp deserves our attention. Knapp's theory does not convince Wolff at all. According to Wolff, in an economic sense, money is not a creature of 'the state'. Ordinary commercial use can accept objects in circulation that do not have the state's blessing as 'money'. There may also be instances where state-produced money is not accepted, although the existence of a strong state in his own time makes this unlikely.[12] He vehemently rejects Knapp's idea that each and every coin or note embodies, or represents, a claim against a central agency so that 'payment' would seem to be an assignment of such a claim.[13] Another matter of controversy between Wolff and Knapp is the 'unit of account'.[14] In Knapp's view, the only way

[9] Wolff, 'Das Geld' (n 4) 570 fn 20.

[10] Georg Friedrich Knapp, *The State Theory of Money* (HM Lucas and J Bonar tr., Macmillan & Co 1924). Translation of the fourth German edition.

[11] On Knapp, see Bertram Schefold, 'Knapp, Georg Friedrich' (1987) 3 The New Palgrave 54–55; Hans-Michael Trautwein, 'G.F. Knapp: An Economist With Institutional Complexion' in Warren Samuels (ed.), *European Economists of the Early 20th Century* (Vol. 2, Edward Elgar 2003) 167–78.

[12] Wolff, 'Das Geld' (n 4) 567.

[13] ibid 568.

[14] ibid 571–73.

to define a unit of account was by reference to a conversion rate with a unit of account that was in use at an earlier time. Only the state could introduce new units of account, and the only way to do this was by way of a historical backward reference (*rekurrenter Anschluss*). Wolff sees Knapp as attaching too much significance to such conversion regulations. Wolff claims that they are only used during a transitional period and hence have no explanatory power for the meaning of 'money' once the transitional phase has passed. Furthermore, definitions of new monetary units can also use units currently in use in foreign systems as their base point of reference. Finally, according to Wolff, not all transitions are accompanied by a fixed conversion regulation, as that conversion can also be left to a free market process.

Wolff summarizes his review of Knapp's work as follows:[15] It is to Knapp's credit that he put an end to the view that the proper way to define monetary units is by reference to a quantity of currency metal and, also, that the units of other currencies can be used for such a definition. In Wolff's view, however, Knapp is mistaken in focusing exclusively on preceding monetary systems as the reference point for establishing the monetary unit currently in use. It would be equally one-sided if one were to postulate that the only way to introduce and define a new monetary unit would be by singling out the exchange rate for specific money of a neighbouring country at a given date.

Turning from the economic to the legal concept of money, Wolff points to the ubiquitous uses and regulations of money across the entire breadth of the legal system. He then introduces a distinction that will then run consistently through his tract. The legal system qualifies money either as 'mandatory' (*zwangsläufiges, aufdrängbares Geld*) or as 'optional' money (*freiläufiges, ablehnbares Geld*).[16] Mandatory money is the equivalent of legal tender. Wolff's key message here is this: objects need not be legal tender for their status as 'money' to be recognized. In other words, 'optional' money is 'real' money, too. One encounters 'optional' money in a variety of cases. Optional money includes fractional coins in quantities in which they are not, or cease to be, mandatory; banknotes issued by private banks; coins of the currency system that have lost their status as mandatory money; and—perhaps most importantly—coins of a foreign origin which nonetheless circulate as money. Trade coins would be of the same nature, but do not seem to be in much use in Wolff's time.

Looking at legal tender kinds of money more closely, Wolff unfolds several distinctions, showing that their non-rejectable quantity can come with different restrictions. Wolff adds other taxonomical classifications of money.[17] All this need not be reproduced here.

[15] ibid 573.

[16] Other terms that Wolff finds in use are *usuelles* or *fakultatives Geld*: customary and facultative money.

[17] Wolff, 'Das Geld' (n 4) 584–92.

Wolff's next chapters describe the historical development of the German monetary system.[18] When Wolff qualified for a German academic career in 1900, he had also been awarded the '*venia legendi*' (the authorization to teach) for German legal history. His supervisor had been the outstanding legal historian, Otto von Gierke. Among his academic teachers were many other legal historians, Karl von Amira, Heinrich Brunner, and, on the Roman law side, Alfred Pernice and Ernst Eck.[19] In 1920, however, Wolff made it a condition of his acceptance of the chair offered to him in the Berlin faculty that 'German Legal History' would be excluded from the denomination of his chair.[20] His chapter on the historical development of German monetary law may stand out as Wolff's main contribution to the field of legal history.[21]

After a chapter on the present-day structure of Germany's monetary system, another chapter deals with the wartime regulations of money, both in Germany and in enemy countries.[22] Wolff next focuses on money in private law, including specifically its use in commercial law. For this, the rules of the German Civil Code and the German Commercial Code provide the frame of reference. Wolff's attention turns first to matters of property law. There he finds particular rules regarding the mixing of money and the acquisition of title on the strength of good faith. The interchangeability of money pieces is of central importance. Another characteristic is their attribute as consumables.

One of the most contested issues in the treatment of money is the discharge of monetary obligations and related difficulties that can arise when there is a change in the currency system. The topic gets a somewhat subdued treatment.[23] Like other authors, Wolff distinguishes different kinds of monetary obligations before focusing on the obligation that requires the payment of a sum of money. He discards a metallistic understanding of this kind of obligation according to which the debtor would always have to deliver coins with constant metal content. In formulating his own definition of a monetary obligation, Wolff returns to his more fundamental deliberation from the introductory part of his work. Here he had set out that, apart from the corporeal object that can be classified as money, the term 'money' is also used to denote an 'asset-power' (*Vermögensmacht*).[24] This is the holder's power to spend the money, whether in the purchase of commodities, discharge of debts, or making a gift. This power is not corporeal, although it is usually present in the form of corporeal money pieces. Wolff uses the term 'abstract money' (*Geld im abstrakten Sinne*). Wolff defends a pragmatic usage of the word

[18] ibid 593–99.
[19] ibid 550.
[20] Gerhard Dannemann, 'Martin Wolff (1872–1953)' in Stefan Grundmann and others (eds) *Festschrift 200 Jahre Juristische Fakultät der Humboldt-Universität zu Berlin* (De Gruyter 2010) 563–64.
[21] Wolff had written expert advice on matters of a historical nature.
[22] Wolff, 'Das Geld' (n 4) 615–23.
[23] ibid 635f.
[24] ibid 569.

money that includes the incorporeal view of money as abstract 'purchasing power'. This leads Wolff to the following definition:

> Delivery of a sum of money means the making available of an incorporeal asset-power of a certain numerical magnitude, or, as one often reads, of a certain 'value'.[25]

The transfer of ownership in corporeal items, such as coins and notes, is '*an und für sich*', in other words, not something that the monetary obligation requires. The transfer of corporeal items is nothing but the means, and indeed the only means suitable, to make available to its holder the 'asset-power' that is the true content of the monetary obligation, in so far as this incorporeal asset-power is represented in corporeal items. Wolff considers that bank transfers are another means to make the abstract asset-power available for a person to use but finds that it is not, or as he cautiously adds 'not yet', fully equivalent.[26] The monetary obligation hence requires the transfer of as many corporeal items as have a nominal value equal to the amount of the monetary obligation. So, nominalism is presented as a consequence of the abstract concept of money that explains the existence of monetary obligations. The main and, in all likelihood, the intended implication of this view is that no distinction needs to be made between paper money and coins. Wolff rejects the view that only 'currency coins' (*Währungsmünzen*) can be used for discharge, a view which had been expounded in the influential writings of Bernhard Windscheid.[27] Should fractional coins have a lower metal content than would be expected for their nominal value, they could be rejected by the creditor. But if they were accepted, they would nonetheless constitute full payment. Wolff here finds a practical application for his distinction between mandatory money and optional money. Should a debtor tender optional money, the creditor may reject the offer without triggering *mora creditoris*. If he accepts, however, this has to be considered a proper discharge by performance, not a discharge on the strength of something received in lieu of performance, a *datio in solutum* (*an Erfüllungs statt*).[28] The same rules apply if the tender is accepted by an agent. Further implications follow, one of which concerns claw-back actions in insolvency.[29] Claw-back on behalf of the insolvent party's estate is possible when the now-insolvent party had made a payment to a creditor that was not due to him. In Wolff's view, a creditor who has received optional money has received his due and is not liable for a claw-back action.

[25] ibid 637: '*Leistung einer Geldsumme bedeutet vielmehr die Verschaffung einer unkörperlichen Vermögensmacht von bestimmter rechnersicher Größe oder, wie oft gesagt wird, eines bestimmten "Wertes"*'. Wolff notes but does not adopt the language of 'value-obligation'.

[26] Wolff, 'Das Geld' (n 4) 637.

[27] Bernhard Windscheid, *Lehrbuch des Pandektenrechts* (Vol. 2, Th Kipp ed., 9th edn, Rütten & Loening 1906) § 256 N. 3.

[28] Wolff, 'Das Geld' (n 4) 638.

[29] ibid 639.

Another notable consequence of the distinction between mandatory and optional coins is the treatment of foreign coins. If accepted, they constitute full payment of the debt, although with the special qualification that it is necessary to calculate the rate of exchange between the foreign coins and the units in which the debt is denominated.

Wolff had so far avoided using the concept of nominalism to define monetary obligations. It is only in the next step of his reasoning that the currency system comes into view, and it is that system, rather than the concept of nominalism, which he uses to express the nature of a monetary obligation. Characteristically for Wolff's approach, the currency system used by the parties can be one of many different types. It may be the domestic system currently in force when the parties conclude their obligation. But it might also be a past system or a foreign one. Since the monetary obligation is about 'asset-power', it can be expressed in different currencies. The currency system that is used to express the monetary obligation—which is about a certain 'asset-power'—does not necessarily determine the currency of payment. Wolff's money tract does not systematically set out all the pertinent conflict of laws issues. Here, however, he tackles Section 244 of the Civil Code, which addresses the matter of the currency of payment for monetary obligations expressed in a foreign (i.e. non-German) currency. He finds that Section 244 of the Civil Code only controls the issue if German civil law governs the obligation. It is not a conflict of laws norm. Twenty-five years later, Wolff changed his view, as will be shown in the next chapter.

Wolff raises the issue of whether domestic conversion rates should also be applied by foreign courts and gives a positive answer. Of the many historical instances where this issue arose, Wolff singles out the Austrian Coupon cases.[30]

Last but not least, Wolff tackles the problem that has been at the centre of civilian monetary thought, due to the endless currency upheavals in continental European history. How do changes in a currency system affect monetary obligations?[31] As items of the old currency will have lost their status as money and can no longer be used for discharging the debt, the resolution of the problem comes down to an issue of conversion between currencies. Usually, that should not be a problem, Wolff finds, since legislators will provide an official tariff for the conversion. The legislator enjoys discretion as to the choice of this conversion rate but should aim at a rough equivalence of the 'asset-power' to avoid unfairness. He mentions that this, from a metallistic viewpoint, is usually seen as the key issue of monetary law. He identifies this as the reason why authors of doctrinal writings have tended toward

[30] ibid 643. On these cases, see Rastko Vrbaski, 'Multiple Currency Clauses and Currency Reform. The Austrian Coupon Cases' in David Fox and Wolfgang Ernst (eds), *Money in the Western Legal Tradition* (OUP 2016) 575–89.

[31] Wolff, 'Das Geld' (n 4) 642f.

an excessively narrow concept of money. He acknowledges that for Knapp the problem vanishes, but siding with Knapp's critic, Helfferich, Wolff finds:

> Some have phrased the fault they find with Knapp's theory in the language that it is a purely 'juristic', not an economic one. But Knapp's theory leaves the lawyer in the lurch as well. The issue, of how the *legislator* should design the conversion norms, may perhaps be classified as 'non-legal', but the problem that Knapp ignores does exist in the interpretation of the general domestic law, as well as in cases where a [statutory] conversion norm is lacking.[32]

Wolff closes this chapter with comments upon another type of monetary obligation which limits the compliant forms of tender to specific kinds of coins or notes (*Geldsortenschuld*).[33]

All in all, Wolff in 1916 sought a legal position that can be characterized as post-metallistic, but anti-Knapp. Wolff's textbook on property law, the first edition of which had come out in 1910 only a little earlier than this money tract,[34] became the ultimate authoritative textbook. It saw 10 editions and was in use as the top textbook in its field well into the 1970s.[35] Of course, 'property law' is considered to be a rather 'static' field of law. Wolff's money tract, however, is all but forgotten. After 1933, the use and citation of the *Handbuch des Handelsrechts* must have become less and less attractive, in view of its Jewish editor-in-chief and the predominantly Jewish authors. In 1939, a two-volume commentary on the Commercial Code was published, edited by the infamous undersecretary of the Reichs Ministry of Justice, Franz Schlegelberger (1876–1970).[36] As the preface tells us, that commentary was inspired by the wish to reflect on the impact that the 'fundamental reformation of law' had on German commercial law. (In substance this amounted to the adaptation of existing legal rules to Nazi doctrines of law.) It was one of many products that sought to provide the legal community with commentaries and textbooks written by authors under the Nazi whip who vouched for ideological correctness, and to systematically exclude the work of authors identified as Jews from the corpus of German legal literature.

For unrelated reasons, Wolff's contribution on money soon became outdated. After the hyperinflation and currency reform of the mid-1920s, the currency

32 ibid 644 (author's translation).

33 ibid 645–48.

34 Martin Wolff, *Das Sachenrecht (Lehrbuch des Bürgerlichen Rechts. Bd. 2, Abt. 1)* (Elwert 1910).

35 In 1957, Ludwig Raiser (1904–1980) re-issued the book with an updated and slightly revised text.

36 On Schlegelberger, see Michael Förster, *Jurist im Dienst des Unrechts: Leben und Werk des ehemaligen Staatssekretärs im Reichsjustizministerium, Franz Schlegelberger, 1876–1970* (Nomos 1995); Sibylle Hofer, 'Franz Schlegelberger: Abschied vom BGB (1937)' in Thorsten Keise and others, *Wege zur Rechtsgeschichte: Die rechtshistorische Exegese* (Böhlau 2022) 480–81; Andreas Thier, 'Schlegelberger, Louis Rudolph Franz' in *Neue Deutsche Biographie* (Vol. 23, Historische Kommission bei der Bayerischen Akademie der Wissenschaften 2007) 44–45; perhaps too apologetic: Arne Wulff, *Staatssekretär Prof. Dr. Dr. h.c. Franz Schlegelberger 1876–1970* (Lang 1991).

exchange regulations of the Nazi and WWII periods, and the introduction of the *Deutsche Mark* in 1948, a return to Wolff's 1917 publication for practising lawyers made no sense. The mantle of the authoritative and comprehensive exposition of monetary law fell on Wilhelm Weber (1887–1969?), a judge who had contributed to the Staudinger commentary on the German Civil Code since 1938.[37] His contribution had about the same style and format as Wolff's. Wilhelm Weber's commentary was taken over, in 1983, by Karsten Schmidt (born 1939).[38] His commentary was also published as a standalone volume.[39] It was Schmidt who freshly reviewed Knapp's work, 80 years after Wolff.[40]

II. Monetary Obligations in *Private International Law*—the German Side (1933)

Wolff's *Internationales Privatrecht* was published in 1933 in the highly prestigious series *Enzyklopädie der Rechts- und Staatswissenschaften*.[41] It is a comprehensive treatise on the German conflict of laws system at the time, paying due regard to the internationality of the book's topic. The book and its counterpart, the English law-focused *Private International Law*, written and published (1945)[42] after Wolff emigrated to England, have long been recognized as milestones in the academic treatment of conflict of laws.[43] There is no need to renew this praise here. Only the chapters devoted to monetary law will be revisited.

We start with the work of 1933. The book contains a chapter on the conflict of laws regarding monetary obligations.[44] Interestingly, Wolff here moves closer to Knapp's theory. Wolff quotes 'Knapp's famous words' (*die berühmten Worte Knapps*), 'Money is a creature of the legal system'. Regarding Knapp's theory, he refers the reader back to his chapter in *Ehrenbergs Handbuch*, with the clarification that Knapp's doctrine would go too far if it were taken from a legal point of view. This, however, had never been his (Wolff's) intention.[45] Wolff here also takes

[37] On Wilhelm Weber, see Heinz Beck, *Neue Juristische Wochenschrift* (1967) 1648.

[38] Cf. Karsten Schmidt, 'Das Geld im BGB und im Staudinger' in Martinek and Sellier (eds), *100 Jahre BGB – 100 Jahre Staudinger* (CH Beck 1999) 76–96.

[39] Karsten Schmidt, *Geldrecht. Geld, Zins und Währung im deutschen Recht* (Sellier 1983).

[40] Karsten Schmidt, 'Die "Staatliche Theorie des Geldes": Jahrhundertwerk oder Makulatur? Ein Streifzug durch Knapps "Staatliche Theorie des Geldes"' in A Weber (ed.), *Währung und Wirtschaft: das Geld im Recht. Festschrift für Prof. Dr. Hugo J. Hahn zum 70. Geburtstag* (Nomos 1997) 81–92.

[41] Martin Wolff, *Internationales Privatrecht* (Springer 1933) (hereafter Wolff, *Internationales Privatrecht*).

[42] Martin Wolff, *Private International Law* (OUP 1945) (hereafter Wolff, *Private International Law*); see below, Section IV.

[43] Gerhard Dannemann, *Rechtsvergleichung im Exil. Martin Wolff und das englische Recht. Antrittsvorlesung 1. Juli 2003* (Humboldt-Universität zu Berlin, Öffentliche Vorlesungen, Heft 135) (Humboldt-Universität Berlin 2004) 9f.

[44] Wolff, *Internationales Privatrecht* (n 41) 96–101.

[45] ibid 98.

up Knapp's term 'chartalism' as a synonym for nominalism: 'Today, "nominalism" (chartalism) rules everywhere.' He then adopts Knapp's concept of the 'recurrent link' (*rekurrenter Anschluss*). Citing Knapp, Wolff finds:

> Every modern currency law regulates the 'recurring link' of the new currency to the old, and—with an exaggeration—it has even been stated that in a nominalist monetarized economy, money can only be defined by its recurrent link: 1 Mark has to be defined as ½ Taler, one Reichsmark as 1 trillion Mark.[46]

Regarding conflict of laws, Wolff addresses the intricate question of whether the 1925 German revaluation that broke the hyperinflation[47] should be characterized as a currency norm or a norm pertaining to the monetary obligation. It was a highly relevant and hotly debated question because it determined which obligations came under the German revaluation law of 1925. According to the 'obligation theory' (*Schuldrechtstheorie*), obligations were revaluated that were controlled by the German law of obligations (*lex causae*). According to 'currency theory' (*Währungstheorie*), obligations were revaluated where the currency for payment was set in Mark (*lex monetae*), regardless of their *lex causae*. Wolff sides with the 'obligation theory', rejecting the 'currency theory'.[48] This approach, Wolff maintains, also controls changes regarding fluctuations in the purchasing power of a specific currency. All this is markedly different, in his view, from cases where changes in the currency itself are at stake. These have to be accepted as being effective wherever that specific currency is contractually chosen.

Wolff here presents a new understanding of Section 244 of the Civil Code.[49] In his view, it is a veiled conflict of laws norm: the place of payment, if located in Germany, leads to the applicability of the German statutory norm of section 244, giving the debtor the option to discharge his debt in marks, even if the obligation is governed by a law other than the German one.[50] Section 244 thus carves out the sole matter of the currency of payment, in this narrow aspect overriding the *lex causae*. Wolff also advocates, by way of analogy, a reverse application of the norm in cases where the place of payment is in a foreign country: if German law controls the obligation, the law of the place of payment is acknowledged, on the strength of

[46] Wolff, *Internationales Privatrecht* (n 41) 99, author's translation: '*Jedes moderne Währungsgesetz regelt den "rekurrenten Anschluss" der neuen Währung an die alte, und man hat (übertreibend) geradezu gesagt, dass in einer nominalistischen Geldwirtschaft das Geld* ***nur*** *durch seinen rekurrenten Anschluss definiert werde: 1 Mark sei zu definieren als ½ Taler, eine Reichsmark als 1 Billion Mark.*'

[47] See Jan Thiessen, 'The German Hyperinflation of the 1920s' in David Fox and Wolfgang Ernst (eds), *Money in the Western Legal Tradition* (OUP 2016) 735–69.

[48] Wolff, *Internationales Privatrecht* (n 41) 99.

[49] At the time, section 244 ran: (1) If a money debt stated in a currency other than the mark is payable within the country, then payment may be made in marks unless payment in the other currency has been expressly agreed. (2) Conversion occurs at the rate of exchange in effect in the place of payment at the time of payment.

[50] Wolff, *Internationales Privatrecht* (n 41) 97.

the controlling German law, to determine any question over the possible choice of different currencies to be used as payment.

III. Wolff's Views in FA Mann's *The Legal Aspect of Money* (1938)

When FA Mann became Wolff's assistant, and Wolff became Mann's supervisor in Berlin, Wolff's money tract in *Ehrenbergs Handbuch* had already been out for a decade and a half. In all likelihood, Mann assisted, or at least accompanied, Wolff when he worked on his *Internationales Privatrecht*, which Wolff finished in August 1933. For his own *The Legal Aspect of Money*, Mann used all of Wolff's money publications. The chapter in *Ehrenbergs Handbuch* is listed under the books 'referred to merely by the author's name'.

Mann, however, reviewed Knapp's theory afresh. One interesting point of contrast is that Mann uses Knapp's approach much more enthusiastically than Wolff. For Mann:

> only those chattels are money to which such character has been attributed by law, i.e. by or with the authority of the state. This is the State theory of money which in modern times has come to be connected with the name of G. F. Knapp, to whose principal work it has given the title.[51]

Mann also registers the widespread academic echo of Knapp's theory:

> It attracted a great deal of discussion among economists, partly exuberant praise, partly the most adverse criticism [. . .] Among jurists for whom Knapp's theory was less revolutionary its essence was readily accepted, although they were emphatic that it not should be regarded as a legal work.[52]

For the last proposition, Mann cites Wolff's money tract and also his *Internationales Privatrecht*. Mann does not see it as 'open to doubt that in this country [England] that prerogative exists, and, accordingly, the State theory of money rules'.[53]

Mann comes to Knapp's defence against the attack by BM Anderson, who had rejected the state theory of money on the ground that it was 'typical of the tendency in German thought to make the State the centre of everything'.[54] To counter this charge, Mann points to the general acceptance of nominalism and the great

[51] FA Mann, *The Legal Aspect of Money* (Clarendon Press 1938) 15 (hereafter Mann, *Legal Aspect*).
[52] ibid 10–11. For the different views of Knapp's work, Mann cites Max Weber on one hand, and Ludwig von Mises on the other hand.
[53] Mann, *Legal Aspect* (n 51) 12.
[54] BM Anderson, *The Value of Money* (Macmillan 1917) 433.

influence of the Austinian jurisprudence.[55] He also sides with Knapp against the proponents of the 'societary' theory of money.[56] Mann takes up Knapp's concept of the historical definition of units of account.[57] He registers criticism, which, however, is discarded:

> Nevertheless, experience shows that in most, if not in all modern cases, a unit of account can in fact be linked to an antecedent unit, and Knapp's doctrine can therefore be adopted as a useful working principle. As Martin Wolff said, in a negative sense it was Knapp's merit not to have defined the unit of account according to the standard metal of the currency system, and positively, we are indebted to him for having explained a unit of account by connecting it with the unit of other systems. That Knapp explains the unit by connecting it with the antecedent unit only may be too narrow, but so long no better definition can be found, his principle, if it is not regarded as an inflexible one, cannot be abandoned.[58]

Mann's reliance on Knapp culminates in the treatment of nominalism. 'The extent of monetary obligations cannot be determined otherwise than by the adoption of *nominalism*.'[59]

Nominalism [. . .], together with the view of money as a creature of law and the 'recurrent link' principle involving the rejection of the metallistic doctrine, form part of the State theory of money as revived by Knapp.[60]

He refers the reader to Wolff's formulation,[61] according to which this principle postulates that monetary obligations are discharged by 'the payment of so many chattels, being legal tender at the time of payment, as, if added together to the nominal values indicated thereon, produce a sum equal to the amount of the debt'.[62] Mann then sets out to show, in a historical excursus, that the nominalistic principle goes back to ancient times, 'although it received fresh force from Knapp's theoretical investigations and his striking formulations'.[63] For all its shortcomings, Knapp's theory here provided a valuable underpinning for the legal principle of nominalism.[64] Somewhat surprisingly, in this work as in the work to be reviewed next, Wolff's transition to fiat money nominalism does not greatly impact the

55 Mann, *Legal Aspect* (n 51) 10–11 fn 7.
56 ibid 19–21.
57 ibid 34.
58 ibid 35. As Mann added, Knapp's theory is of less relevance for England, 'because the history of the pound is a continuous one'.
59 Mann, *Legal Aspect* (n 51) 63.
60 ibid 64.
61 Wolff, 'Das Geld' (n 4) 637.
62 Mann, *Legal Aspect* (n 51) 63.
63 ibid 64.
64 Mann's use of Knapp's state theory is dealt with further in the chapters by Joseph Sommer and Simon Gleeson in this volume.

exposition of the minutiae of monetary law. The gold clause issue may be a notable exception.[65]

IV. Money in Wolff's *Private International Law* (1945)

Wolff's *Private International Law* came out in 1945.[66] Wolff re-uses much of the expertise he had acquired, and the solutions he had proposed, writing his 1933 *Internationales Privatrecht*, merging them with English case law. On quite a few occasions he also cites his contribution to *Ehrenbergs Handbuch*. For the English conflict rules Wolff could rely on Mann's *The Legal Aspect of Money*, which he lauds as 'the main work on the subject'.[67]

Wolff addresses in particular the matter of whether a debt expressed in foreign money has to be discharged by payment in foreign money. Wolff sees the question as one controlled by the proper law of the contract. For English law, this principle undergoes a modification due to the procedural rule that English, as well as American, courts 'have no jurisdiction to order payment of money except in the currency of this country'.[68] For the English law, Wolff supports the adoption of the principle laid down in Section 244 of the Civil Code, which would require allowing the creditor to bring a second action for an eventual increase of value of the foreign currency amount between the time of the judgment and the actual payment.

Turning to the effect of disturbances in the monetary system, Wolff starts with a retrospective report on the problem as it presented itself under the metallistic doctrine, only to find:

> The metallistic doctrine has disappeared entirely, *nominalism* prevails everywhere; i.e. a debtor of money is bound to pay in whatever at the date of payment is legal tender in the country whose money is in issue, and he has to pay so many pieces of that money that if one adds together the units of measurement as indicated on those pieces their sum equals the sum of money owed.[69]

This is fully in line with Mann's definition. The earlier concept of the 'asset-power' (*Vermögensmacht*), which was supposed to be the true content of monetary obligations, has gone overboard altogether.

[65] See Section V; see also David Fox, 'Gold Clauses in the Capital Markets of the Early 20th Century' in this volume.

[66] Wolff, *Private International Law* (n 42). The book is dedicated to the Warden and Fellows of All Souls College, which had provided Wolff with *inter alia* a study and access to the college library.

[67] ibid 484.

[68] ibid 469.

[69] ibid 463.

As to currency reforms, Wolff proposes the same view as in 1933. If a debt is defined in a specific currency, the creditor must take 'the rough with the smooth', even if the proper law of the contract is that of another country. This is his solution for the Austrian Railway Coupon cases, for which he sides with the German courts that had decided them. By contrast, fluctuations in purchasing power, such as those caused by inflation, have a legal effect, if at all, according to the proper law of the contract. (An example would be where a country has enacted specific revalorization laws.) In line with his 1933 work, he sees the revalorization as affecting the obligation as such. A revalorization decreed by a specific country affects the contract only if that country's law is the proper law of the contract. As in 1933, Wolff distinguishes between the legislative exchange of one currency for another, on the one hand, and revalorization measures, on the other. The exchange of the currency affects the debt expressed in units of the older currency and hence is controlled by the *lex pecuniae*, while revalorization measures, as an aspect of the proper law of the contract, affect all debts that are controlled by the law that revalorizes monetary obligations. Wolff elucidates his view using Knapp's concept of 'recurrent link'. The German currency reform of 1924 had defined a new currency (the *Reichsmark*) by a link to the previous *Mark*, setting 1 *Reichsmark* generally at 1,000,000,000,000 *Mark*. The revalorization measure was another matter. For different debts, different revalorization rates were decreed, e.g. a 1917 mortgage of 10,000 *Mark* became a mortgage of 2,500 *Reichsmark*. For the English law, Wolff finds support for this view in the ruling of Atkin LJ, who in *Société des Hôtel Le Touquet Paris Plage v Cummings*[70] had framed the rule that 'it is the debt that is valorized and not the currency'.[71]

In 1950, Wolff saw the second edition go into print. The part on money obligations remained largely unaltered, with the passages on 'Foreign Currency Restrictions' now taking note of the conflict implications of the Bretton Woods agreement.[72] No major changes were made. Addressing the specific issue of the critical moment in time for which the conversion from foreign to domestic currency has to be made, Wolff now refers the reader to the solution Mann had set out.[73] Wolff may well have known about Mann's piece even though it had not yet appeared in print when Wolff delivered his book to the press in 1944.[74]

[70] [1922] 1 KB 451, 463–64.

[71] Further deliberations deal with moratoria and foreign currency restrictions, Wolff, *Private International Law* (n 42) 475–84.

[72] Martin Wolff, *Private International Law* (2nd edn, OUP 1950) 747–45.

[73] ibid 462.

[74] FA Mann, 'Problems of the Rate of Exchange' (1945) 8 ModLR 177.

V. Wolff on Gold Clauses, 1917 to 1953

In 1917, Wolff mentioned gold clauses only briefly.[75] For him, contractual gold clauses created a form of *Geldsortenschuld*, an obligation that requires payment in 'coins' of a certain type.[76] Gold clauses, as used in mortgaging, require payment in a currency that is gold-based, excluding particularly silver coins. He saw the use of gold clauses as a reaction to bimetallism. A gold clause of another type, in his view, is the private banks' institutional duty to redeem their banknotes in gold. At the time Wolff wrote, the war triggered changes in the German currency system. Temporarily, one then hoped, the duty of the Reichsbank and the German state to redeem *Reichskassenscheine* (treasury bonds) and banknotes issued by the Reichsbank was suspended. This had established, as in other belligerent countries, a paper money currency, setting the gold currency aside.[77] Insofar as private banks were under an obligation to redeem their banknotes in gold, they were now allowed to use banknotes issued by the Reichsbank. Wolff elucidated in detail the legal consequences of these measures.

In his *Internationales Privatrecht*, Wolff looks into regulatory interventions in the operation of gold clauses.[78] He comes back to the German WWI statutory instrument (28 September 1914) that invalidated all pre-war gold clauses. The territorial reach of this regulation, Wolff finds, follows from its policy background: the outflux of gold shall be stopped and debtors shall be protected against the dwindling value of paper money. Hence only payments by German nationals and payments to be made on German territory are in the range of the regulation. Payments that have to be made by foreigners in foreign territory are not affected. More importantly, Wolff does not qualify such regulations as currency norms, and hence they are applicable only if they are decreed by the state whose law controls the contract.

As an illustration, Wolff adds the hypothetical that two Germans whose contract, controlled by German law, provides for payment in dollars with a gold clause. In Wolff's view, the United States' invalidation of gold clauses in 1933 had no effect unless the contract provided for payment to be made in the US. Should payment have to be made in New York indeed, a German court would not have to apply the American regulation, as it is not part of the law controlling the contract. However, the debtor cannot be expected to leave unused the legal option granted by the state where he must discharge his obligation,[79] which I understand means that the debtor cannot be barred from discharge in the US using Dollar notes.

[75] On gold clauses see David Fox, 'Gold Clauses in the Capital Markets of the Early Twentieth Century' in this volume.
[76] Wolff, 'Das Geld' (n 4) 646f.
[77] ibid 616–18.
[78] Wolff, *Internationales Privatrecht* (n 41) 100–01.
[79] ibid 57.

Wolff acknowledges that if such a regulation hits foreign creditors the effect may be viewed, from the creditor's perspective, as expropriations without compensation, which he presumes can only be recognized when the obligation seems 'localized' in the regulating state's territory.

The topic gets extensive treatment in *Private International Law*, where Wolff already relies on Mann's treatment of the subject matter.[80] Wolff here distinguishes gold *coin* clauses from gold *value* clauses, referring the reader to the case of Serbian Loans,[81] decided by the Permanent Court of International Justice. Gold coin clauses are frustrated if the coins go out of circulation. The gold value clauses are instruments that determine the amount of payment due (in notes, coins, or other means of payment) to match a certain amount of gold as valued at the time payment is due. It is a matter of construction (taking the methodology from the law controlling the contract) what kind of gold clause a contract entails. He finds that the validity of gold coin clauses in England is open to doubt, whereas gold value clauses are valid unless invalidated by special statutes.

As a matter of policy, Wolff tends to the critical view of gold clauses, thereby taking fiat money nominalism to its extreme. Gold clauses have operative value only in times of a currency shake-up. In such a situation, creditors should be treated alike, whereas gold clauses privilege some creditors to the prejudice of others. Gold clauses, to put it in other words, violate the *par condicio creditorum*. As a consequence, Wolff finds himself not averse to legislation which by abrogating gold clauses puts creditors on equal footing again. Should there have been widespread use of gold clauses in England, when the country went off the gold standard in 1931, the government's policy would have been defeated. The savers' wish to be protected against currency disasters does not deserve unconditional support. Wolff quotes the French lawyer Joseph Hamel (1889–1962), that the best protection for savings is the awareness of the risks involved in owning something and wanting to keep it. Wolff sets the stage for the conflicts analysis by declaring as 'narrow-minded and utterly unsound' the argument, 'developed by shrewd business men and their lawyers, that foreign abrogations of gold clauses must be inapplicable outside the state where they were enacted'.[82] This was not in line with FA Mann's view of the gold clause issue. Mann had set out the law of gold clauses in a wonderfully positivistic manner, trying to fend off, or minimize, anti-gold clause interventions in the contract as negotiated by the parties.[83] Clearly, Mann and Wolff were not *ad idem* on each and every issue of law.

There is but one question that Wolff sees falling squarely in the topic of his conflicts book, namely: 'What law answers the question of whether a court should

[80] Wolff, *Private International Law* (n 42) 475–79.

[81] Payment of Various Serbian Loans Issued in France, *France v Kingdom of the Serbs, Croats, and Slovenes*, Judgment [1929] PCIJ Ser. A No. 20, ICGJ 260 (PCIJ 1929).

[82] Wolff, *Private International Law* (n 42) 477.

[83] Mann, *Legal Aspect* (n 51) 92f., 103f.

apply foreign abrogation laws?'[84] Wolff reviews three possible solutions on display, the *lex pecuniae* (as used in Poland, Germany, and Austria), the *lex loci solutionis*, and the proper law of the contract. In evaluating these, Wolff takes up the distinction between gold coin and gold value clauses. The former has a link to the currency system insofar as the abrogation of gold coins clauses can be seen as interfering with the monetary character of gold coins. Abrogating the latter, however, works as a diminution of the monetary obligation and hence cannot be controlled by the *lex pecuniae*. That leaves the choice between the *lex loci solutionis* and the proper law of the contract. To explain both solutions he uses the case of a Canadian law-controlled loan in Canadian dollars, repayable in London and subject to a gold value clause that was abrogated in 1937. In line with the view Wolff had (scantily) set out in 1933, he explains that the proper law of the contract should control the question. The abrogation of the gold value clause alters the content of the obligation, rather than affecting merely the 'mode and method of payment'. Wolff ponders and criticizes the Court of Appeal, which, in *British & French Trust Corporation v New Brunswick Railway Co.*,[85] had let the law of the place of payment control the measure of payment as well. It is one of the many instances where Wolff, the very German law professor, was not shy to recommend his own view over that of the Court of Appeal.

Wolff asks whether laws abrogating gold clauses could offend the public policy of the forum, as asserted by courts in Germany, the Netherlands, and France. Wolff sides with English courts: 'If what was said above about the economic unsoundness of gold clauses is correct, it is difficult to see why any country should object to their invalidation'.[86] One may take a different view if the abrogation measure solely targets creditors of foreign residence or nationality. Finally, should the conflict rule, as proposed by him, lead to the applicability of the law of a state that abrogated gold clauses, the more minute questions regarding the range and effect of that abrogation must be established by interpretation of said law.

Shortly after the war, Wolff arranged his pre-war book on Germany's conflict of law rules for a second edition.[87] In the preface, he explains that the book published by Oxford University Press and the German product each deal with the rules of one country only. None is the translation or revision of the other. In dealing with the gold clauses, however, the work done in England is reused here. He starts with the critical view of gold clauses, taken directly from the English book, and then turns to the developments in Germany. In 1936, the German Imperial Court, relying on the *ordre public* argument, had negated the applicability of the abrogation of gold clauses in the United States Joint Resolution of 5 June 1933 in the case of a German

[84] Wolff, *Private International Law* (n 42) 477.
[85] [1937] 4 AER 516, 525, 528.
[86] Wolff, *Private International Law* (n 42) 479.
[87] Martin Wolff, *Das Internationale Privatrecht Deutschlands* (2nd edn, Springer 1949) 137–38.

national who was under a duty to pay in the US based on a contract controlled by American law. This was not acceptable, Wolff found. Holders of the same bond with a gold clause would be treated differently based on their nationality alone, all else being equal. Indeed, the German legislator in 1936 reacted and decreed retroactively that concerning foreign currency bonds devaluation measures had to be followed if they originated in the *lex pecuniae* and that no recourse to the *ordre public* could be had against this law.

In the third edition, which came out posthumously in 1953, Wolff added a report on the latest French law development. There, one discussed the distinction between gold clauses payable between local parties in the home jurisdiction and those where the payer was abroad. From a comparative perspective, the case law of the Court de Cassation stood out insofar as it upheld, for international contracts that need to equalize different modes of payment, gold clauses even in face of abrogating enactments, with an argument based on the supremacy of the contracting parties' agreement.[88]

VI. Coming Full Circle

We only can speculate how Wolff and Mann dialogued with each other in the production of Wolff's two works on private international law and of Mann's *The Legal Aspect of Money*. They converge in the adoption (and adaptation) of Knapp's theory, although not without qualifications. For Wolff, this meant a change of heart, as he had been rather critical of Knapp's theory in 1917. Did Mann convince Wolff to give up his reluctance? Or had Wolff already changed his view and shared his new closeness to the 'state theory of money' with his then-assistant Mann?

Wolff died in 1953. One would have expected that Mann would have been given the opportunity to take over Wolff's *Private International Law* for a third and then further editions. This was not to be. Other persons seem to have been considered, but nothing came out of it and no further edition appeared.[89] However, when the second edition (1953) of *The Legal Aspect of Money* was turned into a German book in 1960,[90] Martin Wolff's wife, Marguerite Wolff (neè Jolowicz 1883–1964),[91]

[88] Martin Wolff, *Das Internationale Privatrecht Deutschlands* (3rd edn, Springer 1953) 163.

[89] I rely on information obtained by Gerhard Dannemann in interviews with Kurt Lipstein (1909–2006).

[90] FA Mann, *Das Recht des Geldes: Eine rechtsvergleichende Untersuchung auf der Grundlage des englischen Rechts* (Metzner 1960).

[91] On Marguerite Wolff, see Leonie Breunung and Manfred Walther, 'Martin Wolff' in *Die Emigration deutscher Rechtswissenschaftler ab 1933. Band 1 Westeuropäische Staaten, Türkei, Palästina/Israel, lateinamerikanische Staaten, Südafrikanische Union* (DeGruyter/Saur 2012) 567; Annette B Vogt, 'Marguerite Wolff. 1883–1964' in *Women Scientists in Kaiser Wilhelm Institutes, from A to Z* (Veröffentlichungen aus dem Archiv der Max-Planck-Gesellschaft, Hausreihe vol 12, 2nd enlarged edn, 2008) 163–64. Twenty-five years earlier, Marguerite Wolff had translated Fritz Schulz's 'Principles of Roman Law', cf. Wolfgang Ernst, 'Fritz Schulz (1879–1957)' in Beatson and Zimmermann (eds), *Jurists Uprooted. German-Speaking Émigré Lawyers in Twentieth-Century Britain* (OUP 2004) 131.

together with Dr Lucia Serick,[92] did the translator's work. In a way, matters came full circle.

Bibliography

Anderson BM, *The Value of Money* (Macmillan 1917)

Blaurock U, 'Victor Ehrenberg (1851–1929): – "Vater der Versicherungswissenschaft"' in F Loos (ed.), *Rechtswissenschaft in Göttingen. Göttinger Juristen aus 250 Jahren* (Vandenhoeck & Ruprecht 1987)

Breunung L and Walther M, 'Martin Wolff' in *Die Emigration deutscher Rechtswissenschaftler ab 1933. Band 1 Westeuropäische Staaten, Türkei, Palästina/Israel, lateinamerikanische Staaten, Südafrikanische Union* (DeGruyter/Saur 2012)

Dannemann G, 'Martin Wolff (1872–1953)' in Stefan Grundmann and others (eds), *Festschrift 200 Jahre Juristische Fakultät der Humboldt-Universität zu Berlin* (De Gruyter 2010)

Dannemann G, *Rechtsvergleichung im Exil. Martin Wolff und das englische Recht. Antrittsvorlesung 1. Juli 2003* (Öffentliche Vorlesungen. Heft 135, Humboldt-Universität zu Berlin 2004)

Ehrenberg V (ed.), *Handbuch des gesamten Handelsrechts mit Einschluss des Wechsel-, Scheck-, See- und Binnenschiffahrtsrechts, des Versicherungsrechts sowie des Post- und Telegraphenrechts* (OR Reisland 1913–1929)

Endemann W, *Handbuch des deutschen Handels-, See und Wechselrechts*, vol. 2 (Fues's Verlag 1882)

Ernst W, 'Fritz Schulz (1879–1957)' in Jack Beatson and Reinhard Zimmermann (eds), *Jurists Uprooted: German-Speaking Émigré Lawyers in Twentieth-Century Britain* (OUP 2004)

Förster M, *Jurist im Dienst des Unrechts: Leben und Werk des ehemaligen Staatssekretärs im Reichsjustizministerium, Franz Schlegelberger, 1876–1970* (Nomos 1995)

Hofer S, 'Franz Schlegelberger: Abschied vom BGB (1937)' in Thorsten Keiser and others (eds), *Wege zur Rechtsgeschichte: Die rechtshistorische Exegese* (Böhlau 2022)

Isele HG, 'Zur Erinnerung an Heinrich Titze' (1972) 172 Archiv für die civilistische Praxis 392

Keller C (ed.), *Victor Ehrenberg und Georg Jellinek: Briefwechsel 1872–1911* (Klostermann 2005)

Knapp GF, *The State Theory of Money* (HM Lucas and J Bonar tr., Macmillan & Co. 1924)

Knies K, *Das Geld: Darlegung der Grundlehren von dem Gelde* (2nd edn, Weidmannsche Buchhandlung 1885)

Mann FA, *Das Recht des Geldes. Eine rechtsvergleichende Untersuchung auf der Grundlage des englischen Rechts* (Metzner 1960)

Mann FA, *The Legal Aspect of Money* (3rd edn, Clarendon Press 1971)

Mann FA, 'Problems of the Rate of Exchange' (1945) 8 ModLR 177

Medicus D, 'Martin Wolff (1872–1953): Ein Meister an Klarheit' in Helmut Heinrichs and others (eds), *Deutsche Juristen jüdischer Herkunft* (CH Beck 1993)

[92] Dr iur. Lucia Serick, neè Schottlaender (1923–1991), was the wife of the renowned comparative lawyer Rolf Serick (1922–2000), Professor in Heidelberg.

Möllenhoff G and Schlautmann-Overmeyer R, *Jüdische Familien in Münster 1918 bis 1945. Biographisches Lexikon* (Westfälisches Dampfboot 1995)

Pohl M, 'Koch, Richard' in *Neue Deutsche Biographie* (Vol. 12, Historische Kommission bei der Bayerischen Akademie der Wissenschaften 1980)

Schefold B, 'Knapp, Georg Friedrich' in M Vernengo and others (eds), *The New Palgrave* (Vol. 3, 1987)

Schmidt K, 'Das Geld im BGB und im Staudinger' in M Martinek and PL Sellier (eds), *100 Jahre BGB – 100 Jahre Staudinger* (CH Beck 1999)

Schmidt K, 'Die "Staatliche Theorie des Geldes": Jahrhundertwerk oder Makulatur? Ein Streifzug durch Knapps "Staatliche Theorie des Geldes"' in A Weber (ed.), *Währung und Wirtschaft: das Geld im Recht. Festschrift für Prof. Dr. Hugo J. Hahn zum 70. Geburtstag* (Nomos 1997)

Schmidt K, *Geldrecht. Geld, Zins und Währung im deutschen Recht* (Sellier 1983)

Thier A, 'Schlegelberger, Louis Rudolph Franz' in *Neue Deutsche Biographie* (Vol. 23, Historische Kommission bei der Bayerischen Akademie der Wissenschaften 2007)

Thiessen J, 'The German Hyperinflation of the 1920s' in David Fox and Wolfgang Ernst (eds), *Money in the Western Legal Tradition* (OUP 2016)

Trautwein HM, 'G.F. Knapp: an Economist with Institutional Complexion' in Warren Samuels (ed.), *European Economists of the Early 20th Century* (Vol. 2, Elgar 2003)

Vogt A, 'Marguerite Wolff. 1883–1964' in *Women Scientists in Kaiser Wilhelm Institutes, from A to Z* (Vol. 12, 2nd enlarged edn, Veröffentlichungen aus dem Archiv der Max-Planck-Gesellschaft, Hausreihe 2008)

Vrbaski R, 'Multiple Currency Clauses and Currency Reform. The Austrian Coupon Cases' in David Fox and Wolfgang Ernst (eds), *Money in the Western Legal Tradition* (OUP 2016)

Windscheid B, *Lehrbuch des Pandektenrechts* (Vol. 2, Th Kipp ed., 9th edn, Rütten & Loening 1906)

Wolff M, 'Das Geld' in Victor Ehrenberg (ed.), *Handbuch des Gesamten Handelsrechts mit Einschluss des Wechsel-, Scheck-, See- und Binnenschiffahrtsrechts, des Versicherungsrechts sowie des Post- und Telegraphenrechts*, vol IV/section 1 (OR Reisland 1917)

Wolff M, *Das Internationale Privatrecht Deutschlands* (2nd edn, Springer 1949)

Wolff M, *Das Internationale Privatrecht Deutschlands* (3rd edn, Springer 1953)

Wolff M, *Das Sachenrecht* (Lehrbuch des Bürgerlichen Rechts. Bd. 2, Abt. 1, Elwert 1910)

Wolff M, *Internationales Privatrecht* (Springer 1933)

Wolff M, *Private International Law* (OUP 1945)

Wolff M, *Private International Law* (2nd edn, OUP 1950)

Wulff A, *Staatssekretär Prof. Dr. Dr. h.c. Franz Schlegelberger 1876–1970* (Lang 1991)

9

Gold Clauses in the Capital Markets of the Early 20th Century

David Fox[*]

I. Introduction

The first edition of FA Mann's *The Legal Aspect of Money*[1] is a fairly small book running to 330 main pages and bound in brick-coloured octavo covers. On opening the book, we find that Chapter IV, titled 'Methods of Negativing the Effects of Nominalism', is devoted almost entirely to gold clauses. It runs to 23 pages. Gold clauses come up again in Mann's treatment of foreign money obligations, which runs to another 35 pages. In all, about one-sixth of the book is concerned with litigation over contracts stipulating for monetary payments in gold or for payments fixed at gold values.

Gold clauses were one of the most legally troublesome issues in international contracting during the inter-war years while Mann wrote his first edition. At the time, litigation over gold clauses was a sign that the old monetary order based on

[*] I am grateful for the comments of Hector MacQueen and Richard Nolan; and assistance from Léon Carmona Fontaine and Elspeth Reid. The usual disclaimers apply.

[1] FA Mann, *The Legal Aspect of Money* (OUP 1938) hereafter Mann, *Legal Aspect*.

David Fox, *Gold Clauses in the Capital Markets of the Early 20th Century* In: *FA Mann*. Edited by: Jason Grant Allen and Gerhard Dannemann, Oxford University Press. © David Fox 2024. DOI: 10.1093/oso/9780198881452.003.0010

the international gold standard was breaking down, despite the efforts of national governments and central banks to shore up and restore it. Nearly a century later, it is easy enough to recognize that the decades following the First World War were a transitional period for the world's money. Mann himself recognized this even if he made little of it in his legal exposition.[2] Countries discovered by painful experiments how to operate monetary systems that had only a partial connection with precious metals, or possibly none at all. Like all transitional periods, the significance of the changes did not become apparent until afterwards. From the First World War until the mid-1930s, many governments and commentators still assumed that gold was the natural base for a monetary system.

The aim of this chapter is not to recount the doctrinal rules developed by Mann and other contemporary commentators on the interpretation and implementation of gold clauses in monetary obligations. Those rules settled into a workable shape during the 1920s and 1930s as courts across Europe, the United States, and Great Britain resolved the surge of gold clause litigation generated by the monetary instability of the era. Rather, the chapter scratches beneath the doctrinal analysis to the commercial and political purposes served by gold clauses. It seeks to connect them with the prevailing understanding of money and monetary valuation in the early decades of the 20th century. It considers the gold clause contracts as historical instances of the early international bond markets in operation, and the litigation over them as one reaction to the financial instability of the era. All this was the context that Mann surely knew, even if he chose to separate it from his exposition of the legal doctrine.

The chapter briefly introduces the legal doctrine on gold clauses. It then explains the operation of the international gold standard and the legal measures introduced by some of its leading participants—Great Britain, the United States, and France—to implement it in their national systems. This sets the monetary background to the gold clause litigation. Most of the cases arose from long-term bond contracts made before the First World War but litigated after it. World-wide capital markets developed in the late 19th century as the gold standard stabilized the system of international exchange rates that borrowers and lenders in different countries depended on to ensure the real returns on their contracts. Gold clauses bound the parties to a system of exchange rates which they expected to last for the duration of their contracts.

Everything changed abruptly in 1914. The First World War led to a period of price inflation and instability in the exchanges. The international monetary system remained unstable through the 1920s and 1930s as former gold-standard countries contended with periods of inflation and deflation, and saw their currencies devalued. The gold clauses in long-term contracts no longer corresponded to the

[2] See his discussion of the difficulties of defining a monetary unit of account once a currency system was no longer based on gold: ibid 32–37.

monetary values and exchange rates in force. The legal question in this new era was whether the parties could still enforce the clauses and the past monetary values they rested on. The question went beyond the private law of contract since the valuation of money and monetary obligations touched upon the state's sovereign powers over the monetary system.

The final section of the chapter considers three of the leading cases on gold clauses analysed by Mann. These cases have a larger significance beyond the points of legal doctrine that he found in them. They are rare surviving examples of the way investors and borrowers planned transactions in pre-First World War bond markets. They show events in the larger history of the era impinging on parties' financial dealings and on the legal record.

II. The Legal Doctrine on Gold Clauses

An enormous amount of legal literature on gold clauses developed during the 1920s and 1930s.[3] Chapter IV of Mann's *Legal Aspect* (1938) rested on a foundation of international legal decisions and scholarly writing that was already very deep. Many of the sources originated in France, Germany, and the United States. These were all countries whose special monetary history had made gold clauses a feature of ordinary commercial contracting before the First World War and whose currencies had afterwards been devalued or undergone periods of severe inflation.

Mann's distinctive emphasis, however, was on the laws of England. English decisions on gold clauses were few by comparison. The reason, as Mann noted, was that contractual provisions designed to protect against fluctuations in the value of money were very rare in England, whether in purely internal contracts or in those where the parties were in different jurisdictions. Even Germany's war reparations owed to Britain under the Treaty of Versailles were expressed as nominal sterling

[3] See the sources gathered by Mann in *Legal Aspect* (n 1) 218–19. To list just a small selection from France, Great Britain, and the United States: Jules Valéry, 'Clause Payable en or et le Cours Forcé' (1916) 43 J Dr Int'l 1132 (hereafter Valéry, 'Clause Payable en or et le Cours Forcé'); F Gény, 'La Validité Juridique de la Clause "Payable en Or"' (1926) 25 Revue Trimestrielle du Droit Civil 557 (hereafter Gény, 'Clause "Payable en Or"'); BA Wortley, 'The Gold Clause' (1936) 17 BYBIL 112; Arthur Nussbaum, 'Comparative and International Aspects of American Gold Clause Abrogation' (1934) 44 Yale Law Journal 53; JP Dawson, 'The Gold Clause Decisions' (1935) 33 Michigan Law Review 647. In Mann's preface, he acknowledged his special debt to the writings of Arthur Nussbaum, formerly Professor of Law at the University of Berlin. Like Mann, Nussbaum was an émigré lawyer, who became a Visiting Professor at Columbia University. His work came to fruition one year after the *Legal Aspect* (n 1) in Arthur Nussbaum, *Money in the Law* (Foundation Press 1939) (hereafter Nussbaum, *Money in the Law*). His book devoted over 100 pages to gold clauses. English legal practitioners who might not have had access to all the international sources cited by Mann could consult a casebook: Arpad Plesch, *The Gold Clause: a Collection of International Cases and Opinions* (Stevens 1935) (hereafter Plesch, *The Gold Clause*). Plesch, formerly a practitioner at the Hungarian bar, compiled in English translation some leading cases and expert legal opinions from England, the United States, Sweden, the Netherlands, Germany, and Belgium. Mann criticized the incompleteness of Plesch's collection: Mann, *Legal Aspect* (n 1) 219.

sums rather than in the gold-value amounts that the other Allied governments sought to exact.[4]

Mann did not speculate about the reasons for this difference. They probably stemmed from the common law's long-standing practice of enforcing all debts at nominal values.[5] In contrast, the traditional doctrine of the civil law was that debts were payable according to their gold value when they were first contracted.[6] Sterling had been on a mono-metallic gold standard since at least 1816,[7] which was longer than other Western currencies, including the French franc and the United States dollar.[8] The gold value of the pound had stayed unchanged since then, which was probably as long as commercial memory would have extended. Sterling was the world's main reserve currency in the early 20th century, and many international obligations undertaken by parties abroad were denominated in sterling units. Parties seemed to find it safe enough to bargain for simple pounds sterling.

Legal issues arising from gold clauses divided into three main kinds. The *first* question was whether a payment clause was intended to have any connection at all with gold. A reference to a certain type of coin, such as 'sterling gold coin of the United Kingdom', 'gold dollars', or '*francs or*' might be read to mean the nominal monetary units represented by that type of currency. Thus, a reference in a Chilean contract to 'a rent of 93,500 pesos of 183,057 millionths of a gramme of fine gold' could be interpreted as a 'statutory synonym' inserted by a cautious draftsman for the legally defined peso unit of Chile. The debtor would be free to pay the nominal sum of Chilean currency rather than actual gold coin or the current value of that quantity of coin.[9] The question was one of ascertaining the parties' contractual intentions.

The *second* question was whether a reference to gold fixed the mode of payment (a 'modality clause') or the substance or amount of the debt (a 'value clause'). The distinction went to the difference between the parties' chosen currency of payment and the substantial measure of the debt which that currency was intended to

[4] Mann, *Legal Aspect* (n 1) 91. Mann probably owed this observation to Arthur Nussbaum. Compare Nussbaum, *Money in the Law* (n 3) 305.

[5] The leading decision was *Gilbert v Brett* (1604) Davis 18, discussed in Mann, *Legal Aspect* (n 1) 68–70 in the context of the nominalist principle.

[6] Wolfgang Ernst, 'The Legists' Doctrines on Money and the Law from the Eleventh to Fifteenth Centuries' in David Fox and Wolfgang Ernst (eds), *Money in the Western Legal Tradition: Middle Ages to Bretton Woods* (OUP 2016).

[7] Coinage Act 1816, s. 11. Previously, since 1774, the United Kingdom had run a partial bimetallic coinage system where silver coins were legal tender up to £25: Statute 14 Geo. III, cap. 42, s. 2. Before that, the system had been completely bimetallic, with no upper limit on the legal tender status of any gold or silver coins issued as 'the lawful money of England'.

[8] Angela Redish, *Bimetallism: An Economic and Historical Analysis* (Cambridge 2000) chs 6 and 7.

[9] *St Pierre v South American Stores* [1937] 3 All ER 349 per Greer LJ at 351, discussed in Mann, *Legal Aspect* (n 1) 94, interpreting Chilean Decreto-Ley 406 of 14 October 1925, defining the gold value of the peso monetary unit. Contrast *Case of the Brazilian Federal Loans Issued in France* (1929) 56 J Dr Int'l 977, 1008–29, 1021, dismissing the suggestion that a reference to *francs or* was merely 'une clause de style' or 'une pratique routinière'.

discharge.[10] As Mann noted, the distinction depended 'on the construction of each individual contract, and no hard-and-fast rule [could] be laid down'.[11]

Parties were generally free to stipulate that the creditor should receive coins or notes of a certain national currency. Modality clauses of this kind were important for international bond issues since the investors who subscribed to them were likely to reside in a variety of countries.[12] They subscribed to the bonds with their own national currencies and generally expected to receive their interest and capital payments in the same currency. The value of the debtor's obligation, however, needed to be measured in a single currency unit, which was not necessarily the same as currencies subscribed by the investors.

As events developed in the 1930s, it was unheard of for modality clauses stipulating for gold currency to be enforced literally. Creditors had to be content with the nominal sum in inconvertible bank notes. This was the very result they usually wanted to avoid. By this stage, many countries had withdrawn their gold coins from circulation and devalued their currencies from the original gold parities in place when the contracts were first made.[13] Payment in gold became practically impossible or, as in the United States, legally impossible—after the 1933 Joint Resolution of Congress abrogated gold clauses.[14]

If the court instead interpreted the stipulation as a gold-value clause then the creditor might at least secure the substantial value of the sum due even if it was paid in inconvertible notes. The leading English case was the decision of the House of Lords in *Feist v Société Intercommunale Belge d'Électricité* (1933).[15] In 1928, the Belgian company issued bonds through English agents. The bonds provided that investors were entitled to receive their interest and principal sums due at the agents' London offices 'in sterling in gold coin of the United Kingdom, of or equal to the standard of weight and fineness existing on the 1st day of September, 1928'. The House of Lords accepted the creditor's argument that the clause referred not to the modality of payment but 'the means by which the amount of [its] indebtedness [was] to be measured and ascertained'.[16] The creditor was entitled to legal tender sterling notes equal to the value of gold coin of the standard in force at the date of the contract.

The *third* set of questions arising from gold clauses could be grouped around public policy (*l'ordre publique*).[17] This was where the greatest divergence of views among jurisdictions became apparent. In some cases, including Germany and the

[10] See also Plesch, *The Gold Clause* (n 3) v–vi; and *Case of the Serbian Loans Issued in France* (1929) 56 J Dr Int'l 977, 1003.

[11] Mann, *Legal Aspect* (n 1) 100.

[12] See Section IV.

[13] See Section V.

[14] See Section V.

[15] [1934] AC 161. See Mann, *Legal Aspect* (n 1) 101–03, and Section VI.B.

[16] ibid 172, per Lord Russell.

[17] Mann, *Legal Aspect* (n 1) 103–13.

United Kingdom, stipulations for payment of certain kinds of gold coin or for their value in legal tender were fully compatible with domestic legislation on coinage and legal tender.[18] In others, notably the United States after 1933, gold-coin clauses and gold-value clauses were made void on public policy grounds. The view of the United States courts was that they conflicted with the constitutional power of Congress to control the monetary system according to its view of the national interest.[19]

Mann's view was that there was nothing inherently destabilizing to a monetary system in a creditor stipulating for payment in a certain kind of money—gold or otherwise. While a state might legislate that inconvertible paper currencies were legal tender, it did not necessarily follow that stipulations for payment in gold were impliedly prohibited.

Questions of public policy also had an international dimension. Local courts often enforced gold clause contracts governed by foreign laws or those where payment was to be made in another jurisdiction that had legislated to control them.[20] Here, Mann supported the view taken by the House of Lords in *R v International Trustee for the Protection of Bondholders Aktiengesellschaft* (1937).[21] The American abrogation of gold clauses in 1933 applied to all contracts governed by United States law regardless of the residence of the parties or the place of payment designated by the contract. On this question, Mann queried the soundness of other international and European decisions. These confined the territorial effect of the prohibition to payments made in the United States, among American citizens or corporations, or to contracts made after the Joint Resolution came into effect.[22]

III. The International Gold Standard

A. The legal foundations of the gold standard

The period 1880–1914 marked the classical high point of the international gold standard. By a process of unplanned convergence, the major industrial, lending, and borrowing economies of the world defined their national currency units in terms of gold, and fixed their exchange rates in terms of gold parities.[23] By the lights

18 ibid 104.

19 See Section V.

20 Mann, *Legal Aspect* (n 1) 217–33

21 *R v International Trustee for the Protection of Bondholders Aktiengesellschaft* [1937] AC 500, discussed in Section VI.C.

22 Mann, *Legal Aspect* (n 1) 222–33. He argued against this interpretation of the decisions in the *Case concerning the Serbian Loans* (1929) 56 J Dr Int'l 977 discussed in Section VI.A.

23 See generally Michael Bordo and Angela Redish, 'Putting the "System" in the International Monetary System' in David Fox and Wolfgang Ernst, *Money in the Western Legal Tradition: Middle Ages to Bretton Woods* (OUP 2016) (hereafter Bordo and Redish, 'System'); and for contemporary descriptions, see 'Cunliffe Committee on Currency and Foreign Exchanges after the War' (1918), reproduced

of the time, the gold standard was thought to promote price stability at home and, through its international operation, to transmit that stability across the various trading partners who fixed their currencies in gold. If governments played by its unwritten rules, then the gold standard would maintain an equilibrium where exchange rates stayed within narrow bands and excessive trade imbalances were prevented.

The practical workings of the gold standard were matters of economic policy overseen by central banks or national governments. The legal foundations for its workings were slender. Participating countries enacted coinage legislation that defined their national unit of account in terms of a quantity of gold. They would define the weight and fineness of the foundational coin of their monetary system. The legislation would ascribe a money of account value to the coin, which created a relationship between the monetary unit it represented and the quantity of gold it contained. Thus in the period before 1914, the gold sovereign coin of the United Kingdom, which was struck from 123.27447 grains of gold 91.66 per cent fine, had a legal value in payments of £1;[24] the gold dollar of the United States was defined as containing 25 8/10 grains of gold 9/10 fine;[25] and the French franc a 20th part of 6.45161 grams of gold 9/10 fine.[26]

The definition of various monetary units in terms of a common gold standard fixed the official par of exchange between national currencies. Once both countries were on gold then, as Mann explained, an equation could be established between two monetary units based on the common metallic standard.[27] Thus, the pound sterling had a gold par against the US dollar of 1:4.866, and the franc of 1:25.22 so that the pound was worth about US$4.86½ and Ffr25.22.[28] These rates might vary as seasonal changes in the demand for imports or capital affected the currency price. But if the market rates diverged too far from the official par, national monetary authorities would adjust their interest rates, which changed the internal or external demand for funds and re-stabilized the market prices for currency closer to the par.

Thus in practice, the official parities between currencies were expressed as fractional ratios: 1:4.866 or 1:25.22 or the like. In understanding gold clauses, however, it helps to recall the legal formula on which the parities were based. So long as gold

in Barry Eichengreen (ed.), *The Gold Standard in Theory and History* (Routledge 1985) (hereafter Eichengreen, *Gold Standard*); RG Hawtrey, *Monetary Reconstruction* (2nd edn, Longman, Green and Co. 1927) ch. 3 (hereafter Hawtrey, *Monetary Reconstruction*); K Helfferich, *Money* (L Infield tr., Aldelphi Company 1927), Vol. 2, ch. VI (hereafter Helfferich, *Money*); GDH Cole, *Money: Its Present and Future* (Cassel & Co. 1944), ch. 3.

24 Coinage Act 1870, ss 3, 4, Sch. 1 (UK).
25 US Congressional Act chap. 41, 31 Statutes at Large 45 (1900) s. 1. See further Section VI.C.
26 *Loi sur la fabrication et la vérification des monnaies* (7–17 *germinal an* XI) discussed in Section VI.A.
27 Mann, *Legal Aspect* (n 1) 46.
28 For a summary of the official mint parities among Germany, France, Great Britain, and the United States, see Bordo and Redish, 'System' (n 23) Table 27.2.

coins remained officially in circulation, the national legislation expressed the value of monetary units in a reflexive relationship with gold. The foundational coins of the system—sovereigns or dollars—were the physical representation of monetary units tied to defined quantities of gold. Consequently, a stipulation for £1 or $1 was ambivalent in nature, referring either to an obligation for delivery of a kind of coin on the one hand and a quantity of monetary value on the other.

Gold clauses in contracts had the same effect as the fixed exchange parities that were a feature of the international gold standard. They stipulated for the parties' chosen parity between the various currencies that might be involved in the transaction. Rather than express them as fractional ratios, they stipulated for numbers of coins of a certain legal standard. Quantities of coin expressed the value of the monetary units denominating the debtor's obligation.

B. Valuation of the monetary unit in gold

What did it mean to say that a monetary unit was defined in terms of gold? The outstanding contemporary explanation was that of Ralph Hawtrey (1879–1975). Hawtrey was for most of his career a civil servant at HM Treasury and notably served as a British delegate at the 1922 Genoa Conference on international monetary reconstruction called by the League of Nations. In a paper delivered to the British Association in 1919, he explained the relationship:

> When we speak of a monetary standard we mean that which regulates the value or the purchasing power of the monetary unit. The monetary unit is the unit for the measurement of debts. A debt is an economic relation which requires to be expressed as a number or quantity, and, in order that it may be so expressed, it must be expressed in terms of some unit ... But it is a mistake to suppose that [a monetary standard] is *merely* a standard of value, no more than a unit for the comparison of different items of wealth ... The true function of the monetary standard is so to regulate the unit in which debts are measured as to maintain the stability of that system.[29]

In Hawtrey's view, monetary units such as the pound, the dollar, or the franc were substantively empty units for expressing comparisons among different items of wealth and the debts that stipulated for the transfer of wealth between persons.[30] They enabled quantities of one thing to be aligned in numerical relationships with

[29] Reproduced in Hawtrey, *Monetary Reconstruction* (n 23) 37–38 (emphasis original).

[30] For the classic exposition of the function of the monetary unit in expressing relational values between commodities, see Karl Marx, *Capital: A Critique of Political Economy* (S Moore, E Aveling, and E Untermann tr., Wordworth Editions 2013 [1867]) ch. 3.1.

quantities of another. Value was not something inherent in items of wealth or in the means of payment exchanged for them. As an observed fact of economic experience, payment media were particular instances of a more general purchasing power over items of wealth, whether in the form of commodities or services. But the purchasing power of the means of payment could only be ascertained by a relationship of convertibility between the unit and a certain commodity—gold—which existed in stable quantities and for which there was a universal and constant demand.[31] The relative stability of precious metals compared with other kinds of commodity was a fundamental tenet of the system, and was accepted by economists and lawyers alike.[32] By extension, the value of debts, commodities, and services derived from the possibility of exchanging them for money. Money was itself made from a fixed quantity of gold or was exchangeable for gold at a fixed rate.

Hawtrey's insight was to link the gold standard to debts as well as to monetary means of payment.[33] Both were denominated in units of account, and so debts, like the money that discharged them, could be related to a general purchasing power based on quantities of gold. Although Hawtrey mentions gold clauses nowhere in his writings, he would have understood their effect. Gold clauses specified the fixed quantity of monetary purchasing power that the creditor expected to receive in return for discharging the debt. Rather than leave the bargain open, with the debtor's duty expressed in empty nominal units, the creditor specified for performance linked to the universally recognized representation of purchasing power. The gold clauses mimicked the state's own power by incorporating a standard of value into the contract. They internalized the fixed purchasing power of a national monetary unit into the parties' private bargain.[34]

However, Hawtrey's explanation does not tell quite the whole story. The creditor's specification for a gold value could only ever approximate to the purchasing power that money might afford at any given time. The purchasing power of money varied as inflation or deflation in the creditor's country altered the general level of prices.

[31] For other contemporary rationalizations of gold standard theories of value, see David Barbour, *The Standard of Value* (MacMillan & Co. 1912) chs 4–5; and Gustav Cassel, *Money and Foreign Exchange after 1914* (Constable 1922) 1–8 (hereafter Cassel, *Money and Foreign Exchange*).

[32] For example, see Gény, 'Clause "Payable en Or"' (n 3) 564; and *Bronson v Rodes* (1868) 74 US 229, 249 per Chase CJ. Price stability was identified as a distinctive feature of precious metals, which partly explained why they were universally selected as media of exchange: Carl Menger, 'The Origins of Money' (1892) 2 Economic Journal 239. But the stability of gold values was only relative rather than absolute. Gold depreciated slightly against silver during the 19th century as world production and holdings of gold increased: Helfferich, *Money* (n 23) 123–41, 175–207.

[33] As he explained in the preface to R Hawtrey, *Gold Standard in Theory and Practice* (Longmans 1927): 'Currency is better explained in terms of credit than credit in terms of currency. That is so in theory, in practice and in law. I have here expounded the gold standard in close relation to the theory of banking and credit.'

[34] See the explanation of the Permanent Court of International Justice noted in the *Case of the Serbian Loans Issued in France; and the Case of the Brazilian Federal Loans Issued in France* (1929) 56 J Dr Int'l 977, 996–97, 1022 discussing the '*franc or*'.

As a precaution, a preferred solution might have been to link the debtor's obligation to some external index of prices. In the early decades of the 20th century, however, the use of index clauses in domestic commercial contracts was uncommon. At least in the United States, various price indices were published by the 1930s.[35] Each was based on a different basket of commodities or services. They therefore generated different measures of the price level, any one of which might have approximated more or less satisfactorily to the level of price inflation felt by the debtor or creditor. Index clauses were thought to be unsuitable for securities issued by public utilities, such as railway companies or local municipalities, or for long-term insurance contracts (and these were the very contracts where gold clauses were most favoured). The value of the recurrent income received or assets held by these organizations might not rise or fall at the same rate as the inflation experienced by the creditors to whom they owed their obligations. In short, there was no guarantee that any given price index selected for the contract would operate neutrally between the debtor and the creditor to the obligation.[36]

Besides, even where price indices existed, they might not have worked satisfactorily in contracts with an international element where the debtor and creditor were in different countries. Many bonds were sold to investors abroad. A theory by which price inflation in one country affected its exchange rate with another was only developing in the 1920s.[37] The orthodox understanding remained that exchange rates were primarily determined by gold parities between countries even if the usual conditions for the operation of the international gold standard were no longer in place. None of this would have created the conditions for contracting parties to abandon their familiar practice of stipulating for payments in gold and instead use index clauses to stabilize the value of the debtor's performance.

[35] See JP Dawson and JW Coultrap, 'Contracting by Reference to Price Indices' (1935) 33 Mich L Rev 685 for their use in the USA; and Gény, 'Clause "Payable en Or"' (n 3) 626–30 for the argument from principle. For some of the practical difficulties of preparing reliable price indices in Europe early in the 20th century, see Cassel, *Money and Foreign Exchange* (n 31) 45–51; JM Keynes, *Treatise on Money* (1930) vol. 1, ch. 4 in Austin Robinson and Donald Moggridge, *The Collected Writings of J M Keynes* (3rd edn, Cambridge University Press 2013). The most extreme versions of index clauses fixed the value of a debtor's obligation against a single commodity, such as rye, wheat, or coal since a stable consumer demand for them could be guaranteed. Rye mortgage bonds were issued on this footing during the German hyperinflation of 1922–23: Nussbaum, *Money in the Law* (n 3) 403–06. They were, however, more a symptom of collapse in the monetary system than anything offering a workable alternative to a gold standard.

[36] Compare *Norman v Baltimore and Ohio Railroad Co* (1934) 294 US 240, 318, where the court considered the economic imbalance that would result if the railroad's debts were enforced at their original gold value but its income was determined by the new devalued standard of the dollar.

[37] This was Gustav Cassel's theory of 'purchasing power parity' developed after reflection on the wartime inflations: Gustav Cassel, *Post-War Monetary Stabilization* (Columbia University Press 1928), ch. 1 (hereafter Cassel, *Monetary Stabilization*).

IV. The Gold Standard and Early 20th-Century Capital Markets

Studies of the gold standard generally emphasize its function in regulating the balance of payments among trading partners. The gold clause cases emphasize its role in stabilizing arrangements for international lending and borrowing. The gold standard supported the 'first globalization' of capital markets during the late 19th and early 20th centuries.[38] These centred on the City of London, with sterling as the main reserve currency for settling international payments. Other markets operated out of the leading financial centres of Western Europe: Paris, Berlin, Brussels, and Geneva. The United States developed from being a major borrower in the European capital markets during the 19th century to the dominant international lender during and after the First World War. Its main financial centre was—and remains—New York.

Many of the gold clauses cases arise from debt instruments issued to subscribers by governments, municipalities, and utility companies in developing countries. In return for a fixed-interest return, investors subscribed the loan capital that built ports, mines, railways, power stations, and public transport networks. Taking a small sample from the gold clauses cases, we find the Moroccan government raising a loan in the French and Belgian bond markets in 1904;[39] the City of Tokyo issuing sterling-denominated bonds in 1912 in Britain, France, and the United States to fund its tramway and electric lighting infrastructure;[40] the Argentine port of Rosario issuing bonds between 1903 and 1911 to investors in France;[41] a Belgian electricity company issuing sterling-denominated bonds in 1928;[42] and, most frequently of all, bonds issued to fund the construction of railways in South America or the United States.[43] As a variant on this pattern, special-purpose banks might be incorporated with a European base to raise funds which they would then lend on security to borrowers abroad. One such example was *la Banque hypothécaire franco-argentine*, which channelled funds from French investors to borrowers in Uruguay, Paraguay, and Argentina.[44] A company with its main seat of activity abroad might be incorporated in and directed from a European financial centre. Thus *la Société d'Héraclée*, founded in 1896, had the majority of its directors and

[38] The term belongs to Laure Quennouëlle. See Laure Quennouëlle and Youssef Cassis (eds), *Financial Centres and International Capital Flows in the Nineteenth and Twentieth Centuries* (OUP 2011) 7. For international investment in the gold standard era, see Lance E Davies and Robert E Gallman, *Evolving Financial Markets and International Capital Flows* (Cambridge 2001) chs 1, 2, 7; and GB Magee and AS Thompson, *Empire and Globalisation* (Cambridge University Press 2010) ch. 5.

[39] Cour de cassation (Req), 5 November 1934 (France) (1934) 63 J Dr Int'l 177.

[40] Cour de cassation (Ch civ), 14 January 1931 (France) (1931) 58 J Dr Int'l 126.

[41] Cour de cassation (Civ), 9 July 1930 (France) (1930) 58 J Dr Int'l 124.

[42] *Feist v Société Intercommunale Belge d'Électricité* [1934] AC 161.

[43] Cour de cassation (Civ) 24 January, 14 February 1934 [1934] *Dalloz RP*, I, 73; *Case of the Brazilian Federal Loans Issued in France* (1929) 56 J Dr Int'l 977, 1008–29.

[44] Cour de cassation (Ch civ), 14 January 1934 (France) (1934) 61 J Dr Int'l1202.

shareholders in France but was incorporated to develop the port and coalmines in the Ereğli region in Turkey.[45]

Allied governments during the First World War were forced to look abroad to fund their war efforts. The war could not have been fought without the huge expansion of credit in the neutral countries that supplied food and munitions to the belligerent states.[46] Some of this credit consisted in 20-year, interest-bearing bonds issued by the British government on the New York markets. Britain borrowed for itself and on behalf of its European Allies.

The common feature of so many of these bonds was their long duration and range of countries from which they drew investors. Their typical term was 20 years, but loans of 35 or 40 years' duration were not unknown. The longest was perhaps the 1895 bond floated by the Serbian government in the markets of France, Germany, and Austria—it was repayable over 72 years.[47] The scale of the loans was such that the borrowers could not expect to repay them from just a few years' operating profits. The borrowers therefore committed themselves to making annual amortization payments into sinking funds. These would meet any periodic redemptions by investors and ultimately ensure that the outstanding principal was repaid at the end of the term.[48]

Investors subscribed to the bonds using their own national currencies. They might, for example, pay francs or dollars to acquire bonds where the debtor's obligation was denominated in, or measured by, sterling.[49] For investors' convenience, the bonds usually provided that they would be paid the interest and principal in their own national currency at named banks in the financial centres where the loan was raised. These would often be in London, Paris, or New York. They might also provide for payment at a cognate financial centre, such as Brussels or Geneva, at the prevailing market rate of exchange with the French franc.[50]

Long-term bond issues created formidable problems of internal and external calibration. The borrower needed to ascertain the extent of its annual liabilities to pay interest and contributions to the sinking fund. In a case where the borrower was itself an intermediary on behalf of other ultimate borrowers (who might themselves operate in different countries),[51] it needed to match its anticipated currency

45 Tribunal fédéral suisse (1re section civile), 11 February 1931 (1931) 58 J Dr Int'l 362; Cour de cassation (Civ) 7 July 1931 (France) (1932) 59 J Dr Int'l 267. Similarly, *Derwa v Rio de Janiero Tramway, Light & Power Co* (1928) 4 DLR 542 (Ontario company operating in Brazil issues bonds to subscribers in London, Geneva, Brussels, and Berlin).

46 See generally Hew Strachan, *Financing the First World War* (OUP 2004) (hereafter Strachan, *First World War*); also Sections V and VI.C below.

47 *Case of the Serbian Loans Issued in France* (1929) 56 J Dr Int'l 977, 988 discussed at Section VI.A.

48 For example, the 1912 bond issue by the City of Tokyo: Cour de cassation (Ch civ), 14 January 1931 (France), (1931) 58 J Dr Int'l 126; and *Case of the Brazilian Federal Loans Issued in France* (1929) 56 J Dr Int'l 977, 1008–29, where the amortization and repayment schedule was expressed in the Port of Perambuco, and Federal railways bonds at 1012–16.

49 Cour de cassation (Ch civ), 14 January 1931 (France) (1931) 58 J Dr Int'l 126.

50 For example, le Tribunal fédéral suisse (1re section civile), 11 February 1931 (1931) 58 J Dr Int'l 362.

51 Cour de cassation (Ch civ), 14 January 1934 (France) (1934) 61 J Dr Int'l 1202.

receipts from the borrowers in those different countries to its own annual liabilities. Ultimately, the bondholders expected a payment at home in their local currency which corresponded to the value of their outlay when they first subscribed to the bond.

Gold clauses served as a common standard against which the various currencies in the transaction could be calibrated. Their effect was to base the nominal value of the principal sum due in a quantity of gold ascertainable at fixed date—usually the date of issue. Gold clauses determined the value of any annual payments made by the borrower for interest and sinking fund contributions. If the currency receipts expected from any ultimate borrowers of the funds were themselves expressed through a gold clause, then they too would be at a rate fixed in terms of the common standard. It did not matter whether the ultimate borrowers were, for example, in Uruguay, Paraguay, or Argentina, the bond issuer was in France, and the bondholder in Belgium. Each could pay or be paid in its own currency but the measure of their claims or liabilities was reduced to a common denominator in gold.

Seen in this way, gold clauses were essential to the borrower's planning of the whole transaction. They were as relevant to the immediate present when the bond was first issued as they might have been a precaution against future events. Adapting Ralph Hawtrey's explanation of a national monetary standard quoted earlier, contractual gold clauses based the various debts involved in the transaction on a common standard so 'as to maintain the stability of that system', where the system was the transaction itself.[52] They internalized in the contract the ratios of purchasing power established by the general rules of the gold standard. They did not stipulate for standards that were any different from those generally in force when the contracts were made. Since they were contracting within the existing exchange parities rather than against them, they did not trespass upon any power of the state to control the monetary standard. All going well, the parties would probably not have expected or wanted actual payment in gold. It would be good enough to pay the investors in whatever currency was legal tender at the due date and place of payment.[53]

With hindsight, it may easy to interpret gold clauses as attempts by investors to secure the full repayment of their loans against the risks of price inflation or devaluation of the monetary standard by their governments. As events turned out in the 1930s, this often became their function. But to concentrate on the investors' interests would give too simple a view of the reasons for including them. More pressing were the interests of the bond issuers. They needed a stable monetary standard to plan their business operations and make repayments of capital

[52] See Hawtrey, *Monetary Reconstruction* (n 23) 37–38, discussed in section III.B.

[53] As the Permanent Court of International Justice noted in the *Case of the Serbian Loans Issued in France*; and the *Case of the Brazilian Federal Loans Issued in France* (1929) 56 J Dr Int'l 977, 983, 1024.

and interest. As large governmental or financial institutions, they were strongly placed to set the terms of the transaction. Gold clauses were as important to the debtors as to the creditors, and probably more so.

V. The First World War and its Aftermath

The need of the belligerent states to pay for the First World War overrode the domestic and international rules for operating the gold standard.[54] Once the purchasing power of their national monetary units was no longer determined by a relationship with gold, the usual restraints on price inflation loosened and exchange rates no longer had a reason to stay at their pre-war parities. The war began a period of domestic and international monetary instability that continued for the next 25 years. To quote an observer, writing in 1933:

> Then, in August 1914, the lyrical purr of the whole plant faded away at the behest of governments. Scarcely any public safeguard that can be invented appears to be willing to hamper governmental manipulation of the currency—call it defence if you will—as soon as vital danger threatens the State.[55]

Even those countries that kept up a semblance of the gold standard during the war failed to maintain the conditions that might have ensured its stabilizing effects. The belligerent countries suspended the convertibility of their paper currencies to gold.[56] Their gold coinages disappeared from use. Gold coins accumulated in the reserves of national banks, as if the simple holding of the gold would—without more—maintain the purchasing power of their currencies. To different degrees, the belligerent countries kept their commercial and military economies running by printing as much paper money as they needed. Governments issued short-term

[54] For the financial arrangements across all the belligerent states, see Strachan, *First World War* (n 46); B Eichengreen, *Golden Fetters: The Gold Standard and the Great Depression, 1919–1938* (OUP 1992), ch. 3; For contemporary accounts of war finance and its links to price inflation and a fall in exchange rates, see Cassel, *Money and Foreign Exchange* (n 31) 1–8; Cassel, *Monetary Stabilization* (n 37) 68; and P Einzig, *World Finance Since 1914* (Kegan Paul 1935) chs 2–7, 12 (hereafter Einzig, *World Finance*).

[55] DS Edwards, *A Critical Study of Gold Reserves and the Monetary Standard* (PS King & Son 1933), 23 (hereafter Edwards, *Critical Study*). Edwards was an independent economist with visiting connections at the University of London and New York Chamber of Commerce.

[56] In Great Britain, Bank of England notes remained convertible to gold sovereigns but the government relied on patriotic duty to discourage holders of the notes from cashing them for sovereigns. It introduced legal tender currency notes of £1 and 10s to make up for a dearth of small coinage and the withdrawal of gold sovereigns: Currency and Bank Notes Act 1914, s. 1. See generally AE Feaveayear, *The Pound Sterling* (OUP 1931) ch. 12; M de Cecco, *The International Gold Standard: Money and Empire* (2nd edn, F. Pinter 1984), ch. 7. In France, notes of the Banque de France ceased to be convertible to gold (*cours forcé*) but remained legal tender (*cours légal*): *loi monétaire* (5 August 1914) Art. 3 [1914] *Dalloz RP*, IV, 88. See generally Gény, 'Clause "Payable en Or"' (n 3) 567–68.

credit instruments that circulated as substitutes for cash. They raised loans from their own citizens and from private investors in neutral countries, mainly the United States. The government in Great Britain acquired foreign securities held by its own citizens to use as collateral for its own borrowings in the United States. Manufacturers in neutral countries supplied armaments on credit to the belligerent countries.

The result was a period of sustained inflation in domestic prices. Inflation was a defining economic feature of the war years, and it was by no means confined to the defeated countries of central Europe that suffered the hyperinflations of the early 1920s.[57] Considering only those countries that fared relatively well, in Great Britain the inflation rates from 1914 to 1919 ran at an average of 17.4 per cent (100 in 1914 = 223.5 in 1919); in France at 21 per cent (100 in 1914 = 240 in 1919); and in the United States at 11.1 per cent (100 in 1914 = 187.1 in 1919).[58] Inflation in all three countries increased towards the end of the war. By comparison, inflation rates in Great Britain during the immediate pre-war years had stayed at around 0.0–1.0 per cent per annum. Rates were at similar levels in France, apart from an exceptional spike between 1910 and 1912.

The war also threw the foreign exchanges into disarray. The belligerent countries suspended the free export of gold, either by legislation or by creating practical obstacles that made shipping gold too costly or risky to undertake.[59] They ran trade deficits to provide for the necessities of the war. The usual flows of gold that should have corrected these imbalances ceased to operate. (Even when countries exported some of their gold reserves to pay for imports from abroad, they did not rein in the supply of money at home, as would usually have happened under the gold standard rules.) The value of sterling against the United States dollar fell as low as US$4.50 in September 1915 but was stabilized by the British government in January 1916 at US$4.76 7/16, which was about 2 per cent off its official gold-standard parity of $4.866.[60] The French franc stayed close to its official par with sterling during the

[57] For the hyperinflations, see François Velde, 'Hyperinflations of the Early Twentieth Century' in David Fox and Wolfgang Ernst (eds), *Money in the Western Legal Tradition: Middle Ages to Bretton Woods* (OUP 2016).

[58] For Great Britain, see the UK Office of National Statistics table Inflation_data.xls at <https://www.officialdata.org/UK-inflation> accessed 9 March 2023; for France, see <https://france-inflation.com/calculateur_inflation.php> accessed 9 March 2023; and for the United States, Bureau of Labor Statistics, Table 24, Historical Consumer Price Index for all Urban Consumers at <https://www.bls.gov/cpi/tables/historical-cpi-u-201709.pdf> accessed 9 March 2023.

[59] In principle, gold exports from Great Britain remained possible during the war but licensing rules and the costs of insurance discouraged movements of specie. Exports were legally prohibited in 1919 to prevent speculation on the price arbitrage between London and New York: Proclamation (1 April 1919) Geo V (1 April 1919) *London Gazette* 4209. Gold exports from France, other than by the Banque de France, were prohibited in 1915: *Décret relative à la prohibition de la sortie de l'or* (3 July 1915) [1915] *Dalloz RP*, IV, 172.

[60] See M Friedman and A Jacobson Schwartz, *A Monetary History of the United States 1867–1960* (National Bureau of Economic Research 1960) 196–205 (hereafter Friedman and Schwartz, *A Monetary History of the United States*).

war but quickly depreciated during the early 1920s. By 1925 it was worth just one-fifth of its pre-war value against sterling.[61]

The instability in domestic and international monetary values took a different direction after the war. Those countries that avoided the hyperinflations took measures to stabilize their price levels by bringing their currencies back to their pre-war gold parities or at least stabilizing them at the new market rates at which they had settled: 'It became a matter of financial sanitation and prestige to contemplate anew a freely functioning gold standard.'[62]

The result for many countries was a period of price deflation. In Great Britain, prices fell between 1921 and 1925 in anticipation of returning to the gold standard.[63] £100 in 1925 would have had the same purchasing power as £124.19 in 1921. Prices fell at an average rate of -5.27 per cent a year. Deflation remained the norm in Great Britain until the mid-1930s. In the United States, 1921–1922 saw a sharp reversal of the immediate post-war inflation. This remained the trend through the depression years of 1931–1933. Only in 1934 did the United States see signs of a return to modest price inflation.[64] France presented a different picture. Post-war inflation continued there until the franc was stabilized in 1926 and then restored to the gold standard in 1928.[65]

Throughout this period, most European countries accepted that they had floating currencies that operated outside the formal discipline of the gold standard rules. National governments did, however, intervene in the foreign exchange markets, and pegged their currencies against those of their neighbours or trading partners. Some were pegged against sterling, which still kept its status as a reserve currency and which was seen as a likely candidate for returning to the gold standard at its pre-war parity.[66] These informal systems of currency management were transitional measures until the formal resumption of the gold standard. Testament to this view were the resolutions of the Financial Commission of the League of Nations conference held in Genoa in 1922. Their resolutions identified currency stability as the first essential step in the economic reconstruction in Europe.[67] The Commission resolved that it was desirable for all European countries to be on a

[61] H von Jürgen Schneider, O Schwarzer, and M Denzel (eds), *Währungen der Welt III* (Franz Steiner 1997) 124 (hereafter von Jürgen Schneider, Schwarzer, and Denzel (eds), *Währungen*).

[62] Edwards, *Critical Study* (n 55) 25.

[63] UK Office of National Statistics table Inflation_data.xls at <https://www.officialdata.org/UK-inflation> accessed 9 March 2023.

[64] See Bureau of Labor Statistics, Table 24, Historical Consumer Price Index for all Urban Consumers at <https://www.bls.gov/cpi/tables/historical-cpi-u-201709.pdf> accessed 9 March 2023.

[65] The franc was probably undervalued compared with the currencies of its trading partners: Edwards, *Critical Study* (n 55) 23.

[66] Eichengreen, *Gold Standard* (n 23) Table 4.1, 100–104.

[67] For the resolutions, see *Genoa Financial Commission Report* (Federal Reserve Bulletin June 1922) 678. For contemporary discussion of the Genoa resolutions, see Hawtrey, *Monetary Reconstruction* (n 23) ch. 6; and for their place in attempts at international monetary cooperation, see Eichengreen, *Gold Standard* (n 23) 154–62.

common standard, which it took to mean gold. The Commission left it to individual countries to decide if they would return to gold at their pre-war rate or one that stabilized currencies at their new, depreciated rate. This was the popular view too. Writing in 1933, the financial journalist Paul Einzig said: 'Even during and after the war, the British public regarded the abnormal conditions affecting gold as essentially temporary, and took it for granted that sooner or later the *status quo* would be restored.'[68]

Great Britain acted in 1925. The Gold Standard Act 1925 bound the Bank of England to buy and sell gold ingots at a legal price of £3 17*s* 10½*d* per troy ounce, which corresponded to the former pre-war standard and fixed the par of exchange with the dollar at its traditional rate of 1:4866. The Act abolished the convertibility of Bank of England and currency notes to gold.[69] Its effect was to continue the suspension in circulation of gold sovereign coins, which had practically disappeared in August 1914. The French franc returned to the gold standard in 1928 but at its new depreciated rate of 65.6 milligrams of gold 9/10 fine.[70] The United States remained on the gold standard at its traditional parity of 25 8/10 grains of gold 9/10 fine until the 1933 devaluation.

None of these measures restored the old stability enjoyed during the pre-war period of the gold standard. Monetary retrenchment by the United States Federal Reserve in 1928–1929 transmitted itself through international credit and trading networks. The rate of new money growth across the world fell and in the United States the volume of money in circulation actually shrank. Sources of credit in the international bond markets dried up and central banks' reserves of gold tended to flow towards creditor countries. Banks in the major financial centres found themselves exposed as investors abroad sought to repatriate their funds. Debtor countries and exporters of agricultural produce resorted to devaluations to stimulate demand for their exports.

The result was another break with gold. The Bank of England's gold reserves came under pressure during 1931 and sterling fell sharply against the dollar and the franc. By 19 September 1931, Britain was forced to suspend the gold standard.[71] A series of banking crises in the United States drove the newly elected administration of President Roosevelt to engineer a 41 per cent devaluation of the dollar during 1933.[72] The president issued a decree setting the new gold value of the dollar.[73] A Joint Resolution of Congress nationalized all private holdings of gold

[68] Paul Einzig, *The Future of Gold* (Macmillan & Co. 1934) 1.

[69] Gold Standard Act 1925, s. 1(1), (2). For an international summary of the countries that resumed the gold standard, see Eichengreen, *Gold Standard* (n 23) Table 7.1, 188–9.

[70] *Loi monétaire* (25 June 1928) Arts 1, 2; [1928] *Dalloz RP*, IV, 313.

[71] Gold Standard (Amendment) Act 1931, s. 1.

[72] See generally Eichengreen, *Gold Standard* (n 23) ch. 10; and Friedman and Schwartz, *A Monetary History of the United States* (n 60) ch. 8.

[73] Proclamation (31 January 1934), (No 2072), 31 USCA §821, made pursuant to the Gold Reserve Act of 1934 (48 Stat 337) s. 12 (31 USCA §821).

and gold coin, prohibited the free export of bullion, and barred the enforcement of gold clauses in contracts.[74] The Resolution provided that gold clauses must be paid 'dollar for dollar' at the nominal amount. The United States Supreme Court upheld the constitutionality of these measures as far as they applied private contractual bargains.[75] France, Belgium, the Netherlands, and Switzerland held out in a gold bloc until they too were forced to devalue their currencies in 1936.[76]

By the end of this period, all these currencies were either floating at managed rates or nominally pegged to gold at a depreciated standard. The defining features of the classical gold standard—convertibility of notes, free minting, and free import and export of gold—had ceased.

VI. Mann's Gold Clause Cases

We turn now to some of the leading gold clause cases analysed by Mann in *Legal Aspect*, which he wrote as a young legal scholar and published in England in 1938. Nowadays, all world currencies have broken their connection with gold, so the cases hardly have any direct relevance to practitioners. The current edition of the *Legal Aspect* calls them 'a matter of history' and doubts whether they will ever need to be revived.[77]

The cases do, however, have a larger significance beyond the superseded points of law they stand for. The legal record offers a glimpse into important historical events of the early 20th century, and the way they impinged on the financial arrangements of the governments and commercial actors of the era. They are examples of actual deals done by known historical figures in the pre-First World War financial markets. We see how they planned their transactions to fit the monetary conditions of the time and how they reacted once their assumption that gold was the natural and permanent basis for monetary values fell apart during the economic turbulence of the 1920s and 1930s.

The section explains three of Mann's most important cases: *The Case of the Serbian Loans Issued in France* (1929);[78] *Feist v Société Intercommunale Belge d'Électricité* (1933);[79] and *R v International Trustee for the Protection of Bondholders Aktiengesellschaft* (1937).[80] They all have a rich back story that the legal record—and Mann—did not tell.

[74] For the Joint Resolution, see the decision of the United States Supreme Court in *Norman v Baltimore and Ohio Railroad Co.* [1935] 294 US 240, 291–92.

[75] ibid.

[76] See Einzig, *World Finance* (n 54) chs 2–7, 12, 44–45. France abrogated the gold standard by *loi monétaire* (1 October 1936) Arts 1, 2, 8 [1936] *Dalloz RP*, IV 393. It devalued the franc and subjected all international movements of gold to the control of the Banque de Franc.

[77] FA Mann, *The Legal Aspect of Money* (C Proctor ed., 7th edn, OUP 2012) 11, 06.

[78] (1929) 56 J Dr Int'l 977.

[79] [1934] AC 161.

[80] [1937] AC 500.

A. *Case of the Serbian Loans Issued in France (1929)*

The Case of the Serbian Loans Issued in France (1929)[81] was one the earliest of the inter-war cases on gold clauses. As a decision of the Permanent Court of International Justice in the Hague, its reasoning influenced decisions in the French, English, and United States courts. It was important to Mann's account in the *Legal Aspect* (1938) since it provided a fully reasoned justification for the interpretation of gold clauses on a gold-value basis.[82]

The loans were a series of bonds issued between 1895 and 1913 on the international financial markets. The issuer was the Kingdom of Serbia. By the time of the litigation in 1929, the liabilities on the bonds were owed by the Kingdom of the Serbs, Croats, and Slovenes. It was the territorially expanded successor to Serbia which had been declared after the Armistice of 1918. The government of France brought the claim on behalf of French private investors after a period of diplomatic negotiations failed to resolve disagreements about the legal basis for repaying the loans.[83]

Serbia had gained its full independence from Ottoman rule under the Treaty of Berlin of 1878.[84] The Serbian King Milan Obrenović (1868–1889) then embarked upon a programme of modernization as he sought to transform Serbia from a rural backwater of the Ottoman Empire into a viable nation that could hold its own among the other emerging states of the Balkans region and the established imperial powers, notably Austria-Hungary and Germany. Milan rebuilt the centre of his capital, Belgrade, and began a programme of centralizing the government administration. Expansion of the railways and developing a professionally trained, well-equipped army were important parts of his programme. The 1878 Treaty required Serbia to build a railway line from Austria-Hungary in the direction of Istanbul (it was expected that the contracts for building the line would be awarded to Austrian companies). Territorial expansion was never far from the aims of Milan and his 20th-century successor but one, King Petar Karadjordjević (1903–1918).[85] Serbia intervened in the shifting nationalist conflicts of the early 1900s as the various Balkan peoples resisted the waning Ottoman sovereignty over their territories. These culminated in the First and Second Balkans Wars of 1912 and 1913. A few short months of intense fighting and genocidal atrocities ended in the expulsion of the Turks from Macedonia, Thrace, and Montenegro. Serbia took control of

[81] *The Case of the Serbian Loans Issued in France* (1929) 56 J Dr Int'l 977. For an abbreviated English translation, see Plesch, *The Gold Clause* (n 3) 1.

[82] See Mann, *Legal Aspect* (n 1) 101–02.

[83] It conducted similar negotiations with the government of Brazil, which was also determined in related litigation before the Permanent Court: (1929) 56 J Dr Int'l 977, 1009–29.

[84] See generally LS Stavrianos, *The Balkans since 1453* (New York University Press 1958); M Glenny, *The Balkans 1804–1912* (Granta 2012) on which this historical account draws.

[85] He was preceded by the son of King Milan Obrenović, Alexander I Obrenović (1889–1903).

much of Macedonia and established its administration there. The Second Balkans war of 1913 saw Serbian and Greek forces turn on their former Bulgarian allies.

The first loans of 1895 consolidated existing government debts owed to European banks. The others can be linked to key parts of the Serbian government's policy of the era. The loans of 1906 and 1909 were used for building railways and buying armaments. (The armaments would often have been manufactured in the same countries where the loans were issued so much of the money passed in a circle through Serbia and back to its country of origin.) The loan of 1913 was used directly to pay the debts of the 1912–1913 Balkans wars and to support the extension of Serbian administration into the newly acquired territories in Macedonia. Consistently with the Serbian government's political ambitions, the value of the loans was very great. They varied in value between Ffr60 million and Ffr355 million (about £206 million and £1.3 billion in today's sterling rates). The 1913 bond issue alone was for Ffr250 million.[86]

The terms of the bonds were between 50 and 72 years. They contained the usual arrangements for amortization. They were mainly issued to investors in France, Germany, and Austria, as well as in Serbia itself. Other sales were made in Belgium, Switzerland, the Netherlands, and Russia. In the case of the bonds considered by the court, the principal and interest due under them was denominated explicitly in *francs or*. Some of the German and Austrian issues were denominated in *Reichsmark* or *Schilling* but at their official gold parity with the French franc. Belgian and Swiss investors received their principal and interest payments in their own local currencies at the market rates of exchange with the French franc. Since the Belgian and Swiss francs were on the same gold par as the franc in France, the nominal value of payments in the three countries would not have differed by much.

Thus, the *franc or* was adopted in the bonds as the monetary standard for calibrating the various currency obligations in the bond. It determined the rate at which the Serbian government would have to service its obligations out of its revenues denominated in Serbian dinar. During the First World War, the French investors continued to receive their capital and interest payments in paper notes of the *Banque de France* at nominal values.[87] As we have seen, at the outbreak of the war, France introduced a system of *cours forcé* where its notes were no longer convertible to gold.[88] Officially, nothing happened to depreciate the paper franc against the *franc or* so the investors found no reason to question the substantial value of the Serbian government's obligations secured by the gold clauses. The investors' problem emerged in the first half of the 1920s. As the international value of the French franc fell, the franc:dinar exchange rate fell from Ffr23.88:din100 in

[86] See the summary (1929) 56 J Dr Int'l 977, 981–83.
[87] (1929) 56 J Dr Int'l 977, 1000–01.
[88] *Loi monétaire* (5 August 1914) Art. 3 [1914] *Dalloz RP*, IV, 88, discussed in Section V above.

1921 to Ffr44.65:din100 in 1929.[89] The decision of the French government to rebase the gold value of the franc in 1928 at its new depreciated rate brought home the extent of the investors' loss if they continued to receive paper banknotes for their debts.[90]

The narrow legal question turned on the meaning of the term *franc or* as it appeared in bond contracts. The Serb-Croat-Slovene government contended that it was only bound to pay the loan at nominal rates, which would have thrown the loss of the devaluation on the French investors. Against this, the court held that *franc or* was not just a formulaic reference to the French unit of account regardless of its value in terms of gold. Nor was it a stipulation for payment in French gold currency. If it had been a modality clause of that kind it would have been overridden by the French legislation making banknotes *cours forcé*. The court observed that such an interpretation would have been practically untenable even when the bonds were issued: gold coins did not exist in the small fractional units that the interest payments in the bond coupons stipulated for. It concluded that the clauses only made sense as stipulations for gold values.[91] As a consequence the Serb-Croat-Slovene government had to pay depreciated banknotes at the original gold value of the debts.

Realistically, the court could only have interpreted the gold clause as stipulating for gold values or a nominal sum unrelated to gold.[92] The *franc or* was a legal abstraction rather than an actual coin that had ever been struck, even before 1914. One-franc coins were made from silver, and gold was only used for coins of higher denominations. The court derived the meaning of the *franc or* from the legal definition of the franc unit decreed by Napoleon Bonaparte in 1803. The law promulgated on 7 *germinal an* XI (1803) gave its name to the French monetary standard that remained in force until the devaluation of 1928. The so-called *franc germinal* was a bimetallic unit but one that operated primarily by reference to silver: '*Cinq grammes d'argent, au titre de 9/10ᵉˢ de fin, constitute l'unité monétaire qui conserve le nom de franc.*'[93] Gold coins were issued in pieces of 20 and 40 francs. The law went on to define their weight, which was set in a fixed ratio by weight to silver: 155 20-franc pieces were struck from a kilogram of gold 9/10 fine. The *franc or* was thus a notional weight corresponding to a 20th part of 6.45161 grams.[94]

The court accepted that nothing in the French domestic legislation prevented this conclusion. The legislation was drafted and interpreted to protect the interests of French holders of international debt instruments against the risk of depreciation

[89] Von Jürgen Schneider, Schwarzer, and Denzel (eds), *Währungen* (n 61) 141. Most of the change in the exchanges seems to be explained by the fall in the franc. After 1921, the dinar broadly stabilized against sterling.

[90] *Loi monétaire* (25 June 1928) Art. 2; [1928] *Dalloz RP*, IV, 313.

[91] (1929) 56 J Dr Int'l 977, 993–97.

[92] ibid 996.

[93] *Loi sur la fabrication et la verification des monnaies* (7–17 *germinal an* XI).

[94] ibid, Titre I, Art. 1(8).

in the foreign exchanges. Soon after the notes of the *Banque de France* were made *cours forcé* after the outbreak of the war, a doubt emerged about the effect of the legislation on obligations owed by foreign debtors.[95] If inconvertible banknotes were legal tender did they discharge all debts at nominal rates even those of foreign debtors expressed as gold clauses? Eventually, the view settled that they did not: the *cours forcé* legislation only applied to internal debts. The reasons of *ordre publique* that justified the French government in monopolizing the circulation of gold coins in France did not extend to foreign debtors. They did not apply to international obligations expressed in gold clauses: for them the parties' freedom to contract for gold values was unaffected by the legislation. Later legislation confirmed the same view. The legislation that devalued the franc in 1928 and again in 1936 exempted existing obligations stipulated in *francs or*. They continued to be payable at their original gold values.[96]

The upshot of the decision was that the liability of the Serbian-Croat-Slovene government was now declared to be five times greater than it was during the war years. The court's decision gave the French investors a double benefit. The stipulation for *francs or*, which might have been inserted to protect them against a devaluation of the Serbian dinar against the franc, also protected the investors against their own government's devaluation of the franc. The new nation state of Yugoslavia began its life saddled with onerous debts owed to the former Great Powers to whom it owed its existence some 40 years earlier. Those powers that survived the war, such as France, remained a powerful creditor class. Mann wrote his first edition of the *Legal Aspect* (1938) at the end of two decades of international wrangling over reparations and the legacy of debt created by the First World War.[97] Both presented huge obstacles to economic recovery and international goodwill. But as the outcome of the decision shows, debts incurred by borrower states before the war could be as much a live problem for international relations as those incurred during it. The gold clause ruling in the *Case of the Serbian Loans Issued in France* (1929) reinforced the pre-war relations of economic power and dependence between Europe's established states and their emerging neighbours.

B. *Feist v Société Intercommunale Belge d'Électricité (1933)*

The decision of the House of Lords in *Feist v Société Intercommunale Belge d'Électricité* (1933)[98] is notable for two reasons aside from the legal point that a

[95] See Valéry, 'Clause Payable en or et le Cours Forcé' (n 3); Gény, 'Clause "Payable en Or"' (n 3) 369–71.

[96] *Loi monétaire* (25 June 1928) Art. 2; [1928] *Dalloz RP*, IV, 313; *loi monétaire* (1 October 1936) Art. 6, [1936] *Dalloz RP*, IV 393.

[97] See generally B Eichengreen, *Golden Fetters: The Gold Standard and the Great Depression, 1919–1938* (OUP 1992), ch 5.

[98] [1934] AC 161.

gold-value clause was permissible in English law. It stands out first as a typical example of a gold clause transaction. The case involved a 35-year bond issued by a utility company which was borrowing in the London capital markets, in what still had a claim to be the world's major reserve currency. The second reason is the date of the bond—1928. Unlike many of the other gold clauses cases, which involved contracts made before 1914, the bonds in *Feist* were issued in the uncertain post-war period when contractual parties were putting their faith in the restoration of the gold standard. The proper interpretation of the contract depended on the special monetary conditions in Great Britain between 1926 and 1931 during Britain's short-lived restoration of sterling to a gold-bullion standard.

As its name suggests, the *Société Intercommunale Belge d'Électricité* was a utility company that ran power stations and an electricity network in Belgium. Through a series of acquisitions and mergers after the Second World War, it was absorbed into *Electabel NV*, which is now the main provider of electricity and gas in Belgium.[99] The '*société intercommunale*' was a distinctive form of Belgian corporate entity used for public utility services. The *Société Intercommunale Belge d'Électricité* was in mixed public and private ownership with a share of its capital belonging to private investors.

Mr Feist's bond was styled 'Thirty-Five Year Sinking Fund 5½% Sterling Bond. Due September 1st, 1963'. The terms of the bonds were drafted in English and governed by English law. The issue comprised bonds of £1,000, £500, and £100, all with the same interest rate and maturity date. They had a total value of £500,000, equivalent to some £22 million at today's rates. The company had been extending its distribution grid in the years before the litigation, which may explain why it was looking to raise capital.[100] The bonds went on sale on 26 September 1928.

Marcus Samuel & Co. oversaw the bond issue in London and were designated as the payment agents for the *Société*. They were a British firm who were early players in developing the oil and petroleum markets of the Near and Middle East. The head of the second generation of the firm—Marcus Samuel, Viscount Bearsted (1853–1927)—founded the Shell Transport and Trading Company, which continues today as the familiar oil company.[101] It was a major supplier of petroleum to Britain and the Allies in the First World War. Samuel & Co. broke new ground when they floated the first issue of Japanese government bonds in the London markets in 1897. They made a name for themselves in raising capital for railway and harbour developments as Japan took its first steps towards industrialization. Samuel & Co. would have brought to the *Société* their combined experience of the international

[99] See <https://www.company-histories.com/Electrabel-NV-Company-History.html> accessed 9 March 2023.

[100] See the company's annual reports held by the Leibniz Information Centre for Economics at <https://pm20.zbw.eu/folder/co/0127xx/012797/about.de.html> accessed 9 March 2023.

[101] See R Henriques, *Marcus Samuel: First Viscount Bearsted and Founder of the Shell Trading and Transport Company* (Barrie and Rockliffe 1960) chs 1–5.

capital and energy markets, which doubtless grew in the inter-war years as Western enterprises expanded into the former Ottoman territories of the Middle East.

The payment clauses in the bonds and the interest coupons were in similar form. They bound the company to pay the sums due 'in sterling in gold coin of the United Kingdom, of or equal to the standard of weight and fineness existing on the 1st day of September, 1928'. Mr Feist sought a declaration that it should be interpreted literally as stipulating for actual gold coin or as a gold-value clause. The *Société* argued that the clause only entitled the bondholder to the nominal sums due in the bonds and interest coupons. The House of Lords favoured the gold-value interpretation.[102] The *Société* was bound to pay whatever sum of sterling was needed to buy the requisite quantity of gold in the London markets at the due date of each payment.

When the bonds were issued in 1928, the gold-value interpretation was the only one that would have given practical meaning to the wording of the payment clause. The Gold Standard Act of 1925 confirmed in law what had been true in practice since 1914: Bank of England notes and currency notes were no longer convertible to gold although they were still legal tender.[103] Gold coins had practically disappeared from circulation. If in 1928 the parties had stipulated for gold coins, they would have been contracting for something that was already impossible.

This context strongly supported the interpretation that the clause was intended as a stipulation for gold value. The parties were deliberately putting their faith in the newly restored gold parity between sterling and the Belgian franc. The Belgian franc went back on a gold-bullion standard in 1925 (the same year as sterling), and the exchanges held constant between November 1926 and October 1931. By contrast, the franc had fallen year on year against the pound in the years leading to 1926.[104] It was tenable for the House of Lords to interpret the 'special words' of the clause as intended to lock in the prevailing gold parity between sterling and the Belgian franc.[105]

Whatever faith the *Société* and the bondholders placed in the newly restored monetary order of 1925 proved to be short-lived. The dispute was precipitated by the first half-yearly interest payment due after Britain dropped out of the gold standard in September 1931.[106] Sterling quickly depreciated from its 1925 gold-standard parity, and fell by about 40 per cent against the Belgian franc. The franc

[102] It was influenced by the recent decision of the Permanent Court of International Justice in the *Case of the Serbian Loans Issued in France* (1929) 56 J Dr Int'l 977, considered in Section VI.A.

[103] Gold Standard Act 1925, s. 1(1)(a)–(b).

[104] The market rate of exchange while both currencies were on the gold standard held at about £28.70:Bfr1000.00. The rate fell to a mean of £39.89:Bfr1000.00 during 1932: von Jürgen Schneider, Schwarzer, and Denzel (eds), *Währungen* (n 61) 35–36.

[105] [1934] AC 161, 172 per Lord Russell. A similar change in interpretation happened in the interpretation of international contracts stipulating for 'pounds sterling'. After the devaluation of the Australian and New Zealand currencies in 1931 and 1933, a reference to 'sterling' pointed specifically to the monetary unit of Great Britain: *De Bueger v J Ballantyne & Co Ltd* [1938] AC 452.

[106] See Section V.

was still on gold when Mr Feist issued his originating summons in 1932. But the franc also came under intense pressure soon afterwards. As the litigation in *Feist* was being heard by the House of Lords, economic advisers in Belgium were debating the merits of a devaluation or maintaining the existing policy of deflation in prices and wages. The strong franc was stifling economic activity and was a cause of rising unemployment. After a change in government, Belgium was forced to devalue by 28 per cent in March 1935.[107]

As a consequence of the devaluation, the franc weakened against sterling but its new value was still some 19 per cent below the old gold parity that the parties had stipulated for in the contract. The effect of the Lords' decision was that the franc liability of the *Société* to the bondholders would increase by this amount. We can only conjecture how real that loss might have been to the *Société*. The *Société* might have benefited from the economic stimulus that the devaluation delivered to the Belgian economy. If in the end its business turnover increased, it might have absorbed the additional liability. Identifying the ultimate winners and losers of a currency revaluation is not as straightforward as identifying which party won or lost in the gold clause litigation.

Feist was significant to Mann's treatment in the *Legal Aspect* (1938) because it confirmed that English law found nothing in gold-value clauses that was inherently contrary to the principle of monetary nominalism or to public policy.[108] The decision came just months after the United States Congress had abrogated gold and gold-value clauses in US-dollar contracts on the ground that they interfered with Congress's powers over the monetary system. A similar point seems not to have been argued in *Feist*. Questions of the state's monetary power were conspicuous by their absence. We may speculate how the House of Lords might have resolved them. Any negative consequences that followed from enforcing the clause at its 1925 gold value were borne by the party outside Great Britain and did no damage to the British government's monetary policy at home. Indeed, they probably improved the nominal value of Britain's foreign earnings. Unlike in the United States,[109] gold clauses between internal parties were almost unheard of in Great Britain.[110] The Lords' decision might only have affected contracts with an international element. This distinction between internal and international contracts became common in the legislation and case law of the era. As we have seen, the French legislation of 1928 and 1936 defining the new gold values of the franc preserved the existing monetary standard for international contracts already in force.[111] The policy was that devaluation should not affect gold clauses based on the old standard. The decision in *Feist* achieved the same outcome for sterling.

[107] Eichengreen, *Gold Standard* (n 23) 359–64.
[108] Mann, *Legal Aspect* (n 1) 104, 109.
[109] See Section VI.C.
[110] See Section II above.
[111] See Section VI.A.

C. *R v International Trustee for the Protection of Bondholders Aktiengesellschaft (1937)*

State finance and war debts were fraught questions in the 1930s and not ones that Mann with his positivist style of writing would have raised.[112] We get no hint of any political flavour to the gold clause litigation. Mann presents the disputes as turning mainly on the interpretation of contract terms, which were disembodied from the reasons which might have explained why the contracts were first made and then disputed before the courts. In 1937, however, state finance and war debts emerged as live questions before the House of Lords in *R v International Trustee for the Protection of Bondholders Aktiengesellschaft* (1937).[113] Mann duly explained the legal effect of the decision. The House of Lords held that the bond issue in question was governed by United States law. It confirmed that the United States' abrogation of gold clauses in 1933 extended to all contracts governed by United States law, even those to which the British government was a party. The abrogation applied to contracts made before 1933.[114] The result was that the gold-value clause in the case was not enforced. The British government could pay the dollar debt in the bond at nominal rates rather than at the gold value that the parties stipulated for.

The *Bondholders* case had a political edge that Mann did not investigate. It was a late chapter in the longer story of financing the First World War and the international rancour over war debts that followed in its wake. The House of Lords' decision was a good result for the British government. The decision reduced the international value of its war debts to private investors in the United States by some 41 per cent. The decision bears out the old adage that a government's devaluation of its currency works as a tax on its investor class, although with the twist here that the British government benefited at the expense of investors in the United States.

The case turned on the payment clauses in a series of war bonds floated by the British government on the New York financial markets in the early months of 1917. The eventual form of the loans consisted in 20-year government bonds, paying 5½ per cent interest.[115] Investors were promised principal and interest payable at the investors' option at the offices of JP Morgan and Co. in New York or London.[116] The bonds fell due in 1937.

[112] On the negotiation of war finance in the United States, see K Burk, *Britain, America and Sinews of War 1914–1918* (Routledge 1985) ch. 5; and Zachary Carter, *The Price of Peace: Money, Democracy and the Life of John Maynard Keynes* (Random House 2020) ch. 2.

[113] [1937] AC 500.

[114] Mann, *Legal Aspect* (n 1) 220–21, 227–28.

[115] The loans were originally issued as one-year or two-year notes, convertible to twenty-year bonds. The conversion to long-term debt worked to the government's advantage by postponing the need to raise new short-term finance to repay the notes when they fell due in 1918 or 1919.

[116] JP Morgan had acted as the British government's procurement and finance agents in the United States since 1915. They were also its bankers, providing it with overdraft facilities. JP Morgan profited hugely from commission and interest payments during the war, and used their experience to position themselves as financiers to other European governments after the war.

It is worth pausing to say something about the place of the 1917 bond issue in the larger financing of the war. The total value of the loan was US$250 million, a sum equivalent to some £2.49 billion today. However great that sum may seem, it must be set against British government expenditure in the early months of 1917. Britain was spending about US$250 million every month in the United States on behalf of itself and its European Allies. Loans and credits financed the purchase of essential food and munitions. Every dollar borrowed in the United States spared the Bank of England's gold reserves, which would otherwise have been run down to pay for the government's foreign purchases. Just as importantly, dollar loans enabled the British government to intervene in the foreign currency markets to support the dollar–sterling exchange rate.

The situation was precarious. Early in 1917, America remained technically neutral, and support from the government of President Wilson for Britain and the Allies was equivocal at best. The war was financed from month to month, and late in 1916 the coffers of the British Treasury were nearly empty. In November that year, the United States Federal Reserve had issued formal warnings cautioning banks and private citizens against investing too heavily in short-term foreign government securities. All these events conspired to undermine British attempts to raise money in the financial markets.

In simplified form, the payment clauses in the bonds provided that investors were to receive the principal and interest thereon either in New York 'in gold coin of the United States of America of the standard weight and fineness existing February 1, 1917' or in London 'in sterling money at the fixed rate of $4.86½ to the pound'. The clause fixed the monetary standard in the bonds at the then-prevailing gold value of the dollar and the pre-war par of exchange between the dollar and the pound.[117] The contractual exchange rate in the sterling payment option eliminated the exchange risk for investors who chose to claim their interest and principal repayments in London. During the war, while the international operation of the gold standard was suspended, market rates diverged from the official gold par.[118]

Stipulations for 'gold coin of the United States of America' were common in American bond issues, even those intended to operate internally between United States citizens or corporations.[119] Although the conservative traditions of lawyers' drafting practices were doubtless one reason for their use, gold clauses had a foundation in the diverse composition of the American currency during the 19th century.[120] After the foundation of the Federal mint in 1792, the United States worked

[117] See Section III.A.

[118] See Section V.

[119] For a judicial description of their history, see the first instance decision in *Re Missouri Pacific Railroad Co* 7 F Supp 1, 2-3 (1934), per Faris DJ (railroad bonds issued in 1903 payable in 'gold coin of the United States of the present standard of weight and fineness').

[120] As to which, see generally Friedman and Schwartz, *A Monetary History of the United States* (n 60) ch. 2. The legal history of the dollar standard is described in *Bronson v Rodes* (1868) 74 US 229, 249.

on a bimetallic monetary system, although one that operated primarily in reference to silver.[121] In 1849, the mint was authorized to issue gold coins in dollar units.[122] It was not until 1834 that gold coins became legal tender.[123] To this metallic monetary base were added many paper notes issued by private banks throughout the states. They circulated at varying market rates, which adjusted to the solvency of the issuing banks and the distance from the place of issue. During the Civil War, the Federal Treasury issued its own non-convertible notes—the 'greenbacks'—which were made legal tender by legislation.[124] They, too, passed at a discount from par. A note with a nominal value of $1 might be worth just 75c against a gold dollar. The Federal Treasury resumed the convertibility of the greenbacks in 1879, which had the effect of bringing their market values to par.[125] Matters rested there until 1900 when the United States went definitively on to the gold standard.[126] The dollar consisting of 25 8/10 grains of gold 9/10 fine was fixed as the standard unit of value. This was the dollar standard in force when the British government issued its war bonds in 1917 and which the bonds stipulated for in their payment clauses.

American contract parties in the mid-19th and early 20th centuries drafted payment clauses to match the shifting kinds of money in circulation. They might stipulate for payment in one kind rather than another. American courts recognized the parties' contractual freedom to select whichever kind of legal tender was worth more in the market.[127] This American practice influenced the House of Lords' reading of the payment clause in the case.[128] It became easier to interpret it as a gold-value clause, inserted to guard against the risk of depreciation of the currency. Following *Feist v Société Intercommunale Belge d'Électricité* (1933), it held that the effect of the clause was:

> merely to fix a measure or a scale of payment which will apply where the currency depreciates or is de-valued but the payment of that amount can lawfully and

[121] 1 Statutes at Large 246 (1792) ss. 9, 20. The choice of silver aligned the United States dollar with the Spanish dollar.

[122] 9 Statutes at Large 397 (1849) s. 1.

[123] 5 Statutes at Large 136 (1837) ss. 9, 11 (gold coins issued after 1834 were made legal tender retrospectively).

[124] An additional element to the complexity of the US currency was the banknotes issued by the Confederate government during the Civil War. See JP Dawson and FE Cooper, 'The Effect of Inflation on Private Contracts: United States, 1861–1879' (1935) 33 Mich L Rev 706.

[125] 18 Statutes at Large 296 (1875) s. 3.

[126] 31 Statutes at Large 45 (1900) s. 1.

[127] An 1861 clause for payment 'in specie' meant that only payment in coin was acceptable. It would have excluded payment in the depreciated paper currency, including even the legal tender greenbacks: *Bronson v Rodes* 74 US 229, 251–52 (1868) per Chase CJ. To the same effect was a clause for 'gold or silver coin lawful money of the United States', which had the additional effect of making clear that payment in either kind of coin was equally good (both were legal tender): *Lake County v Oregon* (1868) 74 US 71.

[128] [1937] AC 500, 516–17 per Lord Atkin.

> properly be made in the currency of the day in the country when the obligation falls due.[129]

This interpretation was important. For by 1937, the very events that the House of Lords read the investors as guarding against had come to pass. The United States dollar had been devalued in 1933 by about 41 per cent. The Joint Resolution of Congress had abrogated gold clauses and provided that gold clauses must be paid 'dollar for dollar' at nominal amounts. If the resolution applied to the British government's debts, then they too would be depreciated as surely as gold-value debts between American citizens.

The central legal question was therefore whether the bonds were governed by United States law. The House of Lords were satisfied that the necessary contractual intention could be found. Lord Maugham's speech reads as a blunt assessment of 1917 *Realpolitik*.[130] He listed the political facts and wartime events in the years and months either side of the floatation of the loan, running from the sinking of the *Lusitania* in 1915, to Germany's announcement of unrestricted submarine warfare the very day before the loans were issued, to the recall of the American and German ambassadors shortly afterwards. For Lord Maugham, the entry of the United States into the war was inevitable. Whether or not he was right about this, he clearly considered that the British government had to accept the loan on whatever terms the United States government would tolerate, including subjecting itself to American law.

By 1937, however, the British government must have been glad of this result. As a debtor for a sum measured in United States dollars, it stood to benefit from President Roosevelt's devaluation of the dollar as much as Roosevelt's own government might have. Indeed, the British government seemed to fare even better from the devaluation than its American counterpart. In *Perry v United States* (1935),[131] the Supreme Court held that Congress could not use its constitutional powers to fix the monetary standard to reduce the real value of its own debts owed to investors in wartime Liberty Bonds. By definition, that constitutional protection did not extend to investors enforcing dollar debts against foreign governments. The Constitution did not bind the British Government so the House of Lords' interpretation of the bond contracts reduced the value of Britain's war debts at a stroke. The Lords' deference to foreign monetary sovereignty made for a neat coincidence of public law and public interest.

[129] ibid 519.
[130] [1937] AC 500, 568.
[131] 294 US 330 (1935).

VII. Conclusion

Mann's *Legal Aspect* presents a positivist view of the monetary law of his time. Litigants argued cases before courts on technical points of law and Mann duly gathered them into an ordered system of rules. That is the great value of his work.

Legal doctrine necessarily operates at one remove from the political or economic forces that shape it. The risk to historians who look back at that doctrine is that they lose sight of the personalities, transactions, and wider forces that made it what it was. That is indeed the problem with Mann's presentation of the gold clause cases. They only make sense when we recreate the monetary world which explains why parties inserted gold clauses in their contracts and then litigated their disputes in the courts. Seen in this way, the cases tell a different story. Gold clause litigation was a sign that the pre-war monetary world of the international gold standard was breaking down. All countries were on their way to developing fiat money systems but they carried a legacy of long-term financial contracts made on the assumption that the old gold values of money would remain a permanent feature of the monetary world. The gold clause transactions are period pieces of their time. We see real examples of the world's early capital markets at work.

But the cases can make for uncomfortable reading once we learn the background that informed them. They were part of the recent world events that Mann grew up with, even if he found no reason to explain them in his work. Capital flowed along the channels carved by larger forces of international power relations. The investors who subscribed to the bonds in the financial markets of Europe and America were not just funding railways and electricity networks. They were also providing the capital that made possible the wars and calamitous changes in international politics of the era.

The courts that determined the gold clause cases played their own part in separating the economic winners from the losers in the uncertain inter-war years. As was true of the other debt and reparations obligations of the era, the interests of creditors seemed to prevail over the interests of debtors. But the winners' successes were perhaps only partial. The creditors found that they held their contractual rights subject to states' overriding powers over the monetary system. In the longer term, creditors and debtors might have benefited from the economic revival that generally followed from states' decisions to de-link their currencies from gold. Besides, as world politics deteriorated during the late 1930s, the gold clause cases might only have served as short-term resolutions to the problems of international debt. We can only speculate how many of these debt obligations were actually paid after the next economic calamity, the Second World War.

If for no other reason, the gold clause cases deserve to be remembered as a transition between the old monetary order of the international gold standard and the new order of the Bretton Woods system. They duly kept their place in the second edition of *Legal Aspect*, published in 1953, where Mann's exposition of them was hardly unchanged from the first edition.[132] But their diminishing relevance to the new legal and monetary order that prevailed after the Second World War is obvious from the new Part III of the book. Mann's outline of exchange control and the valuation of foreign currencies ran to 79 pages. These rules derived partly from the treaty obligations binding the United Kingdom and other Member States under the Articles of Agreement of the International Monetary Fund. International obligations, rather than the self-regulating norms of the classical gold standard, now governed the international value of money and its flow across state borders. The old monetary world that required gold clauses to fix the value of cross-border debts was gone.

Bibliography

Burk K, *Britain, America and Sinews of War 1914–1918* (Routledge 1985)

Cassel G, *Money and Foreign Exchange after 1914* (Constable 1922)

Cassel G, *Post-War Monetary Stabilization* (Columbia University Press 1928)

Dawson JP, 'The Gold Clause Decisions' (1935) 33 Michigan Law Review 647

Dawson JP and Coultrap JW, 'Contracting by Reference to Price Indices' (1935) 33 Mich L Rev 685

Eichengreen B, *Golden Fetters: The Gold Standard and the Great Depression, 1919–1938* (OUP 1992)

Einzig P, *The Future of Gold* (Macmillan & Co. 1934)

Fox D and Ernst W (eds), *Money in the Western Legal Tradition: Middle Ages to Bretton Woods* (OUP 2016)

Friedman M and Jacobson SA, *A Monetary History of the United States 1867–1960* (National Bureau of Economic Research 1960)

Gény F, 'La Validité Juridique de la Clause "Payable en Or"' (1926) 25 Revue Trimestrielle du Droit Civil 557

Glenny M, *The Balkans 1804–1912* (Granta 2012)

Hawtrey RG, *Monetary Reconstruction* (2nd edn, Longman, Green and Co. 1927)

Henriques R, *Marcus Samuel: First Viscount Bearsted and Founder of the Shell Trading and Transport Company* (Barrie and Rockliffe 1960)

Helfferich K, *Money* (L Infield tr., Aldelphi Company 1927)

Mann FA, *The Legal Aspect of Money* (OUP 1938)

Nussbaum A, *Money in the Law* (Foundation Press 1939)

Plesch A, *The Gold Clause: A Collection of International Cases and Opinions* (Stevens 1935)

Stavrianos LS, *The Balkans since 1453* (New York University Press 1958)

Strachan H, *Financing the First World War* (OUP 2004)

Valéry J, 'Clause Payable en or et le Cours Forcé' (1916) 43 J Dr Int'l 1132

Von Schneider J and Schwarzer D (eds), *Währungen der Welt III* (Franz Steiner 1997)

[132] FA Mann, *The Legal Aspect of Money* (2nd edn, OUP 1953).

10

FA Mann's Conservative Revolution

Joseph H Sommer

I. Introduction

Let me begin with an author's note, which may highlight the focus and limits of this chapter. I am an American payment lawyer. My profession led me to FA Mann's opus: *The Legal Aspect of Money*.[1] This chapter is about his theory of money, and how it has withstood the test of time. Mann's theory of money is contained in the first few chapters of his book. I will not comment on the remainder of the book, which treats comparative and public international law.

Through this chapter, I argue that Mann's theory of money was so successful because it was so conservative. He had to manage a revolution: purge the gold standard from English law and legal instinct. The United Kingdom had just left the gold standard in 1931. The economics profession may have been prepared for this transition, but the legal profession was not. Mann's revolution was limited. He taught that the value of money has no external metric by which it can be measured. It could only be measured by reference to law. He called this insight 'nominalism'. Otherwise, Mann changed as little as possible. He toppled the mystique of gold, as he had to. But he did not build anew. He put fiat legal tender on the same pedestal

[1] FA Mann, *The Legal Aspect of Money* (5th edn, Clarendon Press 1992) (hereafter Mann, *Legal Aspect*).

Joseph H Sommer, *FA Mann's Conservative Revolution* In: *FA Mann*. Edited by: Jason Grant Allen and Gerhard Dannemann, Oxford University Press. © Joseph H Sommer 2024. DOI: 10.1093/oso/9780198881452.003.0011

that gold had occupied. Nothing else changed. His new god would be worshipped with the same rites as the old one.

Mann's revolution was conservative even by the standards of his day. It is now showing its age as Mann's legal tender god is losing its believers. Paper currency is beloved by criminals, and precludes negative interest rates. It is also unhygienic, and may be on its way out.[2] Private units of account now exist, embedded in electronic media of exchange. Bank money has inconspicuously gained legal tender status. In some contexts, paper money has inconspicuously lost it.

We can still fit the old law and theories to these new monies.[3] But this only means that good lawyers can always provide a rationale when asked. The necessary intellectual techniques are increasingly Procrustean. Today's monies demand better theories. These theories are not hard to find. They have been on the shelf since the Edwardian era.

A few biographical dates are useful, to calibrate the intuition. FA Mann was born in 1907. He was a youth during the German hyperinflation of 1921–1923. He was still a German resident when Germany (along with the United Kingdom, Japan, and others) left the gold standard in 1931. As a young lawyer, in 1933, he joined the German Jewish diaspora in the United Kingdom. This was the same year the United States abandoned the gold standard, followed by Italy (1934) and France (1936).[4] The first edition of *The Legal Aspect of Money* was published in 1938. He died in 1991 and his fifth and final edition was published posthumously in 1992. This work has since undergone three more editions, under the aegis of Charles Proctor. I shall limit myself to Mann's book in this chapter.

One final note before the prologue: *The Legal Aspect of Money* was a legal reaction to the death of the gold standard, and its replacement with fiat sovereign paper money. I stress the word *legal*. The economic causes and consequences of this shift are of little interest to Mann, and similarly of little interest to this paper.

II. Prologue

A. Gold

Mann's great opus destroyed the hold of the gold standard on the legal imagination. Or did it? Nevertheless, we must first discuss the gold standard. For our purposes,

[2] Christian Barontini and Henry Holden, 'Proceeding with Caution—a Survey on Central Bank Digital Currency' (BIS Paper No. 101, January 2019) <https://www.bis.org/publ/bppdf/bispap101.pdf> accessed 16 December 2021 (hereafter Barontini and Holden, 'Proceeding with Caution'). This paper mentions Sweden and Uruguay, specifically.

[3] Simon Gleeson, *The Legal Concept of Money* (OUP 2018) (hereafter Gleeson, *Legal Concept*).

[4] See the chapters in Part I of this volume '"A German Lawyer of Jewish Extraction" in England: FA Mann's Legal Biography'.

the gold standard defined a national unit of account as a weight of gold. This implied only one true international unit of account, with different national media of exchange. 'A note payable in pounds, shillings, and pence made in any country, is but another mode of expressing the amount in dollars and cents.'[5] Internationally, the gold standard was keyed to bullion, used to settle interbank balances. The domestic gold standard was more complex, since it had to deal with both coin—measured by tale—and bullion, measured by weight. Although coin could contain bullion, the two measures were different, the melt value of the coin seldom coinciding with its face value.[6]

There is something naturalistic about the gold standard. It seems to prescribe the value of money in terms of an objective external metric. The rhetoric can soar. Gold is true; gold is stable; gold precedes politics or law. Gold is precious and tangible. Gold protects the individual against the collective (at least, the moneyed individual). Gold is the anchor to which all money is attached. Or slightly more realistically: gold was the only monetary asset that is not somebody else's liability. Plenty of people still believe this package, although some of this faith has transubstantiated to mathematical algorithms. But others have thought differently for a long time.[7] We shall turn to these heresiarchs in a moment.

The lawyers of the gold standard era did not question the primacy of specie, at least in their capacity as lawyers. But they were nonetheless creative, perfecting alternative media of exchange that could meet the needs of commerce. In the mid-18th century, Lord Mansfield's famous opinion in *Miller v Race*[8] asserted the functional equivalence of paper and coin. By the end of the century, a few courts became aware that final payment could be by bank credit, with no physical tender necessary.[9] The first half of the 19th century created the basic law of bank money payments via negotiable instruments.[10] At least in the common law world, credit transfers had to wait—a point to which we shall return.

5 *Thompson v Sloan*, 23 Wendell 71, 75 (NY 1840).

6 This is one of the major themes in English monetary history, which was on a coin standard until the 18th century. Christine Desan, *Making Money: Coin, Currency, and the Coming of Capitalism* (OUP 2014) (hereafter Desan, *Making Money*). On the Continent, coins often passed by name, with a monetary value assigned by law. Arthur Nussbaum, *Money in the Law: National and International* (rev'd edn, Foundation Press 1950) 37–40 (hereafter Nussbaum, *Money in the Law*).

7 Geoffrey Ingham, *The Nature of Money* (Polity Press 2004) 40 (hereafter Ingham, *Nature of Money*); Desan, *Making Money* (n 6) 332–53 (citing 17th- and 18th-century theorists such as Nicholas Barbon and John Locke).

8 1 Burr 452, 97 Eng Rep 398 (KB 1758).

9 *Bolton v Richard*, 6 Durnford & East 139, 101 Eng Rep 477 (KB 1795) (payment finality with bank money); *Levy v Bank of the United States*, 4 US (4 Dall) 234, 1 Binn 27 (Pa 1802) (same).

10 A few landmarks: *Carr v Carr* [1811] 1 Mer 543 (deposits as money substitute); In re *Franklin Bank*, 1 Paige 249 (NY Ch 1828) (deposits as debt); *Bank of the United States v Bank of Georgia*, 23 US (10 Wheat) 333 (1825) (Story J) (final payment via bank credit); *Eyles v Ellis* [1827] 4 Bing 112, 130 Eng Rep 710 (same); *Foley v Hill* [1848] 2 HLC 28, 9 ER 1002 (HL) (deposits as debt); *Baldwin's Bank of Penn Yan v Smith*, 215 NY 76, 109 NE 138 (1915) (payment finality with bank insolvency).

But the Anglo-American lawyers mostly cared about payment plumbing, not monetary theory. Gold could remain the legal aristocrat: the centre of all aspirations. But bank money was the legal tradesperson, doing almost all the useful everyday work. Courts recognized this. Bank money was not legal tender, but courts almost always treated it as such, finding assent to bank money even when it pointedly did not exist.[11] No matter the aspirations toward gold, it figured little in the workaday legal world.

B. Mann's Intellectual Precursors

Revolutions have their prophets, and the fiat money revolution was no exception. I pick four prophets: two German academics and two Britons.[12] I do not pretend to be an intellectual historian. What you read is a law office history, hopefully accurate but woefully incomplete and intended for a specific purpose: to set the stage for Mann's work.

Georg Simmel first. His book, *The Philosophy of Money*, which first came out in 1900, is not easy to read or describe. Any brief explanation of Simmel is invariably a vulgarization. So here is mine. Simmel viewed money as a kind of worldly god, whose existence requires a practicing community of believers. For Simmel, the monetary system contains 'a further element of social-psychological quasi-religious faith. The feeling of personal security that the possession of money gives is perhaps the most concentrated and pointed form and manifestation of confidence in the socio-political organization and order.'[13] In this view, money is 'predominantly a system of meaning rather than an imposition of force'.[14] Only the believing community gives money its value: not gold and not the law. As Simmel wrote:

> When barter is replaced by money transactions a third factor is introduced between the two parties: the community as a whole, which provides a real value corresponding to money ... This is the core of truth in the theory that money is only a claim upon society. ... It has been argued against this theory that metallic

[11] Mann, *Legal Aspect* (n 1) 77; Herman Oliphant, 'The Theory of Money in the Law of Commercial Instruments' (1920) 29 Yale LJ 606, 608 (hereafter Oliphant, 'Theory of Money') ('by an unwarrantable construction of the language used, many of the courts ... reach the practical result that instruments expressed to be payable in *de facto* money are none the less commercial instruments').

[12] Ingham, *Nature of Money* (n 7) discusses all four in more detail than I do. He also takes different lessons from three of them. Martin Wolff, who was Mann's mentor and engaged closely with Simmel and Knapp, may have been another prophet. See Chapter 8 in this volume by Wolfgang Ernst, 'Before FA Mann: Martin Wolff on Monetary Law'.

[13] Georg Simmel, *The Philosophy of Money* (David Frisbie ed., Tom Bottomore and David Frisbie tr., 3rd edn, Routledge 2004) 179 (hereafter Simmel, *Philosophy of Money*).

[14] Robert Cover, 'Nomos and Narrative' (1983) 97 Harvard Law Review 4, 12 (hereafter Cover, 'Nomos and Narrative'). Professor Cover was discussing religious law within a modern secular state, but his words and context are too apt to ignore.

> money involves credit, that credit creates a liability, whereas metallic money payment liquidates any liability; but this argument overlooks the fact that the liquidation of the individual's liability may still involve an obligation for the community ... Viewed from the sociological perspective, there is no doubt that metallic money is also a promise and that it differs from the cheque only with respect to the size of the group which vouches for it being accepted.[15]

Simmel noted that he was not alone. 'In recent times, the interest in the stability of money value has even led to proposals for abolishing the metal reserve against which such notes are issued', although it 'is not yet technically feasible to accomplish what is conceptually correct, namely to transform the money function into a pure token money'.[16]

Secondly, we turn to Georg Knapp, whose first edition of *The State Theory of Money* came out in 1905. Knapp bowed to Simmel, but did not use his work.[17] Knapp begins his text with the following words: 'Money is a creature of law', and '[t]he soul of currency is not in the material of the pieces, but in the legal ordinances which regulate their use'.[18] Too many subsequent readers have gone no further than these sentences.

The title of Knapp's book is important. In the original German, it was *Staatliche Theorie des Geldes*. *Rechtstheorie* ('legal theory') is a perfectly good German compound word, but Knapp did not use it. Nor did he call it the *rechtliche Theorie*. Knapp grounded money in the power of the *state*, more than the mere command of *law*. To Knapp, money included, but was not limited to, any medium of exchange that the state would accept as payment. This stripped property moneys—paper or gold—of all distinction in domestic transactions. Credit money was no different than gold if the state would accept it. Legal tender had no salience. But Knapp went beyond state acceptance. 'Giro' money, invariably private (at the time), was a distinct form of credit money. But even without state acceptance, it was still money. The state was unnecessary: any clearing house would do.[19]

> That a unit of value, the mark banco, was independently established at the Hamburg Giro bank, unconnected with the unit of value for State money, is a particularly instructive circumstance; each pay-group can make a unit of value for

[15] Simmel, *Philosophy of Money* (n 13) 177–78.

[16] ibid 190, 165.

[17] Georg Friedrich Knapp, *The State Theory of Money* (HM Lucas and J Bonar tr., Simon Publications 2003) vii ('As [Simmel] treats only of the sociological side of currency, I do not need to regard my work as competing with his') (hereafter Knapp, *State Theory*). Nussbaum, *Money in the Law* (n 6) 18 praised Simmel ('most spirited and brilliant analysis of money'), but barely used him.

[18] Knapp, *State Theory* (n 17) 1, 2. In the original German, the opening line reads that money is a creature of the *legal order* (*Rechtsordnung*), not *law* (variously *Recht, Gesetz*).

[19] ibid 148.

> itself. The State can do it, because it is a pay-society, not because it is the State. The State is only the most familiar, the oldest society of payers; it is not the only one.

Thus, Knapp argued that the state was sufficient, not necessary. Although he was not always consistent,[20] it is easy to read Knapp as an apostle of Simmel: 'Payment is a transaction which in any case implies a society, whether it be the State or the customers of a bank or any other kind of association of payers.'[21] Knapp's treatment of set-off is particularly useful:

> Each definitive means of payment establishes for the holder a *claim on the central office* which only arises in such event; the holder, at the moment when the *central office makes a claim* on him—but not before or afterwards—has a counter-claim which he brings to light by the delivery of definitive means of payment for the purpose of discharging his debt. This notion of an eventual counter-claim is lacking in our [19th-century German] jurisprudence, while the concept of an absolute counter-claim is quite familiar.
>
> The jurist never refers to an eventual counter-claim. But why should not this concept be introduced? By introducing it we can state the case as follows:
>
> The liquidation of a lytric [i.e. denominated in monetary terms] *claim of the central office* is always carried out by means of a set-off, that is, by bringing a counter-claim into account—either an absolute one, if at the moment there is one ready, or, if there is no absolute counter-claim in existence, by a counter-claim which is only eventual, and that is always possessed by a person who holds a definitive means of payment.[22]

Note that set-off denies the need for any sort of special settlement money outside of ordinary credit, such as gold for interbank transactions or central bank accounts.

We now go to our third prophet: Alfred Mitchell-Innes. He was a far more obscure figure, who wrote on the eve of World War I. He was neither an economist nor lawyer nor academic: just a British diplomat stationed in Washington. Mitchell-Innes believed that money was nothing more or less than any liquid credit which could be offset against debts due. So, he echoed Knapp, although more pithily: 'Debts and credits are perpetually trying to get into touch with one another, so that they may be written off against each other, and it is the business of the banker to bring them together.'[23] He equalized all embodiments of credit: tangible or intangible, public or private; they could all serve as money.[24]

[20] Nussbaum, *Money in the Law* (n 6) 9.
[21] Knapp, *State Theory* (n 17) 158.
[22] ibid 154–55. Emphasis added.
[23] Alfred Mitchell-Innes, 'What is Money?' (1913) 30 Banking Law Journal 377, 402.
[24] Mitchell-Innes, who rarely cited anybody, attributed much of his credit theory to MacLeod. Alfred Mitchell-Innes, 'The Credit Theory of Money' (1914) 31 Banking Law Journal 151, 159 (hereafter Mitchell-Innes, 'The Credit Theory of Money'). However, MacLeod distinguished money from

Mitchell-Innes took Knapp one step further. Knapp observed that international gold standard currencies did not trade at par, despite their common link to bullion. Mitchell-Innes examined the American experience of domestic exchange. American bank money did not quite trade at par, despite the common dollar.[25] This leads to the astonishing inference that each bank issues its own money![26] It takes little more insight to remember that no money is universally accepted. Who buys a house with small notes? A plea of 'legal tender' would likely be ignored, if anybody dared try.[27] By the same token, no corner stand would accept a cheque for a cup of coffee.

These three authors had two things in common. First, they were not interested in either the law of money or monetary policy. They were trying, in their different ways, to imagine money unlinked to specie. Second, they all wrote during the heyday of the gold standard. They did not have to burden themselves with the messy worlds of policy or law. And mostly they did not, although Knapp discussed the international gold standard in some detail, believing it was necessary in a world of competing local moneys.[28]

Our final prophet is Keynes, with his *Treatise on Money*. Keynes' *Treatise* was published in 1930, during the last gasp of the gold standard. Unlike the first three, Keynes wanted to change the world, not just describe it. He wanted to replace gold with fiat money. To do this, he had to break gold's mental hold.

Keynes relied on Knapp. He helped Knapp get a translator for the 1924 English translation.[29] His *Treatise on Money* started with Knapp's mixed social and legal theory of money.[30]

> Now by the mention of contracts and offers, we have introduced Law or Custom, by which they are enforceable; that is to say we have introduced the State or the Community. Furthermore, it is a peculiar characteristic of money contracts that

credit, conventionally viewing money as credit ascribed with legal tender. Henry Dunning MacLeod, *The Theory of Credit* (Longmans, Green 1889) 82–83. Mitchell-Innes refused to do so. And style matters. MacLeod used a ponderous Victorian style. Mitchell-Innes wrote like a sprightly Edwardian.

25 Mitchell-Innes, 'The Credit Theory of Money' (n 24) 154.

26 Par trading of bank money entails substantial social engineering: an early obsession of the Federal Reserve System. George B Vest, 'The Par Collection System of the Federal Reserve Banks' (1940) 27 Fed Res Bull 89; Walter Wyatt, 'The Par Clearance Controversy' (1944) 30 Va L Rev 361. Other triumphs of the engineers' art include: the lender of last resort; deposit insurance; capital and liquidity requirements; licensing restrictions; and prudential supervision. Even today, par trading is only done over a limited range. Interbank exposures are limited by regulation, so banks would not need to price them. 12 CFR § 206.

27 *Suffolk Bank v Lincoln Bank*, 23 F Cas 346, 3 Mas 1 (CCD Me 1821) (Story J) (No 13,590); Commission Recommendation of 22 March 2010 on the scope and effects of legal tender of euro banknotes and coins, <https://eur-lex.europa.eu/legal-content/EN/TXT/PDF/?uri=CELEX:32010H0191&from=EN> (accessed 14 February 2022).

28 Knapp (n 17) 216–303.

29 ibid vi.

30 John Maynard Keynes, *A Treatise on Money* (Harcourt Brace 1930, Martino Publishing 2011) 6.

> it is the State or Community not only which enforces delivery, but also which decides what it is that must be delivered as a lawful or customary discharge of a contract which has been concluded in terms of the money-of-account.

But the very next sentence changed the script. Keynes dropped the Community, apparently forever.

> The State, therefore, comes in first of all as the authority of law which enforces the payment of the thing which corresponds to the name or description in the contract. But it comes in doubly when, in addition, it claims the right to determine and declare *what thing* corresponds to the name, and to vary its declaration from time to time—when, that is to say, it claims the right to re-edit the dictionary. This right is claimed by all modern states and has been so claimed for some four thousand years at least. It is when this stage in the evolution of money has been reached that Knapp's chartalism—the doctrine that money is peculiarly a creation of the State—is fully realised.

He had good reason for his disappearing trick. The Community—naturalistic, customary, organic—was in the thrall of gold. Only the state—rational, national, and compulsory—could wrench money away from gold—or at least do so with enough speed and planned direction. No social theory of money could work for Keynes. His statal theory of money had to be a legal theory, rooted in sovereign command.

III. Mann's Theory

Keynes won. Both gold standards disappeared: the domestic redemption standard immediately, and the international bullion standard with time. The law had to deal with the consequences. These consequences were both domestic and international. Domestic law mostly involved the extent of government power, and managing the legal transition away from convertibility. These problems were mostly of a single time: the 1930s.

The international problems were more complex, and more persistent. Mann's book remains a valuable guide to them today. What is the chosen money? This is not always obvious in the aftermath of territorial or governmental changes. And some contracts are ambiguous. What about payments in foreign currencies? Should they be calculated or enforceable in the foreign currency, or that of the court with jurisdiction? Should one country recognize another's new money? Under what circumstances and with what value? Are choice of law or place of payment relevant? Should one country recognize another country's devaluation, notwithstanding a protective clause in the contract? (*Which* country's devaluation?) What about exchange controls? Who bears the risk of currency fluctuation when the parties, chosen money, and courts are not coincident? Whose law governs which aspects of a debt and its payment? The list goes on.

Many of these international problems predated the end of the gold standard. Currencies were never fully stable, even ballasted by gold. Borders and sovereigns constantly changed. Governments occasionally redenominated their currency against gold. But the 1930s were different. The gold standard was an ideology as much as a set of economic arrangements. It denied politics in favour of naturalism. Accordingly, it minimized sovereignty and exalted a transnational order based on inalterable natural market rules. It preached stability, at least in principle. The new world was one of less stability and naturalism, but more rationalism, nationalism, and state control.

Keynes hinted at this, with his switch from the Community to the state. But Keynes was not a lawyer and did not work out the argument. He simply asserted it: 'Money is simply that which the State declares from time to time to be a good legal discharge of money contracts.'[31] Mann was at least aware of Keynes' work,[32] and sought to put the state at the legal centre of money.

Mann built on two pillars: 'nominalism' and 'money'. He defined 'money' first, putting the state foremost.

A. Mann's Money

Mann's money included 'all chattels which, issued by the authority of the law and denominated with reference to a unit of account, are meant to serve as universal means of exchange in the State of issue'.[33] (For non-legal readers, a 'chattel' is a movable object of property: e.g. a cow or a coin.) His definition did not require legal tender: just state authority.[34]

Mann demanded chattel money. For him, bank money would not do.[35] Mann's argument seemed to be mostly stemming from tradition, not necessity.[36]

> Although at times money was not expressed by any corporeal symbols but was represented by accounts with a bank, which, for the purpose of effecting

[31] John Maynard Keynes, *A Tract on Monetary Reform* (1923, Macmillan & Co 1932) 9.

[32] Mann, *Legal Aspect* (n 1) 14 fn 63. There is another reference to Keynes in the first edition, but this was dropped for editorial reasons. FA Mann, *The Legal Aspect of Money* (Clarendon Press 1938) 31 fn 3 (hereafter Mann, *Legal Aspect First Edition*); Mann, *Legal Aspect* (n 1) 43. There is no correspondence with Keynes in Mann's files.

[33] Mann, *Legal Aspect* (n 1) 8. The words 'in the State of issue' were missing from the first edition. Mann, *Legal Aspect First Edition* (n 32) 8.

[34] Mann, *Legal Aspect* (n 1) 42–43.

[35] 'There is, accordingly, no room in a book on the law of money for a discussion of such problems as bank accounts, deposits ... or negotiable instruments.' See ibid 6 fn 20. This language was missing in the first edition.

[36] ibid 8.

payments, were credited or debited (bank money), yet from primitive periods until the present day men have been accustomed to connect the idea of money with definite symbols, whether these were animals, commodities, quantities of metal, or coins and bank notes, as we today find them in all civilized countries. Money is a chattel personal.

Mann acknowledged other traditions, duly citing Knapp's dematerialized Hamburg *mark banco*.[37] Mann also demanded legal approbation of money: the 'State or Chartalist theory of money which in modern times has come to be connected with the name of G.F. Knapp'.[38] In Mann's first edition, legal approbation was not logically necessary: just a matter of positive English law. 'Whatever one may be inclined to think of [nonstatal money] in theory, it cannot be denied that in this country the State theory rules.'[39] The fifth edition went further. As we shall see, it appeared to repudiate the logical possibility of non-state money, too.

Although Mann did not directly demand that money be legal tender, it still came in through the back door, because only chattels could be invested with legal tender. '*[I]n principle* means of payment other than bank notes or coins may freely be rejected by a creditor to whom they are tendered.'[40] Mann's 'in principle' carries an enormous weight, one which it can no longer bear, since it is no longer the law. We shall return to this in Section C below, when we discuss the legal meaning of legal tender. But first, let us examine Mann's nominalism.

B. Mann's Nominalism

Mann was not the first to define nominalism. Just before Mann's first edition, fellow Berlin émigré Arthur Nussbaum had a definition of his own, which he viewed as the accepted one. '[T]he essence of nominalism consists in the arithmetical relationship of a given money to the pertinent ideal unit (dollar, franc, etc.).'[41] This definition does not require any particular instantiation of money. It works just as well for bank or non-statal moneys.[42] This definition was not good enough for Mann, however.[43] Mann's definition incorporated Nussbaum's, but added

37 Knapp, *State Theory* (n 17).
38 Mann, *Legal Aspect* (n 1) 14.
39 Mann, *Legal Aspect First Edition* (n 32) 12.
40 Mann, *Legal Aspect* (n 1) 6 (emphasis added).
41 Arthur Nussbaum, 'Basic Monetary Conceptions in Law' (1937) 35 Mich L Rev 865, 879. Nussbaum would prefer the word: 'numeralism', but believed that 'nominalism' was already the standard usage.
42 Gleeson, *Legal Concept* (n 3) 120–21.
43 Mann, *Legal Aspect First Edition* (n 32) 63. He dropped the slighting reference to Nussbaum by his fifth edition: Mann, *Legal Aspect* (n 1) 90.

additional constraints. Although the text is all Mann's, the **bold** text is consistent with Nussbaum. The *italic* text represents where Mann diverged from Nussbaum's ideas:[44]

> **The nominalistic principle means that** *a monetary obligation involves the payment of so many chattels, being legal tender at the time of payment, as, if added together according to the nominal value indicated thereon, produce a sum equal to the amount of the debt. In other words,* **the obligation to pay £ 10 is discharged if the creditor receives what at the time of performance are £ 10, regardless of both their intrinsic and their functional value. It follows that a monetary obligation has no other 'value' than that which it expresses.**

In either definition, a liquidated debt is defined by the face value of the liquidated debt. It adverts to nothing else. *Money has no metric but itself.* Money does not represent gold or anything else. This is the law today. A debt for 10 units payable next year is satisfied by a payment of 10 units next year. The units may be specified by the parties, but are outside the parties. Domestic courts will not adjust for inflation or currency devaluation, and foreign courts usually respect this. Nor does the governing law or place of performance matter for the magnitude of the debt, although it may determine its existence or enforceability.

Mann added the italicized language because he believed that his theory of money was prior to nominalism.[45] We shall view this belief as a mystery for the moment, and here discuss the more general notion of nominalism shared by both Mann and Nussbaum.

Nominalism was not new, but still was revolutionary. To arrive at nominalism, Mann rejected both the metric and the ideal of gold, at a time when its allure was strongest, and the injustices wrought by currency debauchery the greatest.[46] Mann chose sovereignty and national economies over globalism and international commerce. This hard choice was not a necessary one. Mann's intellectual world did not deny that money *could* be an abstract representation of its metallic (or other 'true') value. Gold held minds then—and still does today. To Mann, an external reference was possible, but wrong. He based his nominalistic principle on a deliberate policy choice, which we have adopted and retained today in our law. 'Nominalism in this sense is a legal principle, but is empirically derived from a generalization of the normal factual situation.'[47]

[44] Mann, *Legal Aspect* (n 1) 90. In his first edition, Mann only demanded 'delivery of chattels which at the time of delivery are money'. Mann, *Legal Aspect First Edition* (n 32) 63. He added legal tender later.

[45] Mann, *Legal Aspect First Edition* (n 32) 10; Gleeson, *Legal Concept* (n 3) 118–19.

[46] Mann allowed for some rare exceptions, such as hyperinflation. Mann, *Legal Aspect* (n 1) 106–08. See Jan Thiessen, 'The German Hyperinflation of the 1920's' in David Fox and Wolfgang Ernst (eds), *Money in the Western Legal Tradition: Middle Ages to Bretton Woods* (OUP 2016) 735.

[47] Mann, *Legal Aspect* (n 1) 90.

Nominalism is more flexible than it sounds, at least for international cases. The most common flexure is with timing rules governing exchange rates.[48] By picking a date, a court can pick a rate that yields its favoured result. Courts can sometimes even pick a rate as well as a time. The United States seems to prefer black-market rates over official rates. Mann, always an advocate of monetary sovereignty, found this shocking.[49]

C. Legal Tender

Mann based money on legal tender. But legal tender is a modest doctrine, akin to the doctrine of hindrance in contract law. As a general rule, obligees want to be paid, and will not be fussy about any commercially reasonable means of payment. ('Commercially reasonable' probably means 'liquid', conjoined with 'cheap' and 'safe'.) But occasionally, an obligee does not want payment, no matter how reasonable the form. Perhaps a lessor would want to reject a payment, to engineer a default on a burdensome lease renewal. The contractual doctrine of legal tender protects a payor against such a bad faith payee.

The common law permits refusal of all payments in tangible media, including legal tender. But the consequences of refusal depend on what is being tendered. An uncollected cheque is little better than a promise of the payor; a private bank note is no better than the credit of the issuing bank. US law allows the payee to refuse such tenders without penalty, but suspends the obligation to pay for a reasonable time so that the payor may obtain a better payment medium.[50] The payee even has the power to *refuse legal tender*. The refusal might even be reasonable, if the payee suspects a counterfeit. But counterfeits are less likely than bad credit, and rejection of an apparently good note is more likely to be in bad faith. Therefore, the consequences of rejection are different. Rejection of a bad note presented in good faith is similar to other rejections. But rejection of a good legal tender note cannot benefit the rejector if the tenderer remains willing to pay:

> The effects of this [legal tender] attribute are that, if such money is tendered by a debtor in strict compliance with all the numerous and exacting requirements

[48] United States rules vary by the state, with the enforcement date the most common. Uniform Foreign-Money Claims Act § 3. This statute has been adopted by half the states, with a safety valve for extreme events, such as exchange control or revalorizations: Section 12 comm. 2. New York has its own rule. NY Judiciary L § 27. The other states rely on their common law.

[49] Uniform Foreign-Money Claims Act § 1(10); Restatement (Fourth) of the Foreign Relations Law of the United States § 490 Rptr's Note 6 (1987). Compare to Mann, *Legal Aspect* (n 1) 455–56.

[50] *Simmons v Swan*, 275 US 113, 116 (1927); UCC § 2-511; WFK, *The Requisite Medium in a Tender of Performance of an Obligation to Pay Money* (1928) 76 U Pa L Rev 433 (hereafter WFK). Only express contractual terms could alter this. I cannot speak to English law, but Mann seems to view *Simmons* favourably, if not quite replicated in England. Mann, *Legal Aspect* (n 1) 78.

> of a proper tender and the tender is refused, interest as an element of damages ceases to accumulate, the creditor may not thereafter in an action to collect the debt recover his costs, parties secondarily liable are discharged and securities on property are lost.[51]

A rejection of legal tender is still a rejection. The debt remains, stripped of most ancillary remedies and consequences. (Or alternatively, rejected legal tender transforms the old relationship into a simple non-interest-bearing demand debt.) The legal tender notion only applies to antecedent debt—a streetcar, for instance, could insist on tokens rather than coins as a condition of passengers boarding.[52]

This debtor protection framework made sense in 1938, the year of Mann's first edition. But its rationale eroded with time, for two interrelated reasons. First, credit transfers became increasingly practicable: first with the telegraph, then the telex, and now the Internet. In a credit transfer, the *payee* controls its credit risk in the payment process, not the payor. Therefore, the legal tender notion—which still permits rejection—is less justifiable. Why let a payee reject a wire transfer when it has already selected its bank? Mann himself stated the second reason:

> Where large amounts are involved ... payment by legal tender is frequently unthinkable and in many contexts cannot possibly be within the contemplation of the parties, so that a robust process of construction ought to displace the legal principle in most cases.[53]

Mann suggested a clumsy workaround: that 'the creditor would be entitled, not to payment, but to specific performance by way of a credit ... so that the obligation would not be monetary one'.[54] This implies that some obligations denominated in monetary terms are not monetary obligations. This statement may be logically tenable, but it is linguistically violent.

The United States cut this knot in 1989. Uniform Commercial Code (UCC) Article 4A overtly equated a wire transfer to a legal tender payment. The UNCITRAL Model Law on International Credit Transfers followed in 1992.[55] These legal instruments permitted discharge of a payment without the involvement of the

[51] Oliphant, 'Theory of Money' (n 11) 609. *See also* WFK (n 50); Mann, *Legal Aspect* (n 1) 76; Gleeson, *Legal Concept* (n 3) 134.

[52] *Martin v Rhode Island Company*, 32 RI 162, 78 A 548 (1911); *Nemser v New York City Transit Authority*, 140 Misc2d 369, 530 NYS2d 493 (NY Cty 1988).

[53] Mann, *Legal Aspect* (n 1) 77.

[54] ibid 201.

[55] The Official Text of Article 4A dated back to 1989, and it was adopted by the various states over time. The most important state—New York—adopted it in 1991. The New York Court of Appeals held it as 'persuasive authority' in interpreting earlier case law. *Banque Worms v Bankamerica*, 77 NY2d 362, 371, 570 NE2d 189, 568 NYS2d 541 (1991). For the UNCITRAL Model Law, see <https://uncitral.un.org/sites/uncitral.un.org/files/media-documents/uncitral/en/ml-credittrans.pdf> accessed 18 February 2021.

payee. They could even allow discharge against the payee's express opposition.[56] As far as I can tell, current English law allows for discharge once the beneficiary's bank 'accepts the payment and decides to credit the beneficiary unconditionally with the equivalent amount'.[57] If bank money acts as legal tender, why does money still need to be a chattel?

Mann's legal tender is an odd principle of law: modest in intended scope, reluctant to bite, and almost toothless even when it nips. Perhaps the word 'fiction' applies better than 'principle'? If so, the usual question applies—why retain an awkward fiction, full of epicycles, deferents, equants, and eccentricities? And why base a theory of money on it? There must be something more to it than what I have said. To understand Mann's attachment to legal tender, maybe we should listen to its enemies.

D. Legal Tender, Legal Transitions, and Sovereignty

As I have phrased it, the legal tender doctrine seems technical and innocuous. But the term has evoked outrage. 'The truth is indeed that legal tender is simply a legal device to force people to accept in fulfilment of a contract something they never intended when they made the contract'.[58] A legal tender law asserts that the state 'has the power to alter the condition of contracts between private parties, and authorize their payment or discharge in something different from that which the parties stipulated'.[59]

This outrage is misplaced. The legal tender attribute can be consistent with the gold standard or freedom of contract. Indeed, the pre-1931 Bank of England note was both legal tender *and* convertible to gold. And legal tender is merely a default (as opposed to a mandatory) rule, with which contract law abounds. Such rules can be contracted around, and frequently were, with 'gold clauses'.[60] A gold clause could require payment in bullion or coin, or an option of foreign currency, or bullion's worth of legal tender.[61] Legal tender or inconvertibility alone cannot displace the gold standard, at least among those who desire gold or gold's worth.

[56] Article 19 of the UNCITRAL Model Law contained an optional provision equating the payee bank's receipt of a wire transfer to a tender of cash. UCC § 4A-406(b) equates receipt to payment of money unless (1) the payment was forbidden by contract; (2) the creditor promptly objects; and (3) the creditor was harmed by the payment: *e.g.*, immediate bank insolvency or a transfer sent to a jurisdiction with pending creditor process.

[57] Roy Goode and Ewan McKendrick, *Goode on Commercial Law* (5th edn, Penguin 2016) 17, 51.

[58] Friedrich A Hayek, *Denationalisation of Money—The Argument Refined* (3rd edn, Institute of Economic Affairs 1990) 39–40 (hereafter Hayek, *Denationalisation of Money*).

[59] *Juilliard v Greenman*, 110 US 421, 451 (1884) (Field J dissenting).

[60] See Chapter 9 in this volume by David Fox, 'Gold Clauses in the Capital Markets of the Early 20th Century'.

[61] Mann, *Legal Aspect* (n 1) 169–70.

The outrage against legal tender was better directed at the abrogation of the gold clause: the main event of the 1930s. A contract for gold or gold's worth became a contract for money at the official gold exchange rate. Parties could no longer opt for their own monetary regime; they were bound by their state's regime, and their state's revaluations. Abrogation was nearly universal[62] even if not permanent. Abrogation was more important than inconvertibility or legal tender, because it could not be avoided. Mann viewed the gold clause as vitiating 'the effects of nominalism'.[63] This may explain his unusual definition of nominalism, tied closely with the legal tender attribute and precluding gold clauses based on gold or foreign currency. Mann wanted state control of money, and legal tender alone was not enough.

Perhaps realizing that the new monetary order needed some extra support beyond legal tender, Mann turned to law, citing Knapp:[64]

> Only those chattels are money to which such character has been attributed by law: i.e. by or with the authority of the State. This is the State or Chartalist theory of money which in modern times has come to be connected with the name of G.F. Knapp, to whose principal work it has given the title.

As we have seen, this misreads Knapp. Although to be fair, Knapp was ambivalent. Mann then seems to abandon chattels *and* law (as Knapp did), and to look directly to sovereignty:

> The chattel issued by the State is only the external sign of the many aspects of sovereign power over money, from which it is derived. That power involves much more than the mere issue of money in the legal sense. It comprises the whole of monetary, credit, fiscal, and budgetary policy as well as those measures which economists tend to include in the concept of money ... It should be obvious, therefore, that a particular currency is no more than the consequence of political sovereignty.[65]

I certainly endorse this statement.[66] But it is also a non sequitur. Sovereignty does not require chattel money—or legal tender. Nor do Mann's manifestations of

[62] Nussbaum, *Money in the Law* (n 6) 280–81 (listing abrogations). 'Only very few countries, particularly England and Switzerland, have refrained from direct judicial or legislative interference with gold clauses.' See ibid 282.

[63] This is expressed in the titles of Chapter 4 of the first edition, and Chapter 6 of the fifth edition.

[64] Mann, *Legal Aspect* (n 1) 14.

[65] ibid 15.

[66] More meaningfully, so do others. Charles AE Goodhart, 'The Two Concepts of Money: Implications for the Analysis of Optimal Currency Areas' (1998) 14 Eur J Pol Econ 407, 410–11 (hereafter, Goodhart, 'Two Concepts'). Desan, *Making Money* (n 6) applies this principle to the English monetary system, going back before the Norman invasion.

sovereignty draw directly on the unique sovereign attribute—its monopoly of legitimate violence. Sovereign power, as we shall see, can be social rather than legal.

And the connection between sovereignty and money is a delicate one, in any case. Strong currencies are intrepid travellers and easily pass borders, away from the command of the sovereign. Henry VIII had to implore the rulers of the Netherlands and Flanders to 'decree that the English coins [Henry had just debased] should pass at their old values'.[67] Feavearyear does not tell us whether these rulers listened. The United States could never control the Eurodollar. And most courts have taken a very minimalist view of the IMF's exchange control provisions.[68] Conversely, the United States always denied the sovereignty of the Confederacy, but treated the rebel dollar with far more consideration.[69] Even today, the state of New York respects the monetary decrees of any 'dominant authority asserting governmental, military, or police powers of any kind'.[70] This would doubtless include the ISIS dinar. This language would seem to include a modern drug cartel, which nobody views as a sovereign, or even a de facto sovereign. And this is all before cryptocurrency!

IV. Mann and the Edwardians

Mann rejected an alternative theory of money—the social (or 'societary') theory held by Simmel, Knapp, and Mitchell-Innes. It was even adopted by some prominent academic lawyers of the time. Nussbaum was one of them: Herman Oliphant another. Martin Wolff may have been a third.[71]

A. The Social Theory of Money

The social theory maintains that something becomes a medium of exchange because a community treats it as such. The community can also create a unit of account denominating this medium. Unmoored from the sovereign, the social theory of money is a functional theory: more congenial to conventional economic reasoning. It does not require legal tender, or a reliance on property money. It requires no basal medium of exchange for which other media are mere substitutes.

[67] AE Feavearyear, *The Pound Sterling: A History of English Money* (OUP 1931) 51.

[68] Mann, *Legal Aspect* (n 1) 365.

[69] For instance, *Thorington v Smith*, 75 US (8 Wall) 1 (1868); *Bank of Old Dominion v McVeigh*, 61 Va (20 Gratt) 457 (1871).

[70] NY Banking L § 138(1). So does Massachusetts. Mass Gen Stat Tit XXII, Ch. 167D § 20.

[71] Nussbaum, *Money in the Law* (n 6); Oliphant, 'Theory of Money' (n 11). Nussbaum was a renowned specialist in monetary law. Oliphant's adoption was casual—a consequence of his legal realism. See Chapter 8 by Wolfgang Ernst, 'Before Mann: Martin Wolff on Monetary Law' in this volume.

The social theory of money does not deny the central role of the state: something that would require an impressive blindness to fact.[72] But it does not view this role as primarily legal, in the sense of enforceable rules that create money. Instead, it looks to the state's enormous legitimacy and transactional power.[73] Following Knapp, the social theory includes statal moneys as a subset of social money. There is nothing inherently statal about central banking. In a vacuum, any large bank could fit the role, if it chose not to maximize profit. Charles Goodhart thus argues that central banks are a natural extension of clearing houses, and Hayek argued that any bank could create its own unit of account.[74]

Mann rejected the social theory in favour of his legal theory. In his first edition, his rejection was based mostly on his reading of pre-existing English law.[75] His rejection became more fundamental with time. It is brief enough to reproduce, adding bracketed numerals for clarity:

> [The social theory] would be tenable in law only [1] if it could explain the relevance of crises for the legal definition of money, [2] if it were reconcilable with the undeniable monopoly of the modern State over currency, [3] and if it could point to a single case where money in the legal sense was created or lost its character by the will of the community against or without the will of the supreme *de jure* or *de facto* authority. ... [4] [The social theory] is not proved by pointing to cases in which privately issued media of exchange in fact circulated, but their recognition as money for legal questions was never put to the test.[76]

I do not understand his first point and the other three do not stand up to experience or analysis. The state is not quite a monopolist these days, and the social theory of money is perfectly consistent with a state monopoly. The social theory is a theory of transactional power and the state is usually the largest transactor. Mann's next point is tautological, since the 'will of the community' is itself a de facto authority—something recognized in New York law.[77] His final point can be rephrased: the absence of apposite law discredits the social theory. But there is apposite law! The law sometimes privileges private media over legal tender. Both the UK and some US states forbid scrap dealers to pay with cash.[78] For another example, several

[72] Goodhart, 'Two Concepts' (n 66).

[73] Viewed another way, the state is a faith community that has the kind of weak social ties in which the alienating substance of money flourishes. Weak ties and faith community are an unusual combination, which may explain Goodhart's observation that money is generally associated with states.

[74] Charles Goodhart, *The Evolution of Central Banks* (2nd edn, MIT Press 1988) 29–46; Hayek, *Denationalisation of Money* (n 58).

[75] Mann, *Legal Aspect First Edition* (n 32) 12–13.

[76] Mann, *Legal Aspect* (n 1) 23. Nussbaum seems to respond to the same points in a different way. Nussbaum, *Money in the Law* (n 6) 5–8. Mann also expressed his third point in his first edition. Mann, *Legal Aspect First Edition* (n 32) 12.

[77] See text accompanying (n 70).

[78] La RS § 37:1973 (2017); Miss Code Ann § 97-17-71.2 (2017); Legal Aid, Sentencing, and Punishment of Offenders Act 2012, s. 146 (England). An American lawyer might scent a constitutional

states require that towing companies accept credit cards if offered as payment. This makes them as much 'legal tender' as state money, and has held up to constitutional attack.[79] Similarly, the European Union has held that a Member State can sometimes compel payment with bank money, forbidding legal tender euro notes.[80]

B. Why the Legal Theory?

Given Mann's vehement objections to the social theory, he must have been very strongly attached to his legal theory. But why? It is conceptually weak. It has little to do with the legal tender it demanded, although it does support the abrogation of the gold clause. (Ironically, England never abrogated the gold clause.) The social theory was ready on the shelf, thanks to the Edwardian theorists. The social theory agrees that the state's law can destroy a social consensus if it so chooses[81]—the point of abrogating gold clauses. But the social theory denies that the law can create the necessary consensus unaided. The social theory ascribes this creative role to the state's transactional hegemony.

I cannot get inside Mann's mind, but I agree with his choice. A legal theory of money was the right theory for the time. Gold had to go, by any means necessary. And legal means were indeed necessary for the time: irredeemability and abrogation. The social theories could accommodate this, but the legal theory had rhetorical advantages. It was conservative, in both legal form and ideology. Money, in English law, had been English coin and Bank of England notes. All else was a money substitute: a claim to money. Under the gold standard, these notes were redeemable for bullion at the windows of the Bank of England. English law changed nothing but redemption, and neither did Mann. Mann's legal theory resembled the gold standard as far as it could. He projected the new regime onto the old law.

The legal theory had another advantage. Gold had been a naturalistic anchor to which money attached. The legal theory provided another anchor, with a stronger mode of attachment, at least for its time: nationalism. The 1930s was an era of nationalism and state power, not naturalism or social construction. The legal theory was suited to this new era, at least for those attuned to the new ideology.

problem with such statutes at the state level. But an American court would not. *Genesee Scrap & Tin Baling Co v Rochester*, 558 F Supp2d 432 (WDNY 2008).

[79] *Porter v Atlanta*, 259 Ga. 526, 384 S.E.2d 631 (1989); *Cade v Montgomery County*, 83 Md. App. 419, 575 A.2d 744 (1990); *Berry v Hannigan*, 7 Cal. App. 4th 587, 9 Cal. Rptr.2d 213 (Ct. App. 1st App. Dist. 1992). Credit cards provide cheap and effective dispute resolution to the payor: something a consumer could not get from a wrongfully extracted cash payment.

[80] Joined Cases C-422/19, C-423/19 *Johannes Dietrich & Norbert Häring v Hessischer Rundfunk* (26 January 2021), ECLI:EU:C:2021:63. I thank Jason Allen for bringing this case to my attention.

[81] Cover, 'Nomos and Narrative' (n 14) made precisely this point for religious communities, which Simmel suggests resemble monetary ones.

Finally, the legal theory of money also had the advantage of fitting Mann's training and interests. Mann was an *international* lawyer, not a payment lawyer. He separated money—a sovereign emanation—from mere payment law. This let him focus on his main interest: sovereignty in an interconnected world. This in turn reinforced his legal theory: rooted in sovereign power. Mann was also a positivist invested in state sovereignty.

This may explain Mann's first edition of 1938. But I have mostly been citing his fifth edition that was published in 1991. If anything, Mann's state theory of money hardened over time, even as it became less tenable. Bank credit money was becoming irrefusable. Hayek had already demonstrated the possibility of private money unlinked to metal.[82] Markets had begun to eclipse the state. Electronic token monies were beginning to emerge.

V. Conclusion: A Future of Nominalism?

Mann proposed two theories: a legal theory of money, and the concept of nominalism. The legal theory never quite made sense in its own time, is looking worse today, and will look even worse in the future. But nominalism, if not quite Mann's version, was perfect for its time. With a little abstraction, it might also suffice for the future. It may even go further than money—much further.

Let me try to abstract or generalize the idea. To me, 'nominalism' means that a legal result is solely determined by the data content of an authentic message of shared symbolic social meaning.[83] This message could be a dollar bill or a wire transfer. This definition equates all media of exchange, except bullion.[84] It also unifies monetary law with the far more quotidian payment law. Payment law is nominalistic in structure, relying solely on authentic communications involving banks and their customers. Even property monies (see more in the Appendix) are communicative in nature.

This kind of extended nominalism goes beyond money and payment law. It is a general phenomenon. It applies to such things as traffic lights and elections,[85] as well as money. Such nominalistic socio-legal constructs might be the strongest constructs imaginable. If the authentication is good, the shared social meaning

[82] For legal tender, see (n 55); Hayek, *Denationalisation of Money* (n 58). The first edition of Hayek's tract was published in 1976.

[83] Joseph H Sommer, *Where is a Bank Account?* (1998) 57 Maryland L Rev 1, 60–64. Other views of nominalism may be found in Nussbaum, *Money in the Law* (n 6) 17–19; Ingham, *Nature of Money* (n 7) 50–56. We leave aside its meaning in medieval philosophy.

[84] The weight and assay numbers of bullion may be nominalistic, but the payee takes the bullion, not the numbers. Unless the bullion remains in the vaults of a trusted bailee, a subsequent payment might require a new weighing and assay. Gold coin, taken by tale, is nominalistic: a far more useful form of money.

[85] Given the recent American experience with elections, one might doubt the shared social meaning of votes, and the strength of their authentication. But this takes us far afield.

is indisputable, since it relies on nothing but symbols themselves. It has all the strengths of legal formalism, without the suspicion of judicial manipulability. If the authentication is reliable and the rules are based on symbols alone, there is nothing to manipulate. Nominalism may solve a puzzle posed by John Searle:

> I will use the tools we have assembled to give an account that describes the structure [i.e. social construction] not only of money but also of marriage, property, hiring, firing, war, revolutions, cocktail parties, governments, meetings, unions, parliaments, corporations, laws, restaurants, vacations, lawyers, professors, doctors, medieval knights, and taxes, for example. I do not know how to tell the story for each of these with the simplicity of the story about money.[86]

I would submit that Searle's difficulty with other stories owes something to Mann's nominalism, or more generally my own. Most of his other phenomena are not nominalistic. They refer to physical reality, as well as symbols. Physical reality complicates social constructs. Conversely, Searle never included traffic lights or the institution of voting on his list. He might have found them as simple (his word!) as money.

Appendix: On Property Money

Mann's theory of money was a property theory, whose fulcrum was a particular chattel. Simon Gleeson[87] has updated the theory to include intangible objects of property rights, such as cryptocurrency. But even Gleeson seems to insist that credit is not money: just a money substitute—a right to receive property money.

The limitation of money to property has some intuitive attraction. It avoids circularity. With property money, credit is a right to tender of property. No circularity here! Credit money, unmoored from property, becomes circular. Credit is a right to damages. The damages remedy is itself a kind of credit. There is nothing underneath the credits: credits all the way down. Where is the value in credits for . . . other credits? Debt, in this view, refers to nothing but itself. This point was likely foreseen by Keynes:

> When, however, what was merely a debt has become money-proper, it has changed its character and should no longer be reckoned as a debt, since it is *of the essence of a debt to be enforceable in something other than itself*. To regard Representative Money [i.e. central bank money], even when it conforms to an

[86] John R Searle, *The Construction of Social Reality* (Free Press 1995) 79.
[87] Gleeson, *Legal Concept* (n 3) 149–94.

> objective standard [e.g. the gold standard,] as being still a debt will suggest false analogies.[88]

Keynes' enforcement problem is not very serious. A debt is enforced by an involuntary sale of a debtor's assets. Bank money is usually accepted in such sales. True, the bank money is just a right to a sale of the bank's assets after judgment, which is itself merely a right to a sale of another bank's assets . . . But what is wrong with this? A payment of bank money remains a final payment, even though it merely transmutes one debt to another.

Maybe this is the problem? If a payment merely changes the identity of a creditor, can any payment ever be truly settled? Payment is just ceaselessly shifting debt. Isn't an external settlement medium necessary? No. Knapp and Mitchell-Innes already answered the settlement problem. Credits can mutually annihilate in a set-off. One could view banks as a topological construct, reducing $(n^2\text{-}n)/2$ bilateral credit relations to a more tractable set of relations of magnitude 'n'. This would dramatically increase the frequency of set-offs, by concentrating them onto central nodes. With banks, no external settlement medium is required. Central banks, or clearing houses, further concentrate the debts of the banks. It could indeed be credit, all the way down.

We have broken two circles, but still must deal with another. If debt indeed refers to nothing other than itself, how does it refer to itself? Here is where the social theory of money is particularly useful. As Simmel pointed out, every social fact is circular—it exists because we collectively believe that it exists. The *creation* of this social consensus is a vast and mysterious process, but we can subsequently take its *preservation* for granted. That's how social facts work, unless they are strongly contested from the outside.

It may be difficult to create a credit money by pure consensus, but it is doable. The 'Linden Dollar' of the Second Life online game is a credit money, unlike most cryptocurrencies, which take the form of property. Money is community, and the Internet creates communities. But once established, any consensus refers to itself, rather than its founding.[89] It has no need for coin or banknotes, or any other object of property. (Some jurisdictions seem to be abandoning banknotes even now.)[90] Even Bitcoin could ultimately dispense with its crypto-tokens, if the tokens support a credit money long enough.

If credit money is sufficient, why do sophisticated modern commenters like Gleeson still limit 'money' to property? I am not an English lawyer, but I will hazard a guess. As far as I can tell, the English law of restitution operates on substitute

[88] Keynes, *A Treatise on Money* (n 30) 6 (emphasis added).

[89] Mann, *Legal Aspect First Edition* (n 32) 36 and Mann, *Legal Aspect* (n 1) 49 make this point for the pound sterling; a recurrent link to another currency or specie is unnecessary.

[90] See Barontini and Holden, 'Proceeding with Caution' (n 2).

property. Most tracing exercises entail bank accounts. If money is not a form of property, is there anything for English law to operate on?[91]

Bibliography

Barontini C and Holden H, 'Proceeding With Caution—A Survey on Central Bank Digital Currency' (BIS Paper No. 101, January 2019) <https://www.bis.org/publ/bppdf/bispap101.pdf> accessed 16 December 2021

Cover R, 'Nomos and Narrative' (1983) 97 Harv L Rev 4

Desan C, *Making Money: Coin, Currency, and the Coming of Capitalism* (OUP 2014)

Feavearyear AE, *The Pound Sterling: A History of English Money* (OUP 1931)

Gleeson S, *The Legal Concept of Money* (OUP 2018)

Goodhart C, *The Evolution of Central Banks* (2nd edn, MIT Press 1988)

Goodhart C, 'The Two Concepts of Money: Implications for the Analysis of Optimal Currency Areas' (1998) 14 Eur J Pol Econ 407

Goode R and McKendrick E, *Goode on Commercial Law* (5th edn, Penguin 2016)

Hayek FA, *Denationalisation of Money—The Argument Refined* (3rd edn, Institute of Economic Affairs 1990)

Ingham G, *The Nature of Money* (Polity Press 2004)

WFK, 'The Requisite Medium in a Tender of Performance of an Obligation to Pay Money' (1928) 76 U Pa L Rev 433

Keynes JM, *A Tract on Monetary Reform* ([1923], Macmillan & Co 1932 reprint)

Keynes JM, *A Treatise on Money* (Harcourt Brace 1930, Martino Publishing reprint 2011)

Knapp GF, *The State Theory of Money* (HM Lucas and J Bonar tr., Simon Publications 2003)

MacLeod HD, *The Theory of Credit* (Longmans, Green 1889)

Mann FA, *The Legal Aspect of Money* (OUP 1938)

Mann FA, *The Legal Aspect of Money* (5th edn, Clarendon Press 1992)

Mitchell-Innes A, 'The Credit Theory of Money' (1914) 31 Banking L J 151

Mitchell-Innes A, 'What is Money?' (1913) 30 Banking L J 377

Nussbaum A, 'Basic Monetary Conceptions in Law' (1937) 35 Mich L Rev 865

Nussbaum A, *Money in the Law: National and International* (rev'd edn, Foundation Press 1950)

Oliphant H, 'The Theory of Money in the Law of Commercial Instruments' (1920) 29 Yale L J 606

Searle JR, *The Construction of Social Reality* (Free Press 1995)

Simmel G, *The Philosophy of Money* (David Frisbie ed., Tom Bottomore and David Frisbie tr., 3rd enlarged edn, Routledge 2004)

Sommer JH, 'Where is a Bank Account?' (1998) 57 Maryland L Rev 1

Thiessen J, 'The German Hyperinflation of the 1920's' in David Fox and Wolfgang Ernst (eds), *Money in the Western Legal Tradition: Middle Ages to Bretton Woods* (OUP 2016)

Vest GB, 'The Par Collection System of the Federal Reserve Banks' (1940) 27 Fed Res Bull 89

Wyatt W, 'The Par Clearance Controversy' (1944) 30 Va L Rev 361

[91] David Fox, *Property Rights in Money* (OUP 2008). Mann, *Legal Aspect* (n 1) 6, 7 might be acknowledging this point.

11
Constitutional Dimensions of Monetary Authority under the Gold Standard and Bretton Woods

Will Bateman

I. Introduction

The liberal constitutional systems of Western Europe and North America experienced fundamental changes between 1900 and 1950. Parliaments began voting for enormous spending programmes, far in excess of tax revenues, funding the creation of a large system of public administration.[1] Deficit funds were directly injected into the economy and paid to newly employed public servants. The relative and absolute size of executive government radically increased. Judiciaries had to develop new doctrines to apply the rule of law to the rapidly expanded public

[1] Vito Tanzi and Ludger Schuknecht, *Public Spending in the 20th Century: A Global Perspective* (CUP 2000) (hereafter Tanzi and Schuknecht, *Public Spending*); Will Bateman, *Public Finance and Parliamentary Constitutionalism* (CUP 2020) ch. 4 (hereafter Bateman, *Public Finance*).

Will Bateman, *Constitutional Dimensions of Monetary Authority under the Gold Standard and Bretton Woods* In: *FA Mann*. Edited by: Jason Grant Allen and Gerhard Dannemann, Oxford University Press. © Will Bateman 2024.
DOI: 10.1093/oso/9780198881452.003.0012

sector.[2] The public funding explosion was triggered by society-wide mobilization of the two world wars, but then continued under aggregate-demand Keynesian economic policies.[3] To lift employment, wages, and output, those policies provided potent fiscal stimulus in the form of universal social insurance, nationalization of industry, and low rates of interest on public and private credit.

The public monetary system, with central banks and treasuries at the core, was integral to those changes in the size and structure of the constitutional state. The link was explained by JM Keynes before the *General Theory*: 'an increase of output cannot occur unless ... public authority ... be called in aid to create additional current incomes through the expenditure of borrowed or printed money. [O]nly from this factor ... can [we] expect the initial major impulse'.[4] That effect could not be achieved under the Gold Standard, which imposed two terminal constraints on parliamentary fiscal power. The first was intellectual: parliamentarians, central bankers, academic economists, and professional investors believed that public deficit spending must be prohibited as it caused inflation and currency debasement.[5] The other constraint was legal: the legal framework of the Gold Standard forced central banks to adopt operational rules which linked central bank money supply to international payment flows. To preserve the domestic gold stock under a gold-convertible currency regime, the archetypical central bank, the Bank of England, was required to hold the value of its domestic currency (relative to foreign currencies and gold prices) within fixed bands to prevent outflows of gold. When investors predicted a devaluation of sterling, through balance of payments or public deficits, they would sell the currency for higher-valued foreign assets or gold. The default central bank response was to lift interest rates on public and private credit to induce inwards payments, cool the domestic economy, and drive down inflation. Thereby, Gold Standard central banks suppressed economic activity even when fiscal agencies were attempting to address underlying economic dysfunction, such as during financial rescue and welfare state programmes.[6] True it is that Victorian constitutional jurists wrote about a 'system of parliamentary control'

[2] Roscoe Pound, 'The Rule of Law and the Modern Social Welfare State' (1953) 7 Vanderbilt LR 1; Harry W Jones, 'The Rule of Law and the Welfare State' (1958) 58 Columbia LR 143; Bruce Ackerman, *We the People, Volume 2: Transformations* (Bellknap Press 2000) chs 9 and 10.

[3] Tanzi and Schuknecht, *Public Spending* (n 1) chs 2 and 3. For an accessible summary of the aggregate-demand policies, see text accompanying n 45 and following, below.

[4] Letter from John Maynard Keynes to President Roosevelt (30 December 1933) in Donald Moggridge (ed.), *The Collected Writings of John Maynard Keynes* (Vol. 21, Macmillan 1982) 291 (hereafter Moggridge, *JM Keynes*).

[5] Those attitudes are carefully examined in James Ashley Morrison, *England's Cross of Gold: Keynes, Churchill and the Governance of Economic Beliefs* (Cornell University Press 2021) (hereafter Morrison, *England's Cross of Gold*).

[6] Antithetically to Gold Standard logic, those state supports are now understood as 'automatic stabilizers' of the economy: Alisdair McKay and Ricardo Reis, 'Optimal Automatic Stabilizers' (National Bureau of Economic Research Working Paper 22359, 2016) <https://www.nber.org/papers/w22359> accessed 27 April 2023.

which governed 'the collection and expenditure of the revenue, and all things appertaining thereto',[7] but Gold Standard rules attenuated the total quantity of public money available to the parliamentary process.

The monetary system created at the 1944 Bretton Woods conference mostly freed parliaments from those technical constraints.[8] Parliamentary fiscal power was generally free to spend new-money sovereign debt. Government credit policy was free to stimulate the general economy with low interest rates.[9] The foreign exchange value of national currencies was disconnected from domestic monetary policy by express treaty text, domestic legislation, statutory financial institutions, and the quotidian operations executed by central banks and treasuries. Very large fluctuations in the exchange value of national currencies would be solved by the institutional censure of official devaluation, rather than fiscal constraints. The hard limit of this system was reached in 1971, when the hegemonic anchor of the system could not devalue its currency-peg to gold and chose fiscal freedom over monetary constraint. Compared to what came before (and after), Bretton Woods empowered parliaments and treasuries, facilitating extensive state intervention in economic activity, mainly through public spending.

The greatest monetary jurist of the 20th century, FA Mann, published his seminal treatise in the late 1930s—in the pre-war United Kingdom, but drawing substantially on his Continental theoretical and methodological training. That framing allows us to understand why Mann said that 'the peculiar privileges and functions ... of central banks ... fall ... within the scope of constitutional rather than monetary law'.[10] Obeying that taxonomic stipulation, Mann excluded the statutory powers of monetary authorities from his field-defining treatise on monetary law. The aim of this, perhaps heretical, chapter is to explore the constitutional dimension of monetary law during the period Mann rose to fame. Understanding where central banks fitted within the structure of constitutional government complements and enriches our understanding of Mann's comprehensive analysis of the private law of money. It also fills a gap left in his 'legal aspect' of money. Despite adhering to a strongly statist conception of money, Mann's decision to bracket-out central banking and fiscal institutions from his legal analysis surely weakened his contribution to monetary studies and left his work vulnerable to criticisms of under-inclusion. To understand the full extent of states' authority over money it is

[7] AV Dicey, *The Law of the Constitution* (JWF Alllison ed., OUP 2013) 171.

[8] Those legal developments followed the intellectual shift away from viewing monetary scarcity as inexorable: Morrison, *England's Cross of Gold* (n 5) 145–66.

[9] For the most accessible legal analysis of this use of monetary powers during the post-war period, see Eric Monnet, *Controlling Credit: Central Banking and the Planned Economy in Postwar France, 1948–1973* (CUP 2018) (hereafter Monnet, *Controlling Credit*).

[10] FA Mann, *The Legal Aspect of Money* (4th edn, Clarendon Press 1982) 29–30. See the chapter in this volume by Wolfgang Ernst for an analysis of Mann's intellectual priors.

necessary to move beyond judicial law and into the realm of the statutory entities of central banks and sovereign-debt issuing treasuries.

Section II reviews the birth, life, and death of the Gold Standard, with a particular focus on how that monetary system impacted the relative balance of constitutional power between parliaments, executive governments, and central banks. That commodity-convertibility system grew from concerns about the relationship between state-controlled money and price stability in the UK during the early 19th century. Paradoxically, the Gold Standard required extensive state intervention in markets to operate and eventually collapsed under the pressure of public welfare provision and public-sector expansion. That pre-history is necessary to understand the extent of constitutional change wrought by the move from Gold to Bretton Woods, particularly the latter's facilitation of Keynesian economic expansion.

Section III surveys the essential design elements of the Bretton Woods system that permitted Keynesian fiscal expansion by separating international and domestic monetary policy. It begins by presenting the statutory tools used to separate exchange rate management (foreign monetary policy) and inflation management (domestic monetary policy) before the introduction of Bretton Woods: the exchange 'equalisation' and 'stabilization' accounts enacted in 1932–33 which allowed the 'central bank [to] make its short-term interest rates to an actual or potential holder of foreign funds exactly what it chooses, without ever changing the rates chargeable to domestic borrowers'.[11] It then reviews the international obligations contained in the IMF Articles of Agreement which, presupposing the existence of those foreign-exchange funds, provided Member States vast latitude to implement 'domestic social or political policies'[12] with inflationary impacts. It closes by explaining the market operations undertaken by central banks to abide by treaty obligations while expanding domestic monetary policy.

Section IV concludes by reflecting on the extent of latitude afforded to fiscal agencies under the Bretton Woods system and the constitutional implications of that posture. After explaining the fragilities of the Bretton Woods system through the lens of the 'trilemma of international finance' and the creation of the Gold Pool, the chapter then turns to explore a prominent episode of constitutional history at the height of the Bretton Woods years: the 1967 UK 'Sterling Crisis'. That episode of British constitutional and monetary history was the first major 'fundamental disequilibrium' devaluation under the IMF Articles and precipitated substantial alterations to the UK's domestic constitutional order. Ultimately, however, it maintained the priority of domestic over international monetary policy and revealed the substantial flexibility permitted to Bretton Woods Member States to engage in Keynesian fiscal policy. The episode also revealed the time-limited nature of

[11] John Maynard Keynes, 'The Future of the Foreign Exchanges' in Moggridge, *JM Keynes* (n 4) 365.

[12] Articles of Agreement of the International Monetary Fund (Washington, 27 December 1945) 39 UNTS 40, Art. 4(5)(f).

Bretton Woods: the system could not indefinitely maintain fixed exchange rates, capital account liberalization, and independent domestic monetary policy, as evidenced by the eventual collapse of the Bretton Woods system.

The chapter's primary jurisdictional focus is on the UK and the US. As the monetary hegemons and anchors of both Gold Standard and Bretton Woods systems, those systems assume particular importance in a constitutional analysis of 20th-century monetary policy.[13] It draws on and develops the (already sophisticated) body of literature regarding the Bretton Woods system, including its legal foundations, particularly the book-length works of Sayers, Eichengreen, Naef, Schwartz, Humpage, Bordo, and Best.[14] In that sense, this chapter is a work of translational scholarship, designed to bring the findings of a diverse non-legal literature together for a legal audience. The novel contribution emerges from the focus on the shifting balance of power between institutions of the constitutional state created by different monetary regimes, rather than their comparative economic effectiveness. Understanding the constitutional dynamics of money allows a richer appreciation of the interconnections of state and market institutions, thus enriching our understandings of law, economics, and politics.

II. Monetary Authority under the Gold Standard

The constitutional dimensions of Bretton Woods did not emerge from an historical vacuum. The system of fixed exchange rates was designed against the backdrop of the 'classic' Gold Standard.[15] It presupposed the importance of a commodity-anchor for monetary stability and adjustment of money values in response to international payment flows. It was also a 'world' money system in which responsibility was vested in the monetary hegemon.[16] There the similarities stopped. In radical contrast to the Gold Standard, the Bretton Woods system severed international and domestic monetary policy and imposed very weak constraints on parliamentary fiscal power.

[13] The dollar was the de jure reserve currency, while sterling was the 'secondary reserve currency': Alain Naef, *An Exchange Rate History of the United Kingdom: 1945–1992* (CUP 2022) 136 (hereafter Naef, *Exchange Rate History*). Evidently, focusing on those two currencies does not provide the complete story of central banking through the Bretton Woods years: see, e.g., Monnet, *Controlling Credit* (n 9).

[14] RS Sayers, *The Bank of England: 1891–1944* (CUP 1976) (hereafter Sayers, *The Bank of England*); Barry Eichengreen, *Golden Fetters: The Gold Standard and the Great Depression, 1919–1939* (OUP 1996) (hereafter Eichengreen, *Golden Fetters*); Naef, *Exchange Rate History* (n 13); Michael D Bordo, Owen F Humpage, and Anna J Schwartz, *Strained Relations: US Foreign-Exchange Operations and Monetary Policy in the Twentieth Century* (University of Chicago Press 2015) (hereafter Bordo, Humpage, and Schwartz, *Strained Relations*); Jacqualine Best, *The Limits of Transparency: Ambiguity and the History of International Finance* (Cornell University Press 2005).

[15] Scholars of monetary history recognize different forms of 'Gold Standard' including a 'classical' system (from 1844 to 1913) and an 'inter-war' system (from 1919 to 1933): see, e.g., Eichengreen, *Golden Fetters* (n 14). For reasons of space, the core focus here is on the classical system.

[16] cf Eichengreen, *Golden Fetters* (n 14) 5.

To understand the extent of the changes in the constitutional structure of money wrought in 1944 we must revisit the birth, life, and death of the Gold Standard.

A. 'Classic' Gold Standard: constitutional dimensions

The 'classic' Gold Standard was a system of legal monetary constraints that were designed to remove legal control over money creation from parliaments and vest it in a profit-seeking statutory bank that would modulate the money supply according to the balance of external trade and capital flows. That system grew from a time of pure-fiat money and high inflation. During the 'restriction period'[17] parliamentary legislation (i) prohibited the Bank of England from exchanging bank notes for gold coins; (ii) designated paper bank notes as a type of 'legal tender'; (iii) permitted payment of public taxes and dues in paper money; and (iv) required the Bank of England to seek Parliament's consent before undertaking major monetary operations.[18]

A loud complaint about that system was that it reduced the comparative value of British currency and triggered inflation.[19] The ultimate cause of those maladies was identified as the vesting of power over money issuance in 'the state':

> In the present state of the law, [the Bank of England's governing body] have the power, without any control whatever, of increasing or reducing the circulation in any degree they may think proper: a power which should neither be intrusted to the State itself, nor to any body in it; as there can be no security for the uniformity in the value of the currency, when its augmentation or diminution depends solely on the will of the issuers.[20]

Although historians now doubt the premises underlying that thinking,[21] the Gold Standard was designed to cure the problem of state involvement in money issue via

[17] See generally Patrick K O'Brien and Nuno Palma, 'Danger to the Old Lady of Threadneedle Street? The Bank Restriction Act and the regime Shift to Paper Money, 1797–1821' (2020) 24 European Review of Economic History 390 (hereafter O'Brien and Palma, 'Danger to the Old Lady of Threadneedle Street?').

[18] Cash Payments Act 1797 (37 Geo 3 c 45) ss 1 and 2.

[19] Select Committee appointed to Inquire into the Cause of the High Price of Gold Bullion and to take into consideration the State of the Circulating Medium and of the Exchanges Between Great Britain and Foreign Parts, *Report* (1810) 58–75.

[20] David Ricardo, 'On the Principles of Political Economy and Taxation' in Piero Sraffa (ed.), *The Works and Correspondence of David Ricardo* (Liberty Fund 2005) vol. 1, 359. Some modern economic historians contest Ricardo's treatment, writing that 'the Bank never became an agency of the state [during the restriction period], even in wartime' although they also document that 'the Bank did provide high levels of support to the Government during the Restriction Period': O'Brien and Palma, 'Danger to the Old Lady of Threadneedle Street?' (n 17) 411 fn 62.

[21] O'Brien and Palma's quantitative analysis finds that '[t]he timing of inflation does not match that of the expansion of the Bank's notes ... what happened was that payment deficits caused by the war economy caused depreciation of the pound, especially noticeable into the later years of the first decade of the 1800s, as the Continental Blockade and the 1807 American Embargo took effect. The resulting

a self-denying ordinance:[22] Parliament would enact legislation preventing it from future involvement in the issue of money.

Conceptually, the Gold Standard was founded on a simple idea encapsulated in Hume's 'price-specie[money]-flow' mechanism: prices, money quantities, and international trade would remain stable as money flowed between trading nations.[23] If 'specie' (gold) is the money unit in both Britain and the US, then importing a product from the US to Britain will lead to a flow of money out of Britain and towards the US. The quantity of money in the US will increase and cause growth in domestic investment (+money to invest in new businesses), employment/wages (+money to pay labour), and output (+goods and services). The quantity of money in Britain will decrease and cause a reduction in investment (-money to invest), employment/wages (-money to pay wages), and production (-goods and services). Relative price-levels would respond symmetrically: US prices will increase relative to British price falls. Eventually, that process reverses the balance of trade and payments, as US merchants begin importing more British goods than they export. When that occurs, money flows out of the US and into Britain; expanding investment, employment/wages, and production in Britain; and contracting the US economy.

In its most abstract form, that institutional structure would prevent two types of economic harm. First, it would prevent states printing money to fund their operations in ways that caused domestic inflation and adversely affected the bargains of real and financial economy transactions: funding for government programmes would be subject to the same basic monetary rules as transactions between private individuals. Secondly, it would prevent states from depreciating their currencies as a type of disguised subsidy to domestic industry: international trade in goods and services would determine the respective value of domestic monetary units, rather than vice versa.

depreciation of the pound caused domestic prices to rise and created the need for the Bank of England supply enough banknotes to keep the money supply from falling' in O'Brien and Palma, 'Danger to the Old Lady of Threadneedle Street?' (n 17) 407, citing Marie-Thérèse Boyer-Xambeu, Lucien Gillard, and Ghislain Deleplace, 'Régimes monétaires, points d'or et serpent bimétallique de 1770 à 1870' (1994) 45 Revue Économique 1139; Larry Neal, *The Rise of Financial Capitalism: International Capital Markets in the Age of Reason* (CUP 1990); Larry Neal, 'A Tale of Two Revolutions: International Capital Flows 1789–1819' (1991) 43 Bulletin of Economic Research 57, 64; Henry Thornton, *An Enquiry into the Nature and Effects of the Paper Credit of Great Britain* (George Allen and Unwin 1802).

[22] In this sense, Parliament copied its earlier practice of delegating budget formulation to the executive government: Bateman, *Public Finance* (n 1) 51–54.

[23] David Hume, 'Of the Balance of Trade' in *Essays, Moral, Political, and Literary* (Longmans, Green and Co. 1889 [1758]) vol. 1; Eichengreen, *Golden Fetters* (n 14) 32–33.

B. 'Domestic' and 'international' monetary authority under the Gold Standard

Hume's 'homeostatic'[24] model never represented the real world, where money is not chunks of 'gold' but national currencies authorized and regulated by governments.[25] In reality, flows of 'specie' in Gold Standard models are exchange transactions of currency pairs: e.g. sterling ('GBP') for the United States dollar ('USD'). If both currency units are convertible for a fixed weight of gold, then any 'flow' of gold occurs as the differential in the currencies' exchange value and transportation costs.[26] Market-moving holders of GBP (and GBP-denominated assets) will sell them if they predict the currency's value will (or has) depreciated relative to another currency or commodity. Depreciation can derive from trade deficits or domestic inflation and will trigger capital flight: investors sell sterling in favour of a foreign currency or gold as the final safe haven, which further fuels depreciation. Imported goods become more expensive, input costs for import-exposed domestic businesses increase, and additional money-issuance by domestic credit providers and government is required, fuelling further inflation and swelling the volume of gold-convertible money-units. Without redress, under a gold-convertible monetary system, that behaviour will eventually threaten the capacity of the central bank to maintain its gold stock.

Under that system, two major variables will trigger a central bank to react: (i) the quantity and price of the world's marketable gold stock; and (ii) the balance of payments in gold-denominated money. The Bank of England used different operations to target those variables: interest rate policy and direct operations in the gold market.[27] The Bank's most prominent mechanism for holding money-values stable, 'Bank Rate',[28] responded directly to shifts in the foreign exchange value of sterling by raising/lowering the rate of interest it charged for access to credit. To sterilize drains on the gold stock, the Bank of England relied on raising the rate of interest it charged private banks and governments for access to its credit.[29] That manipulation of credit cost had 'international' and 'domestic' effects. The international effect was to induce investors to exchange foreign currency for GBP or

[24] Eichengreen, *Golden Fetters* (n 14) 32.

[25] For a compelling history of British state involvement in creating, distributing, and regulating the monetary unit, see Christine Desan, *Making Money: Coin, Currency, and the Coming of Capitalism* (OUP 2014) (hereafter Desan, *Making Money*).

[26] Eichengreen, *Golden Fetters* (n 14) 37.

[27] Sayers, *The Bank of England* (n 14) vol. 1, 28–53 provides an extensive description and analysis of those operations.

[28] ibid 28–37.

[29] The structure of English (and, thus, world) financial markets during the Gold Standard was complex and does not map easily onto contemporary models of market structure. For an accessible entry-point see Anthony C Hotson, *Respectable Banking: The Search for Stability in London's Money and Credit Markets since 1695* (CUP 2017).

keep their funds in GBP-denominated bank accounts to access the higher rate of return on sterling.[30] More important was the domestic effect, which operated in the following way:

> higher Bank rate would mean curtailment of credit ... the curtailment of credit would diminish enterprise and cause unemployment, and ... unemployment would tend to bring down wages and costs of production generally.[31]

As Eichengreen elaborated: 'the consequent rise in unemployment ... eliminated the excess demand for traded goods, and put downward pressure on prices. Lower prices enhanced the competitiveness of domestic goods and restored balance to the external accounts.'[32]

The major policy variable subordinated in classic Gold Standard models was public-sector expenditure, which reflects the comparatively small size of governmental economic activity during the 19th century.[33] Money quantities within Britain could grow if public spending increased beyond the point of fiscal balance: budget deficits implied the introduction of 'new money' into the economy by governments, dilution of purchasing power, and inflation.[34] Gold standard governments could obtain new-money debt finance from two sources: entirely private banks and quasi-public central banks.[35] Both lines of credit would be influenced by Bank Rate. Private banks would pass on Bank Rate to sovereign borrowers, plus a margin, and central banks could pass Bank Rate directly to treasuries through bilateral credit lines and primary market purchases.[36]

Attenuating money creation for public expenditure was thus a necessary feature of the Gold Standard. Even ignoring the ultimate scarcity rule of the Gold Standard,[37] deficit spending would trigger inflation worries and cause private

[30] As contemporary observers explained, raising Bank Rate 'had the immediate effect of retaining money ... which would otherwise have been remitted abroad and of attracting remittances from abroad to take advantage of the higher rate': Committee on Currency and Foreign Exchanges After the War (Cunliffe Committee), *First Interim Report* (Cmd 9182, 1919) para 4 (hereafter Cunliffe Committee).

[31] Keynes, 'The Future of Foreign Exchanges' (n 11) 367.

[32] Eichengreen, *Golden Fetters* (n 14) 35.

[33] As expounded by the Cunliffe Committee (n 30), 'If a sound monetary position is to be re-established and the Gold Standard to be effectively maintained, it is in our judgement essential that government borrowings should cease at the earliest possible moment'.

[34] As Morrison explains, 'All policy, especially fiscal policy, was subordinated to the need to defend the gold value of the currency' in Morrison, *England's Cross of Gold* (n 5) 147.

[35] This is a simplification of the British primary sovereign-debt market under the Gold Standard. As Allen illustrates, the Bank of England had a dominant role in primary market issues: William A Allen, *The Bank of England and the Government Debt: Operations in the Gilt-Edged Market, 1928–1972* (CUP 2018) 11.

[36] The UK central bank would also directly subsidize public debt via '[l]oans to customers, made at the Government's request, to help them lend to the State': John Clapham, *The Bank of England: A History* (Vol. 2, CUP 1944) 424.

[37] If paper and book-entry money be convertible to gold at a fixed weight, government spending is limited by the portion of the world gold stock it controls.

investors to sell domestic-currency assets, including government bonds, triggering the central bank to lift Bank Rate to induce them to remain onshore. If Bank Rate were not passed to the government through sovereign debt markets, more investors would flee and aggravate inflation, both forecast and realized. Thus, legal constraints indirectly mandated central banks to reduce the supply of money for deficit spending to governments through the cost and quantity of public debt, in the short run, and diminished fiscal receipts, in the longer run. This logic placed central banks in the position of imposing limits on government spending, despite parliamentary voting to the contrary: provoking an obvious clash with constitutional institutions privileging the supremacy of legislative institutions to set fiscal policy and more basal principles of parliamentary supremacy.[38]

C. Welfare state spending, gold's terminus, and Keynesianism

As the size of the public sector grew post-World War One, the conflict of parliamentary fiscal authority and Gold Standard monetary authority reached terminal velocity. The UK's reliance on deficit funding to pay unemployment welfare benefits in 1931 triggered a fiscal and monetary crisis which ended in the parliamentary repeal of the Bank of England's obligation to 'pay' paper notes with any form of metallic commodity:[39] thereby ending the classic Gold Standard in its home jurisdiction. It was replaced by a system of statutory foreign-exchange accounts that facilitated the severance of domestic and international monetary policy and would eventually form the backbone of the Bretton Woods system.[40]

Definitive histories of the Gold Standard's collapse under the weight of British welfarist fiscal policy are told by Eichengreen and Sayers:[41] the almost century-old monetary system perished in roughly 70 days between July and September 1931. During the fiscal year 1931–32, the UK Treasury was obligated to pay unemployment benefits to around 2.5 million people. This triggered a deficit in the government's social insurance system of around GBP 100 million, compared to a general-government deficit of GBP 28 million. Foreign investors were reluctant

[38] For the orthodox constitutional position regarding parliamentary control of fiscal policy around the turn of the 20th century, see Bateman, *Public Finance* (n 1) 3–7.

[39] Gold Standard (Amendment) Act 1931 (21 & 22 Geo 5 c 46) s. 1(1). That Act actually repealed the 'bullion' payment provision in the Gold Standard Act 1925 (15 & 16 Geo 5 c 29) s. 1(2), leaving in force the 'coin' payment provision in s. 1(1)(a) of that 1925 Act: 'The Bank of England, notwithstanding anything in any Act, shall not be bound to pay any note of the Bank . . . in legal coin . . . and bank notes shall not cease to be legal tender by reason that the Bank do not continue to pay bank notes in such legal coin.'

[40] As explained in part III below.

[41] Sayers, *The Bank of England* (n 14) vol. 2, 387–415; Eichengreen, *Golden Fetters* (n 14) 284–85. Given the demands of space, this abridged account omits important parts of the narrative, particularly the role of global liquidity conditions stemming from cascading sovereign-debt crises and the impact of the 1931 US economic crisis. For that detail, see Eichengreen, *Golden Fetters* (n 14) 258–80.

to lend to the UK government due to concerns that large budget deficits would spiral into inflation: any 'American loan to support the pound [was] contingent on budgetary economies in general and reductions in unemployment benefits in particular'.[42] Domestic budget cuts were proposed, including + 20 per cent of obligated unemployment benefits, but political agreement could not be reached and the (Labour) government fell. A new (coalition) government then imposed a 10 per cent reduction in unemployment welfare, which permitted the raising of some debt finance from offshore investors, mainly JP Morgan and foreign central banks.[43] Public-sector salaries were further cut,[44] including those of military employees: naval salaries would be cut by 10 per cent for higher-ranks and 25 per cent for lower-ranks. Those austerity programmes did not convince creditors and capital flight intensified as investors liquidated sterling for both gold and foreign-currency denominated assets. Five days before the Gold Standard fell, the Bank informed the Treasury there was only three weeks of gold left in Britain. Members of the British Navy began protesting, widely reported as a mutiny, against salary cuts. Massive outflows of gold accelerated as investors anticipated further deficit spending. Facing complete depletion of Britain's gold stock, the Bank of England and Treasury formulated a plan to 'go off' the Gold Standard, which was swiftly legislated.[45]

The end of the Gold Standard illustrates the intractable constitutional and economic problems which Bretton Woods was designed to avoid. The Gold Standard's essential logic required central banks to lift interest rates when faced with currency depreciation in foreign-exchange markets, with depreciation proxying for uplift in domestic prices relative to a foreign currency: viz, inflation. The system assumed that the source of depreciation would be balance of payments deficits, and the primary instrument was an increase in the central bank interest rate to attract inflows of foreign currency through investors hunting for yield and balance of payments surplus caused by lower prices in a contracting domestic economy. Currency depreciation could also stem from investor concerns about national government deficit spending. As the size and ambition of public-sector interventions grew in the Gold Standard's final few decades, that monetary system provided no meaningful response to economic plans built on new-money deficits. As Sayers explains about the Gold Standard's death in 1931: 'The biggest element in the lack of foreign confidence, which was the proximate cause of the loss of reserves, was the budget deficit, and no jumps in Bank Rate could have greatly abbreviated the political crisis.'[46]

42 Eichengreen, *Golden Fetters* (n 14) 283.

43 Including the Bank of France and the Federal Reserve Bank of New York: ibid 284–85; Sayers, *The Bank of England* (n 14) vol. 2, 394–99.

44 Sayers, *The Bank of England* (n 14) vol. 2, 404–05.

45 Gold Standard (Amendment) Act 1931 (21 & 22 Geo 5 c 46) s. 1(1).

46 Sayers, *The Bank of England* (n 14) vol. 2, 406.

Until the first decades of the 20th century, budget deficits, inflation, and currency depreciation did not present an enduring problem for the Gold Standard because the need to eliminate public deficits was widely accepted by parliamentarians, central bankers, investors, and economists.[47] The growth of Keynesianism fundamentally altered that position. Keynes' ideas taught that new-money financed deficit spending was a *sine qua non* to national economic growth:

> an increase of output cannot occur unless by the operation of one or other of three factors. Individuals must be induced to spend more out of their existing incomes, or the business world must be induced, either by increased confidence in the prospects or by a lower rate of interest, to create additional current incomes in the hands of their employees, which is what happens when either the working or the fixed capital of the country is being increased; or public authority must be called in aid to create additional current incomes through the expenditure of borrowed or printed money.
>
> In bad times the first factor cannot be expected to work on a sufficient scale. The second factor will only come in as the second wave of attack on the slump, after the tide has been turned by the expenditures of public authority. It is, therefore, only from the third factor that we can expect the initial major impulse.[48]

The full theoretical justification for that thinking can be found in the *General Theory of Employment, Interest and Money* wherein Keynes presented his theory of aggregate-demand economic management built around using fiscal and monetary authority to boost consumption propensity and the inducement to invest. Economies would expand if more people had more money in their hands to buy goods and services and to invest in new enterprises. Additional money for Keynesian aggregate-demand stimulus would come from the central bank:

> Unemployment develops, that is to say, because people want the moon;—men cannot be employed when the object of desire (i.e. money) is something which cannot be produced and the demand for which cannot be readily choked off. There is no remedy but to persuade the public that green cheese is practically the same thing and to have a green cheese factory (i.e. a central bank) under public control.[49]

[47] ibid 390: 'it had become accepted doctrine that an uncorrected budget deficit is the root of forced increase in the supply of money and depreciation of the currency, and that such depreciations become almost if not quite unmanageable. This view was not a mere academic fetish: it permeated the atmosphere in all financial markets.'

[48] Letter from John Maynard Keynes to President Roosevelt (30 December 1933) in Moggridge, *JM Keynes* (n 4) 291.

[49] John Maynard Keynes, *The General Theory of Employment, Interest and Money*, in *The Collected Works Writings of John Maynard Keynes* (Vol. 7, Macmillan 1973) 235.

In that sense, the institutional structure of Keynesianism was fundamentally incompatible with a legal monetary system that imposed an absolute block on the amount of money supplied to the government and private economy. It was, however, entirely compatible with the Bretton Woods monetary system agreed upon in the closing days of World War Two.

III. Money and State Power under the Bretton Woods System

Bretton Woods is often neutrally described as a 'gold-dollar standard' monetary system.[50] While technically correct, that label fails to explain how the Bretton Woods system facilitated the growth of Keynesian state-based economic planning. If IMF members agreed to hold the exchange value of their domestic currencies to the US dollar, and the US dollar was convertible to gold, then, *prima facie*, that system maintained the core logic of the Gold Standard: forcing central banks to respond to inflation by contractionary domestic monetary policy; trumping parliamentary fiscal policy with monetary constraints. That simple logic did play out during the post-war period as welfare and state-centric parliamentary fiscal policy reached their 20th-century zenith. How then, should we understand the constitutional balance of power between parliaments, executive governments, and central banks under the Bretton Woods system? Mann offers us no clear guidance. His decision to exclude that question from the remit of 'monetary law' had the unfortunate consequence of omitting the fascinating interaction of state institutions, money, and financial markets from his state-theoretic account of money. Ironically, the legal and institutional details of monetary authorities during Mann's career powerfully substantiate his broader scholarly claims regarding the juristic foundation of money.

From a constitutional perspective, Bretton Woods' chief innovation was the facilitation of parliamentary fiscal power to engage in new-money deficit spending despite inflationary effects. It achieved this by legally and institutionally segregating domestic and international monetary policy. Central banks were empowered to intervene in foreign-exchange markets to neutralize private-market movements against inflationary (and deflationary) fiscal policy. Impossible to implement under the Gold Standard, this segregation of exchange-rate stability and expansionary fiscal policy was achieved long before the Bretton Woods treaties via statutory foreign-exchange 'stabilization' or 'equalization' funds in the early 1930s.

[50] Michael Kumhof and others, 'Central Bank Money: Liability, Asset, or Equity of the Nation?' (2020) Cornell Legal Studies Research Paper 20–46, 5 <https://papers.ssrn.com/sol3/papers.cfm?abstract_id = 3730608> accessed 27 April 2023 (hereafter Kumhof and others, 'Central Bank Money').

A. Exchange equalization/stabilization

In the Gold Standard's wake, the UK and US legislatures created funds to be controlled by their treasuries to 'equalize' or 'stabilize' their domestic currencies in foreign-exchange markets. Those funds were designed to replace central bank interventions in currency markets to stabilize the exchange value of national currencies under the Gold Standard. In both jurisdictions, the central bank was the 'agent' of the national treasury in executing currency-exchange transactions, but formal legal control remained with the politically accountable treasury. This shifted ultimate responsibility for exchange rate stability from the central bank to the executive government, a major change from balance of institutional power created by the statutes underpinning the Gold Standard regime.

The Finance Act 1932 declared that 'There shall be established an account, to be called "the Exchange Equalisation Account", which shall be under the control of the Treasury'.[51] That fund would be used 'for checking undue fluctuations in the exchange value of sterling'.[52] The Exchange Equalisation Account would be capitalized with periodic sterling injections from the national pool of fiscal and debt receipts (the 'Consolidated Fund') but also funds 'advance[d]' by the Bank of England directly.[53] The Exchange Equalisation Account's first use was to repay the Bank of England for money lost during the 1931 Sterling Crisis.[54] Although not prescribed in statute, the Equalisation Account would be 'operated by the Bank' of England.[55] The Account's balances were closely linked to government borrowing, as sterling-denominated holdings were directly invested in UK government debt:[56] 'Substantial changes in the [Exchange Equalisation Account's] gold and foreign currency holdings would ultimately be reflected in an increase in or a reduction of its capital, by means of a sterling transfer from or to the central government.'[57] That mechanism would prevent operations to arrest sterling depreciation from impacting the domestic money supply: large purchases of sterling for foreign currency would result in the increased funding to UK sovereign-debt issues.[58] From the Gold Standard's quietus until World War Two, the Equalisation Account would

[51] Finance Act 1932 (22 & 23 Geo 5 c 25) s. 24(1).
[52] ibid s. 24(3).
[53] ibid ss 24(4) and (6).
[54] ibid s. 25.
[55] Bank of England, 'The Exchange Equalisation Account: Its Origins and Development' in *Bank of England Quarterly Review, Quarter 4* (1968) 377, 378 (hereafter Bank of England).
[56] This was expressly authorized by statute: 'The Treasury may cause any funds in the Account to be invested in securities or in the purchase of gold in such manner as they think best adapted'. Finance Act 1932 (22 & 23 Geo 5 c 25) s. 24(3).
[57] Bank of England (n 55) 379.
[58] ibid; Naef, *Exchange Rate History* (n 13) 68–69.

buy and sell sterling, gold, and foreign currencies in order to hold the exchange value of sterling within a range of the original gold convertibility price.[59]

A similar exchange 'Stabilization Fund' was created in the US by the Gold Reserve Act of 1934 to be used '[f]or the purpose of stabilizing the exchange value of the dollar' by 'deal[ing] in gold and foreign exchange and such other instruments of credit and securities'.[60] The fund was to be 'under the exclusive control of the Secretary of the Treasury, with the approval of the President, whose decisions shall be final and not be subject to review by any other officer of the United States'.[61] Like the UK, the US Stabilization Fund was linked to public debt issue via the Treasury Secretary's power to use the fund for 'the investment and reinvestment in direct obligations or the United States'.[62] Also like the UK, the US Fund would appoint the central bank as its agent: the Federal Reserve Bank of New York held that role and transacted in foreign-exchange and gold markets for the US.[63] This operational responsibility was limited: 'Central banks were to be demoted to fiscal agency status, executing instructions that finance ministers issued. Stabilization funds . . . had the resources to intervene in the foreign exchange market.'[64]

The vast difference of this regime to the Gold Standard was explained by Keynes over a decade before Bretton Woods. He wrote, '[i]n former days changes in the quantity of bank money mainly depended upon whether gold was flowing into or out of our central reserves. Today these movements, being absorbed by the Exchange Equalisation Fund, have no effect on the quantity of money.'[65] By segregating foreign-currency markets from domestic money quantities, the Exchange Equalisation Account made 'it possible to have an effective bank rate for foreign transactions different from the effective rate of domestic transactions'.[66] Later historians agreed with Keynes that the Exchange Equalisation Account was 'designed to smooth sterling fluctuations and so pave the way for a lower Bank Rate without external factors being allowed to intrude'.[67]

The US Stabilization Fund 'shared a common purpose' with the UK Exchange Equalization Account: it permitted management of foreign exchange rates through a separate mechanism to domestic monetary policy. Indeed, it was motivated to allow the same separation of domestic and international monetary policy in

[59] Bank of England (n 55) 377. Demands of space require us to skirt over the Account's activities during and after the war but see Bank of England (n 55) 382–84.

[60] Gold Reserve Act of 1934, ch. 6, § 10(a), 48 Stat 337, 341.

[61] ibid § 10(b).

[62] ibid.

[63] Anna J Schwartz, 'From Obscurity to Notoriety: A Biography of the Exchange Stabilization Fund' (1997) 29 Journal of Money, Credit and Banking 135, 142 (hereafter Schwartz, 'From Obscurity to Notoriety').

[64] Bordo, Humpage, and Schwartz, *Strained Relations* (n 14) 66.

[65] Letter from John Maynard Keynes to the Editor of the Times (21 February 1936) in Moggridge, *JM Keynes* (n 4) 379.

[66] Keynes, 'The Future of the Foreign Exchanges' (n 11) 364.

[67] Forrest H Capie, Terry C Mills, and Geoffrey E Wood, 'Debt Management and Interest Rates: The British Stock Conversion of 1932' (1986) 18 Applied Economics 1111, 1113.

opposition of the UK's first movement: 'A motive for establishing the ESF was US suspicion that the EEA was created to keep sterling from appreciating relative to the dollar. To make depreciation of the dollar that devaluation had achieved effective, the administration concluded required establishment of a fund comparable to the one the British had.'[68] More importantly, the US Stabilization Fund freed domestic monetary policy of the need to be responsive to fluctuations in the foreign exchange value of money. So much was openly acknowledged in the Federal Open Market Committee: 'the last time the [Federal Reserve] System reacted in its policy decisions primarily because of foreign developments was ... in 1931. At that time, with unemployment constantly increasing and with every element in the domestic economy calling for ease, the System responded by tightening in order to protect the gold supply.'[69] As we shall see, Bretton Woods imposed no comparable institutional constraints on central banks in the face of fiscal expansion.

B. Bretton Woods rules

The legislative innovations which grew from the Gold Standard's collapse in the early 1930s, separating international and domestic monetary policy, are identifiable from the outset of the original IMF Articles of Agreement. The Keynesian latitude afforded to domestic monetary policy would only be limited by a prohibition of malicious currency deprecation designed to injure trading partners. In one sense, the IMF was not 'Keynesian' as it represented the US plan for global monetary stability rather than the British vision which Keynes officially championed.[70] Core features of the IMF's legal framework do, however, bear an eerie similarity to Keynes' proposals, from the 1930s, for the severance of domestic and monetary policy to permit currency depreciation in the service of new-money financed fiscal stimulus.[71]

The treaty's 'purpose' provisions explicitly disconnected exchange rate stability from domestic monetary policy. Opposing the logic of the Gold Standard, the Bretton Woods system was designed 'to give confidence to members by making the Fund's resources available to them under adequate safeguard, thus providing

68 Bordo, Humpage, and Schwartz, *Strained Relations* (n 14) 60.

69 Federal Open Market Committee, Minutes of Meeting on 10 January 1961, 41, quoted in Bordo, Humpage, and Schwartz, *Strained Relations* (n 14) 129.

70 Key differences from the UK's position (championed by Keynes at Bretton Woods) were the absence of an international currency ('Bancor') and a smaller lending facility to allow countries to engage in fiscal policy: James M Boughton, 'Why White, Not Keynes? Inventing the Post-War International Monetary System' in Arie Arnon and Warren Young (eds), *The Open Economy Macromodel: Past, Present and Future* (Springer 2002) (hereafter Boughton, 'Why White, Not Keynes?').

71 For a review of the literature for and against the idea that Keynes' pre-war theorizing materially impacts policy-making, see Morrison, *England's Cross of Gold* (n 5) ch. 10.

them with opportunity to correct maladjustments in their balance of payments without resorting to measures destructive of national or international prosperity'.[72] That system would tolerate disequilibria in international payment flows in ways that would permit domestic monetary policy to stimulate inflation: the aim was to 'shorten [not "eliminate"] the duration and lessen [not "correct"] the degree of disequilibrium in the international balances of payments'.[73] Expressly invoking the language of the treasury-controlled funds which grew in the UK and US after the Gold Standard's death, the Fund would 'promote exchange stability' with the aim of avoiding 'competitive exchange devaluation', with the adjectival focus on competition bearing heavy juristic weight.[74] The core institutional link between the IMF and domestic monetary jurisdictions also assumed the existence of domestic monetary institutions with a special mandate to intervene in foreign-currency markets, rather than domestic monetary policy. Article 5, section 1 provided that 'Each member shall deal with the Fund only through its Treasury, central bank, *stabilization fund*, or other similar fiscal agency and the Fund shall deal only with or through the same agencies'.[75]

The IMF treaty contained two major operational norms for Member States: maintaining the 'par value' peg and drawing on IMF foreign-currency resources. Both preserved enormous levels of discretion for domestic central banks to facilitate expansionary fiscal policy.

The seminal IMF obligation was for members to hold the exchange rate of their currencies within a limited range of 'par value[s] ... expressed in terms of gold ... or ... the United States dollar'.[76] Members were originally required to hold the 'maximum and minimum rates for exchange transactions ... within their territories' within 1 per cent for 'spot transactions' and such 'a margin which exceeds [1 per cent] [that] the Fund considers reasonable' for forwards.[77] This obligation required monetary authorities (equalization funds, treasuries, or central banks) to intervene in their domestic currency-exchange market to hold their currencies within stable ranges. Par values could be changed on proposal by a member 'to correct a fundamental disequilibrium': once changed, the exchange stability obligations would attach to the new par value.[78] Such proposal did not require the IMF's approval within 10 per cent of the initial par value. Changes between 20 per cent and + 30 per cent would be considered by the Fund with a view to 'concurring' or

[72] Articles of Agreement of the International Monetary Fund (Washington, 27 December 1945) 39 UNTS 40 (IMF Articles of Agreement) Art. 1(v).
[73] ibid Art. 1(vi).
[74] ibid Art. 1(iii).
[75] Emphasis added.
[76] IMF Articles of Agreement, Art. 4(1). Initial par values for most IMF members were set in 1947–48: International Monetary Fund, *Annual Report* (1949) 25. These were set in both gold prices and US dollars: International Monetary Fund, *Annual Report* (1947) 72–77.
[77] IMF Articles of Agreement, Art. 4(3).
[78] ibid Art. 4(5)(a).

'objecting' to the change. The Fund was required to 'concur in a proposed change' if it was satisfied that a proposed change of par value was necessary to 'correct a fundamental disequilibrium'. Critically, the Fund was prohibited from objecting 'to a proposed change because of the domestic social or political policies of the member proposing the change'.[79]

The second major IMF norm concerned access to the Fund's resources. The Fund's central transactional function was 'supplying a member, on the initiative of such member, with the currency of another member in exchange for gold or for the currency of the member desiring to make the purchase'.[80] Each IMF member was 'entitled to buy the currency of another member from the Fund in exchange for its own currency' on several conditions.[81] The main evaluative condition was that those purchases were used for domestic operations needed to maintain the par value peg.[82] The quantitative limit set the volume of access to IMF credit by reference to a debtor member's initial quota on several conditions:

> The proposed purchase would not cause the Fund's holdings of the purchasing member's currency to increase by more than twenty-five percent of its quota during the period of twelve months ending on the date of the purchase nor to exceed two hundred percent of its quota, but the twenty-five percent limitation shall apply only to the extent that the Fund's holdings of the member's currency have been brought above seventy-five percent of its quota if they had been below that amount.[83]

This quantitative formula limited access to the Fund resources by reference to each member's 'quota': representing members' share of world trade. This quantitative limit could be 'waived' at the Fund's 'discretion ... especially in the case of members with a record of avoiding large or continuous use of the Fund's resources'.[84]

Both core elements of the IMF scheme had highly discretionary elements which would permit very extensive monetary expansion for 'domestic social and political policies'. Although the IMF's legal framework and institutional practices would develop substantially between 1944 and 1971,[85] this basic structure, with its inbuilt accommodation of Keynesian monetary policy, remained largely intact. The 'secondary role of inflation prevention'[86] was given some normative weight via the

[79] ibid Art. 4(5)(f).
[80] ibid Art. 5(2).
[81] ibid Art. 5(3)(a).
[82] ibid Art. 5(3)(a)(i). Technically, the funds could be used for any of the 'purposes' of the Fund.
[83] ibid Art. 5(3)(a)(ii).
[84] ibid Art. 5(4).
[85] See, e.g., JK Horsefield, *The International Monetary Fund 1945–1965: Twenty Years of International Monetary Cooperation* (IMF 1969) vol. 1.
[86] Boughton, 'Why White, Not Keynes?' (n 70) 86.

assumption that the US dollar would remain convertible into gold at nominated par value. This assumption required certain, pre-Bretton Woods, legal machinery to remain in existence, particularly the legal framework by which the US Treasury would sell gold to foreign purchasers.[87] That mixture of US Congressional and Executive legislation provided the ultimate back-stop to the expansion of public and private credit globally. It was not indefinitely sustainable. The build-up of US dollars outside the US forced the US to choose radical fiscal contraction or removal of the gold-anchor at the base of the Bretton Woods system of pegged exchange rates.[88] Rather than adjust domestic fiscal policy, the US political branches revoked the essential legal foundation of the system.[89]

C. Running the Bretton Woods system

A complete understanding of how Bretton Woods succeeded in severing international and domestic monetary policy requires a brief review of operational details. We are aided in this task by Naef's historical review of British exchange rate policy and Bordo, Humpage, and Schwartz on US foreign exchange measures.[90]

In both jurisdictions, foreign exchange interventions were executed by central banks as agents of treasuries using the exchange equalization/stabilization accounts set up in 1932–33.[91] Both the Bank of England and the Federal Reserve understood their foreign-currency operations as distinct to domestic monetary policy. The UK central bank:

> treated fundamental economic variables as exogenous to its intervention decisions as it could not adjust fundamentals. [Bank currency traders] could do no

[87] Milton Friedman and Anna Schwartz, *A Monetary History of the United States 1867–1960* (Princeton University Press 1963) ch. 8; Bordo, Humpage, and Schwartz, *Strained Relations* (n 14) 57–61; Kenneth W Dam, 'From the Gold Clause Cases to the Gold Commission: A Half Century of American Monetary Law' (1983) 50 U Chi L Rev 504 (hereafter Dam, 'Gold Clause Cases to the Gold Commission').

[88] Michael D Bordo, 'The Operation and Demise of the Bretton Woods System; 1958 to 1971' (National Bureau of Economic Research Working Paper 23189, 2017) <https://www.nber.org/papers/w23189> accessed 28 April 2023.

[89] Dam, 'Gold Clause Cases to the Gold Commission' (n 87) 528–29.

[90] See Naef, *Exchange Rate History* (n 13); Bordo, Humpage, and Schwartz, *Strained Relations* (n 14). Limitations of space require a selective review of these sources: both of which should be consulted to understand the full intricacy and temporal changes in UK and US exchange rate interventions under Bretton Woods. An accessible introduction to some of those complexities can be found in Michael D Bordo, Eric Monnet, and Alain Naef, 'The Gold Pool (1961–1968) and the Fall of the Bretton Woods System: Lessons for Central Bank Cooperation' (National Bureau of Economic Research Working Paper 24016, 2017) <https://www.nber.org/papers/w24016> accessed 28 April 2023 (hereafter Bordo, Monnet, and Naef, 'The Gold Pool').

[91] In the US, the Federal Reserve Bank of New York also executed foreign exchange interventions on its 'own account' from 1961: Bordo, Humpage, and Schwartz, *Strained Relations* (n 14) 137–48.

> more than try to influence the Treasury or government. The Bank did not consider devaluation or changes in interest rates as options. [Bank currency traders] were often forced to intervene in spite of the fundamental value of the currency.[92]

Similarly, the US central bank's interventions in foreign-currency markets were conditioned on the proviso that 'they did not interfere with the domestic objectives of monetary policy'.[93] There was some evidence of domestic tightening 'solely for international considerations', but it was marginal.[94]

The Bank of England's 'first goal' of foreign-currency interventions was 'to keep the exchange rate within the Bretton Woods bands' while the 'second goal' was to 'avoid "undue fluctuations in the exchange value of sterling" '.[95] The US operated in a similar way, but was required to focus on maintaining the price of gold and the total volume of dollars outside the United States to safeguard the US's gold stock, given the convertibility of dollars into gold by foreign central banks.[96]

Executing those goals required market operations with private commercial counterparties and foreign central banks. Naef details how these occurred at the Bank of England in 1961:[97] 'intervention orders were given during business hours by telephone to four retail or commercial banks: Westminster, Lloyds, National Provincial and Société Générale. Westminster received the bulk of the orders. The goal was either to prevent the exchange rate from depreciating too quickly or to encourage or amplify an appreciation.' The Bank of England's foreign-exchange dealers:

> feared both the opening of the market in Paris in the morning and the opening of the New York market at 3 pm. The Bank of England usually gave sterling a final push in the last half-hour of trading. After that, the Bank handed over the responsibility for intervention to the New York Fed in the evening. The Fed's operations were monitored by a 'principal' at the Bank of England. The principal stayed in touch with New York until the market closed late in the evening London time.[98]

The Bank of England predominately used spot transactions while the Federal Reserve Bank of New York used forward transactions to intervene in currency markets.[99] For spot transactions designed to push the exchange rate of the domestic currency (say, sterling) upwards against a foreign currency (say, the dollar), the

[92] Naef, *Exchange Rate History* (n 13) 50.
[93] Bordo, Humpage, and Schwartz, *Strained Relations* (n 14) 138.
[94] ibid 130.
[95] Naef, *Exchange Rate History* (n 13) 47, quoting Finance Act 1932 (22 & 23 Geo 5 c 25) s. 24(3).
[96] This required complex multi-lateral transactions with foreign central banks and domestic-currency dealers: Bordo, Humpage, and Schwartz, *Strained Relations* (n 14) 133–37, 151–60.
[97] Naef, *Exchange Rate History* (n 13) 49.
[98] ibid.
[99] ibid 51; Bordo, Humpage, and Schwartz, *Strained Relations* (n 14) 133.

central bank would sell dollars for sterling until the domestic currency was trading safely in the Bretton Woods range. Forward transactions were more complex and involved buying and selling currencies forward at a premium over spot prices: as forward prices on a foreign currency (say, Deutschmark, 'DM') moved away towards the top of its par value range (say, with USD), the US central bank would sell DM forward until spot and forward rates moved back within range.[100] Both techniques required large reserves of foreign currency, which could be obtained through purchases on private markets, from swap agreements with foreign central banks/treasuries, and from the IMF under Article 3.[101]

IV. Conclusion: Balance of Constitutional Power under Bretton Woods

While central banks had been intervening to hold their currencies within par value ranges from the 1940s, the Bretton Woods system only became wholly operational with the capital account convertibility of the secondary reserve currency, sterling, in 1958.[102] Within three years, North American and European central banks were cooperating to manipulate the world's gold price to prevent its appreciation against the par value of the system's anchor currency: the US dollar. The trigger for potentially de-pegging movement of gold prices against the dollar was expansionary fiscal policy in the US, as was candidly explained by a commodity dealer corresponding with the Federal Reserve:

> [currency speculators] on the Continent and, in particular Switzerland … seem to have decided that Senator Kennedy was going to be elected. They considered that this would bring about more inflation in your Country [the United States] and, as a result, your balance of payments would suffer further. They considered, therefore, that a devaluation of the dollar in the first half of next year was a real possibility...[103]

Those traders began dumping dollars for gold: locking in effective short positions against the dollar they predicted would devalue. Central banks from Europe and America reacted to defend the Bretton Woods system by pooling their gold in the

[100] See Bordo, Humpage, and Schwartz, *Strained Relations* (n 14) 133–37 for detailed examples of forward transactions to hold par values in range.

[101] Domestic currency could always be procured from the central bank, but complex arrangements existed in some countries to draw domestic currency for exchange-equalization operations from other statutory 'funds': for a discussion of the complexities in the UK and US, see Naef, *Exchange Rate History* (n 13) 68–69; Schwartz, 'From Obscurity to Notoriety' (n 63) 145–46.

[102] See, Naef, *Exchange Rate History* (n 13) 6, 92–95 for the different historical definitions of 'convertibility'.

[103] ibid 103.

Bank of England to sell into the UK's gold market when excess gold demand threatened the exchange value of the US dollar.[104] The transactional logic was the same as currency-exchange interventions: when gold prices moved past the par value target ($35) with the USD, the Bank of England (as agent for other Gold Pool central banks) would sell gold into the market for dollars.[105]

The Gold Pool was a stop-gap which was eventually broken by another fiscal-monetary crisis triggered by UK welfare-state spending in the latter 1960s: the 'Sterling Crisis 1964–1967',[106] which we shall explore shortly. It was also an attempt to resolve the 'trilemma of international finance', which indicated that nations could choose (only) two of three policy postures regarding their currency: 'free capital flows; a fixed exchange rate; and monetary policy independence.'[107] If capital could flow freely, then speculators would respond to expansionary monetary policy by running short positions against the depreciating currency which would ultimately de-peg it from the fixed exchange rate to currencies of more contractionary monetary policy zones. If capital controls existed, that mode of arbitrage would be unavailable and currency issuers would have more freedom to maintain relatively expansionary policy with a fixed exchange rate. If multiple countries stapled their domestic economic policies, then expansionary policy would not necessarily trigger depreciation (at least not within the harmonized nations) and the arbitrage opportunity would be largely neutralized, thus allowing the fixed exchange rate to operate.

While that trilemma was first popularized in 1958, the Bretton Woods system proved sufficiently flexible to accommodate all three features of economic policy for a relatively long period of time.[108] Compared to modern monetary policy phases, the 13-year life of Bretton Woods is roughly comparable to the periods of 'conventional' interest-rate setting in the US and UK (1990s[109] to 2008) and the following periods of 'unconventional' quantitative easing (2009–2022). The unique constitutional feature of Bretton Woods was its capacity to allow parliamentary fiscal policy relative freedom while also maintaining a system of fixed exchange rates and a formal monetary peg to gold. This constitutional flexibility can be seen in the episode which would 'eventually end some 150 years of (sometimes interrupted) gold-backed systems':[110] the 1967 sterling devaluation.

104 Bordo, Monnet, and Naef, 'The Gold Pool' (n 90).

105 Before the Gold Pool interventions, the price of gold in London moved as high as $38, but central bank gold sales forced the price back within 1 per cent of the par value: Naef, *Exchange Rate History* (n 13) 102, fig. 7.1.

106 I follow Naef, *Exchange Rate History* (n 13) ch. 9, to date the episode in this way.

107 ibid 92. An illuminating and critical account of this trilemma is contained in Michael D Bordo and Robert N McCauley, 'Triffin: Dilemma or Myth?' (Bank of International Settlements Working Paper 684, 2017) <https://www.bis.org/publ/work684.htm> accessed 28 April 2023.

108 Bordo and McCauley (n 107).

109 Ulrich Bindseil, *Monetary Policy Implementation: Theory, Past, and Present* (OUP 2004) 203. Different accounts will date interest-rate settings in different ways.

110 Naef, *Exchange Rate History* (n 13) 148.

A. Sterling Crisis 1964–1967

Between 1964 and 1967, the secondary currency of the Bretton Woods system, sterling, experienced successive crises that led to a prominent 'fundamental equilibrium' devaluation under the IMF Articles.

The first signs of stress began shortly before the election of the UK centre-left Labour party. Currency traders began selling sterling for dollars in anticipation of depreciation and devaluation caused by 'weak fundamentals'[111] and an 'over-stimulative budget'.[112] Within two weeks of the election victory, the Bank of England was buying sterling for dollars at eight times their historical daily average.[113] After the government's first welfarist budget was introduced, the run on sterling intensified. This had contagious effects on both IMF anchor-monetary units: 'A downward shock to the price of sterling tended to make gold appreciate against the dollar. A shock to sterling led to global instability. This led investors to withdraw from the dollar and invest in gold, which was seen to be a safe haven. This in turn put pressure on US gold reserves, adding to the crisis.'[114] To staunch contagion, foreign central banks, particularly the Federal Reserve, lent large quantities of their local currencies to the Bank of England to allow it to maintain par values.[115] The political branches implemented successive 'stop-go' economic policies of fiscal constraint and expansion.[116]

A point of formal systemic crisis was reached in November 1967 upon the UK's invocation of its right under Article 4(5) of the IMF Articles to propose that the par value of sterling with the dollar be changed to correct a 'fundamental disequilibrium'.[117] A 14.3 per cent reduction against the dollar was proposed. The IMF reviewed the proposal and concurred. Sterling's par value with the US dollar changed from £1:US$2.80 to £1:US$2.40. Fourteen countries with 'close economic relationships with the United Kingdom or severe payment difficulties' also devalued.[118] The UK also received a massive credit-line from the IMF under a US$1.4 billion stand-by agreement to establish 'confidence in the new parity for Sterling': it was fully drawn in June 1968.[119] This injection of dollars was the IMF's largest operation for

[111] ibid 133.

[112] Charles A Coombs, *The Arena of International Finance* (Wiley 1976) 112.

[113] Naef, *Exchange Rate History* (n 13) 134.

[114] ibid 144.

[115] Michael Bordo, Ronald MacDonald, and Michael J Oliver, 'Sterling in Crisis: 1964–1967' (National Bureau of Economic Research Working Paper 14657, 2009) <https://www.nber.org/papers/w14657> accessed 28 April 2023; Naef, *Exchange Rate History* (n 13) 170–79. The extent of the foreign loans was not disclosed to avoid further pressure on sterling.

[116] Bordo, MacDonald, and Oliver (n 113) 5–7; Jim Tomlinson, *The Labour Governments 1964–70, Volume 3: Economic Policy* (Manchester University Press 2004).

[117] International Monetary Fund, *Annual Report* (1968) 17, 97.

[118] ibid 8.

[119] ibid 101.

the fiscal year and used the UK's entire quota.[120] It was increased by another US$1 billion or so in 1969.[121]

The IMF recorded the driver of those changes as 'massive speculative pressure built up against sterling in June and July'.[122] Currency traders were selling large volumes of pounds for dollars because of inflation caused by fiscal and monetary policy. Throughout 1966, public-sector employment and wages rose while central bank credit costs dropped. Despite inflationary pressures and capital flight, Bank Rate was lowered from 7 per cent to 5.5 per cent in the 12 months leading up to official devaluation.[123] A short-term fiscal austerity programme was implemented (where public-sector incomes were brought to a 'standstill'), but prices, employment, and wages grew immediately upon its cessation.[124] This triggered 'a large outflow of funds from London' but 'the British authorities did not raise Bank Rate'. The UK 'sustained large and growing losses of external revenue' and central bank interest rates were raised in dire straits, two weeks before devaluation.[125] Eventually the store of dollars in the Exchange Equalization Account dwindled such that the Bank of England could not defend sterling's par value.

The solution was the combination of a change in par value and massive injections of IMF foreign-currency credit. Post-devaluation and the IMF loan, parliamentary fiscal policy was temporarily tightened. Austerity measures were immediately imposed: 'The main cuts were made in proposed spending on education, health and welfare, housing, and roads. The result was to reduce planned expenditure in 1968/69 by about £300 million and in 1969/70 by over £400 million.'[126] Taxes were raised: 'Higher duties were imposed on alcoholic beverages, tobacco, and mineral oil. Moreover, purchase taxes and vehicle excise taxes were increased, as were the rates for the Selective Employment Tax. The total revenue from all increases in taxation was estimated at nearly £800 million in 1968/69 and at more than £900 million in a full year.'[127]

Monetary policy did not match that fiscal restraint. Concurrently with fiscal austerity, Bank Rate was lowered from 8 per cent to 7.5 per cent, mainly to boost confidence. The Treasury and Bank of England tried to persuade British banks to reduce credit extension, but during the episode bank credit to the private sector rose by some £750 million.[128] In the full year following devaluation, credit extensions to the private sector grew by £590 million, against £530 million in 1967. Public debt fell by £385m, leaving a net increase in total credit created. The 'substantial

[120] International Monetary Fund, *Annual Report* (1969) 34.
[121] ibid 76.
[122] International Monetary Fund, *Annual Report* (1968) 50.
[123] ibid 51.
[124] ibid.
[125] ibid.
[126] International Monetary Fund, *Annual Report* (1969) 74.
[127] ibid 74–5.
[128] ibid 75.

expansionary impact of these domestic factors' was 'partially offset by the external [trade] deficit'. Sterling-denominated money did, however, increase by 6.5 per cent fuelling further sterling devaluation.[129]

B. Constitutional consequences of devaluation

Economically, the 1967 devaluation was a calamity from which the Bretton Woods system would not recover: it ended the Gold Pool and laid the foundations for the Nixon Shock which formally terminated the global system of fixed exchange rates and the dollar–gold peg.[130] Thereby, it can be seen as a failed moment in the UK's economic and monetary history,[131] although whether that failure exceeded the miscalculations of economic policy which led to the Global Financial Crisis is a question deserving of deep study.

Rather than answer that broader question, our concern here has been to understand the balance of constitutional power under the Bretton Woods system. The 1967 sterling devaluation clearly illustrates the constitutional dynamics of that system of global fixed exchange rates: parliamentary voting for expansionary fiscal policy forced (domestic and foreign) monetary authorities to adjust their policy postures and, ultimately, placed the entire system of fixed exchange rates in jeopardy. Those dynamics placed parliaments at the apex of economic and financial policy, leaving central banks in the inferior constitutional role of policy-takers, not policy-makers. When moments of crisis were reached, solutions were political and compromissory, rather than financial and punitive. While official devaluation was a political embarrassment, it did not trigger vast constraints on parliamentary fiscal power, nor did it produce a sudden failure of international cooperation by other monetary authorities.

Compared to what came before, this balance of constitutional power was a transformation. It reversed the constitutional logic of the Gold Standard and facilitated Keynesian economic policies. Novel and cooperative institutional norms and practices were created which were placed under heavy stress and eventually collapsed. For this volume, that trajectory proves Mann right: the unique powers and privileges of central banks should be seen as part of constitutional law. The manner in which those powers are legally structured will fundamentally change the balance of power within the constitutional state. Mann lived and wrote through periods of constitutional history that demonstrated the vastly different ways that monetary and fiscal power can be structured. His professional life saw radically

[129] ibid 76.

[130] See Naef, *Exchange Rate History* (n 13) chs 10–11 and literature cited therein.

[131] Alternative interpretations of the episode emphasizing the impact of international financial developments have been proposed: Scott Newton, 'The Sterling Devaluation of 1967, the International Economy and Post-War Social Democracy' (2010) 125 English Historical Review 912.

different periods of parliamentary constraint and empowerment. After his retirement, the balance of constitutional power changed again. The institution of central bank independence and inflation targeting sought to reverse the balance of power achieved under the Gold Standard, with parliaments subjected to financial constraints imposed by central banks. This model of 'monetary dominance' was clearly explained by central bank officials in the 1980s:

> imagine that monetary policy dominates fiscal policy. Under this coordination scheme, the monetary authority independently sets monetary policy by, for example, announcing growth rates for base money for the current period and all future periods. By doing this, the monetary authority determines the amount of revenue it will supply the fiscal authority through seigniorage. The fiscal authority then faces the constraints imposed by the demand for bonds, since it must set its budgets so that any deficits can be financed by a combination of the seignorage chosen by the monetary authority and bond sales to the public.[132]

Once implemented, that balance of power between parliamentary (fiscal) and technocratic (monetary) institutions correlated with the resolution of one type of disfunction left by the Bretton Woods system: domestic inflation and exchange-rate instability. Eventually, this re-configuration of monetary authority broke under disfunction. In each period, Mann's dictum, declaring central banking within constitutional law, was substantiated. Our historical review of the constitutional aspects of monetary authority does, however, draw into question the theoretical completeness of Mann's 'legal aspect' of money. Both fiscal and monetary institutions (treasuries and central banks) are creatures of legal power. The instruments they issue (sovereign-debt securities and money) have drawn their existence from statutory authority for centuries. The commercial financial institutions that buy debt and borrow new-money rely on those state institutions for their profitable operations over all time horizons. Depending on the structure of those legal institutions, both states and markets will behave in fundamentally different ways. Surely a deep consideration of that collection of legal and constitutional facts would have supported Mann's proximate goal to analyse the legal aspect of money and his ultimate theoretical support for the state theory of money. Forthcoming generations of Mann (and 'money') scholars will, no doubt, pick up where the giant of 20th-century monetary law set off.[133]

[132] Thomas J Sargent and Neil Wallace, 'Some Unpleasant Monetarist Arithmetic' (1981) 5(3) Federal Reserve Bank of Minneapolis Quarterly Review 1, 1–2.

[133] The foundation stones have already been laid: Desan, *Making Money* (n 25); Robert Hockett and Saule Omarova, 'The Finance Franchise' (2017) 102 Cornell Law Review 1143; Rosa Lastra, *International Financial and Monetary Law* (OUP 2006); Simon Gleeson, *The Legal Concept of Money* (OUP 2018); Kumhof and others, 'Central Bank Money' (n 50); Will Bateman and Jason Allen, 'The Law of Central Bank Reserve Creation' (2022) 85 Modern Law Review 401; Will Bateman, 'The Law of Monetary Finance under Unconventional Monetary Policy' (2001) 41 Oxford Journal of Legal Studies 929.

Bibliography

Ackerman B, *We the People, Volume 2: Transformations* (Bellknap Press 2000)

Allen WA, *The Bank of England and the Government Debt: Operations in the Gilt-Edged Market, 1928–1972* (CUP 2018)

Bank of England, 'The Exchange Equalisation Account: Its Origins and Development' in *Bank of England Quarterly Review, Quarter 4* (1968) 377

Bateman W, *Public Finance and Parliamentary Constitutionalism* (CUP 2020)

Bateman W, 'The Law of Monetary Finance under Unconventional Monetary Policy' (2001) 41 Oxford Journal of Legal Studies 929

Bateman W and Allen J, 'The Law of Central Bank Reserve Creation' (2022) 85 Modern Law Review 401

Best J, *The Limits of Transparency: Ambiguity and the History of International Finance* (Cornell University Press 2005)

Bindseil U, *Monetary Policy Implementation: Theory, Past, and Present* (OUP 2004)

Bordo MD, 'The Operation and Demise of the Bretton Woods System: 1958 to 1971' (National Bureau of Economic Research Working Paper 23189, 2017) <https://www.nber.org/papers/w23189> accessed 28 April 2023

Bordo MD, Humpage OF, and Schwartz AJ, *Strained Relations: US Foreign-Exchange Operations and Monetary Policy in the Twentieth Century* (University of Chicago Press 2015)

Bordo MD, MacDonald R, and Oliver MJ, 'Sterling in Crisis: 1964–1967' (National Bureau of Economic Research Working Paper 14657, 2009) <https://www.nber.org/papers/w14657> accessed 28 April 2023

Bordo MD and McCauley RN, 'Triffin: Dilemma or Myth?' (Bank of International Settlements Working Paper 684, 2017) <https://www.bis.org/publ/work684.htm> accessed 28 April 2023

Bordo MD, Monnet E, and Naef A, 'The Gold Pool (1961–1968) and the Fall of the Bretton Woods System: Lessons for Central Bank Cooperation' (National Bureau of Economic Research Working Paper 24016, 2017) <https://www.nber.org/papers/w24016> accessed 28 April 2023

Boughton JM, 'Why White, Not Keynes? Inventing the Post-War International Monetary System' in Arie Arnon and Warren Young (eds), *The Open Economy Macromodel: Past, Present and Future* (Springer 2002)

Boyer-Xambeu MT, Gillard L, and Deleplace G, 'Régimes monétaires, points d'or et serpent bimétallique de 1770 à 1870' (1994) 45 Revue Économique 1139

Capie FH, Mills TC, and Wood GE, 'Debt Management and Interest Rates: The British Stock Conversion of 1932' (1986) 18 Applied Economics 1111

Clapham J, *The Bank of England: A History* (CUP 1944)

Committee on Currency and Foreign Exchanges After the War, *First Interim Report* (Cmd 9182, 1919)

Coombs CA, *The Arena of International Finance* (Wiley 1976)

Dam KW, 'From the Gold Clause Cases to the Gold Commission: A Half Century of American Monetary Law' (1983) 50 U Chi L Rev 504

Desan C, *Making Money: Coin, Currency, and the Coming of Capitalism* (OUP 2014)

Dicey AV, *The Law of the Constitution* (JWF Alllison ed., OUP 2013)

Eichengreen B, *Golden Fetters: The Gold Standard and the Great Depression, 1919–1939* (OUP 1996)

Federal Open Market Committee, Minutes of Meeting on 10 January 1961 <https://www.federalreserve.gov/monetarypolicy/fomchistorical1961.htm> accessed 17 November 2023

Friedman M and Schwartz A, *A Monetary History of the United States 1867–1960* (Princeton University Press 1963)
Hockett RC and Omarova ST, 'The Finance Franchise' (2017) 102 Cornell Law Review 1143
Horsefield JK, *The International Monetary Fund 1945–1965: Twenty Years of International Monetary Cooperation* (IMF 1969)
Hotson AC, *Respectable Banking: The Search for Stability in London's Money and Credit Markets since 1695* (CUP 2017)
Hume D, *Essays, Moral, Political, and Literary* (first published 1758, Longmans, Green and Co. 1889)
International Monetary Fund, *Annual Report* (1968)
International Monetary Fund, *Annual Report* (1969)
Jones HW, 'The Rule of Law and the Welfare State' (1958) 58 Columbia LR 143
Kumhof M and others, 'Central Bank Money: Liability, Asset, or Equity of the Nation?' (2020) Cornell Legal Studies Research Paper 20–46 <https://papers.ssrn.com/sol3/papers.cfm?abstract_id=3730608> accessed 27 April 2023
Lastra RM, *International Financial and Monetary Law* (OUP 2006)
McKay A and Reis R, 'Optimal Automatic Stabilizers' (National Bureau of Economic Research Working Paper 22359, 2016) <https://www.nber.org/papers/w22359> accessed 27 April 2023
Mann FA, *The Legal Aspect of Money* (4th edn, Clarendon Press 1982)
Moggridge D (ed.), *The Collected Writings of John Maynard Keynes* (Macmillan 1971–89)
Monnet E, *Controlling Credit: Central Banking and the Planned Economy in Postwar France, 1948–1973* (CUP 2018)
Morrison JA, *England's Cross of Gold: Keynes, Churchill and the Governance of Economic Beliefs* (Cornell University Press 2021)
Naef A, *An Exchange Rate History of the United Kingdom: 1945–1992* (CUP 2022)
Neal L, *The Rise of Financial Capitalism: International Capital Markets in the Age of Reason* (CUP 1990)
Neal L, 'A Tale of Two Revolutions: International Capital Flows 1789–1819' (1991) 43 Bulletin of Economic Research 57
Newton S, 'The Sterling Devaluation of 1967, the International Economy and Post-War Social Democracy' (2010) 125 English Historical Review 912
O'Brien PK and Palma N, 'Danger to the Old Lady of Threadneedle Street? The Bank Restriction Act and the Regime Shift to Paper Money, 1797–1821' (2020) 24 European Review of Economic History 390
Pound R, 'The Rule of Law and the Modern Social Welfare State' (1953) 7 Vanderbilt LR 1
Sargent TJ and Wallace N, 'Some Unpleasant Monetarist Arithmetic' (1981) 5(3) Federal Reserve Bank of Minneapolis Quarterly Review 1
Sayers RS, *The Bank of England: 1891–1944* (CUP 1976)
Schwartz AJ, 'From Obscurity to Notoriety: A Biography of the Exchange Stabilization Fund' (1997) 29 Journal of Money, Credit and Banking 135
Sraffa P (ed.), *The Works and Correspondence of David Ricardo* (Liberty Fund 2005)
Select Committee appointed to Inquire into the Cause of the High Price of Gold Bullion and to take into consideration the State of the Circulating Medium and of the Exchanges Between Great Britain and Foreign Parts, *Report* (reprinted for J. Johnson and Co. 1810)
Tanzi V and Schuknecht L, *Public Spending in the 20th Century: A Global Perspective* (CUP 2000)
Thornton H, *An Enquiry into the Nature and Effects of the Paper Credit of Great Britain* (James Humphreys 1802)
Tomlinson J, *The Labour Governments 1964–70, Volume 3: Economic Policy* (Manchester University Press 2004)

12

El Aspecto Legal del Dinero

FA Mann's Impact in Latin America

María Emilia Buccella, Rosa María Lastra, and Jason Grant Allen

I. Introduction

FA Mann was the pre-eminent monetary lawyer of his generation. He defined and organized the field of monetary law, notoriously combining a logical approach embedded in the rich German legal and philosophical tradition to the case-oriented and practical common law tradition of his adopted home jurisdiction in England.

This chapter seeks to understand the impact of his magnum opus in Latin America. In particular, the chapter seeks to: (i) contextualize Mann's work by explaining the historical background of its translation into Spanish and the importance of these developments to the evolution of monetary law (and monetary theory) in the 20th century, particularly with reference to the problem of exchange controls in times of crisis; (ii) understand the main implications of FA Mann's work, with emphasis on the literature on exchange controls and sovereign debt; and (iii) investigate the impact of *The Legal Aspect of Money* in the disciplines of law and economics in the Latin American region, and in the Spanish-speaking world in general.

Exploring the dissemination and impact of *The Legal Aspect of Money* in Latin America also provides a historical context within which to critically assess Mann's

María Emilia Buccella, Rosa María Lastra, and Jason Grant Allen, El Aspecto Legal del Dinero In: *FA Mann*. Edited by: Jason Grant Allen and Gerhard Dannemann, Oxford University Press. DOI: 10.1093/oso/9780198881452.003.0013

weighty legacy in monetary law. His approach to the law of exchange controls and, in particular, to the interpretation of Article VIII(2)(b) of the International Monetary Fund (IMF) Articles of Association provides some insight into his perspective on the law of money, particularly its international dimension, and his theoretical (pre)commitments. In this context, archival materials including correspondence regarding the publication of the Spanish translation and correspondence with other international monetary lawyers (such as Sir Joseph Gold of the IMF) come to life.

II. Historical Background: Actors, Institutions, and Economic Realities

FA Mann maintained a fluid dialogue with various Latin American jurists and legal specialists throughout his prolific career.[1] The story of the Spanish translation of FA Mann's magnum opus began in 1981, thanks to a letter sent on 22 May of that same year by Fernando Alejandro Vázquez Pando, a member of the Editorial Committee of the Mexican journal *Jurídica*,[2] who invited Mann to participate in the publication of a special issue to commemorate the journal's 30th anniversary. In this letter, Vázquez Pando expressed his interest in case studies involving foreign public law and their similarities and/or differences with respect to cases typically considered under the orbit of private international law.[3] In a cordial reply about two months later, Mann declined the invitation on the basis that prior commitments would not allow him to undertake this work.[4] Both agreed, however, on the possibility of future collaborations.[5]

The dialogue between Vázquez Pando and FA Mann was resumed towards the end of the following year, a short time after Mexico declared, in August 1982, the moratorium on its foreign debt, which marked the commencement of an international debt crisis that quickly expanded throughout Latin America.[6] In a letter

[1] Among them Andrés A Aramburu-Menchaca, Antonio Boggiano, Emilio J Cárdenas, Gonzalo Parra-Aranguren, Julio E Curutchet and Julio C Otaegui. He regularly met Julio E Curutchet in the MOCOMILA meetings, of which Mann was original rapporteur and Curutchet a member. For an early history of MOCOMILA, see <https://www.mocomila.org/about/history.pdf> written by Lee Buchheit, accessed 6 June 2023.

[2] Jurídica is a scientific journal edited by the Law Department of the Iberoamericana University, Mexico. It was born as a yearbook in 1969, but most recently it became a semi-annual journal. See <https://juridica.ibero.mx/index.php/juridi≥ accessed 6 June 2023.

[3] Fernando A Vázquez Pando to FA Mann (Mann estate, NLMann_0837 41-100, 22 May 1981).

[4] FA Mann to Fernando A Vázquez Pando (Mann estate, NLMann_0837 41-100, 17 July 1981).

[5] Fernando A Vázquez Pando to FA Mann (Mann estate, NLMann_0837 41-100, 25 August 1981); FA Mann to Fernando A Vázquez Pando (Mann estate, NLMann_0837 41-100, 16 September 1981).

[6] See José Antonio Ocampo and others, *La crisis latinoamericana de la deuda desde la perspectiva histórica* (CEPAL 2014) (hereafter Ocampo and others, *La crisis latinoamericana*). For a comprehensive post-mortem analysis, see Karin Lissakers, *Banks, Borrowers and the Establishment: A Revisionist Account of the International Debt Crisis* (Basic Books 1991) (hereafter Lissakers, *Banks, Borrowers and the Establishment*).

dated 22 November 1982, Vázquez Pando highlighted the growing importance that the legal aspects of money and exchange controls subjects were acquiring in Mexico in the face of the crisis. This, together with the scarcity of Mexican legal doctrine on monetary issues, motivated the interest of the publishers of *Jurídica* to incorporate a special section on the legal aspects of money.

In particular, their intention was to include a work of FA Mann on subjects related to the international monetary system, more specifically the IMF and its structure, purposes, and conditionalities. They also suggested the possibility of including a Spanish translation of one of his most recently published articles on monetary matters in case Mann was not available to write an article for that issue.[7]

In response, at the beginning of December, Mann offered the Committee the translation of an article published in the *Swiss Yearbook of International Law* in 1980 on payment challenges associated with foreign money liabilities. He also proposed the translation of one of the chapters of the fourth edition of *The Legal Aspect of Money*, which had been published by Oxford University Press in April 1981. The tumultuous history of the international monetary system in the 20th century (World War I, Gold Standard and its demise, devaluations and protectionism, German reparations and the role of the Bank for International Settlements, World War II), the establishment of the IMF with a dual gold-dollar standard (the par value regime), and the collapse of this par value regime—de facto in 1973 when the so-called gold window was closed, *de iure* in 1978 with the coming into force of the Second Amendment to the IMF Articles of Agreement—had given rise to a whole set of legislation and legal problems, concerning matters such as currency valuation and exchange controls, as well as a body of international treaty law. Naturally, FA Mann had turned his attention to these matters from the second edition (1954) of *The Legal Aspect of Money*.[8]

It is noticeable, however, how Mann's enthusiasm increases as the letter progresses. In the last paragraph of it, and somewhat as a farewell, the lawyer suggested the idea of translating the whole book into Spanish. This probably makes the letter of 7 December 1982 one of the most significant testimonies for the purposes of the present chapter.[9]

Vázquez Pando reacted enthusiastically to both ideas. Regarding the special section in the journal, he proposed the translation of Chapter XII of the third edition of *The Legal Aspect of Money* (Chapter XV of the fourth edition).[10] Furthermore, Vázquez Pando made a proactive commitment to the translation of the book and

[7] Fernando A Vázquez Pando to FA Mann (Mann estate, NLMann_0837 41-100, 22 November 1982).

[8] See generally for a history of international monetary law Chapter 12 of Rosa Lastra, *Legal Foundations of International Monetary Stability* (OUP 2006) (hereafter Lastra, *Legal Foundations*). See, for example, the review of the second edition by Charles Evan in (1956) 32(1) Indiana Law Journal 117.

[9] FA Mann to Fernando A Vázquez Pando (Mann estate, NLMann_0837 41-100, 7 December 1982).

[10] The interest in said chapter is justified by the idea that 'in Mexico nothing had been written so far in relation to the general aspects of private international law of exchange controls'. See Fernando A Vázquez Pando to FA Mann (Mann estate, NLMann_0837 41-100, 20 December 1982).

informed Mann of the steps taken to find a publisher.[11] These efforts continued into 1983, including a meeting with Francisco Borja Martínez, the legal subdirector of the *Banco de México*. Through him, the proposal came to the director of the bank and the director of the *Fondo de Cultura Económica* (FCE),[12] who both agreed with the idea of a co-edition under the sponsorship of the *Banco de México* and the FCE.[13] In two subsequent letters sent in January 1983, Mann approved both translations and clarified that, should the translation of the book finally take place, details would have to be concluded with Oxford University Press.[14]

Chapter XV was eventually published in *Jurídica* in due course,[15] after the completion of the required process of due diligence.[16] For its part, the translation of the book followed a more erratic path. The FCE postponed its decision on publication until June 1983, because of a change in directorship and the need to discuss the proposal with the new authorities.[17] Our interpretation of the archive material suggests that, even without a concrete response from the FCE, Vázquez Pando and the authorities of the *Banco de México* had a strong interest in the materialization of the publication. This is documented in a letter dated 24 August 1983 in which Vázquez Pando seeks to move the negotiations forward, in line with the wishes of the *Banco de México*.[18]

FA Mann, appreciative of these efforts, wrote to Adam Hodgkin, Oxford University Press editor, stating that he was 'anxious to conclude the negotiations with Mexico as quickly as possible in order to ensure an early completion of the

[11] Fernando A Vázquez Pando to FA Mann (Mann estate, NLMann_0837 41-100, 20 December 1982).

[12] Vázquez Pando describes the publisher as the most important in Mexico, with a significant activity in Latin American countries and Spain. He also highlights the peculiarity that the Spanish version had not been previously translated in any other country. This awakened the publisher's interest in having the exclusive rights of publication.

[13] Fernando A Vázquez Pando to FA Mann (Mann estate, NLMann_0837 41-100, 12 January 1983). In a letter written some years later, on 12 June 1986, Vázquez Pando acknowledges that, after Mann's proposal, he reached out to Francisco Borja Martínez, whom he recognizes as one of the most important staff members of the *Banco de México* and a very good friend. They both agreed in trying to get the publication through the FCE. From there, Borja Martínez contacted Jorge Farías Negrete, the General Manager of the *Fondo de Cultura Económica*, who accepted the offer and initiated the necessary steps so that the publication could be carried out. See Fernando A Vázquez Pando to FA Mann (Mann estate, NLMann_0837 1-20, 12 June 1986).

[14] FA Mann to Fernando A Vázquez Pando (Mann estate, NLMann_0837 41-100, 20 January 1983); FA Mann to Fernando A Vázquez Pando (Mann estate, NLMann_0837 41-100, 24 January 1983).

[15] See <https://revistas-colaboracion.juridicas.unam.mx/index.php/juridica/article/view/11016/10072> accessed 6 November 2023.

[16] For correspondence about this, see Fernando A Vázquez Pando to FA Mann (Mann estate, NLMann_0837 41-100, 28 January 1983); FA Mann to Fernando A Vázquez Pando (Mann estate, NLMann 0837 41-100, 18 April 1983); Fernando A Vázquez Pando to FA Mann (Mann estate, NLMann_0837 41-100, 8 June 1983); FA Mann to Fernando A Vázquez Pando (Mann estate, NLMann_0837 41-100, 22 June 1983).

[17] FA Mann to Fernando A Vázquez Pando (Mann estate, NLMann_0837 41-100, 8 March 1983); Fernando A Vázquez Pando to FA Mann (Mann estate, NLMann_0837 41-100, 5 April 1983); Fernando A Vázquez Pando to FA Mann (Mann estate, NLMann_0837 41-100, 8 June 1983).

[18] Fernando A Vázquez Pando to FA Mann (Mann estate, NLMann_0837 41-100, 24 August 1983). In this letter, Vázquez Pando requests information on the conditions of the contract.

translation work'.[19] However, more delays followed, and in due course the unfortunate news came that, due to the budget cuts in response to the unfolding crisis, the FCE (a public trust) and the *Banco de México* lacked the funds necessary to carry out the publication that year and that the costs would be contemplated in the 1984 budget, after the approval from the Congress.[20]

The dialogue quickly resumed in the new year. On 19 January 1984, Vázquez Pando wrote to Mann communicating he had had lunch with Francisco Borja and Jorge Farías Negrete, and that during said lunch, they had been discussing the publication of the book. In said letter he also mentioned that, given the good relationship known to exist between Oxford University Press and the *Fondo de Cultura Económica, el Fondo* was going to contact Oxford University Press to agree to the terms and conditions of the publication.[21]

Obstacles to conclude the agreement remained for a while longer. On the 31st of January 1984, Vázquez Pando received a telephone call from the representative of the FCE, who let him know that he had received a telex from Oxford University Press asking for a fee of £2,000 to make the translation possible. The amount far exceeded, according to Vázquez Pando, the fees that Oxford University Press normally demanded from the FCE, in a context in which the public sector in turn faced severe budgetary restrictions. Vázquez Pando transmitted this to Mann with the intention, at the request of the representative of the FCE, to ask for his help so that the FCE and Oxford University Press could reach an agreement that would be mutually beneficial.[22]

Mann quickly interceded in the negotiations. Via a letter sent to Oxford (along with an attached copy of the letter dated January 31 received from Mexico) he rejected receiving the amount of £ 2,000, emphasizing he was only interested in the translation and possibly royalties. The note culminates with Mann's request to Catherine Johnson-Gilbert to please do all she can to make the translation happen.[23]

[19] FA Mann to Adam Hodgkin (Mann estate, NLMann_0837 41-100, 26 September 1983). For more details regarding the inclusion and involvement of Oxford University Press in completing the translation, see: FA Mann to Adam Hodgkin (Mann estate, NLMann_0837 41-100, 6 September 1983); Adam Hodgkin to FA Mann (Mann estate, NLMann_0837 41-100, 15 September 1983); FA Mann to Adam Hodgkin (Mann estate, NLMann_0837 41-100, 26 September 1983); Adam Hodgkin to FA Mann (Mann estate, NLMann_0837 41-100, 30 September 1983); Catherine Johnson-Gilbert to FA Mann (Mann estate, NLMann_0837 41-100, 6 October 1983).

[20] FA Mann to Catherine Johnson-Gilbert (Mann estate, NLMann_0837 21-40, 28 November 1983); FA Mann to Fernando A Vázquez Pando (Mann estate, NLMann_0837 21-40 28 November 1983); Catherine Johnson-Gilbert to FA Mann (Mann estate, NLMann_0837 21-40, 1 December 1983); Fernando A Vázquez Pando to FA Mann (Mann estate, NLMann_0837 21-40, 9 December 1983).

[21] Fernando A Vázquez Pando to FA Mann (Mann estate, NLMann_0837 21-40, 19 January 1984). A few days after receiving the letter, Mann forwarded it to Johnson-Gilbert in order to accelerate the agreement. See FA Mann to Catherine Johnson-Gilbert (Mann estate, NLMann_0837 21-40, 24 January 1984).

[22] Fernando A Vázquez Pando to FA Mann (Mann estate, NLMann_0837 21-40, 31 January 1984).

[23] FA Mann to Catherine Johnson-Gilbert (Mann estate, NLMann_0837 21-40, 13 February 1984).

Apparently, his intervention contributed to the agreement of the parties. On 15 May 1984, Oxford University Press and the FCE signed a Memorandum of Agreement by which the FCE was granted the exclusive licence to publish *The Legal Aspect of Money* in the Spanish language (in volume form) on a global scale under the title *El Aspecto Legal de Dinero*.[24]

Almost two years later, Mann contacted Vázquez Pando again asking him about the status of the translation.[25] In a letter dated 16 May 1984, he replied that the translation was already ready and that it was expected to arrive in bookstores soon.[26] Five days later, Vázquez Pando sends him a second letter to which he attaches a copy of the translation.[27]

Mann reacted with words of gratitude to Vázquez Pando, the *Banco de México*, and the FCE, as well as the person who worked on the translation, Eduardo L Suárez (whose postal addresses he requested to express his personal appreciation). In his response, Mann also raised two notable issues. First, he highlighted his surprise about the absence in the volume of a description of his professional and academic career. Secondly, he mentioned that, during his holidays in Spain, he had noticed a promising market for the book there and suggested alerting the editors about this.[28]

Regarding the biography, Vázquez Pando let him know that the format varied significantly in Mexico and that, in the case of the FCE, they usually included only the author's name, since the editorial was known for publishing books written by renowned authors on specific subjects. As regards the opportunities in the Spanish market, he argued that the FCE's prestige in the Spanish-speaking world was the reason why he had suggested it as a publisher.

In the same correspondence, Mann received the postal addresses of the persons involved in the whole process, Francisco Borja Martínez, Deputy Director General

[24] The bilateral agreement stated that the volume should be published within 24 months of the date of signing. Furthermore, the FCE undertook to pay Oxford the sum of £1,500 on account (and in anticipation) of a royalty of 7.5 per cent, calculated on the published price of any hardcover or paperbound edition issued by the FCE. This rate would rise to 10 per cent after 3,000 copies sold (all payments would be free of tax and other deductions). See Memorandum of Agreement (Mann estate, NLMann_0837 21-40). In September, Catherine Johnson-Gilbert informed Mann of the cancellation of the advance payment. See Catherine Johnson-Gilbert to FA Mann (Mann estate, NLMann_0837 21-40, 14 September 1984).

[25] They were in contact between January and May 1985, exchanging acknowledgements about Mann's contribution to *Jurídica*, a period in which the jurist also received a copy of volume 16. See Fernando A Vázquez Pando to FA Mann (Mann estate, NLMann_0837 1-20, 8 January 1985); FA Mann to Fernando A Vázquez Pando (Mann estate, NLMann_0837 1-20, 13 March 1985); Fernando A Vázquez Pando to FA Mann (Mann estate, NLMann_0837 1-20, 3 April 1985); FA Mann to Fernando A Vázquez Pando (Mann estate, NLMann_0837 1-20, 2 May 1985); FA Mann to Fernando A Vázquez Pando (Mann estate, NLMann_0837 1-20, 13 May 1985).

[26] Fernando A Vázquez Pando to FA Mann (Mann estate, NLMann_0837 1-20, 16 May 1986).

[27] Fernando A Vázquez Pando to FA Mann (Mann estate, NLMann_0837 1-20, 21 May 1986). This information contrasts with a letter from Oxford University Press which announces that the Spanish edition was published in February of the same year. See Catherine Johnson-Gilbert to FA Mann (Mann estate, NLMann_0837 1-20, 19 June1986).

[28] FA Mann to Fernando A Vázquez Pando (Mann estate, NLMann_0837 1-20, 2 June 1986).

of the *Banco de México*, and Jorge Farías Negrete, General Manager of the FCE.[29] The acknowledgements to both were sent later in separate letters.[30] The archive material only contains Borja Martínez's response, who, with great satisfaction, informed Mann that the book was delivered to all head advisors of the in-house legal departments of the Mexican banks, as well as to prestigious Mexican lawyers and scholars, getting valuable and positive feedback from his work.[31]

III. Expectations and Dissemination of the Work

Almost four years after the publication of the translation, Mann reached out to Julio Ernesto Curutchet, an Argentine legal scholar of monetary law and fellow colleague in the Monetary Committee of the International Law Association (MOCOMILA) to express his concern about the level of sales of his book in Latin America:

> I have recently received a royalty statement for the sum of about £30 sterling. This indicates to me that the sales have been incredibly small. In fact, I understand that the distribution of Mexican books in South American Spanish-speaking countries is very badly organized. I therefore venture to write to you in order to ask whether something can be done about this. I shall be very grateful for any suggestion you can make.[32]

The University of Oxford Press Author Statement Details allow us to understand and explain Mann's concerns:[33] indeed, by the beginning of 1990 fewer than a dozen copies had been sold. However, sales levels soared shortly after, growing by 2,1760 per cent when the period from date of publication to 31 March 1990 is compared to the period from 1 April 1990 to 31 March 1991. It should also be noted that the sales peak of the translation occurred between 1 April 1990 and 31 March 1991.

On the basis of a detailed analysis of the archival material, we also find that the Oxford University Press' sales figures show a correspondence between periods of higher levels of sales and significant events in Latin American economic history and in the global economic scenario associated with international financial

[29] Fernando A Vázquez Pando to FA Mann (Mann estate, NLMann_0837 1-20, 12 June 1986).

[30] FA Mann to Lic. Don Francisco Borja Martínez (Mann estate, NLMann_0837 1-20, 18 June 1986); FA Mann to Lic. Jorge Farías Negrete (Mann estate, NLMann_0837 1-20, 18 June 1986).

[31] Lic. Francisco Borja Martínez to FA Mann (Mann estate, NLMann_0837 1-20, 16 July 1986).

[32] FA Mann to Dr JE Curutchet (Mann estate, NLMann_0837 1-20, 8 January 1990). See <https://www.curutchetodriozola.com.ar/los-abogados/julio-e-curutchet/?lang=en> accessed 6 June 2023.

[33] The further analysis is based on the Author Statement Details for the fourth edition and the number of copies sold by the *Fondo de Cultura Económica* for the Spanish translation. The periodization corresponding to the analysis is taken following the records. The information available goes from 31 March 1982 to 31 March 2006 (RS460_NLMann_0830).

crises. Specifically, the years with the highest levels of sales[34] coincided with: the start of negotiations and concretion of the Brady Plan (1990–1992) in many Latin American countries;[35] the so-called '*Crisis del Tequila*', which also started in Mexico and extended to other Latin American countries (1994–1995); the Asian Financial Crisis (commencing 1997); the Brazilian crisis (1999); and the Argentine Crisis (2001–2002).[36]

All of this allows us to conclude that the impact of *El Aspecto Legal del Dinero* on the Latin American continent has not been minor and that its dissemination has been closely related to episodes of macroeconomic fragility.[37] This evidence in turn leads us to the following questions:

- What have been the main contributions of the work in the Latin American region?
- What debates, if any, has it aroused?
- Which of its points have contributed to the debate on the economic reality of Latin America from time to time?

Addressing these questions, in turn, provides an opportunity to understand the interaction between macroeconomic conditions and monetary law in Latin America during a crucial period in modern monetary history. The implications of this understanding extend beyond Latin America, since the experience of the 1980s in the region, like a canary in a coalmine, offers invaluable insights for monetary theory and practice and for the interaction between money, banking, and sovereign debt markets. In the current economic circumstances, with interest rate rises in the US and other advanced economies including the UK and the EU (in a situation which is reminiscent of the rises that took place under Fed Chairman Paul Volcker), the pressures on many emerging economies that borrowed extensively during the years of 'easy money' (coinciding also with increased lending by China to many countries in Africa[38]) may lead again to sovereign defaults in developing countries.

[34] October 1999–March 2002 constitutes the second most significant period in terms of sales level.

[35] Among them: Mexico, February 1990; Venezuela, March 1990; Costa Rica, May 1990; Uruguay, October 1990. Brazil reached a prior agreement with most of the creditor banks in July 1992, presenting the final restructuring plan at the end of that year. For its part, Argentina submitted the restructuring plan to the banks in mid-1992. See e.g. Roddy Rivas-Llosa M, *Los Bonos Brady* (Universidad del Pacífico 1997) 51–125 <http://hdl.handle.net/11354/104> accessed 8 May 2023.

[36] See <https://www.imf.org/external/np/ieo/2003/arg/index.htm> accessed 6 June 2023.

[37] Another possible research question could have been the comparison between the sales volumes of the original version in English and the Spanish translation. There are, however, different variables that interfere with the analysis, among them, the date of publication, the size of the respective markets, and the number of editions.

[38] For an overview of Chinese Loans to Africa, see <https://www.bu.edu/gdp/chinese-loans-to-africa-database/> accessed 9 May 2023.

IV. The Impact of Mann's Work in Latin America

A. Economics vs law or economics and law and the legal concept of money

Economic debates about the nature of money are well illustrated by Paul Davidson in his work *Money and the Real World* (1972):

> While economists have probably spilled more printers' ink over the topic of money than any other, and while monetary theory impinges on almost every other conceivable branch of economic analysis, confusion over the meaning and nature of money continues to plague the economics profession.[39]

But money is a legal construct. Whether as an object of property or as a credit–debit relationship, money always has a legal dimension. While this dimension is most notable in the law of payments, all money issues must be understood under this prism, as recognized in the first lines of *El Aspecto Legal del Dinero:*

> *La embrollada cuestión de lo que es el dinero ha ocupado tan constantemente la atención de los economistas que un abogado podría vacilar para unirse al esfuerzo de solución. Pero la respuesta verdadera debe determinarse, si ello es posible. Porque el dinero resuelve todas las cosas. Es una noción fundamental, no sólo de la vida económica de la humanidad sino también de todos los departamentos del derecho. En efecto, gran parte del trabajo cotidiano de un abogado gira alrededor del término 'dinero' en sí mismo y de las numerosas transacciones o instituciones basadas en ese término, tales como deuda, daños, valor, pago, precio, capital, interés, impuesto, legado pecuniario.*
>
> [The troublesome question, What is money? Has so constantly engaged the minds of economists that a lawyer might hesitate to join in the attempt to solve it. Yet the true answer must, if possible, be determined. For 'money answereth all things'. It is a fundamental notion not only of the economic life of mankind but also of all departments of law. In fact, a great deal of a lawyer's daily work centers around the term 'money' itself and the many transactions or institutions based on that term, such as debt, damages, value, payment, price, capital, interest, tax, pecuniary legacy.][40]

[39] Paul Davidson, 'Money and the Real World' (1972) 82 The Economic Journal 101, 101 (hereafter Davidson, 'Money and the Real World').

[40] FA Mann, *El Aspecto Legal del Dinero: con referencia especial al derecho internacional privado y público* (Banco de México 1986) 27 [*The Legal Aspect of Money: With Special Reference to Comparative Private and Public International Law* (4th edn, Clarendon Press) 3] (hereafter Mann, *El Aspecto Legal*).

Notwithstanding the importance of the legal dimension, from a doctrinal perspective there was, in Mann's own words, '*una laguna que debe llenarse*' (literally 'a gap to be filled').[41] Accordingly, the first chapter of *El Aspecto Legal del Dinero* is ordered around two questions: '*¿Cuáles son las características en virtud de las cuales se llama a una cosa dinero? (. . .) ¿Cuál es la naturaleza intrínseca del fenómeno descrito por la palabra "dinero?"*' ['What are the characteristics under which a thing is called money? (. . .) What is the intrinsic nature of the phenomenon described by the word "money"?']][42]

If, as Hicks argues, money is defined by its functions,[43] Mann asserts that there is a wide acceptance among jurists that the basic function of money, among those enunciated by economists,[44] is to serve as a universal medium of exchange, and that legal professionals '*tomarán esto en cuenta al definir el dinero en el sentido legal*' ['will take this into account when defining money in the legal sense'].[45] While Mann does not ignore the importance of developments in economic theory on the functions of money, he highlights their inadequacy to explain money in a legal sense, thus '*en general resulta inaceptable para los abogados la noción del economista de que es dinero todo lo que funcione como dinero*' ['the economist's notion that money is all that functions as money is, in general, unacceptable to lawyers'].[46]

The state plays, in particular, an essential role in the definition of money provided in *El Aspecto Legal del Dinero*.[47] Mann draws on the contributions made by GF Knapp, an economist whose influential work, *Die Staatliche Theorie des Geldes*, was published in its original language in 1905.[48] In Mann's own words:

> *Se sugiere que, en el campo del derecho, la calidad del dinero debe atribuirse a todos los bienes que, emitidos por la autoridad de la ley y denominados con referencia a una unidad de cuenta, deberán servir como medios universales de intercambio en el Estado emisor.*
>
> [It is suggested that, in the field of law, the quality of money should be attributed to all goods that, issued by the authority of law and denominated with reference

41 ibid 16.

42 ibid 29.

43 John Richard Hicks, *Critical Essays in Monetary Theory* (Oxford Clarendon Press 1967) 1.

44 In the question about what money is, the traditional theory of money has focused its answer on specifying its functions. See David A Martin, 'The Medium Is Not The Money' (1972) 6 Journal of Economic Issues 67, 67.

45 Mann, *El Aspecto Legal* (n 40) 29.

46 ibid 29–30.

47 For Latin American works that address these issues and reference the book in Spanish, see e.g. Jorge Andrés Torres Calderón, 'Contrato de arrendamiento de entidades estatales con renta en especie: inexistencia- atipicidad' (MPhil thesis, Universidad Santo Tomás de Aquino 2017) for the Colombian case and Jesús de la Fuente Rodríguez, 'Generalidades del Dinero' (2018) 271 Revista de la Facultad de Derecho de México 789, 791–808 for the Mexican case.

48 George Friedrich Knapp, *Die Staatliche Theorie des Geldes* (first published 1905, Makroskop Mediengesellschaft 2018). Its English translation was published in 1924, George Friedrich Knapp, *The State Theory of Money* (HM Lucas and J Bonar tr., Macmillan & Co. 1924).

to a unit of account, should serve as universal means of exchange in the issuing State.][49]

A few pages further, Mann asserts '*Sólo son dinero los bienes a los que la ley haya atribuido tal carácter, es decir, por la autoridad del Estado*' ['Money is only the goods to which the law has attributed such a character, that is, by the authority of the State'].[50] The state theory of money (*lex monetae*) is key to the understanding of money by Mann.[51]

Developments on the legal nature of money as well as the evolution of international monetary law have strongly inspired the work of Latin American jurists.[52] Mann's approach to money has also triggered an interdisciplinary dialogue between economists and lawyers which has been taken up by several Latin American jurists, not only in the study on the conceptualization of money but also in the determination and order of the monetary system,[53] as well as in the study of the legal nature of interest rates.[54]

[49] Mann, *El Aspecto Legal* (n 40) 32. And to this he adds that 'money can only legally lose its character by virtue of a formal demonetisation' at 44.

[50] ibid 38.

[51] In the field of economics, the initial contributions by Knapp, Keynes, and Lerner, among others, have influenced the interpretation of modern post-Keynesian authors about money, which they conceived as a 'creature of the State'. See George Friedrich Knapp, *The State Theory of Money* (first published 1924, Augustus M. Kelley 1973) vii–viii, 7–40, 95–143; John Maynard Keynes, *A Treatise on Money: The Pure Theory of Money* (Vol. 1, first published in 1930, Harcourt Brace & Co. 1976) 3–11; Abba Ptachya Lerner, 'Functional Finance and the Federal Debt' (1943) Social Research 38, 40; Abba Ptachya Lerner, 'Money as a Creature of the State' (1947) 37(2) American Economic Review 312, 313–14. The approach commonly known as Chartalism emphasizes the role of taxes in the creation of money and the sovereignty of the state in the fixing of the unit of account. See Davidson, 'Money and the Real World' (n 39) 101, 106–07; L Randall Wray, *Credit and State Theories of Money* (Edward Elgar Publishing 2004) 12, 243, 245–56; L Randall Wray, 'From the State Theory of Money to Modern Money Theory: An Alternative to Economic Orthodoxy' (Levy Economics Institute of Bard College Working Paper 172, 2014). Within this school of thought, there are authors who, however, without ignoring the importance of the state, argue that banks and other financial institutions have historically played a more relevant role in the creation of money. See for example Luis-Philippe Rochon and Matias Vernengo, 'State Money and the Real World: Or Chartalism and Its Discontents (2003) 26(1) Journal of Post Keynesian Economics 57, 58, 65–66.

[52] See for example Sebastián Boada Morales, 'La naturaleza jurídica de la cuenta bancaria' (2019) 36 Revista de Derecho Privado 171, 178; Jorge Vargas Morgado, 'Observaciones acerca de la naturaleza jurídica del papel moneda' (2009) 5 Revista de la Asociación Internacional de Derecho Administrativo 405, 410–26; Francisco Joaquín Moreno y Gutiérrez, 'Sistema Monetario Mexicano' (DPhil thesis, Universidad Panamericana 2012); Manuel López Escudero, 'El Derecho Monetario Internacional en la Era de la Globalización Financiera' <https://www.ehu.eus/eu/web/cursosderechointernacionalvitoria/-/el-derecho-monetario-internacional-en-la-era-de-la-globalizacion-financiera> accessed 6 June 2023.

[53] For these discussions in the framework of the Constitutional Reform proposed in Peru after the fall of Alberto Fujimori regime, see José García-Pita y Lastres, 'El sistema Financiero Peruano, Ante La Reforma Constitucional: Modelo Constitucional Económico y Sistema Financiero' (2002) 3(3) Revista de Derecho 169, 216–18, 220–22.

[54] See Fernández Cruz for a case study on the 1984 Peruvian Civil Code. Gastón Fernández Cruz, 'La naturaleza jurídica de los intereses: punto de conexión entre derecho y economía' (1991) 45 Derecho PUCP 177, 178, 190–91, 196, 200–07, 211–12.

B. Monetary obligations and the nominalist principle

In the preface to the fourth English edition, Mann describes how some of the most significant economic and legislative developments in Britain and internationally (with particular reference to the IMF) have inspired changes, especially in the first part of his work, with respect to the previous edition:

Desde la publicación de la tercera edición en 1971, ciertos cambios radicales han transformado el derecho monetario: la inflación que depreció el poder de compra interno de la libra en más de 70% entre 1971 y 1981, lo que hizo necesaria la reorganización y ampliación de la primera parte de este libro; el aumento del material comparado, debido en gran medida a la existencia universal de la inflación (. . .); el derrumbe del sistema de valores paritarios del Fondo Monetario Internacional en 1971, la consiguiente flotación de las monedas, incluida la libra esterlina y la ausencia de un sistema monetario internacional efectivo.

[Since the publication of the third edition in 1971, radical changes have transformed the law of money: inflation which resulted in a depreciation of the pound's internal purchasing power by more than 70% between the beginning of 1971 and 1981 and rendered it necessary to reorganize and enlarge the first part of this book; the increase of comparative material, largely due to the universal existence of inflation, (. . .) the collapse of the International Monetary Fund's par value system in 1971, the consequent floating of currencies, including sterling, and the absence of an effective international monetary system.][55]

The problem of inflation is addressed in Chapter IV on monetary obligations in national currency. There Mann explores, among other aspects, the general nature and scope of nominalism, as well as its application in England. Regarding the latter, Mann states:

En Inglaterra nunca se ha puesto en duda el control absoluto del nominalismo. El derecho inglés carece de todo aparato que, en el caso de las sumas líquidas, pudiera conducir a una revisión o un ajuste de la sustancia de la obligación. No se dispone de instrumentos de interpretación como los que se han utilizado en otras partes. Ni siquiera la implicación de los términos podría permitir que el tribunal hiciera un nuevo contrato para las partes. Solo puede concederse algún alivio contra los cambios del valor monetario mediante la adopción de cláusulas protectoras o por la adopción del legislador.

[55] Mann, *El Aspecto Legal* (n 40) 7 [English original version in *The Legal Aspect of Money* (4th edn, OUP 1982) Preface].

> [In England the unimpaired control of nominalism has never been doubted. English law lacks all equipment that, in the case of liquidated sums, could lead to a revision or adjustment of the substance of the obligation. Interpretative devices such as have been resorted to abroad are not available. Even the implication of terms could not permit the court to make a new contract for the parties. Relief against changes in monetary value can only be granted by the adoption of protective clauses or by the legislator.][56]

On this, the author ponders:

> *¿Es la mera reducción del poder de compra del dinero un elemento del daño que la ley reconoce como recuperable, a pesar del principio del nominalismo? ¿O es por lo menos posible la recuperación de la pérdida sufrida por el hecho probado de que, si no hubiese habido mora, el acreedor habría podido comprar alguna propiedad (o circulante extranjero) por menos dinero que en el momento del pago?*
>
> [Is the mere reduction in the purchasing power of money an item of damage which, notwithstanding the principle of nominalism, the law recognizes as recoverable? Or is it at least possible to recover loss suffered by reason of the fact proved by the creditor that, had there been no default, he could and would have bought some property (or foreign currency) more cheaply than at the time of the payment?][57]

The successive periods of monetary instability and inflationary acceleration suffered by Latin American countries in the 1980s and 1990s gave also rise to debate on these issues among jurists in the region. Mann's magnum opus had a demonstrable impact both in addressing these phenomena and in a substantive sense as well.

Some of these issues were framed in the debate proposed by Mann on 'valorism' versus nominalism.[58] As acknowledged, this is one of the fundamental debates in monetary theory: nominalism, the theory to which Mann subscribed, posits that the value of money is 'nominal', i.e., determined by the face value of the monetary instrument. The state theory of money and nominalism are mutually reinforcing in Mann's work, since it is the state that determines what money is. (In the context of national law, an obligation to pay X units in a given currency is discharged by payment of X units in that currency, regardless of any changes in the purchasing power or external value of that currency.)

56 ibid 140–41 [English original version in *The Legal Aspect of Money* (4th edn, OUP 1982) 107].
57 ibid 142 [English original version in *The Legal Aspect of Money* (4th edn, OUP 1982) 108].
58 ibid 112–16. See further Joseph Sommer's chapter in this volume on Mann's attempt to 'dethrone' the gold standard.

'Valorism' is the theory that sees the extent of a monetary obligation determined not by a sum of units of nominal value but by some 'intrinsic' value, for example in precious metal. But this suggests a fluctuating economic value. Mann's commitments to the legal foundations of monetary systems were based on the economic and legal conceptions of money of his times. Much has changed since then, both in the composition of capital markets, in the nature of monetary policy, and in the extension of private money (bank deposits and more recently different versions of digital money). These changes notwithstanding, the purpose of this chapter is to examine the impact of Mann's work in Latin America, and, in that regard, we proceed to survey briefly variations of the nominalist principle in some countries in the region.

In the case of Peru, the country experienced a period of hyperinflation between 1987 and 1990; in that context, there was a wide debate about the relevance of the nominalist principle adopted by the 1984 Civil Code. In a study on monetary obligations in Peru published in 1995, Osterling Parodi and Castillo Freire defend its validity under the idea of the principle as the best guarantor of greater economic stabilization. Despite the severe depreciations suffered by the national currency since the sanction of the Code, the authors argue that nominalism '*en nada ha entorpecido u obstaculizado la contratación*' ['has not hindered or hampered the contracting'].[59]

Pelletier Barberena (1995) reflects on the adoption of the nominalist principle in Mexico and exposes the legal basis for the application of the so-called 'Theory of Unpredictability' as a feasible solution to scenarios of loss of purchasing power of money.[60] For the case of Colombia, Quiróz, Durán, and Villamil (2005) conduct a theoretical-practical study in which they analyse six milestone judgments of the Civil Court of Cassation of the Supreme Court of Justice on the issues of devaluation and indexation of monetary obligations, in order to assess whether there is a jurisprudential trend towards the application of the nominalist or the 'valorist' principle. They conclude that, though there had been uniformity in the recognition of the legal effects caused by inflation and currency depreciation (considered a persistent issue since 1979), the 'valorist' postulate was imposed in any adjustment of the obligations, replacing the postulates of the monetary nominalism.[61]

The second part of *El Aspecto Legal del Dinero* addresses foreign money obligations in the sphere of (English) national law,[62] while the third part focuses on

[59] Felipe Osterling Parodi and Mario Castillo Freire, *Estudios sobre las obligaciones dinerarias en el Perú* (Universidad Nacional Autónoma de México 1995) 52.

[60] Rolland Pelletier Barberena, 'Teoría de la Imprevisión: Remedios contra los efectos de la depreciación monetaria' (1995) 25 Jurídica anuario del Departamento de Derecho de la Universidad Iberoamericana 247, 254, 260–61.

[61] Alejandra María Quiróz Valencia, Claudia Juliana Durán Galvis, and Javier Eduardo Villamil López, 'La corrección monetaria y su aplicación judicial en el campo contractual colombiano' (B.S. thesis, Universidad Autónoma de Bucaramanga 2005).

[62] For a discussion of obligations in foreign currency in Latin America, see for example Giral Pimentel for the Venezuelan case and Ossola for the case of Argentina: José Alfredo Giral Pimentel,

the study of exchange controls and exchange rates. In the introduction to the third part, Mann argues: '*El homo economicus del siglo XX sabe que la tasa de cambio, y la balanza de pagos, se han convertido en su enigma y en una de sus enfermedades principales. El efecto sobre la ley ha sido profundo*' ['The homo economicus of the twentieth century knows that the exchange rate and the balance of payments have become his enigma and one of his main diseases. The effect on the law has been profound'].[63]

The legal understanding of exchange rates and balance of payments, which is at the core of the functions of the IMF and, consequently, at the core of the international monetary system, felt somewhat alien to many lawyers at the time in which Mann started writing his magnum opus in England. While Mann kept a reluctance to engage with the legal aspects of monetary policy (the internal dimension of the conduct of money) he freely engaged with the legal aspects of exchange controls and exchange contracts (the external dimension of the conduct of money). In this latter sphere money is both 'relational'—since the exchange rate is the price of a currency in terms of other currencies—and 'competitive'—since countries compete in the provision of money internationally—with some currencies (notably the US dollar, the quintessential reserve currency in which many international transactions—oil contracts for example—are denominated). Thus, the external concept of money is much more economically fluctuating than the internal concept of money. However, the experience of inflation or hyperinflation tests the limits of the nominalist principle.

What Mann failed to fully grasp is the increasing relevance of the private sector in the international financial system. Mann had lived in a world in which official foreign reserves and the imposition of controls on the transfer of payments and capital were a feature of the dominion (sovereignty) of the state. But in the world of today (following the demise of the par value regime), foreign exchange markets (private) and other private international capital markets dwarf the amounts of official reserves. We refer to these issues in the next section.

'Derecho Internacional Privado Sustantivo de los Títulos de Crédito en Venezuela' (1995) 96 Revista de la Facultad de Ciencias Jurídicas y Políticas de la Universidad Central de Venezuela 83, 141–44; Federico Alejandro Ossola, 'Arts. 746 a 804' in Ricardo Luis Lorenzetti (ed.), *Código Civil y Comercial de la Nación Comentado* (Vol. V, 2015).

A rich literature can also be found for the case of Brazil, which takes up much of Mann's contributions, although it uses different editions of the work in English. See for example Gustavo Henrique Barroso Franco, *O Plano Real e Outros Ensaios* (F Alves 1995) ch. 2; Gustavo Henrique Barroso Franco, *The Real Plan and the Exchange Rate. Essays in International Finance* (International Finance Section, Department of Economics, Princeton University 2000); Camila Villard Duran, 'Jurisprudência comentada (ADPF 77): o debate judicial sobre a disciplina jurídica da moeda como padrão de valor' (2015) 70(18) Revista de Direito Bancário e do Mercado de Capitais (RDB) 294, 9.

[63] Mann, *El Aspecto Legal* (n 40) 411.

C. The importance of exchange controls literature to the economic reality of the region

The 'Lost Decade' (*La Década Perdida*) is the name given to the period from 1982 to roughly 1990 when many countries in Latin America were unable to service their foreign debt.[64] By the beginning of that decade, a large part of the developing world faced external debt problems.[65] The decade triggered a rethink of the international institutional framework on monetary and financial affairs.[66]

The oil crises in the 1970s led to substantial increases in the price of this commodity. The first oil crisis in 1973 was triggered by the oil embargo by the then members of the Organization of Arab Petroleum Exporting Countries (OAPEC, which later became OPEc) targeted at nations that had supported Israel during the Yom Kippur War. The second oil crisis in 1979 was triggered by a drop in oil production in the wake of the Iranian revolution. By the end of the first oil shock, the price of oil had risen nearly 300 per cent from US$3 per barrel to nearly US$12.

The exorbitant profits obtained by oil-exporting countries, the so-called 'recycling of petrodollars',[67] signified that commercial banks from the 'global north' played a pivotal role in granting loans to the 'global south', leading to a lending boom in the region. Private external financing was characterized by the competition between national banks to place resources in the international financial markets, frequently in the form of syndicated loans at variable interest rates. These loans were subject to relatively lax credit assessments by the banks, as Lissakers and others have noted.[68] This was a classic example of a 'boom', which would eventually lead to a 'bust'.

The growth of the Eurodollar market also played a key role in the incentives for US banks to lend to projects in the region. This new phase of financing, with private banking (not official sector lending) as the main line of indebtedness, implied a shift in risk from creditors to debtors, explained by an interest rate scheme subject to that of the interbank market rate (LIBOR). When interest rates changed directions in 1979, with Fed Chairman Paul Volcker raising forcefully interest rates to fight inflation in the USA, developing countries were unable to service the loans.

[64] Though the Lost Decade was disastrous from a financial and economic perspective, it also ushered a fundamental change in the political climate in Latin America, with a shift from military governments to democratically elected civilian governments.

[65] In the autumn of 1983, 40–50 developing countries were engaging in negotiations to restructure their outstanding debt. See Dragoslav Avramoviĉ, 'External Debt of Developing Countries in Late 1983' in Miguel S Wionczek in collaboration with Luciano Tomassini (eds), *Politics and Economics of External Debt Crisis. The Latin American Experience* (Routledge 2019).

[66] Carlos F Díaz-Alejandro, 'Latin American Debt: I Don't Think We Are in Kansas Anymore' (1984) 1984(2) Brookings Papers on Economic Activity 335, 335–36

[67] For an explanation, see e.g. Johannes Wiegand, 'Bank Recycling of Petro Dollars to Emerging Market Economies During the Current Oil Price Boom' (IMF Research Department Working Paper WP/08/180, July 2008).

[68] See Lissakers, *Banks, Borrowers and the Establishment* (n 6).

This 'Volcker shock' in response to the economic consequences for the US of the 'oil shocks' explains the origins of the crisis.

The crisis broke out with the default of Mexico in 1982. The response to the crisis by the regulatory authorities and central banks was first timid and hesitant considering the solvency and stability of the creditor banks, notably in the US. This first phase, the so-called Baker Plan, in 1985 simply postponed the resolution of the problems: borrowing to pay interest on the loans, which in turn led to an expansion in the amount of principal owed to the banks. (Lissakers explains that this was motivated by the regulatory definition of 'non-performing loans' applicable to US banks, and that this simply delayed some much-needed restructuring.[69]) The second phase of the response to the crisis was a recognition of the inevitability of restructuring and debt reduction. Under the so-called Brady Plan in 1989, commercial bank loans were no longer 'rolled over', but instead were transformed into freely tradable securities (so-called Brady Bonds) at a discount (i.e. debt reduction). Through this, '[a] new species of investor—the bond investor—was introduced to the rewards and to the risks of lending to sovereign borrowers'.[70]

This explains part of the history and context in which the translation of The Legal Aspect of Money into Spanish takes place. Certainly, the legal literature on these issues was scarce prior to the 'Lost Decade'. The process of financial liberalization initiated by many Latin American countries in the 1970s was also accompanied by a paradigm change. The seminal works of Ronald McKinnon (1973) and Edward Shaw (1973) advocated for a complete liberalization of financial markets, claiming a direct benefit on the growth rate of the economy.[71] These ideas not only sparked debate within academia, but also gained significant traction in public policy. By the mid-1970s, an increasing number of countries had initiated the liberalization of their capital account (even though the IMF obligation to members only extends to current account liberalization but not capital account liberalization, as further explained below). The dimension of the Debt Crisis gave rise to a rich and abundant literature (by economists, lawyers, and political scientists), much of which identifies Latin America as a distinctive region in the recurrence of financial crises.[72] The most severe crises have been associated with massive capital inflows followed by abrupt and untimely capital outflows.[73] This had been a warning that John Maynard Keynes had expressed vigorously in the negotiations that eventually led

69 ibid.

70 See Lee Buchheit, 'A Quarter Century of Sovereign Debt Management: An Overview' (2004) 35 Georgetown Journal of International Law 637.

71 Ronald I McKinnon, *Money & Capital in Economic Development* (The Brookings Institution 1973) 117–77; Edward S Shaw, *Financial Deepening in Economic Development* (OUP 1973) 9–12.

72 For some of these discussions, see for instance Carlos Díaz-Alejandro, 'Good-Bye Financial Repression, Hello Financial Crash' (1985) 19 Journal of Development Economics 1, 1–2, 20–23; José María Fanelli, 'Liberalización Financiera y Cuenta de Capital: Observaciones Sobre la Experiencia de los Países en Desarrollo' (1998) 38(149) Desarrollo Económico 339, 341–49.

73 Ocampo and others, *La crisis latinoamericana* (n 6).

to the establishment of the IMF.[74] The nature of these crises thus puts into question the desirability of exchange controls (i.e. restrictions of capital transfers and payments).[75] The literature on liberalization of capital flows, drawing, in particular, on the law of the IMF, questions the wisdom and the adequate sequencing of capital account liberalization.[76]

D. Article VIII(2)(b) and the law of exchange controls

Article VIII of the IMF Articles of Agreement (a provision which remains unaltered since its original formulation) imposes 'general obligations' upon member countries with regard to the avoidance of restrictions in current international transactions.[77]

> Exchange contracts which involve the currency of any member and which are contrary to the exchange control regulations of that member maintained or imposed consistently with this Agreement shall be unenforceable in the territories of any member. In addition, members may, by mutual accord, cooperate in measures for the purpose of making the exchange control regulations of either member

[74] Lastra, *Legal Foundations* (n 8) ch. 12. See generally Benn Steil, *The Battle of Bretton Woods, John Maynard Keynes, Harry Dexter White, and the Making of a New World Order* (Princeton University Press 2013).

[75] Exchange controls act as an artificial barrier, intended to 'protect' national credit markets. Once they are abolished, and individuals are free to transfer their funds abroad, domestic direct credit controls are likely to be much less effective as a lever of monetary policy, since they only cover domestic banks. Therefore, a government wishing to use some sort of domestic credit controls (e.g., quantitative credit controls) will be reluctant to remove exchange controls. Without exchange controls, intermediation that is blocked or penalized domestically will simply be re-routed offshore to the detriment of the domestic sector. See Rosa Lastra, *International Financial and Monetary Law* (OUP 2015) 2.79–2.84 (hereafter Lastra, *International Financial and Monetary Law*). See also Charles Goodhart, *Money, Information and Uncertainty* (2nd edn, MacMillan 1989) 374.

[76] Some economists argue that free capital mobility does not lead to an optimal allocation of resources, especially when significant domestic distortions exist. See e.g. Joseph Stiglitz, 'Capital Market Liberalization, Globalization and the IMF' (2005) 20 Oxford Review of Economic Policy 57–71. Controls on short-term capital inflows, as in Chile, have been appraised on the grounds that countries imposing such controls are subject to less volatility than countries with unrestricted capital mobility; if speculators cannot bring money into the country, then capital will not flow out when market sentiment changes. There are certainly dangers in liberalizing capital movements in an economy in which the macroeconomic framework and the financial sector are weak. Before adopting such liberalization, a country needs to prepare its financial sector, often through the restructuring of the financial industry (adequate sequencing of reforms), the strengthening of the capital base of the financial institutions, and the replacement of capital controls by effective prudential regulation and supervision. A report on the Fund's approach to capital liberalization released in May 2005 by the Independent Evaluation Office found that in the absence of a formal mandate, the Fund has not always provided consistent policy advice to its members. See IEO Report on the 'Evaluation of the IMF's Approach to Capital Account Liberalization', 25 May 2005, <http://www.imf.org/ieo> accessed 9 May 2023. See generally Chapter 13, section F of Lastra, *International Financial and Monetary Law* (n 75).

[77] See generally Chapter 13, section F of Lastra, *International Financial and Monetary Law* (n 75).

more effective, provided that such measures and regulations are consistent with this Agreement.

Article VI, section 3 of the IMF Articles of Agreement allows members to exercise 'controls of capital transfers as necessary to regulate international capital movements'. Both Harry Dexter White and John Maynard Keynes (the chief architects of the IMF) had favoured in their proposals the control of capital movements, since short-term capital flows in the 1920s and 1930s were considered a fundamental ill of the inter-war economy. According to Keynes:

> It is widely held that control of capital movements, both inward and outward, should be a permanent feature of the post-war system… If control is to be effective, it probably involves the machinery of exchange control for all transactions, even though a general open license is given to all remittances in respect of current trade.[78]

White had noted that each member country should 'subscribe to the general policies of permitting foreign exchange trading in an open, free and legal market, and to abandon, as rapidly as conditions permit, all restrictions or controls by which various classes of foreign exchange transactions have been prohibited or interfered with'. However, he also pointed out that, in practice, there are situations 'that make inevitable the adoption of controls' on movements of capital.[79]

As noted earlier, a lot has changed since 1944 in terms of volume and composition of capital flows; however, the law of the IMF has not changed in this respect, even though some economists have advocated the need to extend convertibility to capital account.[80] In the European Union and in developed countries generally, capital account liberalization is the norm. But the tide turned following the financial crises in East Asia in the late 1990s and the Global Financial Crisis of 2007–2009, and the momentum to push forward an amendment to the IMF Articles of Agreement to extend the Fund's jurisdiction to 'capital transactions' was lost. Indeed, it is unlikely that 'capital account convertibility' will be adopted *de jure* by the IMF any time soon. The recognition also about the disruptive effects of the speculative short-term flows has influenced IMF policy prescriptions, mainly focused on the management of capital flows.

Article VIII (2) requires members to avoid restrictions on *current* payments and transfers; i.e., members have an obligation to offer unrestricted access to foreign

[78] See paragraph 45 of Keynes's 1942 proposal, reproduced in J Keith Horsefield (ed.), *The International Monetary Fund 1945–1965* (Vol. 3, IMF 1969) 13.

[79] See White's 1942 proposal in ibid 47 and 63.

[80] See, e.g., Stanley Fischer, 'Capital Account Liberalization and the Role of the IMF' in Stanley Fischer and others, *Should the IMF Pursue Capital Account Convertibility?* (Princeton Essays in International Finance No 207, 1998).

exchange to conduct trade in goods and services. This obligation is often referred to as an obligation to maintain 'current account convertibility'. However, the jurisdiction of the IMF extends only to payments and transfers for *current* international transactions, not to *capital* transactions (the regulation of capital movements is left to the Member States). This distinction in the Articles of Agreement between 'current' and 'capital' transactions—largely due to historical considerations—is considered by some to be 'conceptually and operationally awkward'.[81]

It is interesting to link this debate about exchange controls with the early history of MOCOMILA, a body with which Mann was also personally involved; indeed, the history of MOCOMILA also involves the history of Mann, both as a member and as the inspiring figure for future generations of monetary lawyers.

The International Law Association (ILA) was founded in October 1873 and the Monetary Law Committee of the ILA or MOCOMILA was established by the Executive Council of the ILA in 1951. The original rapporteur was FA Mann and its president, Max Gutzwiller.[82] At its 45th Conference in Lucerne in 1952, the ILA instructed MOCOMILA to submit a statement of principles relating to such questions of monetary law as the Committee deemed appropriate. At that first meeting, FA Mann announced that 'our task is to harmonize international monetary law'. In its first report to the ILA, MOCOMILA said that it had resolved:

> [T]o devote its attention primarily to practical questions rather than matters of academic interest ... with a view to developing principles recommended for general acceptance, in particular: (i) the conflict of laws relating to exchange controls, (ii) the law of protective clauses (gold clauses, index clauses, etc.) with special reference to their efficacy in the event of legislative interferences, (iii) the determination of the money of account with special reference to certain types of contracts such as insurance, sale, agency and negotiable instruments, (iv) international investments and their protection by international monetary law, (v) the enforcement of foreign currency obligations, and (vi) international cooperation in monetary matters.[83]

MOCOMILA opined that the 'branch of monetary law which is most urgently in need of international clarification is the conflict of laws relating to exchange controls'. Particular attention was directed at Article VIII(2)(b) of the IMF Articles of Agreement, a provision that the Committee found 'so obscure that it cannot afford any authoritative guidance to the solution of our problem'.[84] Mann led the

[81] See, e.g., Manuel Guitián, *The Unique Nature of the Responsibilities of the International Monetary Fund*, IMF Pamphlet Series No 46 (IMF 1992) 31 <https://www.imf.org/external/pubs/ft/pam/pam46/pam46.pdf> accessed 9 May 2023.

[82] See Lee Buchheit, 'An Early History of MOCOMILA' available at https://www.mocomila.org/about/history.pdf accessed 9 May 2023 (hereafter Buchheit, 'MOCOMILA').

[83] ibid.

[84] Article VIII(2)(b) of the IMF Articles of Agreement reads as follows:

discussions of Article VIII(2)(b) and urged the Committee to treat the IMF Articles of Agreement as a *fait accompli* and to accord them a degree of 'respect, goodwill and loyalty' commensurate with a treaty of such magnitude.[85] Exchange controls, and in particular the implications of Article VIII(2)(b), occupied the attention of MOCOMILA in the 1950s and 1960s, while the global sovereign debt crisis (following Mexico's default in 1982) set much of the agenda for the Committee's meetings in the 1980s.

1. Mann and interpretation of Article VIII(2)(b)

Writing at the turn of the millennium in an homage to Sir Joseph Gold, Werner Ebke described the evolution of Article VIII(2)(b) against the background that neither the drafters of the Agreement nor the legislators of the IMF Member States, when giving effect under their domestic law to it, foresaw the development of the law:

> The past fifty years witnessed a rapid increase in actions in which Article VIII, section 2(b), was invoked as a defense. Infrequent in the 1950s, such actions have ripened into a complex body of law. Article [VIII(2)(b)] must, no doubt, rate as the most profoundly powerful instrument in the hands of courts and administrative agencies of the IMF Member States, designed to foster, within the Fund and between its members, the institutional objectives of international monetary cooperation and collaboration at each stage of international business and finance transactions. Without belittling the role of the judiciary, it is fair to say that legal scholars have contributed greatly to the extraordinary development of the law under Article [VIII(2)(b)].[86]

Mann also played a leading role in this debate. Although the early editions of *The Legal Aspect of Money*—and Arthur Nussbaum's American counterpart text—concentrated on other matters (primarily domestic and comparative law and private international law), following the creation of the IMF both authors added sections dealing with the public international law of money. According to Stephen Zamora, however, both books remain heavily weighted towards the comparative

> Exchange contracts which involve the currency of any member and which are contrary to the exchange control regulations of that member maintained or imposed consistently with this Agreement shall be unenforceable in the territories of any member. In addition, members may, by mutual accord, cooperate in measures for the purpose of making the exchange control regulations of either member more effective, provided that such measures and regulations are consistent with this Agreement.

[85] See Buchheit, 'MOCOMILA' (n 82).

[86] Werner Ebke, 'Sir Joseph Gold and the International Law of Exchange Controls' (2001) 35(4) The International Lawyer 1475, 1475.

law approach rather than focusing on international monetary law *per se*.[87] In the fourth edition, Mann wrote:

> [There] are certainly important rules which international law has grafted upon the municipal law of money. Yet their scope is relatively limited and modest. ... The reason for the absence of a comprehensive international law of money lies not only in the grave practical difficulties which stem from political and economic causes as well as from the fact that in many respects a common standard is lacking, but is also to be found in the widespread impression that the existing body of international law has failed to develop any rules of conduct in monetary affairs.[88]

In the preface to the fifth edition—published posthumously in 1992—Mann sets out his final view in characteristically strident terms:

> Lastly, it is necessary to express regret that Chapter XIII dealing with Article VIII(2)(b) of the [IMF Articles] requires a disproportionate and ever increasing amount of space in order to explain a single provision consisting of a few, largely obscure words. Although correctly understood they are of very limited scope, for more than 40 years they have bedevilled international legal practice and in most countries, including the United Kingdom, led to unsatisfactory results. It is suggested that the United Kingdom should follow the example of Australia, Sweden, and Mexico and eliminate the provision from its municipal law. It ought to have no place in the law of a modern State intent upon upholding international commercial practice.[89]

As noted earlier, Mann acted as an inspiration for future generations of monetary lawyers, both in MOCOMILA and generally in the world of academia, central banking, and international financial institutions. One of us (Lastra) is currently Vice-Chair of MOCOMILA and had drawn inspiration from Mann in the analysis of the international monetary system. Indeed, the books *Legal Foundations of International Monetary Stability* (OUP 2006) and *International Financial and Monetary Law* (OUP 2015) trace the history and evolution of the public international law of money and the regulation of finance. In this regard, building on the legacy of Mann, these two works have become seminal in their own right and portray a far more complicated system than the one that was designed in the 1940s. The system continues to change, and institutional issues have become far

[87] Stephen Zamora, 'Sir Joseph Gold and the Development of International Monetary Law' (1989) 23(4) The International Lawyer 1009, 1010–11.

[88] FA Mann, *The Legal Aspect of Money* (4th edn, OUP 1982) 463 (hereafter Mann, *Legal Aspect Fourth Edition*).

[89] FA Mann, *The Legal Aspect of Money* (5th edn, OUP 1992) vi (hereafter Mann, *Legal Aspect Fifth Edition*).

more relevant. In dialogues with Charles Proctor, the architect and author of the subsequent post-mortem editions of Mann's magnum opus, it is clear that Proctor himself is moving beyond the world of exchange contracts and exchange controls, nominalism, and monetary obligations into a far more complex and multi-dimensional world, where the international monetary system is not as easily identifiable as it was when the IMF was set up and until the abandonment of the Bretton Woods par value regime. In this regard, questions about Article VIII(2)(b) need to be contextualized in the world that Mann lived and that gave rise to the formulation of the IMF Articles of Agreement.

Coming back to Article VIII(2)(b), the key question relates to its interpretation and scope. What exchange control laws fall within the provision? Which domestic and international 'contracts' fall within the definition of 'exchange contracts' and are therefore 'unenforceable'? What is the meaning of 'enforceability' and what are its consequences? Broadly, Mann opposed an approach that gave the provision limited effect in the interests of preserving commercial certainty in international contracting. This was considerably narrower than the approach favoured by other leading lights, including Sir Joseph Gold of the Legal Department of the IMF. However, it was also considerably broader than the approach favoured by Nussbaum, who interpreted the category of 'exchange contracts' very narrowly to mean only 'contracts for the exchange of currency' and no other contracts.[90]

Mann's approach to Article VIII(2)(b) followed from his views on monetary sovereignty: he saw exchange contract problems as a matter of (and for) private international law, without the treaty-based intervention that he interpreted as having doubtful meaning and undesirable consequences for international commerce.[91] Mann and Gold maintained a cordial correspondence over the years, noting their fundamental disagreement on this and similar matters. In a 1969 exchange, for example, Gold noted two points of disagreement on the interpretation of Article IV(6), writing that he hopes Mann will 'accept these comments in the spirit of fun that you have mentioned in your letter'.[92] In the fifth edition, Mann notes that Gold's contributions 'invariably advocate[d] an excessively broad interpretation and scope of the [IMF Articles]'.[93] In a short piece published as an IMF Staff Paper, Gold addresses Mann's position directly:

[90] Charles Evan, 'The Legal Aspects of Money, Second Edition by FA Mann' (1956) 32(1) The Indiana Law Journal 119, 121.

[91] In the fourth edition, he wrote: 'subject to such exceptions as customary international law or treaties have grafted upon the rule, the municipal legislator is free to define the currency of his country, to decide whether or no [sic] it should be based on gold, to depreciate or appreciate its value, to permit or abolish gold clauses, to impose exchange control or to take other measures affecting monetary relations. Customary international law does not normally fetter the municipal legislator's discretion in these matters or characterize his measures as an international wrong for which he could be held responsible... And where international relations arise, customary international law allows each State to devise its own system of private international law and thus to determine the extent to which the monetary laws of foreign States are applicable within its boundaries.' Mann, *Legal Aspect Fourth Edition* (n 88) 465–66.

[92] Joseph Gold to FA Mann (RS149_NLMann_0293, 4 August 1969).

[93] Mann, *Legal Aspect Fifth Edition* (n 89) XX.

> Dr. Mann's distinction in the field of monetary law gives great weight to his views. This is enhanced by his pioneer work—as a contributor to legal periodicals and as Rapporteur of the [MOCOMILA]—in directing the attention of the legal profession to the provision and in analyzing some of its many complexities. Some of the views on the provision expressed by Dr. Mann in his new edition should receive general assent; although other points are more doubtful, there is at least an even chance that he may be right. However, there are some conclusions of a quite fundamental character which should not be accepted.[94]

Gold proceeds to take issue with three propositions. The first is a technical point Mann makes about the construction of Article VIII(2)(b), drawing a distinction between the 'unenforceability' and 'invalidity' of a contract. The second is an equally technical distinction between 'making' an exchange contract and 'performing' one. The third point relates to the application of Article VIII(2)(b) to domestic as well as international contracts.

Their difference of opinion can be illustrated by the case of *Wilson, Smithett & Cope Ltd v Teruzzi*.[95] This case concerned certain members of the London Metal Exchange (LME), who carried on business as dealers and brokers in metals, and Terruzzi, a resident of Italy who dealt in metals. The parties entered into a series of contracts, including six which provided for the delivery of quantities of certain metals. These contracts were all denominated in sterling. Terruzzi was a speculator, who was hoping to sell the metals on immediately and profit from a fall in price that he anticipated in the three months between contracting and delivery. Unfortunately for Terruzzi, the prices rose substantially instead of falling, such that he owed the LME members a significant amount of money. He sought to avoid the contract on the grounds that they were exchange contracts contrary to the regulations imposed in Italy; as such, he argued that the English courts should refuse to enforce them under Article VIII(2)(b).[96]

Mann continued to believe in the broadest possible approach VIII(2)(b)—in effect, he thought that Lord Denning had got it right in *Terruzzi* that it caught contracts which in any way affect a country's exchange resources.

Teruzzi both illustrates Mann's impressive impact on the development of the English law on exchange controls, and its limits. In an earlier case, *Sharif v Azad*,[97] Lord Diplock had held that that Article VIII(2)(b) should be liberally construed, 'having regard to the object of the Bretton Woods Agreement to protect the

[94] Joseph Gold, 'Article VIII, Section 2(b), of the Fund Agreement and the Unenforceability of Certain Exchange Contracts: A Note' (International Monetary Fund Staff Papers) 335–36.

[95] [1976] 1 Lloyd's Rep. 509.

[96] This summary draws on Joseph Gold, 'Exchange Contracts, Exchange Control, and the IME Articles of Agreement: Some Animadversions on *Wilson, Smithett & Cope Ltd. v. Terruzzi*' (1984) 33(4) International & Comparative Law Quarterly 777, 784–85.

[97] [1967] 1 QB 605.

currencies' of the Member States; Lord Denning suggested that the term 'exchange contracts' should be interpreted to mean 'any contracts which *in any way* affect the country's exchange resources'.[98] Gold observed that '[i]n the *Terruzzi* case, Lord Denning, in retreating from his earlier opinion, explained that he had accepted this definition because it had the support of Dr F. A. Mann, and "in the belief that, coming from such a source, it must be right" '.[99] The debate at this point becomes quite technical, relating to the proper approach to construing the words 'exchange contract' in the context of the IMF Articles. The *Teruzzi* court adopted something more consistent with Nussbaum's formulation of 'contracts for the exchange of currency' rather than Mann's preferred approach.

Consequently, most of Mann's additions to the fifth edition in this regard involved his strong disagreement with Lord Diplock's speech in the House of Lords in *United City Merchants v Royal Bank of Canada*[100]—which he, in his inimitable style, suggested should be ignored. The point was that Lord Diplock had confirmed the narrow interpretation of 'exchange contracts' but added to the scope of VIII(2)(b) a new type of contract, effectively 'exchange contracts in disguise'.

In addition to the preface cited above, Mann added a footnote in the fifth edition[101] to the effect that since Australia, Mexico, and Sweden had all become members of the IMF without enacting local legislation enforcing VIII(2)(b), it must therefore be open to the United Kingdom to repeal the relevant provisions of the Bretton Woods Order in Council while remaining an IMF member: 'Article VIII(2)(b) should almost 50 years after the end of the world war be recognised as an aberration. If it cannot be abrogated, the United Kingdom should follow the Australian, Mexican and Swedish example.'[102]

This point seems to have arisen from a brief correspondence with Dr Lars AE Hjerner of the University of Stockholm in May 1991, while Mann was working on the fifth edition. Mann wrote: 'I wonder whether you could help me on the following point. I understand that Sweden has not accepted Article 8(2)(b) of the Articles of Agreement of the International Monetary Fund. Is this correct?' Hjerner confirmed that Sweden did adhere to the IMF Agreement and had made no reservation but took a dualist approach to the effect of international legal instruments in private law and Article VII(2)(b) seems not to have been transposed into Swedish law. Mann replied that this 'gives me the information I require and confirms my belief that a Swedish Court cannot apply Article 8(2)(b), and that, after all, is all that matters'.

98 ibid 615, 618.
99 Gold (n 96) 793.
100 [1982] 2 Lloyd's Rep. 1
101 Mann, *Legal Aspect Fifth Edition* (n 89) 364.
102 FA Mann to LAE Hjerner (Mann estate, RS146_NLMann_0361, 8 May 1991 and 3 June 1991); LAE Hjerner to FA Mann (Mann estate, RS146_NLMann_0361, 30 May 1991).

What this debate illustrates is Mann's engagement with the evolving nature of the legal aspects of money. Though part of such debate feels antiquated in a world in which private capital flows have grown exponentially and in which some financial institutions are larger than many states, part of it remains very relevant for the understanding of the limitations of our institutional legal setting.

V. Conclusion

The history of the Spanish translation of *The Legal Aspect of Money* helps us appreciate the ingenuity and continuous engagement with evolving monetary matters that characterizes the intellectual legacy of Mann and his persistence in getting the translation done. By contextualizing the translation against the economic conditions in Latin America in the 1980s, the chapter casts some light (1) on the influence on Mann in the development of monetary law in the region, (2) on the dialogue between law and economics, and (3) on some specific aspects of the law of exchange controls on the one hand and the law of sovereign debt on the other hand. While the former (exchange controls) is anchored in the power of the state, the latter (sovereign debt) shows the limitations of the powers of states (in particular debtor countries) in the international financial arena. Notwithstanding the important role of the IMF as an arbiter or referee in sovereign debt workouts, debt restructuring remains mostly a contractual matter, albeit one heavily influenced by the confluence of law, geopolitics, markets, and economic realities.

The recurrent nature of crises in Latin America suggests that we need an improved legal and institutional framework to pave the way for sustainable development in the region. Mann invited us through his work to look at the law of money in a systematic way. The law has changed but the invitation remains.

Bibliography

Avramoviĉ D, 'External Debt of Developing Countries in Late 1983' in Miguel S Wionczek in collaboration with Luciano Tomassini (eds), *Politics and Economics of External Debt Crisis. The Latin American Experience* (Routledge 2019)

Barroso Franco GH, *The Real Plan and the Exchange Rate. Essays in International Finance* (Princeton University 2000)

Boada Morales S, 'La naturaleza jurídica de la cuenta bancaria' (2019) 36 Revista de Derecho Privado 171

Davidson P, 'Money and the Real World' (1972) 82 The Economic Journal 101

Díaz-Alejandro CF, 'Latin American Debt: I Don't Think We Are in Kansas Anymore' (1984) 1984(2) Brookings Papers on Economic Activity 335

Díaz-Alejandro CF, 'Good-Bye Financial Repression, Hello Financial Crash' (1985) 19 Journal of Development Economics 1

de la Fuente Rodríguez J, 'Generalidades del Dinero' (2018) 271 Revista de la Facultad de Derecho de México 789

Fanelli JM, 'Liberalización Financiera y Cuenta de Capital: Observaciones Sobre la Experiencia de los Países en Desarrollo' (1998) 38(149) Desarrollo Económico 339

Fernández Cruz G, 'La naturaleza jurídica de los intereses: punto de conexión entre derecho y economía' (1991) 45 Derecho PUCP 177

García-Pita y Lastres J, 'El sistema Financiero Peruano, Ante La Reforma Constitucional: Modelo Constitucional Económico y Sistema Financiero' (2002) 3(3) Revista de Derecho 169

Giral Pimentel JA, 'Derecho Internacional Privado Sustantivo de los Títulos de Crédito en Venezuela' (1995) 96 Revista de la Facultad de Ciencias Jurídicas y Políticas de la Universidad Central de Venezuela 83

Hicks JR, *Critical Essays in Monetary Theory* (Clarendon Press 1967)

Keynes JM, *A Treatise on Money: The Pure Theory of Money* (Vol. 1, first published 1930, Harcourt Brace & Co. 1976)

Knapp GF, *The State Theory of Money* (HM Lucas and J Bonar tr., Macmillan & Co. 1924)

Knapp GF, *The State Theory of Money* (first published 1924, Augustus M. Kelley 1973)

Knapp GF, *Die Staatliche Theorie des Geldes* (first published 1905, Makroskop-Mediengesellschaft 2018)

Lerner AP, 'Functional Finance and the Federal Debt' (1943) 10 Social Research 38

Lerner AP, 'Money as a Creature of the State' (1947) 37(2) American Economic Review 312

Lissakers K, *Banks, Borrowers and the Establishment* (Basic Books 1991)

López Escudero M, 'El Derecho Monetario Internacional en la Era de la Globalización Financiera' (2003) https://www.ehu.eus/eu/web/cursosderechointernacionalvitoria/-/el-derecho-monetario-internacional-en-la-era-de-la-globalizacion-financiera

McKinnon RI, *Money & Capital in Economic Development* (The Brookings Institution 1973)

Mann FA, *El Aspecto Legal del Dinero: con referencia especial al derecho internacional privado y público* [*The Legal Aspect of Money: With Special Reference to Comparative Private and Public International Law*] (Spanish translation of the 4th edn, Fondo de Cultura Económica 1986)

Martin DA, 'The Medium Is Not The Money' (1972) 6 Journal of Economic Issues 67

Moreno y Gutiérrez FJ, 'Sistema Monetario Mexicano' (DPhil thesis, Universidad Panamericana 2012)

Ocampo JA and others, *La crisis latinoamericana de la deuda desde la perspectiva histórica* (CEPAL 2014)

Ossola FA, 'Arts. 746 a 804' in Ricardo Luis Lorenzetti (ed.), *Código Civil y Comercial de la Nación Comentado* (Vol. V, Rubinzal-Culzoni Editores 2015)

Osterling Parodi F and Castillo Freire M, *Estudios sobre las obligaciones dinerarias en el Perú* (Universidad Nacional Autónoma de México 1995)

Pelletier Barberena R, 'Teoría de la Imprevisión: Remedios contra los efectos de la depreciación monetaria' (1995) 25 Jurídica anuario del Departamento de Derecho de la Universidad Iberoamericana 247

Quiróz Valencia AM, Durán Galvis CJ, and Villamil López JE, 'La corrección monetaria y su aplicación judicial en el campo contractual colombiano' (B.S. thesis, Universidad Autónoma de Bucaramanga 2005)

Rochon L-P and Vernengo M, 'State Money and the Real World: Or Chartalism and Its Discontents' (2003) 26(1) Journal of Post Keynesian Economics 57

Shaw ES, *Financial Deepening in Economic Development* (OUP 1973)

Torres Calderón JA, 'Contrato de arrendamiento de entidades estatales con renta en especie: inexistencia- atipicidad' (MPhil thesis, Universidad Santo Tomás de Aquino 2017)

Vargas Morgado J, 'Observaciones acerca de la naturaleza jurídica del papel moneda' (2009) 5 Revista de la Asociación Internacional de Derecho Administrativo 405

Villard Duran C, 'Jurisprudência comentada (ADPF 77): o debate judicial sobre a disciplina jurídica da moeda como padrão de valor' (2015) 70(18) Revista de Direito Bancário e do Mercado de Capitais (RDB) 294

Wiegand J, *Bank Recycling of Petro Dollars to Emerging Market Economies During the Current Oil Price Boom* (IMF Research Department Working Paper WP/08/180, July 2008)

Wray LR, *Credit and State Theories of Money* (Edward Elgar Publishing 2004)

Wray LR, *From the State Theory of Money to Modern Money Theory: An Alternative to Economic Orthodoxy* (Levy Economics Institute of Bard College Working Paper 172, 2014)

13

Mann on Cryptocurrency

Simon Gleeson

I. Introduction

What legal rights does the producer of a money token have over that token after it passes into circulation? And how are those rights different depending on whether the producer of the money token is or is not a sovereign? This chapter addresses (but does not resolve) these questions.

FA Mann defined money as a chattel 'issued by the authority of law'[1] and, if he had held religiously to that view, these questions would have had no meaning for him. However, he resiled from this definition in practice; it was as clear to him[2] as it was to Arthur Nussbaum[3] that sometimes things created other than by the state circulated as currency, sometimes backed by the full force of law with the positive

[1] FA Mann, *The Legal Aspect of Money* (5th edn, OUP 1992) 8 (hereafter Mann, *Legal Aspect*). The reason for citing this edition is that much of Mann's material relating to exchange control has been removed from later editions as the discipline has fallen into practical desuetude.

[2] ibid 19.

[3] Arthur Nussbaum, *Money in the Law—National and International* (2nd edn, Foundation Press 1950) 34–6 (hereafter Nussbaum, *Money in the Law*).

Simon Gleeson, *Mann on Cryptocurrency* In: *FA Mann*. Edited by: Jason Grant Allen and Gerhard Dannemann, Oxford University Press. © Simon Gleeson 2024. DOI: 10.1093/oso/9780198881452.003.0014

status of recognized legal tender, and at other times deriving their legal status as money from nothing more than the fact of their widespread circulation.[4] There is more to money than the law.

Mann was adamant that the powers of a sovereign creator of a money token over the use of that token extended beyond the mere right to determine its value ('nominalism') and included some degree of control over the subsequent use of that money. The most common form of such controls is the imposition of exchange controls. This is in practice an attempt by the creator of a currency to provide that, as between two parties otherwise unconnected with it, that currency may be used in some transactions but not others. This is a now largely forgotten battlefield, although it was one on which Mann fought many battles. Mann took the view that a currency creator had an inherent right to impose exchange control restrictions or to take other measures affecting monetary relations,[5] and that such restrictions should in principle be respected and enforced by other states.

The question as to what the nature of these rights might be, and in particular whether they are manifestations of public or private law, is of some considerable difficulty. Mann elided the point by suggesting the existence of a *lex monetae*—broadly the idea that money itself has a proper law which should be applied to some transactions involving it. However, the nature of such a *lex monetae* is numinous. What gives a currency unit the attribute of a *lex monetae*? Is it the fact that it is recognized as 'currency', or is it the fact that it is created by a 'sovereign'? Is the concept of *lex monetae* prescriptive or descriptive?

The reason that this matters is that current developments in the field of computer science and payment practice seem to be trending towards the production and circulation of private monies. In principle there is nothing novel about private money per se—notes issued by commercial banks have at one time or another circulated in most major economies and been treated as money. The question that needs to be answered in this regard is what the differences are between the powers of a sovereign issuer of money over that money and the powers of a private issuer of money over that money.

One way of addressing this question is to ask whether privately issued money would have its own *lex monetae*. Considered as a simple yes/no question, the answer to this question is clearly no—whether or not *lex monetae* is a purely public law doctrine, it unquestionably has a public law element to it, which cannot be simply mapped across to a private issuer. However, the question is in fact more nuanced than this in two ways. The first nuance is as to whether it might be possible, through the doctrines of private law, to impose restrictions on the use of a private monetary instrument which are similar to those imposed by a *lex monetae*.

[4] For instance, California gold coins. See ibid, 12; *Chapman v Cole* [1858] 78 Mass. (12 Gray) 141; and for Mann see Mann, *Legal Aspect* (n 1) 19.

[5] Mann, *Legal Aspect* (n 1) 461.

The second is as to what degree of connection might be required between a private monetary instrument and a state to bring that instrument within the scope of the public law of that state, and what such a hybrid *lex monetae* might look like.

The starting point for these enquiries must be a more detailed examination of the nature of *lex monetae* than is generally considered useful. This must begin with consideration of which rights of a money creator are generally recognized, and on what juridical basis.

II. The Rights of a Sovereign Over Its Money

A. Nominalism

One of the essential rights of the creator of a thing is to *designate* that thing. Assume that a car manufacturer has three models, called the 100, the 200, and the 300. I have an agreement with a garage to purchase, next year, a model 200. Now assume that the manufacturer, as part of a rebranding exercise, redesignates the cars so that they are now called the 200, the 300, and the 400. What have I agreed to buy? It seems entirely clear that if I have agreed to buy a 200, I have agreed to buy whatever vehicle the manufacturer designates as a 200. I will not get what I thought I was going to get, but, having identified the thing I wanted by reference to the manufacturer's designation, there is no scope for arguing that I should get anything other than the thing that the manufacturer so designates.

All of this is axiomatic, and none of it requires the postulation of a *lex automobilia*. Why is the position different for money?

The answer to some extent is that money is legislated for, and where a thing is the subject of legislation that legislation tends to be considered as part of dealings with it. However, this takes us back to a debate which has existed within monetary theory for a very long time. The question may be posed thus: is money a thing which exists, and is separately recognized in law, or is it something whose existence is the result of its recognition in law?

This point was one of the fundamental disagreements between Mann and Nussbaum. Mann, coming from legal culture in which money had been a state responsibility for centuries, had no doubt that money derived its status as such through the will of the sovereign. Nussbaum, a Berlin émigré like Mann to the US but also a historian of the US economy,[6] was absolutely clear that money had existed in many forms across the American states well before the Federal legislature took an interest in the subject, and was equally clear that monetary legislation regulated existing payment mechanisms but did not create them.

[6] Arthur Nussbaum, *A History of the Dollar* (Columbia University Press 1957).

This is not the place to resolve this debate. However, its existence must be borne in mind as we approach the idea of *lex monetae*. For Mann, money was a creature of law. In recognizing a thing as money, one necessarily recognizes the law which creates it. This raises what might be described as the paradox of *lex monetae*: monetary law is necessarily public law, and the courts of one country in general do not recognize the public law of other countries. However, in dealing with monetary obligations, the principle of nominalism requires exactly that recognition.

Assume that a purely private body creates and issues a payment instrument. The instrument has no formal legislative recognition in any legal system, but circulates widely, and contracting parties regularly specify it as a payment medium. How should courts approach obligations to deliver it? The principle of nominalism would seem to apply to it in exactly the same way that it applied to the car in the earlier example. It may be recalled that the original Facebook 'Libra' of 2019[7] proposal involved the establishment of a value for each Libra coin based on an index of other currencies. It seems entirely clear that parties who had contracted for payment in Libra would be obliged to accept Libra in the form which its producer specified, such that if Facebook had changed the balance of the currencies used to compile the index, the value of Libra would thereafter have to be taken to be that resulting from the newly rebalanced index.

What, therefore, is the difference between the ideas of *lex monetae* and nominalism? Or, put another way, are there aspects of *lex monetae* which go beyond the concepts necessarily implied by nominalism?

B. Beyond nominalism

The idea that the rights of a state over its currency go beyond a simple power to specify that currency is commonly encountered in both academic writing and judicial decision-making. As the International Court of Justice said in the *Serbian Loans Case*,[8] 'it is indeed a generally accepted principle that a state is entitled to regulate its own currency', and the concept of regulation in this context clearly goes beyond simple specification.

A state is entitled to regulate anything within its own borders through the exercise of its police powers, and the ordinary monetary powers which are ascribed to a state—the power to define the currency of its territory, to devalue or revalue the currency, and to allow or reject the use of foreign currencies within its borders—derive from those police powers. Viewed from this perspective, a *lex monetae*

[7] See e.g. Clifford Chance, 'Facebook's Libra - an Exciting but Challenging Road Ahead' (27 June 2019) <https://www.cliffordchance.com/briefings/2019/06/facebook_s_libra-anexcitingbutchallengin.html> accessed 22 May 2023.

[8] *Serbian and Brazilian Loans Case* [1929] PCIJ Ser. A No. 20.

has no domestic application: these domestic rights—what Mann called 'internal' sovereignty[9]—are nothing to do with monetary law. The essence of a *lex monetae* is that the state may determine a set of attributes which are to be applied to its currency—which should be recognized and accepted *beyond its borders*. These are the rights which Mann suggests are 'external' rights. He argues that 'the obligation to recognise the monetary sovereignty of other states lies at the heart of the *lex monetae* principle'.[10] In identifying the essence of *lex monetae*, we therefore have to begin by asking which powers of a sovereign over its currency are recognized in the territory of other sovereigns.

The key point here is that a private creator of a monetary unit does not have police powers. It therefore follows that, by identifying the rights which a sovereign has over its currency outside its borders, we can identify the greatest extent of the powers which are available to a *non-state* creator of a monetary unit in any territory.[11] This is because it is an established principle of public international law that states do not enforce the public policy of other states within their territories. Thus any rights of a state over its currency which are in fact recognized by the courts of other jurisdictions cannot—*ex hypothesi*—be purely public law rights, and, if they are not public law rights, they could be attributable to a non-state actor.

The rule that states do not enforce the public laws of other states is well established: Rule 20 of *Dicey, Morris and Collins*[12] states in terms that:

> English courts have no jurisdiction to entertain an action: (1) for the enforcement, either directly or indirectly, of a penal, revenue or other public law of a foreign State; or (2) founded upon an act of state.[13]

In *Government of India v Taylor*,[14] Viscount Simonds observed[15] that the rule was already well established when Lord Mansfield CJ repeated the formula 'for no country ever takes notice of the revenue laws of another' in a series of cases in the 18th century.[16] Lord Keith explained that this is not a mere prejudice against revenue laws, but an articulation of a deeper principle, since the enforcement of a claim for taxes is an extension of the sovereign power which imposed the taxes, and that an assertion of sovereign authority by one state within the territory of another, as distinct from a patrimonial claim by a foreign sovereign, is (treaty or convention

[9] Mann, *Legal Aspect* (n 1) 527.
[10] ibid 276.
[11] By which we mean *state* territory, assuming that there are no significant non-state or interstitial territories today.
[12] Lord Collins and Jonathan Harris (eds), *Dicey, Morris & Collins on the Conflict of Laws* (16th edn, Sweet & Maxwell 2022).
[13] ibid.
[14] [1955] AC 491.
[15] ibid 504.
[16] *Planché v Fletcher* [1779] 1 Doug 251, 253; *Holman v Johnson* [1775] 1 Cowp 341, 343; and *Lever v Fletcher* [1780] unreported.

apart) contrary to all concepts of independent sovereignties. Hence, it is said, the exertion by a sovereign power of its sovereign jurisdiction can happen only within its sovereign territory, and can have no legal effect in any other jurisdiction.

If the creation of money were a purely sovereign act of state, this principle would prevent the monetary laws of any other country being exercised in the UK. However, that is not the law. In *Ottoman Bank v Chakarian (No 2)*,[17] exactly this argument was put before the Privy Council as regards a revaluation of the Turkish currency. Lord Wright dealt with it as follows:

> A further point put forward by Sir William Jowitt was based upon the construction of the Turkish statute which authorized the issue of currency notes and made them legal tender. These statutes were in terms limited to Turkish currency in Turkey. Sir William has contended that outside Turkey pre-war currency law remained in effect, so that the legal tender outside Turkey remained the Turkish gold pound. Their Lordships are unable to accept this contention. The currency in any particular country must be determined by the law of that country, and that law is naturally in terms limited to defining what is legal tender in that country. But when that is fixed by the local law it determines what is the legal tender of that country for purposes of transactions in any other country, so that a foreign Court will, when such questions come before it, give effect to the proper law of legal tender so determined. There is no foundation in their Lordships' judgment for the argument that Turkish paper is only legal tender as equivalent to gold *sub modo*, that is, within the territorial limits of Turkish jurisdiction.[18]

It is therefore clear that there is more to a *lex monetae* than a simple assertion of the nominalistic principle—what is being applied here is not simply the Turkish state's definition of its currency, but the 'proper law' of the currency *per se*. On this basis, English law—and the law of almost every other country—will recognize the jurisdiction of a state over its own money. This jurisdiction therefore cannot be simply a result of an act of state.[19]

If the extraterritorial powers of a state over its own money are not a product purely of private law, then what are they? This turns out to be a difficult question. Arthur Nussbaum correctly says that 'the rules relating to money are scattered over the various fields of law—contract, administrative, constitutional, criminal, procedural, international law etc [such that] an absolute classification seems inappropriate'.[20] It is arguable (and Nussbaum *does* argue) that the endowment of coins or notes with the character of legal tender is an act of sovereignty, and hence of public

[17] [1938] AC 260.
[18] [1938] AC 260 at 278.
[19] This, of course, begs the question as to whether, if it *were* an act of state, what sort of act of state it would be, see FA Mann, 'The Foreign Act of State' in *Foreign Affairs in English Courts* (OUP 1986) 164.
[20] Nussbaum, *Money in the Law* (n 3) 35–36.

law. However, foreign courts will consider the domestic legal status of a currency in deciding whether to recognize certain aspects of its legal nature which go well beyond its legal tender status (and, indeed, are necessarily irrelevant to that status, since legal tender legislation is necessarily purely territorial).

C. The territoriality of money

One possible explanation for the idea that the jurisdiction of a state extends to dealings with its currency outside its territory is the idea that money 'never leaves home'. The argument here is that, as Knapp has been interpreted as suggesting, all sovereign money is ultimately a claim on the sovereign power which created it. That sovereign can only be found, and can only be sued, in its own jurisdiction. In modern finance law, it is customary to regard all payments in a currency as ultimately settled through the domestic payment system (usually ultimately through the central bank) of the country of issue, and therefore to be potentially subject to the legislation of the sovereign of that country. The point of this argument is that the recognition of the *lex monetae* does not in fact represent the recognition of the public policy of the issuing state in the territory of another state, but simply a recognition by the courts of that other state that the transaction is ultimately executed on the territory of the home state, and therefore subject to its laws. The question of extraterritoriality therefore never arises.

The problem with this argument is that it elides the currency and the transaction. Where two people in the UK transact in US dollars, it is stretching language and logic to say that the transaction in fact occurs in the US. This argument becomes even weaker if the settlement of the transaction is effected by the transfer of physical cash, or by the delivery of a negotiable instrument of some form. Indeed, if this argument were correct, the whole idea of exchange control restrictions would be otiose, since countries would be indifferent to the physical location of their money. We must therefore conclude that the territoriality of physical money should be determined in the same way as for any other physical thing.

D. *Lex monetae* as protection of a public interest

The issue of the powers of a prince with respect to money outside his territory was examined in the English courts in the case of *Emperor of Austria v Day and Kossuth*.[21] The facts of this case were unusual. Kossuth was a revolutionary, who aimed to foment revolution in Hungary against the Austro-Hungarian emperor

[21] (1861) 2 Giff 628, 3 DE G F & J 216.

and to establish it as an independent country. As part of his preparations for that endeavour, he had commissioned from Day (a banknote printer in London) a series of banknotes purporting to be issued by the independent State of Hungary and bearing his signature. The notes bore no resemblance to any note circulating in the Austro-Hungarian empire, so no issue of forgery arose.

The emperor applied for an injunction restraining the defendants from continuing to manufacture the bank notes. His case was put on three grounds: (i) violation of his rights and prerogatives as king of Hungary 'by promotion of revolution and disorder and otherwise'; (ii) injury to the state of Hungary by the introduction of a spurious circulation into that kingdom; and (iii) injury to the subjects of the emperor in Hungary by the same cause.

There was no doubt that the English court did not have jurisdiction to interfere on the grounds that the notes were intended to be used for the purpose of promoting revolution and disorder. The court also rejected the second ground, holding that the right of coining and issuing paper money is the prerogative of a sovereign: 'so far, therefore, as this bill is founded upon the prerogative rights of the Plaintiff, or upon the political rights of his subjects' the injunction should be refused, since 'the prerogative rights of sovereigns seem to me, as at present advised, to stand very much upon the same footing as acts of State and matters of that description, with which the municipal courts of this country do not and cannot interfere'.[22]

However, the court upheld the injunction on the third ground. The Lord Chancellor, Lord Campbell, opined that 'if the acts meditated by the defendants and forbidden by this injunction were actually done, a pecuniary loss would be sustained by the plaintiff and by all his subjects, holders of the existing currency'.[23] He therefore concluded that the court had jurisdiction to protect property from an act which, *if* completed, *would* give a right of action. Lord Justice Turner said that the third ground on which the bill was based alleged a case of injury to the subjects of the kingdom, 'an injury not to the political but to the private rights of the plaintiff's subjects'. He concluded: 'I agree that the jurisdiction of this Court in a case of this nature rests upon injury to property actual or prospective, and that this Court has no jurisdiction to prevent the commission of acts which are merely criminal or merely illegal, and do not affect any rights of property, but I think there are here rights of property quite sufficient to found jurisdiction in this Court.'[24]

The important thing about this case is what it does not say. As Mann correctly observed, it found that it is *not* the case that 'customary public international law imposes upon the State the general duty of affording protection to the monetary systems of the other members of the family of nations'.[25] Courts will intervene in

[22] ibid 252.
[23] ibid 237.
[24] ibid 253–54.
[25] Mann, *Legal Aspect* (n 1) 479.

order to protect the private rights of a sovereign's subjects, but not the sovereign's public rights.

This establishes that, where a monetary token is in widespread circulation, the creator of that token will retain some rights in respect of it. The logic of the *Emperor of Austria* decision seems to be that, although the sovereign cannot sue to protect its own rights, the sovereign acts in its capacity as the representative of the people, and if the 'private' interests of the people are harmed, then those rights should be protected. The proposition thus established is that an autocrat cannot make peremptory rules in respect of currency and look to have them obeyed, but where the action which he is seeking to take can be established to be *bona fide* for the benefit of the people of the country over which he rules, that action will be recognized.[26]

The implication of this argument is that the state which creates an item of currency has some rights in respect of that item. However, those rights arise from its position not as a state issuer of currency but as the voice of the users of a currency, whose interests would otherwise be injured by a particular act in relation to it. This is, in principle, exactly on all fours with the position of a private creator of a non-state token. However, the House of Lords in the *Emperor of Austria* case clearly attached great significance to the fact that the bringer of the action was the sovereign authority—it was on this basis that the Emperor derived his ability to bring an action to protect the people of the state over which he was the sovereign. It is by no means unarguable that the private provider of a money token might be able to bring a similar action on a similar basis, but the point must for now remain undetermined.

III. A Quasi-*Lex Monetae*?

A. Quasi-*lex monetae* through private property law?

It may be noted at this point that one could suggest that a private provider of a money token might derive powers over transactions involving that token on a much more straightforward basis; that is, by virtue of its status as the token's creator, it retains some sort of possessory or proprietary interest in the token.

This idea has been regularly explored as a potential basis for state monetary sovereignty. The theoretical underpinnings of the sovereign theory of money are to be found in French 16th-century thought. This heavily advocated the proposition that because the prince had the sole right to coin money—the *ius cuidendae*

[26] I am grateful to Jason Allen for pointing out to me that this issue has arisen in a number of colonial and post-colonial Privy Council cases which dealt with the power of territorial authorities to make laws for the 'peace, order, and good governance' of the territory in question. See *R v Secretary of State for Foreign and Commonwealth Affairs, ex parte Bancoult (No 2)* [2008] UKHL 61 (the Chagos Islanders case) for an extreme example.

monetae—the money he created must ultimately belong to him, [27] or must at least be his '*ius et proprietas*'. This, it should be emphasized, was not an argument to the effect that the prince might take that money at will, but it was an argument that the prince had a residual interest in the money in circulation (a position which may seem extreme today, but in fact sits with a doctrine of monarchical absolutism which enjoyed considerable clerical support at the time[28]) which entitled him to assert some rights in respect of it—most notably, the right to have it called in and reissued in different denominations. The existence of this residual right does not seem to have been seriously challenged at any point, and was regularly asserted across Europe during the various recoinages.

However, there is a significant difference between the idea of residual rights and the idea of complete ownership. Nicolas Oresme (1320–1382) was clearly of the view that the provision of money to the community was a public function akin to the provision of justice or security. The prince was therefore not only entitled to provide money to his country, but also *obliged* to do so. However, did that make all money the prince's property? Oresme was clear that it did not, and in his commentary on the matter he came as near as he could to disagreeing with Jesus. In his Chapter VI, entitled 'Who owns the Money?', he says this:

> Although it is the duty of the prince to put his stamp on the money for the common good, he is not the lord or owner of the money current in his principality. For money is a balancing instrument for the exchange of natural wealth, as appears in Chapter I. It is therefore the property of those who possess such wealth. For if a man gives bread or bodily labour in exchange for money, the money he receives is as much his as the bread or bodily labour of which he (unless he were a slave) was free to dispose. For it was not to princes alone that God gave freedom to possess property, but to our first parents and all their offspring, as it is in Genesis. Money, therefore, does not belong to the prince alone. But if anyone object that our Saviour, when a penny was shown Him, asked: 'Whose is this image and superscription?' and when it was answered 'Caesar's', gave judgment: 'Render therefore unto Caesar the things which are Caesar's, and unto God the things that are God's' (as though He meant 'The coin is Caesar's because Caesar's image is stamped upon it'), it is clear to anyone who reads the context that He does not say that the money was due to Caesar because it bore Caesar's image, but because it was 'tribute'. For, as the apostle says: 'Tribute to whom tribute is due; custom to whom custom.' Christ therefore showed that the stamp was the means of knowing

[27] Bodin, *Six Livres de la Republique* (1576) I, Chap 11, 213. See Andreas Zimmermann, *A Contemporary Concept of Monetary Sovereignty* (OUP 2013) 9–12 and, for more detail, Rosa Lastra, *International Financial and Monetary Law* (OUP 2015) 13–20.

[28] See for example the quasi-absolutist ideas of Augustinius Triumphus of Ancona. The whole position as regards the nature and role of the state is well described in Michael Wilks, *The Problem of Sovereignty in the Later Middle Ages* (Cambridge University Press 2008).

> to whom the tribute was due, namely the person who fought the battles of the state, and by reason of his dominion had the right to coin money. Thus, money belongs to the community and to individuals. And so say Aristotle in the seventh book of the Politics 4 and Cicero about the end of the old Rhetoric.[29]

It is very hard not to side with Oresme in this argument. The whole point of money is that it is a universal medium which 'passes freely from hand to hand throughout the community',[30] and it is hard to square free circulation with an inherent limitation on ownership or use. It is also noteworthy that, if Mann is correct that money is to be analysed as if it were a chattel, there is no mechanism by which any such ownership right could be asserted under private law. The principle of *numerus clausus* which applies to chattels has it that title to chattels is broadly indivisible.[31] If it is said that the creator of a money token retains any sort of proprietary right to a token, it must be said that that proprietary right is one of complete ownership. As a result, it must be concluded that the only right which a holder of such a token can have is a temporary right to possession—akin to seisin of land—of a thing absolute ownership of which is vested in the state. This idea cuts so directly across one of the most fundamental concepts of the law of money—that transfer of possession conveys complete and unchallengeable title[32]—that it must be rejected in the context of private tokens.[33] It should also be pointed out that it is possible for a private creator of a chattel to impose contractual restrictions on its use by the immediate transferee, and there are some arguments to the effect that these restrictions may in some circumstances bind subsequent transferees—in particular where the asset transferred is a chose in action.[34] However, this proposition is debatable, and has recently (and entirely validly) been criticized by the Court of Appeal.[35] The conclusion is therefore that if it is not clear that any such retention of title could be accomplished under private law, and there is no explicit provision creating it under public law, it cannot easily be said to exist.

B. Quasi-*lex monetae* through private law generally

The absence of any proprietary right, however, does not imply the absence of any right at all. At this point, it is helpful to consider what rights the creator of a money

[29] Nicholas Oresme, *De Moneta* (C Johnson tr., Thomas Nelson & Sons 1956) ch. 7, 11.

[30] Per F.A. Walker, as approved in *Moss v Hancock* [1899] 2 QB 111, 116. However, Mann noted that the German Federal Supreme Court took a different view in Mann, *Legal Aspect* (n 1) 8.

[31] Michael Bridge and others, *The Law of Personal Property* (3rd edn, OUP 2022) paras 1–60.

[32] *Higgs v Holiday* (1600) Cro. Eliz. 746; also see Mann, *Legal Aspect* (n 1) 9.

[33] Restrictions on use can be imposed by private parties through contractual means.

[34] See *Linden Gardens Trust Ltd v Lenesta Sludge Disposals Ltd* [1994] 1 AC 85, especially at 108.

[35] *First Abu Dhabi Bank PJSC V BP Oil International Limited* [2018] EWCA Civ 14.

token absolutely and unquestionably *does* have, and they certainly include the right to determine its value. If, as a medieval merchant, I have in my purse a particular coin, the coin in my purse is mine, but the prince who issued it may at any time decide that it is worth something different from what I gave for it. There are two very different ways in which this may occur. One is in relation to the other coins which the prince has issued: if, for example, the prince has issued both silver and gold coins, he may in his absolute discretion assert that a gold coin which was previously worth 10 silver coins is now worth 12. The other is in relation to other coins: he may wish to decree that the gold coin that he issues is worth half of a gold coin issued by some other issuer.

The ability to determine the value of a unit of currency is, however, only one manifestation of the power of a sovereign over it. True dominion is ultimately demonstrated by the ability to *derecognize* it. This is convincingly and comprehensively demonstrated by the fact that the member states of the euro area effectively abolished their pre-euro domestic currencies by a simple legislative act. This did not simply result in the cessation of the circulation of pre-euro notes; it abolished the very concept of the predecessor currencies as ideal units. On the day after the changeover, a French franc balance maintained by (say) a Sudanese depositor with (say) a Malawian bank became a euro balance without either party having any say in the matter.

This is nominalism in action at its most muscular, but it is worth considering how it comes to be that an act of state of this kind can have this sort of extraterritorial effect. The point is that when we speak of a claim for money, we think in terms of a legal fiction whereby a money claim is a claim for delivery of a physical thing created by its issuer. If that issuer stopped creating that thing, delivery would become impossible, and the payment contract would be frustrated. Mann understood this, which is why he famously described money as a physical thing: specifically, a chattel personal.[36] He explained that 'from primitive periods until the present day men have been accustomed to connect the idea of money with definite symbols, whether these were animals, commodities, quantities of metal, or coins and bank notes'.[37] There is nothing wrong with legal fictions.[38] However, the idea that money is a physical thing is more a 'practical fiction'—a way of thinking about a situation which is universally applied even by those who know that it is incorrect.[39] This is why we speak of money as being 'created' by its issuer. However, it is not argued that a state ceases to have any involvement in its monetary units

[36] Mann, *Legal Aspect* (n 1) 8.
[37] ibid.
[38] Lon Fuller's 'legal fictions'.
[39] As an example, even specialist electrical engineers are inclined to think of electricity as 'flowing' around a circuit like water, although they are perfectly aware that as a matter of physics it does no such thing.

once created—if only because, as noted above, the state retains at least the residual power to derecognize those units.

IV. Exchange Control Powers

A. *The sovereign's power to restrain use of its currency*

It is reasonably easy to see how the idea that the sovereign has a right to determine by legislation the value of its currency within its territory morphed in the minds of governments into the idea that the sovereign had a right to determine by legislation the value of its currency as against the currency of other sovereigns. Thus was born the idea of exchange control through legislation. The monetary history of the 20th century can be seen as a titanic contest of strength between sovereigns, on the one hand, and people (or 'market forces'), on the other, to see how effectively and for how long governments could 'buck the market' in terms of the value of their own currencies. As with any struggle between sovereign power and market forces, the long-term outcome was never in doubt; it is now clear that this was a doomed venture which brought significant human suffering in its wake. However, in order to understand the authorities, it is necessary to remember that there were times when the idea that a government had a right to control the value of its currency appeared indisputable.

The earliest battles in this arena arose in respect of attempts by government to regulate the exchange of their currencies for gold. The most public trials of strength arose out of the 1933 'Joint Resolution to assure uniform value to the Coins and Currencies of the United States',[40] which inter alia prohibited any clause in any contract which required payment of a sum of US dollars assessed by reference to the dollar value of gold. In *Norman v Baltimore & Ohio Railroad Co*,[41] the US Supreme Court held that the intrinsic sovereign power of the United States extended to prohibiting certain transactions under US law where those transactions involved a dealing in US dollars which contravened the sovereign power of the Congress. The Supreme Court did not rely on any specific provision of the US Constitution, but explained that the right of Congress to vary the value of the US dollar was an inherent aspect of state sovereignty. Chief Justice Hughes said:

> [T]he source of that authority in all the related powers conferred upon the Congress and appropriate to achieve 'the great objects for which the government was framed'—'a national government, with sovereign powers'. [. . .] The broad and comprehensive national authority over the subjects of revenue, finance, and

[40] 73rd Congress Session 1, Chapter 48: Pub. Res. No. 10.
[41] 294 US 240 (1934).

> currency is derived from the aggregate of the powers granted to the Congress, embracing the powers to lay and collect taxes, to borrow money, to regulate commerce with foreign nations and among the several states, to coin money, regulate the value thereof, and of foreign coin, and fix the standards of weights and measures, and the added express power 'to make all laws which shall be necessary and proper for carrying into execution' the other enumerated powers.[42]

Although the issue involved a private transaction, the court concluded that:

> [T]he same reasoning applies to the constitutional authority of the Congress to regulate the currency and to establish the monetary system of the country. If the gold clauses now before us interfere with the policy of the Congress in the exercise of that authority, they cannot stand.[43]

This seems to be fairly clear—by virtue of its power to create the currency, the Supreme Court believed that the state has the inherent power to restrict its usage. Thus, if the creator of a currency wishes to provide that it cannot be used for a particular purpose, his right to do so derives not from his police power, but from his status as the creator of that currency.

B. *The extent of exchange control powers*

We therefore need to ask what the limits are of this residual power. Mann took the view that a currency creator had an inherent right to impose exchange control restrictions or to take other measures affecting monetary relations,[44] and that such restrictions should be respected and enforced by other states—provided that they were not contrary to the public policy of those states. It seems that he took the view that these powers arose out of the *lex monetae*.

This was, unsurprisingly, a controversial position. Nussbaum[45] took the view that exchange control restrictions were simply incapable of international private law recognition on grounds of public policy. Mann disagreed, taking the view that (a) exchange control restrictions were not aspects of state public policy, and were therefore not barred from recognition in the UK as acts of state, and (b) that that there was no other principle of UK public policy which absolutely prohibited the recognition of such laws.

42 294 US 241. The court cited *Juilliard v Greenman* 110 US 439–40.
43 ibid 312.
44 Mann, *Legal Aspect* (n 1) 461.
45 Nussbaum, *Money in the Law* (n 3) 461.

Mann argued that exchange control laws are unlike revenue laws, in that they are not mere manifestations of sovereign policy. His logic was that exchange control laws are equivalent to export and import restrictions or customs duties,[46] arguing that:

> If goods are sold from Brazil to France and France introduces import restrictions, judges will examine the effects of any impossibility which thus arises without regard to an alleged principle of public policy; if France introduces exchange control and makes payment of the price impossible, the approach cannot be different.[47]

Hence, he argued, if governments are entitled to pass laws restricting the import and export of physical goods, and those laws are respected in other jurisdictions, why should they not be equally able to pass laws restricting the import, export, and use of their own currency, with those restrictions also being respected in other jurisdictions.

Part of the problem with this argument is that it is an apples-to-oranges comparison—import restrictions do not pretend to have extraterritorial effect. It is also now not entirely clear that this is correct even in relation to import restrictions. In *Government of the Islamic Republic of Iran v The Barakat Galleries Ltd*,[48] the Court of Appeal confirmed that laws of another country which involve the exercise or assertion of a sovereign right or seek to enforce governmental interests will not be enforced in the UK. However, it also set out to explore where the borders of that class of rules might be. Importantly for our purposes, it observed that exchange control legislation was clearly within that class, and therefore unenforceable in the UK.[49] However, it also considered that it is possible, but by no means certain, that export restrictions also fall within it. For example, in *King of Italy v Marquis Cosimo de Medici Tornaquinci*[50] it was said that an Italian law prohibiting the removal of certain assets from Italy applied to those assets only whilst they remained in Italy, but did not restrict their disposal thereafter. It seems clear that if such legal restrictions do not apply to items constituting part of the national patrimony outside the jurisdiction, it is unlikely that similar restrictions could apply to national currency outside the jurisdiction, even if imposed by national law.

Mann also accepted that even if the exchange control laws of other jurisdictions were in principle capable of being enforced by the UK courts, there is an important public policy test to be applied before any such enforcement is ordered.[51]

[46] Mann, *Legal Aspect* (n 1) 401.

[47] ibid. This conclusion is at least questionable in the light of *King of the Hellenes v Brostrom* (1923) 16 LL LR 167. However, for a case where such arrangements were respected, see *Re Regazzoni v KC Sethia (1944) Ltd* (1958) AC 301 (HL).

[48] [2007] EWCA Civ 1374.

[49] para 127.

[50] (1918) 34 TLR 623. To be fair, in *King of the Hellenes* Lord Phillips observed that 'The case is not fully reported and is of little assistance'.

[51] Mann, *Legal Aspect* (n 1) 478.

His position was that there are numerous situations in which the design or effects of foreign exchange controls are such that the English courts should not enforce them. Here again, it is important to remember *when* Mann was writing. In the run-up to the Second World War, a number of restrictions were introduced by foreign states (notably Nazi Germany) in respect of cross-border transactions whose aim was explicitly to disadvantage a particular target group. In such circumstances, it is clear that the public policy of the forum may bar the recognition of any sovereign right that might otherwise exist. As Upjohn J said in *In Re Claim by Helbert Wagg & Co Ltd*:[52]

> [T]his court is entitled to be satisfied that the foreign law is a genuine foreign exchange law, that is, a law passed with the genuine intention of protecting its economy in times of national stress, and for that purpose regulating (*inter alia*) the rights of foreign creditors, and it is not a law passed ostensibly with that object but in reality with some object not in accordance with the usage of nations.

Mann's list of the objects encompassed in this last phrase[53] includes legislation which is ostensibly oppressive or discriminatory in character or application, or obviously preparatory or incidental to acts of illegal warfare, or of trade warfare, or contrary to the fundamental rights of man's personal freedom, or otherwise opposed to the policy of English law.[54] From this, his position is clearly that although there is no public policy reason why the English courts should necessarily and automatically refuse to recognize sovereign restrictions on the use of their currency, there is equally no public policy reason why those courts should necessarily and automatically give effect to such restrictions. Provisions of this latter kind will be rejected as a 'spoliative encroachment'.[55]

The conclusion that follows is that a state which creates a monetary unit retains some degree of control over the subsequent use and transmission of that unit simply by virtue of its status as the unit's creator, and independent of its status as a sovereign power. This, of course, raises some interesting questions as to whether and to what extent any such rights are reserved (or created) by a non-state actor. However, before we come to that question it is necessary to investigate a preliminary issue which sounds almost facile when articulated, but which in fact raises some profound and difficult questions of monetary law: When is a currency unit 'the currency of a state'?

[52] [1956] Ch 323, 351.
[53] Mann, *Legal Aspect* (n 1) 472–78.
[54] Mann, *Legal Aspect* (n 1) 406.
[55] See the decision of the Swiss Federal Tribunal of 8 October 1935 *Amtliche Sammelung* 61 II 242 at 248.

V. What Money Is Public Money?

A. When is money public money?

During and after the First World War, German cities and industrial undertakings issued private money (*Notgeld*, lit. 'emergency money'). Such instruments were issued entirely without the sanction (or even the knowledge) of the relevant government. However, the German Supreme Court held that they were nonetheless 'money', in that persons forging them were guilty of counterfeiting.[56] The court explained that this was not a departure from the principle that money only exists by authority of the state, on the basis that the state had retrospectively sanctioned the issue of such money by *tolerating* it.[57] This is broadly the same position as Knapp's argument that money is money by reason of its accommodation as such within the legal order, primarily by acceptance at the state pay offices.

Mann's position is therefore that the state theory of money, properly analysed, amounts to the proposition that a circulating medium is money if the state in some way accommodates the use of that medium as such. What does 'accommodation' mean in this regard? Knapp correctly identifies that the most basic form of 'accommodation' in this regard is acceptance in payment. Anything that the state routinely accepts in payment of money debts is, on this argument, money. This already broadens the definition considerably, and recent developments have placed even greater stress on the idea of 'accommodation'. Accommodation is a considerably broader concept than simple recognition in law. Joseph Sommer's essay in this volume[58] helpfully clarifies the basis of Mann's 'legal theory' of money and explains how it operated as a tool to facilitate the abandonment of monetary gold standards. However, he also clarifies that in reality the role of the state in the 'creation' of money arises not from its power as legislator, still less from any formal declaration (e.g. of legal tender status), but from what he describes as its 'enormous legitimacy and transactional power'.

Assume that a state wishes to encourage the circulation of crypto tokens which perform the function of money within its territory.[59] How does it go about 'accommodating' such a crypto currency, and when does such accommodation extend to constituting that crypto token as a form of sovereign money? A first approximation might be to give the tokens the status of legal tender. However, merely specifying that a monetary unit constitutes legal tender in your territory does not make that monetary unit 'yours'—when Zimbabwe adopted the US dollar as legal tender in 2014, the US dollar did not thereby become the currency of Zimbabwe. More is

56 14 June 1937, JW. 1937, 2381.
57 28 November 1923, RGZ. 107, 78 and see Mann, *Legal Aspect* (n 1) 19.
58 See Chapter 10 in this volume by Joseph Sommer, 'FA Mann's Conservative Revolution'.
59 As has recently been the case in El Salvador and the Central African Republic.

needed. The simplest approach is to follow the logic of Knapp and for the state simply to announce that it will systematically accept those crypto tokens in payment of obligations due to it. A further step might be to give the token provider an account with the central bank of the state concerned, and require it to operate on the basis that every token issued is backed by an equivalent deposit with that central bank (this is the basis on which Scottish currency is issued by private commercial banks today).

There are at least four possible fact-patterns here:

1) A state issues its own crypto coins which circulate alongside its ordinary money (generally referred to as 'Central Bank Digital Currency', or 'CBDC');
2) A private operator issues a coin which is tied to the state's own currency (generally referred to as a 'stablecoin') with the approval and cooperation of the state concerned;
3) A private issuer issues a private coin with its own value, but that coin is adopted by a sovereign authority as legal tender in its territory (as has recently happened in El Salvador and the Central African Republic); and
4) A private issuer issues a private coin, with no formal state adoption, but the coin becomes a widely circulating medium in the state concerned and is accepted by that state in payment of public debts.

It is probably not possible to answer the question of where the line is to be drawn as to what counts as 'accommodation' with certainty. However, what does seem certain is that once a state has taken sufficient steps in this direction, there will come a point at which the token is identifiably its own sovereign currency. This matters, because at this point public international law becomes engaged.

VI. Interaction of Private Currencies and the Treaty Law of Money

A. *Public international law of money and the IMF Treaty*

Article VIII of the Articles of Agreement of the International Monetary Fund (IMF) imposes on its member states a series of obligations. The most important, contained in Article VIII(2)(a), is not to impose restrictions on the making of payments and transfers for current international transactions. However, as regards capital transactions, the imposition of exchange controls is permitted. Most importantly, VIII(2)(b) provides:

> Exchange contracts which involve the currency of any member and which are contrary to the exchange control regulations of that member maintained or

> imposed consistently with this Agreement shall be unenforceable in the territories of any member.

Much of the discussion concerning this provision turns on the definition of 'exchange contract'. However, for this purpose we are interested in the meaning of the term 'involve the currency of any member'. Exchange control regimes generally apply to much more than the currency of the imposing country—for example, the Exchange Control Act 1947 in the UK applied to transactions involving gold, travellers' cheques, bills of exchange, and securities, as well as foreign currency. Mann took the view that this was entirely legitimate. He believed that a transaction 'involved the currency' of a particular state if it affected the financial area within which the transaction had economic effects. He said:

> 'Currency' should be construed in the broad sense of economics rather than the strictly legal sense. The term may include gold, securities of whatever denomination, even land, movables or intangibles; the transfer of such property may 'involve the currency' of a member state.[60]

As an example, he gave the French case of *De Boer v Ducro et al.*[61] In that case, a sale by a Dutch resident of shares in a French company to a German buyer for French francs was held to be contrary to the exchange control legislation of the Netherlands. The argument was that the transaction had the effect of reducing the capital stock of the Netherlands, and was therefore a contract involving the currency of the Netherlands. This interpretation has been supported by the IMF:

> A country's currency would be involved, and therefore its exchange controls would be protected by Article VIII, Section 2(b), if...
>
> (1) one of the parties to the contract was a resident of that country. For instance, in the case of a loan by a New York commercial bank to an Argentine public enterprise, the currency of the country of the debtor (Argentina) would be involved as well as the currency of the country of the creditor (the United States), or
> (2) the contract is to be performed with assets located in that country's territory. For example, if the loan to the Argentine enterprise by the commercial bank in New York contemplated the making of a payment with assets held by the Argentine debtor on an account of the debtor with a bank in Frankfurt, the currencies of Argentina, the United States, and the Federal

[60] Mann, *Legal Aspect* (n 1) 386.

[61] Paris Court of Appeal, 20 June 1961, reported in International Law Reports, Volume 47, 1974, 46–52.

> Republic of Germany would all be involved for purposes of Article VIII, Section 2(b), and their exchange controls, if any, regulating such loans could all be protected by the provision. In contrast, the currency of payment of the loan would not be relevant to determining whether a member's currency was involved.[62]

This is a massive expansion of the definition of 'currency', and one which probably has no direct application outside the field of the interpretation of the IMF agreement. However, it does indicate quite strongly that the power to impose restrictions on *money-like* objects extends well beyond the universe of tokens directly created by the sovereign itself. The conclusion which appears to flow from this is that, for Article VIII(2)(b) purposes at least, all of the crypto items identified above—including those which are privately created but *accommodated* by the state—should be regarded as the 'currency of the state'.

That brings us to a question: if an IMF signatory country has adopted a crypto token (including by accommodation), and seeks to impose exchange control restrictions on transactions involving that crypto token, are other countries required to give effect to such restrictions by reason of the domestic effect of Article VII(2)(b)?

Mann's logic suggests that, provided that the exchange control restrictions were properly imposed (i.e. to combat a sudden outflow of capital from the state concerned) they should be given effect. However, it is very difficult to envisage any set of circumstances in which the imposition of controls on crypto tokens which was not accompanied by restrictions on all payment media would be recognized as 'exchange control' measures for this purpose.

This question becomes harder still when we come to central bank digital currencies. There is no doubt that a CBDC is the money of the country concerned—it represents a claim on the relevant central bank, and it differs from such claims no more than two banknotes of different denominations differ from each other. In this case, however, the question is slightly different—if such a country were to impose restrictions on the transferability of its CBDCs but not on the transferability of other monetary assets (such as notes, coins, and bank claims), would such restrictions be enforceable in a third country under Article VIII(2)(b)? The answer here, again, seems to be determined by an investigation of the basis of the imposition of the restrictions. If the state imposing the restriction was facing a capital outflow, and had taken a series of concerted measures which included the placing restriction on transactions in its CBDCs, it is very hard to see that any other state would be able to resist the application of its national implementation of VII(2)(b) to such

[62] Francotte, comment on 'The Fund Agreement in the Courts' in *Current Legal Issues Affecting Central Banks* (IMF 1992) 22.

transactions on the basis that the CBDCs were not in fact the 'currency' of the state concerned.

It should be noted that the question of whether or not a particular instrument is legal tender is not as determinative of these issues as might be hoped. In general, it is of course the case that the instrument which is legal tender in a country is the currency of that country. However, there have been cases where a country's currency has not been formally declared to be legal tender—for example the German *Rentenmark* of 1923–24—but this does not make that currency any less the currency of the state if it is issued by the government concerned for the purposes of passing as currency. More importantly, it is perfectly possible for a state to declare the currency of another state to be its legal tender. The fact that a state's currency may have collapsed to such an extent that the currency of some other state is the predominant circulating medium is somewhat familiar. It is entirely possible that an authority in such a position might simply recognize the facts on the ground and constitute that currency as legal tender. However, if I declare your currency legal tender in my country, that does not make your currency my own. Thus if such an adopting country purported to impose restrictions on the adopted currency, it can be confidently predicted that those restrictions would not be recognized by third states under Article VIII(2)(b).

VII. Contractual Restrictions on Private Tokens

It is clear that the creator of an entirely private medium would retain all of the private rights to which he was entitled, regardless of whether the currency concerned was adopted by a sovereign or not. It is therefore necessary to consider what private rights might exist.

Clearly, as a matter of English law, the creator of a payment obligation can condition that obligation such that it can only be transferred in certain ways and/or to certain persons.[63] There has been some academic debate as to whether this principle applies only to restrictions on assignment of debts or as to whether it goes further than that and in effect recreates a doctrine of estates as regards intangible property.[64] However, it is broadly agreed that where an obligation is created by contract, if the terms of that contract are that the obligation thereby created cannot be transferred to a person of a particular kind, that provision is effective.

[63] See *Barbados Trust Company Ltd v Bank of Zambia* [2007] EWCA Civ 148, applying *Linden Gardens* (n 34).

[64] In other words, determining that the *numerus clausus* principle applies to tangible but not intangible personal property. Professor Sir Roy Goode has argued strenuously against this conclusion; see 'Contractual Prohibitions Against Assignment' [2009] Lloyd's Mar. & Com LQ 300, 303–04. See also *Goode & Gullifer on Legal Problems of Credit and Security* (7th edn, Sweet & Maxwell 2023) 3-38 to 3-40.

However, when we say 'effective' in this case, it is important to note that the thing which is being given effect is the contract by which the obligation is created. In *Barbados Trust*,[65] Lord Waller approved the observation of Professor Goode in his article[66] to the effect that 'even in cases of assignment the court must focus on which contract it is dealing with. The contract under which A assigns a debt of C to B may well be enforceable as between A and B, even if, when B seeks to sue C he may fail.' The question in this case is as to whether, if B assigns to D, D to E, and E to F, C has any defence against F? There is a perfectly respectable argument that this is the case—in particular, if C can challenge the initial transfer to B, then it may be argued that it should be unaffected by any subsequent transfer, as its liability remains a liability only to A.

This is not, however, a problem. The position as regards a crypto token of this form is no different from that as regards a crossed cheque. A crossed cheque cannot be transferred from hand to hand, since such a transfer does not give the transferee any rights against the drawee. It is useful only as a payment instruction to the drawee to make a particular payment in a particular way to the banker of a particular person. What this means is that it is, indisputably, no form of 'currency'. The essence of the idea of currency is that it should be capable of being circulated, and that, if it is circulated, its circulation is unrestricted.

The easiest way to approach the idea of circulation as currency is, oddly, through the law of bills of exchange. The modern law of bills of exchange sprang up in the 19th century in an era of massive shortage of other monetary instruments, largely driven by the existence of metallic money standards. Its purpose, shortly stated, was to enable payment through the creation of private instruments which would, so nearly as possible, perform the function of circulating money. By great good fortune, the English law of bills of exchange was codified in 1882, and that codification sets out the law relating to circulating money to the extent that it endeavours to give such bills as nearly as possible the characteristics which that circulating money has in law. One of the primary essentials of that code was the idea that any instrument which was in any way conditional should fall outside its scope. This emphasizes one of the most fundamental rules of recognition which exists within the system: anything which cannot be freely transferred is not money.

This does not, of course, mean that issuers must wholly lose control of their instruments. If I issue instruments to a group of buyers, and contract with these buyers that none of them will transfer any of those instruments to a man named Smith,[67] I can reasonably expect that they will comply with my stipulation, and sue

[65] [2007] EWCA Civ 148.

[66] R Goode, 'Inalienable Rights?' (1979) 42 MLR 533.

[67] Or, more pragmatically, to anyone who has not verified their identity under the money laundering regime.

them for damages if they do not. What I cannot do is to refuse to pay a holder in due course named Smith who presents an instrument for payment.

The upshot of all of this is that it is perfectly possible for private issuers to create instruments whose transferability is limited. There is nothing unusual about this. However, such instruments are, by definition, neither currency nor capable of being currency. The basic definition of currency is precisely and exactly that it 'passes freely from hand to hand'.

The significance of this is as follows. It would be perfectly possible for a private issuer to create a payment instrument which was restricted in terms of its transfer. A sovereign could create an instrument with those same characteristics, since a sovereign must have all the legal capacities which a subject could have.[68] However, what that sovereign could not do would be to designate such an instrument as a form of *currency*, since an instrument with any sort of restricted transferability does not satisfy the basic definition of currency.

The attempt to evade this issue by arguing that the instrument itself is fully transferrable, but the restrictions on its transfer are matters of private contract, falls some way wide of the mark. One of the problems which payments law presents to contract lawyers is specifically the issue that—almost by definition—the recipient of a transferable payment instrument does *not* have a contractual right against the payor under the instrument.[69] Once an instrument has passed into conventional usage, and is generally accepted as a payment medium and passed from hand to hand, the idea that the relationship between the current holder and the creator of the instrument is the result of some ineffable implied contract between them cannot stand.

However, this leaves an important question. When a creator places such a token in circulation, do they relinquish all of their rights and controls over it, or do they retain some right as its creator which is in some way cognate to the position of a state creator of money under the *lex monetae*? This brings us back to the underlying concept of *lex monetae*. If a sovereign can create an instrument with restricted transferability, but such an instrument will not be acknowledged as currency under the ordinary canons of civil law, the two questions remain: (a) can a sovereign designate such an instrument as its own currency, and (b) if it does so, are other sovereigns compelled or required to recognize that status?

[68] This proposition is neither absolute nor as unequivocal as it is set out here. For a more nuanced discussion see e.g. 'The Crown as Corporation' in Jason Grant Allen, *Non-Statutory Executive Powers and Judicial Review* (CUP 2022) ch. 5.

[69] As regards bills of exchange, the argument that such rights are the result of the Bills of Exchange Act 1882 fall, on the basis that such claims were recognized in law many centuries before that act was passed. As regards transferrable letters of credit, no coherent English contract law explanation has ever been advanced as to why the claims of the beneficiary under the letter of credit should be legally enforceable, and yet they are universally treated as such—see Ali Malek and David Quest, *Jack: Documentary Credits* (4th edn, Tottel 2009) 6–7.

VIII. Conclusion

We can conclude this investigation by way of an illustration, which shows both what we know and the open questions that remain. Let us assume that a large authoritarian state creates a cryptocurrency. Assume further that the terms of issue of this currency are that it shall not be owned or controlled by persons whom the issuing government regards as 'subversive'. A person in the United Kingdom transfers, under an English law governed contract, units of this cryptocurrency to another person in the United Kingdom who is a citizen of the large authoritarian state and is considered by that country to be 'subversive'. As a matter of English law, does the transferee of the cryptocoins own them?

There are two preliminary points which must be disposed of. The first is that a number of such projects appear to be in development; however, their focus is not on legal analysis, but on programming the limits on transferability into the tokens themselves. This may or may not be possible, but is outside the scope of legal enquiry. The second is that this is exactly the sort of situation where Mann proposed that English law should not recognize any such restriction on the basis that it is discriminatory. However, inherent in his position is the idea that such a restriction is *prima facie* enforceable but should not be enforced for English public policy reasons. For present purposes, we leave public policy aside, and look only at the basic question of *prima facie* enforceability.

We approach the question first from a property law perspective. If I ask whether a sculptor can create a statue which cannot be sold to a man named Smith, the idea seems faintly preposterous. This kind of restriction would be somehow inconsistent with the nature of ownership of a chattel. However, If I create by contract an intangible asset, and the terms of the contract which creates it are that the person to whom I owe the contractual obligation concerned cannot be transferred to a man named Smith, any such transfer will be ineffective.[70] This therefore brings us back to the question as to the nature of the token—is it more like an intangible asset, or an item of personal property?

The answer to this is reasonably straightforward. If a token were to be regarded as a contractual claim, then it could only be transferred by assignment or novation. The whole point of the distributed ledger technology is that there need be no contract (or any other relationship) between the transferor and the transferee. If that is true, then the transfer cannot be a transfer of a contractual right against the issuer. We must therefore regard the token to be transferred as an item of 'property'.

Imagine that A sells a chattel to B, but agrees with B that that chattel will not be sold to C. That agreement is legally binding, and A could obtain an injunction to restrain B selling the asset to C if necessary. However, what if B then sells the asset

[70] *Linden Gardens Trust v Lenesta Sludge Disposals Ltd* [1993] UKHL 4.

to D? The law of England is remarkably clear on this point: D is not bound by any such restriction, whether he had notice of it or not. The position might be different if A retained an ownership right in the property, such that B was a mere lessee. However, there is no mechanism at English common law[71] by which A can both divest himself of the ownership of the property and at the same time retain a right of control as to its subsequent ownership. It is not the case that no such mechanism exists—the law of real property caters for exactly this class of rights.[72] However, the law of personal property does not, and the property that we are dealing with here is not real property.

The position is, therefore, the same as it would be if a car manufacturer sold a car on the contractual basis that it should not be driven at more than 70 miles per hour. Such a provision in the contract of sale would be enforceable against the immediate purchaser. However, once the car had been sold to a third party, that third party would not be bound by that covenant, and could drive at whatever speed he liked.

This brings us to our conclusion. It seems to be the case that a sovereign cannot, as a matter of either public or private law, assert any kind of ownership over the currency which he issues. He may, *qua* sovereign, impose penalties on those of his citizens who deal with his currency in a way of which he disapproves, but that is the exercise of his police power and has nothing to do with monetary law. There is therefore no aspect of monetary law which grants any inherent right to an issuer of a currency to restrain its circulation as a matter of law. If this is true for public authorities, it must be equally true for private issuers. There is no private '*lex monetae*'. More importantly, this will be true (a) whether or not the private issuer seeks to impose restrictions on the transferability of the tokens which it issues, and (b) whether or not the tokens so issued are accepted by one or more sovereigns as legal tender. It is accepted that it may be possible for issuers of such tokens to impose practical (i.e. technical) restrictions on the transferability of such tokens. However, such restrictions cannot be enforced as a matter of law in any other jurisdiction, whether under Article VIII(2)(b) of the IMF agreement or under customary international law.

Mann (and Nussbaum) correctly categorized the *lex monetae* as a congeries of legal principles which embraces public and private law doctrines. It is an uncertain concept, and some of the more extensive claims made for its scope during the debates over the establishment of the euro do not stand up to scrutiny. However, it is unquestionably a hybrid of private and public law doctrines. Thus, although a private creator of money tokens may be able to replicate some of the attributes of a *lex monetae* by contract, there is no *lex monetae* of purely private money tokens that has not been in some way adopted by the state.

[71] For the time being we disregard Equity.
[72] The class of property known as 'incorporeal hereditaments'.

Bibliography

Allen JG, *The Crown as Corporation in Non-Statutory Executive Powers and Judicial Review* (CUP 2022).

Bodin, *Six Livres de la Republique* (1576; trans M Tooley as *The Six Books of the Commonwealth*, Blackwell 1967)

Bridge M and others, *The Law of Personal Property* (3rd edn, OUP 2022)

Collins L and Harris J (eds), *Dicey, Morris & Collins on the Conflict of Laws* (16th edn, Sweet & Maxwell 2022)

Francotte, comment on 'The Fund Agreement in the Courts' in *Current Legal Issues Affecting Central Banks* (IMF 1992)

Goode R, 'Contractual Prohibitions Against Assignment' [2009] Lloyd's Mar & Com LQ 300.

Goode R and Gullifer G, *Goode & Gullifer on Legal Problems of Credit and Security* (7th edn, Sweet & Maxwell 2023)

Lastra R, *International Financial and Monetary Law* (OUP 2015)

Malek A and Quest D, *Jack: Documentary Credits* (4th edn, Tottel 2009)

Mann FA, 'The Foreign Act of State' in *Foreign Affairs in English Courts* (OUP 1986)

Mann FA, *The Legal Aspect of Money* (5th edn, OUP 1992)

Nussbaum A, *A History of the Dollar* (Columbia University Press 1957).

Nussbaum A, *Money in the Law—National and International* (2nd edn, Foundation Press 1950)

Oresme N, *De Moneta* (C Johnson tr., Thomas Nelson & Sons 1956)

Wilks M, *The Problem of Sovereignty in the Later Middle Ages* (Cambridge University Press 2008)

Zimmermann A, *A Contemporary Concept of Monetary Sovereignty* (OUP 2013)

14

A New and Unsolved Riddle in Monetary Law

The Complex Case of Central Bank Digital Currency

*Christian Hofmann**

I. Introduction

FA Mann saw many changes throughout his lifetime (1907–1991), including sea changes in the financial industry. Technology progressed dramatically in the 20th century and revolutionized the ways in which financial intermediaries offer an ever-growing variety of services to the public. Crises occurred and revealed to financial regulators that their approaches had been insufficient. The history of financial services is a history of a learning process by default, in which regulation reacts to failures by introducing new sets of rules. Over time, layers of regulatory restrictions build up, prompting the financial industry to innovate in their quest to improve their services and products and, occasionally, to bypass these restrictions. The concept of money, the supply of currency, and the execution of payment

* The chapter draws on the author's articles 'Which Markets Need Central Bank Digital Currency?' (2023) 18(3) Capital Markets Law Journal 281; 'The Impact of a Digital Dollar on Singapore's Society, Banking Sector and Monetary System' (2023) 39(3) Banking and Finance Law Review 381; 'Unlimited Central Bank Digital Currency: The Case for a Public Good in the Euro Area and its Regulatory (and De-regulatory) Implications for Modern Finance' (co-authored with Iris Chiu) (2023) 48(1) North Carolina Journal of International Law 1.

Christian Hofmann, *A New and Unsolved Riddle in Monetary Law* In: *FA Mann*. Edited by: Jason Grant Allen and Gerhard Dannemann, Oxford University Press. © Christian Hofmann 2024. DOI: 10.1093/oso/9780198881452.003.0015

transactions were core aspects of change in the 20th century, and FA Mann drove discussion of the legal aspects of these developments like no other.

The 21st century has started with what has been termed the fourth industrial revolution. This revolution is yet again an era of change driven by technological innovation, and one of the objectives of this innovation is to find ways to bypass the traditional channels for cashless payments and stores of value. Distributed ledger technology is used to generate cryptoassets, which have morphed from creative experiments into serious investments in the course of only a few years and hold the potential to grow into a shadow payment, a shadow banking, and even a shadow central banking industry. Regulators and central banks are alarmed and look for measures that might help them counter potential risks to financial and monetary stability. In our search for guidance on how to assess these developments, we turn to the works of influential scholars.

FA Mann and others have defined the concept of money in general terms such that we can use their definitions to determine under which prerequisites novel 'monetary' objects such as cryptoassets could morph into a new type of private money. Today, we also know enough about store of value and means of payment generated by licensed and regulated private institutions, above all commercial banks, and the interaction of public and private money, especially the anchor function of central bank money, to decide in which instances new forms of store of value and means of payment promise to serve the public or threaten the stability of the financial and monetary system. Equipped with such guidance, we can tackle the challenges that result from the constant changes in the financial world resulting from technological advancement and innovative powers of the financial industry.

This chapter contributes to the discussion that addresses the changes resulting from cryptoassets by taking a closer look at the concept of Central Bank Digital Currency (CBDC). Much has already been written about CBDC. Central banks themselves and the Bank for International Settlements (BIS) have made substantial contributions in which they have analysed the benefits and risks of this new type of central bank money. We draw on these findings in Section II, which presents the characteristics of CBDC. However, not all questions have been answered. The leading sources on CBDC base their analyses on the assumption that all financial markets are the same. However, that is not the case, as this chapter argues. We take a closer look at the situation in specific jurisdictions and markets in Section III, which reveals that CBDC could be a net positive for all of them, although for different reasons.

We look at China, where no long tradition of private banking exists and the central bank exercises strong control over capital flows and targets the oligopolistic market powers of Alibaba's Alipay and Tencent's WeChat Pay. We briefly touch on the situation in the euro area where, until recently, banks were haunted by negative interest rates for excess reserves and the public faced an erosion of the store of value function of their bank deposits. The situation of countries with low levels of financial inclusion where large parts of society have no access to conventional store of value opportunities and cashless payment systems are also mostly neglected by the current debate driven by the BIS and the central banks of wealthy nations.

II. CBDC as a Promising New Development at the Interface of Money, Banking, and Central Banking

In today's monetary landscape, several forms of money exist, including cash, private money, and the deposits held by commercial banks in reserve accounts with central banks. Together, these elements form the national monetary system, wherein the competent authorities oversee the creation, distribution, and intrinsic value of money. Cash, which includes banknotes issued by central banks and government-issued coins, represents the most traditional form of money.[1] It possesses the key attributes commonly associated with money: the ability to retain its value for future use, the basis for measuring the value of goods and services, and wide acceptance as a medium of exchange in transactions.[2] However, in the majority of modern economies, cash holdings play a subordinate role as individuals tend to store the majority of their wealth in deposit accounts held with commercial banks. Although these holdings in bank accounts are technically data entries in the ledgers of the banks and represent account holders' claims against the banks, they are considered a form of money, at least if they are instantly accessible for withdrawals and payment transactions.[3] The primary source of liquidity for commercial banks is the reserve accounts they maintain with central banks. This reserve money constitutes the second type of central bank money, and it is accessible exclusively to commercial banks and governmental entities.[4]

[1] In more detail on cash Corinne Zellweger-Gutknecht, Bemjamin Geva, and Seraina N Grünewald, 'Digital Euro, Monetary Objects and Price Stability—A Legal Analysis' (2021) 7(2) Journal of Financial Regulation 284, 300 (hereafter Zellweger-Gutknecht, Geva, and Grünewald, 'Digital Euro').

[2] For these three components of money Charles Proctor, *Mann on the Legal Aspect of Money* (7th edn, OUP 2012) paras 1.49–1.60 (hereafter Proctor, *Mann on Money*); A Sáinz de Vicuna, 'An Institutional Theory of Money' in M Giovanoli and D Devos (eds), *International Monetary and Financial Law: The Global Crisis* (OUP 2010) paras 25.04–25.14; T Cargill, *The Financial System, Financial Regulation and Central Bank Policy* (CUP 2017) 30–32 (hereafter Cargill, *The Financial System*).

[3] For details see Bank of England, 'Central Bank Digital Currency Opportunities, Challenges and Design' (Bank of England Discussion Paper, 2020) para. 1.1 (hereafter Bank of England, 'Central Bank Digital Currency'); Proctor, *Mann on Money* (n 2) para. 3.17; Zellweger-Gutknecht, Geva, and Grünewald, 'Digital Euro' (n 1) 285, 317. The types of money available to the public are identical with what is termed as 'broad money' because it consists of all monies circulating in the economy and available to the public for their transactions, i.e. cash including banknotes and coins and commercial bank money stored in deposit accounts, see Michael McLeay, Amar Radia, and Ryland Thomas, 'Money in the Modern Economy: An Introduction' (Bank of England Quarterly Bulletin, Q1, 2014) 4, 7, 11 (hereafter McLeay, Radia, and Thomas, 'Money in the Modern Economy').

[4] For this reserve money, see Ulrich Bindseil, 'Issuing a Digital Euro' (ESCB Legal Conference, 2020) 172 (hereafter Bindseil, 'Issuing a Digital Euro'); Seraina N Grunewald, Corinne Zellweger-Gutknecht, and Benjamin Geva, 'Digital Euro and ECB Powers' (2021) 58(4) Common Market Law Review 1029; McLeay, Radia, and Thomas, 'Money in the Modern Economy' (n 3) 11.

For his part, Mann attempted to maintain a narrower conception of money until his death, though he was aware that the narrowness of his approach would cause economists and commercial men to object.[5] As Joseph Sommer explains in Chapter 10 of this volume, Mann limited the legal concept of money to tangible money. Mann's reservations against the concept of commercial bank money were rooted in his strong defence of the state theory of money against any efforts of diluting it in favour of a more effect-focused move in the direction of the 'societary theory' of money.

However, in most economies today, these concerns are no longer valid. The push towards cashless societies, which has led to the prominence of commercial bank money, is not primarily driven by societal demands but rather an agenda pursued by central banks and other government authorities. Commercial bank money serves as a liquidity multiplier used by central banks to implement their monetary policy objectives across the entire economy. Central banks themselves rely on intangible money as the foundation for supplying liquidity to markets and as a tool to transmit their monetary policy objectives. Reserve money, which is simply a data entry reflecting commercial banks' claims against central banks, fuels the operations of banks. Commercial bank money amplifies the impact of central banks' policies, particularly in expansionary environments where central banks aim to inject liquidity into markets.[6]

As a result, commercial bank money has become an indirect tool of central banks, driving investments and spending to achieve their monetary policy objectives. In contrast, physical money has lost its significance for monetary policy purposes. For as long as cash has not been phased out but is still being seen as a necessary part of payment systems, central banks still issue banknotes to support their statutory obligations in ensuring smooth payment operations.[7] However, when it comes to central banks' pursuit of monetary policy goals, their role is negligible.

Furthermore, bank regulators and supervisors exert strict control over the creation and usage of commercial bank money. Commercial bank money is only created and transferred for as long as commercial banks fully comply with stringent regulatory frameworks imposed upon them. The recent wave of regulatory reforms known as Basel III and the implementation of the Financial Stability Board's Key Attributes of Effective Resolution Regimes for Financial Institutions[8]

[5] See FA Mann, *The Legal Aspect of Money* (5th edn, OUP 1992) 6. See also Bank of England, 'Central Bank Digital Currency' (n 3) para. 1.1; Proctor, *Mann on Money* (n 2) para. 3.17; Zellweger-Gutknecht, Geva, and Grünewald, 'Digital Euro' (n 1) 285 and 317. The types of money available to the public are identical with what is termed as 'broad money' because it consists of all monies circulating in the economy and available to the public for their transactions, i.e. cash including banknotes and coins and commercial bank money stored in deposit accounts, see McLeay, Radia, and Thomas, 'Money in the Modern Economy' (n 3) 4, 7, 11.

[6] For the effects of changes to the reserve money on the liquidity supply in markets, Cargill, *The Financial System* (n 2) ch. 13.

[7] For example, Art. 3.1, 16 of the Statute of the ECB and ESCB.

[8] 'Basel Principles on Bank Supervision' in Basel Committee on Banking Supervision, *Basel III: A Global Regulatory Framework for More Resilient Banks and Banking Systems* (rev'd edn, Bank for

have strengthened the interventionary powers of state authorities and thereby further aligned commercial bank money with the core concepts of the state theory of money.

In light of these realities, legal professionals now generally accept that data entries in bank ledgers constitute money, joining economists in this understanding.[9] The legal discourse has shifted towards examining the conditions and requirements for the existence and transfer of proprietary rights related to different forms of intangible money, a topic explored by Simon Gleeson in Chapter 13 of this volume, albeit not elaborated upon here.

This exercise of official control over commercial bank money contributes to the willingness of private individuals to exchange central bank-issued cash for repayment claims directed at commercial banks. In this exchange, depositors relinquish their ownership of currency in favour of claims against private debtors, receiving promises of repayment upon demand or at a future date. Depositors accept the associated default risks if banks were to become insolvent.[10]

The growth in acceptance of commercial bank money can also be attributed to the transition of money from representative money to fiat money. Unlike the previous Bretton Woods system (which Will Bateman discusses in Chapter 11 of this volume in detail) or historical metallic standards, where central banks were obligated to redeem banknotes with precious metals or commodities of equivalent value, the current fiat money system no longer requires such backing. Nowadays, central banks merely promise to exchange one of their issued banknotes against another,[11] making swaps of central bank-issued cash into commercial bank money appear less disadvantageous than in erstwhile scenarios.

In the present time, what holds significance is the effective management of fiat currencies by central banks, primarily through a focus on maintaining price stability to uphold the store of value aspect of money. The trust in the monetary system is further reinforced by various mechanisms such as deposit guarantee schemes and the ability to exchange commercial bank money for cash at par value. Additionally, stringent safeguards such as prudential regulation and supervision

International Settlements, June 2011); Basel Committee on Banking Supervision, *Finalising Basel III in Brief—2010 to 2017 Reforms* (Bank for International Settlements 2017); Basel Committee on Banking Supervision, *Basel III: The Liquidity Coverage Ratio and Liquidity Risk Monitoring Tools* (Bank for International Settlements 2013); Financial Stability Board, *Key Attributes of Effective Resolution Regimes for Financial Institutions* <https://www.fsb.org/2014/10/key-attributes-of-effective-resolution-regimes-for-financial-institutions-2/> accessed 9 June 2023.

[9] See references at n 5.

[10] On this process in general terms, see José Gabilondo, *Bank Funding, Liquidity, and Capital Adequacy: A Law and Finance Approach* (Edward Elgar Publishing 2016) 11–22 and 27–37; John Armour and others, *Principles of Financial Regulation* (OUP 2016) 290–93.

[11] See, for instance, the Decision of the European Central Bank of 13 December 2010 on the issue of euro banknotes, Art. 3(2) (ECB/2010/29) [2011] OJ L35/26: 'NCBs shall accept all euro banknotes on the request of the holder for exchange against euro banknotes of the same value or, in the case of account holders, to be credited to accounts held at the recipient NCB.'

provide added assurance. As a result of these protective measures, trust in the banking system is generally high, and most depositors do not make a legal distinction between central bank-issued cash and claims against commercial banks.[12]

Despite its widespread public acceptance, the current monetary system has struggled to adapt to the evolving financial landscape. As cash usage diminishes in favour of electronic payment transactions and commercial bank money experiences rapid growth, the holdings of central bank money by the public are rapidly declining. Nevertheless, central banks have shown limited concern for these developments thus far. While they have responded to the decline of cash by creating their own form of intangible money, its availability has been restricted to commercial banks, with no access granted to private households and the non-financial sector.

The introduction of CBDC would bring about a revolutionary transformation. A widely accessible retail CBDC would enable the public to access electronic money issued and guaranteed by central banks, thereby ending the dual privilege enjoyed by commercial banks. They would no longer hold exclusive control over both access to intangible central bank money and the provision of intangible money to the public.

At this juncture, the significance of Mann's outright dismissal of the notion of intangible private money becomes pertinent once more. Mann's hesitation to acknowledge the legitimacy of data entries in private entities' ledgers stemmed from concerns that considering them as a form of money would expose the public to various risks. However, the introduction of CBDC could provide a means to reconcile Mann's standpoint with the present necessity for intangible forms of money. Currently, it is a significant concern that the public relies on claims against entities that are susceptible to insolvency and liquidity risks when seeking to preserve their store of value.

A retail CBDC that allowed the public to profit from all the benefits inherent in central bank money would provide a solution for this dilemma.[13] As it is widely acknowledged within the central banking community that the introduction of wholesale CBDC would yield overall benefits, especially for cross-border transactions and countries with less developed interbank payment systems,[14] this

[12] McLeay, Radia, and Thomas, 'Money in the Modern Economy' (n 3) 10.

[13] For detailed discussions of retail CBDC, see Cecilia Skingsley, 'Should the Riksbank Issue e-Krona?' (Fintech 2016 Conference, Stockholm, 16 November 2016); Javier Guzmán Calafell, 'Some Considerations on Central Bank Digital Currencies' (Federal Reserve Bank of St. Louis symposium, 'The Next Decade of Finance: Assessing Priorities and Implications for Society, Politics and Economics', Missouri, 11 July 2019); Michael Kumhof and Clare Noone, 'Central Bank Digital Currencies—Design Principles and Balance Sheet Implications' (Bank of England Staff Working Paper No. 725, 2018) 10; Aleksander Berentsen and Fabian Schär, 'The Case for Central Bank Electronic Money and the Non-case for Central Bank Cryptocurrencies' (2018) 100(2) Federal Reserve Bank of St. Louis Review 97, 103–04; Tobias Adrian and Tommaso Mancini-Griffoli, *The Rise of Digital Money* (International Monetary Fund 2019).

[14] For details on digital solutions for wholesale settlements, see Bank for International Settlements, 'Wholesale Digital Tokens' (Committee on Payments and Market Infrastructures Paper, 2019). See

chapter focuses on retail CBDC. While a domestic wholesale CBDC can be seen as analogous to central bank reserves, a domestic retail CBDC does not have a direct equivalent in any economy. Assessing the cost-benefit analysis for retail CBDC is therefore more complex, given that it would entail substantial transformations in financial markets.

The objective of this chapter is to shed light on the implications of the introduction of retail CBDC. Since aspects related to CBDC technology are not central to the core arguments presented here, the focus is on exploring the intersection between law and monetary economics. The discussions primarily concentrate on the overarching justification for the implementation of retail CBDC (start of Section III) and the anticipated advantages in two regions that have made significant progress in CBDC pilot projects: China (Section III.A) and the euro area (Section III.B). Additionally, the analysis extends to regions characterized by lower levels of financial regulation (Section III.C) before concluding the chapter.

III. The Risks and Benefits of CBDC in Selected Markets

It would probably not take the public long to understand that CBDC is their best option for store of value and access to cashless payments. CBDC would obviously improve the retail customers' position in a financial crisis. Currently, panicking retail customers have only the option to withdraw their account holdings in cash,[15] which is a slow and burdensome process because it requires physical withdrawals in bank branches or at ATMs and comes with all the disadvantages of holding cash, especially the high risk of loss. Alternatively, fast and convenient transfers between bank accounts would allow retail customers to terminate their exposures to individual banks, but not to run from 'fallible' private into 'infallible' public money.

Runs of retail customers into CBDC would likely occur in a banking or general financial stability crisis. In the absence of such crisis scenarios, retail depositors would likely see no good reason for leaving any money in deposit accounts unless commercial banks adequately compensated the risk of default inherent in any form of private money. As a result, CBDC could disrupt the funding models of commercial banks, but during non-crisis times only if banks continued to rely on their monopolistic position as sole providers of a combination of store of value

also Bank of England, 'Central Bank Digital Currency' (n 3) para. 5.1; Ashley Lannquist, 'Central Bank Digital Currency Policy-Maker Toolkit' (World Economic Forum Centre for the Fourth Industrial Revolution, Blockchain and Distributed Ledger Technology Platform, January 2020) 6–7.

[15] Hanna Armelius, Carl Claussen, and Hendry Scott, 'Is Central Bank Currency Fundamental to the Monetary System?' (2020) 2 Sveriges Riksbank Economic Review 19, 29 <https://www.riksbank.se/globalassets/media/rapporter/pov/artiklar/engelska/2020/200618/2020_2-is-central-bank-currency-fundamental-to-the-monetary-system.pdf> accessed 26 October 2023.

and access to electronic payment systems. With CBDC offering exactly that as well, banks would need to provide incentives for depositors in the form of compensation that is commensurate with the risks inherent in a swap of central bank money for commercial bank money.

We have argued elsewhere that this could be seen as a welcome development. If CBDC provided the public with access to a free and entirely safe store of value option which also gave access to efficient cashless payments options, bank deposits would become no more than one of many store of value options for the public. This would boost competition in financial markets and create space for market entries of new types of financial intermediaries, especially in the lending sector. Furthermore, it would allow policy makers to start serious conversations about ending the 'too big to fail' dilemma. If commercial banks were no longer essential for providing the critical financial functions (store of value in deposit accounts, access to widely accepted electronic payment systems, and lending to all parts of society), their roles for societies and economies could be re-assessed and thresholds of acceptable and intolerable levels of systemic risk recalibrated.[16] We have also argued that CBDC comes with a significant advantage for financial stability, by eradicating the need for flights into cash or erratic moves of commercial bank money from one bank to another by poorly informed depositors, and instead allows for a seamless move from private into central bank money in times of market insecurities.[17] In addition, we would like to emphasize that CBDC would finally bring retail central bank money technologically up to par with commercial bank money. Commercial bank money is already entirely electronic, and banks are constantly striving to make its usage safer, faster, and more efficient.

However, here we accept the negative outlooks stipulated by some central banks and authors who argue that the introduction of CBDC might prompt banks to pass on their increased financing costs by raising the prices for their services, especially for lending. Such developments might then conflict with central banks' monetary policy objectives in sluggish markets which call for expansionary measures. If central banks wanted to keep liquidity in markets abundant and cheap, they would have to provide it themselves, likely by a combination of two measures: by

[16] Christian Hofmann, 'Digital Euro: An Assessment of the First Two Progress Reports: The Case for Unlimited Holdings of Digital Euros', European Parliament: In-Depth Analysis Requested by the ECON Committee (2023) <https://www.europarl.europa.eu/RegData/etudes/IDAN/2023/741511/IPOL_IDA(2023)741511_EN.pdf> accessed 9 June 2023 (hereafter Hofmann, 'Digital Euro'). See also Todd Keister and Cyril Monnet, 'Central Bank Digital Currency: Stability and Information' (2022) 142 Journal of Economic Dynamics and Control; Iris Chiu and Christian Hofmann, 'Unlimited Central Bank Digital Currency: The Case for a Public Good in the Euro Area and its Regulatory (and Deregulatory) Implications for Modern Finance' (2023) 48(1) North Carolina Journal of International Law 1 (hereafter Chiu and Hofmann, 'Unlimited Central Bank Digital Currency'); Dirk Niepelt, 'Money and Banking with Reserves and CBDC', University of Bern Discussion Papers, No. 22-12.

[17] Hofmann, 'Digital Euro' (n 16). This point has also been emphasized by Monetary Authority of Singapore, *A Retail Central Bank Digital Currency: Economic Considerations in the Singapore Context* (Economic Policy Group November 2021) 30.

replacing commercial banks' dried-up base of cheap deposit funding from retail customers (i.e. by lending massively to commercial banks for less than the interest expected by CBDC-favouring depositors), and by engaging in secondary market purchases of assets such as highly rated bonds and other lower risk securities to channel liquidity directly into the markets.[18] In essence, these critics of CBDC expect landslide shifts from deposits to CBDC which might require central banks to massively increase the volumes of their open market transactions. The results could be higher exposures to default and price risks for central banks and serious implications for prices in secondary markets for financial instruments.[19] Commercial banks could be forced to focus on the suitability of assets for purposes of collateralizing their transactions with central banks,[20] and assets favoured by central banks for their secondary market operations would profit from increased market demand, especially top-rated sovereign and corporate bonds.[21] However, we argue here that even if we accept this negative outlook on the consequences of a CBDC for the banking industry and liquidity interventions by central banks, the magnitude of these negative effects and the overall risk-benefit analysis depends on the specifics of the markets in which CBDCs are introduced, and in particular the banking landscape and the monetary policy objectives and measures of implementation of central banks, as well as the intentions that drive central banks' CBDC plans. The following discussions look at the probable impact of CBDC in three categories of markets for which the current discussion about the potential negatives of a CBDC introduction is only relevant to limited extents. First, China is a very specific place in which a duopoly of e-money providers (rather than commercial banks) dominate the market for store of value and payments. Secondly, the euro area is marked by the effects of years of expansionary monetary policy measures of the eurosystem, which have led to substantial deviations from the typical funding model of commercial banks. Finally, countries with low levels of inclusion have no banking industry to worry about but instead have large parts of society that are cut off from financial services.

[18] Bank of England, 'Central Bank Digital Currency' (n 3) para. 5.2; European Central Bank, 'Report on a Digital Euro' (2020) 16 <https://www.ecb.europa.eu/pub/pdf/other/Report_on_a_digital_euro~4d7268b458.en.pdf> accessed 26 October 2023; Ulrich Bindseil, 'Tiered CBDC and the Financial System' (European Central Bank Working Paper Series No 2351, January 2020) 10 (hereafter Bindseil, 'Tiered CBDC').

[19] In general terms on market transactions of central banks in conventional and crisis times see European Central Bank, 'The Implementation of Monetary Policy in the Eurozone' (European Central Bank, February 2011) 31–41; José Gabilondo, 'Central Banks, Systemic Lending, and Collateral Markets' in Matthias Haentjens and Bob Wessels (eds), *Research Handbook on Crisis Management in the Banking Sector* (Edward Elgar Publishing 2015) 24–41.

[20] For principles of collateralization of central bank lending, see Ulrich Bindseil and others, 'The Eurosystem Collateral Framework Explained' (ECB Occasional Paper No 189, May 2017).

[21] Similarly, Bank of England, 'Central Bank Digital Currency' (n 3) para. 5.3; ECB, *Report on a Digital Euro* (n 18) 16ff.; Bindseil, 'Tiered CBDC' (n 18) 10.

A. China

China's CBDC initiative is the most advanced among major economies. In 2020, the People's Bank of China (PBOC) launched a pilot project in selected locations within the country.[22] Since the PBOC appears to be unimpressed by the typical concerns hampering CBDC projects discussed above, it is worth exploring the factors that make China's position unique.

The first factor is that the PBOC pursues specific objectives that stem from China's distinctive characteristics. The country's policy of capital controls necessitates a robust response to cryptocurrencies and stablecoins to prevent capital transfers outside regulated channels. Introducing a CBDC that the public perceives as convenient and effective can help China justify restrictions or bans on coin schemes, such as prohibiting privately created digital coins from being pegged to the Renminbi (RMB).[23] Additionally, China aims to decrease its reliance on the USD and hopes that a digital RMB will facilitate further internationalization of its currency.[24]

Furthermore, a digital RMB could enable the PBOC to secure victory in its ongoing domestic competition against private payment service providers.[25] Currently, Alibaba's Alipay and Tencent's WeChat Pay dominate electronic payment transactions in China, accounting for over 94 per cent of such transactions.[26]

[22] For all of the below information, see Ke Da, 'Law School of Peking University, The Ideal and Reality of Digital RMB—Based on the Observation of Shenzhen Digital RMB Pilot Activities' (in Chinese) (2020) 104(3) Financial Law Forum 166; Michelle Qi, 'What Would be the Impact of China's Digital Currency?' (Eastspring Investments, November 2020) <https://www.eastspring.com/insights/what-would-be-the-impact-of-china-s-digital-currency> accessed 9 June 2023(hereafter Qi, 'What Would be the Impact of China's Digital Currency?'); Mian Xia, 'In Search of The Perfect Coin: China's Approach towards Cryptocurrency and Its Own Central Bank Digital Currency' (2021) 36(3) BFLR 419, 447–49 (hereafter Mian Xia, 'In Search of the Perfect Coin').

[23] Art. 22 of the People's Bank of China Act, see Vipin Bharathan, 'People's Bank of China Draft Law' (*Forbes*, October 2020) <https://www.forbes.com/sites/vipinbharathan/2020/10/24/peoples-bank-of-china-draft-law-provides-a-legal-basis-for-digital-currency-electronic-payments-dcep-and-bans-all-stablecoins-backed-by-renminbi-reserves/?sh=2b43299b4c0d> accessed 9 June 2023; Mian Xia, 'In Search of the Perfect Coin' (n 22) 437–38.

[24] Chi Hung Kwan, 'China Aiming to Issue Central Bank Digital Currency—Expected Macro-Level Effects' (in Japanese) (27 December 2019). The same hopes are drivers of plans for a digital euro, see European Central Bank, 'Digital Euro Experimentation Scope and Key Learnings' (2021) 9 <https://www.ecb.europa.eu/pub/pdf/other/ecb.digitaleuroscopekeylearnings202107~564d89045e.en.pdf> accessed 26 October 2023 9. So far, China's efforts to make the RMB a leading reserve currency have had limited success, see Dipinder S Randhawa, *China's Central Bank Digital Currency: Implications for ASEAN* (S. Rajaratnam School of International Studies Policy Report 2020) 6.

[25] These reasons are prominently featured in the list of motivations for a digital RMB, see Yifei Fan, 'Analysis on the Policy Implications of the M0 Positioning of Digital RMB' (*Financial Times*, 14 September 2020), No. 001 <https://www.financialnews.com.cn/pl/zj/202009/t20200915_200890.html> accessed 26 October 2023.

[26] 'China Crushed Jack Ma, and his Fintech Rivals are Next' (*Bloomberg Businessweek*, 25 June 2021); Yao Qian, 'Central Bank Digital Currency: Optimization of the Currency System and its Issuance Design' (2019) 12(1) China Economic Journal 1, 3 (hereafter Yao Qian, 'Central Bank Digital Currency'). For details on their payment systems, see Anton Didenko, Dirk Zetzsche, Douglas Arner,

These platforms, through their extensive offerings and integrated payment systems, are seen by users as fast, efficient, and trendy. Alipay and WeChat Pay possess market power that surpasses traditional e-money issuers and consequently have the capability to render bank accounts and commercial bank money redundant. The reason is that Alipay and WeChat Pay not only dominate the electronic payment market but also provide a range of additional financial services. These platforms are interconnected with other financial platforms to which they transfer e-money from their customers' payment wallets. With their pervasive presence and expanding user base, customers may increasingly rely exclusively on Alibaba and Tencent, gradually dismissing the need for other financial services providers.[27]

The primary distinction between the current situation and their potential supremacy over the domestic financial sector lies in the legal nature of their issued means of payment. As long as they issue e-money that depends on underlying bank accounts and facilitates transfers of commercial bank money, they remain tied to the highly regulated banking sector and the monetary order controlled by the central bank.[28]

However, customers are generally unaware of the legal differences between e-money and digital coins. In China, and possibly elsewhere, customers are likely to remain loyal to their trusted payment service providers, regardless of the legal nature of the services and the regulatory control imposed on them. Consequently, there exists a possibility that Alipay and WeChat Pay could transition from regulated and account-linked e-money to unregulated digital tokens, akin to how Visa and MasterCard could theoretically do so in the US and Europe. Such developments are deemed undesirable because only central banks issue money as a public service. Issuers of private money primarily serve their stakeholders and pursue profits, which is acceptable only when their activities are regulated and controlled.

and Ross Buckley, 'After Libra, Digital Yuan and COVID-19: Central Bank Digital Currencies and the New World of Money and Payment Systems' (2020) European Banking Institute Working Paper Series 65/2020, 15.

[27] On the first aspect, see Yao Qian, 'Central Bank Digital Currency' (n 26) 4; People's Bank of China, '中国 民银行关于印发《非银行支付机构重大事项报告管理办法》的通知 (银发 [2021] 198号)' ['Notice of the People's Bank of China on Printing and Distributing the "Administrative Measures on Major Matters of Non-bank Payment Institutions" (Yinfa [2021] No. 198)'] (The People's Bank of China, 23 July 2021); '市场监管总局依法对阿里巴巴集团控股有限公司在中国境内网络零售平台服务市场实施"二选一"垄断行为作出行政处罚' ['The State Administration for Market Regulation imposed administrative penalties on Alibaba Group Holdings Co. Ltd.'s "two-choice-one" monopoly in the online retail platform service market in China in accordance with the law'] *People's Daily* (China, 10 April 2021). On the second aspect, see Qi, 'What Would be the Impact of China's Digital Currency?' (n 22).

[28] For the legal concept of e-money, see Proctor, *Mann on Money* (n 2) para. 1.80.

Recognizing the imminent loss of control over certain segments of the e-commerce industry, Chinese authorities have implemented a range of regulations that restrict the financial operations of major non-bank financial service providers like Alipay and WeChat Pay. These measures primarily address concerns related to competition and shadow banking.[29] The new rules subject companies like Ant Group to higher transparency and accountability standards, criminalize the abuse of market power, and limit or terminate the practice of financial intermediaries venturing into unlicensed services. By focusing on business activities and associated risks, these reforms require payment services providers to either limit their operations to money transfers or apply for banking licences and adhere to the resulting requirements.[30] If they choose the first option, their bank-like behaviour comes to an end.

The second factor relates to the risks that are typically associated with the introduction of CBDC. China has less reason to be concerned about the impact of CBDC on its banking system compared to other countries. China's banking sector differs from those in countries with a long history of commercial banking. In China, the traditional model of intermediation seen in the banking sector did not exist until the 21st century. This explains why the bank–customer relationship, which is a significant pillar of banks' funding models in North America, Europe, and most of Asia, is not as prevalent in China. Commercial banks have never played a pivotal role in driving economic growth in China, unlike in other parts of the world for the past century.[31]

The third factor concerns the issue of central bank mandates. Unlike in other parts of the world, the PBOC does not operate under a narrowly defined mandate. Its wide mandate encompasses multiple objectives and a large range of tasks. In addition to maintaining price stability and promoting economic growth through monetary policy operations, the PBOC pursues macro-prudential policies

[29] For definitions and detailed analyses of the shadow banking phenomenon, see International Monetary Fund, *Global Financial Stability Report: Risk Taking, Liquidity, and Shadow Banking—Curbing Excess while Promoting Growth* (IMF 2014) 66–68; Emilios Avgouleas, *Governance of Global Financial Markets: The Law, the Economics, the Politics* (CUP 2012) 51ff; Tobias Adrian and Adam B Ashcraft, 'Shadow Banking Regulation' (Federal Reserve Bank of New York Staff Report No 559, 2012) 5–8.

[30] See the answers given to journalists' questions by Pan Gongsheng, the Deputy Governor of the People's Bank of China, in 'Pan Gongsheng, Deputy Governor of the People's Bank of China, Answered Reporters' Questions About the Financial Management Department's Re-Interview with the Ant Group' (People's Bank of China, 12 April 2021).

[31] For the development of a private banking system no earlier than the 1980s and the important role of shadow banks, see Simin Gao, 'Anti-'Grey Rhino': Prudential Regulation and Bank Resolution in China' in Douglas W Arner and others (eds), *Research Handbook on Asian Financial Law* (Edward Elgar Publishing 2020) 275–77. For details regarding shadow banks in China, see Wei Shen, 'China's Puzzling Banking and Shadow Banking Sectors After the Global Financial Crisis' in Douglas W Arner and others (eds), *Research Handbook on Asian Financial Law* (Edward Elgar Publishing 2020) 293ff.

targeted at ensuring financial stability.[32] With such a broad mandate, the PBOC would hardly risk overstepping any legal boundaries if the introduction of a digital RMB required it to provide more liquidity to specific sectors of the financial industry or directly to financial markets.

B. The euro area

Every textbook on banking law emphasizes the reliance of commercial banks on funding from retail depositors. However, it is important to acknowledge that, in certain regions, this traditional banking model has undergone significant changes due to unconventional monetary strategies implemented by central banks in response to complex market conditions.[33] This transformation is particularly noticeable in negative interest rate environments. For several years, the eurosystem and Switzerland imposed punitive interest rates of -0.5 per cent and -0.75 per cent on commercial banks for holding excess reserves, while simultaneously expanding the money supply.

Consequently, banks found themselves in a peculiar situation. Cheap liquidity was readily available to them,[34] but storing excess liquidity in reserve accounts had become a significant cost factor. In negative interest rate economies, retail customers who deposited large sums in bank accounts had turned into a costly burden for banks. Other sources of funding allowed banks to adjust their commitments flexibly and reduce borrowing when they saw no profitable opportunities for allocating excess liquidity, but retail deposits were sticky. Banks attempted to dissuade customers from depositing large amounts by implementing negative interest rates and account servicing fees.[35] However, such measures are prone to fail if retail

[32] For the latest version of China's Central Bank Act, see People's Bank of China, '中华人民共和国中国人民银行法 (修订草案)' ['Law of the People's Republic of China on the People's Bank of China (Revision Draft for Comments)'] (The People's Bank of China, 23 October 2020), Arts. 2–5 and 8.

[33] For the 'old normal' of central bank operations with commercial banks, see Jean-Victor Louis, 'The Monetary Authority of the Euro Area' (2009) 2 Eur Banking & Fin LJ 277; Bernd Krauskopf and Christine Steven, 'The Institutional Framework of the European System of Central Banks: Legal Issues in the Practice of the First Ten Years of its Existence' (2009) 46(4) Common Market Law Review 1143. For the most recent set of measures in response to the Covid-19 pandemic, see Christian Hofmann, 'Central Banks and Their Limits in a Pandemic' in Victor V Ramraj (ed.), *Covid-19 in Asia: Law and Policy Contexts* (OUP 2021) 97–112.

[34] Just how cheap it has become for commercial banks to fund their activities with liabilities, above all central bank loans, shows the comparison of funding costs for euro area commercial banks in the time period 2009–2018 compared with 2003–2008 in Bindseil, 'Tiered CBDC' (n 18) 11, tables 2a-2b.

[35] For the implications of negative interest applied to excess reserves and deposits, see Committee on Economic and Monetary Affairs, *What are the Effects of the ECB's Negative Interest Rate Policy?* (European Parliament Monetary Dialogue Paper, June 2021).

customers are compelled to stay despite the costs due to a lack of alternative options for storing value.

The interest rate environment in the euro area experienced a shift in July 2022 when the Governing Council of the European Central Bank (ECB) began raising interest rates and set the interest rate for excess reserves at zero per cent. As of 14 September 2023, these rates are at 4 per cent.[36] While this might encourage some banks to temporarily remove punitive interest rates on customer deposits,[37] the underlying structural issues in the euro area persist, and a return to negative interest rate practices at all levels seems possible, if not likely, once inflation pressures subside.[38]

CBDC would provide an opportunity for depositors to escape these costs, allowing banks to treat depositors similarly to other funding sources. Banks could adjust interest rates on deposits above the levels offered by CBDC, depending on their need for additional funding sources, and lower them to reduce excess liquidity. Furthermore, CBDC would provide central banks with an additional mechanism to implement their monetary policies.[39] They could directly engage with the public and incentivize spending or saving. Particularly in complex situations such as the recent pandemic, where inflation in the eurozone coincided with diminished economic prospects due to disrupted supply chains and halted production,[40] adjusting interest rates for CBDC holdings could enable central banks to swiftly inject or withdraw liquidity into or from the markets.[41]

[36] ECB, *Key ECB interest rates, Interest Rates* <https://www.ecb.europa.eu/stats/policy_and_exchange_rates/key_ecb_interest_rates/html/index.en.html> accessed 9 June 2023.

[37] However, German banks show a surprising reluctance to share the benefits of a higher interest environment with their depositors, see Olaf Storbeck, 'German Banks Accused of Short-Changing Savers with Low Rates—Europe's Largest Retail Deposit Broker Says Country's Lenders Will Make €40bn in "Unfair" Profits this Year' *Financial Times* (6 March 2023) <https://www.ft.com/content/0b185970-c99d-4a5a-9e84-9dfa98c9bea9> accessed 9 June 2023. It should be noted that German banks do not hold reserves with the ECB, but with the Bundesbank as the competent national central bank of the eurosystem.

[38] As of December 2022, the interest rates in the euro area stand at 2 per cent for the deposit facility, which reflects the interest that eurosystem central banks pay for excess reserves. See the constantly updated rates of the eurosystem at <https://www.ecb.europa.eu/stats/policy_and_exchange_rates/key_ecb_interest_rates/html/index.en.html> accessed 9 June 2023. For more detail on these issues and forecast future developments, see Chiu and Hofmann, 'Unlimited Central Bank Digital Currency' (n 16).

[39] For monetary policy considerations as a reason for the introduction of a digital euro, see also Bindseil, 'Issuing a Digital Euro' (n 4) 173.

[40] The eurozone inflation stands at 5.1 per cent in January 2022, see Eurostat, 'Inflation in the Eurozone', <https://ec.europa.eu/eurostat/statistics-explained/index.php?title=Inflation_in_the_euro_area> accessed 9 June 2023.

[41] On further aspects, especially the opportunities that CBDC would offer to de-regulate a banking industry that no longer provides the most elementary store of value and means of payment service to the public, see Chiu and Hofmann, 'Unlimited Central Bank Digital Currency' (n 16).

C. Markets with low levels of financial inclusion

Apart from established financial markets, there exists a group of nations that are interested in CBDC primarily to enhance financial inclusion. In these countries, large segments of the population lack access to financial services, particularly bank accounts and electronic payment systems. Private institutions often avoid operating in these predominantly rural regions due to perceived unprofitability. CBDC has the potential to facilitate access to store of value services and improve the accessibility and efficiency of cashless payments for the unbanked or underbanked regions in these countries.[42]

The concerns discussed earlier regarding the introduction of CBDC do not apply to this group of countries. Enhancing public access to financial services would not jeopardize the stability of the mostly non-existent banking system. Additionally, central banks' mandates would not be in conflict since providing the public with convenient access to central bank money and electronic payment systems are essential tasks of central banks worldwide.[43] In countries where efficient intermediation channels are lacking, central banks either delegate these tasks to reliable and supervised private institutions or undertake them independently. The need for significant expansions of central banks' lending and asset purchasing operations, which are of concern in highly developed financial markets, would not arise. On the contrary, CBDC could potentially enable central banks in countries with limited financial integration to enhance the effectiveness of their monetary policy operations.

While the added value for society is therefore evident in countries with low financial inclusion, introducing CBDC often poses challenges. The absence of commercial banks and financial intermediaries capable of providing store of value services and electronic payment systems to all segments of society necessitates central banks to establish CBDC schemes themselves. No private institutions are available to offer accounts or wallets for storing CBDC or to facilitate payment transactions.[44]

This means that, during the initial phase, central banks would be responsible for offering account or wallet services to everyone and developing the necessary

[42] Bank for International Settlements, 'Central Bank Digital Currencies: Foundational Principles and Core Features, Report No 1 in a Series of Collaborations from a Group of Central Banks' (2020) paras 2.1.2, 2.1.4 <https://www.bis.org/publ/othp33.pdf> accessed 26 October 2023; Bank of England, 'Central Bank Digital Currency' (n 3) para. 2.4.

[43] See Benjamin Geva, Seraina N Grunewald, and Corinne Zellweger-Gutknecht, 'The E-Banknote as a "Banknote": A Monetary Law Interpreted' (2021) 41(4) Osgoode Legal Studies Research Paper 14–15; Protocol (No 4) on the Statute of the European System of Central Banks and of the European Central Bank [2016] OJ C202/230, Art. 3.1.

[44] On this point, see Bank of England, 'Central Bank Digital Currency' (n 3) para. 3.3.

mobile apps for initiating transfers. Furthermore, central banks would need to establish a physical presence in all parts of the country to enable the rural population, which primarily relies on cash as the only form of money in underbanked regions, to convert their cash into CBDC. However, the same factors that contribute to the absence of commercial banks, such as underdeveloped infrastructure and financial constraints, pose significant challenges to central banks' plans. Progress in CBDC research and increased investor interest following successful CBDC launches can potentially support these nations.

Sufficiently wealthy countries with dispersed populations, where central banks recognize the need to establish their own payment system to reach even the most remote parts of the country, form the exception of the exception. These are countries in which large parts of the society are insufficiently included in the services that the financial sector provides, but thanks to the country's wealth the infrastructure is sufficiently strong to support the introduction of a CBDC. The Bahamas serves as a prime example, as its central bank recently introduced the Sand Dollar, a retail CBDC, due to the widespread distribution of the population across the archipelago and the reluctance of commercial banks and payment service providers to serve the more rural islands, particularly those frequently affected by hurricanes.[45]

IV. Conclusion

We have argued in this chapter that the data recorded in commercial banks' ledgers, which represents commercial bank money, should be considered as 'money proper'. It has not only become the most widely used store of value and means of payment in markets with high levels of financial inclusion; it ultimately also meets the criteria of the state theory of money despite not being physical and not issued by central banks. This is because central banks and other state authorities have significant control over the creation, allocation, and transfers of commercial bank money. They even actively support the replacement of cash with commercial bank money. This has prompted us to speculate that even Mann, who previously opposed classifying commercial bank money as 'money proper', may no longer object to this classification given the changed realities. However, we have also conceded that the current situation is suboptimal because the public is de facto forced to rely on private money.

[45] Jim Wyss, 'How the Tiny Bahamas Beat Global Giants in the E-Currency Race' (*Financial Post*, 20 May 2021) <https://financialpost.com/pmn/business-pmn/how-the-tiny-bahamas-beat-global-giants-in-the-e-currency-race> accessed 9 June 2023.

This would change with the introduction of Central Bank Digital Currency since it would enable universal access to central bank money for all members of society, providing a secure store of value and efficient cashless payment options. We have argued that this development presents an opportunity for societies to address the lack of options for store of value and the insidious decline in relevance of central bank money for the public resulting from the dwindling use of cash in payment transactions.

The introduction of CBDC would thereby allow for a revival of Mann's restrictive view on commercial bank money, as the existence of CBDC would reinstate the public's freedom of choice between secure central bank money and riskier deposits with commercial banks. However, the limitation of money to tangible items proposed by Mann (i.e. chattels) would remain obsolete, as CBDC would clearly demonstrate the existence of intangible forms of money, more explicitly than any previous technological changes.

In the chapter's brief assessment of specific financial situations in three different types of markets worldwide, it is generally assumed that CBDC may present challenges for the banking industry. However, it is concluded that there would be net benefits for China, the euro area, and regions with low levels of financial inclusion resulting from the introduction of CBDC.

Bibliography

Adrian T and Ashcraft AB, 'Shadow Banking Regulation' (Federal Reserve Bank of New York Staff Report No 559, 2012)

Adrian T and Mancini-Griffoli T, *The Rise of Digital Money* (International Monetary Fund 2019)

Armour J and others, *Principles of Financial Regulation* (OUP 2016)

Arner DW and others (eds), *Research Handbook on Asian Financial Law* (Edward Elgar Publishing 2020)

Avgouleas E, *Governance of Global Financial Markets: The Law, the Economics, the Politics* (CUP 2012)

Bank for International Settlements, 'Wholesale Digital Tokens' (Committee on Payments and Market Infrastructures Paper, 2019)

Berentsen A and Schär F, 'The Case for Central Bank Electronic Money and the Non-case for Central Bank Cryptocurrencies' (2018) 100(2) Federal Reserve Bank of St. Louis Review 97

Bindseil U and others, 'The Eurosystem Collateral Framework Explained' (ECB Occasional Paper No 189, May 2017).

Bindseil U, 'Issuing a Digital Euro' (ESCB Legal Conference, 2020) 172

Bindseil U, 'Tiered CBDC and the Financial System' (European Central Bank Working Paper Series No 2351, January 2020)

Cargill T, *The Financial System, Financial Regulation and Central Bank Policy* (CUP 2017)

Chiu I and Hofmann C, 'Unlimited Central Bank Digital Currency: The Case for a Public Good in the Euro Area and its Regulatory (and De-regulatory) Implications for Modern Finance' (2023) 48(1) North Carolina Journal of International Law 1

European Central Bank, *The Implementation of Monetary Policy in the Eurozone* (European Central Bank, February 2011)

Gabilondo J, 'Central Banks, Systemic Lending, and Collateral Markets' in M Haentjens and B Wessels (eds), *Research Handbook on Crisis Management in the Banking Sector* (Edward Elgar Publishing 2015)

Gabilondo J, *Bank Funding, Liquidity, and Capital Adequacy: A Law and Finance Approach* (Edward Elgar Publishing 2016)

Grunewald SN, Zellweger-Gutknecht C, and Geva B, 'Digital Euro and ECB Powers' (2021) 58(4) Common Market Law Review 1029

Hofmann C, 'Central Banks and Their Limits in a Pandemic' in Victor V Ramraj (ed.), *Covid-19 in Asia: Law and Policy Contexts* (OUP 2021)

Hofmann C, 'Digital Euro: An Assessment of the First Two Progress Reports: the Case for Unlimited Holdings of Digital Euros', European Parliament: In-Depth Analysis Requested by the ECON Committee (2023) <https://www.europarl.europa.eu/RegData/etudes/IDAN/2023/741511/IPOL_IDA(2023)741511_EN.pdf> accessed 26 October 2023

Ke Da, 'Law School of Peking University, The Ideal and Reality of Digital RMB—Based on the Observation of Shenzhen Digital RMB Pilot Activities' (in Chinese) (2020) 104(3) Financial Law Forum 166

Keister T and Monnet C, 'Central Bank Digital Currency: Stability and Information' (2022) 142 Journal of Economic Dynamics and Control <https://www.sciencedirect.com/science/article/abs/pii/S0165188922002056> accessed 26 October 2023

Krauskopf B and Steven C, 'The Institutional Framework of the European System of Central Banks: Legal Issues in the Practice of the First Ten Years of its Existence' (2009) 46(4) Common Market Law Review 1143

Kumhof M and Noone C, 'Central Bank Digital Currencies—Design Principles and Balance Sheet Implications' (Bank of England Staff Working Paper No. 725, 2018)

Lannquist A, *Central Bank Digital Currency Policy-Maker Toolkit* (World Economic Forum Centre for the Fourth Industrial Revolution, Blockchain and Distributed Ledger Technology Platform, January 2020)

Louis JV, 'The Monetary Authority of the Euro Area' (2009) 2 Eur Banking & Fin LJ 277

Mann FA, *The Legal Aspect of Money* (5th edn, OUP 1992)

McLeay M, Radia A, and Thomas R, 'Money in the Modern Economy: An Introduction' (2014) Q1 Bank of England Quarterly Bulletin 4

Niepelt D, 'Money and Banking with Reserves and CBDC', University of Bern Discussion Papers, No. 22-12 (2022)

Proctor C, *Mann on the Legal Aspect of Money* (7th edn, OUP 2012)

Qi M, 'What Would be the Impact of China's Digital Currency?' (Eastspring Investments, November 2020) <https://www.eastspring.com/insights/what-would-be-the-impact-of-china-s-digital-currency> accessed 9 June 2023

Qian Y, 'Central Bank Digital Currency: Optimization of the Currency System and its Issuance Design' (2019) 12(1) China Economic Journal 1

Randhawa DS, *China's Central Bank Digital Currency: Implications for ASEAN* (S. Rajaratnam School of International Studies Policy Report 2020)

Sáinz de Vicuna A, 'An Institutional Theory of Money' in M Giovanoli and D Devos (eds), *International Monetary and Financial Law: The Global Crisis* (OUP 2010)

Skingsley C, 'Should the Riksbank Issue e-Krona?' (Fintech 2016 Conference, Stockholm, 16 November 2016)

Xia M, 'In Search of The Perfect Coin: China's Approach towards Cryptocurrency and Its Own Central Bank Digital Currency' (2021) 36(3) BFLR 419

Zellweger-Gutknecht C and Weber R, 'Digital Money—Taxonomy and Regulatory Approaches' (2022) 24(6) Zeutschrift für Europarecht (EuZ) G8

Zellweger-Gutknecht C, Geva B, and Grünewald SN, 'Digital Euro, Monetary Objects and Price Stability—A Legal Analysis' (2021) 7(2) Journal of Financial Regulation 284

Conclusions

Gerhard Dannemann and Jason Grant Allen

Part I: Biography

As a biographical subject, Mann is imposing. The scion of venerable banking families and a third-generation lawyer, Mann studied and worked with the great and good at some of the leading law faculties of his time, starting a network of professional connections that would last him a lifetime. He left Germany in time to ensure his own and his family's safety. Because of this dislocation and the associated adversities in settling into a new country, Mann established a life in England where he gained a higher degree, started a family, built a legal practice, and published a leading text—all by a comparatively early age. He attended the Nuremberg trials as a British officer, corresponded regularly with household names across the globe, acted in headline-grabbing international cases (often with a high political aspect), and helped to grow a traditional solicitors' practice to be the model of a modern city law firm. Through it all, he published prolifically at the highest standard—putting many full-time academics to shame. To the extent it can be divorced from his experience of forced migration to England, Mann's biography is that of someone who crossed boundaries: moving from Germany to England; building a career spanning legal practice and legal academia in a manner quite atypical for either legal tradition; working in sub-disciplines within the law that are often humbling in their breadth, from banking law to the recognition of foreign states.

With all of this and more to be said about Mann as a very extraordinary individual, why are three of the four chapters in Part I (pre)occupied with the 'Jewish Question'? One conclusion from this project is that a group of 20-odd experts, brought together to discuss the life and legacy of an émigré lawyer, will inevitably

Gerhard Dannemann and Jason Grant Allen, *Conclusions* In: *FA Mann*. Edited by: Jason Grant Allen and Gerhard Dannemann, Oxford University Press. © Gerhard Dannemann and Jason Grant Allen 2024. DOI: 10.1093/oso/9780198881452.003.0016

hold some discussions on what it means to be Jewish in any given social and historical context, and how exactly that fact is or is not relevant to a description of their life in a project like this.

Our experience was that this set of questions ran deeper, but yielded less concrete answers, than we had expected. Some in our group came into the project with a keen interest in the 'Jewish dimension' of Mann's life and legacy. Others came into the project without prior knowledge that he was Jewish at all, or any notion that it might be relevant to assessing his life and legacy. Others again—including those who knew Mann as a person and as a professional—remained of the opinion that being Jewish had little bearing on his life and legacy beyond being the catalyst for his migration.

Identity is always complex, and Jewish identity particularly so. It is not always realistic to expect consensus on all of these points; in fact, sometimes it is even difficult to find a common frame of reference. In this volume, we decided to document the discussion and make some observations on it, even at the risk of apparent imbalance in the mix of chapters. We have been careful to avoid giving the false impression that Mann was a religiously observant Jew, or that he himself made too much of his Jewish background and identity. We would stress that point again here for the record. Equally, however, we have not shied away from asking what might have been distinctively 'Jewish' about Mann's life, his contribution to the law, and his legacy, rather than stopping at saying something or other about being 'more German than the Germans'.

As Mecklenburg's examination of the 'Golden Years' in Chapter 2 has shown, the rise of German-speaking Jews in a few brief decades was extraordinary. In short, it is a social phenomenon (still) in search of an explanation. Putting this phenomenon in its proper context is important, as it speaks both about Jewish and non-Jewish German-speaking culture, and indeed German society in the relevant period. Each individual biography provides a context in which to do that. What was it about conditions in German-speaking Europe that permitted this remarkable rise? What lasting structures and positive elements might remain despite its equally remarkable demise?

König's Chapter 3 places emphasis on the transnational aspect of Mann's life. He argues that Mann's work, particularly his style of thinking and writing, is influenced by the fact that he transcended borders and that his transnational biography provides an important context to understanding the evolution of the 'legal science' in both English and German legal systems.

In Chapter 4, Paz adopts the idea of 'socialization' in various stages and the idea of a *Denkstil* or *Denkkultur* ('style' and 'culture' of thought, respectively) to articulate the relevance of Mann's Jewish background to his professional occupation with money. This feels intuitively uncomfortable: the nexus between Jews, capitalism, and finance is historically well-documented, and there is an extensive literature exploring how this background, closely intertwined with European antisemitism, has informed the professional interests of many German-Jewish scholars.[1] Mann was

[1] The sources would be too numerous to list here. For a recent example of a very good biography of a 'not very Jewish Jew', Karl Marx, see Shlomo Avineri, *Karl Marx: Philosophy and Revolution* (Yale

the scion of two prominent banking families, and he lived during a time of foment in which *antisemitic* and *anti-financial* rhetoric was implicitly bound up.[2]

Although it is provocative, Paz's investigation of a possible 'Jewish' dimension to Mann's monetary theory and the parallels she draws between Mann and other Jewish (but not very 'Jewish') thinkers such as Karl Marx and Georg Simmel is an important one. Charles Kadushin observes that Simmel was identified as a Jew, and identified himself as a Jew, despite his parents' conversion to Christianity. Incidentally, he and the other 'father' of network research (Emil Durkheim) were both Jewish; Kadushin sets out some of the ways in which their experience as 19th-century Jews may have informed their research interests. In particular, from the background of ghetto and *shtetl* settlements in the Middle Ages and early modernity, following emancipation the network boundaries for Jews expanded: 'Social circles, first described by Simmel, are characteristic of modern mass society and serve to integrate apparently disconnected groups such as Jews into larger societies'.[3] The engagement of German Jews into broader societies (in Germany and in England) was the precise social dynamic we are here engaged with.

Allen's Chapter 1 attempted to frame this Part and achieve a sense of balance. This highly personal chapter draws on a decade of experience living and working in German-speaking Europe and attempts to understand and explain the complexities of Holocaust historiography and the project of building a genuine *Erinnerungskultur* with empathy for the non-Jewish German perspective. At the same time, it is candid about the problems with that project, the uncomfortable cultural dynamics that have played out over the past decades, and the worrisome trends evident in Europe today. While engaging with Mann, this chapter is equally focussed on what it means to write about the legacy of a 20th-century German Jew and how this volume implicitly contributes to the project of the *Erinnerungskultur*. As Allen argues, it is necessary to ensure that we write about Mann and his contemporaries in a way that makes a positive contribution to that project and in a way that cannot be instrumentalized in a stylized 'theatre of reconciliation'.

University Press 2019). See generally Jerry Z Muller, *Capitalism and the Jews* (Princeton University Press 2010), who observes that the nexus between Jews and Capitalism has been more often explored by anti-Semites and apologists than by Jewish Studies scholars.

[2] See, for example, Gideon Reuveni and Sarah Wobick-Segev, *The Economy in Jewish History: New Perspectives on the Interrelationship Between Ethnicity and Economic Life* (Berghahn Books 2010); Abraham Foxman, *Jews & Money: The Story of a Stereotype* (Palgrave Macmillan 2010). A recent study has even found that areas with a higher rate of historical antisemitism have lower rates of utilization of financial services, such as home loans: see Francesco D'Acunto, Marcel Prokopczuk, and Michael Weber, 'Historical Antisemitism, Ethnic Specialisation, and Financial Development' (Working Paper No. 2018-19, Becker Friedman Institute for Economics at the University of Chicago, March 2018) <https://bfi.uchicago.edu/wp-content/uploads/WP_2018-19.pdf> accessed 12 June 2023.

[3] Charles Kadushin, 'Social Networks and Jews' (2011) 31 Contemporary Jewry 55, 60.

Part II: The International Lawyer

Mann is unique as a wanderer between several legal worlds—the German and English legal spheres, legal scholarship, and legal practice, but also between public international law, private international law, and domestic laws. Part II explores Mann as international lawyer in three different aspects: the act of state doctrine and enforcement of foreign public law (Chapter 5), the connection between public and private international law (Chapter 6), and how international commercial contracts and arbitration fit into the framework of public international law, private international law, and domestic law (Chapter 7). It is planned that these three chapters will eventually be complemented by two articles written by project contributors which for time constraints will be published separately, namely Campbell McLachlan's presentation on 'Foreign Relations Law Revisited' as the 44th FA Mann lecture in November 2022, and Wolfgang Schön's presentation at the final project conference on 'International Jurisdiction to Tax: The Legacy of F.A. Mann in International Tax Law'.

Jurisdiction figures prominently in all three of these explorations. For Mann, jurisdiction is a key issue in defining the degree to which courts may be bound by an act of a foreign state or may enforce foreign public law. Public international law notions of jurisdiction, according to Mann, must also shape private international law notions of jurisdiction. And jurisdiction is also key to Mann's insistence that international commercial contracts and international arbitration are not delocalized phenomena which operate outside of the boundaries of domestic laws: it is by being seated in a particular state, and by having to enforce awards in the same or another state, that both litigation before state courts and international arbitration are necessarily connected with one or more domestic laws.

Mann was a very influential practising lawyer, but inevitably with mixed success in his international litigation. One of his greatest disappointments was having ended up on the losing side in the *Barcelona Traction* case, whereas he was on the winning side in other important international cases including the *Young Loan* case.[4] As Part II demonstrates, his legacy on international law as a scholar is very considerable, but also somewhat mixed. Collins shows in Chapter 5 how Mann's seminal 1943 article, 'The Sacrosanctity of Foreign Act of State',[5] went from presenting an outlier position which seemed to rally against received wisdom to becoming mainstream and eventually the basis of modern case law in several common law countries, in a process which continues until today.

When Mann wrote the article, it was generally believed that domestic courts must not question the validity of the acts of foreign states when these surface in

[4] See Introduction, Section I.

[5] (1943) 59 LQR 42 and 155. Mann elaborated on this in various later publications, see Chapters 5 (II.B) and 6 (IV.C).

domestic proceedings; today, it is recognized that domestic courts will scrutinize foreign acts as to whether they are in conformity with public international law. This trajectory included Mann's triumph on a related question in the celebrated 1976 case of *Oppenheimer v Cattermole*.[6] The House of Lords, who were set to allow the appeal, changed their mind after having been pointed to an article published by Mann, re-opened deliberations, and eventually referred the case back for further fact finding.[7] Collins shows a continued influence of Mann's work in subsequent judgments on the related topic of enforcing foreign public law, including *Attorney-General of New Zealand v Ortiz*,[8] *Kuwait Airways Corp v Iraqi Airways Co*,[9] and most recently *Skatteforvaltningen v Solo Capital Partners LLP*,[10] all of which judgments cite extensively Mann's work. The Australian case of *Moti v R*[11] furthermore shows that Mann's influence on this subject is not limited to English law. That Mann's influence continues more than three decades after his death in 1991 is particularly evident in this area of law.

In Chapter 6, Dannemann shows how Mann's influential work on the relationship between public international law notions of jurisdiction and the corresponding private international law notions remain relevant until today, including his celebrated Hague Lectures on the subject.[12] Had he been allowed to continue Martin Wolff's treatise on private international law, or had he written the planned book on jurisdiction in which OUP had shown great interest, his influence on the topic would have been even greater by developing his thoughts further into a general doctrine of public international law influences on private international law. As Dannemann shows, this would have accommodated and could have provided a further basis for his pronounced views on excessive jurisdiction, mandatory overriding provisions, and expropriation. Dannemann also finds it likely that Mann would have discovered in this process that, next to territorial and personal sovereignty, there is also sovereign exercise of state power as a public international law principle which can determine, shape, or limit private international law rules—in particular since the rule that each state regulates its own currency may be the best example for such a conflicts rule based on state power sovereignty. But Mann's correspondence also reveals that he became somewhat reluctant to venture further into private international law jurisdiction. His English solicitor perspective on legal certainty might also have been somewhat in the way, as this made him apprehensive of legal change, international harmonization, and in particular any

6 *Oppenheimer v Cattermole (HM Inspector of Taxes)* [1976] AC 249.
7 ibid 268 (Lord Cross); FA Mann, 'The Present Validity of Nazi Nationality Laws' (1973) 89 LQR 194.
8 [1982] QB 349, aff'd [1984] AC 1 (CA and HL).
9 [2002] UKHL 19.
10 [2021] EWHC 974 (Comm), rev'd [2022] EWCA Civ 234.
11 [2011] HCA 50, (2011) 245 CLR 456.
12 FA Mann, 'The Doctrine of Jurisdiction in International Law' (1963) 111 Recueil des Cours 1; FA Mann, 'The Doctrine of Jurisdiction in International Law Revisited After Twenty Years' (1984) 186 Recueil des Cours 9.

binding interpretation of harmonized norms through international courts. Mann's important legacy in this area is that he identified a very considerable gap between public and private international law, and that he succeeded in closing some of this gap. More work still needs to be done.

In Chapter 7, Cordero Moss evaluates the ongoing influence of Mann on the delocalization debate in commercial law and arbitration law. Mann was a strong supporter of the traditional localized approach, namely that private law disputes are necessarily governed by one or several domestic laws, which are invoked by private international law rules. The opposite view wants to delocalize international private law disputes by resorting to some international *lex mercatoria* or other rules which are not connected to domestic legal systems. This delocalization approach has found considerable support in the scholarly debate while Mann was alive, and remains influential until today. In international commercial practice, model contracts, often based on common law terminology and drafting style, are frequently used with little regard to the domestic law in which they are intended to operate. Likewise, arbiters may have enjoyed the additional legroom which the delocalized approach provides. Cordero Moss shows that, as far as international commercial contracts are concerned, a very similar debate continues until today between two groups of practising lawyers: those who draft international commercial agreements and who often prefer delocalization, standardization, and generally flexibility, and those who litigate issues arising from international commercial agreements, who are faced with domestic rules on jurisdiction, mandatory norms, recognition and enforcement of arbitration awards, who often prefer certainty over flexibility, and who therefore are much closer to Mann's views. She furthermore shows recent trends in arbitration which show a small renaissance of the localized approach. So this debate is still very much ongoing, and while Mann's views have not triumphed, he remains as a main proponent of the localized approach which shows continued relevance both for the present and for future developments.

Part III: Money

Monetary law is the field of Mann's magnum opus—his first and major text in the English language, an apparently self-contained reference book that assumed canonical status in his own lifetime. *The Legal Aspect of Money* often assumes oversize proportions in his legacy. While it should not be allowed to overshadow his considerable contributions to other areas of law, because monetary law has again become a topic of current practical and scholarly interest, Part III of this volume has assumed commensurate proportions. This is not wholly unwelcome, however; as we have seen, Mann's work in monetary law also showcases his learning in other areas (such as international law public and private) and how his polymathic legal knowledge contributed to his status as a monetary lawyer.

The chapters in Part III demonstrate Mann's venerable legacy and continuing relevance as a monetary lawyer. They also reveal certain areas in which his contributions have become of historical interest as history marches onward. Much of the current interest in Mann's work on money relates to the raft of question raised by new technological developments, particularly so-called 'cryptocurrencies' and the possibility that central banks will start issuing electronic tokens directly or mediately to the public in the form of 'central bank digital currencies'. We cannot hold it against Mann that he did not pre-empt these current developments. However, they do provide a test-case for his conception of money, and from them we can observe that his concept of money was overly narrow in certain respects. In short, Mann's dogmatic definition of money as a 'chattel' (the English legal term for a tangible object of property rights that is not 'land') issued by a state was unsustainable by the time he wrote the fifth edition (1992), completed shortly before his death in 1991.

Mann opened his treatise with the 'troublesome question' (i.e. 'What is money?') and the powerful claim that, despite the abundance of economic enquiries into it, the notion of money is equally fundamental to law.[13] He goes on to list a number of concrete scenarios in which the definition of money is of acute practical importance, for example the distinction between a contract of sale (i.e. for a price stated in money terms) and barter. The law seems to provide different answers to the troublesome question in different contexts (e.g. adopting one definition in the law of contract and another in the criminal law) rather than yielding a single, coherent answer.

There are, he says, really two questions to be asked of the 'concrete form' and the 'abstract conception' of money. Of the former we ask, 'What are the characteristics in virtue of which a thing is called money?' Of the latter we ask, 'What is the intrinsic nature of the phenomenon described by the word "money"?'[14] This sets the stage for a major methodological claim:

> In answering these two questions economic theory is unlikely to assist the lawyer to any appreciable extent. Lawyers, it is true, accept that, among all the functions of money which economists have analysed, the basic function is that of serving as a universal medium of exchange, and will take this into account when defining money in the legal sense. Yet such problems as monetary policy, the management of supply, the quantity and soundness of money are no concern of the lawyer. He will benefit more from the economist's view that [various forms of 'bank money', *monnaie scripturale*, *Buchgeld*] may well be treated by the law as money. As a rule, however, the economists view that everything is money that functions as money is unacceptable to lawyers.[15]

[13] FA Mann, *The Legal Aspect of Money* (5th edn, OUP 1992>>) 3.
[14] ibid 5.
[15] ibid 5.

In law, 'the quality of money is to be attributed to all *chattels* which, issued by *authority of the law* and denominated by reference to a *unit of account*, are meant to serve as universal *means of exchange* in the State of issue'[16] even though 'most modern economists, all commercial men and some lawyers cavil at the alleged narrowness of the legal approach'.[17]

With this in mind, one might justifiably wonder whether Mann's legal concept of money is really fit to take us into the 21st century, in which non-chattel money appears to amount and in which non-state issued tokens appear to be making a credible bid for monetary status. In fact, it is often difficult to untangle these two questions—the 'dematerialization' of money tokens and the 'privatization' of their issuance. For the past several decades at least, the dominant form of money has been electronic tokens of a creditor–debtor relationship with a private commercial bank. The move was, first, to 'book money' and secondly to book money kept in electronic databases rather than bankers' books.

But it is all more complex than that, as discussion in the various chapters of Part III show. In conclusion, we can tease out a few points for critical engagement with Mann. First, private banks have become imbricated within a central banking model in which the prerogative of money issuance has been 'franchised' out by the central bank—so much so, that central banks rely on private financial intermediaries for important mechanisms of monetary policy transmission.[18] As we have seen from Bateman's Chapter 11, Mann declined to engage in the law of central banking on the basis that it was a branch of constitutional law rather than monetary law. In turn, he could not engage with the constitutional dimensions of the private commercial banking system, and his methodological and ideological outlook would likely have made him disinclined to do so, in any case.

A second point of criticism relates to Mann's methodological exclusion of economic perspectives. Some argue that a comprehensive understanding of monetary law requires a closer integration of economic principles and considerations, which Mann's work explicitly rejected. An illustration of this is Mann's refusal to engage with Keynesian political economy in his treatise. This approach defined monetary law during much of Mann's lifetime, as JM Keynes was one of the major architects of the Bretton Woods system. Further, Keynes was personally involved in the translation into English of a major source in Mann's own work, Georg Knapp's *Staatliche Theorie des Geldes*, in 1923. It is conjectural, but perhaps his antipathy had to do with the problematical 1936 German edition of Keynes' *General Theory* and the

[16] ibid 6.
[17] ibid 6.
[18] See Will Bateman and JG Allen, 'The Law of Central Bank Reserve Creation' (2022) 81(2) Modern Law Review 401; see also RC Hockett and ST Omarova, 'The Finance Franchise' (2017) 102 Cornell Law Review 1143.

affinity between Keynesianism and Hitlerite economy policy under Hjalmar Schacht.[19]

This was not missed by Mann's contemporaries: in a cordial exchange of letters with Mann, Sir Joseph Gold (then at the Legal Department of the IMF) wrote in 1969 words to the effect that Mann's aversion to Keynes was 'rather sad' and 'particularly unfortunate' in view of Mann's neglect of certain Bretton Woods documents which supported Keynes' view and refuted Mann's. In sum, Sir Joseph expressed the view that Mann had 'not grasped the economics of Keynes' position' that drove the legal compromise.[20] Perhaps as a result of this exchange, the third edition (1971) of *The Legal Aspect of Money* contains one footnote to Keynes' *Treatise of Money* (1930) (without commentary) and one footnote to Keynes' speech (as Lord Keynes in the British Parliament) to the effect that Bretton Woods did not involve any kind of gold standard because it used gold merely as a common denominator for determining the relative value of national currencies without binding them to it.[21] One tends to share Sir Joseph's view that Mann may have been uncomfortable writing beyond his area of expertise as well as his methodological commitment to the idea that 'law' was a product of judicial decisions rather than the non-justiciable operations of central banks.[22]

This leads to a third point. Despite his nominalism, Mann insisted that only money whose token was a chattel was 'real' money; money that remained in the ethereal realm of a banker's book entry was not 'money' properly so called. And yet, insofar as book money conforms to the Knappian requirement of being accepted by the state pay offices in satisfaction of debts denominated in the proper unit of account, it would seem that Mann *ought* to have accepted book money. As Joseph Sommer and Wolfgang Ernst's chapters make clear, Mann was nominally a Knappian but in fact developed his own approach under the Knappian banner. Knapp's 'State Theory' of money is more permissive of privately issued forms of chartal money than Mann's interpretation of that theory.

Although Mann professed to follow Knapp's framework, he actually went further than Knapp in requiring an exercise of state legal authority to create money. For Knapp, 'accommodation' (for example, acceptance at the state pay offices of a privately issued token) was enough to make a token 'real' money. Current debates about the monetary status of cryptocurrencies put strain on Mann's legalist 'State Theory' of money and put a new spin on debates between that theory and market-based and 'societary' theories of money that stress the social rather than state-legal

[19] See generally Bertram Schefold, 'The General Theory for A Totalitarian State? A Note on Keynes's Preface to the German Edition of 1936' (1980) 4(2) Cambridge Journal of Economics 175. See also David Lipka and Dan Šťastný, 'John Maynard Keynes, Socialism and Economic Policy of Nazi Germany [John Maynard Keynes, socialismus a hospodářská politika nacistického Německa]' Acta Oeconomica Pragensia (2008) 1 Prague University of Economics and Business 108–16.

[20] Sir Joseph Gold to FA Mann (Mann estate, RS149_NLMann_0293, 4 August 1969).

[21] FA Mann, *The Legal Aspect of Money* (3rd edn, OUP 1971) 14, 35.

[22] This point emerged from discussion with Will Bateman on his chapter.

basis of money phenomena. Their 'social' theories of money, mostly created before World War I, fit today's monetary order better than Mann's legal theory. As Sommer argues in Chapter 10, such theories rely on social consensus secured by symbols, and perhaps a transactional hegemon; they are potent to explain non-statal monies, immaterial monies, extraterritorial monies, evolving monies, and the quasi-legal tender status of credit transfers in a way that Mann's conventional theory cannot. When facing these monetary (or money-like) phenomena, as in Gleeson and Hofmann's Chapters 13 and 14 respectively, Mann's account leaves us with questions as well as answers.

Note, in this context, that in discussing the 'chattel question' the role of the state has become a central question. In this aspect, too, Mann's approach to money is somewhat less straightforward that it seems at first blush. This in fact brings us around to the first point, relating to Mann's exclusion of the constitutional dimensions of monetary law. Although he dealt with the proliferating public international law of money in the decades of the Bretton Woods era following the Second World War, his refusal to deal with the domestic public law aspects remained problematic at the core. As Bateman argues, Mann's decision to exclude such questions from the remit of 'monetary law' had the unfortunate consequence of omitting the fascinating interaction of state institutions, money, and financial markets from his state-theoretic account of money. Ironically, however, the legal and institutional details of monetary authorities during Mann's career substantiate his broader claims about the legal foundations of money.

Some of these difficulties emerge clearly from an examination of his text in the hands of its contemporary editor, Charles Proctor, who faced the rather difficult task of squaring the circles Mann had drawn around the concept of money. The sixth edition (2005) started on a subtly but importantly different note. There is a weakening of the methodological firewall between 'law' and 'economics':

> [M]oney is a fundamental notion within the economic life and activities of mankind. It seems to follow that an attempt to formulate a *legal* definition of money cannot proceed in isolation, but must take at least some account of economic theory. In addition, as will be seen, technological and other developments over recent years do have consequences for an attempt to formulate a legal definition of 'money'—as the available means of payment multiply, the meaning of 'money' must correspondingly broaden.[23]

According to Proctor, this requires 'at least some consideration' of money's economic functions, which are typically identified as (i) a medium of exchange, (ii) a measure of value or a standard for contractual obligations, (iii) a store of value or

[23] Charles Proctor, *Mann on the Legal Aspect of Money* (6th edn, OUP 2005) 9.

wealth, and (iv) a unit of account. Although the emphasis placed by economists on each of these functions has changed over time, the function as a medium of exchange is key, and Proctor's proposed legal definition 'reflects some of these considerations'.[24] Noting a number of classical legal definitions that adopt a functional approach, and noting the importance of the concept of monetary sovereignty, Proctor concludes:

> With these considerations in mind, it becomes attractive to adopt a functional approach—money is that which serves as a means of exchange—subject to the proviso that its functions must have the formal and mandatory backing of the domestic legal system in the State or area in which it circulates. For anything which is treated as 'money' purely in consequence of local custom or the consent of the parties does not represent or reflect an exercise of monetary sovereignty and thus cannot be considered 'money' in a legal sense. It is necessary to conclude that a definition of 'money' in law must recognise both the functions of money and the legal framework within which it must be created.[25]

In this treatment, Proctor makes several important departures from Mann. First, he abandons the requirement that 'money' be a chattel, i.e. a physical object capable of possession.[26] This is an overdue response to the reality that most money now exists in digital ledgers, not as notes and coins. Secondly, where Mann's editions of the book set out the tenets of the State Theory and then provide a detailed discussion of those tenets, Proctor compares and contrasts the State Theory with the 'Societary Theory'. This approach looks to custom and usage within the market where the State Theory looks only at whether a chattel is issued under the sovereign authority of a state.

Mann disavowed the Societary Theory consistently, whether for right or wrong. Ultimately, Proctor confesses fidelity to a moderated version of the State Theory. He defines 'money' as a *unit of account* prescribed under the *authority of a state* (or state-like[27] political organization—perhaps allowing room for cases like Somaliland) and intended to serve as the generally accepted *measure of value* and *means of exchange* within the relevant territory.[28] His position between the theories is, however, somewhat uneasy, and it is the Societary Theory that seems to do the heavy lifting with regards to new money candidates:

> [T]he State theory—in the somewhat attenuated form proposed above—provides the definition of money in its abstract sense, whilst the Societary theory

24 ibid 10.
25 ibid 14.
26 ibid 27.
27 ibid 23–24.
28 ibid 35–36.

contributes to a description of money as a means of payment, and the development of new forms of 'money'.[29]

In particular, Proctor recognizes in terms that private forms of money such as bank deposits and e-money 'may be used as a means of payment, and may thus be regarded as forms of "money" in a legal sense'.[30]

It is beyond the scope of this text to engage with the subsequent editions of *Mann on the Legal Aspect of Money*, which has grown to be a very different—and much longer—text than Mann's own.

To summarize, then, Mann's enormous contribution to the field of monetary law continues to enrich our understanding of this complex and dynamic field of law today. One of the most valuable contributions of the chapters in Part III is the way that they explain some of the legal and economic history of the 20th century that is necessary to understand our contemporary monetary system. Increasingly, scholars and laypersons alike are engaging with monetary theory without knowledge of how we got to our complex status quo. In our century, Mann's seminal text can hardly be expected to hold all the answers. But his systematization and rigorous legal approach to a subject of fundamental importance continues to enrich our engagement with money and monetary systems today, even if we must depart from some of his methodological and taxonomic stipulations.

Bibliography

Avineri S, *Karl Marx: Philosophy and Revolution* (Yale University Press 2019)

Bateman W and Allen JG, 'The Law of Central Bank Reserve Creation' (2022) 81(2) Modern Law Review 401

D'Acunto F, Prokopczuk M, and Weber M, 'Historical Antisemitism, Ethnic Specialisation, and Financial Development' (Working Paper No. 2018-19, Becker Friedman Institute for Economics at the University of Chicago, March 2018), https://bfi.uchicago.edu/wp-content/uploads/WP_2018-19.pdf accessed 12 June 2023

Foxman A, *Jews & Money: The Story of a Stereotype* (Palgrave Macmillan 2010)

Hockett RC and Omarova ST, 'The Finance Franchise' (2017) 102 Cornell Law Review 1143

Kadushin C, 'Social Networks and Jews' (2011) 31 Contemporary Jewry 55

Lipka D and Šťastný S, 'John Maynard Keynes, Socialism and Economic Policy of Nazi Germany [John Maynard Keynes, socialismus a hospodářská politika nacistického Německa]' Acta Oeconomica Pragensia (2008) 1 Prague University of Economics and Business 108

Mann FA, 'The Doctrine of Jurisdiction in International Law' (1963) 111 Recueil des Cours 1

Mann FA, *The Legal Aspect of Money* (3rd edn, OUP 1971)

Mann FA, 'The Present Validity of Nazi Nationality Laws' (1973) 89 LQR 194

[29] ibid 37.

[30] ibid 37, 43.

Mann FA, 'The Doctrine of Jurisdiction in International Law Revisited After Twenty Years' (1984) 186 Recueil des Cours 9
Mann FA, *The Legal Aspect of Money* (5th edn, OUP 1992)
Muller JZ, *Capitalism and the Jews* (Princeton University Press 2010)
Proctor C, *Mann on the Legal Aspect of Money* (6th edn, OUP 2005)
Reuveni G and Wobick-Segev S, *The Economy in Jewish History: New Perspectives on the Interrelationship Between Ethnicity and Economic Life* (Berghahn Books 2010)
Schefold B, 'The General Theory for A Totalitarian State? A Note on Keynes's Preface to the German Edition of 1936' (1980) 4(2) Cambridge Journal of Economics 175

Index

For the benefit of digital users, indexed terms that span two pages (e.g., 52–53) may, on occasion, appear on only one of those pages.